ANNUAL REVIEW OF ANTHROPOLOGY

EDITORIAL COMMITTEE

ANNUAL REVIEW OF ANTHROPOLOGY

BERNARD J. SIEGEL, *Editor*
Stanford University

ALAN R. BEALS, *Associate Editor*
University of California, Riverside

STEPHEN A. TYLER, *Associate Editor*
Rice University

VOLUME 2

1973

ANNUAL REVIEWS INC.   4139 EL CAMINO WAY   PALO ALTO, CALIFORNIA 94306

ANNUAL REVIEWS INC.
Palo Alto, California USA

COPYRIGHT © 1973 BY ANNUAL REVIEWS INC.

International Standard Book Number: 0-8243-1902-8
Library of Congress Catalog Card Number: 72-82136

Assistant Editor	Jean Heavener
Indexers	Mary A. Glass
	Leigh Dowling
	Susan Tinker
Subject Indexer	Dorothy Read

PRINTED AND BOUND IN THE UNITED STATES OF AMERICA

PREFACE

The second volume of the *Annual Review of Anthropology* reflects continuity with the first as well as several new directions. Bennett et al, for social anthropology, and Flannery, for archeology, carry forward environmental-ecological concerns. The review of human paleontology by Tobias covers substantive work in two important areas to complement the analysis (in Volume 1) by Campbell of conceptual progress in this field. The chapters here on linguistics, on the other hand, break new ground. We have picked up significant new work in the fields of economic anthropology (last covered in the *Biennial Review of Anthropology, 1965*), sociocultural change (social and political movements), and applied anthropology (educational anthropology). One section of the chapter on ecology also deals with contributions to medical studies in anthropology. And finally, this volume initiates a set of reviews of methodology and a critical evaluation of recent publications on the ethnology and archeology of a specific area (the American Southwest).

If you missed the first *Annual Review of Anthropology,* please examine the detailed and thoughtful commentary on Volume 1 prepared by Dr. Henry A. Selby of the Department of Anthropology, Temple University, and published in *Science* (Vol. 180, 1355, 29 June 1973). He writes with approval about the length and scope of the "essays on the state of the art in those areas where something significant or interesting is going on."

Dr. Selby then outlines the areas covered in the initial volume, and concludes his review with words that are gratifying to everyone who has been involved in the task of planning and launching this new series of Annual Reviews: "Altogether this is a successful volume, and manages to convey in a clearer fashion than before the scope of thinking in contemporary Anthropology."

The chapter titles we have utilized in Volumes 1 and 2 (and will suggest to future authors) reflect, to the best of our ability, the principal ways in which anthropologists have come to conceptualize their discipline. They also are meant to assure proper coverage of important subfields and to enable contributors to cope with the growing literature in each field within manageable limits. By the time our fifth volume is published, we hope to have reviewed all of the current subfields and perspectives of anthropology. The next major task of the editorial committee will be to assess the frequency of subjects reviewed, in terms of quality as well as quantity of output in any given period, and to draw up a projection of topics to be covered over the next five-year period.

THE EDITORS AND THE EDITORIAL COMMITTEE

CONTENTS

Margaret Mead.

CHANGING STYLES OF ANTHROPOLOGICAL WORK

❖ 9516

Margaret Mead

The American Museum of Natural History, New York City, NY

The last 20 years have seen an enormous growth of institutions devoted to anthropological enterprises, membership within the discipline, and students, textbooks, and paraphernalia. From a tiny scholarly group that could easily be fitted into a couple of buses, and most of whom knew each other, we have grown into a group of tremendous, anonymous milling crowds, meeting at large hotels where there are so many sessions that people do well to find those of their colleagues who are interested in the same specialty. Today we look something like the other social science disciplines, suffering some of the same malaise, and becoming cynical about slave markets and worried when grants and jobs seem to be declining.

It has been a period of excessive growth; it is astonishing, looking back, to recount how many large enterprises have been undertaken. The year 1953 marked the end of the Korean war and the final exodus from Washington of almost all the remaining anthropologists who had lingered on to make the kind of contribution to national affairs that had developed in wartime. Most of the ventures that had been specifically influenced by the immediate post-World War II world drew to a close: Columbia University Research in Contemporary Cultures, Studies in Soviet Culture, American Museum of Natural History Research in Contemporary Cultures A and B, (189, 213), the Coordinated Investigations of Micronesian Anthropology, the period of affluence in the Foreign Service Institute, the intensive exploitation of the Human Relations Area Files, and the preparation of manuals and directives for participation in technical assistance and foreign aid (13, 191, 269). A few anthropologists stayed on for several more years, but activities of the House Un-American Activities Committee had disillusioned anthropologists with government, and as their participation in government shrank, so did the receptiveness of government agencies to anthropological contributions because there was no one to inaugurate them, receive them, or interpret them.

Anthropologists came out of the war years with several important new orientations. They had learned that their skills could be applied fruitfully to problems affecting modern societies and the deliberations of national governments and nation

1

states. They had learned to apply themselves to problems they had not themselves chosen, and to work with members of other disciplines. While this was most conspicuously true in the United States, the English style of operational research involved anthropologists in many unfamiliar fields, and some of the theoretical approaches of the French underground also meant a novel use of anthropology. A rationale for the kind of contribution that anthropologists could make to problems of national and worldwide scope was developed (171). But, at the same time, the experience of anthropologists during the war was summed up in the dictum, "you can't advise an adviser." If anthropologists were to participate in public activities, it meant some of them had to accept positions within various parts of the establishment, and this they became increasingly unwilling to do. The contradiction between a willingness during World War II to become involved and a disinclination to become involved later has not yet been resolved. This, in addition to the rejection of the Vietnam war, may account for the rather meager participation of anthropologists in the last 20 years in problems involving technical assistance, modernization, arms control, the prevention of nuclear warfare, peaceful uses of atomic energy, population control, and the environmental crisis (122).

In the earlier years, anthropology was so slightly established that the usual academic punishment for unorthodoxy was confined to excluding from it those who expressed very large heresies, such as the racist approach or an overemphasis on the dependence of American Indian culture on importations from Asia. After the war, although such major unorthodoxies persisted to a certain extent, the scene shifted to rewarding those who took part in currently popular minor theoretical discussions. Students were advised to concentrate on very recent polemics, and small, specific discussions of kinship, or variations in response to Lévi-Strauss (144, 160), became the road to academic advancement.

This exodus from any situation connected with national policy coincided with a tremendous growth in research opportunities and academic appointments. The National Institutes of Mental Health and National Science Foundation programs, and in the 1960s the development of programs vaguely conceived as foreign aid that would be relevant to political purposes abroad, such as the Ford Foundation Area Studies programs, all provided funding for academically phrased research. There were not enough funds for the tasks that needed doing, but there were more than enough for the strength and capabilities of those who were mature enough to lead and direct these programs.

An enormous number of new possibilities opened up in the United States through the establishment of new departments in old universities, transformation by upgrading old institutions, and a proliferation of new institutions. The establishment of new universities in the United Kingdom, new forms of cooperation in Paris (through coordination provided by the Sixieme Section de L'Ecole Pratique des Hautes Etudes and the Maison de la Science de l'Homme), and the new universities in Australia, India, and the new countries of Africa and Oceania also widened the field.

Movement from academic post to project to a different academic post was very rapid, and in the scramble for projects and posts there was little time for writing up the large amount of field work that was being funded. A great many young men and women wrote their dissertations, their three short papers, did a few reviews, presented a paper or so, and went on to a tenured appointment with very little opportunity to show their mettle. As the period of educational expansion slows down, it may well be that one legacy from those years will be a layer of middle management, the members of which reached their positions by a kind of gamesmanship that is no longer as relevant to a world where stringency, frugality, and specific capacities critically appraised are again in vogue.

Internationally, there have been a series of large enterprises: the Wenner-Gren Conference of 1952, which held us together for another decade (150, 280); *Current Anthropology,* with its network of associates and commentators; the big University of Chicago symposium on evolution (279); the Wenner-Gren Conferences at Burg Wartenstein and in the United States, the International Congresses of Anthropology and Ethnology, and a strong anthropological presence at the Pacific Science Congresses; the development of the Center for the Study of Man at the Smithsonian; the Laboratoire d'Anthropologie Sociale in Paris; the New Guinea Research Unit of the Australian National University; and the present (culminating) effort for the Ninth Congress of Anthropological and Ethnological Sciences to be held in Chicago in September 1973. These clusters of impressive activities owe a great deal to the imagination and energy of three people: Sol Tax, Editor of *Current Anthropology;* Lita Osmundsen, Director of the Wenner-Gren Foundation; and Clemens Heller of the Ecole Pratique des Hautes Etudes, in Paris. As available openings for research, personnel, and funds have been identified and deployed around the world, these people have enlisted the cooperation of many institutions and seized opportunities for amplifying organizational efforts.

This has also been a period of large research programs, varying from the Caribbean program of the Institute for the Study of Man, the continuing area-based projects, like the Chiapas project (296), Watson's New Guinea project (297), Goldschmidt's African project (114), the associated sets of fellowships and activities of the East-West Center in Hawaii, the New Guinea Research Unit of the Australian National University, the Arctic Institute of North America, Vayda's ecology project on the New Guinea Rainforest, the widespread studies emanating from the University of Manchester, the cluster of studies in French West Africa and French Oceania, integration of studies on political and social organization in the Netherlands at the Hague, and the Australian Institute of Aboriginal Studies. And there are many, many more programs in which there has been an attempt to bring together groups interested in an area with various related anthropological specialties. The large scale long term projects have had, I think, no higher rate of failure —failure to complete work, write it up, or integrate results—than other social science projects which had less complicated logistical problems (177).

The catholicity of anthropology, with its ideological insistence on the psychic unity of man, and its traditional disregard of race, ethnicity, age, and sex as criteria for academic posts or research capabilities, combined with the political instabilities of the post-World War II world, has resulted in another form of international cooperation and interpenetration of different nationally based anthropological traditions. When I was a graduate student, Jochelson, a refugee from the new Russia, was writing the last of his volumes on the Koryak (148) in the tower of the American Museum of Natural History, and an Ansa African student from the Gold Coast (187) was giving us lessons on how Africans viewed their own kinship systems. During these early years, a Nez Perce American Indian left Columbia to be welcomed in the Soviet Union as a member of a persecuted minority, and Boas and Manuel Gamio were planning joint studies in the United States and Mexico. In the early 1930s Radcliffe-Brown was teaching at the University of Chicago and—to the great disapproval of his American colleagues—was being considered for the directorship of a large international effort. Since World War II, the mix of students, students as informants, and faculty members drawn from all over the world, partly due to political upheavals, partly due to the great number of foreign fellowships available, has increased enormously. Americans teach in Japan, Frenchmen in India, Indians in the United States, Ceylonese in Australia, and the number of anthropologists from the new African, Asian, and Oceanic countries has increased. The vociferous group making political demands for more representation of Third World points of view has almost completely ignored this movement of scholars between countries, which has also included Third World political leaders who have studied anthropology in some Euro-American country. It is true that anthropology was born among the Euro-American metropolitan powers and flourished most vigorously among countries with colonial interests or identifiable minorities within their gates. But it is also true that this very anthropological emphasis has brought with it an insistence upon the comparable capacities for political and social development of all the members of *Homo sapiens,* and so has made a substantial intellectual contribution to the process of political democratization in different parts of the world. The current emphasis upon the symbolic processes found in primitive man (166), while it stems (at least within the French tradition) from Lévy-Bruhl, nevertheless reflects just as much interest in the existence of primary process thinking in modern man and the importance of symbolism and ritual in modern life as it does an emphasis on the more vivid and bizarre elements of the culture of preliterate peoples (28, 49–51, 73, 74, 101, 236, 288, 289). One of the belated effects of criticism of Freud's *Totem and Taboo* (88, 195) has been to establish that primitive man could think in ways as rational as modern man, as Boas maintained, and that primitive children might be more rational than primitive adults, and that civilized adults might display the kind of egocentric thinking of civilized children (190, 278). With this it has been established that it is necessary to rethink our whole overevaluation of rational linear thinking, with its dependence upon script and script-like processes (24, 28, 47, 178, 260). There has also been a new interest in cross-cultural studies of cognition and perception (61, 261, 290) and a return to a study of multimedia contexts.

At the same time, there are ways in which anthropologists have remained almost incredibly ethnocentric. Forty years ago Radcliffe-Brown suggested a system of kinship nomenclature that was not only cross-cultural but also a way in which kinship relationships could be read back as reciprocals (242). (I put this system on my typewriter in 1931.) Yet in 1972 Conrad Arensberg (12) can call for real "scientific models" and still express beautifully generated kinship relations as abbreviations of English terms *fa si da* or *mo br da*. We do little better in archeology, or physical anthropology, and only slightly better in linguistics. It is true that we need an agreed-upon terminology, but it is equally true that we need terminology that is not ethnocentric, favoring members of one linguistic group or world religion over another.

The last 25 years has also been a period of massive individual enterprises. These have included: Murdock's progressive exploitation of the Human Relations Area Files, first in *Social Organization* (218) and later in his *Ethnographic Atlas* (219); Lévi-Strauss' enormous and detailed study of the myths of the world (166); Yehudi Cohen's intensive use of cross-cultural comparisons and systematic attempts to grapple with the complexities of large areas (58–60), combining field work and integration of the literature; the Whitings' continued cross-cultural studies (304); Mandelbaum on India (182); Goldman's *Ancient Polynesian Society* (112); Leach's *Social Systems of Highland Burma* (159); and the Geertz's work on Indonesia and Morocco (97, 99, 102). These activities are comparable to the syntheses of an earlier day in which art, folklore, and material culture were organized within theoretical frameworks for the benefit of other students. They are notable for the way in which the individual integrating intelligence, handling vast amounts of material collected by hand, is still the prevalent style, only slightly helped by IBM cards or computers.

Traditionally, the sciences have advanced with the help of complementary interrelations between theory, instrumentation, and the stimulating or diverting effects of the climate of opinion within which their practitioners were working. There has been an increasing amount of critical and historical work on anthropological theory, such as Stocking's very distinguished work on Boas (273) combined with a series of trivial father-killing attacks (251, 302), reassessments of Malinowski to the point of boredom of all those participating, Marvin Harris's portenteous evaluation of everyone else (130), and the interesting experiment of using biography as a method of assessment of periods and national schools of anthropology in the *International Encyclopedia of the Social Sciences* (201). Encyclopedias have become one of the ways that the anthropological ideas which originated in the West have been incorporated into the thinking of other parts of the world, e.g. the *Educational Encyclopedia* published in Hebrew (77) and the Japanese version of the *Encyclopedia Britannica*. But the Wenner-Gren conference on The Nature and Function of Anthropological Tradition, held in 1968, which attempted to delineate the various national streams in anthropology failed both to draw together a sufficiently representative group and to integrate the results (162).

Biography, in a more personal sense than the theoretical evaluations, has also flourished: *Alfred Kroeber* by Theodora Kroeber (151), *Franz Boas* by Herskovits (135), the new series edited by Charles Wagley on Columbia anthropologists (173, 222), *An Anthropologist at Work, Writings of Ruth Benedict* (192) are examples. Autobiographies of various sorts include (166, 185, 271), *High Valley* (244), *Return to Laughter* (42), *Women in the Field* (111), and *Blackberry Winter* (206). There have also been passionate ethnologies like Jules Henry's *Culture Against Man* (132), and Colin Turnbull's *The Mountain People* (287). The furor over the publication of Malinowski's *Diary* (181) represents a low point in the discipline's degree of sophistication. In the inflamed political atmosphere of the 1960s, Malinowski was attacked because of his private diary, which records his tribulations and miseries as he did his magnificent field work. A Polish word, which he used for the Trobrianders when he was most emphatically fed up with them, was translated as "nigger." The increase in self-evaluation and puzzled, troubled exposure of difficulties in the field has not been accompanied, as it might have been, with greater charity or detachment. Anthropologists have continued to be highly personal, unskilled in separating their own affects from their material, polemic, given to *ad hominen* arguments and, as if they were all members of one giant extended family, personal rather than relevant nit-picking.

The question of whether anthropology should be regarded as a self-sufficient science, and as such be required to generate its own propositions and hypotheses without the use either of concepts or the findings of other human or social sciences, remains a subject of controversy (220). At the Wenner-Gren Conference in 1952, David Mandelbaum demanded that the field of culture and personality should make its own contributions and validate its own premises (280), and this same demand has been made by psychoanalysts, because they objected to the importation of physiological data into the validation of their discoveries, as in the famous study of Benedek & Rubenstein (35) in which the findings of the analysts are juxtaposed and validated by records of endocrinological occurrences. Importations from other sciences, whether social and human or biological, are treated by Arensberg (12) as analogies, and yet what he wished to identify as anthropology is "interaction theory," with a heavy dependence on physiological theory and measurement (55).

The argument has several facets. Should there be more than one science concerned with the behavior of human beings, as individuals, in groups, as carriers of culture? Are we not enormously hindered when sociologists, social psychologists, clinical psychologists, psychiatrists, or ethologists attack the same problems as anthropologists, and develop their own set of terminologies, methods, and literature? Shouldn't we all be branches of one human science, which would include human biology, evolution, history and prehistory, distinguished by our methods rather than by the areas or fields that we study? How can we compensate for the damage done by attempts to synthesize a science of human behavior that relies on secondary sources, as Freud did in *Totem and Taboo* (188, 195), as George Land is doing in *Transformation* (157), or on a smaller scale as Barkun (18) is doing in his study of millenarian movements? As long as each subdiscipline of the human sciences persists in its myopic, academically bounded contemplation of its own navel, we will have over-reliance on secondary sources, because access to all the small self-contained subdisciplines will be impossible for the synthesizer.

In addition to the objections that can be raised equally to any of the discussions within the human sciences, there are special conditions in anthropology which complicate the matter even further. One of these is the circumstance that we are dealing with vanishing materials; primitive cultures are swallowed up, remote, isolated human populations interbreed, rare languages vanish when the last two old women who speak them die, archeological remains are destroyed by road-building and dam construction. The data can never be re-collected in the light of later paradigms. Thomas Kuhn's illuminating discussion of the way paradigms are finally replaced in the natural sciences (153) simply does not apply to any branch of anthropology, and only to a limited degree to some of the other human sciences. True, a Bavelas experiment may be repeated on a later group of MIT students (30) or Bell Telephone employees, but won't the difference in period contaminate the experiment, as the later subjects have been reared in a different social milieu, eaten different food, breathed different air? The explicit demand of the natural sciences that an experiment be replicable is simply impossible in anthropology. The nearest approach we can make to it is to preserve observations in as complete a form as possible. Sound-synch film today is the closest we can come to the preservation of a complex event which will be subject to later analysis in the light of new hypotheses. With a 360° sound-synch camera we will come even closer. But replicability we cannot produce. The anthropologist must take earlier data into account; he cannot simply wipe the slate clean and begin all over again as the physical scientist can, and he must therefore continue to use the kind of tools and understandings that will enable him to work with data collected under very different conditions in the past (16).

Furthermore, anthropology shares with other field sciences, with ethology and geology, an extraordinary degree of interpenetration between particular sets of data and theory. Anthropology continues to have such special and peculiar characteristics which on the one hand provide the cement that holds us together as a discipline and on the other hand limit and define our work by the conditions under which it is done. In the laboratory sciences, one laboratory is very like another, better or worse equipped and endowed, but nevertheless laboratory scientists in Japan, Africa, Germany, and the Americas are linked by common methodologies, and scientists can move easily from one country to another. But in the field sciences, the actual conditions of work, bound in as they are with the geography, cultural areal style, politics, logistics, and state of equipment, are so intimately related to the discipline that while the processes of dealing with them provides a basic bond of sympathy between ethnologists a world apart in theory and national origin, they also preserve the extraordinarily idiosyncratic, apprentice style of the discipline.

But this close relationship between the nature of a particular area and the temperament, capabilities, and theoretical orientation of individual field workers has certain other consequences. As anthropology has expanded, the literature has proliferated to such an extent that it is almost impossible to keep up with publications in one's own area, so that an area of specialization shrinks accordingly from the Pacific, to Melanesia, to the Solomon Islands, for example; from New Guinea, to the Highlands, to a part of the Highlands; from Mesoamerica to Mexico; from South America to jungle dwellers only. We do not, on the whole, relinquish our close relationship to our own field materials, and most theoretical work that matters is tightly bound, although sometimes rather remotely, as in the case of Lévi-Strauss, or Radcliffe-Brown in his later years, to the individual's own field work. But the sense of scope which it was possible for Boas, or Kroeber, or Lowie, or Haddon to have is becoming lost under the torrent of publications, many of them unpredictably trivial or unidentifiably magnificent. It is not, I believe, the kind of loss that we anticipated a generation ago, when the 1952 Wenner-Gren conference (150) was designed to hold together the diverging classical fields of archeology, linguistics, ethnology, and physical anthropology. Instead of a split into these larger fields, as we feared, there has been a kind of fragmentation, by areas, by schools, by instruments used, by approaches preferred, by style of work, into subfields which are as complex as whole cultures seen in their complete ecological settings. This fragmentation may perhaps reflect the greater sense of holistic imperatives just as much as it does the sort of narrowing of approaches that one finds in biology—the development of embryology, the merging effect found in biochemistry, or the development of experimental ethology.

There has been an increased but still rather limited response to general systems theory, as variously reflected in the work of Bateson (24), Vayda (293), Rappaport (243), Adams (3), and an interest in the use of computers, programming, matrices, etc (105). But the interaction between general systems theory [as represented, for example, by the theoretical work of Von Bertalanffy (33, 39)] has been compromised, partly by the state of field data, extraordinarily incomparable as it inevitably is, as well as historical anthropological methods of dealing with wholes. General systems theory has taken its impetus from the excitement of discovering larger and larger contexts (163), on the one hand, and a kind of microprobing into fine detail within a system, on the other (41, 258). Both of these activities are intrinsic to anthropology to the extent that field work in living societies has been the basic disciplinary method. It is no revelation to any field-experienced anthropologist that everything is related to everything else, or that whether the entire sociocultural setting can be studied in detail or not, it has to be known in general outline. General systems theory, in a sense, is no news at all, as Von Foerster found out when he attempted to organize a conference of general systems people and anthropologists (162). In a sense, the situation is comparable to that found by the Committee for the Study of Mankind, in which a committee that included Robert Redfield tried to get each discipline to consider its relationship to the concept of Mankind. Anthropologists replied, "we are related already," and so they were. Something similar may be said of attempts to date in mathematical anthropology (107, 149). The kind of information that a computer program can finally provide, on a level of a particular culture, is simply a reflection of how detailed field work has been done, and to the careful field worker, on kinship, for example, it provides no illumination. This is, however, in strong contrast to the uses to which computer programming can be put, as in the work of Alan Lomax (174, 175), where it has been possible to map world styles in song and dance, combining Murdock's technologically defined areas (219) with analysis of films, records, and tapes made by many field workers in many parts of the world.

Without the kind of unification that might be provided by a recourse to some sort of agreed-upon complex mathematical analysis, which would include information retrieval, prediction, and genuine standardization of data collection, the discipline fragments in the way in which Bali, for example, has been studied. Anthropologists have taken samples of one village in detail and studied trance in selected spots. Orchestral music has been recorded and defined for the whole island. Temple ceremonial has been studied at different levels of complexity, and there have been restudies of specific spots. The construction of one ceremonial object found in many ceremonies has been detailed, photographic records of various aspects of the culture have been made, along with cinematographic studies of artistic behavior, etc. Such methods of unsystematically interrelated probes, some taxonomic, some following older categories of analysis, some searching for large chunks of unanalyzed materials, relate each field worker to a different network of interdisciplinary fellow scholars and scientists. One has only to mention the names of Bateson & Mead (25, 26), Kunst (154), Jane Belo (33, 34), Colin McPhee (179), H. J. Franken (86), C. Holt (142), C. and H. Geertz (96, 100, 103), to illustrate this.

So we have had such incomparable, cross-cutting developments as the Society for the Study of Oceania and the Society for Visual Anthropology, Urban Anthropology, and Structural Anthropology. There are those who have developed *festschrifts* for Boas, Herskovits, Radin, Bateson, and the group in applied anthropology who worked on interaction theory (12). And there are those archeologists who combine archeology and ethnology; those who combine primatology and the study of hunters and gatherers; anthropologists who are using video tape; those who are interested in the study of child development, or millenary movements, or ethnohistory, or blood types, ethnoscience, latent structures, and somatotyping. Any given anthropologist of any experience today will be found to have his interests anchored and flourishing in half a dozen fields. So, for example, the late Oscar Lewis was interested in: Mexico (163, 169, 170), Puerto Rico (171), and Cuba; restudies (168), poverty (172), urbanism; the use of tape, multiple familial interviewing, collection, transcription, translation, and integration by one field worker (169), integration of interviews collected and transcribed by many field workers (171); relationship of recorded ethnographic materials and those whose lives are recorded; photography, projective tests, child-rearing, and effects of social revolution. Journals read and articles written span such a variety of fields that it is not surprising that when I asked 80 colleagues, variously selected from many areas and lines of association, to name the five most important books of the last 5 years, only four books were mentioned more than twice. Each respondent revealed his deep involvement in one or more sets of overlapping fields. The interpretation that one informant placed on it, that nothing of very much importance has really happened in the last 5 years, is simply inaccurate. A great deal has happened, but no consensus can be reached, because of the extraordinary diversity within the subject.

This diversity is somewhat paralleled by the increasingly rapid oscillation between the search for universals and the emphasis on diversity. Kluckhohn signaled the search for universals, and the whole series of value studies, eagerly grasped at by other disciplines, represents attempts to find cross-cultural units of analysis which lose the depth of the cultures from which they come. The earlier period of *etic* research, in which etic or cross-culturally viable units that disregarded the specific cultural unities of the cultures within which they were found, has given place to a much more sophisticated use of comparisons. We contrast, for example, the earlier correlation studies from the Human Relations Area Files, their criticism by Norbeck (228), and Mead & Newton (215), and Cohen (58), the substitution of very detailed studies of clusters of cultures, Vizedom (295), and Textor's type of "more" or "less" associations (281). This trend is beautifully summed up in Levi-Strauss' Gildersleeve Lecture (167) in 1972, in which he says:

> Should we insist on sticking to the "etic"/"emic" distinction, this can only be done by reversing the acceptances currently given to those terms. It is the "etic" level, too long taken for granted by mechanistic materialism and sensualist philosophy, which we should consider as an artefact. On the contrary, the "emic" level is the one where the material operation of the senses and the more intellectual activities of the mind can meet, and altogether match with the inner nature of reality itself. Structural arrangements are not a mere product of mental operations; the sense organs also function structurally, and outside us, there are structures in atoms, molecules, cells, and organisms. . . . . When the mind processes the empirical data which it receives previously processed by the sense organs, it goes on working out structurally what at the outset was already structural. And it can only do so inasmuch as the mind, the body to which the mind belongs, and the things which body and mind perceive, are part and parcel of one and the same reality.

At the same time, anthropological interest in diversity has been given a boost by the worldwide responses to such homogenizing trends as the green revolution, which sums up both tendencies. At the same time that there is a drawing together of a huge genetic pool of human experiments in the domestication of a particular grain and the development of synthetic types appropriate for the assumed average growing conditions, there is the rediscovery of the dangers of monocrops and a return to the previous uses of diversity in the horticulture of such areas of poor soil as East Africa (46) and the ecologically varied slopes of the mountainsides of Peru or Guatemala. This renewed enthusiasm for diversity—which is after all our particular concern and heritage—was demonstrated by the symposium held at Brown in the spring of 1971 (240).

Today there is a growing movement towards ecological synthesis and systematization of world materials (8, 284). This is evidenced by the considerations of the planetary environment, the simulations of the Club of Rome (217), the search for an Index for the Quality of Life, the development of a Law of the Seas, the search for appropriate regulation and provision of cross-culturally usable soft-ware in the satellite program, the design of new towns and regions, the development of new energy sources, the invention of new life styles, the revision of education to fit a world of rapid cultural change, and the extreme divergence that exists at present between the experience of the generation in power and the young people under 30 (204).

The more that anthropologists respond to these movements, the more they are almost inevitably forced into narrower specializations, as they try to keep up with the specialized vocabulary of the area of worldwide problems with which they are dealing, the places within anthropological literature where the particular area is being tackled, and those anthropologists—who may be at the moment anywhere in the world—who are concentrating on one aspect of the whole. Who would have expected one of the most brilliant pieces of research relevant to planetary political organization to be developed by a field worker in the Congo (307) and published initially in an African newsletter, or that we would be able to tie it in easily with

Morton Fried's paper at the NYAS on tribalism (89) and Adams' discussion (3) of Central American national political structures? Would we have expected that in the field of urbanization it would be difficult for a student of social integration in the city, who follows work at the Athens Ekistical Institute with graduate work in Sydney, to be at once conversant with legislative proposals for utility corridors and attempts to think about the present status of unemployed youth; or that in the field of child development, it is equally difficult to integrate Lawrence Malcolm's studies of protein deficiencies in New Guinea (180) to the Society for Social Anthropology's gingerly approach to problems of childhood by way of studies of socialization (186)?

There is another set of these clusters which centers about the use of specific instruments, either psychological or technical, and still another of those who are interested in particular theoretical approaches. One of the great advances of recent decades has come in the whole field of semiotics, ushered in by the conference at Indiana University (260). We now have the well-developed fields of Kinesics (41), Proxemics (126–128), Choreometrics and Cantometrics (174), and Paralinguistics (260), all dependent upon a fine scale analysis based on film and tape, and more recently on video tape. These specialities overlap with the interaction studies of Arensberg (12), Bateson (23, 26), Oliver (231), and the interaction chronograph of Eliot Chapple (55), which in turn overlap with cybernetically oriented field studies like Rappaport's (243), studies in Psychiatry (24) and Primatology (71), and studies of conference techniques and reporting (203, 208).

Other groups are formed around the use of psychological instruments, a sophisticated use of Human Relations Area Files (172, 219, 224, 281), the Whitings' continued studies of judgments of selected anecdotes (156, 304), use of questionnaires on mother-child behavior (5), Rorschachs, Raven Matrices, Mosaics, etc. Each user has to have at least a working knowledge of what is being done by others using the same instruments, and these uses are likely to cross every other subdivision, geographical or subdisciplinary.

Another consequence of the proliferation of data is that each theorist became so tied in with the particular field experience within which his theoretical stance became clarified for him—but not for others—that there has developed a complementary tendency to ignore other people's work and start from scratch. It is perhaps not accidental that in *The Nature of Cultural Things* (129), Marvin Harris only uses the work of a social psychologist, Roger Barker (17), who himself insisted on starting from scratch, ignoring all previous work that had been done in the same field. So we have insights, some of them developed decades ago, which prove periodically illuminating to a new generation, such as Bateson's *Naven* (23) or Chapple's *Interaction* chronograph (12). And finally we have books about books about books, like Murphy's *The Dialectics of Social Life* (221), and those by Barnes (19) and Jarvie (147). However, one distinctive feature of the present day set of attack and counterattack is the willingness to discuss, analyze, dissect, propound, and expound the findings of Lévi-Strauss during the course of his work, where in previous periods, except for book reviews, very little of this was done until a master was dead (160).

It is not surprising that there has been such a proliferation of field manuals and field work reports, and quasi-autobiographical discussion of field problems, such as *In the Company of Man* (48), *Crossing Cultural Boundaries* (298), Hilger's story of an Araucanian (138), Golde's *Women in the Field* (111), Williams' *Field Methods in the Study of Culture (305)*, Freilich's *Marginal Natives* (87), and including the mammoth and outrageously delayed handbook by Naroll & Cohen (225). But the writers of most of these manuals have to rely on methods that are not very much of an improvement over those of the 1920s and 1930s. They expose a student to intimate and detailed accounts of the troubles and struggles that other anthropologists have had, just as we expose a student to exercises in a variety of languages and accounts of a variety of kinship systems, with the hope that somehow they will be able to incorporate a sense of how to do their field work with different equipment and under quite different conditions. The traditional tendency to avoid teaching concrete methods of field research has been exacerbated by the extremely rapid changes in technology of taping, filming, photographing, preserving, developing, viewing, retrieving, and preparing materials for suitable forms of publication and exposition. When to this is added the complexity of preparing for a field trip, in terms of selecting and testing equipment, and the length of time it takes to process grant applications, it is perhaps not surprising that efforts to do any systematic teaching in the use of both kinds of instruments break down. But when we add to this a lack of training, and the requirement that predoctoral students elect a narrow problem that often precludes their making the absolutely essential study of the culture first, it is not surprising that a great deal of incomplete work has come out of the areas which have been popular for predoctoral study. It is even possible that the present financial stringency may keep a certain number of graduate students at home, doing book theses and learning how to organize materials before they plunge prematurely into an area which they may only learn to dislike.

There have been curious discrepancies in the application of anthropology also. Ecology became fashionable over a decade ago, and a whole school has grown around the meticulous reporting of terrain, crop, land ownership, ethnobotanical knowledge, soil fertility, and relative shares of food allotted to families of men of different rank. One might have expected that as the environmental crisis deepened there would be contributions from the field of anthropological ecology. Equally, it might have been expected that a field so deeply concerned with the study of kinship and related problems might have contributed to the whole question of population control. In fact, there are only a handful of workers in either field.

It also might have been expected that those who had clamored most loudly for a scientific and objective approach would have eagerly availed themselves of the new exactness of recording provided by film and tape (1, 2, 14, 16, 26, 94, 189). Actually, it was not until video tape appeared that this kind of instrumentation received much approval, and this, I believe, is because video tape will permit the anthropologist to join the sociologist and social psychologist in distancing himself from his data. Someone else, several someone elses, can code the hours and hours of video tape, and the traditional close tie between observation and recording is broken. Those who demand that anthropology be objective and scientific for the most part have been uninterested in improving upon the pencil as a recorder of anecdotes, subsequently given a rank order by three trained observers. So, in spite of the very greatly increased number of anthropologists, both the funds and the personnel needed to make records of existing primitive peoples are missing, and those who emphasize the use of film are likely to be told they aren't doing real anthropology.

The post-World War II period has been characterized by two kinds of turning towards high cultures: intensive work in countries like India and Japan; and attention to subgroups within our own society, such as transvestites, drug addicts, those living in communes, and ethnic minorities. However, work on the white majority is still somewhat suspect; the demand that anthropology should be comparative seems often to be translated into the demand that there must be something strange and other worldly about the people whom the anthropologist studies. This provision was originally not only a way of fulfilling our responsibility to record vanishing cultures, but was also believed by Boas to be a way of attaining a limited degree of objectivity. Boas did not believe that objectivity was possible or even desirable within one's own culture, where the responsible anthropologist, like any responsible citizen, had to take sides on matters of social justice. He believed it was possible to learn that a member of another culture, far away physically and in technological level, might smack his lips aloud as a sign that he had eaten well, and that this was good manners, and still be critical of the manners of ill-bred persons in our midst. But we would, he used to tell his students, be a little more tolerant as we came to understand that manners were learned cultural behavior and not matters of absolute right and wrong.

However, this achievement of a scientific objectivity, and even the achievement of the ethically desirable stance of tolerance, looks very different today from the way it did 50 years ago. Those who are studied, whether they be members of other races, other ethnic groups, the poor, the oppressed, the imprisoned, feel that to use their lives to obtain a kind of objectivity is to treat them as objects, not as subjects (65, 292). And all over the world the previously dispossessed and ignored are actively demanding an identity which the rest of mankind must respect. For many anthropologists, the recognition of these new demands has coincided with new situations which they welcomed, such as the greater ability of previously nonliterate people to participate in research, to write about their own cultures (20), to become ethnologists themselves, and to engage in a mutual interchange, instead of an exchange in which one side was at least partially ignorant of the motivations of the other (234). But such recognition has not by any means been universal; in many divisions of the human sciences, human beings are spoken of as digits, as middle-aged white ethnic males, or black unemployed females; nameless, faceless, they appear as statistics, or as individuals described in terms that the reporter has taken no pains to make bearable. The protests of English-speaking "objects of study" became merged with various forms of political protest and partisanship for the oppressed (291). The possessive "my people" or "my village" appears arrogant where once it appeared affectionate and personal. In fact, the application of anthropological methods to our own society, especially when they are applied to groups other than our own, contaminates the study of other peoples, who become, not the primitive peoples whom we fully respected as representatives of whole cultures, but instead members of disadvantaged groups contending for a place in the sun (291, 292). And the anthropologist, who has developed the idea of culture, in the name of which they are pleading their case, is simultaneously attacked for having somehow been responsible for their primitive state, which they now wish to redefine or repudiate (64). When this is combined with the identification of applied anthropology in fields like technical assistance or community development, as colonial, neocolonial, or imperialistic maneuvers, the whole ethic of research and applied research becomes ambiguous (123, 124).

Another of the current ambiguities in anthropology is the question of the new feminism. Anthropology has traditionally been very receptive to the participation of women. In England, in France, in the United States, and more recently in Japan, women students have been given opportunities to do research, in spite of the objections of introducing women into parts of the world where there are many physical dangers. Yet today there is a lively movement among young women anthropologists against their own departments, against the paucity of data on the primitive societies that have been studied on matters of interest to women: pregnancy, childbirth, women's health, the menopause, etc. There is also a movement against theories of the early division of labor between men and women, which they assert neglect the contributions that prehistoric women made to the development of culture. Too often none of these claims and accusations are analyzed with the degree of cultural sophistication which anthropology should provide. Scarcity of data on women in primitive cultures is due primarily to the fact that most women anthropologists were more interested in doing the same kind of work that men did, rather than studying women and children. Early theories of the consequences of the division of labor, which assigned disproportionate roles to man the hunter, had to wait for correction until studies made on hunters and gatherers provided data on the relative contributions of each sex to subsistence, now estimated at something like 80 percent produced by women. (There is, it is true, one major discovery which had to have been made by women, and that is the discovery of the role of paternity; only women were in a position to make it.) But the revival of discredited speculations about previous matriarchies does no credit to historical perspective and threatens to cloud discussions which should proceed on a different level. University establishments do discriminate against women in all departments. We have been short of data on the female contribution to food supply, and we know far less than we would like to about many aspects of women's lives in primitive societies. "Male" speculations about matriarchies may make attractive daydreams, just as the widely spread myth of the island of women—a male nightmare fear that women could get along without them —is at present being turned into a feminine daydream by some feminist extremists. But as in the question of race, it is a great mistake to let contemporary partisan politics distort a disciplined look at the facts as we now know them.

I wish to return again to the subject of applied anthropology. Applied anthropology involves working with interdisciplinary teams and administrators and politicians. This field, so highly and promisingly developed during and immediately after World War II, has languished during the last two decades (214). A number of conditions have contributed to this decline: loss of interest in psychoanalysis—

which mediated between the field of mental health and anthropology (66, 68, 193, 267, 268); disillusionment with government where many such projects originated; easily found, well-paying jobs in academia and the realization that anthropology is becoming an academic-based discipline with rather rigid hierarchical relationships, from the prestigious universities, through a series of lower echelons, all academic, and the awareness that the ambitious young anthropologist is likely to be penalized for working outside these frozen hierarchies. Anthropology was a vocation until World War II; when it became a field that men and women entered instead with high sensitivity to their career hopes and problems and posts which would fulfill their professional ambitions, something was lost. It may be that the contrast between the relations of pre-World War II field workers and the people they studied or attempted to help in a variety of ways, and the postwar inflation of the field by those who thought of it as just one way of making a living, may also be somewhat responsible for some of the extravagant political accusations of the last decade.

Anthropology, like all the social sciences, has been subjected to intentional politicizing, by the demands of minorities, including students and women, by a questioning about the relationship of scientific work to the state of the world, the inequities of the establishment, the hope of revolution, the mysticism about the people themselves. For anthropology, the intense polarization about these issues has been intensified by a number of special problems: (a) almost all of our field work has been done on the cultures of those who are now subsumed under the term Third World; (b) almost all of our field work involves complicated relationships with some form of officialdom—foreign offices, district officers, Indian agents, or customs officers—and we are also likely to encounter movements and activities which are illegal, from methods of burying the dead, the illegal cultivation of opium, and militant nativistic cults, to politicized rebellions and conspiracies. Furthermore, we have been the discipline concerned with race, with the comparable abilities of all members of the human species, with records of past glory or past primitiveness, with problems of language—dialects, developments of national languages, new orthographies. In a world that is teeming with the rising expectations of minorities, with new nations, and revolutionized or modernized old nations, almost every anthropologist stands somewhere in a crossfire position, knowing too much about the renascence of old customs, or providing information that may be used by some agency of modernization, suppression, or militarization, etc.

The original response to anthropologists participating in national activities during World War II culminated in the code of ethics developed by the Society for Applied Anthropology in 1953 (209), with its insistence on anthropologists taking responsibility for all foreseeable effects. Since then, there have been a succession of crises. There were objections to participation in secret research which was to be guarded against by open publication as represented in the Beals report (31). This was followed by the seemingly contradictory demand that information be hidden from government agencies that might misuse it, which resulted in the Thailand investigation in 1971 (10a, 10b, 11a, 11b) and the recognition that anthropologists not only had to protect their informants and the cultures they studied, but also identifiable communities which might become targets. They are also called upon to become more active protectors of threatened minority primitive peoples around the world, such as the aboriginal peoples in the Amazon valley who are being threatened at present.

The question of the participation by a people in studies of their culture has been raised in many ways: in demands that the Indians receive a percentage of research grants, on the grounds that someone, anthropologist or society, was exploiting them for gain; the assertion that only an ethnic group was equipped to study itself; and proposals, notably by Alan Lomax, that the material collected by anthropologists —especially on music and dance and folklore—be fed back to the people themselves as an element in their cultural renewal. These demands parallel the discussions in medicine which ranged through a suggestion of giving experimental subjects the status of coinvestigator in a relationship of collegiality (123), to a recognition that the aims of the investigator and experimental subject might be so different that only organization on the part of the proposed subjects would meet the situation. The classical position of trust and cooperation between an anthropologist and his informants, no matter how disparate their education, in which both were devoted to recording a vanishing culture and assuring the safety of its artifacts, has now been replaced by a relationship in which the anthropologist must sometimes either espouse the cause of some ethnic group within a revolutionary formula, or be forced to acknowledge that there are no longer such shared values.

It has been a period of minimal detachment and capacity for cultural self-consciousness and loyalty. We could pride ourselves that no anthropologist denounced a fellow anthropologist in the various anticommunist witch hunts of the late 1930s and early 1950s. But the 1960s have involved us in a mass of denunciations and counter-denunciations, in the failure of seniors to recognize the implications of the generation gap, or in a refusal to consider any discussions whatsoever of racial differences, some of which, like the campaign against Carleton Coon's book (62) and the extreme views expressed in the symposium on Science and Race (210), do us little credit.

Intellectual ferment has taken as many and as diverse forms as the formation of clusters of co-workers and recognition of subgoals. Evolution, formerly a battle cry which assumed lines drawn up on both sides, has become a respectable central object of discussion (6, 196, 230, 264, 303), illuminated by studies of the behavior of primates in the wild (115) and attempts at teaching chimpanzees to communicate (238), studies of the brain (43, 239, 241, 300), and by the claims of the various types of structuralists for a basic brain-based grammar (56, 164) and dialectics of opposites (166). While the study of evolution has been enriched by the new kinds of archeology—which united thousands of years of selective adjustment to the same terrain, or by the combinations of studies of living hunters and gatherers and associated primates and ungulates—it has also been given extra urgency by considerations of the present technological crisis. A serious consideration of man-made crises and the need for a middle technology has revived interest in material culture, for example, and the role of museums, and attempts to understand earlier artifacts by making them. It also brings into focus the role of conscious purpose in our increasingly man-made, interdependent world (28).

Ethology has seriously entered into the theoretical considerations of anthropologists only during the last two decades (255), and comparative studies of man and other creatures, the arguments over aggression and war (91, 119, 176, 203, 264) and a reconsideration of the degree of patterning of instinctive behavior have proceeded in parallel with discussions of the structure of the brain and its products (248). Here again, political ideology has clouded the issue and the clarity of the arguments; new findings (235) call for drastic revisions in over-elaborate schemata of human development. The specter of behavior modification, of the loss of autonomy and freedom, not only haunts any discussion of biological engineering, but also hinders investigation into the functioning of the brain, the effects of psychedelic drugs, and the interpretation of insights provided by natural and laboratory experiments with animals (165). There seems little doubt that cross-disciplinary research in the wild, taking in wider and wider considerations of the total environment (78, 238), is a more promising field for anthropological cooperation with other sciences than patching together results of isolated laboratory procedures. The very circumstance that recent studies of the brain involve the whole brain (300) reinforces the traditional anthropological preference for the study of whole cultures and whole societies, with the integrative capacity of our major scientific resource, single human minds (197).

The peculiar history of anthropological field work has introduced a new dimension into the discipline, as field workers have been able to make restudies of earlier work, especially their own. The limitations of purely synchronic records of a people at a given moment in time, and subjects who had the same speed of movement and life-span as the investigator, has been mitigated by the rapidity of culture change. When people studied at 20 or 30-year intervals are changing within a world scene where everything else is changing as well, new opportunities for research have been automatically introduced, as new tools, new concepts, and new conditions enable the field worker to study quite new problems. Boas inaugurated this kind of thing when he took recording and film equipment to the Kwakiutl when he was in his sixties (192), and since then we have had a long series of restudies: by Oscar Lewis (170), Redfield (246, 247), Firth (81), Mead (199), to mention only a few. The possibility of studying fully identified groups over a long period has enormously increased the capacity of anthropology to include individual differences and continuities of personality within statements of cultural regularities. This in turn has made it possible to distinguish levels of analysis more sharply. Taking Lévi-Strauss' categories into the field may illuminate field research, but importing far more detailed studies of myth-making or myth-telling into Lévi-Strauss' work would only be disruptive.

Anthropology is entering a new era, the flesh pots are emptier, the difficulties of doing field work increase geometrically as the equipment grows more elaborate and the political situation in many parts of the world becomes more unsettled. In such meager times as these, anthropology can take several directions: an increased interest in professional careers that involve professional competence in related fields, like town planning, health, nutrition, and political organization; an intensive reexamination of existing materials (where Lévi-Strauss has erected such a challenging theoretical structure); concentration on audio-visual recordings in an attempt to obtain the new kind of records of still living cultures with film and tape (14, 16, 94, 95); a renewed dedication to the preservation of cultural diversity; and a greater involvement in an increasingly endangered planet. The problem remains of how to keep so many extraordinarily diverse and discrepant foci of interest and competence in active interrelationship. The very peculiarity of the task may be what will make it possible.

Literature Cited[1]

1. Adair, J., Worth, S. 1967. The Navajo as filmmaker: A brief report of research in the cross-cultural aspects of film communication. *Am. Anthropol.* 69: 76–78

2. Adair, P., Boyd, B. 1967. *Holy Ghost People.* 16 mm black & white film, sound (60 min). New York: McGraw-Hill

3. Adams, R. N. 1970. *Crucifixion by Power: Essays on Guatemalan National Social Structure, 1944–1966.* Austin: Univ. Texas Press

4. Adams, R. N., Preiss, J. J., Eds. 1960. *Human Organization Research.* Homewood: Dorsey

5. Ainsworth, M. D. 1967. *Infancy in Uganda.* Baltimore: Johns Hopkins Univ. Press

6. Alland, A. 1967. *Evolution and Human Behavior.* New York: Natural History Press

7. Alland, A. 1971. *Human Diversity.* New York: Columbia Univ. Press

8.* Albertson, P., Barnett, M., Eds. 1971. *Environment and Society in Transition.* NY Acad. Sci.

9.* Albisetti, C., Venturelli, A. J. 1968–1969. *Enciclopedia Bororo.* Compo Grande, Mato Grosso, Brasil: Museu Regional Dom Bosco (first volume publ. 1962)

10a. Am. Anthropol. Assoc., M. Mead, chairman, 1971. Charge to the ad hoc committee to evaluate the controversy concerning anthropological activities in relation to Thailand. *Newsletter Am. Anthropol. Assoc.* 12, No. 3

10b. Am. Anthropol. Assoc. 1971. Report of the ad hoc committee to evaluate the controversy concerning anthropological activities in relation to Thailand, Sept. 27, 1971. Part I: Anthropological

Activities in Thailand; Part II: Guidelines on Future Policy

11a. Am. Antrhopol. Assoc. 1972. Council rejects Thai controversy committee's report. *Newsletter Am. Anthropol. Assoc.* 13, No.1:1,9

11b. Am. Anthropol. Assoc., M. Mead, 1972. Thailand controversy response to the board's response to the discussion. *Newsletter Am. Anthropol. Assoc.* 13, No.2:1,6

12. Arensberg, C. M. 1972. Culture as behavior: Structure and emergence. *Ann. Rev. Anthropol.* 1:1–26

13. Arensberg, C. M., Niehoff, A. H. 1964. *Introducing Social Change: A Manual for Americans Overseas.* Chicago: Aldine

14. Asch, T., Chagnon, N., Neel, J. V. 1971. *Yanomama.* 16 mm color film, sound (43 min). Center for Documentary Anthropology, Brandeis Univ.

15.* Balandier, G. 1971. *Political Anthropology.* New York: Pantheon

16. Balikci, A. 1969. *Netsilik Eskimos of the Pelly Bay Region of Canada.* 9 films, 16 mm color, sound (approx. 30 min each). New York: Universal Education and Visual Arts

17. Barker, R. G., Wright, H. F. 1971. *Midwest and Its Children.* Hamden: Shoe String Press (first publ. 1954)

18. Barkun, M. *Disaster and the Millenium.* To be published

19.* Barnes, J. A. 1971. *Three Styles—The Study of Kinship.* Berkeley: Univ. California Press

20.* Barnett, D. L., Mjama, K. 1966. *Mau Mau from Within.* New York: Monthly Review Press

21.* Barth, F., Ed. 1969. *Ethnic Groups and Boundaries.* Boston: Little, Brown

[1]The following kinds of references are included: (*a*) literature cited in text; (*b*) publications which were suggested by one or more of the author's colleagues (starred); (*c*) books the author considers especially interesting; (*d*) references to the author's own work, particularly articles which have extensive bibliographies.

22. Bateson, G. 1956. The message "this is play." In *Group Processes,* ed. B. Schaffner, 2:145–242. New York: Macy Found.
23. Bateson, G. 1958. *Naven.* Stanford Univ. Press. 2nd ed.
24. Bateson, G. 1972. *Steps to an Ecology of Mind.* San Francisco: Chandler
25. Bateson, G., Mead, M. 1962. *Balinese Character: A Photographic Analysis.* N.Y. Acad. Sci. (first publ. 1942)
26. Bateson, B., Mead, M. 1952. *Character Formation in Different Cultures* series. 6 films, 16 mm, black & white, sound. New York Univ. Film Library
    a. *A Balinese Family* (17 min)
    b. *Bathing Babies in Three Cultures* (9 min)
    c. *Childhood Rivalry in Bali and New Guinea* (20 min)
    d. *First Days in the Life of a New Guinea Baby* (19 min)
    e. *Karba's First Years* (20 min)
    f. *Trance and Dance in Bali* (20 min)
27. Bateson, M. C. 1970. *Structural continuity in poetry.* PhD thesis. Harvard Univ., Cambridge
28. Bateson, M. C. 1972. *Our Own Metaphor.* New York: Knopf
29. Bateson, M. C. 1973. Ritualization: A study in texture and texture change. In *Pragmatic Religions,* ed. I. Zaretsky, M. Leone. Princeton Univ. Press
30. Bavelas, A. 1951. Communication patterns in task-oriented groups. In *The Policy Sciences,* ed. H. D. Laswell, D. Lerner, 193–202. Stanford Univ. Press
31. Beals, R. L. 1969. *Politics of Social Research: An Inquiry into the Ethics and Responsibilities of Social Scientists.* Chicago: Aldine-Atherton
32. *Behavioral Science* 1956 to date. Mental Health Res. Inst. Univ. Michigan, Ann Arbor
33. Belo, J. 1960. *Trance in Bali.* New York: Columbia Univ. Press
34. Belo, J. 1970. *Traditional Balinese Culture.* New York: Columbia Univ. Press
35. Benedek, T., Rubenstein, B. 1939. Correlations between ovarian activity and psychodynamic processes: I. The ovulative phase; II. The menstrual phase. *Psychosom. Med.* 1:245 ff., 461 ff.
36.* Bennett, J. W. 1969. *The Northern Plainsmen.* Chicago: Aldine
37.* Berger, P., Luckmann, T. 1966. *Social Construction of Reality.* Garden City: Doubleday
38.* Berlin, B. 1970. A universalist-evolutionary approach in ethnographic semantics. In *Current Directions in Anthropology,* ed. A. Fischer. *Bull. Am. Anthropol. Assoc.* 3:3–18
39. Bertalanffy, L. von 1969. *General System Theory: Essays on Its Foundation and Development.* New York: Braziller
40.* Binford, L. R., Binford, S. R., Eds. 1968. *New Perspectives in Archeology.* Chicago: Aldine-Atherton
41. Birdwhistell, R. L. 1970. *Kinesics and Context.* Philadelphia: Univ. Pennsylvania Press
42. Bowen, E. S. 1964. *Return to Laughter.* Natural History Library 36. Garden City: Doubleday (first publ. 1954)
43. Braud, L. W., Braud, W. G. 1972. Biochemical transfer of relational responding (transposition). *Science* 176:942–44
44. Brown, D. 1971. *Bury My Heart at Wounded Knee.* New York: Holt, Rinehart & Winston
45.* Butzer, K. 1971. *Environment and Archeology.* Chicago: Aldine-Atherton
46. Campbell, J. 1971. *Agricultural development in East Africa: A problem in cultural ecology.* PhD thesis. Columbia Univ., New York
47. Carpenter, E. 1970. *They Became What They Beheld.* New York: Outerbridge & Dienstfrey
48. Casagrande, J. B., Ed. 1960. *In the Company of Man.* New York: Harper
49. Castaneda, C. 1968. *Teaching of Don Juan: Yaki Way of Knowledge.* Berkeley: Univ. California Press
50. Castaneda, C. 1971. *Separate Reality.* New York: Simon & Schuster
51. Castaneda, C. 1972. *Journey to Ixtlan: The Lessons of Don Juan.* New York: Simon & Schuster
52. Caudill, W., Lin, Tsung-Yi, Eds. 1969. *Mental Health Research in Asia and the Pacific.* Honolulu: Univ. Hawaii Press
53. Caudill, W., Weinstein, H. 1969. Maternal care and infant behavior in Japan and America. *Psychiatry* 32:12–43
54. Chagnon, N. A. 1968. *Yanomamo: The Fierce People.* New York: Holt, Rinehart & Winston
55. Chapple, E. D. 1970. *Cultural and Biological Man: Explorations in Behavioral Anthropology.* New York: Holt, Rinehart & Winston
56. Chomsky, N. 1972. *Language and Mind,* enl. ed. New York: Harcourt, Brace, Jovanovich
57.* Clastres, P. 1972. *Chronique des Indiens Guayaki.* Paris: Plon
58. Cohen, Y. A. 1964. *The Transition from Childhood to Adolescence: Cross-*

Cultural Studies of Initiation Ceremonies, Legal Systems, and Incest Taboos. Chicago: Aldine

59. Cohen, Y. A. 1968. *Man in Adaptation: The Cultural Present.* Chicago: Aldine

60. Cohen, Y. A. 1971. *Man in Adaptation: The Institutional Framework.* Chicago: Aldine

61. Cole, M., Gay, J., Glick, J. A., Sharp, D. W. 1971. *The Cultural Contexts of Learning and Thinking: An Exploration of Experimental Anthropolgy.* New York: Basic Books

62. Coon, C. S. 1962. *The Origin of Races.* New York: Knopf

63.*De Laguna, F. 1960. *The Story of a Tlingit Community: A Problem in the Relationship Between Archeological, Ethnological, and Historical Methods.* Washington, D.C.: GPO

64. Deloria, V. Jr. 1969. *Custer Died for Your Sins.* New York: Macmillan

65. Deloria, V. Jr. 1970. *We Talk, You Listen.* New York: Macmillan

66. De Reuck, A. V. S., Porter, R., Eds. 1965. *Transcultural Psychiatry: A Ciba Foundation Symposium.* London: Churchill

67. Deutsch, K. W. 1966. *Nationalism and Social Communication.* Cambridge: MIT. 2nd ed.

68. Devereux, G. 1967. *From Anxiety to Method in the Behavioral Sciences.* The Hague:Mouton

69. Devereux, G. 1968. *Reality and Dream.* New York: Doubleday (first publ. 1951.) 2nd ed.

70. Devereux, G. *Dreams in Greek Tragedy.* Oxford: Blackwell. In press

71. DeVere, I., Ed. 1965. *Primate Behavior.* New York: Holt, Rinehart & Winston

72. Dillon, W. S. 1968. *Gifts and Nations: The Obligation to Give, Receive and Repay.* New York: Humanities Press

73. Douglas, M. 1966. *Purity and Danger.* New York: Praeger

74. Douglas, M. 1970. *Natural Symbols.* New York: Pantheon

75.*Duchet, M. 1971. *Anthropologie et Histoire au Siecle des Lumières: Buffon, Voltaire, Rousseau, Helvetius, Diderot.* Paris: Maspero

76.*Dumont, L. 1970. *Homo Hierarchicus: The Caste System and Its Implications.* Univ. Chicago Press

77. Educational Encyclopedia (Hebrew) 1959–61. Thesaurus of Jewish and general education, ed. M. M. Buber, Vol. 1, 2. Jerusalem: Ministry of Education and Culture, and the Bialik Institute

78. Eisenberg, J. F., Dillon, W. S., Eds. 1971. *Man and Beast: Comparative Social Behavior.* Washington: Smithsonian Inst. Press

79.*Epstein, T. S. 1962. *Economic Development and Social Change in South India.* New York: Humanities Press

80. Erikson, E. H. 1969. *Gandhi's Truth: On the Origins of Militant Nonviolence.* New York: Norton

81. Firth, R. 1967. *Tikopia: Ritual and Belief.* London: Allen & Unwin

82. Firth, R., Ed. 1967. *Themes in Economic Anthropology.* New York: Barnes & Noble

83. Foerster, H. von, Ed. 1950–1956. *Cybernetics.* New York: Macy Found. 5 vols.

84. Fortes, M. 1969. *Kinship and the Social Order.* Chicago: Aldine

85.*Fox, R. 1968. *Kinship and Marriage: An Anthropological Perspective.* New York: Penguin

86. Franken, H. J. et al 1960. *Bali: Studies in Life, Thought and Ritual.* The Hague: van Hoeve

87. Freilich, M., Ed. 1970. *Marginal Natives: Anthropologists at Work.* New York: Harper & Row

88. Freud, S. 1960. *Totem and Taboo.* Transl. A. A. Brill. New York: Random House (first publ. 1918)

89. Fried, M. H. 1966. On the concepts of 'Tribe' and 'Tribal Society.' *Trans. N.Y. Acad. Sci.* 28:527–40

90. Fried, M. H. 1972. *The Study of Anthropology.* New York: Crowell

91. Fried, M., Harris, M., Murphy, R., Eds. 1968. *War: The Anthropology of Armed Conflict and Aggression.* Garden City: Natural History Press

92. Fromm, E., Maccoby, M. 1970. *Social Character in a Mexican Village.* Englewood Cliffs: Prentice Hall

93. Gans, H. J. 1962. *Urban Villagers.* New York: Free Press

94. Gardner, R. 1964. *Dead Birds.* 16 mm color film, sound (83 min). Cambridge: Peabody Museum, Harvard Univ. Distributed by Contemporary Films, New York

95. Gardner, R., Heider, K. G. 1968. *Gardens of War.* New York: Random House

96. Geertz, C. 1959. Form and variation in Balinese village structure. *Am. Anthropol.* 61:991–1012

97. Geertz, C. 1963. *Agricultural Involution: the Process of Ecological Change in Indonesia.* Berkeley: Univ. California Press

98. Geertz, C. 1964. *The Religion of Java.* Glencoe: Free Press (first publ. 1960)
99. Geertz, C. 1968. *Islam Observed: Religious Development in Morocco and Indonesia.* New Haven: Yale Univ. Press
100. Geertz, C. 1972. Deep Play: Notes on the Balinese cockfight. *Daedalus* Winter: 1–37
101. Geertz, C., Ed. 1972. *Myth, Symbol and Culture.* New York: Norton
102. Geertz, H. 1961. *Javanese Family.* Glencoe: Free Press
103. Geertz, H., Geertz, C. 1964. Teknonymy in Bali: Parenthood, age grading and genealogical amnesia. *J. Roy. Anthropol. Inst. Gt. Brit. Ireland* 94: 94–108
104.* Gellner, E. A. 1969. *Saints of the Atlas.* Univ. Chicago Press
105. General Systems Yearbook of the Society for General Systems Research 1956 to date, ed. L. von Bertalanffy, A. Rapoport. Washington: Soc. Gen. Syst. Res.
106. Gilbert, C. 1968. *Margaret Mead's New Guinea Journal.* 16 mm color film, sound (90 min). New York: Nat. Educ. Telev.
107.* Gillespie, J. V., Nesvold, B. Eds. 1970. *Macro-Quantitative Analysis.* Beverly Hills: Sage Publ.
108. Gluckman, M. 1964. *Custom and Conflict in Africa.* New York: Barnes & Noble (first publ. 1955)
109. Gluckman, M., Ed. 1964. *Closed Systems and Open Minds: The Limits of Naivety in Social Anthropology.* Chicago: Aldine
110. Gluckman, M. 1965. *Politics, Law and Ritual in Tribal Society.* Chicago: Aldine
111. Golde, P., Ed. 1970. *Women in the Field.* Chicago: Aldine
112. Goldman, I. 1970. *Ancient Polynesian Society.* Univ. Chicago Press
113. Goldschmidt, W. 1971. *Exploring the Ways of Mankind.* New York: Holt Rinehart & Winston
114. Goldschmidt, W., et al 1965. Variation and adaptability of culture. *Am. Anthropol.* 67:400–47
115. Goodall, J. V. L. 1971. *In the Shadow of Man.* Boston: Houghton Mifflin
116.* Goodenough, W. H. 1970. *Description and Comparison in Cultural Anthropology.* Chicago: Aldine
117. Gorer, G. 1965. *Death, Grief and Mourning.* Garden City: Doubleday
118. Gorer, G. 1966. *The Danger of Equality.* London: Cressett
119. Gorer, G. 1966. Man has no killer instinct. *New York Times Magazine,* Nov. 27:47ff.
120. Gorer, G. 1971. *Sex and Marriage in England Today.* London: Nelson
121. Gould, R. A. 1969. *The Yiwara: Foragers of the Australian Desert.* New York: Scribner
122. Graubard, S. R., Ed. 1965. Science and culture. *Daedalus* Winter issue
123. Graubard, S. R., Ed. 1969. Ethical aspects of experimentation with human subjects. *Daedalus* Spring issue
124. Gwaltney, J. L. 1970. *Thrice Shy: Cultural Accommodations to Blindness and Other Disasters in a Mexican Community.* New York: Columbia Univ. Press
125. Hagen, E. E. 1962. *On the Theory of Social Change.* Homewood: Dorsey
126. Hall, E. T. 1961. *The Silent Language.* New York: Fawcett (first publ. 1959)
127. Hall, E. T. 1963. A system for the notation of proxemic behavior. *Am. Anthropol.* 65:1003–26
128. Hall, E. T. 1966. *The Hidden Dimension.* Garden City: Doubleday
129. Harris, M. 1964. *The Nature of Cultural Things.* New York: Random House
130.* Harris, M. 1968. *The Rise of Anthropological Theory: A History of Theories of Culture.* New York: Crowell
131. Heider, K. G. 1970. *Dugun Dani.* Chicago: Aldine
132. Henry, J. 1963. *Culture Against Man.* New York: Random House
133. Henry, J. 1972. *Pathways to Madness.* New York: Random House
134. Henry, N. B., Ed. 1959. *Community Education.* Nat. Soc. Study Educ. 58th Yearb., part 1. Univ. Chicago Press
135. Herskovits, M. J. 1953. *Franz Boas.* New York: Scribner
136.* Heusch, L. de 1972. *Le Roi Ivre ou L'Origine de L'Etat* (Les Essais CLXXIII). Paris: Gallimard
137. Hilger, M. I. 1954. An ethnographic field method. In *Method and Perspective in Anthropology,* ed. F. Spencer. Minneapolis: Univ. Minnesota Press
138. Hilger, M. I. 1966. *Huenun Namku: an Araucanian Indian of the Andes Remembers the Past.* Norman: Univ. Oklahoma Press
139. Hill, R. B. 1972. *The Strengths of Black Families.* New York: Emerson Hall
140.* Hodgen, M. T. 1964. *Early Anthropology in the Sixteenth and Seventeenth Centuries.* Philadelphia: Univ. Pennsylvania Press

141. Hogbin, I. 1970. *The Island of Menstruating Men.* Scranton: Chandler
142. Holt, C. 1967. *Art in Indonesia.* Ithaca: Cornell Univ. Press
143. Holt, C. 1972. *Culture and Politics in Indonesia.* Cornell Univ. Press
144. Homans, G. C., Schneider, D. M., 1955. *Marriage, Authority, and Final Causes.* Glencoe: Free Press
145.*Horton, R. 1960. A definition of religion and its uses. *J. Roy. Anthropol. Inst. Gt. Brit. Ireland* 90:201–26
146. Ianni, F. A. 1972. *A Family Business: Kinship and Social Control in Organized Crime.* New York: Sage Found.
147.*Jarvie, I. C. 1964. *The Revolution in Anthropology.* New York: Humanities Press
148. Jochelson, W. 1908. *Material Culture and Social Organization of the Koryak.* Mem. Am. Mus. Natur. Hist. 10, part 2. Leiden: Brill
149.*Kay, P., Ed. 1971. *Explorations in Mathematical Anthropology.* Cambridge: MIT Press
150. Kroeber, A. L., Ed. 1953. *Anthropology Today.* Univ. Chicago Press
151. Kroeber, T. 1970. *Alfred Kroeber.* Berkeley: Univ. California Press
152.*Kronenberg, A. 1972. *Logik und Leben.* Wiesbaden: Steiner Verlag
153. Kuhn, T. S. 1968. *The Structure of Scientific Revolution.* Univ. Chicago Press
154. Kunst, J. 1949. *The Cultural Background of Indonesian Music.* Amsterdam: Indish Inst.
155. Kunz, R. M., Fehr, H., Eds. 1972. *The Challenge of Life.* Basel, Stuttgart: Birkhäuser Verlag
156. Lambert, W. M., Minturn, L. 1964. *Mothers of Six Cultures: Antecedence of Child Rearing.* New York, London: Wiley
157. Land, G. *Transformation.* New York: Random House. In press
158. Lawrence, P. 1964. *Road Belong Cargo.* New York: Humanities Press
159. Leach, E. R. 1965. *Political Systems of Highland Burma.* New York: Beacon (first publ. 1954)
160. Leach, E. R. 1970. *Claude Lévi-Strauss.* New York: Viking
161. Lee, R. B., De Vore, I., Eds. 1968. *Man the Hunter.* Chicago: Aldine
162. Leeds, A., von Foerster, H., Eds. 1965. *The Potentiality of Systems Theory for Anthropological Inquiry.* New York: Wenner-Gren Found. Anthropol. Res.
163. Lehman, F. K. 1959. *Some anthropological parameters of a civilization: The ecology and evolution of India's high culture.* PhD thesis. Columbia Univ., New York. 2 vols.
164.*Lenneberg, E. H. 1967. *The Biological Foundations of Language.* New York: Wiley
165. Lévi-Strauss, C. 1961. *Tristes Tropiques: An Anthropological Study of Primitive Societies In Brazil.* New York: Atheneum (first publ. 1961 as *A World on the Wane*)
166. Lévi-Strauss, C. 1964–1971. *Mythologiques.* 4 vols. Paris: Plon.
     Vol.1: *Le Cru et le Cuit*
     Vol.2: *Du Miel aux Cendres*
     Vol.3: *L'Origine des Manières de Table*
     Vol.4: *L'Homme Nu*
167. Lévi-Strauss, C. 1972. Structuralism and ecology. *Barnard Alumnae* Spring issue: 6–14
168. Lewis, O. 1960. *Tepoztlan: Village in Mexico.* New York: Holt, Rinehart & Winston
169. Lewis, O. 1961. *The Children of Sanchez.* New York: Random House
170. Lewis, O. 1963. *Life in a Mexican Village: Tepoztlan Restudied.* Urbana: Univ. Illinois Press (first publ. 1951)
171. Lewis, O. 1966. *La Vida.* New York: Random House
172. Lewis, O. 1966. The culture of poverty. *Sci. Am.* 215:19–25
173. Linton, A., Wagley, C. 1971. *Ralph Linton.* New York: Columbia Univ. Press
174. Lomax, A., Ed. 1968. *Folksong Style and Culture* (Symp. Vol. 88). Washington: Am. Assoc. Advan. Sci.
175. Lomax, A. 1972. The evolutionary taxonomy of culture. *Science* 177:228–39
176. Lorenz, K. 1971. *Studies in Animal and Human Behavior,* vol. 2. Cambridge: Harvard Univ. Press
177. Luszki, M. B. 1958. *Interdisciplinary Team Research: Methods and Problems.* New York: University Press
178. McLuhan, M. 1962. *The Gutenberg Galaxy.* Univ. Toronto Press
179. McPhee, C. 1966. *Music in Bali.* New Haven, London: Yale Univ. Press
180. Malcolm, L. A. 1969. Growth and development of the New Guinea child. *Papua and New Guinea J.* 6:23–32
181. Malinowski, B. 1967. *A Diary in the Strict Sense of the Term.* New York: Harcourt, Brace
182. Mandelbaum, D. G. 1970. *Society in India.* Berkeley: Univ. California Press. 2 vols.
183.*Marshack, A. 1972. *The Roots of Civilization.* New York: McGraw-Hill

184. Marshall, J., Gardner, R. 1958. *The Hunters.* 16 mm color film, sound (72 min). Cambridge: Film Study Center Peabody Mus., Harvard Univ.
185. Maybury-Lewis, D. 1968. *The Savage and the Innocent.* Boston: Beacon Press (first publ. 1965)
186. Mayer, P., Ed. 1970. *Socialization.* Scranton: Barnes & Noble
187. Mead, M. 1937. A Twi relationship system. *J. Roy. Anthropol. Inst. Gt. Brit. Ireland* 67:297–304
188. Mead, M. 1950. The comparative study of cultures and the purposive cultivation of democratic values, 1941–1949. In *Perspectives on a Troubled Decade: Science, Philosophy, and Religion, 1939–1949,* ed. L. Bryson, L. Finkelstein, R. M. McIver, 87–108. New York: Harper & Row
189. Mead, M. 1951. *Soviet Attitudes Toward Authority.* New York: McGraw-Hill
190. Mead, M. 1954. Research on primitive children. In *Manual of Child Psychology,* ed. L. Carmichael, 735–80. New York: Wiley. 2nd ed.
191. Mead, M., Ed. 1955. *Cultural Patterns and Technical Change.* Mentor Books. New York: New Am. Libr. (first publ. 1953)
192. Mead, M. 1959. *An Anthropologist at Work: Writings of Ruth Benedict.* Boston: Houghton Mifflin
193. Mead, M. 1961. Psychiatry and ethnology. In *Psychiatrie der Gegenwart: Forschung und Praxis, III:Soziale und Angewandte Psychiatrie,* ed. H. W. Gruhle et al, 452–70. Berlin: Springer
194. Mead, M. 1963. Anthropology and the camera. In *The Encyclopedia of Photography,* ed. W. D. Morgan, 166–84. New York: Greystone
195. Mead, M. 1963. *Totem and Taboo* reconsidered with respect. *Bull. Menninger Clin.* 27:185–99
196. Mead, M. 1964. *Continuities in Cultural Evolution.* New Haven: Yale Univ. Press
197. Mead, M. 1964. Vicissitudes of the study of the total communication process. In *Approaches to Semiotics,* ed. T. A. Sebeok, A. S. Hayes, M. C. Bateson, 277–87. The Hague: Mouton
198. Mead, M. 1966. *The Changing Culture of an Indian Tribe.* Cap Giant 266, New York: Putnam (first publ. 1932)
199. Mead, M. 1966. *New Lives for Old: Cultural Transformation—Manus 1928–1953,* with new preface. Apollo Editions. New York: Morrow (first publ. 1956)
200. Mead, M. 1968. Cybernetics of cybernetics. In *Purposive Systems: Processes of the First Annual Symposium of the American Society for Cybernetics,* ed. H. von Foerster et al, 1–11. New York, Washington: Spartan Books
201. Mead, M. 1968. Incest. In *International Encyclopedia of the Social Sciences,* ed. D. L. Sills, 7: 115–22. New York: Macmillan. 17 vols.
202. Mead, M. 1969. Crossing boundaries in social science communication. *Soc. Sci. Inform.* 8:7–15
203. Mead, M. 1969. From intuition to analysis in communication research. *Semiotica* 1:13–25
204. Mead, M. 1970. *Culture and Commitment: A Study of the Generation Gap.* Garden City: Natural History Press & Doubleday
205. Mead, M. 1970. *Ethnicity and Anthropology in America.* Wenner-Gren Conf. Ethnic-Identity, Burg Wartenstein Symp. 51. To be published
206. Mead, M. 1972. *Blackberry Winter: My Earlier Years.* New York: Morrow
207. Mead, M. Systems analysis and metacommunication. In *The World System,* ed. E. Laszlo. New York: Braziller. In press
208. Mead, M., Byers, P. 1968. *The Small Conference: An Innovation in Communication.* Paris, The Hague: Mouton
209. Mead, M., Chapple, E. D., Brown, G. G. 1949. Report of the committee on ethics. *Hum. Org.* 8:20–21
210. Mead, M., Dobzhansky, T., Tobach, E., Light, R. E., Eds. 1968. *Science and the Concept of Race.* New York, London: Columbia Univ. Press
211. Mead, M., Heyman, K. 1965. *Family.* New York: Macmillan
212. Mead, M., Macgregor, F. C. 1951. *Growth and Culture: A Photographic Study of Balinese Childhood.* New York: Putnam
213. Mead, M., Metraux, R., Eds. 1953. *The Study of Culture at a Distance.* Univ. Chicago Press
214. Mead, M., Metraux, R. 1965. The anthropology of human conflict. In *The Nature of Human Conflict,* ed. E. B. McNeil, 116–38. Englewood Cliffs: Prentice Hall
215. Mead, M., Newton, N. 1967. Cultural patterning of perinatal behavior. In *Childbearing—Its Social and Psychological Aspects,* ed. S. A. Richardson, A. F. Guttmacher, 142–244. Baltimore: Williams & Wilkins
216. Mead, M., Schwartz, T. 1960. The cult as a condensed social process. In *Group*

Processes: Transactions of the Fifth Conference, October 12–15, 1958, ed. Bertram Schaffner, 85–187. New York: Macy Found.

217. Meadows, D. et al 1972. *The Limits to Growth.* Washington: Potomac Assoc.

218. Murdock, G. P. 1949. *Social Structure.* New York: Macmillan

219. Murdock, G. P. 1967. *Ethnographic Atlas.* Univ. Pittsburgh Press

220. Murdock, G. P. 1972. Anthropology's mythology. *Proc. Roy. Anthropol. Inst. Grt. Brit. Ireland for 1971*, 17–24

221. Murphy, R. F. 1971. *The Dialectics of Social Life: Alarms and Excursions in Anthropological Theory.* New York: Basic Books

222. Murphy, R. F. 1972. *Robert Lowie.* New York: Columbia Univ. Press

223.*Nader, L., Ed. 1969. *Law in Culture and Society.* Chicago: Aldine-Atherton.

224. Naroll, R. 1970. What we have learned from cross-cultural surveys. *Am. Anthropol.* 72:1227–88

225. Naroll, R., Cohen, R., Eds. 1970. *A Handbook of Method in Cultural Anthropology.* Garden City: Natural History Press

226. Norbeck, E. 1970. *Religion and Society in Modern Japan: Continuity and Change.* Houston: Rice Univ.

227. Norbeck, E. 1971. Man at play. *Natur. Hist. Mag.* 80:48–53

228. Norbeck, E., Walker, D. G., Cohen, M. 1962. The interpretation of Data: Puberty rites. *Am. Anthropol.* 64:463–85

229. Norbeck, E. et al, Eds. 1968. *The Study of Personality.* New York: Holt, Rinehart & Winston

230.*Nurge, E., Ed. 1970. *Modern Sioux.* Lincoln: Univ. Nebraska Press

231. Oliver, D. L. 1955. *A Solomon Island Society.* Cambridge: Harvard Univ. Press

232.*Ortiz, A. 1969. *The Tewa World.* Univ. Chicago Press

233.*Otterbein, K. F. 1970. *The Evolution of War: A Cross-Cultural Study.* New Haven: Human Relations Area Files Press

234.*Owusu, M. 1970. *Uses and Abuses of Political Power.* Univ. Chicago Press

235. Payne, M. M. 1973. The Leakey tradition lives on. *Nat. Geogr. Mag.* 143:143–44

236.*Peacock, J. L. 1968. *Rites of Modernization.* Univ. Chicago Press

237.*Pelto, P. J. 1970. *Anthropological Research: The Structure of Inquiry.* New York: Harper & Row

238. Pfeiffer, J. E. 1972. *The Emergence of Man.* New York: Harper & Row (first publ. 1969)

239. Pietsch, P., Schneider, C. W. 1969. Brain transplantation in salamanders: An approach to memory transfer. *Brain Res.* 14:707–15

240. Poggie, J., Lynch, R., Eds. *Modernization: Anthropological Approaches to Contemporary Socio-Cultural Change.* Westport: Greenwood. In press

241. Pribram, K. H. 1969. The neurophysiology of remembering. *Sci. Am.* 220:73–86

242. Radcliffe-Brown, A. R. 1930. A system of notation for relationships. *Man* 30:121–22

243. Rappaport, R. A. 1968. *Pigs for the Ancestors.* New Haven: Yale Univ. Press

244. Read, K. E. 1965. *The High Valley.* New York: Scribner

245. Redfield, R. 1930. *Tepoztlan: A Mexican Village.* Univ. Chicago Press

246. Redfield, R. 1962. *A Village that Chose Progress: Chan Kom Revisited.* Univ. Chicago Press (first publ. 1950)

247. Redfield, R., Villa Rojas, A. 1962. *Chan Kom: A Maya Village,* abr. ed. Univ. Chicago Press

248. Richardson, F. L. W., Ed. *Allegience and Hostility: Man's Mammalian Heritage.* To be published

249.*Rigby, P. J. 1969. *Cattle and Kinship Among the Gogo.* Cornell Univ. Press

250.*Rivière, P. 1969. *Marriage Among the Trio.* London: Clarendon

251. Rohner, R. P., Ed. 1969. *The Ethnography of Franz Boas.* Univ. Chicago Press

252. Romanucci, L. *Violence, Morality and Conflict.* Palo Alto: National Press Books. In press

253.*Rosman, A., Rubel, P. G. 1971. *Feasting With Mine Enemy.* New York: Columbia Univ. Press

254.*Sahlins, M. 1972. *Stone Age Economics.* Chicago: Aldine-Atherton

255. Schaffner, B., Ed. 1955–1960. *Group Processes.* New York: Macy Found. 5 vols.

256.*Schlegel, A. 1972. *Male Dominance and Female Autonomy.* New Haven: Human Relations Area Files Press

257. Schneider, D. M. 1968. *The American Kinship.* Englewood Cliffs: Prentice Hall

258. Schwartz, T. 1962. *The Paliau Movement in the Admiralty Islands, 1946–1954.* Anthropol. Papers Am. Mus. Natur. Hist. 49, Part 2

259. Schwartz, T. 1963. Systems of aerial integration: Some considerations based

on the Admiralty Islands of Northern Melanesia. *Anthropol. Forum* 1:26–97

260. Sebeok, T. A., Hayes, A. S., Bateson, M. C., Eds. 1964. *Approaches to Semiotics.* The Hague: Mouton
261. Segall, M. H., Campbell, D. T., Herskovits, M. J. 1966. *The Influence of Culture on Visual Perception.* Indianapolis, New York: Bobbs-Merrill
262.*Selby, H. A. 1970. Continuities and prospects in anthropological studies. In *Current Directions in Anthropology,* ed. A. Fischer. *Bull. Am. Anthropol. Assoc.* 3:35–53
263.*Silverman, M. G. 1971. *Disconcerting Issue.* Univ. Chicago Press
264.*Simons, E. L. 1972. *Primate Evolution: An Introduction to Man's Place in Nature.* New York: Macmillan
265.*Singer, M. B. 1972. *When a Great Tradition Modernizes: An Anthropological Approach to Indian Civilization.* New York: Praeger
266.*Sinha, S. 1970. *Science, Technology, and Culture: A Study of the Cultural Traditions and Institutions of India and Ceylon in Relation to Science and Technology.* New Delhi: Res. Counc. Cult. Stud., Munshiram Manoharlal
267. Soddy, K., Ed. 1961. *Identity; Mental Health and Value Systems.* London: Tavistock
268. Soddy, K., Ahrenfeldt, R. H. 1965. *Mental Health in a Changing World.* London: Tavistock
269. Spicer, E. H. 1952. *Human Problems in Technological Change: A Casebook.* New York: Sage Found.
270. Spindler, G. D., Ed. 1955. *Education and Anthropology.* Stanford Univ. Press
271. Spindler, G. D. 1970. *Being an Anthropologist: Fieldwork in Eleven Cultures.* New York: Holt, Rinehart & Winston
272. Steiner, S. 1968. *The New Indians.* New York: Harper & Row
273. Stocking, G. W. Jr. 1968. *Race, Culture and Evolution.* New York: Free Press
274.*Strathern, M. 1972. *Women in Between: Female Roles in a Male World, Mount Hagen, New Guinea.* New York: Seminar Press (Academic)
275.*Sturtevant, W. C. 1964. Studies in ethnoscience. *Am. Anthropol.* 66:99–131
276.*Sudnow, D., Ed. 1972. *Studies in Social Interaction.* New York: Free Press
277. Swidler, W. W. 1972. Some demographic factors regulating the formation of flocks and camps among the

Brahui of Baluchistan. In *Perspectives on Nomadism,* ed. W. Irons, N. Dyson-Hudson. Leiden: Brill
278. Tanner, J. M., Inhelder, B., Eds. 1956–1960. *Discussions on Child Development.* London: Tavistock. 4 vols.
279. Tax, S., Ed. 1960. *Evolution After Darwin.* Univ. Chicago Press. 3 vols.
280. Tax, S. et al, Eds. 1953. *An Appraisal of Anthropology Today.* Univ. Chicago Press
281. Texter, R. B., Ed. 1967. *Cross-Cultural Summary.* New Haven: Human Relations Area Files Press
282.*Thomas, K. 1971. *Religion and the Decline of Magic.* New York: Scribner
283.*Tiger, L., Fox, R. 1971. *The Imperial Animal.* New York: Holt, Rinehart & Winston
284. Tiselius, A., Nilsson, S., Eds. 1970. *The Place of Value in a World of Facts.* Nobel Symp. 14. New York: Wiley
285.*Tuden, A., Plotnicov, L. 1970. *Social Stratification in Africa.* New York: Free Press
286. Turnbull, C. M. 1961. *The Forest People.* New York: Simon & Schuster
287. Turnbull, C. M. 1972. *The Mountain People.* New York: Simon & Schuster
288. Turner, V. W. 1967. *Forest of Symbols: Aspects of Ndembu Ritual.* Cornell Univ. Press
289. Turner, V. W. 1969. *The Ritual Process: Structure and Anti-Structure.* Chicago: Aldine
290.*Tyler, S. A. 1969. *Cognitive Anthropology.* New York: Holt, Rinehart & Winston
291. Valentine, C. A. 1968. *Culture and Poverty: Critique and Counter-Proposals.* Univ. Chicago Press
292. Valentine, C. A. 1972. *Black Studies and Anthropology: Scholarly and Political Interests in Afro-American Culture.* Reading, Mass.: Modular Publ.
293. Vayda, A. P. 1969. An ecologist in cultural anthropology. *Bucknell Rev.* March issue
294. Vincent, J. 1971. *African Elite.* New York: Columbia Univ. Press
295. Vizedom, M. B. 1963. *The concept of rites of passage in the light of data from fifteen cultures.* PhD thesis. Columbia Univ., New York
296. Vogt, E. 1961. *A model for the study of ceremonial organization in highland Chiapas.* Presented at 60th Ann. Meet. Am. Anthropol. Assoc., Philadelphia
297. Watson, J. B. 1963. A micro-evolution study in New Guinea. *J. Polynesian Soc.* 72:188–92

298. Watson, J. B., Kimball, S. T., Eds. 1971. *Crossing Cultural Boundaries.* San Francisco: Chandler

299. Wax, M. L., Diamond, S., Gearing, F., Eds. 1971. *Anthropological Perspectives on Education.* New York, London: Basic Books

300. Westlake, P. R. 1970. The possibilities of neural holographic processes within the brain. *Kybernetik* 7:129–53

301. White, L. A. 1959. *Evolution of Culture.* New York: McGraw Hill

302. White, L. A. 1963. *The Ethnography and Ethnology of Franz Boas.* Austin: Memorial Mus. Univ. Texas

303. White, L. A. 1966. *The Science of Culture: A Study of Man and Civilization.* New York: Grove Press (first publ. 1949)

304. Whiting, B. B., Ed. 1963. *Six Cultures: Studies of Child Rearing.* New York, London: Wiley

305. Williams, R. R. 1967. *Field Methods in the Study of Culture.* New York: Holt, Rinehart & Winston

306. Williams, T. R. 1972. *Introduction to Socialization: Human Culture Transmitted.* St. Louis: Mosby

307. Wolfe, A. W. 1963. The African mineral industry: Evolution of a supranational level of integration. *Soc. Probl.* 11:153–64

308.* Young, M. W. 1972. *Fighting with Food.* Cambridge Univ. Press

THE IMPACT OF HUMAN ACTIVITIES ON THE PHYSICAL AND SOCIAL ENVIRONMENTS: NEW DIRECTIONS IN ANTHROPOLOGICAL ECOLOGY

❖ 9517

A symposium by:

Edward Montgomery, John W. Bennett, and Thayer Scudder

Foreword[1]

The rapidly accumulating evidence of danger associated with the human use of the earth has caught most of the sciences unprepared to mount the intensive and necessarily collaborative attack on the problem. Underlying the lack of preparation is the anthropocentric viewpoint of our industrial civilization: that the earth exists for the satisfaction of human needs and wants. Anthropology is no stranger to this idea: for a century, anthropological theory has visualized technological development and the growth of civilization as a triumph of human endeavor; culture has been defined as man's chief mode of adaptation to the natural environment, but for "adaptation," one must often read "exploitation."

Anthropology's insensitivity to the issue has special roots. The proclivity of anthropologists to study tribal and peasant communities has meant that the dramatic effects of industrial man's activities on Nature [for a summary, see Paul B. Sears' paper in the 1956 Wenner-Gren symposium, *Man's Role in Changing the Face of the Earth* (167, 180)] have been of little concern to the discipline. However, even if these effects have been less immediate or dramatic, they are apparent nonetheless, and a careful search of the anthropological literature brings them to light.

Thus, even the most elementary technologies, like stone implements and fire, can have extensive effects on vegetation if the applications are persevering (108). Hunting may have contributed to mammalian extinctions (118, 127). Burning of Western

---

[1]Prepared by J. W. Bennett, who also served as general editor of the symposium. The three contributions were written separately, then circulated among the three authors. All the papers have benefited greatly from this exchange.

grasslands by Indians in connection with bison drives, although well known, was believed by anthropologists to have had no lasting effect on vegetation (194), but recent research by paleoclimatologists indicates that these firings may have significantly reduced the tree cover of sections of the Great Plains (197). Extensive areas of forest in northern Europe (35, 171) were cleared by pre-Neolithic and Neolithic inhabitants for hunting and agricultural purposes, initiating complex cycles of deterioration and recovery. Comparable events may have occurred in aboriginal northeastern North America (54, 139). The beginnings of cultivation and pastoralism in the drier parts of southwest Asia appear to have extensively remodelled the vegetation cover of large areas, preventing, among other things, the regeneration of wild edible grains (76). S. F. Cook (49) analyzed serious soil erosion in Mexican valleys, tracing the damage to pre-Columbian inhabitants. The irrigation schemes developed by Neolithic and Bronze age societies may have degraded the environment very slowly (2, 99), but certainly decisively. Simple tribal agricultures, like swiddening, may be ecologically optimal so long as outside pressures do not induce their practitioners to shorten the interval between crops, or to clear unsuitable soils in drier climates, thus inducing erosion and the widespread replacement of forest by grasses (77). These and many other examples accumulating in the literature suggest that the topic of impact on the physical environment by tribal and peasant societies can no longer be neglected by ecological anthropologists.

However, the issue may be an academic one, since isolated tribal groups are disappearing faster than they can be intensively studied. The big problems lie elsewhere: in former tribal and peasant populations whose subsistence systems have been transformed by the penetration of industrial technology and commercial methods, including those who, due to the "big projects" discussed by Scudder in this symposium, have been forcibly transplanted to new habitats.

The important point is that man's interventions in Nature always imply important changes in human society as well. The social, economic, and health consequences of large dam building are perhaps of no greater magnitude than the changes resulting from the prehistoric development of large-scale irrigation in Southwest Asia and Mesoamerica (1, 76). The causes of population fluctuation in human societies are related to the energy potential of various technological arrangements, and the allocation of increasing energy supplies, and material wealth, will affect the culture and history of societies.

There is no doubt that the topic of the symposium is represented more by promises and expectations than accomplishment. Anthropologists will eventually move toward studies of ecological consequences because these are pressing realities, and because of their own emerging frames of reference will require it. The most important of these is "ecosystem," which refers to the complex reciprocal effects of all factors—physical, biological, behavioral—in any defined reality context, but especially subsistence. Although in biology the major objectives of research on ecosystems may emphasize stability and homeostatic information flows (103), in human situations more attention must be given to adaptive or coping behavior which seeks to change systems, and which certainly modifies systems so that future needs for change and adaptive response are established (18). Once anthropologists fully comprehend the nature of adaptive behavior in man, they will be certain to launch a major inquiry into the effects of human interventions in Nature on the environment and on man himself. (For appraisals of systems analysis in anthropology, see: 75, 93, 121, 168, 186, 192).

The topics selected for this symposium reflect the authors' interests, but hopefully also single out key areas where anthropological work on ecological impact and feedback is progressing. Some major topics are of course omitted: perhaps the most important concerns work on population dynamics, especially fertility. Since anthropological work on population has been the subject of several recent papers and a symposium (11, 96, 144, 145, 176), we were encouraged to omit it.

Montgomery's contribution concerns physiological aspects of the impact of human activities on man, especially in the context of health and nutritional status. The increasing desire of anthropologists in this field for technical data and adequate measurement signifies a movement toward the natural sciences and a need for younger workers to acquire professional training in adjunct disciplines. Bennett's paper concerns one of his major fields of interest: the ecology of agriculture. Here the effects of man's interventions involve the entire ecosystem: Nature, human biology, and sociocultural phenomena. The paper focuses on swiddening agriculture as the field in which most of the anthropological work on impact has centered. Scudder's contribution deals with his major field of research: the study of human consequences of large dam and lake construction in the tropics. In these projects, the effects of massive interventions are compressed into a short time period, and the requirements for readaptation of displaced tribal-peasant populations provide a laboratory for the study of ecological and cultural process.[2]

The literature cited in all three papers includes many items by researchers from fields other than anthropology. However, in most cases the work reviewed was done in conjunction with anthropologists; or the anthropologists were members of research teams or institutes doing collaborative research. There is little doubt that this type of specialized role will become a common one for anthropologists, although it is not yet entirely clear just how the role will be defined vis-à-vis the other disciplines.

[2]For additional reviews of water development projects in the tropics, and anthropological research on water resources generally, see a forthcoming paper by J. W. Bennett, Anthropological Contributions to the Cultural Ecology and Management of Water Resources, in *Man and Water,* ed. L. D. James. Lexington: University of Kentucky Press and Center for Development Change. To be published late 1973.

Section 1:

ECOLOGICAL ASPECTS OF HEALTH AND DISEASE IN LOCAL POPULATIONS

Edward Montgomery
Washington University at St. Louis, Missouri

Observations concerning health and disease are of critical importance in an ecological perspective on human affairs. In this contribution it will be our concern to indicate several significant aspects of such observations. Selected examples of recent work by anthropological, nutritional, and medical researchers are coordinated to highlight the conceptual, theoretical, and practical implications of health and disease data for an ecological anthropology. Since this essay emphasizes needs as well as accomplishments, it attempts at once a review and a preview of the subject.

The general notion that health varies relative to changes in the environment is not new. Rousseau took a long-term view of the matter when positing that "illness of every kind . . . belongs chiefly to man in a state of society" (quoted in 154). In recent years, anthropologists have been rather well informed about the intricate evolutionary relationships of changing disease patterns as concomitants of human history (e.g. 12, 29, 38, 39, 60, 65, 73, 80, 130, 142, 143, 146, 170). However, an understanding of the significance of health and disease in the short-run view of human events is considerably less well developed. This essay examines the emergence of a more explicitly ecological view of health and disease. One prominent aspect of this framework is the development of an ecologically relevant definition of the two key terms, health and disease. Another is the emphasis given to variations of health and disease within particular segments of local populations. A third aspect is the attention given to influential environmental features of local habitats and ecosystems. A fourth is the concern placed upon changes in social and environmental contexts which may be related systematically to changes in patterns of health. A fifth aspect of this emerging ecological view is the consideration which is being given to the implications of health and disease patterns for related systems and subsystems in the local population and local ecosystem. Each of these aspects will be examined in turn.

An Ecological View of Health and Disease

The concepts of health and disease recently have been discussed in ways which help to clarify their theoretical relevance to anthropology and human ecology. Wylie (198) has pointed out that the widely used asymptotic or open-ended definition of health in the Preamble to the Constitution of the World Health Organization

("Health is a state of complete physical, mental, and social well-being and not merely the absence of disease or infirmity.") has no explanatory power. In his words, this sort of definition fails to specify "what health does to organisms or how it may be measured." (198). A particularly important contribution by Audy (9) gives the concepts of health and disease explanatory strength by framing them ecologically. Audy defines health "as a continuing property, potentially measurable by the individual's ability to rally from insults, whether chemical, physical, infectious, psychological, or social" (9). And complementarily, "the concept of disease, necessarily modified by this concept of health, may, for the moment, be regarded as representing episodes during which the property of health is being challenged: most disease is an expression of the rallying, the coping process, but the measurable ability to rally is there all the time" (9). In other words, health and disease can be seen as varying states of an individual's dynamic relations with an environment. Measurement of an individual's level of health depends upon identifying the challenges to that individual, and Audy proposes that an Index of Health be developed which can subsume the multiplicity of positive and negative insults and their cumulative effects. At present we are limited to working with the accepted definitions of diseases, but these do allow for instructive inquiry into the distributions of health variations within and between populations.

Differential Distributions of Diseases in Human Populations

Observations of health conditions may reveal information about the impacts of a population upon its environment or about impacts of some segments of a population upon other of its segments. Nutritional diseases, for example, usually are specific to some sections of a society (115). The dimensions along which differentials of nutritional and infectious diseases may be detected are indicated here with examples from several recent studies.

Some of the most instructive contributions concerning localized distributions of disease in human populations come from workers who have concentrated on the health and disease of infants and young children. From a series of inquiries some general patterns have begun to emerge. It is clear that adequate nutrition and protection from exposure to infection are requisites for reducing the risks of illness during the particularly vulnerable first two years of life. One report, which outlines these features in minimal terms, attributes the generally good health of the children of the Hadza hunters of northern Tanzania to prolonged breast feeding, early supplementation with a range of foods including meat chewed to softness by the mother, and a reduced risk of exposure to intestinal parasites due, at least partially, to the group's continual nomadic movements (112). The key aspects are breast feeding, adequate supplementary nutrition, and protection from possible infections. In other populations such as the Navaho (78) and the western Alaskan Eskimo (131) where both breast feeding and bottle feeding are practiced, the bottle-fed infants have been found to have significantly more illness. While both the nutritional status and the exposure to pathogens for these infants may at least partially account for the findings, there is also an accumulation of evidence that feeding infants with breast milk confers some resistance to infection (111, 129). Studies from rural Punjab, northern India (85) and rural Guatemala (86) have shown that inadequate supplementary nutrition increases the risk of illness, particularly diarrheal disease. Further, infections with parasitic diseases may reduce general resistence and increase the likelihood of illness. It has been argued that a high prevalence of diarrheal disease among infants is a syndrome which reflects the interaction of nutrition and infection (85) and that variations in the second year death rates are largely attributable to the strength of impact of these two factors.

Children beyond infancy and the second year may receive the brunt of the impacts of infections or undernutrition in some populations. For example, among the children of the Karamojong pastoralists, malarial infections are found to be most frequent among children aged 2 to 5, and malnutrition seems to be focused on those aged about 5 to 8 years (110). Similarly, in an agricultural village population in Tamilnadu, southern India, children show generally good health at least through their second year, and thereafter the likelihood of parasitic infections, particularly hookworm, and protein-calorie undernutrition tends to increase through the preschool and early school age years (114, 134). In a central Liberian agricultural population, children aged 5 years and younger show the highest proportion of poor nutrition, and those between 6 and 12 have the highest frequencies of parasitic infections (90).

The identification of differentials of health among adults is particularly complex in that factors of age and behavior are often confounded with other factors pertaining to occupation, social position, economic position, and so on. Aged adults, however, are a group wherein impacts on health are clearly distinguishable in some populations. For example, in a recent nutritional study of the British Columbia Nootka and Chilcotin Indians, it has been reported that the elderly face risks of nutritional problems since traditional foods of more difficult access—such as salmon, marine invertebrates, deer, wild duck, and wild berries—continue to be important in the local diet (21, 55, 123). A study of the health of the aged in three villages in northern India has revealed that rates of illness increase significantly with age (148).

If contrasts in health according to sex are considered, some interesting patterns can be pointed out just from the studies referred to so far. In the rural south India village population, for example, the adult women tend to show a markedly higher proportion of the low serum albumin values, indicative of protein undernutrition (134). The position of teenagers in the same population tends to be reversed, with the girls showing better nutritional health than the boys in the years at and just following onset of puberty. Among the British Columbian Indians, both women and teenage girls are the groups in the population who show clinical and biochemical evidence of significant iron deficiency anemia (55). In the study of the aged in northern India, the men tend to have significantly higher morbidity rates than the women (148).

Health differentials correlated with economic and social position also have been documented and some examples can be cited. The recent study in northeastern Brazil by Gross & Underwood (89) points out that nutritional differences for children and wives vary according to the economic group of the study families. In Nepal, diets and rates of calorie malnutrition have been found to vary significantly according to caste (and socioeconomic) position (30). Several studies in India have reported health differentials according to caste or class position (see bibliography in 134), and recently the studies of Borun (23) and Montgomery (134) have investigated the local sociocultural contexts of these differentials in greater detail. Examples have been reported for populations in Ethiopia and New Guinea in which endogamous divisions have developed in response to endemic infections (155). The process of this health-related social differentiation has been studied by Gorlin in New Guinea (87). At the microsocial level, there is also some interesting evidence that nutritional health and family size can be interrelated, with children in the fourth or later birth order positions showing significantly greater incidence of malnutrition (187).

Accounting for Differentials of Health

In an ecological perspective on health and disease there are three general domains about which we would like to be informed when differentials of health are to be accounted for. In the most general terms, we can ask for adequate information about the environmental context, about man-environment relations, and about social relations. None of the studies cited in the preceding section aimed at explaining health in an explicit ecological framework. However, they and some additional examples can be instructively considered for their respective contributions to any of these three domains of ecologically relevant information.

Studies concerned with differentials of health which have given much attention either to the ecological context or to man-environment relations are relatively scarce. One important contribution which does give careful consideration to both these areas is the recent work of Dunn (61). In his study of the patterns of parasitic infections of several Malayan aboriginal groups, a number of epidemiologically relevant components are considered in the analysis of the variations of habitats. These components include altitude, humidity, temperature, soil type, and presence of scavenging domestic animals. Dunn's earlier demonstration that the numbers of parasitic species infecting hunter-gatherer populations vary with the diversity and complexity of the ecosystem may be recalled in this regard (60). Dunn's additional contribution in the Malayan study is the formulation of a "sanitary status score," which is a composite of values for semiquantitative variables of behavior affecting sanitation. The scored variables include village population density, village population size, land availability around the village, community mobility, subsistence strategies, house types, and the environmental variables referred to above. As Dunn points out, the composite scoring of such behaviors prevents the determination of the specific man-environment links which are involved in the contrasting parasitic infections of the different ethnic groups. This attention to behavioral factors which are related to the probability of infections is similar in many respects to the emphases which have been given to this subject by Alland (7, 8), especially in chapters 3 and 4 of *Adaptation in Cultural Evolution: An Approach to Medical Anthropology.* One study which has attempted to identify the specific behaviors and environmental factors implicated in contrasting parasitic infections is that of John, Montgomery & Jayabal (114) of children in rural and urban southern India.

Most of the studies which were cited as examples indicating differentials in distributions of health have focused upon the social behaviors which are implicated, explicitly or implicitly, in the disease patterns. The specified social dimensions include mother-child relations (78, 85, 112, 131), employer-laborer relations (12, 89, 134), male-female role relations (89, 134), intercaste relations (12, 134, 135), interclass relations (89), and active adults-aged adults relations. The epidemiologically relevant content of such relations is, however, largely presumed. The subleties of discrimination in the differential distribution of foods which may account for variations in nutritional health remain to be explored. Also, the probabilities of social interactions along such dimensions are, in most instances, assumed. A more precise defining of such probabilities within the structural possibilities has yet to be achieved with regard to health-relevant social dimensions. Hausfeld's (97) formulation of a matrix of epidemiologically relevant social interactions for a New Guinea population deserves consideration by those working in this problem area.

The issue of "change" is of a special importance in accounting for differentials of health. The general definition of health commended earlier presumes a continual flow of challenges and a fluctuating level of health which is a product of perpetual changes. In the examples under review this dynamic perspective is not well represented, but rather some particular process or sets of processes have been posited or presumed to account for the observed health patterns. The kinds of processes which have been considered include microsocial differentiation (87), economic transition from subsistence to cash cropping (89), stratification-system elaboration (134), and pervasive ecosystemic changes (61). Such changes as these, which represent challenges to a particular level of health, may be gradual and subtle or blunt and catastrophic in effect. As is indicated by Scudder in his contribution to follow, and by Hughes & Hunter (105) in their review of the health consequences of "development" schemes, declines in health tend to be unanticipated. However, the health consequences of such subtle factors as shifts in diets as in fat consumption patterns (92, 151) and in patterns of amino acid utilization (117, 170), shifts in life expectancies and dependency ratios (142), variations in the fetal environment such as the weight of the mother (51) and even fetal infections (128)—to cite a few examples where the health effects are becoming better known—also have been largely unanticipated. An interesting case for a population familiar to anthropologists is the recent report (132) that the unusually healthy iron nutritional status of the !Kung Bushmen seems to be a relatively new situation. Metz, Hart & Harpending have shown that the extremely low incidence of anemia among Bushmen needs to be explained in terms of supplementary dietary iron in view of the inadequate iron intakes from the foods. The source of supplementation seems to be iron cooking pots, which have been used in the area only since about 1957. The contrast between blunt and subtle challenges to health can be thought of in Audy's (9) terms, that is, that the blunt and hence sometimes catastrophic challenges tend to have more pervasive implications for reduced capacity for response.

Another dimension of contemporary research into ecological aspects of health concerns the work on the implications and interlinkages of disease patterns to various systems and subsystems of societies. There is much interesting work now available and in progress in this area, and only a few examples need be cited to convey the systemic import of such inquiri‿. A number of investigators, including Alland (8), Dunn (62), Leslie (125), and Polunin (146), have given attention to the relationships between characteristic disease patterns and medical systems. Colson's (40) work focuses on the related problem of disease preventive behaviors. Townsend (181) and Weiss (196) have been concerned with the place of health variables related to population regulation, and Weiss has shown that mortality has become steadily less important relative to fertility in the control of population growth. Others, including Rappaport (150) and Shack (169), are working to relate ritual systems to ecological variables. Another promising problem area concerns relating health levels with economic behaviors, and further efforts hopefully will clarify the apparent puzzle inherent in those measurements of carrying capacities in which the enumerated populations have been found at levels no more than 32% to 42% of the calculated expected populations (e.g. 16, 33). Weiner (195) has recently suggested that a health-related factor termed "working capacity" be included in the formula for calculating carrying capacities, but the procedures for estimating this factor are not specified. Kunstadter (120) has described an interesting case in which a temporary lowering of a northwestern Thai village population's health level led to partial crop failures because many families were unable to weed their fields while children were ill. Of course, a satisfactory demonstration of systematic linkages between any of these subsystems will necessarily depend on obtaining sufficiently precise observations of fluctuations in values in one subsystem which can be tested for correlation with varying values of health levels.

Implications for Anthropology

The implications for anthropology of an ecological perspective on health and disease already extend beyond familiarization with the requisite terminology, theory, and models of data interrelationships. Increasing numbers of professional anthropologists are utilizing their talents and areas of expertise to address health-related issues. However, familiarization with the perspective remains an important first step for many, and obtaining an adequate awareness of the highly specialized and often disputed nature of health variables is critical in facilitating communications with fellow researchers in the nutritional and medical sciences. For example, the multiplicity of methods for establishing different aspects of nutritional status (e.g. 44, 109) requires an attentiveness to details often overlooked in anthropological research. Reliance on perhaps too few of the available methods can lead to indeterminate results, as in the case of the nutritional observations on the !Kung Bushmen in which the weight-for-height observations could be interpreted to indicate either undernutrition or an adaptation to a lean body build (124, 182, 183). In short, anthropologists have to become attuned to expectations and assumptions concerning behavioral variations often radically different from those which they ordinarily use. Effective research in this broad area must almost necessarily be interdisciplinary team research, and if anthropologists can see their way clear to integrate the results of such work into an ecological and a general anthropology, a growing number of important contributions can be anticipated in this subject area in the next few years.

Section 2:

ECOSYSTEMIC EFFECTS OF EXTENSIVE AGRICULTURE

John W. Bennett

Washington University at St. Louis, Missouri

Introductory

The environmental impact of agricultural practices is a topic of growing importance, due to the dangers associated with large-scale, intensive production implemented by use of man-made chemical substances and powered machinery (e.g. 4, 156). Anthropologists, concerned primarily with subsistence agriculture and only partly commercialized regimes in peasant enclaves, have conceived of agroecological research largely in theoretical terms, and only recently have become concerned with the feedbacks on society and Nature associated with shifting cultivation and nomadic livestock production. In both cases, the beginning of an interest in policy-relevant questions has emerged out of the contact of formerly isolated agricultural systems with agricultural development programs in tropical and arid lands.

Historical and evolutionary interests constitute the starting point for anthropological studies of subsistence agriculture; specifically, the precise circumstances of the domestication of plants and animals. The accumulated evidence for all parts of the world—southwest Asia, southeast Asia, and Mesoamerica—indicates that domestication and systemic food production arise out of complex food-collecting regimes. Lewis Binford (20) has, for the southwest Asia area, called these "broad spectrum" techniques, implying thorough exploitation of nearly every available foodstuff just short of actual domestication and cultivation.[3] The movement of peoples with such techniques out of a well-endowed habitat into less well-endowed regions, as a consequence of population pressure, would result in the introduction of some of the collected species to new habitats. Subsequent genetic change in these species—partly through natural selection, partly the result of human selective efforts—would lead to "domestication." Domestication, involving in essence the growing of plants on man-selected habitats, would then become co-terminous with "agriculture." However, agriculture can be more or less intensive—that is, differing degrees of adherence to the technique of growing crops and raising animals on the same land year after year. An "extensive" agricultural regime is simply one that falls short of permanent annual cropping, and to the extent that it does, its practitioners display distinctive settlement patterns.

[3]The term "Mesolithic" has been used more commonly to describe these mixed, partly sedentary adaptations.

In a recent attempt to summarize the relationship of population and settlement patterns in subsistence agriculture, P. E. L. Smith (173) notes that agricultural societies generally have several subsystemic versions of their "subsistence pose" (p. 421), and that the question of the precise influence of any factor must take into account all of the possible subsystems. These subsystems will wax and wane depending on changing conditions; that is, they constitute *choices* which confer adaptive flexibility on the entire "system." The present author wishes to add that this element of choice constitutes the point where ecosystem and natural systems generally fail as adequate models for human systems. In the latter, the dynamism associated with choice means that the system tends to change by modifying both the internal and external factors involved, creating new systems, rather than by returning the system back to some pre-existing state. This means also that the effect of various forms of subsistence or types of settlement of population will be difficult to determine without knowledge of all relevant factors, requiring multi-disciplinary cooperative research.

David Harris (93) discusses the differences between major forms of subsistence in ecosystemic terms, viewing "agricultural *systems,* whether they are forms of primitive, palaeotechnic cultivation or of modern, neotechnic farming, simply as distinctive types of man-modified ecosystems" (p. 3). He states that the advantage to this viewpoint is that it focuses "attention on the properties they [agricultural systems] share with all other systems, i.e. structure, function, equilibrium, and change" (93, p. 3). He distinguishes between "generalized" and "specialized" ecosystems, noting that the former, having great diversity of species and many alternative feedback channels and nutritional sources, are more stable or homeostatic. Food-collecting subsistence systems, swiddening, and vegetative or root agricultures generally are closer to generalized or diverse systems, hence more stable and geographically restricted; whereas seed-crop-animal agricultures push toward domestication and geographical expansion as highly specialized, high energy-producing systems.

While the comparison of human subsistence systems to natural ecosystems does clarify central issues, it also tends to obscure some of the fundamental differences between them. The greater dynamism of the human systems means that hunters, swiddeners and other "palaeotechnic" adaptors can in certain cases create just as many problems for man and Nature as the "neotechnic" specialized adaptations. The missing variable in Harris's analogies is the innovative and high-want aspect of human behavior, which can exert severe pressure on all environments as a result of demands emerging out of the social system, and without regard for any currently existing ecosystemic properties.

Swiddening

Anthroecological research on extensive agriculture has consisted of a few studies of pastoralism and a large number of studies of shifting cultivation (also called "slash-and-burn," or "swiddening"; the latter term will be used in this contribution). Swiddening is a particular form of extensive agriculture practiced in the tropics on soils of marginal fertility and depth. In most early typological work in cultural ecology, swiddening was conceived in historical terms as the early stage in the development of agricultural technology from crude, extensive methods to intensive cultivation of the same fields year after year (199). In this sense, swiddening was viewed as an incomplete or arrested stage of development and not as an adaptive system in its own right. Nor was it realized that tribal and peasant groups were capable of shifting from intensive to extensive systems (as in the case of Scudder's Tonga, or Netting's Kofyar, both discussed later.)

Studies of swiddening began in the early 1950s, often stimulated by agricultural development programs [Conklin (48) summarizes the first period of research]. One theme of this early work was an argument for the relative efficiency and ecological integrity of this form of agriculture. In a 1965 book (6), William Allan, an agronomist associated with anthropologists, emphasized the depth and range of knowledge of local resources possessed by swiddeners, noting that the form of cultivation was a specialized adaptation to particular types of soils and not simply undeveloped agriculture. Allan also noted that the critical factor in explaining the many varieties of swiddening was the "ratio between the length of time the soil will sustain cultivation with satisfactory results and the period required for the restoration of fertility" (p. 5).

Allan's 1965 book (and an important early paper: 5) was concerned with a second theme: the attempt to measure the carrying capacity or critical human population density of various forms of swiddening cultivation in Africa. His definition of carrying capacity was implicitly formulated as the largest number of people who could be supported indefinitely by a given system of cultivation without permanent or accumulating injury to the soil. This concept of carrying capacity influenced other earlier swiddening studies, many of which were aimed at showing that swiddening might be capable of supporting more humans than sedentary-intensive cropping (e.g. 47, 59, 88, 122). The work of this period is criticized in a brief paper by the geographer, J. M. Street (177).

Street notes that anthropologists (e.g. 28, 46) were not making "any serious effort" (p. 104) to determine whether degradation of the soil and land surface was in fact occurring; the assumption in much of the literature was that it was *not* occurring. Street remarks that since anthropologists tended to assume that agricultural practices of swidden peoples were permanent and unvarying, they therefore did not examine methods of resource renewal or conservation.

Robert Carneiro's (33) and Richard Salisbury's (152) studies of Amazonian and New Guinea swiddening systems are cited as examples of these deficiencies: the former apparently simply averaged the number of years the villagers let their fields lie fallow, and the latter simply asserted that soil "impoverishment" need not occur since the "ratio of cultivation to fallow" was favorable, i.e. intervals of several years. In neither case was an attempt made to observe the variations in fallowing intervals over time, or to study the actual conditions of the soil which result from specific methods of tillage and fallowing.

While Allan's definition of carrying capacity is logical, Street (177) regards it as extremely difficult to apply. He notes that deterioration of the soil is a slow process, "and short term changes may be so slight as to be exceeded by errors in measurement" (p. 105); and that while measurements of nutrients (e.g. phosphorus) in soil are possible, the *availability* of the nutrient to the plant depends on many other factors which are not observed by anthropologists and remain resistant to specialized agronomic analysis. Cowgill's (50) study of soil fertility under presumed or reconstructed prehistoric Maya cultivation methods is cited by Street as an example: determination of the phosphorus status of various fields under differing periods of fallow and cultivation was invalid, especially for retrospective prediction, because she did not know the nutrient status of the fields at the time of abandonment, and because she was unable to distinguish between existent and available phosphorus.

Street approves of the pioneer studies of swiddening by Freeman (77) in Borneo, and Löffler (126) in India, in that specific efforts were made in both to determine the consequences of swiddening for land degradation, modification of plant cover, and changes in crop output. Freeman found that cropping 2 years in succession caused serious erosion and introduced highly combustible savanna grasses into the forest. Löffler found that progressive shortening of the fallow period was associated with a rise in output. Simonett (172) shows how swiddening in New Guinea has introduced large areas of grasslands into former forest, and Nye & Greenland (140) and Watters (193) summarize the evidence for and against harmful consequences of swiddening in various countries (see also 10, 175).

Street is concerned that anthropologists have a tendency to become "enamored of the object of their scrutiny": in particular, to assume that swiddening tribalists are ideally adapted to the environment on a sustained-yield basis. More limiting than this attitude, perhaps, are the relatively short periods of field work, which make it difficult to spot irregularly recurring events, such as the tendency for some Thai tribes to burn grasslands for fun (82); the serious soil erosion caused by swiddening among the Chimbu of New Guinea (13); or the soil exhaustion problems of the Kara of Lake Victoria, Africa (177, p. 105).[4]

Coordinated investigations of sociocultural matters and swiddening have been carried out on the Maring people in the Central Highlands of New Guinea. Andrew Vayda has done studies of warfare and settlement patterns (185); Roy Rappaport of ceremonials and subsistence activities (149); and the most recent, a study of the physical environment and agricultural resources by geographer William C. Clarke (37). These studies of the same tribal group have been informed by the concept of ecosystem: "the total sum of organisms in a biotic community, the nonliving elements of their environment, and all the interactions that occur among these components of the system" (37, p. 18). Clarke's study is responsive to the criticisms of Street concerning the absence of scientific studies of soil and the impact upon it of

[4]On this point concerning the need for studies of subsistence agriculture (or any agriculture) through time, Scudder noted, in the course of our collaboration on this symposium, that the best way to assess the impact of bush fallow systems is through long-term studies. At Henderson Research Station outside Salisbury, Rhodesia, certain experimental plots have been farmed without any fallowing, green manuring, rotation, fertilization, or animal manuring. Over the years yields gradually drop until they level out at 200-400 lbs. of harvested grain. This yield then continues, as if the recycling of stover, weeds, etc is sufficient to maintain that yield. Assuming 400 lbs. grain harvested will support one person for 12 months, 1–2 acres land cultivated per capita will suffice if fallowing does not occur. The unknown question is whether or not after a number of years yields drop off again to almost zero. But the situation is complicated; more complicated than even Street (177) notes. While the fallowing interval is crucial, very little is known about what happens to the soil, weed growth, etc as a result of changes in this interval; and some agricultural systems may be adapted to a low yield economy where population increase precludes fallowing and where intensification has not occurred.

particular cultivation techniques. Clarke was able to ascertain with a fair degree of probability that the observed Maring swidden system, in interaction with the described habitat, is one of sustained yield, but he acknowledges uncertainties in the analysis. In an illuminating appendix (pp. 199–206), he discusses the impressive difficulties of collecting the amount of data needed for adequate ecosystem analysis involving human activities. Thus far, these investigations among the Maring people have produced some stimulating hypotheses about homeostasis between man and nature, and especially within human activities themselves, but there are many ambiguities, lacunae, and an absence of analysis through time.

Another appraisal of the swiddening technique was made by Clifford Geertz, in his book on *Agricultural Involution* in Indonesia (83, chapter 2). Geertz makes an incisive comparison between swiddening and wet-rice cultivation in ecological and sociocultural terms. Swiddening is represented as an analog to the natural ecosystem of the forest: direct cycling of nutrients from soil to plants, and then back to soil, takes place through the technique of clearance by burning (although a certain amount is lost by burning and harvesting). In rice paddy agriculture, on the other hand, the nutrients are brought to the site by man-engineered flowing water, and successful rice cultivation can be practiced on "unbelievably poor soils" (p. 30). The paddy is therefore a man-made "ecosystem," and it is not geared into natural systems. Anticipating Street's criticisms, Geertz noted that swiddening is harmful to the natural environment only when its practitioners: burn too much; clear unsuitable soils, especially in overly dry climatic zones, thereby encouraging grass replacement; or adhere to too short an interval between plantings. Rice paddy, on the other hand, is nearly indestructible and capable of indefinite extension of productivity. Its chief hazard is its tendency to encourage human population growth, due precisely to its efficiency and susceptibility to marginal productive extensions. Such growth creates a large rural population dependent on agriculture, and the paddy system is peculiarly adapted to indefinite absorption of additional labor inputs.

Michael Moerman (133, pp. 81–84) assesses some of Geertz's conclusions about paddy and notes that Geertz did not take into account the effects of machines and chemicals in enhancing rice yields. Moerman also discusses Geertz' conclusions regarding the relationship between rice agriculture and human population density, noting that the issue is more complex, since population is "large" or dense only relative to amount of food produced, the pattern of ownership (as vs the number living on the land), and the nutritional status of the population (pp. 84–87).

A recent cursory survey of the swiddening literature is provided by Robert Netting (137). No new research along the lines recommended by Street is cited, but an emphasis on time-depth studies and detailed data collection on critical issues such as soil degradation and nutrient status is becoming visible. There is recognition that the fallowing interval is a critical problem, and that this varies and is always subject to pressure from population increase, shifts to a cash economy, and social factors.

The most recent review of the consequences of swiddening in Latin America (193; see also 22, 147) underlines the distinction between "traditional shifting cultivation" and "shifting cultivation imposed by necessity" (pp. 6–12). The former refers to the work of farmers tied to an existing social community and bound by its customs and rules concerning the conservation of a known territory, while the latter refers to pioneers or displaced tribalists, in some cases "land-hungry" people who crop free land for extra income, treating this land less carefully than their own. This finding is of particular importance since it underlines the importance of viewing environmental impact in the context of feedbacks from social and community systems.

A third phase of the swiddening studies in anthropology was inaugurated by Ester Boserup's exposition of her theory that agricultural intensification is generated by population growth (24). Her thesis challenges the assumption long held by anthropologists and others that population increase is a consequence of agricultural yield improvements. To elaborate her argument that intensification is less productive per man-hour than extensive systems, Boserup required a detailed classification of methods of cultivation, beginning with the simplest, occasional forest-clearing type, and continuing up through the various swiddening routines to continuous cropping. Aside from the demographic and productivity arguments, this classification has been of utility in sorting out the many detailed case studies of agroecology and putting them into a coherent frame (see 137, p. 20) and makes possible controlled comparative studies of impact. William C. Clarke's paper on the succession of cultivation systems in New Guinea (36) was one of the first agroecological studies to use the Boserup scheme.

While the Boserup thesis has potential value in providing a framework for physical-environmental impact assessment, some researchers using it have been more concerned with the impact on the social environment in terms of labor, leisure time, and "quality of life." Thus Clarke, in his study cited above, concludes that the shift toward intensive cultivation and increase in gross production resulted in a loss of variety and nutrition in foods and an increase in labor expenditures per unit of food produced. Thus "this change does not bring economic efficiency or secure the agriculturalist from a more toilsome life" (p. 258). Aside from the nutritional issue, no evidence is provided to indicate how he determined the welfare values: whether the tribalists themselves perceived the change in these negative terms, or whether they viewed it as a trade-off between gratification and survival. Assessment of human impact must deal objectively with attitude and percept data just as assessments of physical impact must deal with the biological and material. The question is complex, since there probably *are* absolute parameters of individual adaptability and tolerance, but these are poorly defined, and in any case Clarke does not develop his argument in such terms.

Aside from the question of how tribal and peasant populations may perceive quality of life, possibilities for measurement of changes in work output and energy expended in labor do exist and provide some sort of assessment of impact of econocological changes. The consensus of a number of studies of tropical agriculture, in line with the Boserup thesis, seems to be that subsistence agriculturalists of all types are able to provide for most needs by expending less than the 40-hour work week, and that full intensification—presumably commercialized—may produce more food but at less per-man or per-hour output. On the other hand, some studies seem to show that a shift from one style to another may be accompanied by readjustments in social structure and activities which might be considered by the people themselves as well as the anthropologist to be a gain, offsetting productivity costs. Netting's work on the Kofyar (136) shows, among other things, that with a change toward more extensive methods, intrafamilial tension was lessened due to the fact that an expansion of the number of fields cultivated permitted sons to develop their own enterprises in cooperation with their father, and this reduced family quarrels and disputes over division of the harvest as food and money became more abundant.

David Harris (94) agrees with Boserup that while swiddening requires relatively large amounts of land per person, the productivity of the land per unit of labor is high—in many cases, higher than in sedentary cropping systems. However, Harris concludes that the demographic potential (and the degree of mobility or sedentariness) of swiddening peoples is a variable, related to ". . . ecological factors, particularly the nature of the crop complexes involved" (pp. 258–259). More specifically, swiddeners emphasizing *seed*-crops have low populations and unstable settlement; while *root*-croppers manifest stable settlement and possess the potential for increase. Generalizing from this intermediate (and complex) adaptation of swiddening, it would appear that population, settlement pattern, and the impact of these on natural resources, are related to many factors, and generalizations at the elementary level of "subsistence technology" are inappropriate.

A recent study of swiddening in relation to the Boserup thesis is Eric Waddell's account for a highland New Guinea tribe (188). Like Clarke, Waddell studied a series of related communities with varying degrees of intensification, and could not find that "extensive systems are inherently more productive than intensive ones" (p. 218).[5] Echoing Harris' conclusion, Waddell notes that Boserup failed to include

[5]It is indicative of the imprecision of much anthropological research and commentary concerning Boserup's thesis that a recent appraisal of the Waddell findings by P. E. L. Smith (173) comes to the opposite conclusion; namely, that Waddell showed that the "evolution of agricultural settlement patterns in the highlands follows a broad agricultural sequence in which changes in population density played an important role much as Boserup outlined" (p. 421). A study for Africa with some of the same dimensions of Waddell's (one tribe; separate sections practicing shifting and intensive village agriculture) by Basehart (15) illustrates some of the ambiguities: while he presents statistics on population and social organization for his two types, he acknowledges that the "intensive" group is not as "intensive" as the Kofyar, for example, since they permit a 7 to 13 month fallow interval. He feels that his data confirm the Boserup thesis of more concentrated population settlements for intensive agriculture, although the shifting-cultivation villages have larger total population. He associates different types of homesteads with the two modes of cultivation, but the classification is overlapping. Historical data in the article indicate that the extensive and intensive forms of cultivation represent a recent historical divergence based on intertribal warfare and other factors, rather than long-term subsystemic alternatives. A theoretical viewpoint featuring adaptive or cost-gain behavioral strategies seems more appropriate to these dynamic cases than the Boserup typological perspective (e.g. 19). On the other hand, the value of Boserup's thesis for prehistoric studies, involving longer spans of time and larger areas, is illustrated by Smith & Young's (174) paper on sequences of agricultural and population development in Mesopotamia.

"physical and biological variables in the ecosystem" (p. 219) which would modify productivity in complex combination with the various agricultural techniques. There is a suggestion here that anthropologists would do well to treat Boserup's thesis for what it is: a broad, free-ranging generalization, biased toward technological determinism, and with heuristic, but not precise, diagnostic value. That is, it is no substitute for the meticulous, multi-dimensional technical and comparative studies which need to be made in order to ascertain impacts and causal relationships. [For a critique of Boserup see Bronson (27); he questions her logical sequence of agricultural types and, in particular, her association of given population magnitudes with them, noting that density and mobility are in many cases independent variables, responding to factors other than the agricultural or technological.]

Ecological Aspects of Tribal Livestock Systems

A study of the Karimojong of Uganda by Rada and Neville Dyson-Hudson (63, 64) provides other facets of the problem of agrarian impact on both the physical and social environments. The Karimojong are pastoralists, exploiting a region of variable and uncertain moisture, with many parasitic insects and natural hazards. Movement with the herds to locate suitable grazing and other conditions varies in terms of many factors and is adjusted to the varying resource potential. The authors appear to feel that sedentary cropping or stock-raising would be difficult or impossible in such a natural environment, as has been demonstrated by the difficulties such regimes have experienced under agrarian development programs in this or similar parts of Africa. The Karimojong strategy for livestock production does not maximize the size and quality of the herds for sale at a profit, minimizing the human labor involved in managing them, as is the case in "developed" systems. Instead, their strategy is to maintain a reasonable food supply for the largest number of people and a goodly quantity of animals of indifferent quality for wealth and prestige purposes. While no detailed calculations are provided, the authors conclude that the Karimojong, with their flexible and pragmatic system, manage to support a larger number of humans than would be the case if their range was converted to a profit-maximizing agriculture. As suggested previously, similar arguments have been adduced in favor of swiddening systems over against sedentary cropping in the tropics.

The impact on the physical environment associated with the Karimojong system of livestock management involves frequent short-term abuse of pastures, with long-term recovery. No particular conservationist program is known or followed, but the constant movement of herds, and the recurrent losses of animals and humans due to disease, tend to reduce impact on flora. The poor genetic stock means that the animals are not especially productive, and the lack of rational culling means survival of large numbers of these substandard animals. By maximization standards, this seems irrational and nonconservationist, but the Dyson-Hudsons regard the system as suited to the physical and social environments and reasonably conservationist in effect, if not in practice.

These arguments cannot be discarded offhand, since it is possible that these methods permit sustained yield and optimal human population at the trade-off of the advantages of sedentarism and individual gratification and wealth. Still, the issue is extremely complex, and in the absence of controlled experiments on various alternatives to the existing system, it is difficult to accept a status quo argument. Marvin Harris introduced a similar argument (95) concerning the wandering "sacred" cattle of India, which he views as a vital resource, permitting ecological survival of the Indian population and maintenance of its life-sustaining activities. Harris, like the Dyson-Hudsons, tends to accept the on-going system as functional, and therefore good, but in neither case is there an attempt to make long-range assessments of impact and change, or to test possible alternatives. The dictum of Street, concerning the frequent slowness of deteriorational tendencies and the small increments of change being equal to the error factor in observations, continues to apply (for critical reviews of the Harris piece, see 17, 100; a favorable review is 141).

Nomadic livestock regimes received considerable attention by anthropologists and agricultural specialists in the late 1950s and early 1960s as a result of attempts by southwest Asian and some African countries to sedentarize nomadic tribes. The most comprehensive review of the period was Symposium on Nomads (178); the current summary, including more recent research, is by Darling et al (52). Papers in the latter publication emphasize the consequences for the nomads, for the physical environment of arid and semiarid lands, and for sedentary peoples partly dependent on nomad livestock. Also described are attempts to settle these people and their herds in environments which are exploited best by mobile settlement and pasture rotation. Several writers (e.g. 53, 56, 57) report serious health and nutritional problems among sedentarized nomads, and equivalent difficulties for their herds, which are deprived of the seasonal round of forage or exposed to new diseases and deprived of adaptational defenses. Heady (98) found overgrazing and abuse of water sources in Arabia, resulting from settlement of Bedouin in connection with the oil industry. Talbot (179) described comparable effects of Masai sedentarization and argues for more effective control of pasturage and water if nomads are to be settled. Intersections of nomadic ecology, tourism, and wildlife are also discussed. All writers mention the loss of animal protein that frequently results from moving nomads away from their intensive livestock production. Many of the experiments of the 1950s have, at least temporarily, been dropped in favor of a return to a modified nomadic pastoralism.

While anthropological research has not contributed notably to this record, there is no question that the early insights of Barth (14) and subsequent studies emphasizing the cultural ecology of nomadic pastoralists laid a foundation for a correct ecological understanding of the adaptation; namely, the tendency for nomads to make extremely fine calibrations of resources, and to use available and friable-marginal resources in rotation, encouraging sustained yield.

The opportunities for anthropology arising out of pursuit of the research topics reviewed in this contribution lie in the evident fact that the theoretical relevance of agroecology studies is strengthened by a concern for policy implications. This is so because the latter requires studies taking place over relatively long periods of time in order to be certain of the feedback effects. Since one of the deficiencies of standard ethnological approaches to cultural ecology has been the tendency to confine research to short time periods, thus failing to observe man-environment relations over the (often) relatively long cyclical change patterns, anthropologists are being encouraged to extend their research across years instead of months. The same need for more rigorous demonstration is pushing anthropologists into technical contexts of analysis which require them either to obtain specialized training or to work in tandem with technical specialists. With the larger bodies of data acquired by such methods, research on extensive agriculture is coming to have impressive implications for ecological, demographic, and social-organizational theories.

Section 3:

THE HUMAN ECOLOGY OF BIG PROJECTS: RIVER BASIN DEVELOPMENT AND RESETTLEMENT

Thayer Scudder[6]

California Institute of Technology, Pasadena

In this era of national planning, the big development project is commonplace. In Hirschman's words, "the term 'development project' connotes purposefulness, some minimum size, a specific location, the introduction of something qualitatively new, and the expectation that a sequence of further development moves will be set in motion" (102, p. 1). Big projects constitute development from above; they are superimposed by national or regional agencies upon a local population which has virtually no say during the stages of feasibility studies, planning, and implementation. This generalization is especially applicable to big dams which continue to have

[6]I wish to thank my colleagues Robert H. Bates, David Brokensha, Elizabeth Colson, and Lance Davis for reading and commenting on an earlier draft. I am especially indebted to Elizabeth Colson. Though I take individual responsibility for the contents of this paper, so closely have we worked together over the past 17 years that it is impossible to know with whom certain ideas originated.

a special appeal to planners and politicians alike. Though river basin development and hydroelectric power are usually given as the economic justifications, an aura frequently surrounds dams which takes on intangible but important political and psychological attributes.

In Africa, Kariba was the first dam in the world to create a reservoir of over 100 million acre feet in storage capacity. Pushed to completion by leaders of the former Central African Federation to correct a power shortage, it was also seen as a symbol of modernization which would serve to cement together the territories of Northern and Southern Rhodesia (now Zambia and Rhodesia). In the words of the Federation's first Prime Minister, Kariba's "size and all that sort of thing makes such a popular appeal and it will be an excellent advertisement for the whole Federal area" (quoted in 91, p. 162). Since Kariba's completion in 1958, other big dams have been completed in Ghana (Volta), Egypt (Aswan High), Nigeria (Kainji) and the Ivory Coast (Kossou). Throughout the period of construction each was the most expensive project within the nation's development plan and each was associated directly with the Head of State who personally pushed completion as a symbol of national achievement. Though seldom documented by anthropologists, this "dam euphoria" has been described by Gonzalez (84) in a recent article on the Tavera Dam in the Dominican Republic.

Big dams are a product of technological changes that occurred during the early part of the present century (157, p. 14). In distribution they are found on all continents and in both low and high income nations. As for the reservoirs backed up behind them, by 1970 there were 260 with a surface area of 100 to 1000 square kilometers (72). Man-made lakes of this magnitude have a profound influence on the physical, biotic, and sociocultural systems of their basins, while the dams themselves alter the ecology of river systems below their walls (71, pp. 155–348). While eliminating floods and meeting important economic and psychopolitical needs, the Aswan High Dam, for example, will increase the incidence of bilharzia in Upper Egypt and facilitate the encroachment of the Mediterranean and hence of salinity into the Nile delta which constitutes the heartland of the nation (116, p. 187).

Man's creation of dams and large artificial reservoirs constitutes ecosystem modification on a grand scale. Unfortunately, far too little is known about the long term implications of such modification in different environmental zones. In the United States, for example, no major water project "has been studied with sufficient care and precision to determine its full effects on the systems of water, soil, plants, and human activity which it has altered. Few smaller projects have been examined in enough detail to judge whether they have attained the purposes for which they were intended" (45, p. 15).

Though there are no broad-based cost-benefit analyses which take into consideration ecological changes in the nonhuman environment as well as social costs for any of the African dams (and quite possibly this generalization could be applied to all major dams), their utility would be limited even if they existed, simply because river basins are dynamic ecosystems which have been profoundly altered by damming. Obviously man-made lakes are new water bodies. As such they will take years to stabilize. Throughout the period of stabilization profound ecological changes will continue to occur. The same applies to the river system below the dam. Some of these changes cannot be foreseen at present. The modeling of the physical and biotic aspects of altered river basins and man-made lakes is in its infancy (157), while the inclusion of sociocultural systems within such models has yet to begin. As Bennett has already pointed out in this symposium, human systems not only are more dynamic than nonhuman ecosystems, but their persistence is characterized more by changes in the relationships of the components than by return to original patterns.

Although those undergoing resettlement (the relocatees) constitute just one component of the man-made lakes' ecosystem, the study of human resettlement presents the anthropologist with an exceptional opportunity to carry out long term research within a very broad ecological frame of reference which could have major policy and theoretical implications (161). Even where they fail to meet expected cost-benefit criteria, dams incorporate the relocatees within a wider regional and even national entity (67; 161, p. 34; 190). They also increase opportunity during the implementation and stabilization stages of the project by providing new occupations, often accompanied by job training (58, p. 121; 158) and by widening the markets available for local produce through the provision of improved roads and waterways. In other words, by virtue of its very existence, dam construction accelerates change in certain areas of human behavior. Where suitable baseline studies are completed before relocation occurs, changes can be identified with their implications traced through subsequent restudies. But reservoir resettlement facilitates the study not only of the dynamics of change and continuity among specific human populations, but it also can lead to the generation of hypotheses dealing comparatively with a number of populations. In this sense the anthropologist is provided with a laboratory type situation in which one can study the extent to which different river basin populations respond in similar ways to compulsory resettlement and to incorporation within a new ecological setting.

An anthropology of compulsory resettlement (25, p. 286) also has important policy implications. Although long-run alterations in the physical and biotic nature of river basins may assume greater costs, to date resettlement probably has been the least satisfactory aspect of dam construction—both from the viewpoint of the local people and government planners. This is especially the case where the numbers of relocatees exceed 50,000 as at Kariba, Volta, Aswan, and Kossou (164). The compulsory resettlement of large numbers of people is an incredibly complex process since it requires shifting whole populations. Where government policy is to move people as communities, new settlements also must be created. No settler selection is possible since everyone—young and old, conservative and progressive alike—must be moved. Though resettlement agencies have been fairly successful in providing improved housing and social services, the record in regard to the emergence of viable land and water use systems is dismal (34; 157, pp. 30–31; 164). Though resettlement occurred over 7 years ago in both the Volta and Aswan cases, food relief is still necessary while the most comprehensive manual for resettlement (32) assumes as a matter of course that most governments will need to apply to the World Food Program (WFP) for emergency rations over an extended time period. The need to rely on food relief and other governmental assistance can easily produce a dependency syndrome among the relocatees, especially if the more innovative members of the community opt to leave the resettlement areas entirely. Added to such problems is the need for adjusting to a new habitat, including not just a new physical and biotic environment but also the previous inhabitants (or hosts), many of whom tend to resent the newcomers because of the attention shown them by resettlement officials and because their very presence increases land pressure.

Few governments are aware of this complexity until after the resettlement exercise begins. As a result, inadequate funds, personnel, and equipment are allocated for the task. In connection with the major African reservoirs, for example, final resettlement costs were two or three times the amount that was originally budgeted (113), while the personnel involved seldom have had previous experience with resettlement. To make a difficult task even harder, planning for resettlement rarely begins until after preparatory works have begun at the dam site, and in some cases not until after construction on the dam itself has begun. At that late date there is insufficient time to plan and execute a satisfactory transition from old to new habitats (159, p. 100); as a result resettlement becomes a crash program—full of stress for all involved including the administrators (104)—to remove people before the dam is sealed.

While this unfortunate situation continues to occur, increasingly planners are becoming aware of the need to deal systematically with resettlement during the initial feasibility studies. In good part this growing awareness is the result of the research and especially the publications of a number of anthropologists including Brokensha (25), Brokensha & Scudder (26), Butcher (32), Chambers (34), Colson (41, 42), Fahim (66–69), Fernea & Kennedy (74), Ingersoll (107), Jenness (113), Scudder (159, 160, 163, 164), and Scudder & Colson (165). Several of these investigators have worked in the field with UN specialized agencies (ECAFE, FAO, UNDP, and WHO) while others have been associated with a variety of agencies with a concern for the integrated development of river basins which may or may not involve the construction of main stream dams (see, for example, 157). Because of the combined results of such efforts, planners are finally paying more attention to resettlement during the initial stage of feasibility studies. This is especially gratifying in connection with the planning undertaken by the Mekong Secretariat (located in Bangkok) since the financial and social costs of resettlement in connection with such main stream dams as Pa Mong, where over 250,000 people might require removal, may be so great as to switch attention to other development alternatives. Not only are the opportunity costs of such projects high, but the construction of large-scale dams can easily lock a country into a particular pattern of subsequent development. The risks involved can be very great especially in smaller countries like Egypt, Ghana, the Ivory Coast and those of Southeast Asia which have access to only one major river system.

Detailed studies of the impacts of reservoir relocation by anthropologists and other behavioral scientists did not begin until the 1950s. Though long-term studies were predated by short-term social surveys sponsored by resettlement administrations to obtain census type data on future relocatees before removal, until recently neither planning agencies nor scholars have showed much interest in what happens to people following relocation. In the Tennessee Valley, for example, the world famous TVA has constructed over 20 dams since the 1930s. While these have required the compulsory relocation of over 14,000 families (half of which were share-croppers), I am aware of no follow-up studies other than two MA theses (neither subsequently published) by students at the University of Tennessee (31, 138).

The most systematic study of reservoir resettlement to date is that carried out by Colson and myself among the Gwembe Tonga, 57,000 of whom were relocated between 1957 and 1959 in connection with the Kariba Dam Project.[7] Though our initial baseline study in 1956–57 and first major restudy in 1962–63 dealt with the people on both the Zambian and Rhodesian sides of the river, our other visits (Colson in 1960, 1965, 1968, and 1972 and Scudder in 1967, 1970, 1971, and 1972) dealt only with the Zambian relocatees who numbered 34,000 in 1957. In analyzing our data we have noticed a number of regularities which we think may characterize other populations undergoing reservoir resettlement and perhaps any population faced with compulsory removal. Though an increasing number of anthropologists, sociologists, and geographers have begun to study reservoir resettlement, their field work is recent, and publications dealing with research both before and after relocation are few. The time is ripe, therefore, to present some working hypotheses as to how people will respond to compulsory relocation in the hope that others will test their wider applicability.

In his contribution, Montgomery accepts Audy's definition of health "as a continuing property, potentially measurable by the individual's ability to rally from insults, whether chemical, physical, infectious, psychological or social" (9). In this section I will be using the same definition except that the word "community" will be substituted for "individual." The "community" consists primarily of the relocatees; the "insults" follow from compulsory resettlement and dam construction. There are two broad types of insult: those of shorter duration which are associated with the resettlement process and long-term insults which affect a larger number of people since they result from the impact of the dam on both the lake basin and the downriver areas—in other words, from major modifications in the river basin ecosystem. Though my concern is with the former, an example of the latter type of insult is the increasing prevalence of bilharzia or schistosomiasis. Whereas the incidence of malaria throughout the world has decreased as a result of effective control measures, the incidence of bilharzia has increased until today it is the number one public health problem in the tropics (157, p. 36). This increase in large part is associated with the creation of reservoirs and irrigation projects, both of which tend to provide a favorable habitat for those species of snail which serve as intermediate hosts. Large-scale man-made lakes are no exception.

Prior to the construction of the Aswan High Dam, Van der Schalie (184, p. 63) commented on the possibility that the costs associated with an expected increase in

[7]Through 1963 this research was sponsored by the Rhodes-Livingstone Institute (now the Institute for Social Research of the University of Zambia). While the Institute has continued to provide us with substantial assistance until the present, financial support since 1965 has come from the Social Science Research Council, the American Council of Learned Societies, the Food and Agriculture Organization of the United Nations, the University of California (Berkeley), the California Institute of Technology, and the National Science Foundation.

the incidence of bilharzia in Upper Egypt could offset the benefits associated with the dam. While this prediction seems unduly pessimistic today, the incidence of bilharzia is increasing among fishermen on the lake (153) and no doubt below the dam where fields are converted from basin to perennial irrigation and where irrigation is extended to previously uncultivated desert areas. Though the spread of bilharzia around the shores of Lake Kariba has been slower, Hira (101, pp. 670–672) found 53 out of 77 (69%) school children examined at Siavonga in 1968–1969 to be infected with *Schistosoma haematobium,* while 12 of 77 were positive for *Schistosoma mansoni.* At Volta, the host snails for *Schistosoma haematobium* had yet to be found in the construction area in the early 1960s (Hughes 106, quoted in 189, p. 93). Yet by 1972 the incidence among over 1000 children in a lakeside study area within 10 miles of the dam exceeded 70% (1973 WHO communication to the author). Similar increases can be expected at both Lake Kainji and Lake Kossou.

In contrast to long-term insults like bilharzia, those associated with the resettlement process are of relatively short-term duration. They occur during a period of transition which is the time span for my analysis. This begins when the first rumors about the possibility of relocation circulate among the people. Though insults to the future relocatees commence at that time, they peak immediately prior to, during, and after physical removal. And they end, as measurable effects, only *(a)* after the relocatees once again see themselves as economically self-sufficient, and *(b)* when they feel at home in their new habitat—at which time the transition period ends. Though the emphasis is on the perceptions of the relocatees themselves, the observer can check these against baseline data to form his own independent view on when the relocatees have regained their former standard of living. As for feeling at home in the new habitat, here a variety of indicators can be used to assess adjustment to the physical and biotic environment, on the one hand, and to the hosts on the other.[8]

In connection with the major African reservoirs, the transition period that characterizes the resettlement process has extended for at least a year following physical removal. In the Kariba case most people were relocated in 1958 with the transition period coming to an end during 1964. Though a resettlement mythology continued to exist thereafter, our techniques were not powerful enough to analyze ongoing activities or their absence in terms of insults associated with the resettlement experience. As with their neighbors, the relocatees after 1963 were being influenced by events that pertained not so much to relocation but to the modernization of Zambia. Throughout the transition period, their ecological frame of reference was dominated by the lake basin and the downriver resettlement areas. Thereafter they were increasingly incorporated within an extended ecosystem which included not just the lake basin, but also the line of rail and the major urban centers on the Zambian Plateau (43).

I assume that compulsory resettlement is a traumatic experience which precipitates stress and leads to a crisis of cultural identity. Without exception populations

[8]In the Kariba case, we have emphasized, for example, the resumption of full funeral ceremonial, the reconstruction of household and other shrines, and a return to earlier rates of homestead and village fission.

involved in dam projects resist removal. When resettlement subsequently occurs, people know that they have suffered a terrible defeat because of the inability of their actions (mediated through their leaders and institutions and explicable in terms of their culture) to protect fundamental interests. In sum, it is hard to imagine a more dramatic way to illustrate impotence than to forcibly eject people from a preferred habitat against their will.

The concept of stress is critical to the hypotheses presented in this paper. Although analytically I see human societies as open-ended coping systems in which revitalization (191) can and does occur, those undergoing relocation behave as if a society was a closed system. As a result I hypothesize that revitalization movements [or what Kuhn rather ambiguously calls "paradigm change" in his *The Structure of Scientific Revolutions* (119)] will not occur during the transition stage associated with the resettlement process (see also 40, p. 2). While this may seem puzzling to anthropologists since compulsory resettlement would seem to create the type of conflict situation favorable to revitalization, I suspect that the stress of resettlement is so great as to restrict the capacity for major innovations during the transition period. Rather, people adopt a security orientation; they attempt to cope with uncertainty and to eliminate further risks by clinging to old behavioral patterns, old institutions, and old goals. Where these appear unsuited to the new habitat, they will either be dropped (perhaps entirely, perhaps temporarily) or altered incrementally.[9] Because the new habitat may be quite different, years later the accumulative result of such incremental changes might strike the informed observer as major innovations. Had he not observed the relocatees throughout that portion of the transition period which follows resettlement, this observer might not realize that the innovations represented the summation of a process of incremental change among a people who, in attempting to maintain the familiar and to keep change to the minimum, changed only so much as necessary to pursue old goals in a new habitat.

Analytically, the stress of resettlement can be viewed as a multidimensional insult with psychological, physiological, and sociocultural components. In the minds of the relocatees, relocation is associated with increased hardship and death. Fried's "grieving for a lost home" syndrome (79) is particularly hard on the elderly and on those whose contact with outside areas is limited. At Kariba women bemoaned the fact that they would have to leave the gardens, and especially the garden shelters, that had passed through the female line over generations. Shrine custodians feared that sickness would follow them if they left the areas with which their ancestors' authority was associated. Adults did not wish to leave the graves of their ancestors and complained that they were being thrown away by government into an unfamiliar and hostile hinterland far from their beloved Zambezi River.

As these examples indicate, the stress of resettlement in terms of perceived hardship begins well before the actual removal. It continues in the new relocation areas where the people find themselves as unwilling pioneers. In the major African dam

[9]See (42). Scudder (160) gives a brief description of how Kariba relocatees modified two existing institutions (possession dances and bond friendships) to come to terms with their new physical and biotic environment and its hosts in the major resettlement area below the dam.

projects water supplies in the new homes were initially unsatisfactory, a particularly difficult situation for those resettled at Kariba and Aswan since their former villages usually were within a few hundred yards of the Zambezi and the Nile. Even worse, new land use systems were not ready at the time of relocation so that government-supported food relief was essential to support the relocatees. As a result the people found themselves facing the additional insult of being dependent on the very government that they blamed for uprooting them in the first place. Dependency was further increased by an erosion of local leadership. Local leaders lost status regardless of whether or not they supported or opposed relocation since in the former case they were discredited by the mass of the relocatees and in the latter the execution of resettlement showed their impotence. In relating to local leaders, government officials were unwilling to entrust them with the large sums of money allocated for rehabilitation (42, pp. 184–86) or with a major say in planning the rehabilitation program.

Physiological stress can be best measured in terms of altered morbidity and mortality rates during the transition period. Though quantitative evidence is lacking, because of the absence of baseline surveys of public health prior to relocation, the people's association of resettlement with ill health may be an accurate reflection of reality. At Aswan, for example, Fernea & Kennedy reported that "communicable diseases such as dysentery, measles, and a form of encephalitis quickly spread in the suddenly condensed population. These conditions, aggravated by the high summer temperatures typical of the region, caused a rapid rise in mortality, especially among the very young and the very old" (74, p. 350). At Kariba, an outbreak of human sleeping sickness reached epidemic proportions in one resettlement area, while 41 children of the 1600 people resettled on the Central African Plateau (and hence several thousand feet about their old Valley habitat) died within a single 3-month period. In the Lusitu area below the dam, dysentery ravaged the population with approximately 100 of the 6000 relocatees dying during the first months after the move. A year later 53 women and children died in the same area of an acute condition whose etiology is still obscure, although the best explanation pertains to the consumption of toxic wild plants during a period of food shortage (81, 162). Though Colson's and my statistics show no appreciable increase in mortality among the elderly following relocation, this may be because resettlement's impact upon them was cushioned by being moved as part of a whole community.

A priori there is good reason to expect higher morbidity and mortality rates following relocation, and hence increased physiological stress. Aside from the psychological stress of removal, the increased population density which characterizes most resettlement (since governments try to aggregate people in order to provide better services) increases the risk of epidemic diseases, especially among children. Where new water supplies are inadequate, dysentery may be especially prevalent, while the absense of improved sanitary facilities can result in raised parasite loads. Hunger, caused by reduced agriculture productivity in the years immediately following relocation, has an adverse effect on health, while relocation to a different habitat may bring people into contact with new diseases or disease strains. The new lake itself can be expected to cause changes in the incidence of disease including bilharzia and malaria, the impact of which can be expected to continue long after the transition period associated with resettlement has come to an end. Sociocultural stress is inferred from the way in which people react to the implementation of resettlement. Though I assume that the absence of revitalization during the transition period is correlated with stress, such negative evidence is not very satisfactory. The conditions with which revitalization movements are associated occur with frequency during recent millennia, yet revitalization itself appears to be a relatively rare phenomenon. As Jenness has pointed out (personal communication, 1972), the compulsory relocation of entire communities is also comparatively rare, so that the odds are against the association of the two kinds of events even if compulsory relocation was in fact conducive to revitalization.

I have already hypothesized that those undergoing reservoir relocation behave as if they were part of a closed system. Certain aspects of their behavior during the transition period can be correlated with stress, while other aspects would appear to increase further the degree of stress. In responding to stress, the relocatees attempt to cling to the familiar through what I call a process of cultural involution. Not only do they stick to old routines, but they also adopt a defensive stance by falling back on a core group of supportive personnel with whom they intensify interaction during the period of most intense insults. In the Kariba case, these were kin and other dependents with whom one shared, or had previously shared, a common residence (42).

During our baseline studies, both Colson and I observed fission in our sample settlements during 1956 and 1957. As was the case in the past and is the case today, the goal of adult males was to establish independent homesteads and to increase their control over dependents, land, and livestock. As a result, enterprising men were continually splitting off from existing village homesteads to establish their own. At the same time, new villages were occasionally formed, while old villages fissioned as a result of sorcery accusations, soil exhaustion, and land degradation. During the years immediately following relocation, however, this normal tendency toward fission was reversed through the process of cultural involution.

In the resettlement areas very few villagers chose to use relocation as a chance to remove themselves and a select group of followers from an existing settlement by founding a new village. Not only were old villages reestablished as they were, but within the village, kin who had split off to establish separate homesteads immediately prior to relocation once again built together (see 42, pp. 75–82). A case in point was the history of Mazulu village during the years immediately preceding and following relocation. In 1956 the village consisted of four residential clusters totaling over 100 people. Three of these lay side by side with no discernible boundary between them, while the fourth lay a short distance away—separated by a large Indian Tamarind tree. During the next 12 months the heir-to-be of the head of the separated cluster split off to establish his own independent homestead at a distance of approximately 200 yards. Subsequently the head of another homestead died, and his senior son separated from his three married brothers and also established an independent homestead, while the headman, though a homestead head in his own right, built a new homestead which effectively set him off from the other villagers.

Though these people had been told that resettlement was imminent, and were worried about the possibility, at the time they did not really believe that the government would force them to move. So they continued the age-old process of homestead fission and settlement dispersal in response to entrenched goals. Following relocation this process was temporarily reversed. When new Mazulu was built below the dam, the four brothers built together, and again the headman built his homestead beside that of his fellows so that boundaries were indistinguishable. While the heir of the head of the fourth residential cluster rebuilt separately, his new homestead was now only about 10 yards away from that of his benefactor and less than 30 yards from the headman's. This situation continued through 1963, after which the process of fission once again took over so that by 1972 the village included 12 spatially separated residential clusters.

Another apparent characteristic or regularity associated with compulsory resettlement would appear to increase stress. This is a reduction in cultural inventory, and hence a simplification of the social system immediately following relocation. This occurs for two reasons. First, certain behavior patterns may appear to be irrelevant in the relocation areas and hence are dropped. A case in point are Nile rituals which involved the contemporary Nubian residents of Kom Ombo (and particularly the womenfolk) when they lived in their former homes close to the river prior to the second raising of the old Aswan Dam in 1933. After relocation these rituals fell into abeyance, presumably because the new settlements were sited in an austere desert area several miles inland from the Nile (70). Second, other behavioral patterns are dropped through fear of ridicule by the hosts and of other adverse repercussions in the resettlement areas. In the Kariba case, for example, the Lusitu relocatees hesitated about reestablishing individual, lineage, and neighborhood shrines for fear of alienating the spirits of their new environment and the mediating hosts. It was the latter who advised the relocatees to truncate their funeral ceremonial.

By analogy to ecosystems, simplification increases the vulnerability of social systems. Though I once uncritically utilized this analogy, its application presents major problems. Relocation may, for example, provide the opportunity for people to drop forms of behavior which have decreasing relevance and which even constrain them from following new goals because of inherent conflicts. Kennedy (personal communication) has forcibly made this point in connection with time-and capital-consuming sheiks cults among the Nubians (which were cut back following relocation), while Colson and I have noted the drastically reduced importance of neighborhood agricultural ritual among the Kariba relocatees following resettlement. While neighborhood ritual in the latter case facilitated the formation of a community consensus on when to carry out traditional agricultural activities, the sanctions involved did not encourage certain types of individual initiative. Especially constrained was the initiation of first planting and other seasonal activities before the neighborhood ritual leader had led the way. If such rituals had been carried over into the resettlement areas, the slowly increasing number of improved farmers would have had to choose between following community ritual or the advice of agricultural experts who recommended early planting under lake basin conditions. Though agricultural ritual was losing importance prior to resettlement, partly because of the influence of mission-operated schools, it was resettlement which delivered the fatal blow, and which, for better or worse, opened up the agricultural system to an array of new influences.

Simplification of a complex and relatively rigid institution (in this case the agricultural ritual) or social system may make it easier for people eventually to switch to new forms of behavior. In the case of compulsory relocation, the term "eventually" has increased meaning since I have already hypothesized that the capacity for innovation is reduced during the transition period. At that time the temporary or permanent cessation of certain behavioral patterns can be presumed to cause further stress. In the case of agricultural ritual in the Kariba Lake Basin, the number of people affected was relatively small; in the case of truncated funerals and increased uncertainty over the cause of misfortune, the large majority of the relocatees was involved. By removing familiar routines, the acting out of which give people a feeling of security, reduction in cultural inventory during the transition period can be expected to increase societal stress and reduce even further the capacity for innovative change at that time. This is especially the case with routines that alleviate uncertainty associated with a wide range of misfortunes including death and unfavorable agricultural conditions.

If the assumptions and hypotheses presented in this section are applicable to other populations undergoing compulsory relocation, we have made a step toward formulating a predictive model with both theoretical and policy implications. If, for example, the stress of resettlement reduces the relocatees' capacity for innovation during the transition period, resettlement authorities should keep their plans simple, they should emphasize the familiar, and they should encourage the people to get back on their own feet at the earliest possible moment. This does not mean, however, that a limited number of carefully selected changes cannot be introduced at the time of relocation through a cautious process of planning and implementation. Nor does it mean that the ground work cannot be laid during the transition period for a planned program of rapid change thereafter. Though emphasizing the need to keep resettlement separate from development as well as the need for simplicity, Butcher, for example, recommends (32, p. 7) the introduction of innovations in land tenure at the time of resettlement not only to give the relocatees a sense of security in their new habitat, but also to facilitate agricultural development at a later date.

The resettlement strategy suggested above is very different from that pursued by a number of governments which have attempted to use relocation as an opportunity to intensify agriculture and to introduce new organizational forms among the relocatees (see, for example, 3 and 34 in connection with the Volta case). To date no governments have shown the capacity to deal effectively with the complexities associated with compulsory resettlement (26, 32, 164), especially when a complex development program is initiated at the same time. Even if they did have the skills, attempts to combine resettlement with ambitious development increase the degree of stress as well as the dependency of the people on government; they also prolong the transition period. For the moment, the lesson for developers and social engineers is that compulsory resettlement is a drastic step, inevitably accompanied by a transitional period of suffering. It should be used as a development strategy only after an intelligent and extensive examination of alternatives has been completed.

Literature Cited

1. Adams, R. McC. 1966. *The Evolution of Urban Society.* Chicago: Aldine
2. Adams, R. McC., Jacobsen, T. 1958. Salt and silt in ancient Mesopotamia. *Science* 128:1251–58
3. Afriyie, E. K. 1971. *Resettlement Agriculture: An Experiment in Innovation at Volta Lake, Ghana.* Submitted to Int. Symp. Man-made Lakes, Knoxville, Tenn.: ICSU
4. Aldrich, S. R. 1972. Some effects of crop-production technology on environmental quality. *Bioscience* 22: 90–95
5. Allan, W. 1949. *Studies in African Land Usage in Northern Rhodesia. Rhodes Livingstone Papers No. 15*
6. Allan, W. 1965. *The African Husbandman.* New York: Barnes and Noble
7. Alland, A. 1968. Ecology and adaptation to parasitic diseases. In *Environment and Cultural Behavior,* ed. A. P. Vayda. Garden City: Nat. Hist. Press
8. Alland, A. 1970. *Adaptation in Cultural Evolution: An Approach to Medical Anthropology.* New York: Columbia Univ. Press
9. Audy, J. R. 1971. Measurement and diagnosis of health. In *Environ-Mental,* ed. P. Shepard, D. McKinley. Boston: Houghton Mifflin
10. Bailey, K. V., Bailey, M. J. 1960. Cause and Effect of Soil Erosion in Indonesia. *Symposium on the Impact of Primitive Man on Humid Tropics Vegetation.* Goroka: UNESCO
11. Baker, P. T., Sanders, W. T. 1972. Demographic studies in anthropology. *Ann. Rev. Anthropol.* 1:151–78
12. Barnicot, N. A. 1969. Human nutrition: evolutionary perspectives. In *The Domestication and Exploitation of Plants and Animals,* ed. P. J. Ucko, G. W. Dimbleby. Chicago: Aldine
13. Barrie, J. W. 1956. Population—land investigation in the Chimbu District. *Papua and New Guinea Agr. J.* 11
14. Barth, F. 1956. Ecologic relationships of ethnic groups in Swat, North Pakistan. *Am. Anthropol.* 58:1079–89
15. Basehart, H. W. 1973. Cultivation intensity, settlement patterns, and homestead forms among the Matengo of Tanzania. *Ethnology* 12:57–74
16. Bender, D. R. 1971. Population and productivity in tropical forest bush fallow agriculture. See Ref. 144, 32–45
17. Bennett, J. W. 1967. On the cultural ecology of Indian cattle. *Curr. Anthropol.* 8:251–52
18. Bennett, J. W. 1968. The significance of the concept of adaptation for contemporary socio-cultural anthropology. *Proc. 8th Int. Congr. Anthropol. Ethnol. Sci.* 3:237–41. Tokyo
19. Bennett, J. W. 1969. *Northern Plainsmen: Adaptive Strategy and Agrarian Life.* Chicago: Aldine
20. Binford, L. R. 1968. Post-Pleistocene adaptations. In *New Perspectives in Archeology,* ed. S. R. Binford, L. R. Binford. Chicago: Aldine
21. Birkbeck, J. A., Lee, M., Myers, G. S., Alfred, B. M. 1971. Nutritional status of British Columbia Indians: 2. Anthropometric measurements, physical and dental examinations at Ahousat and Anaham. *Can. J. Public Health* 62: 403–14
22. Blaut, J. M., Blaut, R. P., Harman, N., Moerman, M. 1959. A study of cultural determinants of soil erosion and conservation in the Blue Mountains of Jamaica. *Soc. Econ. Stud.* 8:403–20
23. Borun, M. 1972. *Health and Wealth of Two Untouchable Groups.* Presented at Am. Anthropol. Assoc. Meet., Toronto
24. Boserup, E. 1965. *The Conditions of Agricultural Growth.* Chicago: Aldine
25. Brokensha, D. 1965. Volta resettlement and anthropological research. *Hum. Organ.* 22:286–90
26. Brokensha, D., Scudder, T. 1968. Resettlement. In *Dams in Africa: An Interdisciplinary Study of Man-made Lakes in Africa.* London: Cass
27. Bronson, B. 1972. Farm labor and the evolution of food production. See Ref. 176, 190–218
28. Brookfield, H. C., Brown, P. 1963. *Struggle for Land: Agriculture and Group Territories Among the Chimbu of the New Guinea Highlands.* Melbourne: Oxford Univ. Press
29. Brothwell, D. R., Sandison, A. T., Eds. 1967. *Diseases in Antiquity: A Survey of the Diseases, Injuries, and Surgery of Early Populations.* Springfield: Thomas
30. Brown, M. L., Worth, R. M., Shah, N. K. 1968. Food habits and food intake in Nepal. *Trop. Geogr. Med.* 20: 217–24
31. Brown, R. G. 1951. *Family removal in the Tennessee Valley.* MA thesis. Univ. Tennessee, Knoxville
32. Butcher, D. 1971. *An Operational Manual for Resettlement: A Systematic Approach to the Resettlement Problem Created by Man-made Lakes, With Spe-*

cial Reference to West Africa. Rome: FAO
33. Carneiro, R. L. 1960. Slash-and-burn agriculture: a closer look at its implications for settlement patterns. In *Men and Cultures,* ed. A.F.C. Wallace. Philadelphia: Univ. Pennsylvania Press
34. Chambers, R., Ed. 1970. *The Volta Resettlement Experience.* London: Pall Mall Press
35. Clark, J. G. D. 1945. Farmers and forests in Neolithic Europe. *Antiquity* 19: 57–71
36. Clarke, W. C. 1966. From extensive to intensive shifting cultivation. *Ethnology* 5:347–59
37. Clarke, W. C. 1971. *Place and People.* Berkeley: Univ. California Press
38. Clements, F. W. 1970. Some effects of different diets. In *The Impact of Civilization on the Biology of Man,* ed. S. V. Boyden, 109–41. Univ. Toronto Press
39. Cockburn, T. A. 1971. Infectious diseases in ancient populations. *Curr. Anthropol.* 12:45–62
40. Colson, A. C. 1971. *The Prevention of Illness in a Malay Village: An Analysis of Concepts and Behavior.* Overseas Res. Cent., Developing Nations Monogr. Ser. 2, No. 1. Wake Forest Univ.
41. Colson, E. 1960. *The Social Organization of the Gwembe Tonga.* Kariba Studies, Vol. 1. Manchester Univ. Press
42. Colson, E. 1971. *The Social Consequences of Resettlement.* Kariba Studies, Vol. 4. Manchester Univ. Press
43. Colson, E., Scudder, T. 1972. *New Economic Relationships Between the Gwembe Valley and the Line of Rail.* Conf. Proc. 11th Seminar on Town and Country in Central and Eastern Africa. Int. Afr. Inst.
44. Committee on Procedures for Appraisal of Protein-Calorie Malnutrition of the International Union of Nutritional Sciences 1970. Assessment of protein nutritional status: a committee report. *Am. J. Clin. Nutr.* 23:807–19
45. Committee on Water, NAS-NRC 1966. *Alternatives in Water Management,* publ. 1408. Washington, D.C.: NAS-NRC
46. Conklin, H. C. 1954. Shifting cultivation. *Trans. NY Acad. Sci. II,* 17: 133–42
47. Conklin, H. C. 1957. *Hanunoo Agriculture.* FAO Forest. Develop. Pap. No. 12. Rome: FAO
48. Conklin, H. C. 1961. The study of shifting cultivation. *Curr. Anthropol.* 1: 27–61
49. Cook, S. F. 1949. Soil erosion and population in central Mexico. *Ibero-Americana* 34
50. Cowgill, U. M. 1961. Soil fertility of the ancient Maya. *Trans. Conn. Acad. Arts Sci.* 42
51. Cravioto, J., Birch, H. G., De Licardie, E., Rosales, L., Vega, L. 1969. The ecology of growth and development in a Mexican preindustrial community, report 1: method and findings from birth to one month of age. *Monogr. Soc. Res. Child Develop.* 34.5:1–76
52. Darling, F. F. et al 1972. Intensification of animal productivity. See Ref. 71, 667–790
53. Darling, F. F., Farvar, M. A. 1972. Ecological consequences of sedentarization of nomads. See Ref. 71, 671–82
54. Day, G. M. 1953. The Indian as a factor in the north-eastern forest. *Ecology* 34: 329–46
55. Desai, I.D., Lee, M. 1971. Nutritional status of British Columbia Indians: 3. Biochemical studies at Ahousat and Anaham reserves. *Can. J. Public Health* 62:526–36
56. Deshler, W. 1960. Livestock trypanosomiasis and human settlement in northeastern Uganda. *Geogr. Rev.* 50: 541–54
57. Ibid 1963. Cattle in Africa: distribution types and problems. 53:52–58
58. Doughty, P. L. 1972. Engineers and energy in the Andes. In *Technology and Social Change,* ed. H. R. Bernard, P. Pelto. New York: Macmillan
59. Dumond, D. E. 1965. Population growth and cultural change. *Southwest. J. Anthropol.* 21:302–24
60. Dunn, F. L. 1968. Epidemiological factors: health and disease in hunter-gatherers. In *Man the Hunter,* ed. R. B. Lee, I. DeVore. Chicago: Aldine
61. Dunn, F. L. 1972. Intestinal parasitism in Malayan aborigines (Orang Asli). *Bull. World Health Organ.* 46:99–113
62. Dunn, F. L. Traditional Asian medicine and cosmopolitan medicine as adaptive systems. See Ref. 125
63. Dyson-Hudson, R., Dyson-Hudson, N. 1969. Subsistence herding in Uganda. *Sci. Am.* 220:76–89
64. Dyson-Hudson, N. 1970. The food production system of a semi-nomadic society: the Karimojong, Uganda. In *African Food Production Systems,* ed. P. F. M. McLoughlin. Baltimore: Johns Hopkins Univ. Press
65. Edholm, O. G. 1970. The changing pattern of human activity. *Ergonomics* 13:625–43
66. Fahim, H. M. 1968. *The resettlement of Egyptian Nubians, a case study in de-*

velopment change. PhD thesis. Univ. California, Berkeley
67. Fahim, H. M. 1970. *Cultural Pluralism and the Development of Resettled Nubian Communities.* Presented at Soc. Appl. Anthropol. Meet.
68. Fahim, H. M. 1971. *The Evaluative Research of the Egyptian Scheme of Nubian Resettlement.* Presented at Soc. Appl. Anthropol. Meet.
69. Fahim, H. M. 1971. *Nubian Resettlement in the Sudan.* Unpublished
70. Fahim, H. M. *Change in Religion in a Resettled Nubian Community, Upper Egypt.* Unpublished
71. Farvar, M. T., Milton, J. P., Eds. 1972. *The Careless Technology: Ecology and International Development.* Garden City: Nat. Hist. Press
72. Fels, E. 1970. Die grossen staussen der erde. *Z. Wirtschaftsgeographie* 14: 229–44
73. Fenner, F. 1970. The effects of changing social organization on the infectious diseases of man. See Ref. 38, 48–76
74. Fernea, R. A., Kennedy, J. G. 1966. Initial adaptations to resettlement: a new life for Egyptian Nubians. *Curr. Anthropol.* 7:139–54
75. Flannery, K. V. 1968. Archeological systems theory and early Meso-America. In *Anthropological Archeology in the Americas,* ed. B. J. Meggers. Washington, D.C.: Anthropol. Soc. Washington
76. Flannery, K. V. 1969. Origins and ecological effects of early domestication in Iran and the Near East. See Ref. 12, 73–100
77. Freeman, J. D. 1955. *Iban Agriculture.* London: HMSO
78. French, J. G. 1967. Relationship of morbidity to the feeding patterns of Navajo children from birth through twenty-four months. *Am. J. Clin. Nutr.* 20:375–85
79. Fried, M. 1963. Grieving for a lost home. In *The Urban Condition,* ed. L. J. Duhl. New York: Basic Books
80. Furnass, S. B. 1970. Changes in noninfectious diseases associated with the processes of civilization. See Ref. 38, 77–108
81. Gadd, K. G., Nixon, L. C., Taube, E., Webster, M. H. 1962. The Lusitu tragedy. *Cent. Afr. J. Med.* 8 suppl.
82. Geddes, W. R. 1963. Discussion. *Symposium on the Impact of Primitive Man on Humid Tropics Vegetation.* Goroka: UNESCO
83. Geertz, C. 1963. Two types of ecosystems. In *Agricultural Involution: The Processes of Ecological Change in Indonesia.* Berkeley: Univ. California Press
84. Gonzalez, N. L. 1972. The sociology of a dam. *Hum. Organ.* 31:353–60
85. Gordon, J. E., Chitkara, I. D., Wyon, J. B. 1963. Weanling diarrhea. *Am. J. Med. Sci.* 245:345–77
86. Gordon, J. E., Wyon, J. B., Ascoli, W. 1967. The second year death rate in less developed countries. *Am. J. Med. Sci.* 254:357–80
87. Gorlin, P. 1972. *Health, wealth, and agnation in Abelam: the beginnings of social stratification in New Guinea.* PhD thesis. Columbia Univ., New York
88. Gourou, P. 1956. The quality of landuse of tropical cultivators. See Ref. 180, 336–49
89. Gross, D., Underwood, B. A. 1971. Technological change and caloric costs: sisal agriculture in northeastern Brazil. *Am. Anthropol.* 73:725–40
90. Haas, J., Riddell, J. C., Kingsbury, R. T., Wallace, W. 1969. Health profile and physical capabilities in a rural Liberian town. *Z. Tropenmed. Parasit.* 20:231–40
91. Hall, R. 1965. *Zambia.* New York: Praeger
92. Hankin, J., Reed, D., Labarthe, D., Nichaman, M., Stallones, R. 1970. Dietary and disease patterns among Micronesians. *Am. J. Clin. Nutr.* 23:346–57
93. Harris, D. R. 1969. Agricultural systems, ecosystems and the origins of agriculture. See Ref. 12, 3–15
94. Harris, D. R. 1972. Swidden systems and settlement. In *Man, Settlement and Urbanism,* ed. P. J. Ucko. R. Tringham, G. W. Dimbleby, Cambridge: Schenkman
95. Harris, M. 1966. The cultural ecology of India's sacred cattle. *Curr. Anthropol.* 7:51–66
96. Harrison, G. A., Boyce, A. J., Eds. 1972. *The Structure of Human Populations.* Oxford: Clarendon
97. Hausfeld, R. G. 1970. An anthropological method for measuring exposure to leprosy in a leprosy-endemic population at Karimui, New Guinea. *Bull. World Health Organ.* 43:863–77
98. Heady, H. F. 1972. Ecological consequences of Bedouin settlement in Saudi Arabia. See Ref. 71, 683–93
99. Helbaek, H. 1969. Appendix 1. In *Prehistory and Human Ecology of the Deh Luran Plain,* ed. F. Hole et al. Mem. Mus. Anthropol. No. 1. Ann Arbor: Univ. Michigan Press
100. Heston, A. 1971. An approach to the

sacred cow of India. *Curr. Anthropol.* 12:191–210

101. Hira, P. R. 1969. Transmission of schistosomiasis in Lake Kariba, Zambia. *Nature* 224:670–72

102. Hirschman, A. O. 1967. *Development Projects Observed.* Washington, D.C.: Brookings Inst.

103. Holling, C. S. 1969. Stability in ecological and social systems. In *Diversity and Stability in Ecological Systems.* Report of Symposium held May 26–28, 1969. Upton, N. Y.: Brookhaven Nat. Lab. Biol. Dep.

104. Howarth, D. 1961. *The Shadow of the Dam.* London: Collins

105. Hughes, C. C., Hunter, J. M. 1972. The role of technological development in promoting disease in Africa. See Ref. 71, 69–101

106. Hughes, J. P. 1964. Health aspects of the Volta River Project in Ghana. *Ind. Trop. Health* 5

107. Ingersoll, J. 1968. Mekong river basin development: anthropology in a new setting. *Anthropol. Quart.* 41:147–67

108. Iversen, J. 1949. The influence of prehistoric man on vegetation. *Danmarks Geologiske Undersogelse* 3.6:5–25

109. Jelliffe, D. B. 1966. The assessment of the nutritional status of the community. *World Health Organ. Monogr. Ser. 53.* Geneva: WHO

110. Jelliffe, D. B., Bennett, F. J., Jelliffe, E. F. P., White, R. H. R. 1964. Ecology of childhood disease in the Karamojong of Uganda. *Arch. Environ. Health* 9: 25–36

111. Jelliffe, D. B., Jelliffe, E. F. P. 1971. The uniqueness of human milk: an overview. *Am. J. Clin. Nutr.* 24:1013–24

112. Jelliffe, D. B., Woodburn, J., Bennett, F. J., Jelliffe, E. F. P. 1962. The children of the Hadza hunters. *J. Pediat.* 60: 907–13

113. Jenness, J. 1969. *Reservoir Resettlement in Africa.* Rome: FAO

114. John, T. J., Montgomery, E., Jayabal, P. 1971. The prevalence of intestinal parasitism and its relation to diarrhoea in children. *Ind. Pediat.* 8:137–41

115. Kallen, D. J. 1971. Nutrition and society. *J. Am. Med. Assoc.* 215:94–100

116. Kassas, M. 1972. Impact of river control schemes on the shoreline of the Nile Delta. See Ref. 71, 179–88

117. Kofranyi, E. 1970. The minimum protein requirements of humans, tested with mixtures of whole egg plus potato and maize plus beans. *Hoppe-Seyler's Z. Physiol. Chem.* 351:1485–93

118. Krantz, G. S. 1970. Human activities and megafaunal extinctions. *Am. Sci.* 58:164–70

119. Kuhn, T. S. 1962. *The Structure of Scientific Revolutions.* Univ. Chicago Press

120. Kunstadter, P. 1972. Demography, ecology, social structure, and settlement patterns. See Ref. 96, 313–51

121. Kushner, G. 1970. A consideration of some processual designs for archaeology as anthropology. *Am. Antiq.* 35: 125–32

122. Leach, E. R. 1959. Some economic advantages of shifting cultivation. *Proc. 9th Pac. Sci. Congr.* 7:64–66. Bangkok

123. Lee, M., Reyburn, R., Carrow, A. 1971. Nutritional status of British Columbia Indians: 1. dietary studies at Ahousat and Anaham reserves. *Can. J. Public Health* 62:285–96

124. Lee, R. B. 1969 (Correspondence). *S. Afr. J. Med.* 43:48

125. Leslie, C., Ed. *Comparative Studies of Asian Medicine.* Berkeley: Univ. California Press. In press

126. Löffler, L. G. 1960, Bodenbedarf und Ertragsfaktor im Brandrodungsbau. *Tribus* 9:39–43

127. Martin, P. S. 1973. The discovery of America. *Science* 179:969–74

128. Mata, L. J., Urrutia, J. J., Lechtig, A. 1971. Infection and nutrition of children of a low socioeconomic rural community. *Am. J. Clin. Nutr.* 24:249–59

129. Mata, L. J., Wyatt, R. G. 1971. Host resistence to infection. *Am. J. Clin. Nutr.* 24:976–86

130. Mayer, J. 1967. Nutrition and civilization. *Trans. NY Acad. Sci. II,* 29: 1014–32

131. Maynard, J. E., Hammes, L. M. 1970. A study of growth, morbidity, and mortality among Eskimo infants of western Alaska. *Bull. World Health Organ.* 42: 613–22

132. Metz, J., Hart, D., Harpending, H. C. 1971. Iron, folate, and vitamin B-12 nutrition in a hunter-gatherer people: a study of the !Kung Bushmen. *Am. J. Clin. Nutr.* 24:229–42

133. Moerman, M. 1968. *Agricultural Change and Peasant Choice in a Thai Village.* Berkeley: Univ. California Press

134. Montgomery, E. 1972. *Stratification and nutrition in a population in southern India.* PhD thesis. Columbia Univ., New York. 196 pp.

135. Montgomery, E. 1972. The significance of nutritional data in sociocultural research: examples from southern India.

In *Proceedings of the First Asian Congress of Nutrition,* ed. P. G. Tulpule, K. S. Jaya Rao. Hyderabad, India: Nutr. Soc. India, Nat. Inst. Nutr.

136. Netting, R. McC. 1968. *Hill farmers of Nigeria: The Cultural Ecology of the Kofyar of the Jos Plateau.* Seattle: Univ. Washington Press

137. Netting, R. McC. 1971. *The Ecological Approach in Cultural Study.* Reading, Mass.: McCaleb Module, Addison-Wesley

138. Nielson, R. L. 1940. *Socio-economic readjustment of farm families in Norris area.* MA thesis. Univ. Tennessee, Knoxville

139. Niering, W. A., Goodwin, R. H. 1962. Ecological studies in the Connecticut Arboretum natural area. 1. introduction and survey of vegetation types. *Ecology* 43:41–54

140. Nye, P. H., Greenland, D. J. 1960. *The soil under shifting cultivation. Commonwealth Bur. Soils, Tech. Commun. No. 51.* Farnham Royal, Bucks, England: Commonwealth Agr. Bur.

141. Odend'hal, S. 1972. Energetics of Indian cattle in their environment. *Hum. Ecol.* 1:3–22

142. Omran, A. R. 1971. The epidemiologic transition: a theory of the epidemiology of population change. *Milbank Mem. Fund Quart.* 49:509–38

143. Polgar, S. 1964. Evolution and the ills of mankind. In *Horizons of Anthropology,* ed. S. Tax. Chicago: Aldine

144. Polgar, S., Ed. 1971. *Culture and Population: A Collection of Current Studies.* Cambridge: Schenkman

145. Polgar, S. et al 1972. Anthropology and population problems. *Curr. Anthropol.* 13:203–78

146. Polunin, I. The ecology and evolution of disease in the Chinese, Hindu, and Arab worlds. See Ref. 125

147. Popenoe, H. 1959. The influence of the shifting cultivation cycle on soil properties in Central America. *Proc. 9th Pac. Sci. Congr.* 7:72–7

148. Raj, B., Prasad, B. G. 1970. Health status of the aged in India: a study in three villages. *Geriatrics* 25:142–58

149. Rappaport, R. A. 1967. *Pigs for the Ancestors.* New Haven: Yale Univ.

150. Rappaport, R. A. 1971. The sacred in human evolution. *Ann. Rev. Ecol. Syst.* 2:23–44

151. Reed, D., Labarthe, D., Stallones, R. 1970. Health effects of westernization and migration among Chamorros. *Am. J. Epidem.* 92:94–112

152. Salisbury, R. F. 1964. Changes in land use and tenure among the Siane of the New Guinea Highlands (1952–1961). *Pac. Viewpoint* 5.1:1–10

153. Satti, M. H. 1971. Health hazards from endemic diseases at Lake Nasser, UAR. Abstracted in *Abstr. Pap.: Int. Symp. Man-made Lakes.* Knoxville, Tenn.: ICSU

154. Schiller, F. 1971. Health aspects of the noble savage. *Clio Med.* 6:253–73

155. Schofield, F. D. 1970. Some relations between social isolation and specific communicable diseases. *Am. J. Trop. Med. Hyg.* 19:167–69

156. Schuphan, W. 1972. Nitrate problems and nitrite hazards as influenced by ecological conditions and by fertilization of plants. See Ref. 71, 577–90

157. SCOPE Report No. 2. 1972. *Man-made Lakes as Modified Ecosystems.* Paris: ICSU

158. Scudder, T. 1965. The Kariba case: man-made lakes and resource development in Africa. *Bull. At. Sci.* 21:6–11

159. Scudder, T. 1966. Man-made lakes and population resettlement in Africa. In *Man-made Lakes,* ed. R. H. Lowe-McConnell. London: Academic Press for Institute of Biology

160. Scudder, T. 1968. Social anthropology, man-made lakes and population relocation in Africa. *Anthropol. Quart.* 41:168–76

161. Scudder, T. 1969. Relocation, agricultural intensification and anthropological research. In *The Anthropology of Development in sub-Saharan Africa,* ed. D. Brokensha, M. Pearsall. Soc. Appl. Anthropol. Monogr. No. 10: 31–39

162. Scudder, T. 1971. Gathering among African woodland savannah cultivators—a case study: the Gwembe Tonga. *Zambian Papers No. 5*

163. Scudder, T. 1972. Ecological bottlenecks and the development of the Kariba Lake Basin. See Ref. 71, 206–35

164. Scudder, T. Resettlement. *Proc. Int. Symp. Man-made Lakes,* Knoxville, Tenn.: AGU for ICSU, Washington, D.C. In press

165. Scudder, T., Colson, E. 1972. The Kariba Dam Project: resettlement and local initiative. In *Technology and Social Change,* ed. H. R. Bernard, P. Pelto. New York: Macmillan

166. Scudder, T. et al 1972. Irrigation and water development. See Ref. 71, 155–367

167. Sears, P. B. 1956. The processes of environmental change by man. See Ref. 180

168. Selby, H. A. 1972. Social organization. *Bienn. Rev. Anthropol. 1971:* 283–325
169. Shack, W. 1971. Hunger, anxiety, and ritual: deprivation and spirit possession among the Gurage of Ethiopia. *Man* 6:30–43
170. Shatin, R. 1967. The transition from food-gathering to food-production in evolution and disease. *Int. J. Vitalstoffe-Zivilisationskrankheiten* 12:104–7
171. Simmons, I. G. 1969. Evidence for vegetation changes associated with Mesolithic man in Britain. See Ref. 12, 111–19
172. Simonett, D. S. 1963. *Soil Erosion in the Eastern Highlands of New Guinea.* Presented at Soil Sci. Soc. Am. Meet.
173. Smith, P. E. L. 1972. Land-use, settlement patterns and subsistence agriculture: a demographic perspective. See Ref. 94
174. Smith, P. E. L., Young, T. C. Jr. 1972. The evolution of early agriculture and culture in Mesopotamia: a trial model. See Ref. 176, 1–59
175. Spencer, J. E. 1959. Introduction. Symposium: effects of shifting agriculture on natural resources with special reference to problems in southeast Asia. *Proc. 9th Pac. Sci. Congr.* 7:51–80
176. Spooner, B., Ed. 1972. *Population Growth: Anthropological Implications.* Cambridge: MIT
177. Street, J. M. 1969. An evaluation of the concept of carrying capacity. *Prof. Geogr.* 21:104–7
178. Symposium on Nomads and Nomadism in the Arid Zone. 1959. *Int. Soc. Sci. J.* 11:481–585
179. Talbot, L. M. 1972. Ecological consequences of rangeland development in Masailand, East Africa. See Ref. 71, 694–711
180. Thomas, W. L. Jr., Ed. 1956. *Man's Role in Changing the Face of the Earth.* Univ. Chicago Press
181. Townsend, P. K. 1971. New Guinea sago gatherers: a study of demography in relation to subsistence. *Ecol. Food Nutr.* 1:19–24
182. Truswell, A. S., Hansen, J. D. L. 1968. Medical and nutritional studies of !Kung Bushmen in North-West Botswana: a preliminary report. *S. Afr. Med. J.* 42:1338
183. Truswell, A. S., Hansen, J. D. L., Wannenburg, P., Sellmeyer, E. 1969. Nutritional status of adult Bushmen in the northern Kalahari, Botswana. *S. Afr. Med. J.* 43:1157–58
184. Van der Schalie, H. 1960. Egypt's new high dam: asset or liability? *The Biologist* 42:63–70
185. Vayda, A. P. 1971. Phases of the process of war and peace among the Marings of New Guinea. *Oceania* 42: 1–24
186. Vayda, A. P., Rappaport, R. A. 1968. Ecology, cultural and noncultural. In *Introduction to Cultural Anthropology,* ed. J. A. Clifton. Boston: Houghton Mifflin
187. Rao, K. V., Gopalan, C. 1969. Nutrition and family size. *J. Nutr. Diet.* 6: 258–66
188. Waddell, E. 1972. *The Mound Builders: Agricultural Practices, Environment, and Society in the Central Highlands of New Guinea.* Seattle: Univ. Washington Press
189. Waddy, B. B. 1966. Medical problems arising from the making of lakes in the tropics. See Ref. 159, 87–94
190. Walker, D. E. Jr. 1970. *Politico-economic Effects of Columbia River Dams on Indians of the North West.* Presented at Am. Anthropol. Assoc. Meet., San Diego
191. Wallace, A. F. C. 1967. Revitalization movements in development. In *The Challenge of Development,* ed. R. J. Ward. Chicago: Aldine
192. Watson, P. J., LeBlanc, S. A., Redman, C. L. 1971. *Explanation in Archeology.* New York: Columbia Univ. Press
193. Watters, R. F. 1971. Shifting cultivation in Latin America. *FAO Forest. Develop. Pap. No. 17.* Rome: FAO
194. Wedel, W. R. 1960. The Central North American grassland: man-made or natural. In *Studies in Human Ecology.* Washington, D.C.: Pan American Union
195. Weiner, J. S. 1972. Tropical ecology and population structure. See Ref. 96, 393–410
196. Weiss, K. 1972. A general measure of human population growth regulation. *Am. J. Phys. Anthropol.* 37:337–44
197. Wells, P. V. 1969. Postglacial vegetational history of the Great Plains. *Science* 167:1574–81
198. Wylie, C. M. 1970. The definition and measurement of health and disease. *Public Health Rep.* 85:100–4
199. Yengoyan, A. 1966. Ecological analysis and agriculture. *Comp. Stud. Soc. Hist.* 9:105–17

SOCIAL AND POLITICAL MOVEMENTS

❖ 9518

Ralph W. Nicholas[1]

Department of Anthropology, The University of Chicago

The use of the word "movement" to refer to social and political phenomena first appeared in English in the early nineteenth century. The large-scale social changes and new forms of human distress that came with early industrialism were accompanied by a semantic reevaluation of such terms as "capitalism," "ideology," "masses," "culture," "revolutionary," and many more (Williams 44, pp. 16–17). "Movement" came to be used to describe group responses to the social and cultural crises produced by the conditions of factory labor and urban life during the industrial revolution.

There were, of course, recognizable movements in preindustrial societies. The archetypal movements in Western cultural tradition are the great Biblical ones: the movement of the Jews out of Egypt, led by Moses, and their return to the Promised Land; and the spread of early Christianity. These ancient movements have provided persistent paradigms for movements in the West and have been made available to other cultural traditions by Christian missionaries and European colonialism, by the expansion of Islam, and by the diaspora of the Jews. Thus, many of the recurrent features of movements—patterns of prophecy and eschatology—have a common cultural origin. These constant features, however, are imbedded in a wide variety of unique ideological formulations. Each ideology expresses the unique situation of a people whose life has been unalterably changed, makes this change intelligible, and prescribes action appropriate to the changed world.

[1] I am indebted to a number of colleagues whose contributions cannot fully be reflected in the literature cited: to Victor Turner, who gave me many ideas about movements in his seminar on symbolism; to Ronald Inden, with whom I have worked closely on the analysis of Bengali and South Asian cultural systems; to Shepard Forman and M. S. A. Rao, for fruitful discussions of the concepts used here; and to Paul Friedrich, David Aberle, and Marta Nicholas, who carefully read and criticized an earlier version of this paper. Ideas of Bernard Cohn, Lloyd Fallers, David Schneider, and others are present without acknowledgment. However, it was the heroic movement of the people of Bangladesh—even though they receive little explicit attention here—that impelled me to take up this subject, and it is to them and to the people of West Bengal that I am most deeply in debt.

Social and political movements issue some of the same challenges to anthropological theory and method that were raised by factions (Nicholas 25, pp. 21–23). Like factions, movements are often structurally simple and unstable; and they are functionally paradoxical in that they can be seen as at the same time "disruptive" (of a stable social order) and "adaptive" (to a changing social order). But the similarity stops here. The persons who make up a faction are recruited by a leader on the basis of his particular ties with them as individuals; the persons who constitute a movement are a moral collectivity, united by a common ideological commitment. The faction leader is usually a pragmatic politician whose legitimacy rests on short-run effectiveness; the leader of a movement is usually an extraordinary figure whose legitimacy rests on charisma. The coherence and persistence of a faction, which are often unexpectedly great, depend upon the continuation of the political struggle that is its *raison d'être;* movements are sociologically and ideologically evanescent, rarely appearing the same for more than a short span of time. Although factional contests sometimes appear to be fought over ideological issues, ideology is most often used as an acceptable disguise for an unacceptable struggle over personal power; movements, however, exist for and by their ideologies, and a successful challenge to ideology transforms or terminates a movement.

Like many of the problems that advance theory and method in anthropology, the problem of understanding movements is rooted in an empirical ethnographic problem. Anthropologists collect their data and test their theories through "fieldwork" and through comparisons with the results of other fieldwork. The techniques of fieldwork are adapted to microsocial settings, yet increasingly it is clear that the tribes, peasant villages, and nowadays cities or urban neighborhoods studied by anthropologists are only "part-societies with part-cultures," as Kroeber said of peasant communities. Moreover, we do not know if the units of our research are "representative" of anything larger than themselves and, if so, what that something is. The study of movements in contemporary societies poses the problem of macrosociology and whole-cultural analysis in proportions that anthropologists can grasp.

Winckler's (45) comprehensive survey and analysis of a decade of work on political problems by anthropologists is a conclusive demonstration of the progress toward solving the "conceptual problems" that Easton (9, p. 210) saw standing in the way of the development of a distinctly "political" anthropology. At the same time, examining anthropological analysis from the perspective of a political scientist's concepts of system and process, Winckler detects major gaps. Commenting on group (particularly factional) "inputs" into the political process (45, pp. 333–34), he notes a peculiar absence of attention to "the political issues at stake." And he is hopeful (45, pp. 347–48) that anthropologists will turn their attention and their new analytical methods to ideologies and political cultures. Factions and the small-scale arenas in which they occur are poor contexts for the study of issues, ideologies, and political culture. However, with movements, exactly the opposite is the case.

What is Political?

When Fortes & Evans-Pritchard (13) laid the foundations of political anthropology, they abjured the theories of "political philosophers" in favor of inductive empirical science. They placed great confidence in generalizations based on "observed behavior." To reach general propositions about political behavior assumes a general theory of politics that is applicable to all societies. The effort to devise such a theory has gone on continuously in the social sciences. What is common among most recent attempts is a belief that the empirical referents of the theory must be observable human actions—"behavior" is the official term. It is assumed that if we can observe some "behavior" we can figure out what it means—whether it is about politics, economics, kinship, religion, or law, or it is "multiplex," as Gluckman puts it, or "functionally diffuse," in Parsons' terms.

Searching for a theory to explain the peculiar position of political power in relation to religious authority in classical India, Louis Dumont (6, 7) reexamined the work of Indian "political philosophers." He found a conception of hierarchical subordination without which many thousands of instances of observed behavior could not be understood. This discovery has recently led him (Dumont 8) to reconsider Western social and political theories. He argues that so far as religion, politics, and economics are concerned, "our current definitions express our own culture, and our own culture—I would say our own ideology—embodies an *exceptional development*" (8, p. 31).

Viewed from a universal perspective, the cultural systems of the contemporary West (Dumont says simply "modern ideology") is eccentric in its valuation of the individual. For most societies and for most of history, the qualities distinctive of humanity were derived from society; it is only a recent and somewhat peculiar ideological development from Christianity in the West that sees society as a collection of individuals. Individualism has had a number of important consequences in Western social thought, and these consequences form largely unconsidered assumptions in contemporary social science. Dumont says (8, p. 32):

> Generalising, perhaps rashly, from India, I posit that in most societies the configuration of values has a hierarchical form where the all-embracing normative consideration which we usually call religion contains and limits whatever other social considerations are recognized. To draw only one consequence, politics as we know it is not, as is often assumed, a universal category, and, I believe, not a category capable of being generalised.

If Dumont is right, as I think he is, then we must examine again what is to be the subject matter of political anthropology (as well as the other "political" disciplines). We can define a political function, as in the past, in such a way as to find it in every society, although performed by an array of different structures and processes. However, if we are also to study culture, to understand the meanings by which persons define and differentiate their universes, then we must be prepared to recognize that there are some whole, integral cultural systems that define politics in a seemingly odd way or do not include a political domain even though we can find forms of action in the corresponding societies that strongly resemble what we, from our peculiar cultural perspective, call "politics."

What I refer to in the title as "social and political movements" may now be seen in a different perspective. "Movements" are "social" in the obvious sense that they take place in society and, at one level, they are a phenomenon of social organization. But they are also "social" in that they strive toward goals or values that are of major significance for the whole society. "Public goals" and "values" are key elements of two of the most widely used socially universal definitions of politics, those of Swartz et al (32, p. 7) and of Easton (10, p. 21). Easton, for example, defines the political system of a society as "those interactions through which values are authoritatively allocated for a society." More restricted movements aimed at limited social reform rather than a major social transformation appear infrequently in anthropologists' research, so most of the movements dealt with here are "political" under a definition like Easton's.

At the same time, most of the movements studied by anthropologists are commonly regarded as "religious" phenomena because they involve mystical beliefs, they invoke supernatural powers, they project eschatological fantasies, or have some other characteristic that belongs to our cultural category "religion." Dumont's (8, p. 32) point about the ideological consequences of individualism in the modern West is just as important with respect to religion as it is to politics. We see religion as one among a number of more or less equally important, autonomous realms, of which politics and economics loom largest. For most societies, however, what we call religion encompasses the whole society by providing the ultimate values to which "secular" values and norms have reference; it is *the* domain of authority. Thus, to refer to these movements as "religious," unless this term is to be used in its all-embracing sense, is just as misleading as to refer to them as simply "political."

These preliminary considerations, defining our subject matter and trying to distinguish our own folk categories from those of the people whom we study, arise from a reconsideration of what we can learn from "political philosophy" or "social theory" in its broadest sense, a reconsideration that I think is only at a beginning.

It is not difficult to understand why the distinction between the "religious" and the "political" has been so difficult to draw. Analysts have grappled with the problem in a variety of ingenious ways. Burridge (4, pp. 6–7), who emphasizes the "redemptive process" in movements, argues that the boundary is inevitably indistinct because both religion and politics are centrally concerned with "power." Shils (30, p. 68) holds that since "ideologies are concerned with authority, both transcendent and earthly," they are almost always "political" and, "whether nominally religious or anti-religious," ideologies are always "concerned with the sacred." In a perceptive summary and critique of research on millennarian religious movements, Yonina Talmon (36, pp. 140–44) notes that such movements have often been seen as precursors of secular political organization and as "preparatory schools" for political revolutionaries. Starting from the empirical cases of a number of new states in Africa and Asia, Apter (2, p. 61) has described "political religion in the new nations" as "no ordinary ideology" but "a more powerful symbolic force, less rational, although it may include rational ends." Apter relies upon the work of J. L. Talmon (33–35), who traces the origin and development, in Western political thought, of what he calls "political Messianism," which posits the inevitability of a future perfect society and replaces religion with politics, or rather, fuses the two.

The approach that I take here does not assume that there is necessarily a distinction among political, religious, or other kinds of movements. In some of the "simpler" societies with which anthropologists deal, the absence of a state, a government, or a king, or council in which a differentiated political function might be lodged is now a well-established fact. The dichotomy between sacred and secular or spiritual and temporal, which is crucial to the definition of "the political" in Western cultures, is not drawn (or is drawn very differently) in the civilizations of China and India. Such cultural differences have tended to be obscured by the apparatus of states and governments that have been erected in Asia and Africa since 1947. "Culture" has been invoked mainly to explain away aberrations from the expected patterns of "political development" rather than treated as fundamental to an understanding of what politics is conceived to be by the citizens of the new nations. "A tense conjunction of cultural conservatism and political radicalism is at the nerve of new state nationalism," according to Clifford Geertz (17, p. 328). Western social science is conceptually well prepared to deal with political radicalism, particularly in sociological terms, but is almost helpless when it comes to the cultural component, the structure of meanings that evaluate political symbols and political acts. Studying political movements places us squarely in the middle of the problem of meaning in politics.

The Concept of Movement

In its most general sense, "movement" is used in English to refer to a distinguishing feature of discrete bodies, the action of propulsion. Since a body is a distinct entity, its movement has the property of "direction" relative to other bodies and immobile objects. We distinguish between heavenly bodies, which we think are propelled largely by forces outside themselves (whether gravitation or the hand of God), and living bodies, which we think are propelled autonomously, largely by forces within themselves. Analysts of social movements occasionally write in language suggestive of the determinate quality of astronomical movement, as if the vectoral forces of external bodies impel the body of the movement, with a gravitational field set by its own "mass," to go in a certain direction. Usually, like an asteroid, it ends in a brief meteoric flash. However, most social scientists speak of the social body of a movement as if it were a living body, influenced by external forces but capable of a significant degree of autonomy in setting its own direction.

What is common to these conceptions—and underlies much Western social and political theory—is the notion that persons are united in a social *body,* a *corpus,* which moves or acts as an entity. The "body" is a symbol that has been used in specific ways in the cultural systems of the Christian West. The idea of Jesus Christ as God in a human body was translated into the Church as the mystical body of Christ made up of Christ as the "head" and of "members" who participate in the body by consuming the body of Christ in the sacrament of the eucharist. The symbol of the undying mystical body was brought into the domain of politics in the medieval European kingdoms. Jurists in Elizabethan England ruled that the King had two bodies, a "Body natural and a Body politic," the latter comprised of the King as "head" and his subjects as "members," mutually "incorporated" with one another (Kantorowicz 21, pp. 7–13).

The ramification of body symbolism in Euro-American cultures is very extensive and usually not much considered either by anthropologists or by students of politics.

The "body politic," the "head" of state or of a community, the "corporate" group and its "members" are so much a part of our vocabulary that it seems almost impossible to get along without them. Yet, like our concepts of politics and religion, our notion of human collectivities as "bodies" is part of a folk theory, and it is universally applicable only with explicit and self-conscious warning.

As an example of an alternative cultural construction, I cite the concept of "movement" as a symbol in Bengali culture. The body is used as a symbol in Hindu culture, but it is not usually conceived of as differentiated into a "head" and "members"; rather, it is characterized as an undifferentiated physiological unity. What distinguishes a human body from other generic types of bodies is the ability to discriminate, particularly between "right" and "wrong" conduct. The Bengali term that corresponds most closely to our conception of "political movement" is *āndolan,* a noun denoting three characteristics that seem quite disparate from a Western perspective: (*a*) movement or agitation, especially in the sense of swinging back and forth or oscillating; (*b*) exercise, study, and repeated practice; (*c*) discussion, criticism, debate, and controversy. Thus, instead of our general notion that a movement is unidirectional, (preferably "forward") the Bengali conception emphasizes movement that restores a previous situation. *Āndolan* places discipline and rationality where our concept might emphasize fervor and commitment. This is not to say that participants in Bengali movements lack fervor and commitment, or that discipline and rationality are not valued in Western movements, but that "movement" and *āndolan* are quite different conceptions. When we speak of "political movement" there is implicit a reference to common action with respect to a social body, the "body politic." When Bengalis speak of *āndolan* the reference is to the action of an individual human body with respect to "one's own country" *(swadesh),* "one's own rule" *(swarāj),* or that most individual of all goals, personal "liberation" *(mukti).*

DEFINITIONS   To return to the cultural constructs of anthropologists, the organismic analogy that likens a society to a living body in which the various organs or members must perform their "functions" if the body is to remain viable has figured largely in our thinking. From Durkheim through Radcliffe-Brown down to the present it has been regularly employed, usually accompanied by a warning about the dangers that come from carrying an analogy too far. A. F. C. Wallace (40) uses the organismic analogy to develop a comprehensive theory for the "movements" most familiar to anthropologists. He calls them "revitalization movements," with explicit reference to their attempted re-enlivening of both individual and collective bodies. He defines a revitalization movement "as a deliberate, organized, conscious effort by members of a society to construct a more satisfying culture" (40, p. 265). There are some problems in this definition—e.g. just what it is that adherents of a movement are "conscious" of and whether the satisfaction they seek is cultural, social, or personal—but Wallace's approach is generally neutral on the question of whether a particular movement is to be regarded as religious, political, or economic (although he uses the term "religious revitalization") (40, p. 264).

The advantage of Wallace's definition over that of Heberle (20, p. 6), which is designed mainly to cover "modern" political movements, is immediately clear: "The main criterion of social movement . . . is that it aims to bring about fundamental changes in the social order, especially in the basic institutions of property and labor relationships." Heberle's conception betrays its Western bias in singling out "property" and "labor" for special attention. A recent anthropological attempt at definition shows a similar bias, emphasizing evangelism and progress. Gerlach & Hine (18, p. xvi) define a movement as:

a group of people who are organized for, ideologically motivated by, and committed to a purpose which implements some form of personal or social change; who are actively engaged in the recruitment of others; and whose influence is spreading in opposition to the established order within which it originated.

Bias aside, their promising stress on the importance of ideology leads to disappointment when they announce (18, p. 159) that they do not intend to analyze ideologies ("belief systems") but only to discuss the functions of ideologies for movements.

A criterial definition of "movement" has recently been formulated by Paul Wilkinson (43, p. 27). While he aims at a sociologically universal type of definition, his criteria are based upon consideration of an exceptionally wide array of cases, and his formulation is intended to be of use to all of the social sciences.

1. A social movement is a deliberate collective endeavor to promote change in any direction and by any means, not excluding violence, illegality, revolution or withdrawal into 'utopian' community.
2. A social movement must evince a minimal degree of organization, though this may range from a loose, informal or partial level of organization to the highly institutionalized and bureaucratized movement and the corporate group.
3. A social movement's commitment to change and the *raison d'etre* of its organization are founded upon the conscious volition, normative commitment to the movement's aims or beliefs, and active participation on the part of followers or members.

In the absence of a good sample of cultural constructs parallel to the Western symbol of "movement," Wilkinson's criterial definition or something similar can serve to orient comparative research. However, the notions of deliberateness and consciousness must be broadly interpreted, particularly in revolutionary situations. In addition, Wilkinson speaks only of a "movement's aims or beliefs," suggesting the possibility that movements may be guided by something less than a coherent and comprehensive ideology, and he is critical (43, pp. 60–63) of the concept of "charismatic leadership," which I think is indispensable to understanding movements of social transformation.

TIME AND PROCESS   Movements bear a double relationship to time. From the point of view of the observer, each movement has a natural history or a "career" (Gusfield 19, pp. 447–49). Both socially and culturally, movements are processes, not of the regularly repetitive type that restore and maintain a social structure with reference to a persisting shared symbolic system, but rather of the type that lead to a qualitatively altered structure with reference to a changed pattern of meaning (Nicholas 26, pp. 296–99). Such processes are "liminal," in Victor Turner's (39, pp. 93–111) sense; that is, there is a "passage" between two radically different states of persons and societies.

From the perspective of movement participants also, the movement is liminal: it is a period of vanquishing evil and injustice, the interim between the end of the old and the beginning of the new. The movement may be conceived as marking the end of time as it was previously known and the beginning of eternity, or as the transition to the good and just society, or as the return to the uncontaminated life of the ancestors. The ideology of a movement projects an image of a new life that is outside ordinary experience and for which persons must take preparatory action.

While movements have widely varying degrees of success as defined by their ideologically envisioned goals, they leave behind them societies that are never quite the same as they were previously. The resultants range from the large-scale transformation of successful revolution to the abject demoralization of a pitifully unrealistic movement crushed by superior force. Nevertheless, no matter what the outcome, movements appear to become both *contagious* and *successive*. As news of a cargo cult spread from one area to another in Melanesia, people in the newly affected area began to have prophetic dreams and to experience seizures, even in the absence of overt evangelism or demonstrated success. At the other end of the continuum, the propensity of revolutionaries from one country to propagate their analyses, strategies, and goals in other countries, on the model of Christian missionaries, is well known. By "succession" I mean the tendency for earlier movements to become paradigms for later ones within a single society, as in the "prophetic tradition" of ancient Israel, the recurrence of Crusades in medieval Europe, and of peasant revolts in Russia since the seventeenth century, or the continuous lineage of messianic movements, dating perhaps from preconquest times in Brazil. In many societies, movements of particular types become a patterned form of response to roughly equivalent circumstances over sustained periods of time.

Despite the continuously transformative character of movements over any particular period of time, analysts have found in them discernible sequences of phases, either of the historic-analytic type with respect to individual movements, or of the generalizing-synthetic type with respect to a range of different movements. Theodore Schwartz's (29) account of the Paliau movement on the south coast of the Admiralty Islands is an outstanding example of historic-analytic periodization, covering the period from 1946 through 1954 intensively, although he also examines the pre-War roots of the movement.

In the immediate wake of World War II, during what Schwartz calls the "local phase," a number of leaders made efforts at social and cultural change. While they were comprehensive in their criticism of the old way of life, they offered only partial solutions to perceived problems. When the leader Paliau returned from New Guinea to the islands in 1946, he inaugurated the "first movement phase" by formulating a total program, the "Newfela Fashion," designed to bring a more European culture and society to the Admiralties by largely secular and pragmatic means. The movement was interrupted for three months in 1947 by a rapidly spread cargo cult that envisioned the imminent arrival of Jesus, the ancestors, and a cargo of European goods. Although the cult collapsed when its predictions were entirely unfulfilled, it had involved an unprecedentedly wide range of distinct communities, and it left behind a new unity upon which Paliau and his followers built the "organizational phase" of the movement, anticipating the extension of native courts, councils, and cooperatives to their area by the Australian government. During the period from roughly 1950 to 1953, the "Newfela Fashion" appeared unrewarding and the movement came onto a "plateau phase," characterized by a good deal of "backsliding." A "second cult phase" developed during this plateau and, unlike the first cult, engendered a coherent opposition among movement supporters who eventually defeated the cult. Schwartz's analysis concludes at this point, but he takes account of an additional "officialization phase" in which the anticipated administration-sponsored elected Council was established in 1954.

Schwartz's analysis, well supported by detailed evidence, is based upon the theory that preceding phases strongly condition succeeding ones. Smelser (31) has elaborated a theory of the careers of movements based upon a similar idea, the economic concept of "value-added." He aims at analysis of the temporal process of specific movements in generalizing-synthetic terms. While specifiable preconditions must exist for any kind of episode of collective behavior to occur, the nature, strength, and sequencing of conditions determine the character and career of a movement. The holistic type of movement considered here is termed by Smelser (31, pp. 313–81) "the value-oriented movement": "a collective attempt to restore, protect, modify, or create values in the name of a generalized belief." Smelser's conditions are a mixture of predisposing factors, preconditions, and developmental phases, which he terms (a) structural conduciveness, (b) strain, (c) the crystallization of beliefs, (d) precipitating factors, (e) mobilization for action, and (f) social control.

An example of purely generalizing-synthetic distinctions among movement phases is Burridge's (4, pp. 105–16) three-part periodization, based upon a limited comparison of millennarian movements. Phase 1 of a movement is marked by a recognition of "disenfranchisement" by the affected group, a recognition that precipitates a crisis of understanding, a loss of the sense of personal worth, and "a ferment of intellectual endeavor" directed toward finding "a new integrity." The beginning of Phase 2 is marked by a tentative testing in action of the intellectually achieved solutions reached in Phase 1. Purely political and economic solutions often appear as unsuccessful because they do not touch "fundamental assumptions." The role of the prophet, who either appears in this phase or not at all, is to place the new solutions in a larger "revealed" context and to symbolize in himself the "new man" that all seek to become. Phase 3 is termed "the aftermath." The movement may be successful in achieving its new solutions and become "enfranchised," it may become encysted as a distinct sect, or, as is commonly the case with what come to be seen as anticipatory prophets, it launches a new Phase 1.

Social science has experienced continuing difficulty in the analysis of non-recurring processes. We are adept at handling processes that maintain social systems and at demonstrating the long-term stability of symbolic systems. But, if the easy determinisms of vulgar Marxism and Hegelianism are dismissed, frameworks for analyzing cultural and social change are either so complex as to make an analysis little different from a unique history or so general as to lose sight of most of the data. It is clear that even the isolated, "stable" societies of an earlier generation of anthropological writing never achieved equilibrium. What is less clear is the relationship between culture and disequilibrium.

RELATIVE DEPRIVATION AND ETIOLOGY   There is a general consensus among scholars of different theoretical perspectives that movements take place largely among poor, oppressed, demoralized people. The Seneca prophet Handsome Lake began to preach his "Good Message" only after the Iroquois had been utterly defeated, their once-powerful Confederacy shattered, people driven into wretched encampments where hunger, cold, disease, and pestilence cut away at their population. Alcoholism, suicidal tendencies, fear of witchcraft, and factionalism plagued those who remained. It was from this context that the "Good Message" movement came to give a new birth to the Seneca and to many other Iroquois (Wallace 41). It was from the uprooted and marginal population of medieval Europe—landless peasants, insecure craftsmen, beggars, and vagabonds—that "revolutionary millennarianism drew its strength" (Cohn 5, p. 282). Lanternari (22) refers to such movements as "the religions of the oppressed." Politically, it is the relatively powerless who become the mass basis of movements; it is they who have a grievance, whether it is articulated by bourgeois ideologues or by leaders thrown up from their own ranks. Explanations intended to cover the whole range of movements have taken several forms (Thrupp 37, pp. 25–27).

The concept of "relative deprivation" provides the basis for a comprehensive explanation of the etiology of movements. Whether it appears as oppression and exploitation, or as the withholding of benefits, or as rising expectations, some form of relative deprivation precedes every social movement. Drawing on a great deal of earlier research, David Aberle (1, pp. 315–33) has developed the fullest version now available of the relative deprivation hypothesis. He defines a social movement as "an organized effort by a group of human beings to effect change in the face of resistance by other human beings" (1, p. 315). Movements are classified according to the locus of the desired change (individual or supra-individual) and whether a total or partial change is sought (1, p. 316). Aberle pays little attention to what he calls "reformative" and "alterative" movements which aim at partial changes. He is primarily concerned with "transformative" movements directed toward "total change in supra-individual systems" and "redemptive" movements, which "aim at a total change in individuals" (1, p. 317).

No movements occur in the absence of perceived "relative deprivation," a social psychological concept that summarizes various forms of distress and discontent as "a negative discrepancy between legitimate expectation and actuality, or between legitimate expectation and anticipated actuality, or both" (1, p. 323). He classifies relative deprivations under four headings: "possessions, status, behavior, and worth" (1, p. 326). Relative deprivation does not always lead to the development of a movement, and particular types of deprivation do not lead to certain types of movement. The development of a movement is dependent upon "the context of social relationships of the deprived group" and its "diagnosis of the source of its deprivations" (1, p. 329). Movements seeking total changes tend to occur among deprived groups that lack access to power, often because of social or political subordination or the threat of subordination. Transformative movements are most frequent where the deprived group is socially or spatially isolated from the superordinate group, while redemptive movements are most common among deprived groups that are to some extent integrated in a larger society, although in an altered position of subordination (1, p. 330).

Aberle's explanation is an important theoretical advance, but it does not draw all of the implications from the relative deprivation hypothesis because he blurs the distinction between the social and cultural systems and because he focuses on the "experience of relative deprivation" at the expense of other psychological processes that accompany the phenomenon (1, p. 323).

Sociologically, we can identify many instances in which new relationships of super- and subordination are established. Whether or not a subordinate group is relatively deprived is defined by its culture, that is, by the meaning that a group places on its new relationship. Where the superordinate group is from a technologically advanced Western country and the subordinate one is a small non-Western society without a competitive technology, the new relationship is often initially anomalous, lacking in any known meaning, and thus a challenge to the authoritativeness of the indigenous culture. What appears socially as powerful alien domination often appears culturally, at least at the outset, as a contradiction of the most authoritative meanings: the foreigners do everything wrong and still get their own way. The early "culture contact" situation of subordinate groups of this type is often characterized as "demoralization."

Demoralization is simultaneously a psychological, social, and cultural phenomenon. As Wallace (40, pp. 268–75) puts it, individuals in a society or social group experience increasing stress, comonly leading to increasing incidence of alcoholism, passivity, indolence, violence, irresponsibility, etc. Wallace refers to such a phase as "cultural distortion." Demoralization and distortion usually persist for a period of years, although the duration and outcome are affected by a number of variables that I cannot discuss here. The creative response to demoralization and distortion appears culturally as a symbolic reformulation, a new ideology that gives meaning to the changed situation and, by doing so, entails innovative patterns of action. Psychologically, this creative response appears as what Wallace calls a "mazeway reformulation," a coherent restructuring of what is known, believed, or accepted in the society. Such a "new synthesis of values and meanings" typically occurs to a single person as an inspiration or revelation, often in a dream or vision. This person emerges as a prophet or messiah, the charismatic leader of what appears socially as a movement.

This summary ignores a number of important determinants of the shape of new ideologies, movements, and leaders. For example, the presence of Christian missionaries, the social organization of the subordinate group and its leadership pattern are among the factors that give a distinctive form to every movement. Also, the nature of movements that develop among relatively deprived groups which share a common culture with their superordinate groups is different from movements that develop where cultural differences are great. In particular, the new ideology of the latter type (great cultural difference) invariably incorporates new symbols and meanings borrowed from the dominant group, while in the former type (same culture) the new ideology involves a reevaluation and changed emphasis on shared symbols (e.g. the Holy Ghost is emphasized over Christ, or equality over liberty). However, this discussion indicates the elements that I think necessary to make Aberle's hypothesis complete. The next two sections take up the problems of ideology and charismatic leadership.

Culture and Ideology

To make explicit the view of culture and the assumptions underlying the preceding discussion: I regard a culture as a system of symbols shared and transmitted by a group of people. In most cases, the group of people is a society. There are segmental, dependent symbolic systems shared among persons who constitute definable parts of whole societies (e.g. classes, professional groups) but these do not concern us here. A culture provides a person with categories (concepts) against which to match perceptions; that is, a culture provides the meaning for human experience. As they grow up, individuals learn these categories or meanings, largely in the social contexts in which they are used; and they develop the capacity to communicate with others on the basis of common meanings represented mostly by verbal symbols. This bare statement would be accepted by many (but by no means all) anthropologists. Space does not permit a full argument for this view and against competing views, so it may be regarded as a definition and set of related assumptions. Among those who accept this definition of culture there is no agreement about how a culture is to be "analyzed" or "understood."

If the lexicon of a language is used as an index, it is apparent that any culture contains a very large number of meanings. In what sense can such a set of meanings be said to constitute a "system"? Relations among meanings are not anything like the relations among persons in society. Regular patterns of social interaction have meaning, are describable in cultural categories, and are often culturally evaluated, that is, categorized as proper or improper. Human social interaction cannot be devoid of symbolic content, but the orderliness of the group of meanings that constitute a culture cannot be found in social interaction.

Ruth Benedict is the principal author of the anthropological notion that individual cultures have unique patterns of integration. Recent research (e.g. Dumont 6, Geertz 16, Schneider 27, Turner 39) has greatly refined the methods of cultural analysis and demonstrated that cultures may fruitfully be treated as coherent symbolic systems. It now appears that cultural systems are integrated in two ways: "horizontally" with respect to discrete meanings, and "hierarchically" with respect to the ultimate ground of authority of a culture. "Horizontal" integration subsists in a coherence among meanings. Discrepant interpretations of the same phenomenon and inconsistent or contradictory meanings given to related phenomena tend not to persist within a single system. The logical rules of consistency and contradiction are different in different cultures but, given these differences, I would argue for the existence of a universal process of Weberian "rationalization" and against Lévy-Bruhl's (23, p. 90) contention that "primitives" (or anyone else) might be "indifferent as a rule to the law of contradiction." The cultural process of eliminating inconsistent meanings must go on continuously and universally because of the human capacity for culturally unprecedented experiences or discoveries and because of what we may posit as a human need, rooted in the capacity for and dependence upon culture, to give meaning to or to "explain" everything. New experiences often call for a symbolic reformulation that leads to ramifying changes in the symbols and meanings of a culture—a horizontal reintegration.

Extensive change in a cultural system, demanded by the massive significance of such unprecedented experiences as the arrival of a vastly superior colonizing power or a social revolution, creates doubt about the ultimate basis of authority, the "religion" in Dumont's sense. Anthropologists have recently developed a number of concepts referring, in somewhat different terms, to the notion that cultural systems are hierarchically integrated. Schneider's (27) "central symbols" are concepts that define large areas of related meanings ("cultural domains") and differentiate those meanings by distinguishing their symbolic representation from one another. Geertz's (15, p. 66) use of expressions such as "synoptic paradigm" focuses on the great semantic and evaluative load that is carried by some symbols, which may be regarded as summarizing meanings drawn from many cultural domains. Victor Turner (39) speaks of the "dominant symbols" of rituals as being multivocal or polysemic, as conveying a range of meanings which at one end touches on the most crucial values of a society and at the other is related to emotionally charged "grossly physiological" substances and actions (e.g. blood, semen, sexual intercourse).

Whichever approach is taken, the hierarchical pattern of cultural integration appears as a relation between a small number of semantically complex symbols, which often have a "sacred" quality and are frequently used in rituals and myths, and a relatively large number of dependent symbols which are semantically simpler and are used in ordinary contexts. "Central" or "dominant" symbols may broadly be said to be religious symbols, although in the context of Dumont's "individualistic universe" the sacredness of political symbols (the Constitution), economic symbols (the Free Enterprise System), or kinship symbols (sexual intercourse) may not at first be apparent.

Geertz (16, p. 4) argues that "religious symbols formulate a basic congruence between a particular style of life and a specific (if, most often, implicit) metaphysic, and in so doing sustain each with the borrowed authority of the other." The psychological experience of relative deprivation and the corresponding social condition, a new pattern of subordination, forcibly alter the style of life of the subordinated people. There is an incongruity between style of life and metaphysic which challenges the authoritativeness of both and sets in train the process of rationalization or symbolic reformulation; it is the crisis that brings forth both an ideology and its charismatic voice.

IDEOLOGY   "Ideology" is a term heavily charged with connotations of falsity and fanaticism; it is often used in ways that suggest that it is the very opposite of objective, reasoned understanding. However, if we take the view that objective, reasoned understanding is achieved only in terms of authoritatively given cultural constructs, meanings, and categories, the sharpness of the distinction between ideology and objectivity begins to blur. Like a culture taken as a whole, an ideology is a symbolic system. As Geertz (15, p. 62) puts it, along with other systems of symbols ("culture patterns"), ideologies "provide a template or blueprint for the organization of social and psychological processes." An ideology is persuasive in that it uses existing symbols, either indigenous or alien, to create new configurations that startle, provoke, or awaken persons, while providing them with a credible diagnosis of what has gone wrong with their lives and an authoritative prescription for innovative action. To say that such new images and associations are "distortions" misses their main point: it is to dismiss Marx and Engels because they believed in ghosts ("A spectre is haunting Europe . . .").

A fundamental part of the ideology of the Paliau movement illustrates the formulation of persuasive new images, the use of central symbols, and the synthesis of symbols from different cultures. Admiralty Islanders generally believed that white men, particularly missionaries, had lied to black men by revealing only one meaning of Jesus' message while concealing its inner significance, which would have brought them a white standard of life (Schwartz 29, p. 249). Jesus decided to give the natives the whole revelation and so, one night during the war, appeared to Paliau in a dream.

> Jesus showed Paliau a book. It was the original book *tabu,* the Bible. It had been encased in concrete, and the book itself was half metal, half stone. No one could open it, and no hack saw could have made an impression on the metal. Such was the knowledge that had been concealed from the natives. Now Paliau was given part of this knowledge. All the content of the early meetings is said to have been revealed to him at this time (29, p. 257).

A wide range of distress and discontent is explained in a powerful synthetic image composed of native and foreign elements centered around the authoritative and sacred symbol of the Bible.

Ideological systems are prey to the same problems of coherence and authority as are other cultural systems. Apter (3, pp. 26–28) notes the tension between the themes of nationalism and socialism in new state ideologies; he finds a general oscillation between extremes of these two goals during the pre-independence, independence, and post-independence phases in many new nations. Such oscillations seen in symbolic terms consist of the reevaluation of older symbols and the elevation of one symbol to a place of importance over another which had previously been foremost. The movements first for Indian independence, then for Pakistan, and most recently for Bangladesh illustrate similar ideological processes.

As the Indian independence movement grew during the first three decades of this century, appeals made to large audiences increasingly involved Hindu symbols. A section of the Indian Muslim elite declared that independence for India would not free the Muslims, who would remain subordinate in a Hindu-dominated state.

Despite protests from the largely secular leadership of the Indian National Congress, Muslim leaders began to agitate for a separate homeland in the Muslim-majority areas of northwestern India. There was another area of Muslim majority on India's eastern extremity. Although most of the peasantry of the Province of Bengal were Muslims, they typically cultivated lands that were controlled by high-caste Hindus. The call for a separate Muslim homeland, raised by upcountry Muslims who were in other respects alien to the distinctive culture of Bengal, resonated among the tiny elite of Bengali Muslims, who carried the Pakistan agitation to the countryside. Islam became the dominant symbol among Bengali Muslims, suppressing the previously powerful symbols of the Bengali language and the Bengali country *(Bangla-desh)* that had been the central symbols of Bengali unity.

Soon after Pakistan was created in 1947, the Bengali leadership, representing a majority of the population of the new nation, began to object to the second-class status accorded their province by the dominant West Pakistani elite. This grievance first erupted in the struggle over a national language and, even after Bengali had been made a national language along with Urdu, the problem was not fully resolved. Significant official opinion held that Bengali was a Hindu-tainted language. This opinion was later generalized among West Pakistanis as a belief that Bengalis were Hindu-tainted Muslims, which underlay many atrocities committed by Pakistani troops in Bangladesh.

In 1966, when the Bengali leader Sheikh Mujibur Rahman announced his "Six-point Formula" (subtitled "Our Right to Live"), the people of East Bengal still overwhelmingly identified themselves as Pakistanis (Schuman 28). The "six points" dealt primarily with problems of economic and political parity for East Pakistan. In the December 1970 elections, the Bengali Awami League won an absolute majority in the new National Assembly (and thus deciding power on a new constitution and control over the government). The West Pakistani leadership delayed the meeting of the Assembly in hopes of getting a compromise from the Bengalis. A symbol that had been rising in importance during the election period suddenly appeared as the preeminent symbol of the unity and identity of the Bengalis—the "country of Bengal" *(Bangla-desh)* itself emerged to subordinate the Islamic symbol of Pakistan. The barbarous army "crackdown" on Bengali separatists, begun at midnight on March 25, 1971, sealed the meaning of this symbol: What had been a movement for regional autonomy became a movement for national independence. The frequently fatal heroism that this symbol and its ideology inspired is well documented (M. Nicholas, Oldenburg 24).

When Bangladesh became an independent nation, with secularism and socialism as official goals, the symbols of the movement period began to pale. Sheikh Mujib ordered the silhouette map of eastern Bengal removed from the national flag, arguing that no country puts its map on its flag. In fact, the very name of the country raises the uncomfortable fact that Bangladesh is not the whole of the "country of Bengal," but only the portion in which Muslims are a majority. Hindu-majority West Bengal remains in India. Islam as a symbol has to be conjoined with the symbol of the land in order to define Bangladesh nationality. Although Sheikh Mujib has fought to make Bangladesh a secular state, he is himself a pious Muslim and cannot oppose the recrudescence of Islam in Bengal except when the attendant anti-Hindu sentiments become overt.

The agrarian ideology of Mexican peasants is quite different in content from those of Paliau and the Bengali nationalists. Paul Friedrich (14) gives a detailed historical account of the development of such an ideology in individual, social, and cultural settings. The origin of the movement lay in the 1880s with the alienation of most of the land of the Tarascan Indian village of Naranja to two Spaniards. The ensuing experience of relative deprivation was also one of absolute deprivation, as living standards fell below anything the villagers had previously known. Agitation for agrarian reform was begun on a small scale as early as 1888 by a villager named Joaquín de la Cruz, who had completed part of a legal education. By the time of his assassination in 1919, "the agrarian movement had already achieved momentum in the region"; there were "active local groups" and "a revolutionary ideology was taking place in peoples' minds." Friedrich (14, pp. 56–57) traces this ideology to four principal sources: the specific experience of losing land; outside political forces, particularly the Mexican Revolution; "the spread of socialistic ideas concerning poverty"; and the personal devotion of committed men such as Joaquín.

This was the setting to which an extraordinary young villager named Primo Tapia returned after 14 years in the United States. While in the U.S. Primo had apprenticed himself to the anarcho-syndicalist Flores Magón brothers, where he imbibed the ideas of Bakunin, Kropotkin, Malatesta, and Tolstoy, ideas that were harmonious with "his agrarian concerns, . . . his hatred of the bourgeoisie, . . . his acceptance of revolutionary violence, . . . his millennarian fervor, and . . . his inflammatory style" (14, p. 65). He worked at many jobs in the western U.S. and acted as an organizer for the Industrial Workers of the World. In 1920 he returned to Naranja, at what was an opportune time, having "internalized an elaborate and emotionally charged ideology" (14, p. 74). It might appear that, as an ideologist, Primo Tapia was unoriginal, his formulations were mainly derivative; but in the specific context of Naranja and the Tarascan-speaking area, it was he "who catalyzed and synthesized the preconditions of revolt into the realization of revolt" (14, p. 140). The unspoken values respecting the land and kinship that Primo shared with his fellow Indians constituted the implicit underpinning of the agrarian ideology he articulated. When this ideology represented the alienation of the village's land as "the rape of the pueblo" (14, p. 137), it spoke to these values in unmistakable, emotionally powerful symbolism.

Friedrich (14, pp. 136–39) argues for the critical role of the ideology in the success of the movement. Neither effective organization nor physical violence undirected by ideology could ever succeed. However, effective legal and political action at supravillage levels was also essential to their final victory. The case of the Brazilian peasant movement led by Francisco Julião provides an instructive contrast with the Mexican case (Forman 12). The Brazilian peasantry existed in poverty for centuries before the demand for land reform was articulated in peasant movements. Julião relied on urban organizers, often students, to forge his Peasant Leagues. Although he occasionally demonstrated a flair for appealing propaganda, Julião's "Ten Commandments of the Peasant Leagues for the Liberation of the Peasant from the

Oppression of the Latifundia" appear as so many businesslike statements about progressive taxation, compensation for expropriated lands, cooperative formation, etc (12, pp. 12–13).

Despite the fact that Julião was a charismatic leader to many thousands of peasant followers, he did not provide them with a coherent ideology. The peasants may have been more radical than their leader (12, p. 14). The Leagues were disbanded after the military coup in 1964 and Julião is exiled, so we cannot know whether the movement would have developed an ideology suited to the needs of its adherents. Great and clearly perceived inequalities in landholding persist, however, and Forman (14, p. 24) suggests that "unless the present government undertakes a thoroughgoing agrarian reform, [discontent] could lead the rural masses into a terrifying unity."

Ideologies bring about unity through the creation of a community of believers, persons who accept in common an ultimate value or goal. In any culture there are only a few values or goals that can be endowed with the ultimate significance necessary to engage commitment. Comprehensive ideologies that succeed in creating united movements are characterized by three qualities which so reinforce one another that they can be distinguished only analytically: they are credible, persuasive, and authoritative.

The credibility of an ideology derives from its demonstration of a coherence between meanings shared by a group and its new perception of subordination and relative deprivation. Paliau's ideology rested on the widely held belief that white men had concealed crucial information from Admiralty Islanders. Jesus' revelation to Paliau was believable in this light. The formulations of the peasant leaders Julião and Tapia, that the large landholders were responsible for the distress of the rural masses, was congruous with the facts as the peasants perceived them. Their prescriptions for action were acceptable because the premise was already accepted. Sheikh Mujib's explanation for the backwardness of East Pakistan in West Pakistani exploitation made sense to millions of Bengalis who had personal experience of arrogant, powerful non-Bengali Muslims in their country. His demand for provincial autonomy seemed the obvious solution to the problem.

The persuasiveness of an ideology derives from the striking quality of its innovative symbolic formulation. The same discontents have been voiced by generations of downtrodden people without ever raising a call for action. When Paliau depicted a book of stone and metal encased in concrete, when Primo Tapia spoke of "the rape of the pueblo," or when Sheikh Mujib linked the economic and political autonomy of East Pakistan with the "right to live," they created forceful metaphors that persuaded persons to act in accord with their prescriptions. Geertz (15, p. 59) describes the effect of metaphor in ideology:

> The power of a metaphor derives precisely from the interplay between the discordant meanings it symbolically coerces into a unitary conceptual framework and from the degree to which that coercion is successful in overcoming the psychic resistance such semantic tension inevitably generates in anyone in a position to perceive it. When it works, a metaphor transforms a false identification . . . into an apt analogy; when it misfires, it is a mere extravagance.

The persuasiveness of an ideology may come from a new synthesis of powerful symbols drawn from different experiential realms. When Paliau depicted a book made from the strong substances of white men, metal and concrete, and of Admiralty Islanders, stone, he symbolized the union of two cultural systems in terms drawn from direct experience. The reevaluation of existing symbols and their hierarchical rearrangement also creates startling new formulations. Sheikh Mujib placed the people and land of Bengal above the unity of the Islamic state of Pakistan and shocked both East and West Pakistanis into unprecedented action.

The problem of authority is the most intransigent difficulty in ideologies and movements. If a movement seeks a positive goal, a total social, political, and economic restructuring, it does so in the face of opposition from the powers that be. Authority is already lodged elsewhere, in a colonial administration, a military regime, the church, or an established government. To overcome this fact, an ideology must be based upon a higher authority. Where a movement is grounded on religion, it can claim to speak from divine authority which is higher than mere temporal authority. Paliau based his appeal on a higher religious authority than that provided by the missionaries: the whole Bible revealed directly by Jesus rather than a part of the Bible brought by men. While religious justification was invoked by both the pious Sheikh Mujib and the sceptical Primo Tapia, their basis of authority was primarily a conception of "the rights of men" which had been elevated to the realm of transcendental values by the theory of political democracy. Whatever the ultimate ground of authority in a culture, the general tendency in ideology is to draw an absolute antithesis between the prevailing secular authority and the authority on which the movement is based, between absolute evil and absolute good. Manichean imagery is a common feature of ideologies; it endows an ideology with absolute authority by demonizing its opposition. The problem of authority brings us to the last topic to be considered here: leadership and charismatic legitimation.

Charismatic Authority

Much of what has already been said here has necessarily dealt with aspects of charismatic leadership. Movements that seek large-scale social transformation are regularly led by charismatic figures. It is the charismatic leader who synthesizes and articulates the ideology of a movement. The connection between leader and ideology is so close that it is difficult to disentangle the loyalties of the adherents. Followers often tend to merge the physical person of the leader and his ideology, attributing divine or superhuman qualities to both.

The movement as a social entity and the charismatic leader are mutually dependent upon one another. There are numerous examples of peoples in distress who suffered many years of demoralization because they had no one who could break the spell. The same peoples—defeated and dislocated Iroquois Indians, bewildered Melanesians, the rootless unemployed of medieval Europe, or land-poor Mexican peasants—have been shocked into unprecedented unity and revolutionary forms of action by the visionary syntheses of charismatic leaders. This is not to argue for a "great man" theory but to put the extraordinary cultural and social achievements of great men into the proper cultural and social contexts.

Max Weber (42, pp. 1111–20) took the term *charisma,* "gift of grace," from church history and applied it to a general social process. Although there has been much criticism of the concept, it is clear that it identifies a phenomenon of very widespread significance. Many social scientists have found it difficult to use charisma in the value-free sense on which Weber insisted. Grouping St. Paul, Lenin, and Hitler, prophets, demagogues, and valiant military leaders into a single category has appeared to many analysts as misleading and often obnoxious. Nevertheless, Weber's original, if somewhat unsystematic, generalizations on charismatic authority have been confirmed and reconfirmed in hundreds of empirical cases. It is true that Weber led himself into a contradiction when he spoke of the "routinization" and "depersonalization" of charisma (Weber 42, pp. 1121–38; Tucker 38, pp. 753–54), but this problem does not concern us here.

Weber saw charismatic authority as consisting of two indispensable components: (a) a sense of extraordinary calling, revelation, or mental or physical gift on the part of the leader; and (b) a recognition of the extraordinary gift by the people to whom the leader thinks himself to be called. Should the leader's sense of special mission disappear, or should his social recognition be withdrawn, his claim to legitimacy collapses.

Specifying the nature of charismatic authority on the basis of a richly detailed study of the Jamaa movement in Katanga, Johannes Fabian (11, pp. 6–7) emphasizes its "intentional, orientational character." Commenting on Weber's observation that charismatic leadership demands unconditional faith, Fabian says:

... This so-called unconditional faith means acceptance of a *total system* of orientation. A charismatic leader does not gain influence by giving piecemeal advice in particular situations. He has his impact because he offers an all-embracing definition of the situation. It is because his message is total and "logical" that the behavior of his followers is not erratic and "curious" (as movements appeared to many observers not long ago) but consistent and observable as a *distinct social reality.*

What Fabian calls a "total system of orientation" is what I have called an ideology. The qualities of credibility, persuasiveness, and authority which are essential to ideology at the cultural level are mirrored at the social level in the charismatic leader, the articulator of the ideology.

A comparative examination of charismatic leadership must take account of differences in the cultural constructions of leadership in different societies. For example, the Seneca prophet Handsome Lake was a "triumphant success" in propagating his new religious message, while . . .

In the politics of the chiefs' council, despite the eminence of his titles, Handsome Lake failed, mired in personal jealousies and tribal factionalism and unable to call upon an efficient bureaucracy for the administration of his policies. Such a failure, indeed, was in a sense ordained by Iroquois culture, for a correlate of the theme of freedom was an extreme sensitivity to issues involving personal dominance (Wallace 41, p. 296).

So far as originality and organizational skills were concerned, Paliau and Handsome Lake appear quite similar. Both relied upon revelation mixed with practical wisdom to develop their movements. Both synthesized alien and indigenous ideas in the creation of their new ideologies. However, Paliau was successful in both religious and political terms and behind his success lay "the older pattern of leadership by 'big men' which had prevailed throughout much of Melanesia" (Schwartz 29, p. 398).

> The extension of political relations beyond the village was rare, effected by a few "big men" of legendary great prestige. The Paliau Movement had created a political unit of a size and complexity of structure that were unprecedented in the Admiralties. The creation of this unit and its organization centered around the person and leadership of Paliau. Although his role as leader involved a vast expansion of its functional content beyond the scope of native precedent, and although this role was based in part on a fusion of European models, there was still much that suggested the "big man" of the past (29, p. 398).

Differences in the cultural construction of leadership also result from differences in what is regarded as the ultimate ground of authority. Authority that is conceived to flow from an omnipotent, omniscient deity may be conceived as absolute and unchallengeable, while authority that is thought to be based upon the popular will may be regarded as limited, situationally relative, and fallible. Discussing charismatic leadership with particular reference to Lenin, Robert Tucker (38, p. 736) argues:

> Followers can be under the spell of a leader and can accept him as supremely authoritative without necessarily agreeing with him on all occasions or refraining from argument with him. In the highly argumentative atmosphere of a modern radical party, for example, a leader can be both charismatic and contested on specific points, as Lenin often was by his close followers. Indeed, he can even manifest some of his charisma in the inspired way in which he conquers dissent by the sheer power of his political discourse.

The relationship between "movement" and "party" raises one final issue, which is the problem of the sociology of movements. I can say very little about this problem here. An adequate account of movement sociology would have to deal both with the extreme of organizational instability, as for example, in a short-lived cargo cult, and with a high level of organizational stability, as in a contemporary totalitarian party. At the same time, while movements in small-scale societies may be unitary organizations, such phenomena as "working class movements" or "nationalist movements" usually involve a simultaneous and successive diversity of organizational forms. Thus, the range of movements typically studied by anthropologists would have to be considerably broadened to permit satisfactory generalization; space does not permit this here.

Weber's (42, pp. 1114–17) discussion of the instability and revolutionary character of charismatic authority suggests further lines of comparative enquiry. The processes of economic and political rationalization that take place in successful movements, tending to transform them into sects, parties, or whole polities, is one such line. Another concerns the internal social processes of growth, faction, and schism in movements. However, these must remain subjects for another paper.

Literature Cited

1. Aberle, D. F. 1967. *The Peyote Religion Among the Navaho.* Chicago: Aldine. 2nd printing
2. Apter, D. E. 1963. Political religion in the new nations. In *Old Societies and New States,* ed. C. Geertz, 57–104. New York: Free Press. 310 pp.
3. Apter, D. E., Ed. 1964. Introduction. *Ideology and Discontent,* 15–46. New York: Free Press. 342 pp.
4. Burridge, K. 1969. *New Heaven, New Earth.* New York: Schocken
5. Cohn, N. 1961. *The Pursuit of the Millennium.* New York: Oxford Univ. Press. Rev. ed.
6. Dumont, L. 1970. *Homo Hierarchicus.* Univ. Chicago Press
7. Dumont, L. 1970. *Religion/Politics and History in India.* Paris: Mouton
8. Dumont, L. 1971. Religion, politics, and society in the individualistic universe. *Proc. Roy. Anthropol. Inst.* 1970: 31–41
9. Easton, D. 1959. Political anthropology. *Bien, Rev. Anthropol.* 210–62
10. Easton, D. 1965. *A Systems Analysis of Political Life.* New York: Wiley
11. Fabian, J. 1971. *Jamaa: A Charismatic Movement in Katanga.* Evanston: Northwestern Univ. Press
12. Forman, S. 1971. Disunity and discontent: a study of peasant political movements in Brazil. *J. Latin Am. Stud.* 3:3–24
13. Fortes, M., Evans-Pritchard, E. E., Eds. 1940. *African Political Systems.* London: Oxford Univ. Press
14. Friedrich, P. 1970. *Agrarian Revolt in a Mexican Village.* Englewood Cliffs: Prentice-Hall
15. Geertz, C. 1964. Ideology as a cultural system. See Ref. 3, 47–76
16. Geertz, C. 1966. Religion as a cultural system. In *Anthropological Approaches to the Study of Religion,* ed. M. Banton, 1–46. London: Tavistock. 176 pp.
17. Geertz, C. 1972. Afterword: the politics of meaning. In *Culture and Politics in Indonesia,* ed. C. Holt et al, 319–35. Ithaca: Cornell Univ. Press. 348 pp.
18. Gerlach, L. P., Hine, V. H. 1970. *People, Power, Change.* Indianapolis: Bobbs-Merrill
19. Gusfield, J. R. 1968. The study of social movements. *Int. Encycl. Soc. Sci.* 14: 445–52
20. Heberle, R. 1951. *Social Movements.* New York: Appleton-Century-Crofts
21. Kantorowicz, E. H. 1957. *The King's Two Bodies.* Princeton Univ. Press
22. Lanternari, V. 1963. *The Religions of the Oppressed,* transl. L. Sergio. New York: Knopf
23. Lévy-Bruhl, L. 1966. *Primitive Mentality,* transl. L. A. Clare. Boston: Beacon
24. Nicholas, M., Oldenburg, P., compilers. 1972. *Bangladesh: The Birth of a Nation.* Madras: Seshachalam
25. Nicholas, R. W. 1965. Factions: a comparative analysis. In *Political Systems and the Distribution of Power,* ed. M. Banton, 21–61. London: Tavistock. 142 pp.
26. Nicholas, R. W. 1968. Rules, resources, and political activity. In *Local-Level Politics,* ed. M. J. Swartz, 295–321. Chicago: Aldine. 437 pp.
27. Schneider, D. M. 1968. *American Kinship: A Cultural Account.* Englewood Cliffs: Prentice-Hall
28. Schuman, H. 1972. A note on the rapid rise of mass Bengali nationalism in East Pakistan. *Am. J. Sociol.* 78:290–98
29. Schwartz, T. 1962. The Paliau Movement in the Admiralty Islands, 1946–1954. *Anthropol. Pap. Am. Mus. Nat. Hist.* 49:207–421
30. Shils, E. 1968. The concept and function of ideology. *Int. Encycl. Soc. Sci.* 7: 66–76
31. Smelser, N. J. 1963. *Theory of Collective Behavior.* New York: Free Press
32. Swartz, M. J., Turner, V. W., Tuden, A., Eds. 1966. *Political Anthropology.* Chicago: Aldine
33. Talmon, J. L. 1952. *The Rise of Totalitarian Democracy.* Boston: Beacon
34. Talmon, J. L. 1957. *Utopianism and Politics.* London: Conservative Political Centre
35. Talmon, J. L. 1960. *Political Messianism: The Romantic Phase.* New York: Praeger
36. Talmon, Y. 1962. Pursuit of the millennium: the relation between religious and social change. *Archiv. Europ. Sociol.* 3: 125–48
37. Thrupp, S. L., Ed. 1970. *Millennial Dreams in Action.* New York: Schocken
38. Tucker, R. C. 1968. The theory of charismatic leadership. *Daedalus* 97: 731–56
39. Turner, V. W. 1967. *The Forest of Symbols.* Ithaca: Cornell Univ. Press
40. Wallace, A. F. C. 1956. Revitalization movements. *Am. Anthropol.* 58:264–81
41. Wallace, A. F. C. 1970. *The Death and Rebirth of the Seneca.* New York: Knopf

42. Weber, M. 1968. *Economy and Society,* ed. G. Roth, C. Wittich. New York: Bedminster. 3 vols.

43. Wilkinson, P. 1971. *Social Movement.* New York: Praeger

44. Williams, R. 1961. *Culture and Society, 1780–1950.* Harmondsworth: Penguin

45. Winckler, E. A. 1970. Political Anthropology. *Bien. Rev. Anthropol.* 1969:301–92

ECONOMIC ANTHROPOLOGY ❖ 9519

Richard F. Salisbury

Anthropology of Development, McGill University, Montreal, Quebec, Canada

In 1965, a review of economic anthropology, authored by Manning Nash, appeared in the *Biennial Review of Anthropology*. Since then there have been articles by Dalton (12) and Firth (15) and a book by LeClair & Schneider (23), summarizing earlier materials. LeClair & Schneider also presented the arguments in the major 1967 controversy between substantivists and formalists. A concluding assessment by the present author (31) saw the controversy as fruitless. Substantive analyses of production and distribution were clearly needed to permit formal analysis of choices made in the allocation of resources. Neither approach alone could predict behavior in new situations. Classifying economies in substantivist terms yielded a static (or comparatively static) analysis portraying economies either as in equilibrium or as between two equilibrium states. Assuming that all decisions aim at maximizing production (as formalists were accused of doing), or are "rational," ignores the vast literature on societies pursuing multiple cultural goals. The two approaches need to be fused—we need total models of economic systems in which decision making, particularly by the peasant or the worker, is seen as producing the observed behavior and its derived model. Barth (6) formulated an essentially similar view of social change as requiring both systemic studies and studies of personal decisions which generated the systems.

Since 1967, unfortunately, the debate has continued, but materials presented in strictly dialectic terms of substantivist-formalist have yielded little of value. A spate of articles, for example, on the characteristics of "primitive money" have not added to the analyses widely current by the mid-1950s. They have illustrated their writers' lack of knowledge of the existing literature. Melitz (25) has also shown how the idea that specialized forms of exchange items are found only in "primitive" societies is based on a naive analysis of what happens in "modern" societies.

The present review ignores these post-mortem spasms of the substantivist-formalist debate and considers three fields of economic anthropology where "live" work has been published since 1967: marketing, production, and entrepreneurial organization. The concern is with an issue implicit in Barth's formulation and explicit in my own—how far the decision processes at the local level "generate" the system,

85

and how far they reflect a "system" determined otherwise. As of 1972 the most salient theoretical controversy lies between environmental determinists and those who see anthropology as showing human culture and knowledge as influencing behavior. The final section reviews relations between economic anthropology and cultural ecology.

Marketing

Studies of peasant marketing of foodstuffs and export commodities had by 1967 developed models of total systems and of individual decision making by marketers. The model was of a multilevel network of markets and traders through which individually produced goods were bulked and transported, while bulk imports of manufactures were distributed into progressively smaller units. Individual decision analysis had focused on the fixing of prices, how long-term relationships between sellers and buyers entered into price decisions, and the degree of rationality of sellers in calculating their returns.

Two systemic models have dominated the last 5 years—(a) the ecological analysis of how regional complementarity determines market systems, and (b) the central place and location theory model, derived ultimately from von Thünen's work of the early nineteenth century, where relative positions of towns and their hinterlands are seen as determinant.

Harding (19) makes an ecological analysis of long-distance canoe trading in the Vitiaz Strait area of New Guinea, which long antedated pacification and political unification of the area, and which has only modified itself with modern changes in crops and the availability of manufactured goods. Ecological complementarity is highly significant, as between island communities, coastal communities, and inland communities, and between communities with seasonal shortages occurring at different periods of the year. Trading permits more local specialization in such areas, which are not forced to diversify production inefficiently in order to avoid the risks of periodic scarcity. Yet the specialization between independent communities appeared almost to have gone to extremes—coastal villages possessed no large canoes for long-distance voyaging, while pigs and dogs were seen as almost exclusively products of particular regions. Several islands with relatively large populations and very little land depended almost entirely on middleman profits, coupled with the manufacture of pots or carving (often from materials obtained in trade).

Societal differentiation has thus proceeded far beyond the level indicated by ecological variation. In explaining how such specialization originally began, how the existing differentiation is maintained, and how it is spread to new communities, Harding (19) considers the relationship between trading and "big-man" feast giving. He shows how specific trading voyages are motivated by the desire of individuals to accumulate goods required for gaining prestige within their own village by giving feasts. It is their activity which establishes the network of trade friendships, and it is their innovativeness which introduces new commodities into the system. They amplify the system, but at a rate regulated by their limited arena for prestige competition. The system needed ecological diversity to emerge, but its present form is conditioned by the decisions of the traders.

Other studies of non-monetary trade show how social and cultural factors constrain decisions within the potential provided by ecological diversity. Salisbury (32), for example, shows how New Britain women's attitude to trade has affected their response to the advent of expatriate buyers. Traditional trade using shell money as a medium of exchange was based on a system of nominally "fixed equivalent" prices. Exchanges were viewed as "delayed barter" with no profit involved, although varying size of units did make for limited price variation. This attitude did cushion against immense price variations for highly seasonal products when long-term supplies were balanced. Relatively few local producers have entered the market to supply expatriates with vegetables, since this is risky and no ideology has been developed to eliminate risk. By contrast an open, price-fixing market has developed to supply the steady demand for nonseasonal foodstuffs by native peri-urban villages.

The central place and location theory model of geographers has only recently been adopted by anthropologists. Studies by Hill & Smith (21) for Africa, Smith (33) for Latin America, and Brookfield (10) for the Pacific provide good introductions to the field. General consideration of the costs of transportation, for example, suggest that on a flat plain they will be at a minimum if second-order centers for trading rural products against manufactures are symmetrically grouped around major centers, and that the location of third-order centers are symmetrically located with respect to the other centers. Mapping shows that if modifications are made for situations that do not correspond to the ideal "flat plain," most systems of marketing centers fit this spatial model reasonably well.

Can one then conclude that transportation costs are the deciding factor in determining the location of centers and where market women sell their goods? Smith (33) points out how the costs of land, the problems of maintaining highly productive but not full-time occupations, and difficulties of maintaining cultural identity, in fact, account for the distribution of Guatemalan Indian rural marketing centers. Hodder & Hassall (22) reanalyze the location of Roman administrative centers in England, which were located, not in relation to the distribution of the indigenous population, but arbitrarily on a hexagonal grid to facilitate regional administration. It was only subsequently that many of them developed into market centers. Brookfield (10), while starting from a spatial model, explicitly looks for cultural factors that might explain deviations from such a model. He finds "fixed unit" selling general in the Pacific. There is also a general nonemergence of the predicted zones of close-in market gardening and distant pastoralism. Instead, areas distant from markets specialize in export crops. The limited purchasing of indigenous foodstuffs by expatriates in administrative towns, as in New Britain, would explain the former, and visiting of towns by islanders only to obtain cash would explain the latter. Whether or not towns play the role indicated by the spatial model is clearly affected by cultural factors.

Gladwin & Gladwin (17) explicitly study the criteria used by market women in Ghana to decide where to sell fish. It is common knowledge (at least among the 27 successful traders interviewed) that there is a threshold size of catch below which it is unprofitable to transport fish to inland markets, as the spatial model would predict. But they also share knowledge of how to estimate profits when the state of demand is unknown (and risky) but the supply is known. They can estimate profits for about 12 conditions of supply and risk, and it is these estimates which determine where they go. It would be a Herculean task to determine what the risks are objectively, even for a social scientist. Folk categories, in fact, determine behavior, and it is relatively simple to produce a *descriptive* model predicting actual behavior from a knowledge of folk categories.

The fact that folk models of relatively simple nature have analogs in complex formal mathematical terms has been recognized in other areas. Norvell & Thompson (26) show that Jamaican higglers talking in terms of catering to preferred customers, specializing in particular commodities, and expecting partners to share unexpected losses are making the calculations that would be appropriate in a formal mathematical model derived from the assumption that there exists only a limited number of "places" in any market, and sellers must aim to preserve their "place." Plattner (29) uses multiple regression analyses and production functions to show what factors affect the profits of itinerant peddlers in Southern Mexico. It turns out that amount of capital, number of mules used, and the route traveled do affect profits, but quite as important is what traders explicitly say is significant—"knowing one's customers." Plattner shows that an indirect measure of knowledge—the mark-up a trader can get away with—correlates most highly with profits.

Production

Before 1967 the charge was often made that anthropologists ignored production and concentrated on exchange. While this has never been true regarding food production, a group including Sahlins and headed by Godelier and Meillassoux, based in Paris, has deliberately attempted to develop a general neo-Marxian model of "primitive production." They try to correct errors due to Marx' nineteenth century view of primitive society, while confirming that in subsistence economies "what counts is that there should be enough to satisfy the needs."

Sahlins (30) follows Chayanov's 1927 analysis of peasant production in Czarist Russia, asserting that in domestic production a worker works as hard as is needed to supply his dependents rather than to maximize returns. Sahlins calls this "intensity of production" and sees how far it follows Chayanov's rule in societies with available data—Gwembe Tonga, Tiv, Kapauku, Moala, and Maring. The first approximately follows the rule, but the last three show many deviant households which produce far more than they need for their dependents. In Moala the chiefly lineages produce a surplus, in Kapauku the "big men" do, while in Maring the scatter is extreme. The societies that reveal most scatter are those producing most above the bare-subsistence level, accumulating the surplus as capital in the form of animals to be "converted ultimately into social and political benefits." The strongest incentive there for intensive production would appear to be the desire for prestige or political power.

Sahlins seems to consider Chayanov's rule still valid, if one ignores overproducers. His data show, however, that in two of the five societies the correlation between intensity and the ratio of dependents is opposite to that predicted by Chayanov, and in no case is the correlation significant—it is "inappropriate as a predictive relationship" (30, p. 45). Nonetheless, even if the results are unclear, they point to a new way to study production incentives in non-monetary societies.

Godelier's (18) most available work for anglophones analyzes the determinants of exchange rates for locally produced salt in a part of New Guinea only recently brought into a monetary economy. He tests the Marxian hypothesis that rates would parallel labor costs, and finds this untrue. The Baruya group, who monopolize salt production, obtain a twofold advantage in exchanges. To explain why they do not charge more, why allies may use salt-producing facilities without payment, and why "big men" give salt to widows and orphans, Godelier says that "in trade between groups what counts is reciprocal satisfaction of their needs rather than an even balance in their labor output" (18, p. 69). They are not motivated by profit.

Again the conclusion is naive. One break in the Baruya monopoly brought bitter rage and a cut in the rate of one third; the cost of travel clearly forces distant groups to accept even worse rates; the high valuation of leisure by the Baruya (who work only one-third of the time) indicates production restriction; "big men" build political support by calculated generosity. The observed level of production and pricing seems nicely adjusted to labor costs, transport costs, monopoly advantages, and political power. Baruya appear typically human, using very familiar techniques of economic decision making.

Polly Hill (20) has continued to advocate studies of non-Western but monetary production. Her case studies of enterprises in Ghana, which use minimal amounts of cash and operate predominantly on kin relationships, show how each factor of production—land, capital in various forms, and organization—may be provided by different parties. Returns are allocated independently to each factor (or party), using traditional forms. Thus, for example, Accra is supplied with milk from cows owned by Ga-speakers, herded by Fulani, in kraals owned by other Ga. Expansion has followed economic opportunity without requiring employer-employee relationships. Ewe fishermen form "companies" for seasonal seine fishing, but divide the catch to reward the factors. After the workers are fed and the net repaired, the balance is divided into fixed "shares" for the workers, the net owner, the bos'n, and the entrepreneur who recruited and "staked" the company. It would appear that such co-adventurer systems of "shares" in fishing are worldwide. The Ewe companies are distinctively formal, even excluding the wives of crew men who must "buy" fish to market it, and distinctively they separate the role of net-owner and crew member. Nonfishermen among the Ewe accumulate wealth by building up numbers of nets owned. As her title shows, Polly Hill focuses on the variant ways in which capital accumulations are built up in non-monetary forms.

Fishing has been the subject of studies in Norway, Newfoundland, and Great Britain, stimulated in part by Barth's (4) work on crew organization. Anderson & Wadel (2) collect several of these to show how technological change has had variable effects on "traditional" production organizations. Nineteenth century inshore fishing from small out-ports used simple gear and small boats, adapted to family production units. The same unit accumulated, controlled, and maintained capital, recruited and trained labor, and handed down knowledge. Fission in crews and steady expansion in numbers of boats were part of the family growth cycle. Engines, deep-water seines, and electronic fish-finding equipment require organizational changes. Crews are larger, the costly capital items cannot be maintained by crew members alone, skippers need greater knowledge to be effective, and the risk of loss from faulty or poorly informed decisions is greater. The diversity of needed skills places a premium on stable crews, yet the previous organization for ensuring stability no longer works.

Very different patterns emerge in each locality in reaction to local ecology, local culture, local government measures, and the structure of international trade. Skipper-crew relations vary with the uncertainty of catches; divisions into "shares" and relations between owners and skippers vary with technology; family and affinal patterns vary with the types of information flow and mobility of crews. The overall economy of world fishing may be sharply constrained by the marine food chain and by factory-ship technology, but within this global constraint, a multitude of variables of local origin condition what is actually produced.

Entrepreneurship

The local social condition that has most commonly been seen in the past as distinguishing "modern" societies from "traditional" ones has been the relative prevalence of "entrepreneurship." A number of articles dealing with "entrepreneurship" as a psychological trait have appeared during the past 5 years. Also, there has been an increasing amount of literature indicating that "enterprise" is by no means uncommon in "traditional" societies, even if it takes forms other than the creation of private businesses oriented to monetary profit making.

The studies of Hill (20) and Salisbury (32) have already been mentioned. Other examples include: Forman's (16) study of raft fishermen in Brazil; studies of village manufacturers in Mexico by Acheson (1), M. Belshaw (7), and Cook (11); the report by Owens (27) on engineering firms near Calcutta; Marris & Somerset (24) on Tanzanian businessmen; Pitt's (28) study of tradition and progress in Samoa; Finney's (14) and Strathern's (34) work on entrepreneurs in New Guinea.

Two major themes emerge. The first, from the work of Finney, Salisbury, and Pitt, and from the earlier work of Cyril Belshaw and Geertz, is the way in which entrepreneurs can be motivated, not by goals of personal profit but by desires to advance the status of a larger grouping. Where this is the case, the operation of their enterprise takes a distinctive form. The larger grouping combines to contribute capital for the enterprise, whether this is in the form of land, or labor to make buildings or improvements to land, or directly as cash. Local labor is used where possible, and generation of employment is seen as an aim of the enterprise. Returns may be made to the grouping in the form of intangible services, while accounting may aim either at increasing the capital assets of the group or at making no profits but providing services at low cost.

The second theme, stemming from Benedict's (8) seminal article, is that these small-scale enterprises are analyzable in much the same terms as "family firms" have been in the economic literature. Implicit in this approach is the idea that they present an intermediary "stage" between individual enterprise and the emergence of large "universalistic" firms (either state or corporately owned). The previously mentioned studies of Ewe and North Atlantic fishermen clearly fit in this field, and indicate the problems that such firms face in acquiring capital stocks, in keeping up wide-ranging relationships with outsiders, and in mobilizing labor when special skills are required.

Owens (27) in particular considers the limits on the expansion of such firms by studying the households of engineering entrepreneurs near Calcutta. Entrepreneurs live in larger, more joint-family households than do non-entrepreneurs. Capital stocks can be kept together if the owning "co-parsenary" group lives together (is "commensal"), and a major skill of entrepreneurs is averting domestic splits which would lower stocks below critical levels. However, this is significant only while the firm is expanding and joint living can reduce consumption expenditures to permit capital accumulation. Joint-family households, and by implication family firms, become less useful when the firm has exceeded a critical size. At this point joint living is raising the level of too many nonproductive family members, while reducing too greatly the level of the entrepreneur. At that point he usually builds his own single-family house.

Entrepreneurship, in short, is an ability that is extremely widely dispersed and is by no means restricted to monetary societies or to joint stock corporations. The innovative organizer of production or distribution must adapt his enterprise to his existing social milieu as much as to existing nonsocial resources, and what one empirically finds is a wide range of organization forms. Barth's (3, 5) specification of two social niches to which entrepreneurs can adapt their enterprises—the brokerage niche when two cultural groups are in interaction, and the conversion niche, when a society formally has discrete spheres of exchange—does not exhaust the adaptations made by entrepreneurs.

Ecology and Economics

Two themes—the environmental constraints on human behavior to which humans adapt, and the way in which human decisions are made voluntarily in awareness of many of the constraints but also arbitrarily—have run through the listing of studies in earlier sections. In the past 5 years these themes have tended to become phrased as polar positions in a debate between "cultural ecologists" and "formalist" anthropologists. The intensification of work on the resources available to nonindustrial societies has added much to our understanding of the relationship at particular points in time of cultural behavior to available resources. Extremists have phrased this either in a variant of Radcliffe-Brownian functionalism, as though *every* element of behavior contributed to the maintenance of the society in its existing form, or as *adaptation* to the surrounding natural resources which are taken as given. It is a short step from such a stance to one of environmental determinism.

In the opposite direction the great increase in mathematical analysis and model building that has characterized recent formalist economic anthropology has led to a tendency to argue that models built on the basis of decisions taken at the individual level "explain" the operation of the system as a whole. This concentration on individual decision making has been reinforced even more by the development of techniques for eliciting statements from the decision makers themselves about how they make decisions. Models so based seem psychologically real, at the same time that they appear to fulfil Barth's (6) demand for being "generative."

The possibility for sterile debate is clearly present, if polarization proceeds further. What may be ignored is the degree of complementarity between the analyses. For the social scientist, as for people who live in a particular environment, "natural" resources do exist and do provide a basis for human action; these resources need closer study. But they provide only part of the total resources available. Other humans, and their potentialities for being organized in different ways, provide yet another resource base, while knowledge, technology, and human cognition provide other resources. Davis (13) has shown, for example, that over £ 140 million of consumer expenditure in the United Kingdom is generated by the gift economy.

However, it is impossible to segregate the role of "resources" and the role of individual decisions in determining the level of an economy *at one point in time*. All one can do is to say that all elements are interrelated. Where, over time, a group of humans has remained in the same environment but has changed in terms of knowledge and/or organization, and has also changed its level of production, one can begin to analyze the effects of environment and decisions. So, too, when different groups of humans inhabit the same environment but utilize it differently, one can analyze what factors are determinant and what are permissive.

Among the New Guinea Tolai, Salisbury (32) has documented how four major technological innovations have been adopted over the hundred years since first European contact. The initial adoption of each innovation occurred because individuals were able to evaluate the likely gains from it in terms of their existing knowledge and experience. Though each innovation was in fact not used most efficiently at its initial introduction, a political ferment at the time of introduction permitted this inefficiency to pass unnoticed, and enabled modifications in social organization to occur later and permit the new technology to operate efficiently. Existing economic concepts and the structure of local opportunity costs are crucial determinants of whether change will occur, as is the existence of political ferment. Many alternative levels of production are possible with the same availability of natural resources, but which level in fact occurs is determined by local decisions about technology and sociopolitical organization. Especially is this true when a local political unit can maintain its autonomy in decision making and can prevent itself becoming entirely dependent on decisions made by larger political units which are unaware of the local structure of opportunity costs.

John Bennett (9) analyzes the ways in which four distinct cultural groups— Hutterites, Indians, farmers, and ranchers—utilize the same available resources on the Saskatchewan prairies. Each uses a different *adaptive strategy,* or pattern of resource use, chosen by evaluating the costs of alternative uses so as to meet goals set in cultural and human terms. Over time, however, a selective process occurs whereby a strategy that can be viewed as adaptive to the resources available at one time actually changes the total resources. Hutterite communal living, for example, that was initially valued as a means of preserving a way of life, creates large family units which can smooth out the riskiness of prairies farming, while by giving children less schooling it lowers the opportunity costs of labor. They flourish far from towns, while small farmers have developed close relationships with town centers and depend on collective political action to avoid risks, and so have tended to gather around towns. What has thus happened is an *adaptive process* (9, p. 14) in which new specializations of society and microenvironments occur at the initiation of cultural factors.

In short, provided one is aware of the need for analyzing the other side of the equation, it does not matter whether one starts by studying human strategies and organizations or by looking at resources. The economic anthropologist who focuses on how humans cognize their resources, organize for their use, and plan for the long term can profitably and equitably share the field with the cultural ecologist. The more sophisticated he becomes in developing a decision model of behavior, the more likely his work is to mesh with the work of a cultural ecologist.

Literature Cited

1. Acheson, J. M. 1972. Limited good or limited goods: Response to economic opportunity in a Tarascan pueblo. *Am. Anthropol.* 74:1152–69
2. Anderson, R., Wadel, C., Eds. 1972. *North Atlantic Fishermen.* Newfoundland Soc. Econ. Pap. No. 5. Memorial Univ. Newfoundland
3. Barth, F. 1963. *The Role of the Entrepreneur in Social Change in Northern Norway.* Bergen: Norwegian Univ. Press
4. Barth, F. 1966. *Models of Social Organization. Occas. Pap. Roy. Anthropol. Inst. London 23*
5. Barth, F. 1967. Economic spheres in Darfur. See Ref. 15, 149–74
6. Barth, F. 1967. On the study of social change. *Am. Anthropol.* 69:661–69
7. Belshaw, M. 1967. *A Village Economy: Land and People of Huecorio.* New York: Columbia Univ.
8. Benedict, B. 1968. Family firms and economic development. *Southwest. J. Anthropol.* 24:1–19
9. Bennett, J. W. 1969. *Northern Plainsmen.* Chicago: Aldine
10. Brookfield, H. C. 1969. *Pacific Marketplaces.* Canberra: Australian Nat. Univ.
11. Cook, S. 1970. Price and output variability in a peasant-artisan stone-working industry in Oaxaca. *Am. Anthropol.* 72:776–801
12. Dalton, G. 1967. *Tribal and Peasant Economies.* Garden City, NY: Natural History Press
13. Davis, J. 1972. Gifts and the U.K. economy. *Man* 7:408–29
14. Finney, B. 1968. Big-fellow man belong business in New Guinea. *Ethnology* 4: 394–410
15. Firth, R. 1967. *Themes in Economic Anthropology. A.S.A. Monogr. 6.* London: Tavistock
16. Forman, S. 1970. *The Raft Fishermen: Tradition and Change in the Brazilian Peasant Economy.* Bloomington: Indiana Univ.
17. Gladwin, H., Gladwin, C. 1971. Estimating market conditions and profit expectations of fish-sellers at Cape Coast. In *Studies in Economic Anthropology,* ed. G. Dalton, 123–43. Am. Anthropol. Assoc.
18. Godelier, M. 1971. "Salt currency" and the circulation of commodities among the Baruya of New Guinea. See Ref. 17, 52–73
19. Harding, T. G. 1967. *Voyagers of the Vitiaz Strait.* Seattle: Univ. Washington
20. Hill, P. 1970. *Studies in Rural Capitalism in West Africa.* Cambridge Univ. Press
21. Hill, P., Smith, R. H. T. 1972. Spatial and temporal synchronization of periodic markets: Evidence from four emirates in Northern Nigeria. *Econ. Geogr.* 48:345–55
22. Hodder, I., Hassall, M. 1971. The nonrandom spacing of Romano-British walled towns. *Man* 6:391–407
23. LeClair, E., Schneider, H. K. 1968. *Economic Anthropology.* New York: Holt, Rinehart & Winston
24. Marris, P., Somerset, A. 1971. *African Businessmen: A Study of Entrepreneurship and Development in Tanzania.* London: Routledge and Kegan Paul.
25. Melitz, J. 1970. The Polanyi School of Anthropology on money. *Am. Anthropol.* 72:1020–40

26. Norvell, D. G., Thompson, M. 1968. Higglering in Jamaica and the mystique of pure competition. *Soc. Econ. Stud.* 17:407–16

27. Owens, R. 1971. Industrialization and the Indian joint family. *Ethnology* 10: 223–50

28. Pitt, D. 1970. *Tradition and Economic Progress in Samoa.* London: Oxford

29. Plattner, S. 1969. *Peddlers, Pigs and Profits. Itinerant Trading in Southeastern Mexico.* PhD dissertation. Stanford Univ.

30. Sahlins, M. 1971. The intensity of domestic production in primitive societies. See Ref. 17, 30–51

31. Salisbury, R. F. 1968. Anthropology and economics. See Ref. 23, 477–85

32. Salisbury, R. F. 1969. *Vunamami: Economic Transformation in a Traditional Society.* Berkeley: Univ. California

33. Smith, C. 1972. *Production in Western Guatemala; the Interaction of Markets, Distance and Geographical Givens.* Presented at Conf. Math. Econ. Anthropol., St. Louis

34. Strathern, A. 1972. The entrepreneurial model of social change. *Ethnology* 11: 368–79

ANTHROPOLOGICAL STUDIES OF THE EDUCATIONAL PROCESS ❖ 9520

Frederick O. Gearing and B. Allan Tindall[1]

Department of Anthropology, State University of New York at Buffalo

A first annual review poses obvious problems of selection. We confine ourselves to works published in 1971 and 1972 almost exclusively. We further confine ourselves to works which report empirical research and which deal with or directly bear on processes of cultural transmission insofar as those processes are treated as *inter*-psychic events. This is an interpretive review, an attempt at synthesis around selected themes we deem especially significant. The reader is invited to consult other recent reviews (Gearing 10, Lindquist 23, Sindell 36, Wolcott 44) and is additionally invited to consult five recent collections of works (Cazden, John & Hymes 4; Gumperz & Hymes 15; Ianni & Storey 18; Lindquist 22; Middleton 24; M. Wax, Diamond & Gearing 43).[2]

[1] The authors wish to thank Thomas G. Carroll, Wayne D. Hughes, Walter E. Precourt, and Leta B. Richter, who as members of the Project in Ethnography in Education, Department of Anthropology, State University of New York at Buffalo—Frederick O. Gearing, Director —assisted in the readings and discussions which led to this report.

[2] Excluded are: programmatic research statements; works drawing on extant literature and principally pointed to policy questions; a rather large body of materials for and about the teaching of anthropology at various school and college levels; finally, items contained in the above-named collections are not here treated with two exceptions, through simple parenthetical reference is made at junctures. A few empirical works by anthropologists not included in this review are included in the bibliography, with asterisks. Excluded from these discussions, rather arbitrarily, are intrapsychic concerns even though these are sometimes intermixed in the studies included. An intrapsychic proposition is one which asserts that, in some organism, where one specified mental event occurs another specified mental event will follow, or various reversals, negations, and compounded propositions of that kind. Inter-psychic propositions are silent as to such connections. For example, the term "equivalence of meaning" as between the perceptions of two or more parties is often used in these pages, but commitment to the intrapsychic notion of dissonance, typically integral in discussion of equivalence, is here avoided. Intra- and interpsychic propositions are of course complementary, not competitive.

95

In all human communities babes are born innocent, and in most communities virtually all end up acting and thinking much as their parental generation acts and thinks. That this regularly happens is an awesome fact; it may also be an often depressing fact (in Jules Henry's angry phrase, it entails "learning stupidity"). In any event, precisely how this cultural transmission happens is largely mystery.

The processes of cultural transmission as here defined are constituted in regularly occurring patterns of encounter, wherein are transacted various *equivalences of meaning*, which equivalences together form a network and are the cultural system of the community in question. A network of equivalent meanings is constituted by similarities of shared perception and, as Wallace has argued (41), by organized diversity of perception, the similar and the diverse together, each in its way, enabling the members of the society adequately to predict each other's behavior. We are here concerned with how such networks of equivalence get recreated over the generations and with how that fails to occur. Studies which directly bear have one or more of the following features: they carefully examine the content of a people's perceptions and patterns of variability among those perceptions; they closely examine who encounters and communicates with whom; they examine how in the course of those encounters transactions of equivalences proceed.

What Is Transmitted?

Anthropological studies of culturally patterned perception go back at least as far as Boas, follow several strong traditions including many studies of kinship and social structure (where these are seen as code) and almost all studies of religion, and draw directly on the more recent endeavors of ethnoscience and cognitive anthropology more generally. The ethnographic problem has been, and remains, carefully to discern how a people sort their world into their system of categories. Among the large body of contemporary works, we here select for brief mention but five: two directly examine systematic variability of perception; one examines apparent variability which on examination is not that; and two directly examine how peoples perceive their world to be connected or connectable, part with part, the "logics" half of ethnoscience.

Berreman (2) asks, among other things, how men (in urban Dehra Dun, Northern India) identify each other as to social categories. He finds and charts patterns of variability: low in respect to ascribing identity as to religious group, and increasingly variable as to regional-linguistic-national-racial group, to caste, and to social class. All these identity ascriptions vary according to who is speaking with whom in what situation. For one example, all men use the term "untouchable" in respect to some others, but no man uses it to refer to his own caste-group. Similarly, Sankoff (33, 34) charts cognitive variability (among the Buang of New Guinea) as to ascriptions of membership in the several existing decent groups, the *dgwa,* and as to the ownership of land plots by these *dgwa.* He additionally suggests a key methodological device, the "average cognitive model" which is a cognitive construct drawn by the observer, average in the sense of a midpoint among a variable array. With that construct he is able to infer that any individual's cognitive model will depart from the average insofar as such departure enhances the status of his *dgwa.*

Provencher (28) examines variability in styles of interaction in Malaysia, which styles would seem to vary as to urban center and rural hinterland and thus imply cognitive variation in these regards as between those populations. On closer examination he finds a complex code, shared generally, which defines the two interaction styles: one *(halus)* is formal, the other *(kasar)* informal; the first attentive to social status, the second inattentive; the first invoked in settings where one often encounters unfamiliar persons, the second in settings where one often encounters intimates; both invoked in both urban and rural regions according to situation but in contrasting frequencies.

Cole et al (5, 6, 9) examine aspects of cognitive mappings (of the Kpelle of Liberia) including the logics by which connections among things are perceived, and they conclude,

> These connectives parallel those used in formal logic, in all but one case . . . They find disjunction easiest; in order of increasing difficulty are conjunction, negation, and implication. Equivalence [i.e. the notion in formal logic] they find very difficult. This pattern contrasts significantly with American behavior, and many of the differences seem to reflect differences in linguistic structure between Kpelle and English (9, p. 83).

Additionally, Cole and his colleagues (6) examine the methodological issue of contrived testing in cross-cultural situations and conclude that in such cognitive studies testing must complement observation of naturally occurring events, but that nonperformance on a test does not, by itself, imply the absence of the involved cognitive process; this, because repeatedly they found, after some modification of the test, often a chance modification, the processes apparently missing were in fact evoked. They conclude, "cultural differences in cognition reside more in the situations to which particular cognitive processes are applied than in the existence of a process in one group and its absence in another" (p. 233). If this conclusion holds up in future research, it will constitute a significant breakthrough in studies of cultural transmission. The reports contain much data on variability, and patterns are noted, as between literate and nonliterate, for example; but the patterns are not further examined.

In similar fashion Gladwin (11) seeks to examine the cognitive processes by which men (of Puluwat atoll) accomplish the logically complex task of navigating across open waters, and he concludes that the cognitive processes involved are both noninnovative and abstract (an uncommon combination among middle-class Americans). He further ponders the generally poor performance of these men on I.Q. tests and, devising an inference test, concludes that the I.Q. tests do not, as had been generally supposed, sort as to capacities for abstract thought, but sort as to presence or absence of a "heuristic strategy," the presence of which designers of I.Q. tests have taken for granted. (See also Leacock, Bernstein, Boggs, John in Cazden et al 4.)

These studies bear on, though they do not principally and directly examine, processes of cultural transmission. These and many others of this kind bear in that they attempt carefully to elicit the cognitive mappings by which perceptions are structured and may do so with special attention to patterned variability. Most do not directly examine cultural transmission (Cole et al and Gladwin provide the principal exceptions) in that there is no systematic attention as to who in the societies in question regularly encounters whom, nor how in such encounters transaction proceeds.

Before turning to works which directly address these matters, we want to point out one set of observations which emerges from these five studies collectively. The contents of cognitive mappings include three analytically separable realms, identifiable in the articles. First, men bring to encounters some sense of setting, some mapping of categories of situation which defines for each of them any particular encounter as to its kind. Provencher's report strongly suggests two large categories of event, as perceived by members of that society, which respectively evoke the formal and informal styles, but only suggests, for of course mappings as to those categories must independently be elicited. Perhaps in many societies there exist discoverable categories as roughly suggested by the words sacred and profane or categories of ritual as against nonritual, and so on.

Second, parties bring to an encounter some mapped sense of the nature of the world about them, human and nonhuman—the categories into which things fall and the ways such parts are connected, the unreflecting or folk sciences, as it were, of the two parties. As to categories of nonhuman things, both the Cole and Gladwin studies deal with such categories in aspects of their studies not mentioned above, and both deal with connections among things as was discussed.

Third, parties bring to encounters mappings as to a crucial subset of the above, the ways men generally are sorted into categories of social identity and how such categories are connected in role relationships, of differential power and the like. The Berreman and Sankoff studies deal directly with these phenomena.

Beyond these realms of cognitive mapping, another realm, not cognitive in nature, may be analytically separated: skills must necessarily be acquired. Cognitive mappings allow one to know about entities and their connections; skills allow one to put that into practice. All the above studies refer to how men deploy their knowledge; the Cole and Gladwin studies significantly use this distinction, knowledge and its use, in their analyses.

Who Transacts with Whom?

Anthropological studies of processes of cultural transmission tend strongly toward holistic conception: all encounters which regularly occur are in principle entailed, not only encounters of adults with young and not only encounters in explicitly instructional contexts. This conception is of course correct, however remotely attainable it may in fact be.

Of the recent studies before us, Leis (21) most systematically describes the society in view (an Ijaw village of Nigeria) as a system of regularly occurring encounters as between categories of persons: children by ages 0–4 (including a subset, 2–4), then for girls and boys together and separately 5–8, 9–13, and 14–17, and adults— encounters among all these in all regularly occurring combinations. Call such an image of a society an encounter profile. In that patterned sequence of encounters, it is shown, the young acquire identities in terms of sex, kinship, friendship, and additionally adopt behavior patterns describable by the values, sharing, honesty, and hard work. Leis does not characterize encounters among adults. Analogously, though less completely, Ward (42) draws an encounter profile of a rural black community in Louisiana, USA, and on that basis analyzes the learning of language in that community. More broadly, but thinly in detail of reported data, Epstein (7) for Peru and Keifer (19) for Japan chart encounter profiles in family, local commu- nity, national bureaucratic organization, and respectively trace emerging orienta- tions to mestizo culture and developing national loyalties.

It seems evident that for studies of cultural transmission, systematically drawn encounter profiles are both necessary and possible. Possible, by careful use of the societies' own categories of age, sex, and social strata; so drawn as to create cells for each thinkable kind of encounter (some several hundred cells, probably, in most societies or in any manageable sector of an industrialized society); and possible, as an initial step, by estimating relative frequencies of such kinds of encounter, and useful subsets within these. Necessary, because such a profile would provide a gross mapping of density of encounters as these vary along a life career axis; for males in contrast to females, for persons of high strata against others of low strata. Such a mapping would clearly reduce sampling error, the risk of overgeneralization, and perhaps other ethnographic error, and would generally establish sound bases for analysis of cultural transmission.

Goldschmidt (13) has suggested an "ethnography of encounters" as a data base for virtually the full range of anthropological endeavor. He does not suggest the systematic assembling of encounter profiles. However, the use of an encounter profile as a basis for any ethnography of encounters would seem to provide some insurance against the ethnographic errors named above, whatever the focus or theoretical purpose. [See also collection by Gumperz & Hymes (15); we have not ourselves reviewed the items in that collection.]

How Do Transactions Proceed?

Of the preceding studies, Leis most systematically reports the kinds of transactional activity by which cultural transmission occurs. He plots encounter categories and shows what is transacted in each, as we saw; and, to our current purpose, he additionally describes a good deal of the patterning of transactional activity accord- ing to those encounters: in one kind of encounter, observation and experiment; in another, imitative play; in another, participation in work-tasks; in still others, admonition, physical punishment, and praise. In some detail, Ward similarly de- scribes the transactional events through which language is learned. Similarly, Glad- win's study describes in some detail how, through formal instruction on land and guided experimentation at sea, the novice learns navigation. Hostetler & Huntington (17) describe, in less detail than the above, the processes (example and imitation, memorization) by which parents and the schools conjointly mold Old Order Amish youth according to Amish standards. (See also Wylie in Lindquist 22; Fortes, Firth & Williams in Middleton 24.)

In three of these, it is either presumed (Hostetler & Huntington 17) or shown (Gladwin 11, Ward 42) that what is occurring is convergence of maps, specifically cognitive changes on the part of the young toward the adults. But cultural systems consist also, following Wallace (41), of organized diversity of thought; thus cultural transmission presumptively includes transactional processes wherein maps diverge and wherein parties, on the basis of divergent perceptions, come nevertheless to correctly predict one another's behavior. An array of fascinating ethnographic studies strongly imply, though they do not as they stand clearly show, this process whereby divergent equivalences are regularly generated in transactions between old and young in some classes of situation.

In 1968 a book appeared which had a large impact in educational circles, *Pygmalion in the Classroom* by Rosenthal & Jacobson (32). The study demonstrated that the beliefs teachers entertain as to the varying levels of ability of their students set in motion transactions such that the students come to perform academically according to those levels. In the experiment, as reported in the study, those initial beliefs were implanted by false (randomly assigned) information about the students. The study had obvious implication for education of the children of the poor, and a host of studies were mounted to replicate the results, in almost all of which the results were not replicated. Very recently, Finn (8) has reviewed that array, argued that the statistical procedures doomed them, and mounted an analogous small study himself, using multivariate statistical analysis, wherein the initial "Pygmalion" results were in part confirmed. It should be noted in passing that multivariate analysis permits simultaneous handling of multiple independent and multiple dependent variables, and would thus appear to permit statistical analysis of what to an ethnographer begins to resemble the real world. That world is partly grasped in the anthropological studies which follow, all of which emerged in those intervening months, all addressed to variations on the "Pygmalion" theme.

Rist (29) did an ethnography of a kindergarten (black teacher, black students) in which he noted that in the very early weeks the teacher had sorted the children into ability groups. He asked himself what information the teacher then had to accomplish that sorting, discovered that she had various information as to the children's social classes but little else, and found that she had in fact sorted them by social class. There was no movement of children between the ability groups during the year, and the children in fact performed at those levels.

Analogously Rosenfeld (30), on the basis of 4½ years of teaching in a predominantly black ghetto school in Harlem, traces similar self-fulfilling prophesies by which students come to conform to the expectations of the teachers (predominantly white). By virtue of his position and by doing ethnography, he was further able to intervene in his own classroom. He observed and plotted the social structure of the students (their alliances and oppositions, etc), allowed those groupings to operate at academic tasks, and generally retransacted roles as between himself and the students. The students raised their scores on standardized achievement tests across the range of subject areas, but this change was read by the staff at large as the result of a trick of some mysterious kind.

Still further, Leacock (20) compared schools of respectively lower and middle class students and, cross-cutting, black and white students, and found expectation-and-performance levels to vary as to economic class but not to vary in respect to race. Brophy & Good (3) examined expectation and performance as it varied between male and female and between high achievers and low. Still further, Talbert (38) examined patterns of spatial movement toward the periphery of the classroom by children in two kindergartens as these movements were affected by teacher behaviors and as these spatial locations in turn affected interaction; she also examined interaction as this varied as to sex and through time during the school year.

Leis's study (above) reports, and these "Pygmalion" studies may report (and also may not) that second kind of cultural transmission process above-named where mappings diverge. Clearly parties are being sorted and their behaviors are diverging accordingly, and clearly these parties regularly come correctly to predict each other's behavior. Whether they so predict on the basis of increasingly similar or increasingly dissimilar mappings cannot convincingly be said: to these purposes all are half-studies, for we learn much about aspects of the cognitive maps of the teachers, but we learn very little (except indirectly by remote inference) about the analogous mappings by the students or about changes in those mappings over time. We suppose that there is little similarity in the ways Rist's teachers cognitively map "teacher" and "slow learner" and the way those students map those same identities —we suppose but we do not know. (See also Raum in Middleton 24.)

Entailed is another perhaps critical dimension of transaction which can be called "transacting agendas." The parties in the reported encounters are evidently engaged in negotiation and renegotiation with each other as to their respective positionings vis-à-vis one another and their critical audiences and as to their respective immediate purposes. Agenda transaction is the dimension of personal operationalization in any encounter: What do I want? How important is that? What does he want and how badly? What are my options? How do these others relate?

Among those reported, some verbal interchanges are such that each party seriously wants "to understand" the other, but some are debates wherein it is useful to willfully misunderstand; the difference lies in the way the parties position themselves in respect to one another. Or one party, after watching another behave, identifies and imitates; in another encounter a party watches and mocks.

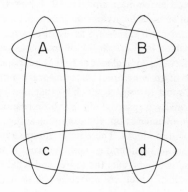

Two simple models seem usefully to sort complex phenomena into manageable simplicity. First, one party to an encounter, A, transacts with a second party, B; they imagine two critical audiences, each constituted of one party or many, physically present or not, c and d. Whatever else the encounter of A with B may be about—necessarily some exchange drawing upon or affecting their perceptions of setting and folk science and formal identity and perhaps some testing of skills—A is also actively negotiating how he is positioned vis-à-vis B and how those audiences are positioned in relation to them: who are "we" and who are "they"? By this model, A has only two options: he and B are "we," in opposition to c and d, who are "they"; or he and c are "we" and B and d are "they." B of course has the parallel options. The second model is a variant: A and B compete for the allegiance of a single audience, c. [We, of course, draw here from the work of Goffman (12) and others working in the traditions of small group sociology and social psychology.]

From the several reports it seems dimly evident that in the course of such positioning and repositioning, parties to these encounters have selectively preempted other aspects of the transaction (the three R's included) in the service of this negotiation, which is another way of describing the "Pygmalion" effect.

Agenda may in fact prove to be the "growing tip" of many or all transactions, thus of cultural transmission. A future research implication seems evident: a key dimension of transaction to watch, with the finest grained analysis possible, is the transaction of equivalences and the failures of transaction of equivalence in respect to agenda. The key questions become two: Do A and d settle upon some stable way to define their relationships of alliance and apposition in respect to one another and their critical audiences, and if so, how? And what other aspects of their mapping have they put into the service of this negotiation and this resolution, and how?

Testing as Equivalence

A fact has been frequently examined, though not by any of the recent anthropological studies before us: in large societies, one of the central functions which fall to formal education systems at all levels is gatekeeping. Gatekeeping decisions in the schools are made in substantial part through testing: I.Q. testing, performance testing at all levels, credentialling exams, etc. At surface level, a test is a measure of equivalence: testor and testee map similarly "2 + 2 = 4," or they do not. It is also evident that the full array of behaviors and relationships entailed in any testing is also being covertly measured. Gladwin's study discovered that I.Q. tests assume a "heuristic strategy" which is discrepant with analogous procedures practiced by those islanders. Put otherwise, equivalence as to that heuristic strategy is commonly transacted in the course of growing up in some cultural communities including that of the test makers and most testees, so much so that they are oblivious to it. But that strategy is not normally transacted among those islanders (it is not necessary or useful in their mode of navigation, for example) and probably in many other places including some within blocks. There no doubt are a host of such underlying features: as to time, as to the nonliteral game-like nature of the questions, as to the surrounding social structure (who gets the scores and what they then do), etc, etc, equivalent mapping of all of which are normally transacted in some communities but not in others. (See also: Leacock in Cazden et al 4; R. Cohen in Ianni & Storey 18; Hymes in M. Wax et al 43.)

Mass Society and Power

Thomas & Wahrhaftig (39), among the studies before us, uniquely treat in detail and directly the massive influences which can be generated by historical movements in the society at large, which influences, they show, can simply overwhelm transactional processes that might otherwise occur in local communities, as among conservative Cherokees and white "hillbillies" in Eastern Oklahoma specifically. The historical movements treated include: the freezing in virtue of technological developments of the long-operating pattern of collective social mobility of immigrant ethnic groups, the numerical burgeoning of the middle class and its life styles and values; and as a result, and centrally, the crystallization of thought about the schools and the consolidation of power over the schools by the middle class, which monopolizations are so far advanced that it becomes literally unthinkable by school men that the schools could have a function other than training students for life by middle-class occupations, styles, values. Thomas & Wahrhaftig show that these developments are so strong as simply to preclude communication, and the young and old members of these communities withdraw. Both communities, but especially the Cherokees, once had strong and productive involvements with their institutions of formal education. Now they are thoroughly alienated as, say the authors, are many other "out-of-it" communities across the country. Anthropologists often profit from a characteristic myopia, but also suffer in failing to see clearly and appreciate the power of such massive influences on the local scenes they directly observe. Students of cultural transmission should welcome this convincing reminder. (See also: Kimball in Ianni & Storey 18; R. Wax, Dumont & M. Wax in Lindquist 22; Mead, R. & E. Hunt in Middleton 24; Y. Cohen in M. Wax et al 43.)

"Hidden Curriculum"

In the Rist study and in the Pygmalion studies generally, in Gladwin's treatment of testing, in Thomas & Wahrhaftig's descriptions of "out-of-it" communities, there consistently runs the theme that schools have failed, as indeed by obvious humane measures these schools conspicuously have. The question, however, is whether such failures are aberrancies of some kind or whether, from some understanding of the nature of cultural transmission generally, one would predict precisely what in these studies is reported. Evidently, the latter is true.

In most places, most of the time, in respect to most aspects of culture, societies do replicate themselves over the generations. A heuristic notion, "hidden curriculum," is frequently encountered: to us it means those behaviors which unfold in formal education settings, typically at the initiative of adults in those institutions that enjoy power relative to the young but early becoming a kind of inadvertent co-conspiracy between and among old and young, whereby in classroom and school are replicated the structural forms of the wider society. Hidden curriculums are seen unfolding in all these studies of failure; they can also be seen unfolding as conspicuously in "good" schools. What in fact is happening is that the society is reproducing itself—caste system, class system, sex roles, and all—and through actions which in some substantial part the actors themselves are only dimly aware of and actions which they, in full awareness, would often deplore. One could as easily say that the cultural transmission processes seen here awesomely succeed. (See also: P. & H. Byers, Gumperz & Hernandez-Chavez, Kochman, Dumont, Philips in Cazden et al 4; Wallace, Burnett, Lacey, Comitas, Ramcharan in Ianni & Storey 18.)

Comparative (Hologeistic) Studies: A Note

The years 1971–72 reveal a curious trough in respect to broadly comparative studies of cultural transmission. We have before us 2 books and 14 articles from the late 1950s and 1960s and approximately equivalent numbers appear to be currently in various stages of development, but in the period in question nothing appeared in print to our knowledge. In 1970, however, one methodological work which most directly bears did appear, Goodenough's (14) discussion of the emic-etic problem, which problem arises most conspicuously in hologeistic studies. Goodenough argues that etic language must be derived inductively from emic languages, that a system of etic categories must contain discriminations which mark the emic boundaries as perceived by each cultural system under examination, that an etic system must, that is, be able to describe each emic system and violate none of them. And he shows that this is possible, in respect to some aspects of cognitive mappings at least; for example, categories of age, sex, kinship, social strata as these combine in deference to role behavior.

Studies of cultural transmission are necessarily involved in matters of cognitive mapping. For such studies especially, Goodenough's discussion has cleared away obstacles and sketched the future course which is clear in principle, however difficult it may often prove to be in the doing. In short, one may expect a surge of hologeistically organized research on cultural transmission and may hope for interesting results in the early future.

Literature Cited

1.* Baty, R. M. 1972. *Reeducating Teachers for Cultural Awareness: Preparation for Educating Mexican-American Children in Northern California.* New York: Praeger

2. Berreman, G. D. 1972. Social categories and social interaction in urban India. *Am. Anthropol.* 74:567–86

3. Brophy, J. E., Good, T. L. 1970. Teachers' communication of differential expectations for children's classroom performance. *J. Educ. Psychol.* 61:365–74

4. Cazden, C. B., John, V. P., Hymes, D., Eds. 1972. *Functions of Language in the Classroom.* New York: Teachers College Press

5. Cole, M., Gay, J. 1972. Culture and memory. *Am. Anthropol.* 74:1066–84

6. Cole, M., Gay, J., Glick, J. A., Sharp, D. W. 1971. *The Cultural Context of Learning and Thinking.* New York: Basic Books

7. Epstein, E. H. 1971. Education and Peruanidad: internal colonialism in the Peruvian highlands. *Comp. Educ. Rev.* 15:188–201

8. Finn, J. D. 1972. Expectations and the educational environment. *Rev. Educ. Res.* 42:387–410

9. Gay, J., Cole, M. 1967. *The New Mathematics and an Old Culture.* New York: Holt, Rinehart & Winston

10. Gearing, F. O. 1973. Anthropology and education. In *Sourcebook in Social and Cultural Anthropology,* ed. J. Honigmann. Chicago: Rand McNally

11. Gladwin, T. 1970. *East in a Big Bird.* Cambridge: Harvard Univ. Press

12. Goffman, E. 1959. *The Presentation of Self in Everyday Life.* Garden City, NY: Doubleday

13. Goldschmidt, W. 1972. An ethnography of encounters: a methodology for the enquiry into the relation between the individual and society. *Curr. Anthropol.* 13:59–71

14. Goodenough, W. H. 1970. *Description and Comparison in Cultural Anthropology.* Chicago: Aldine
15. Gumperz, J. J., Hymes, D., Eds. 1972. *Directions in Sociolinguistics: The Ethnography of Communication.* New York: Holt, Rinehart & Winston
16.* Grindal, B. T. 1972. *Growing Up in Two Worlds: Education and Transition Among the Sisala of Northern Ghana.* New York: Holt, Rinehart & Winston
17. Hostetler, J. A., Huntington, G. E. 1971. *Children in Amish Society: Socialization and Community Acculturation.* New York: Holt, Rinehart & Winston
18. Ianni, F. A. J., Story, E., Eds. 1973. *Cultural Relevance and Educational Issues: A Reader in Anthropology and Education.* Boston: Little, Brown
19. Keifer, C. W. 1970. The psychological interdependence of family, school and bureaucracy in Japan. *Am. Anthropol.* 72:66–75
20. Leacock, E. B. 1971. Theoretical and methodological problems in the study of schools. See Ref. 43, 169–79
21. Leis, P. E. 1972. *Enculturation and Socialization in an Ijaw Village.* New York: Holt, Rinehart & Winston
22. Lindquist, H. M., Ed. 1970. *Education: Readings in the Process of Cultural Transmission.* Boston: Houghton Mifflin
23. Lindquist, H. M. 1971. World bibliography of anthropology and education with annotations. See Ref. 43, 307–84
24. Middleton, J., Ed. 1970. *From Child to Adult: Studies in the Anthropology of Education.* Garden City, NY: Natural History Press
25.* Nash, M. 1972. Ethnicity, centrality and education in Pasir Mas, Kelantan. *Comp. Educ. Rev.* 16:4–15
26.* Pashkin, A. 1972. *Kanuri School Children: Education and Social Mobilization in Nigeria.* New York: Holt, Rinehart & Winston
27.* Paulston, R. G. 1972. Cultural revitalization and educational change in Cuba. *Comp. Educ. Rev.* 16:474–85
28. Provencher, R. 1972. Comparisons of social interaction styles: urban and rural Malay culture. In *The Anthropology of*

Urban Environments, ed. T. Weaver, D. White, 69–75. Soc. Appl. Anthropol. Monogr. 11
29. Rist, R. C. 1970. Student social class and teacher expectation: the self-fulfilling prophecy in ghetto education. *Harvard Educ. Rev.* 40:411–51
30. Rosenfeld, G. 1972. *"Shut Those Thick Lips!" A Study of Slum School Failure.* New York: Holt, Rinehart & Winston
31.* Rosentiel, A. 1971. The changing focus of native education in Alaska. *Artic & Alpine Res.* 3:187–97
32. Rosenthal, R., Jacobson, L. 1968. *Pygmalion in the Classroom.* New York: Holt, Rinehart & Winston
33. Sankoff, G. 1971. Quantitative analysis of sharing and variability in a cognitive model. *Ethnology* 10:389–408
34. Sankoff, G. 1972. Cognitive variability and New Guinea social organization: the Buang Dgwa. *Am. Anthropol.* 74:555–66
35.* Shimahara, N. 1971. *Burakumin: A Japanese Minority and Education.* The Hague: Martinus Nijhoff
36. Sindell, P. S. 1969. Anthropological approaches to the study of education. *Rev. Educ. Res.* 39:593–605
37.* Slobin, D. I. 1971. *Psycholinguistics.* Glenview, Ill.: Scott, Foresman
38. Talbert, C. 1970. Interaction and adaptation in 2 negro kindergartens. *Hum. Organ.* 29:103–14
39. Thomas, R. K., Wahrhaftig, A. L. 1971. Indians, hillbillies, and the education problem. See Ref. 43, 230–51
40.* Valentine, C. A. 1971. Deficit, difference, and bicultural models of Afro-American behavior. *Harvard Educ. Rev.* 41:137–51
41. Wallace, A. F. C. 1970. *Culture and Personality.* New York: Random House. 2nd ed.
42. Ward, M. C. 1971. *Them Children: A Study in Language Learning.* New York: Holt, Rinehart & Winston
43. Wax, M. L., Diamond, S., Gearing, F. O., Eds. 1971. *Anthropological Perspectives on Education.* New York: Basic Books
44. Wolcott, H. F. 1967. Anthropology and education. *Rev. Educ. Res.* 37:82–92

MYTHOLOGY AND FOLKLORE ❖ 9521

Richard M. Dorson

Folklore Institute, Indiana University, Bloomington, Indiana

While the terms mythology and folklore are frequently linked together in both lay and academic discourse, the students of the two subject matters have steadily grown apart. In the eighteenth century mythology was its own science, but today it has become an uneasy adjunct to anthropology, classics, literature, and theology. None of the recent writers on mythology cited below are folklorists by primary allegiance, and while all make gestures toward folklore, they appear surprisingly ill-informed on current folklore scholarship. In their scanty references they refer to the old standbys of a past generation—Boas, Stith Thompson, Archer Taylor—and make no mention of, say, the *Journal of the Folklore Institute* or the *Folktales of the World* series, both initiated in 1963. Still the study of mythology continues to attract powerful minds and to produce stimulating works.

Conversely, folklore has within the past two decades achieved the status of an independent discipline in the United States, with close to a hundred doctorates being granted by Indiana University and the University of Pennsylvania. These folklorists chiefly concern themselves with traditions within their own cultures, where myth as a form has disappeared.

Because of the scope and vast, uneven literature on these topics, the present review will eschew journal articles and deal only with books, in English, mainly from the past 3 years but reaching back a year or two more if they fit into a theme under discussion. The aim has been to select titles that illustrate theoretical and research trends in studies of mythology and folklore.

Current interest in myth and mythology has extended to an historical concern with past interest, and in *The Rise of Modern Mythology 1680–1860* two associate professors of English, Feldman & Richardson (17), constructed a bounteous history-cum-anthology. They chose their dates to encompass immediate predecessors of the well-known modern philosophers of myth, and they selected their authors to illustrate the widely eclectic variety of writings about myth during the period. In the Enlightenment era the upsurge of rationalistic inquiry coupled with the new literature of exploration and travel induced a reexamination of pagan and heathen myths. Feldman & Richardson point out that by the nineteenth century myths had become invested with qualities of creative literary art and spiritualizing religious principles.

107

Meanwhile mythology, formerly an independent study devoted to Greek and Roman myths, had broadened to cover myths of many peoples but had lost its status as a separate branch of learning and become an adjunct to various subdivisions of the humanities and social sciences.

To illustrate this development Feldman & Richardson resort to a compromise between an intellectual history and an anthology. They preface each selection or group of selections with succinct brief essays placing the myth writer in his philosophical setting. These essays, with their bibliographical notes, maintain a high standard of scholarly excellence and illuminate the excerpts. In their net Feldman & Richardson catch a host of German, French, English, and American antiquaries, churchmen, philologists, poets, critics, historians, social theorists, and professed mythologists, the great and the obscure, united all in a sensitivity to the force of myth. Essays and selections indicate how myth is directed by Jacob Grimm toward folklore, by Marx toward ideology, by Goethe into literature, by Wagner into musical drama, by Bulfinch into bowdlerized fairy tales, by Blake into poetic symbolism, and so on through scores of ingenious commentaries. Only in their last section, The Nineteenth Century to 1860, do the editors attempt more than chronological sequences, with headings on German, English, and American romanticism and myth, and only in the romantic movement—a loose enough designation—does a unitary attitude toward myth as a high mode of truth achieve some dominance in a given period.

The myth writing of yesteryear seems very far removed from that of today. In the 1970s the scholarly impulse to interpret and even to create myth finds its foremost exponents in Joseph Campbell, an American professor of literature, and Claude Lévi-Strauss, the French anthropologist. Another mythologist, Raphael Patai, in *Myth and Modern Man* (36) describes both men as mythopoets, makers as well as students of myth, and quotes Lévi-Strauss as calling his book *The Raw and the Cooked* (27) a myth of its own, "the myth of mythology." In terms of style, the ornate, rhapsodic prose of Campbell and the relentlessly logical narrative of Lévi-Strauss suggest creative rather than pedagogical writings.

Since completing his tetralogy on world mythology, *The Masks of God,* in 1968, Campbell has brought out two volumes of papers and talks elaborating his mythological system. In 1970 he published *The Flight of the Wild Gander, Explorations in the Mythological Dimension* (2), assembling pieces written and read between 1944 and 1968. Two years later he presented in *Myths to Live By* (3) transcripts of tape-recorded talks he delivered at the Cooper Union Forum in New York City from 1958 to 1971. Campbell's lurid body of work is highly repetitive, and one essay or book melts into another. He admires Jung and the Jungian view of omnipresent archetypal symbols, and he sees recurrent themes—theft of fire, virgin birth, incarnation, the returning hero—linking the world's folktales, legends, and myths and reflecting basic human biological and psychological demands. His pronouncements verge on the mystical. "Mythology is the womb of mankind's initiation to life and death," he writes in *The Flight of the Wild Gander* (2); mythology is "dreamlike and, like dream, a spontaneous product of the psyche" (p. 251). Toward the particularism of field anthropologists and their American Anthropological Society (*sic,* p.

46) he betrays a defensive edginess, and praises Bastian for placing universal elementary ideas ahead of local factors. The psychoanalytical keys of Freud and Jung added to Bastian's thesis give Campbell his springboard.

In *Myths to Live By,* Campbell (3) moves from the role of mythographer to the role of prophet. While stressing the psychic unity of mankind, he dwells on the ideal of self-obliteration in the East as contrasted with the assertive individualism of the West. Regarding religious mythologies of the West as outdated and sterile, he advises the churches to dispense with talk and renew their rituals. In this same vein he chides Frazer for assuming that a rationalist exposure of superstitious customs would lead to their disappearance. In his mystical posture, Campbell retells myths in the form of pretty fables and inflates his rhetoric in an incantatory pitch. Lowering his voice, he descends to down-to-earth homilies about the boy at the lunch counter who had boldly defied the fundamentalism of his teacher and mother. Then he is off again, dazzling his audience with quotations from the *Upanishads* and the *Bhagavad Gita.* Yet for a modern Occidental man, as he prides himself, he finds the youth culture regressive and schizophrenic, untuned to the vibrations of the true mystics.

Campbell appeals firstly to a literary constituency, Lévi-Strauss to an anthropological constituency, although they have reached far wider audiences. The myths that Campbell cites from variegated sources are literary and artistic reworkings of the oral originals or fluent renderings of field sources. For the illustrations of his books he chooses artistic devices representing mythic themes. In *The Raw and the Cooked, Introduction to a Science of Mythology: I,* Lévi-Strauss (27) exclusively cites field-collected oral myth texts of Brazilian and other South American Indian tribes, among whom he himself has done extensive fieldwork. He illustrates his work with photographs and drawings of Indians and their environment. Yet if they start from opposite ends, Campbell from the prehistoric and classical and Lévi-Strauss from the contemporary tribal, they move toward the same central goal, a universal system of mythology. Campbell (3) says: "Essentially the same mythological motifs are to be found throughout the world . . . such images stem from the psyche . . . they cannot be interpreted properly as references . . . to local historical events or personages" (p. 253). Lévi-Strauss (27) writes: "The layered structure of myth . . . allows us to look upon myth as a matrix of meanings, which are arranged in lines or columns, but in which each level always refers to some other level, whichever way the myth is read. Similarly, each matrix of meanings refers to another matrix, each myth to other myths" (pp. 340–41). Their ultimate meaning lies in the mind that generates them and in the image of the world perceived by that mind.

So Lévi-Strauss begins with one Bororo myth and works his way through 186 more, diagramming the binary oppositions of such empirical categories as the "raw and the cooked, the fresh and the decayed, the moistened and the burned" (p. 1). Everything fits beautifully, under the master's touch, into tables of opposites, and if a piece seems to be missing, he gently guides the reader to its restoration. Thus when one myth apparently lacks an incest episode, he shows that the act of a grandmother squatting over the head of her sleeping grandson and farting in his face is properly to be interpreted as inverted incest (p. 64). One recalls the mythological schemes of the solar and the sexual mythologists who interpreted all myths with similar neat finality and excited such admiration in their day.

Raphael Patai, the prolific Judaic scholar who collaborated on *Hebrew Myths* with Robert Graves in 1964, seeks not to unlock the world's myths with a new key in *Myth and the Modern Man* (36) but to show their relationship to cigarette ads, Mickey Mouse cartoons, and James Bond movies. After summarily reviewing schools of myth interpretation, he turns to consider mythologizing tendencies in America of the 1960s. His aim is twofold: to demonstrate first that contemporary Americans develop myths much as did the ancient Greeks, and second that these myths respond to the psychic needs of particular followings. Thus Mickey Mouse of the Disney animated cartoons cavorts through a series of encounters with a monster cat in which he emerges triumphant through cunning and agility. As middle America identified with Mickey, so did the Greeks of old identify with Herakles, likewise a buffoon-hero, in his series of mighty labors. One sector of black Americans accepted the myth of the Godhead with which Father Divine invested himself. Contrary to customary myth process, he managed to become a legend in his lifetime, and, through the manipulation of his wife, to transcend the fact of death. Radical student activists at the peak of SDS violence chose for their mythic hero a fantasized 5-year-old, whom they named Marion Delgado and invested with their own infantile spleen toward, and imagined power over, the authoritarian system. They selected a superchild because in permissive America the errant child never gets punished.

Various aspects of American popular culture suggest mythological themes to Patai. Television commercials for cigarettes and soft drinks recall for him the Greek myths surrounding nectar and ambrosia. *Playboy* magazine and its clubs and bunnies foster a new "sex myth" of a virile, dominant, but blasé male fending off hyper-mammalian young women. The *Playboy* rabbit evokes images of sexuality and seeming weakness that, like Mickey Mouse, conceal inner strength. Madison Avenue admen endow the washing machine with a mana that befits this "most powerful, active, and aggressive of all major household appliances" and emphasize its "masculine, phallic aspect" (p. 257) before delighted housewives. In forced analogies such as these between classical myths and the blandishments of mass culture Patai has strained the concept of myth beyond any recognizable meaning. Mickey Mouse is nobody's demigod.

In *Myth, Its Meaning and Functions in Ancient and Other Cultures,* Geoffrey S. Kirk (25) refuses to deal with "modern myths," although he concedes that a proper comprehension of these "bastard modern forms" may be aided by a study of the genuine article. Himself a professor of classics at the University of Bristol, and the deliverer of the Sather classical lectures at the University of California on which this book is based, Kirk takes a refreshingly broad view of his subject by exposing classical myths to light from folklore and anthropology. An initial chapter considers and rejects prevalent conceptions of myth that associate myths exclusively with gods, or rituals, or religion. Kirk contends, quite correctly, that myth narratives cannot be precisely categorized since they flow into other kinds of folk narratives such as fairy tales and legends. Most folklorists would agree with his assertion that myth implies no more than a traditional story, which may deal with deities or explain origins or involve religious matters or sanction customs. Recognizing that myths contain folktale elements and reflect the styles of individual storytellers is a large step forward in comparative mythological study.

A second chapter offers an astute analysis of Lévi-Strauss's structural theory as applied to South American myths. Kirk proposes certain plausible modifications: that Lévi-Strauss not attempt to fit all myths into his model of polarities resolved by a mediator; that he seek meaning in content as well as structure; that he allow for the nonstructural elements contributed by narrators, and indeed begin his analysis by empirical observation of myth tellers rather than with a priori dogma about the structure of the human mind. In the main Kirk gives high marks to Lévi-Strauss for advancing the state of mythological study beyond all previous systems, and for his convincing analysis of how Brazilian myths functioned to mediate between the contradictions of nature and culture.

In subsequent chapters Kirk brings to bear folklore perspective and Lévi-Straussian structural theory on Sumerian, Akkadian, and Greek myths. His approach yields fresh rewards, as when he perceives the nature-culture contrast in the Gilgamesh epic, but not among the Greeks, for whom the natural environment posed no formidable problems. He sees a special quality of Greek myth in its emphasis on heroes—elsewhere usually found in legend—and a flaw in its poverty of fantasy. Subsequently, Kirk extends his comparative treatment to Germanic, Egyptian, and Hindu myths and finds their relationships with the mythic expression of ancient Greece less meaningful than with that of Mesopotamia. A final chapter weighs certain theories of mythic formulation, particularly those of Cassirer and Jung, and proposes a myth typology based on narrative, operative, and speculative functions. He himself supports the thesis that many myths can be classed as speculative in their concerns with man's life, death, culture, and environment. Kirk's own work represents a high level of speculative scholarship resting on a sound comparative and folkloric base.

FOLKLORE

History of Folkloristics

One sign of the coming of age of folklore studies is the appearance of historical and biographical explorations of the great nineteenth century folklorists who developed the subject. The past 5 years have seen histories of Finnish and British folkloristics, two biographies of the brothers Grimm, a biography of the Serbian folklorist and linguist Vuk Karadzić, and a volume of biographical essays on the Scandinavian folklorists. Hitherto the most elementary information about the pioneer collectors and scholars of folklore has been lacking in English-language sources.

Finland occupies a special position in the history of folklore scholarship. In the late nineteenth and early twentieth centuries Finns took the lead in collecting and explicating oral peasant traditions and developing an analytic system which attracted international attention, the so-called Finnish historical-geographical method. The monograph of Jouko Hautala, *Finnish Folklore Research 1828–1918*

(21), sets the illustrious figures now so well known—Elias Lönnrot, collector of the Kalevala poems, Julius Krohn and his son Kaarle, who formulated the Finnish method, and Antti Aarne, pioneer tale cataloguer—in a full perspective. It was the collections of oral epic poems, mainly from Carelia in eastern Finland, published by the country doctor Lönnrot in 1835 as the *Kalevala*, that inspired cultural drives toward a Finnish national civilization and formed the foundation for the Finnish achievement in folklore studies. To ensure that ample variants were available for comparative folklore studies, Kaarle Krohn stimulated the Finnish Literature Society to increase their archival holdings, which rose from 43,000 items in 1877 to over half a million by 1930. (Today they approach three million.) In his Finnish folklore seminar at the University of Helsinki, Kaarle trained dozens of young scholars, as Antti Aarne, who propagated his methods.

Less familiar names also come into view: A. E. Ahlquist, the first outspoken critic of Lönnrot's *Kalevala* scholarship; M. A. Castrén, theorist of Finnish mythology; E. Salmelainen, the first major Finnish collector and scholar of folktales; V. Salminen, who collected and compared Ingrian wedding songs; and E. N. Setälä, critic of the historic-geographic method and exponent of the mythical interpretation of ancient Finnish poetry. For the American scholar, the information on these and other relatively unknown figures is especially useful. Hautala's history turns into a catalog of Finnish folklorists and a summary, often with extensive quotations, of their publications. This is a digest of academic scholarship by a member of the guild. One dissertation after another on a folklore subject produced at the University of Helsinki is mentioned and synopsized. Hautala recognizes the major trends of folklore theory, from early nineteenth century romantic nationalism through nature mythology and positivistic evolutionism to the historical-geographical methodology, and he comments temperately on their weaknesses. But lacking is any human side of scholarship or of the Finnish folk who are being so assiduously studied.

The story that unfolds in Dorson's *The British Folklorists, a History* (6) is almost wholly a nonacademic chronicle. Some points of parallelism are notable. While the central magnet of the *Kalevala* is absent, the successive waves of interest in folkloric matters by antiquaries, nature mythologists, evolutionists, and diffusionists wash over Britain as well as Finland. But literary and antiquarian societies, culminating in 1878 in the Folk-Lore Society, and not universities supported folklore research in England, a situation that accounts for its decline after the first World War and for the anomaly of an American writing the history of British folklore. The "Great Team" of the Folk-Lore Society that carried its prestige to a peak in the International Folklore Congress held in London in 1891 were all private scholars: Andrew Lang, a free-lance writer; George Laurence Gomme, a London civil servant; Edwin Sidney Hartland, a solicitor; Edward Clodd, a banker; and Alfred Nutt, a publisher. Unlike the Finns, none engaged in any field collecting, although their large body of theoretical writings, suggesting analogies between the beliefs of peasants and contemporary aboriginals, did generate collecting activities in the English counties and throughout the Empire. In Scotland, Ireland, and Wales impulses of cultural nationalism have in the twentieth century led to institutional folklore centers that sponsor considerable fieldwork. *The British Folklorists* endeavors to trace the vigorous but largely forgotten efforts of folklore enthusiasts who built upon each other's labors from the first national history of William Camden in 1586 up to Edward B. Tylor and the "Great Team" of anthropological folklorists whom he so powerfully influenced. Tylor established anthropology firmly at Oxford, but folklore never gained entry into Oxford and Cambridge.

Selections from the major figures in *The British Folklorists,* aimed at presenting the continuous development and spirited controversies of British folklore theory in the nineteenth century, were edited by Dorson in a two-volume anthology, *Peasant Customs and Savage Myths* (7). Writing for a general rather than a scholarly audience, although maintaining high standards of research methods as they sought to construct a "science" of folklore, the Victorians expressed themselves with grace, fluency, and zeal, and, in the cases of Lang and Clodd, with wit and charm. Yet their work has vanished from the scene. At international folklore congresses the names of the "Great Team" and their associates are rarely mentioned, while the Finns on their much narrower academic and cultural base have maintained their eminence. In England social anthropology has rejected folklore and new developments in folklore have come in the name of social history and oral literature. The moral is obvious; in the twentieth century the fate of folklore studies has for better or worse rested with the academic professional and his university sponsor.

Complementing and to some extent overlapping with Hautala's history is a volume of collective biographical sketches dedicated to him on his sixtieth birthday, *Biographica, Nordic Folklorists of the Past,* edited by Strömbäck (39) and others. Twenty-four folklore scholars of Finland, Sweden, Denmark, Norway, the Faroe Islands, and Iceland (the last two with single representatives) reviewed the accomplishments of 26 of their predecessors, some internationally known, like von Sydow, Svend Grundtvig, the Krohns, and Axel Olrik, and others of local reputation. This volume testifies to the vigorous and continuous activities, past and present, of Scandinavian and Finnish folklorists who held chairs at the universities of Copenhagen, Oslo, Lund, and Helsinki, museum curatorships, pastorates, and teaching positions from which they embarked on lifelong collecting and publishing careers. Unlike the inner circle of the English Folk-Lore Society, the Nordic folklore enthusiasts almost without exception possessed roots in the country soil and engaged in frequent field trips. A number, like the indefatigable Evald Tang Kristensen of Denmark and Jón Árnason of Iceland, expended their energies in amassing rather than theorizing about oral traditions.

While more personal and revealing than Hautala's wooden history, *Biographica* displays the unevenness one can expect from two dozen humanists turning their hands to the critical biographical sketch. Some essays, like Tillhagen's on the folk-medicine expert Reichborn-Kjennerud, Nesheim's on the Lappish collector Qvigstad, and Strömbäck's on the talented but unproductive Moltke Moe, do little more than abstract or quote from the writings of their subjects. Conscious of dealing with an unknown, A. A. Koskerjaako, overshadowed by his great Finnish colleagues, Kuusi writes persuasively that "in the history of scholarship, fame seems to be a cumulative affair: he who has, gets more" (p. 67) and makes a case as a neglected pioneer for the headmaster who abjured popularization or sweeping sensational theories and who wrote only in Finnish, and little at that, on a neglected subject, legal proverbs. For the most part the essays avoid filiopietism and often indulge in hard-hitting criticism. In her sketch of Henning Feilberg, the Danish teacher, minister, and compiler of the dictionary of the vernacular language of Jutland, Bente Alver challenges the assumptions of his 1904 study *Jul*, interpreting Christmas customs as a festival of death. Alver finds his methods deficient in source criticism and genre analysis and in failure to distinguish between individual and collective elements of tradition. In a solid essay appraising Axel Olrik's scholarship, Bengt Holbek, who contributes a judicious preface to the volume, declares that for all Olrik's esteemed writings on Danish heroic poetry, Scandinavian mythology, and theories of folk-epic composition, he customarily overlooked the individual informant.

The Nordic folklorists have chiefly ploughed their own vineyards and influenced each other. Yet they have advanced folklore studies to a greater degree than any other body of regional scholars. This tentative volume affords some clues to their thought and motivations.

In the history of folkloristics the role of the brothers Jacob and Wilhelm Grimm is crucial, and two biographies have recently appeared in English. Since the brothers were born a year apart and died within 4 years of each other (Jacob's dates are 1785–1863, Wilhelm's 1786–1859) and since they collaborated on much of their scholarly work and shared their professional lives, one biography inevitably serves both. *The Brothers Grimm*, an impressionistic portrait by Ruth Michaelis-Jena (33), who had previously edited lesser known folktales collected by the brothers, paints in homely details of their lives, drawn in large part from published correspondence and materials, iconographic as well as printed, from the Brüder Grimm Museum in Kassel. *Paths Through the Forest, A Biography of the Brothers Grimm* by Murray Peppard (37), chairman of the German department at Amherst College, is far more the academic biography with a surer command of the historical and intellectual setting. Both biographies retell the basic narrative of the brothers' youth in Steinau, their college days at Marburg, their posts as librarians in Cassel, their move to the university at Göttingen when denied promotion by the Elector of Hesse, their defiance of King Ernest Augustus of Hannover on his repeal of the liberal constitution of 1833 and Jacob's subsequent exiling, and the final phase as revered lecturers at Berlin University. Bachelor Jacob emerges as a research mole, vexed at every interruption to his labors, such as the Congress of Vienna in 1815, which he was obliged to attend as a minor functionary. More outgoing, and finally marrying at 39, Wilhelm achieved somewhat less as an original scholar. What strikes the modern academic is the similarity of his problems with those of the Grimms: the struggles for a position, advancement, recognition, academic freedom, scholarly principles versus commercial rewards. The opus that won them their greatest fame, the *Kinder- und Hausmärchen*, was the one on which through successive editions they steadily compromised with the demands of the marketplace.

Both biographers are deplorably ignorant of folkloric scholarship. Michaelis-Jena barely rises above the level of reciting titles and repeating clichés about the brothers' works. Because he pretends to more authority, Peppard fails even more dismally to comment intelligently on their folklore publications. His translation of *Sagen* as "Folk Tales" and his constant comparisons between the "Fairy Tales" (Märchen) and the "Folk Tales" (*Sagen*), which every folklorist refers to as legends, make a mockery of basic folklore terminology. His statement that the "true fairy tale . . . will be characterized by prudery" (p. 64) is another shocking piece of ignorance. It is the old story of the competent literary scholar who lacks any basic training in folklore. Campbell for all his rhapsodizing gives a much more preferable brief treatment of the work of the Grimm brothers on the folktale, with a crisp definition of *Sagen*, in a 1944 essay, The Fairy Tale, reprinted in *The Flight of the Wild Gander* (2).

Like Jacob Grimm, whom he met and with whose ideas he sympathized, Vuk Karadzić devoted his lifelong energies to propagating a national language and folklore. His biographer, Duncan Wilson (42), has written in *Vuk Stafanović Karadzić 1787–1864*, "The various branches of Vuk's work were all undertaken with the one aim in view of reviving the Serb popular language for the greater use and glory of the Serb nation" (p. 7). Toward this end Vuk collected and published oral poetry and folktales sung and recited in the folk dialects that he knew from his own village childhood, while in his *Dictionary* of the Serb popular tongue (1818), as well as in his posthumous *Life and Customs of the Serb People* (1867), he recorded many folk beliefs and rituals. Accordingly, Vuk takes rank as one of the founding fathers of national folklore studies in early nineteenth century Europe, and Wilson gives full recognition to Vuk's folkloric and ethnographic activities. While disclaiming any pretense to new knowledge, and excusing himself as a working diplomat, Wilson provides a highly informative, scholarly biography based on Vuk's extensive writings and on secondary studies in Serbian, French, German, and English. Wilson's narrative combines the political-chronological account of Vuk's career in Serbia under the Turks and in Vienna under the Austrian Empire with his ethnographic activities in Croatia, Dalmatia, and Montenegro. For the folklorist there are vignettes of heroic singers, such as Tešan Podrugović, a destitute reed-cutter in the Srem who recited a hundred heroic songs about outlaw leaders; discussion of the favoring conditions in Vuk's early life for the folk creation of heroic poetry about the wars of liberation against the Turks; examples of Vuk's stylistic revision of folktales; and appendices of translated texts of traditional poems, tales, and beliefs collected by Vuk, and Jacob Grimm's sympathetic review of Vuk's 1823 collection of Serb popular songs. Biographical studies of this caliber are sorely needed for the Grimms and for other major European folklorists of the nineteenth century.

General and Theoretical Works

While no single theory or school has emerged from the younger generation of American folklorists, a definite point of view and community of interest are recognizable and have found expression in a special issue of the *Journal of American Folklore* separately issued as a book titled *Toward New Perspectives in Folklore* (35). Co-editors are the editor of the *Journal,* Paredes, and his colleague at the University of Texas, Bauman, who conceives of the symposium as emphasizing the "event" rather than the "item" aspect of folklore. Of the 13 contributors, 8 hold doctorates in folklore, one in American studies, one in psychology, and three are anthropologists. They evince strong interest in linguistics communication theory, the sociology of small-group interaction, developmental psychology, and structural and symbolic forms of analysis. To a large extent they conceive of folklore as communication. Ben-Amos states that "folklore is a communicative process," and he eliminates from his definition the long-established criteria of tradition and oral transmission. If a popular song or anecdote enters into the communication of a small group, it should be treated as folklore, and if a traditional tale or ballad appears on television, it ceases to be folklore. Bauman emphasizes the use of folklore in "communicative reaction." Hymes sees the new perspective as a "focus on the communicative event." Elli Maranda begins her analysis of Lau riddle texts with the "hypothesis that verbal art is a form of communication."

Another favorite term is performance. To Abrahams, "Folklore is folklore only when performed." Goldstein contends that a given individual actively performs only certain items in his repertoire, and that performance, not passive knowledge, is the test of whether a tradition can be labeled active or inactive. Bauman argues that attention to "folklore as doing . . . folklore performance" holds the key to the future of empirical folklore studies.

Still another approved term is continuum, with its suggested transcendence of the conventional categories of the genres and space-time divisions. Working on a corpus of Israeli legends, Heda Jason redefines the Grimms' definition of historical and local legends into a "linear continuum" with separate tales distributed along the continuum. In seeking to develop a methodology for analyzing festival behavior, Robert J. Smith prepared a "simple hedonic continuum" to determine normative and actual affective responses to two folktales. Defining folklore in context, Ben-Amos asserts that "the narrator, his story, and his audience are all related to each other as components of a single continuum." Attempting to point out related interests of folklore and linguistics, Hymes describes speech in terms of genres and of esthetic quality, and allows that "folklorists will be most concerned with the more highly organized, more expressive end of the two continua." Gossen views Chamula oral tradition in holistic terms rather than under the rubrics of European genres. So too Sutton-Smith examines various expressive forms "such as dreams, stories, folktales, rhymes, cartoons, and games as if they could all be part of the same conceptual domain," and arrives at what he considers an "expressive profile" of a youthful age group. In these studies the tendency is to soften not only the genre distinctions within folklore but also the boundaries between folkloric and nonfolkloric expressive behavior. The article by Alan Dundes on Folk Ideas as Units of World View—refreshingly jargon-free, in contrast to the balance of the papers—steps outside the genres to suggest that folklorists record traditional attitudes, often referred to as myth in the derogatory sense, which represent inherited values and fallacies in the folk community. Such values may be expressed in proverbial form —"money talks"—or in ordinary discourse.

In the end there is little that is novel in *New Perspectives.* The contributors have for the most part written previously on the points they make here. Attention to "artistic verbal performance" is already becoming something of a cliché, and rather than enlarging the scope of folkloric investigation the concept excludes material culture and all nonverbal folk forms. The anthropologists included continue as in the past to interpret the one culture in which they have done their fieldwork. Perhaps the most valuable contribution, involving no new perspective but a refinement of method, is Tedlock's proposal for more faithful translation of Zuñi oral narratives by attention to all linguistic and paralinguistic features. One curious byproduct of the "new perspective" is the disappearance from view of the folk, who are shunted aside in favor of models, graphs, and social-science terminology.

Two volumes of essays devoted to structural theory have recently been issued by Elli Köngäs Maranda and Pierre Maranda (31, 32). They co-edited *Structural Analysis of Oral Tradition* (32), heavily weighted toward the analytic method of Lévi-Strauss, who supplies one chapter explicating three Guianese myths. Although all the essays deal with folklore materials—tribal folktales and ritual, Finnish riddles, Javanese folk drama, cross-cultural folksongs—they belong to the discipline of structural linguistics rather than folkloristics. Only 3 of the 13 contributors—Köngäs Maranda, Dundes, and Lomax—are folklorists, and the folk whom they study make few appearances in these papers full of diagrams and computer statistics. Commenting on the necessity to identify before interpreting folk narrative, Dundes points out that "to someone trained in folklore, it is clear that the narrative [a Sherente myth] is not simply a retelling of Genesis. It is in fact a standard European narrative, a tale found in the Grimm collection . . ." (p. 295), and he furnishes the type and motif numbers. Responding, the ethnographer Maybury-Lewis concedes his ignorance of the folktale type he had collected and accepts the label of a "folkloristically naive anthropologist" (p. 316). Lévi-Strauss frankly states that the need for ethnographic knowledge recedes as the semantic universe of the myth becomes clearer (p. xxix). The Marandas recognize that the papers they have assembled "show that the structural and semantic anthropological approach to oral tradition is different from traditional folkloristics" (p. xxix).

Also in 1971 the Marandas published *Structural Models in Folklore and Transformational Essays* (31), reprinting a 1962 essay they had jointly written and adding a transformational myth analysis by Pierre and a transformational riddle analysis by Elli Köngäs. The few vivid pages describing their recent field experience recording Lau folklore in Melanesia, "where myth and ritual are fully alive and form the core of the culture," contrast with the main content of the diagrammatic papers.

At the opposite end of the folklore spectrum fall two volumes of collected articles by Dorson (8, 9), *American Folklore and the Historian* (see under "American Folklore") and *Folklore, Selected Essays*. In the humanistic tradition these essays discuss questions of oral narrative style, concepts of myth and legend, the historicity of tradition, and the future of folklore as an academic discipline. A folklorist of the "new perspectives" school reviewing these volumes would point out the absence of computerized conclusions and models of communicative behavior.

Two contrasting attempts were made in the past 2 years to survey the subject matter of folklore comprehensively. In *Folklore and Folklife, an Introduction,* edited by Dorson (11), 16 contributors deal with specific folklore genres and research techniques, and the editor discusses 12 schools of folklore theory in an introduction. The faculty and former students of the Folklore Institute of Indiana University constitute the core of the authors, reinforced by three specialists from Britain and one from Switzerland. Recognizing the extension of the folklore concept to cover material culture as currently acknowledged by European and American folklorists, the volume gives attention to folk costume, folk cuisine, folk architecture, and folk crafts. In between the clear-cut areas of oral folklore and physical artifacts are placed the performing arts of folk drama, folk dance, and folk music, and such matters of social belief and custom as folk medicine and folk religion. Nonliterate and non-Western cultures are omitted from discussion.

Conversely, they receive considerable attention in *Lore, An Introduction to the Science of Folklore and Literature* by Munro S. Edmonson (13), who calls his book "an introduction to the science of lore . . . commonly described by such terms as *folklore* or *comparative literature,* here defined as the study of connotative meaning." No professional folklorists use these terms in these ways, or deal with materials in his manner. He tabulates all the world's cultures and all the world's literatures, oral and written, from prehistoric times to the present, under the rubrics of Speech, Song, Story, Plays, and Style, and in a lengthy Chronological Outline of the World's Written Traditions. His examples come indiscriminately from everywhere. Thus under "Plays" he presents excerpts from a Filipino riddling game, an American Negro Street-corner obscene taunting contest, Vietnamese courtship verses, the Middle American ritual ball game Tlachtli, a hypothetical Reindeer Dance ritual drama of Cro-Magnon hunters, a ceremonial preparation of Alacaluf whalers of southern South America, a Mayala Negrito ritual drama for propitiating mountain spirits, a New Year's ritual in Kuntunso in Ghana dedicated to the god Tano the Hyena, a Pueblo Indian raingod ceremonial (in which the text has the Chief Raingod striking the first clown with his yucca whip to elicit the response, "Ouch, goddam, that hurts!"), and so on. In providing his miscellaneous texts of speech, song, story, and play, Edmonson intends to illustrate the power and range of metaphor. He sees "connotative relationships" as metaphors, and he believes that "some part of the building of a world political structure rests on the development of comprehensible and acceptable metaphors on which to base it—in short, it awaits the further elaboration of a world literature" (p. 234). This work seems to be the stuff rather than the study of folklore.

British Folklore

The most exciting folkloric studies of the past 5 years have come from an unexpected direction. They are written by two English social historians familiar with British social anthropology and working closely together. Keith Thomas (40), author of *Religion and the Decline of Magic,* directed the dissertation at Oxford University of Alan Macfarlane (29), published as *Witchcraft in Tudor and Stuart England,* and both express deep debt to the other's work. Thomas's history is the more comprehensive and philosophic, a densely annotated, panoramic examination of the supernatural belief systems within and without the church in sixteenth and seventeenth century England. Macfarlane concentrates on beliefs in witchcraft in three Essex villages—Hatfield Peverel, Boreham, and Little Baddow—in the same period. Their joint work goes far beyond anything in print in delineating the social functions of magical beliefs in pre-industrial England. Thomas and Macfarlane seek to establish —one on a national, the other on a local scale—the precise manner in which ideas now regarded as superstitions operated in English society after the Reformation. Where folklorists customarily list and describe beliefs in general terms, Macfarlane and Thomas are determined to pin down as far as possible the nature, extent, genesis, and social utility of supernatural concepts. On witchcraft, for example, they ask who in the community held such beliefs, over what periods of time, exactly what the villagers believed, what counter-measures they pursued, from magical to legal, and to what kinds of individuals they imputed their charges. Thomas reports that an accusation against a witch for riding a broomstick occurs only once in an English trial. The wealth and orderliness of the information they have presented, and the convincing nature of their evidence, make these volumes landmarks in a field plagued by popularizers and dilettantes.

Ironically Thomas and Macfarlane have approached the study of folklore materials not from the great humanistic tradition of the Victorian folklorists, whose day ran out with the first World War, but through what they consider hard-nosed social sciences of today, quantitative history and social anthropology. It is only plausible that, folklore never having gained a foothold at Oxford and Cambridge, these historians of witchcraft should exchange notes with anthropologists of witchcraft at the High Table, and so add a comparative dimension to their insular concerns. Thomas incorporated into his work a paper he presented to the Association of Social Anthropologists on The Relevance of Social Anthropology to the Historical Study of English Witchcraft, and Macfarlane includes three chapters of anthropological field data. Avant-garde too in historical method, they pursue statistical conclusions and Thomas defers to the computer that has made the "historian's traditional method of presentation by example and counter-example . . . the intellectual equivalent of the bow and arrow in a nuclear age" (p. x).

Yet the success of these studies rests on time-honored methods rather than new magic formulas. Thomas has done what a good historian must do: he has mastered an enormous, complex literature of primary and secondary writings, and he has analyzed them to show lines of force and change. His canvas covers the magical system within the medieval and Protestant Church, exemplified by acts of divine providence and the efficacy of prayer; the folk magic of healers and "cunning men"; the intellectually fashionable dependence on astrology; the role of witchcraft and related beliefs in ghosts and fairies, auguries and apparitions. Always he seeks to explain the social reasons for the emergence, persistence, and decline of supernatural ideas. Thus he accounts for the abandonment of the once-popular belief in lucky and unlucky days by the changing conception of time contingent on the shift from a seasonal agricultural calendar to a more technological routine, the acceptance of Newtonian time regularity, and the invention in 1657 of the pendulum clock. Widespread sentiments of rebellion at the time of the Reformation and the Civil War induced the belief in prophecies, Thomas contends, rather than prophecies stimulating rebellion. To answer the question why witchcraft reached a peak in the 120 years after the accession of Elizabeth I in 1559, he suggests that in this period it assumed a particularly menacing aspect because the continental theological concept of witch-craft as heretical Devil-worship fused with the English popular notion of witchcraft as malevolent magic. Such conclusions represent processes of historical reasoning, buttressed by substantial evidence. But the new tools contribute little. Thomas concedes the unavailability of firm statistics for the large questions he is covering. As for insights from social anthropology, he considers Malinowski's thesis that magical ideas decline when technological advances render the old magical rites for controlling phenomena unnecessary, and finds it wanting. The eighteenth century had moved away from the sixteenth century's reliance on magic, and magical techniques had lost their appeal well before new technical solutions had come to hand. The key, Thomas finds, lay not in new achievement but in new aspirations, in an altered mental set that stressed self-help.

If he deplored his own pursuance of conventional historical method, Thomas still could praise the statistical and anthropological mold of *Witchcraft in Tudor and Stuart England,* the work of his disciple. Macfarlane's (29) reworked dissertation bristles with maps, tables, figures, diagrams. Every item of information that can be tabulated about witchcraft is given its statistical identity. We learn that 473 indict-ments of 299 persons accused of witchcraft in Essex in the Home Circuit resulted in 112 executions between 1560 and 1700; that 23 of 49 husbands of accused witches reported in the Essex Assizes between 1560 and 1680 were alleged victims; that in the three Essex villages under survey between 1560 and 1599 witchcraft lagged behind sexual offences and nonattendance at church but considerably exceeded murder and drunkenness; that assize indictments from 1560 to 1680 recorded the bewitchment of 124 pigs, 123 sheep, 110 cows, 63 horses, and 11 chickens valued from fourpence to four pounds. Besides this scrupulous amassing of documentary data, Macfarlane adds to his pot summary statements of beliefs about witches in African tribal societies and among the Navaho. And where does it all end? "A close examination of the records for one English county has shown that witchcraft beliefs were an important part of village life" (pp. 250–51). When Macfarlane turns from specifics to generalities, he admits that his hypotheses about the rise and decline of English witchcraft require knowledge of "the total intellectual and social back-ground of sixteenth—and seventeenth—century England" (p. 206). He defers to Thomas as Thomas deferred to him. As for the new light to be shed from anthropo-logical field studies, well, Macfarlane muses, some suggest a correlation between social change and witchcraft fears—and some do not. He regrets the lack of studies of witchcraft in African towns which could offer possible analogies with Tudor and Stuart England. In the end the evidence that remains most firmly in the reader's mind is the individual oral testimony sought by the folklorist, as in this outburst over a garden fence by a parson railing at a suspected witch, recorded in a pamphlet of 1582: "I am glad you are here you vield strumpet (saying) I do think you have bewitched my wife, and as truly as God doth live, if I can perceive yt she be troubled any more as she hath been, I will not leave a whole bone about thee, and besides I will seeke to have thee hanged" (p. 107). This is the authentic voice of the folk, not the whir of the computer.

An invaluable resource for the folklorist is the four-volume *Dictionary of British Folktales* (omitting Celtic examples), assembled by Katharine Briggs (1). Hitherto England has appeared woefully lean in oral traditional narratives, compared to the treasures in Ireland, Scotland, and on the continent. By diligent sleuthing of myriad printed sources that have captured traditional narratives in texts close to the spoken word, and by giving due recognition to the legend and jest, Briggs has confounded disparagers of the English storytelling tradition.

Ewart Evans (15) continues his informative interviewing of traditional craftsmen and farmworkers in East Anglia in *Where Beards Wag All, The Relevance of the Oral Tradition*. In associating himself with David Thomson in an old-fashioned work stringing together comparative myths and folklore about the hare, and suggesting their debt to man's observations on the hare's enigmatic behavior, Evans (16) is less successful.

American Folklore

American folklore as a subject-matter field has been characterized by lack of a theoretical base, random field collecting often following vogues of the moment, and the dominance of commercial over academic goals. The past few years have seen some reversals of these trends. An attempt at formulating A Theory for American Folklore grounded in the social realities of American history was first presented by Dorson in 1957 in a paper, reprinted with other of his pieces supporting the argument in *American Folklore and the Historian* (8). A conference devoted to the genre most closely linking American history and folklore produced an unusually coherent and stimulating set of papers, published as *American Folk Legend, A Symposium*, edited by Wayland D. Hand (20). The 14 participants, all professional folklorists, in exploring general and specific legendary themes arrived at a surprising consensus on the need to recast the concept of legend in North America. Rather than the static notion of a simple narrative summarized on a 3X5 card, the participants one after another spoke for a fluid, complex form coalescing with other genres, dipping into the popular culture, susceptible to psychological and functional analyses. In terms of suggestive theory and vivid empirical data covering Pennsylvania—German, Mormon, Navaho, Kentucky mountain, Mexican, and urban legendry, this work merits high praise.

Imaginative regional fieldwork beyond single-genre collecting still lags in the United States, but the recent period has registered one notable credit in George Carey's *A Faraway Time and Place, Lore of the Eastern Shore* (4). Carey concentrated on the white watermen of the lower Eastern Shore of Maryland's Chesapeake Bay between the Nanticoke and Pocomoke Rivers. These "proggers" living off the crabs, oysters, terrapin, ells, ducks, and other creatures of the bay and marshes possessed a distinctive subculture filled with a traditional lore of anecdote, legend, tall tale, jest, belief tale, folk speech, and folk naming that Carey has captured in a fluently written ethnography. As in any such collection, many familiar narratives and folk beliefs can be recognized, and it is deeply regrettable that the publisher, Robert B. Luce, excided the author's appendix of tale types and motifs. This is a perennial problem for the folklore scholar who must battle with publishers to explain the necessity for including comparative notes and identifying motifs.

Another work of regional collecting, but with an emphasis on the traditions of material culture rather than of oral expression, is *The Foxfire Book* (41), which became something of a national phenomenon on its publication in 1972. Articles in national magazines have repeated the success story of Eliot Wigginton (41), the Cornell graduate who went to teach at Rabun Gap-Nacoochee School deep in the Southern Appalachians of Georgia and, finding his students bored and hostile, set them to interviewing their grandparents and collecting folklore which they printed in a magazine called *Foxfire*. The students became deeply excited, the magazine prospered marvelously, and *The Foxfire Book* emerged as a best-selling selection from its files. Its astonishing appeal lies in satisfying certain current vogues: the interest in ecology and primal nature, the revival of manual skills, the nostalgia for the good old simple ways and days. Much of the book proves to be a do-it-yourself guide to building a log cabin, making chairs and baskets out of split oak, cooking mountain recipes on wood stoves and in Dutch ovens, even constructing a moonshine still. Oral lore is represented in realistic tales of hunting turkeys and bears, accounts of the properties of snakes, faith-healing experiences of bloodstopping, burn healing, and curing thrash, and statements on planting by the signs. Photographs of the mountain people and their artifacts supply a valid visual documentation of these topics.

For a product of high-school pupils and a teacher untrained in folklore *The Foxfire Book* does surprisingly well. It presents accurate tape-recorded texts, graphic informant sketches, and genuine examples of Appalachian cultural traditions. But as a whole it seriously misrepresents folklore. The *Foxfire* premise rests on the old discredited cliché that the old lore must be gathered speedily from the aged before it vanishes, and ignores the fact that folklore belongs as well to the young and to the present even more than to the past. Wigginton romanticizes mountain folkways in stereotypic fashion: "There is something about a quilt that says people, friendship, community, family, home, and love" (p. 144). He renders mountain speech in unnecessarily folksy dialect (what is the purpose of spelling "the" as "th"?). He provides no conspectus of the community with which he is dealing, and no comparative information to indicate that much of the Foxfire material has been collected elsewhere. Some of the main genres of Appalachian folklore—e.g. the local historical legend—are almost wholly unrepresented. The stress on the applied folklore of chimney-building and straw-mattress making suits a homeowner's manual rather than a serious cultural study. These criticisms would not be needed if *The Foxfire Book* had not received such wide acclamation as a folklore work and the Foxfire concept a 2-year Ford Foundation grant of $196,000 for its application to 11 other student groups in disadvantaged areas.

Three first-rate treatments of what might be called cultural histories of American popular folk music all deal with the period since the 1920s when electronic media and political ideology reshaped traditional folksongs. In *Country Music, U.S.A.,* Bill C. Malone (30) considered the history of American rural southern music sung and performed for gain. His narrative covers such favorite musical styles as hillbilly,

country, mountain, western, honkytonk, and bluegrass, and such celebrated performers as Jimmie Rodgers, Vernon Dalhart, the Carter Family, Roy Acuff, Hank
Williams, Bill Monroe, and Earl Scruggs, who profoundly influenced these styles.
Malone demonstrates the importance to the folklorist of these and other popular
singers and instrumentalists who disseminated many traditional songs through
recordings, radio and television shows such as the Grand Ole Opry, and cabaret,
tent-show, vaudeville, and honky-tonk appearances. He is alert to the distinctions
between folk and nonfolk music, and astutely points out that in the 1930s left-
leaning urban intellectuals appropriated the term "folk music" for composed urban
protest songs far removed from folk tradition, while the "hillbilly music" disparaged
by city intellectuals remained firmly within a folk milieu. Also, Malone recognizes
that southern country music reflects industrial and social changes in northern cities,
that the South itself changes, and pastoral images yield to moralizing songs about
railroad wrecks and truck-driving.

In a more specialized vein, Archie Green (19) in *Only a Miner* has investigated
the tangled histories of coal-mining songs recorded on 10-inch discs at 78 rpm by
a variety of recording artists ranging from local traditional singers to the celebrities
of country music. He unravels the genealogies of such pieces as "Only a Miner,"
which he calls "the American miner's national anthem," and "Nine Pound Ham-
mer," popularized by Merle Travis, in intricate but lucid accounts of field and
commercial recordings, white and Negro sources, and emotional and technological
ingredients. A new kind of research is opened here, based on recording company
files, interviews with technicians, artists, and executives of the companies, and the
fugitive song literature of the recordings themselves. Green also addresses himself
to larger questions of folklore theory, such as the impact of electronic culture on
the folk society, and differences between traditional and popular songs. Bibliographical and discographical check lists appended to each chapter and well-chosen illustrations of miners and musicians enhance the work.

Complementing Malone's history of country music, R. Serge Denisoff in *Great
Day Coming, Folk Music and the American Left* (5) concentrates on the urban
intellectuals from the 1930s to the present who have actively associated protest and
dissent with the singing of purported folksongs. Here is a different cast of characters,
featuring Woody Guthrie, Pete Seeger and the Almanac Singers, Alan Lomax, Paul
Robeson, Bob Dylan, Burl Ives, and Irwin Silber, editor of *Sing Out!*, the organ of
the movement. This is an ironic story of frustration, internal splits, and ideological
doubts as these talented and in many ways successful singer-socialists failed almost
completely to win an audience committed to their objectives. They idealized a
working class but evoked little response from the labor unions; they vainly sought
to attach European communist values to American traditions; they anguished over
the problem of commercialism and forfeited opportunities they desperately needed,
as when the Almanac Singers refused to wear Lil' Abner costumes and so lost a
coveted Rainbow Room contract in New York.

Denisoff maintains an impartial stance in handling these sensitive issues, but he
does not hesitate to make value judgments. He sees Guthrie as a unique hybrid of
rural and urban cultures, none of whose protest dustbowl songs were sung by the

Okies and Arkies he represented. Burl Ives emerges as a turncoat playing the "innocent dupe" role before the McCarran Committee in the Senate, when investigation of communist folksingers threatened his career. Using the term "folk enterpreneur" to denote a conscious spokesman for proletarian values and a composer of "agit-prop" song, Denisoff avoids confusing traditional singers with reform-minded performers.

Afro-American folklore continues to flourish as a subfield of American folklore. For the volume and sensitivity of its raw data on Negro hoodoo beliefs, the publication of Hyatt (22), a retired Episcopalian clergyman, has no match in American folklore. Noteworthy collections of blues from Louisiana prisons and worksongs from Texas prisons have been issued by Oster (34) and Jackson (24). An oversize volume by Lovell (28), bringing together a miscellany of information on the spiritual and its worldwide impact, badly needs the pruning of an editor and consultations with a folklorist on basic concepts. Valuable for its theoretical statements by both black and white scholars is the anthology of previously published but widely scattered writings on many aspects of Afro-American folklore assembled by Dundes (12).

What might be called the great bamboozle in American folklore, namely the effort of author and commercial publisher to reach the mass market with sentimentalized folklore claiming scholarly value, is exemplified in Emrich's *Folklore on the American Land* (14). This kind of production, superficial and chauvinistic in its selections and comments and ludicrous in its concepts (the author singles out Santa Claus and The Cowboy as the two chief American legends), damages folklore studies in the eyes of other disciplines.

At the other extreme lies the laborious research monograph undertaken in a limited regional area, represented by Randolph's (38) monumental bibiography of Ozark folklore. The great field collector has here produced a model regional inventory, culling every kind of printed source from novels to newspapers, organizing his entries by coherent genres, and enriching them with flavorsome and judicious annotations. This is a pioneer work in revealing the wealth of printed sources available to the American folklorist.

African Folklore

In recent years Africa has moved from a position of marginal folklore activity conducted by practitioners in other disciplines—anthropologists, linguists, political scientists, historians—to one ever closer to the professional center. In the 1960s the Oxford Library of African Literature, under the general editorship of E. E. Evans-Pritchard, G. Lienhardt, and W. Whiteley, published a dozen volumes of traditional oral poetry and prose. The volume editors deal with the materials of folklore but employ the methods of the literary scholar or the ethnologist. A climax and synthesis to this approach appeared in Ruth Finnegan's *Oral Literature in Africa* (18). Finnegan addressed herself to the full range of oral expressive forms throughout sub-Saharan Africa, and adeptly utilized the accumulated monographs of tribal ethnographers to present a depth survey with copious examples. At every point she stressed the performance situation of the particular oral genre: praise poems, dirges, hymns, divining songs, hunters' songs, war songs, political songs, children's game songs, and folktales. This emphasis on social context wins the folklorist's approval, but he regrets the downgrading of oral narrative forms, the absence of comparative annotation—characteristic of the whole Library of African Literature series—and the unfamiliarity with current folklore theories and methods. Finnegan seeks to apply the techniques of literary criticism to her materials when her own evidence fully demonstrates the gulf between written and oral literature and the need to formulate distinctive criteria for appraising verbal performances.

A conscious contrast to Finnegan's point of view is proposed in *African Folklore,* edited by Dorson (10), which espouses a folkloristic approach to African cultural traditions. This volume developed from a Conference on African Folklore held at Indiana University in 1970, at which Africans and Americans presented research papers on a variety of oral genres. Sixteen of these papers, dealing with aspects of the folktale, the proverb, tongue twisters, the heroic epic and heroic songs, folk drama, visions, oral history, and literary uses of folklore, formed Part II of the volume. An extended essay on Africa and the Folklorist by the editor formed Part I, and field-collected texts furnished by the contributors and annotated by the editor formed Part III.

Indexes

Useful indexes of traditional narratives were issued by Kirtley (26) for Polynesian folktale motifs and by Ikeda (23) for types and motifs of Japanese folktales. It is regrettable that no such indexes have yet been published for African oral narrative, although several exist in dissertation form.

Literature Cited

1. Briggs, K. M. 1970–71. *A Dictionary of British Folk-Tales.* Bloomington: Indiana Univ. Press. 4 vols.: 580, 580, 623, 774 pp.
2. Campbell, J. 1969. *The Flight of the Wild Gander.* New York: Viking. 248 pp.
3. Campbell, J. 1972. *Myths to Live By.* New York: Viking. 276 pp.
4. Carey, G. 1971. *A Faraway Time and Place.* Washington, New York: Luce. 256 pp.
5. Denisoff, R. S. 1971. *Great Day Coming.* Urbana, Chicago, London: Univ. Illinois Press. 219 pp.
6. Dorson, R. M. 1968. *The British Folklorists, a History.* Univ. Chicago Press. 518 pp.
7. Dorson. R. M., Ed. 1968. *Peasant Customs and Savage Myths.* Univ. Chicago Press. 2 vols. 751 pp.
8. Dorson, R. M. 1971. *American Folklore and the Historian.* Univ. Chicago Press. 239 pp.
9. Dorson, R. M. 1972. *Folklore, Selected Essays.* Bloomington: Indiana Univ. Press. 311 pp.
10. Dorson, R. M., Ed. *African Folklore.* 1972. Garden City, N.Y.: Doubleday Anchor. 587 pp. Hardback ed. by Indiana Univ. Press
11. Dorson, R. M., Ed. 1972. *Folklore and Folklife, an Introduction.* Univ. Chicago Press. 561 pp.
12. Dundes, A., Ed. 1973. *Mother Wit from the Laughing Barrel.* Englewood Cliffs, NJ: Prentice-Hall. 673 pp.
13. Edmonson. M. S. *Lore, An Introduction to the Science of Folklore and Literature.* New York: Holt, Rinehart & Winston. 456 pp.
14. Emrich, D. 1972. *Folklore on the American Land.* Boston, Toronto: Little, Brown. 707 pp.
15. Evans, G. E. 1970. *Where Beards Wag All.* London: Faber & Faber. 296 pp.
16. Evans, G. E., Thompson, D. 1972. *The Leaping Hare.* London: Faber & Faber. 262 pp.
17. Feldman, B., Richardson, R. D. 1972.

The Rise of Modern Mythology 1680–1860. Bloomington, London: Indiana Univ. Press. 564 pp.

18. Finnegan, R. 1970. *Oral Literature in Africa.* Oxford: Clarendon. 558 pp.

19. Green, A. 1972. *Only a Miner.* Urbana: Univ. Illinois Press. 504 pp.

20. Hand, W. D., Ed. 1971. *American Folk Legend, A Symposium.* Berkeley, Los Angeles, London: Univ. California Press. 237 pp.

21. Hautala, J. 1968. *Finnish Folklore Research 1828–1918.* Helsinki: Finnish Acad. Sci. 197 pp.

22. Hyatt, H. M. 1970. *Hoodoo-Conjuration-Witchcraft-Rootwork.* Memoirs of the Alma Egan Hyatt Foundation. Hannibal, Mo.: Western Publ. 2 vols. 1843 pp.

23. Ikeda, H. 1971. *A Type and Motif Index of Japanese Folk-Literature.* Helsinksi: Suomalainen Tiedeakatemia Academia Scientiarum Fennica. 375 pp.

24. Jackson, B. 1972. *Wake Up Dead Man: Afro-American Worksongs from Texas Prisons.* Cambridge: Harvard Univ. Press. 326 pp.

25. Kirk, G. S. 1971. *Myth.* Berkeley, Los Angeles, Cambridge: Univ. California Press. 299 pp.

26. Kirtley, B. F. 1971. *A Motif-Index of Polynesian Narratives.* Honolulu: Univ. Hawaii Press. 486 pp.

27. Lévi-Strauss, C. 1969. *The Raw and the Cooked.* Transl. from French by J. and D. Weightman. New York: Harper & Row. 387 pp. First publ. 1964 in France under title *Le Cru et le Cuit*

28. Lovell, J. 1972. *Black Song: The Forge and the Flame.* New York: Macmillan. 686 pp.

29. Macfarlane, A. 1970. *Witchcraft in Tudor and Stuart England.* New York: Harper & Row. 334 pp.

30. Malone, B. C. 1968. *Country Music, U.S.A.* Austin, London: Univ. Texas Press for Am. Folklore Soc. 422 pp.

31. Maranda, E. K., Maranda, P. 1971. *Structural Models in Folklore and Transformational Essays.* The Hague: Mouton. 145 pp.

32. Maranda, P., Maranda, E. K., Eds. 1971. *Structural Analysis of Oral Tradition.* Philadelphia: Univ. Pennsylvania Press. 324 pp.

33. Michaelis-Jena, R. 1970. *The Brothers Grimm.* London: Routledge & Kegan Paul. 212 pp.

34. Oster, H. 1969. *Living Country Blues.* Detroit: Folklore Assoc. 464 pp.

35. Paredes, A., Bauman, R., Eds. 1972. *Toward New Perspectives in Folklore.* Austin, London: Univ. Texas Press for Am. Folklore Soc. 181 pp.

36. Patai, R. 1972. *Myth and Modern Man.* Englewood Cliffs: Prentice-Hall. 359 pp.

37. Peppard, M. B. 1971. *Paths Through the Forest, a Biography of the Brothers Grimm.* New York: Holt, Rinehart & Winston. 266 pp.

38. Randolph, V. 1972. *Ozark Folklore, a Bibliography.* Bloomington: Indiana Univ. Folklore Inst. Monogr. Ser. 24. 572 pp.

39. Strömbäck, D., Alver, B., Holbek, B., Virtanen, L., Eds. 1971. *Biographica, Nordic Folklorists of the Past.* Copenhagen: Nord. Inst. Folkedigtning. 452 pp.

40. Thomas, K. 1971. *Religion and the Decline of Magic.* New York: Scribner's. 716 pp.

41. Wiggington, E., Ed. 1972. *The Foxfire Book.* Garden City, NY: Doubleday Anchor. 384 pp.

42. Wilson, D. 1970. *The Life and Times of Vuk Stefanović Karadzić 1787–1864.* Oxford: Clarendon. 415 pp.

REVIEW OF CHILD LANGUAGE ❖ 9522

Thomas Roeper and David McNeill[1]

Department of Psychology, University of Chicago

A French child—like children everywhere—begins to communicate by fitting his[2] few words to new meanings. "Bebe" first refers to himself, but then includes: photos of himself, all photos, all pictures and all books. He cannot fail to know that these perceptually diverse objects are not identical, but he does not give each object a different name. When a perceptual disposition is evident, it is not linked to particular objects but rather to a dimension: "fly" means fly, specks of dust, and bread crumbs. Other perceptual categories that appear are: movement, shape, sound, and texture (Clark 16). From the first word we can see that a child's language involves more than just naming and more than just words for perceptions. A child follows semantic principles which demonstrate consistency, but which often prove difficult for adults to state.

These principles become obvious only through observation of a child in context (plus the use of hard thought and much conjecture). Without context, a child's communication generally fails. The concentrated inferential powers of adults often prove inadequate to the discovery of what a child means. This fact testifies (*a*) to the subtlety of a child's semantic intention, and (*b*) to a need (whether or not evident to him) for the child to improve his system of communication to the point where it is essentially context-free. No one doubts, fortunately, that a child has human sorts of meanings in mind when he seeks to communicate. This in itself is remarkable and requires explanation. In a later section, we shall contrast what a child chooses to mean with the choices made by apes.

What sort of a system does the child acquire? Language has at least three components: phonology, syntax, and semantics. The first two are clearly separate; the latter two show important differences but the degree of their interconnectedness is currently a matter of debate (Chomsky 15, Fillmore 19, Lakoff 30, McCawley 32). In any case, during the period of acquisition all three components undergo develop-

---

[1]Preparation of this report was supported by grants from NSF and NIE to David McNeill.

[2]The masculine pronoun is used in the generic sense to indicate a child of either sex. Until a suitable term of reference is found that will encompass all human beings in a similarly concise manner, we shall continue to use this terminology (Editor's note).

127

ment at once. A child's knowledge of language is not limited to the meanings of words; he must also understand the use of language for purposes of social interaction. These questions fall in the domain of pragmatics or sociolinguistics. A child uses speech to draw attention to himself, and it is clear that a 5-year-old has several speech styles, although the subtlety of the notion of "style" makes it difficult to trace its ontogenesis. [Black children, for example, use more final consonant clusters in the presence of whites than in the presence of blacks (Labov 29, Wolfram 58).]

The claim that motivates acquisition research is not simply that children learn an adult system of language, but that their speech displays a series of evolutionary systems and constructions that lead to adult grammar (Brown 9, Brown & Bellugi 10, Brown & Hanlon 11, Miller & Ervin 35). A child's system, no less than an adult's, may be defined at a fairly abstract level. Consider one of the most famous examples: the overgeneralization of past tense -ed endings. The most frequent verbs in the language happen to be strong verbs whose vowels shift to indicate past tense: come/came; see/saw. It can be just these verbs to which the child first applies the past tense -ed (Ervin 18). Therefore, a child does not even begin by repeating a new form from an adult model. When the child recognizes the -ed ending as a marker of past tense for some verbs in the parents' usage, he immediately attaches this ending to verbs in his own usage, using it for strong (come) verbs, weak ones (try), and those that take no ending (hit—hitted), only gradually restricting it to its proper domain of applicability: weak verbs. Notice that the inflection seems to be obtained more or less instantly on a verb and never is seen as a pecularity of some verbs (as went is the peculiar past for go). This example reveals how a child establishes hypotheses within diverse constraints.

A similar conclusion can be drawn from the observations of Weir (56), who taped the speech of her child at night and found that the child systematically reviewed phonological and syntactic paradigms. One such example was: go for glasses, go for them, go to the top, go throw, go for blouse, pants, go for shoes. It is evident here that the child was relating successive words to a grammatical structure that he held clearly in mind. There also appears to be a semantic series interwoven into the sequence with blouse, pants, shoes.

Many of the languages of the world explicitly encode through endings a number of fundamental semantic relations between objects: possessive, agentive, locative, objective, indirect object, actor, and others. (All languages implicitly encode these relations.) Children demonstrate knowledge of these relationships at the single word stage well before they show any attention to grammatical markers (e.g. that -er means agent). For instance, when a child suddenly points to a shoe and says Daddy, we interpret this to mean "Daddy's shoe" (possessive). That just this relation occurs in numerous cases suggests that it represents a distinct semantic concept—a semantic prime. That it emerges in different languages without reference to their structures suggests it is universal and therefore an intrinsic factor in the ontogenesis of the child. The efficiency of our communicative system is dependent upon our capacity to encode most of our thoughts in these fundamental relations, and the capacity of our language to make them recognizable.

A new development in the study of child language has been the discovery of an orderly evolution of semantic relations during the period when all recognizable speech is limited to single words (Bloom 5; Greenfield 23; Greenfield, Smith & Laufer 24; Smith 53). It has generally been assumed that language structure emerges when a baby first combines two or more words in a single utterance. Before 18 months of age or so, children are usually thought to be building up and refining a vocabulary of words. But it is now clear that they also use these words to encode distinct semantic structures: agent of action, recipient of action, location, and the like. Indeed, the single word stage already contains just those relations that become syntactically explicit in children's early word combinations.

According to Greenfield et al (24), the earliest vocalizations to serve a recognizable linguistic function are various "performatives" at 10 or 11 months (*hi, bye-bye, mm*—all uttered as an integral part of an action). These are soon joined (12 months or so) by the names of people *(dada, ma)*, which at first are used only when the person is not in view but can be heard. Vocatives appear at about 15 months (Child: *Mommy.* Mother: *what?* Child: *down*). Slightly later (16 to 18 months) the child begins to use single words to indicate the object of a demand (*maw,* "milk"), and then (19 months) to indicate the object of a direct action (*poon,* "spoon," as mother removes a spoon), and still later (21 months) to indicate the instrument of an action (*poon,* "spoon," as child watches someone eat with a spoon). In all, Greenfield et al document the emergence of 14 such semantic relations. Often the same word occurs successively in new relational uses, as in the example of "spoon." This fact is one major argument for accepting the evidence of single word speech as indicating a true developmental process; why otherwise would *poon* not have been used as an instrument, for example, when it was already used as an object of a direct action? The course of development generally proceeds from simpler, more egocentric, more concrete uses to more complex, more other-centered, more abstract uses. Thus, naming a person who is present to view precedes the use of the very same name vocatively. The use of a word to indicate the object of the child's demand arises before use of the same word as object of a direct action.

Perhaps the strongest evidence for the development of semantic relationships during the single word period is that when a new usage occurs with one particular word, it quickly spreads to other words. This rapid extension can be understood only if a new semantic relationship has become available to the child. For instance, within 2 weeks after using the word *fan* as the first object of a demand, one child described by Smith (53) had extended this usage to four other words (a substantial proportion of his vocabulary at the time).

A controversy has sprung up between Bloom (5) and Greenfield et al (24) over the origin and explanation of the relations that occur during the single-word period. Greenfield et al made use of a modified version of Fillmore's (19) case grammar to describe their observations, a formulation that implies continuity between the single-word stage of development and the semantic structures of later patterned speech. Bloom, however, has argued that the "semantic" relations of the single word period are only trivially linguistic in character. Rather, they reflect the child's underlying cognitive development (as observed by Piaget 41). Thus, the fact that a word is used as an object of a demand before being used as an object of a direct action can be explained by the child's greater cognitive egocentrism at the younger age. In our view, this controversy is almost totally lacking in substance. To choose between a linguistic description (case grammar) and a nonlinguistic description (stages of cognitive growth) implies that there is some way to state one description in terms of the other; to state, for example, that the relations of case grammar are the relations produced through cognitive growth. We do not see how this can be done. Certainly it has not yet been done by Bloom or other cognitivists (see the section below on the cognitive basis of language acquisition).

The upsurge of work in child language during the past decade was first motivated by Chomsky's demonstration that language structure was far more complex and "abstract" than hitherto supposed. These "abstractions" which describe adult capabilities with astonishing elegance are presumably what a child must acquire. They are sufficiently remote from the surface features of language that Chomsky was able to demonstrate that no system of inference would allow a child to decide on the appropriate grammar for his language within just a few years (e.g. Chomsky 13). Yet children do master most of their native tongue between 2 and 5 years of age. We are led then to the hypothesis that some of a child's language ability is innate.

Chomsky's grammar is syntactically based and builds on the notion that language has levels (phonology, syntax, semantics). The interfaces between levels may be intricate and not obvious, but they do not affect the basic structure of each component. Since the original formulations of transformational grammar, there has been a denial of the proposition that syntax and semantics are separable. There is now a parallel development within linguistics and psycholinguistics: semantic relations are fundamental both to syntactic relations and to a child's earliest utterances. A number of researchers have found that much of a child's first corpus can be described in terms of actor, action, possession, location, etc (e.g. Bloom 4, Bowerman 7). These categories, though they may have syntactic correlates in inflections, are fundamentally semantic. From this work grew a new regard for the Piagetian viewpoint that language is a logical outgrowth of cognitive maturation. In brief, Piaget claims that an active relationship to an object precedes an effort to encode that relationship in words (Piaget 42). We think that Chomsky's position can be seen as perfectly compatible with this notion: the child's search for linguistic structures may be set in motion by semantic motivations and by an awareness of context, but those structures are not equivalent to nor can they all be derived from semantic structure.

Since we speak in surface structures, how does a child know what form the deep structure of his language has? Because the deep structure configuration of verb, adverb, negative, adjective may vary from language to language, children commit errors. For a certain period, children treat passives as if they were actives. That is, they perform a superficial analysis in which *Jim* is the actor in *Jim is liked by John.* To account for a child's knowledge of language, we must attribute to him not only some a priori knowledge of what language is like but some method for evaluating possible grammars, that is, for determining which language he is trying to learn.

This capacity has been called LAD (Chomsky 14, McNeill 33) or the Language Acquisition Device. To what extent the contents of such a device includes exclusively linguistic knowledge and to what extent it may include general properties of cognition is unknown, although recent evidence and the speculation based on Piagetian theory has steadily increased the role of general cognition in linguistic explanations. On the other hand, Roeper (45, 46) has suggested that a purely linguistic factor is involved in learning deep structure order: a child may know that subordinate clauses retain deep structure order.

What are some examples of universal and nonuniversal features? 1. Consider the acquisition of tag questions in English (Brown & Hanlon 11). At one point, suddenly a child will begin to use sentences such as *John went home, didn't he* where he adds *didn't he* instead of *huh*. This small addition involves a number of transformations: negative, pronominalization, and subject-verb inversion. The most interesting fact is that tags emerge just when each of these transformations has appeared elsewhere in the child's speech. While showing the emergence of a nonuniversal aspect of grammar, this is evidence for the *psychological reality* of the transformations, and it reveals a rather natural developmental process: transformations first occur in isolation before they occur in combination. 2. Sinclair & Chipman (personal communication) report that children understand sentences such as (*a*) *John saw the boy whom I like* more easily than they understand (*b*) *John saw the boy who likes me*. Example *a* is transformationally more difficult than *b* because the object has been moved to a position before the subject, but it may be understood more easily because the cognitive status of the noun *boy* does not change; it is the object of the action *(see, like)* in both component sentences. This form of nonlinguistic but cognitive simplicity may be universal. 3. A last example suggests that linguistic theory may still be insufficiently abstract. Languages may have a deeper coherence than we have yet been able to fathom. A language with a final verb is likely to be right-branching (English sentences flow to the right, an intuition captured in rightward branching of a standard tree diagram), have prenominal adjectives, and "gap" forward (e.g. English permits *John ate steak and Bill beef* but not *John steak and Bill ate beef*). There is no evidence that children make the kind of wildly inappropriate hypotheses that would suggest that these factors are being treated separately (although evidence is sparse). If there is a universal which links these facts, then we may have to attribute to the child knowledge of that universal to explain the absence of a certain set of errors. Because the factors involved look purely linguistic in nature, it is difficult to imagine how they would be resolved into general cognitive rules.

The increasing emphasis on the cognitive basis of language acquisition is part of a new movement toward a more explanatory treatment of child language. While not every aspect of child language lends itself to explanation in terms of cognitive development, many universals are derivable from known facts of children's cognitive development. For example, the universal tendency for the grammatical subjects of early sentences to be animate agents can be understood in terms of the wider tendency toward animism in children's thinking at the same time. The process shown in example 2, above, where a sentence with a double-function word is more difficult than a sentence with a single-function word, has been related by Bever (3) to a general perceptual difficulty with double functioning. It is virtually impossible, for example, to see the center line in ☐ as being simultaneously the side of both the left and right figures. Bever has similarly speculated that the restriction on order of adjectives in English and other languages *(the large red plastic spoon,* but not *the plastic red large spoon)* is a special case of a general perceptual rule: as long as a constant perceptual relationship holds within a series, the series is seen as continuous. If there is a reversal, the series is broken. This rule applies to a series of lines of steadily increasing height, as well as to a series of adjectives in which successive members are more concrete and noun-like. Hence, *the plastic red large spoon* is unacceptable because it is perceptually broken. Martin & Molfese (31), however, have criticized this theory.

Bloom (5) and Sinclair (50) have argued that children acquire only linguistic structures that encode conceptual relations already evolved as part of cognitive development. Slobin (51) has similarly argued that cognitive difficulty determines the order of acquisition of language, writing that, ". . . the pacesetter in linguistic growth is the child's cognitive growth" (p. 184). An example is the occurence of locative expressions in the speech of bilingual children. When one language (e.g. Hungarian) provides an easily mastered inflectional system for marking the locative case and another (e.g. Serbo-Croatian) forces the child to master a complex system, the bilingual child begins to encode locative relations at the *same* time in both languages. A similar theoretical position has been taken by Schlesinger (48) and Parisi & Antinucci (37).

The approach to child language shared by various authors mentioned here—viz a desire to explain language acquisition by reference to cognition—is daring and exciting in its prospects. Claims of progress, however, in our view are clouded by the failure of any cognitive theory to make actual contact with linguistic theory. Does some notion of *location* comparable to the meaning of the grammatical locative exist when a child reaches for a hidden object? Does visual (or haptic) cognition have different principles of organization from comunicative or linear cognition? The danger in this area lies in the ease of empty abstraction. What is needed is a deeper theory that solves the classic puzzle of the relation between language and thought. The goal of explanation under present conditions may very well be premature. The two examples from Bever are exceptions in this regard in that they appear to offer actual explanations. To our knowledge, however, these examples are unique, even in Bever's own writings.

Crucial evidence for the validation of any hypotheses about the importance of universals in language learning must come from cross-cultural comparison. If patterns of acquisition are repeated in other languages whose structures make somewhat different demands, then the common features of all children acquiring language should point to universals. At present there is still far more evidence about English than any other language, but evidence has been gathering quickly from other languages such as: Luo (Blount 6); Samoan (Kernan 27); Tzeltal (Stross 55); Finnish (Bowerman 7). Slobin (51) has begun to sift out acquisition procedures from this data. Among the universals we can observe are these: exceptions to rules are avoided; discontinuous morphemes are avoided; new rules are overgeneralized beyond their true domain of applicability; the ends of words are more easily learned than the beginnings; there is a preference not to mark a semantic category by a zero morpheme.

The data gathered from cross-linguistic studies suffers from the fact that there are no adult grammars available for many languages. Nevertheless it is clear that the patterns of acquisition fall within the predicted universal limits, though the manifestations of universals are often unique. For instance, the discontinuous Arabic negative /ma . . . s/ is acquired later than the prefixed negative /mis/ by Egyptian children, although both are equally frequent. The discontinuous /ma . . . s/ is never substituted for /mis/ but the opposite often occurs (Omar 36). Similarly, in French the discontinuous negative morpheme ne . . . pas is not acquired at once, but rather occurs first simply as pas. These facts illustrate the same principle that we find in verb-particle constructions in English: children avoid the separation of elements (e.g. pick up it instead of pick it up).

An exciting series of discoveries has been made by Gardner & Gardner (21) and Premack (43) regarding language in another species. That language is possible for non-humans has long been denied on theoretical grounds. The mental processes necessary for language have been thought unique to our own species. There had been ample empirical confirmation of this view in the list of failed efforts to teach chimpanzees a human language (e.g. Hayes 25, Kellogg 26). (Chimpanzee has always been the species of choice for these experiments.)

Gardner & Gardner (22) and Premack (44) more or less simultaneously pointed out that the cause of these failures may have been relatively uninteresting. The chimpanzee had been expected to produce articulate speech. In contrast, Gardner & Gardner used ASL, American Sign Language, the gesture language employed by deaf persons in North America. Premack (43) invented an artificial language that could be "written" on a surface with bits of colored plastic. The visual-manual mode of communication is clearly superior for the chimpanzee.

Washoe (the Gardners' subject) was raised in a manner that approximated that of a human child. She lived at the Gardners' home and spent many hours each day in the company of human handlers. She was subjected to some vocabulary drill, but also to a good deal of spontaneous conversation. All messages in her presence used ASL. While ASL as employed by the deaf differs from spoken English in a number of important respects (cf. Bellugi & Fischer 1), Washoe's handlers were for the most part not deaf and tended to convert English sentences into sign, including the major regularities of word order (Gardner & Gardner 21, p. 176). This is fortunate since it makes comparisons to child speech more plausible. Washoe developed a substantial vocabulary of signs and spontaneously began to combine these into sequences of two, three and even more signs. It is this latter development that is so remarkable and exciting.

Unfortunately the Gardners usually disregarded the order in which Washoe made sequences of signs. Apparently order changes were frequent. Although Washoe is reported to have produced nearly 300 different combinations (by 1971), the order of signs is reported for only 90 of these (Gardner & Gardner 21). Even with this frustrating obfuscation of the data, however, it is possible to find certain regularities.

McNeill (34) has analyzed these examples and concluded that the principle which best summarizes Washoe's production is that words for addressees occur before action words, and words for nonaddressees occur after action words. Both patterns are exemplified in *you tickle Washoe* and *you out me* (each word glossing a sign). Washoe's patterns do *not* support the claim that she encoded the semantic relations of agent-action or action-recipient with word order, although the conceptualization of agent, action, and recipient is implicit in the content of her messages. Thus, the structural (grammatical) meaning of *you tickle Washoe* in addressee-action-nonaddressee, in which agent-action-recipient is nonstructurally expressed. The string with two agents *you out me,* which was made as Washoe and her handler went out of doors together, has the same grammatical meaning within her system, directly encoding addressee-action-nonaddressee and nonstructurally encoding agent-action-agent. Thus, Washoe appears spontaneously to have adopted a novel (from the point of view of human language) grammatical principle: the structural meaning of strings is *social* in character. It is conceivable that free ranging chimpanzees already make use of similar grammatical system.

It is quite impressive that Washoe did this on the basis of linguistic specimens that encoded, from the point of view of her human handlers, conceptual relations among agents, actions, and recipients. It is evident from Washoe's grasp of these conceptual relations and her ability to express them nonstructurally that chimpanzees have the mental processes necessary for language. That she imposed a radically different solution (social rather than conceptual) suggests the existence in children of a capacity for encoding conceptual relationships into sequences of symbols which chimpanzees lack. Such a capacity would give rise to specifically linguistic universals (as suggested earlier).

Premack's chimpanzee, Sarah, was subjected to a rigorous and carefully programmed training regime. In contrast to Washoe, there was meticulous attention paid to the encoding of negation, questions, and the conceptual relations of agent and recipient. The results seem to us fairly convincing: Sarah was able to master a number of the linguistic forms that Washoe missed. For example, Sarah spontaneously combined the symbol for "not" with the symbol for "same" to express the notion "different" (whereas Washoe never used negation in combination with other symbols, although she used negation alone). What explains this difference between the two chimpanzees? Premack's method was such that Sarah never was exposed to more than one unknown grammatical feature at a time. Washoe, on the other hand, was in a situation more nearly comparable to a child's. Several aspects of any given message could be unfamiliar. Sarah did not on her own have to find the significant aspects of new messages, therefore, but Washoe did. Apparently, chimpanzees are not able to perceive the conceptual significance of various syntactic devices on their own, although they can do so with assistance. One aspect of *Homo sapiens'* capacity for language may therefore be a high sensitivity to grammatical forms that are used for encoding cognitive relations.

The question of the input to children's acquisition has attracted a good deal of attention in recent years. This line of work can be traced back to Cazden's (12) experiment on "expansions"—the tendency of adults to repeat and complete ("expand") the telegraphic utterances of small children. It is now clear that expansions are only one of many special features that appear in adult speech to young children. Studies by Brown et al (8), Drach (17), Friedlander et al (20), Kobashigawa (28), Pfuderer (39), Phillips (40), Slobin (52), and Snow (54) have shown that adults make linguistic adjustments across a wide range of parameters. They restrict themselves to simpler constructions and vocabulary, repeat themselves and the child, isolate grammatically significant constituents, and avoid imposing a heavy semantic load. In part, the special adjustments adults make arise from a conviction that repetition and drill will help the child, but there is also an attempt to simulate the speech of young children. The most common utterances recorded by Bloom (5) in the speech of one mother to her young child were verbatim repetitions, including all telegraphic aspects. From the data available, this simulation is on the whole fairly successful, even including a rise in pitch. The assumption adults tacitly make is thus that children understand best speech that fits their own current grammatical system. However, this assumption may be systematically in error. According to Shipley et al (49), children best understand speech that is one stage ahead of their own level.

In the Berkeley cross-cultural studies (Blount 6, Kernan 27), it was noted that information about language is transmitted mainly within peer groups. Many other societies appear to use a similar means of transmission and in preindustrialized America and England peer group transmission may also have been fairly common. On the other hand, most studies of language development have been restricted to situations in which language is transmitted from adults to children. Thus, what has been discovered of the acquisition process rests on a cultural and historical parochialism of unknown magnitude. Recent studies by Bennett (2), Passonneau (38), Scharf (47), and Welsh (57) suggest that important differences exist between the adult-to-child and child-to-child modes of transmission.

Several of the studies of adult speech to children appear to have been motivated by a desire to refute the claim in Chomsky (13, 14) that the data on which children base language acquisition are "degenerate." These authors apparently believe that if adults can be demonstrated to respond to the special communication problems posed by small children, adult speech will not be shown to be "degenerate." But this argument is the result of a misunderstanding. Chomsky (13, p. 38) showed that the so-called transformational cycle, for example, cannot (in principle) be induced by a language learner from any actually available sample of speech. Since there is evidence for the transformational cycle in the linguistic competence of adults, one must logically agree that the linguistic data these adults obtained as children was "degenerate" with respect to the cycle. Whether it was simplified, repeated or what not, is thus irrelevant.

In conclusion, the convergence of findings from linguistic theory, child language, Piagetian theory, the study of nonhuman primate communications, and linguistic interactions suggests both the correctness of current research trends and the possibility that epiphenomena have been generated because the various systems are too loosely formulated. Thus prospects are both tantalizing and perhaps chimerical.

Literature Cited

1. Bellugi, U., Fischer, S. 1973. A comparison of sign language and spoken language. *Cognition* 1:173–200
2. Bennett, S. 1973. *Linguistic Interactions in the Process of Language Acquisition —Semantic Factors.* Unpublished paper. Univ. Chicago Dep. Psychol.
3. Bever, T. G. 1970. The cognitive basis for linguistic structures. In *Cognition and the Development of Language,* ed. J. R. Hayes. New York: Wiley
4. Bloom, L. 1970. *Language Development: Form and Function in Emerging Grammars.* Cambridge: MIT Press
5. Bloom, L. 1973. *One Word At a Time.* The Hague: Mouton
6. Blount, B. G. 1969. *Acquisition of Language by Luo Children.* PhD thesis. Univ. California, Berkeley. Working paper #19, Language Behav. Res. Lab.
7. Bowerman, M. 1973. *Early Syntactic Development.* New York: Cambridge Univ. Press
8. Brown, Robert, Salerno, R. A., Sachs, J. 1972. *Some Characteristics of Adults' Speech to Children.* Univ. Connecticut Language Acquisition Lab. Rep. #6
9. Brown, Roger, 1973. *A First Language.* Cambridge: Harvard Univ. Press
10. Brown, Roger, Bellugi, U. 1964. Three processes in the child's acquisition of syntax. *Harvard Educ. Rev.* 34:133–51
11. Brown, Roger, Hanlon, C. 1970. Derivational complexity and order of acquisition in child speech. See Ref. 3, 11–55
12. Cazden, C. B. 1965. *Environmental Assistance to the Child's Acquisition of Grammar.* PhD thesis. Harvard Univ. Grad. Sch. Educ.
13. Chomsky, N. 1968. *Language and Mind.* New York: Harcourt, Brace, Jovanovich
14. Chomsky, N. 1957. *Syntactic Structures.* The Hague: Mouton
15. Chomsky, N. 1972. *Studies on Semantics in Generative Grammar.* The Hague: Mouton
16. Clark, E. What's in a word? On the child's acquisition of semantics in his first language. In *Cognitive Development and the Acquisition of Language,* ed. T. Moore. New York: Academic
17. Drach, K. 1969. *The Language of the Parent: a Pilot Study.* Univ. California, Berkeley. Language Behav. Res. Lab. paper #14
18. Ervin, S. M. 1964. Imitation and structural change in children's language. In *New Directions in the Study of Language,* ed. E. H. Lenneberg. Cambridge: MIT Press

19. Fillmore, C. J. 1968. The case for Case. In *Universals in Linguistic Theory,* ed. E. Bach, R. T. Harms. New York: Holt
20. Friedlander, B. Z., Jacobs, A. C., Davis, B. B., Whetstone, H. S. 1972. Time-sampling analysis of infants' natural language environments in the home. *Child Develop.* 43:730–40
21. Gardner, B. T., Gardner, R. A. 1971. Two-way communication with an infant chimpanzee. In *Behavior of Nonhuman Primates,* ed. A. M. Schrier, F. Stollnitz, Vol. 4. New York: Academic
22. Gardner, R. A., Gardner, B. T. 1969. Teaching sign language to a chimpanzee. *Science* 165:664–72
23. Greenfield, P. M. 1968. *Development of the Holophrase.* Harvard Univ. Center for Cognitive Studies. Unpublished
24. Greenfield, P. M., Smith, J., Laufer, B. *Communication and the Beginnings of Language.* Stanford Univ., Dep. Psychol. In preparation
25. Hayes, C. 1951. *The Ape in Our House.* New York: Harper
26. Kellogg, W. N. 1968. Communication and language in the home-raised chimpanzee. *Science* 162:423–27
27. Kernan, K. T. 1969. *The Acquisition of Language by Samoan Children.* PhD thesis. Univ. California, Berkeley. Working paper #21, Language Behav. Res. Lab.
28. Kobashigawa, B. 1969. *Repetitions in a Mother's Speech to Her Child.* Univ. California, Berkeley. Language Behav. Res. Lab. paper #14
29. Labov, W. 1966. *The Social Stratification of English in NYC.* Washington, D.C.: Center for Appl. Ling.
30. Lakoff, G. 1971. On generative semantics. In *Semantics: An Interdisciplinary Reader,* ed. D. Steinberg, L. Jacobowits. Cambridge Univ. Press
31. Martin, J. E., Molfese, D. L. 1972. Preferred adjective ordering in very young children. *J. Verb. Learn. Verb. Behav.* 11:287–92
32. McCawley, J. Syntactic and logical arguments for semantic structures. *Proc. 5th Int. Seminar Theor. Ling.* Tokyo: TEC Corp. In preparation
33. McNeill, D. 1966. Developmental psycholinguistics. In *The Genesis of Language,* ed. F. Smith, G. A. Miller. Cambridge: MIT Press
34. McNeill, D. Sentence structures in chimpanzee communication. In *Competence in Infancy,* ed. J. S. Bruner, K. Connolly. New York: Academic. In press

35. Miller, W., Ervin, S. 1964. The development of grammar in child language. In *The Acquisition of Language*, ed. U. Bellugi, R. Brown. *Monogr. Soc. Res. Child Develop.* 29:9–34

36. Omar, M. K. *The Acquisition of Egyptian Arabic as a Native Language*. PhD thesis. Georgetown Univ. In preparation

37. Parisi, D., Antinucci, F. 1970. Lexical competence. In *Advances in Psycholinguistics*, ed. G. B. F. D'Arcais, W. J. M. Levelt. Amsterdam: North-Holland

38. Passonneau, R. 1973. *Functional Categories of Child-to-Child Speech*. Univ. Chicago Dep. Psychol. Unpublished

39. Pfuderer, C. 1969. *Some Suggestions for a Syntactic Characterization of Baby-Talk Style*. Univ. California, Berkeley. Language Behav. Res. Lab. paper #14

40. Phillips, J. R. 1970. *Formal Characteristics of Speech which Mothers Address to their Young Children*. PhD thesis. Johns Hopkins Univ.

41. Piaget, J. 1952. *The Origins of Intelligence in Children*. New York: Norton Library

42. Piaget, J. 1968. Quantification, conservation, and nativism. *Science* 162:976–81

43. Premack, D. 1971. On the assessment of language competence in the chimpanzee. See Ref. 21

44. Premack, D. 1966. Preparations for discussing behaviorism with chimpanzee. See Ref. 33

45. Roeper, T. 1973. *Approaches to a Theory of Language Acquisition with Examples from German Children*. PhD thesis. Harvard Univ.

46. Roeper, T. Connecting child language and linguistic theory. See Ref. 16

47. Scharf, E. 1973. *Aspects of Child-to-Child and Child-to-Adult Speech: a Preliminary Study*. Unpublished paper. Univ. Chicago Dep. Psychol.

48. Schlesinger, I. M. 1971. Production of utterances and language acquisition. In *The Ontogenesis of Grammar: Facts and Theories*, ed. D. I. Slobin. New York: Academic

49. Shipley, E. F., Smith, C. S., Gleitman, L. F. 1969. A study in the acquisition of language: Free responses to commands. *Language* 45:322–42

50. Sinclair, H. 1970. The transition from sensory-motor behavior to symbolic activity. *Interchange* 1:119–26

51. Slobin, D. I. 1973. Cognitive prerequisites for the development of grammar. In *Studies in Child Language Development*, ed. C. Ferguson, D. I. Slobin. New York: Holt, Rinehart & Winston

52. Slobin, D. I. 1969. *Questions of Language Development in Cross-Cultural Perspective*. Univ. California, Berkeley, Language Behav. Res. Lab. paper #14

53. Smith, J. 1970. *The Development and Structure of Holophrases*. Unpublished honors thesis. Harvard Univ. Dep. Ling.

54. Snow, C. E. 1972. Mothers' speech to children learning language. *Child Develop.* 43:549–66

55. Stross, B. 1969. *Language Acquisition by Tenejapa Tzeltal Children*. PhD thesis. Univ. California, Berkeley. Working paper #21, Language Behav. Res. Lab.

56. Weir, R. 1962. *Language in the Crib*. The Hague: Mouton

57. Welsh, A. 1973. *Child-Child Speech: A Preliminary Analysis*. Univ. Chicago Dep. Psychol. Unpublished

58. Wolfram, J. 1969. *Detroit Negro Speech*. Washington, D.C.: Center for Appl. Ling.

RECENT CLASSIFICATIONS OF GENETIC RELATIONSHIPS

❖ 9523

C. F. Voegelin and F. M. Voegelin

Department of Anthropology, Indiana University, Bloomington

The stability in method, theory, and results of genetic relationship classification in the better known language families—as Indo-European, Uralic, and Semitic—has been generalized as characteristic of genetic classifications for most of the world in contrast to fluctuations in method and theory, and results in synchronic or noncomparative linguistic work. Thus Garvin (17): "What has remained constant throughout the development of historical linguistics is a heritage of comparative method. Irrespective of many disputes about details, there is a core of incontrovertible general principles which is as valid today as it was when these principles were first introduced in the past century."

But the "comparative method" that Garvin alludes to can be applied only between languages whose grammars are adequately described; when less than this is available—as in parts of Oceania and Africa, and most of South America—recourse is necessarily made to comparing presumptive cognates by the methods of lexicostatistics, mass comparisons, and the like.

Our impression, from having surveyed the classifications of the "Languages of the World" for the *Encyclopaedia Britannica* (in press), is that it is useful (in order to accommodate much data in brief space) to divide the world into major regions. For the Euroasiatic world the major regions are Europe, South Asia, North Asia, Southwest Asia, East Asia, and Southeast Asia. Two major regions are linguistically as well as geographically peripheral in the Old World—sub-Saharan Africa and the parts of Oceania that are non-Austronesian. New World language families are as disconnected from the languages in the connected regions of the Old World as are languages in the regions peripheral to it. Before colonialism all language families except those in peripheral regions and those in the New World were in some sort of contact with languages in neighboring regions of the Old World—e.g. Japanese with Korean, Korean with Altaic, Altaic with Indo-European.

The question of genetic relationship (or common descent from a single proto language for each language family) is not always possible to disentangle from numerous questions of typology, universals, and borrowing or stimulus diffusion among languages in contact. From a strictly genetic point of view, languages in contact are often enough unrelated languages. They may indeed be genetically unrelated; even so, they are not necessarily unrelated historically.

Even among languages that are genetically related, as the North Germanic group, long contact between subgroups leads to diffusion which might obscure the paths of descent. (The descent in this case was no more distant than from proto-Germanic.) In terms of genetic relationship, Norwegian before the modern period would have been grouped with Icelandic and Faroese, but today the latter two (Insular Scandinavian) are mutually intelligible, but are no longer so with Norwegian, which has come to share intelligibility (or semi-intelligibility) with Danish and Swedish (Continental Scandinavian). It was during the modern period (1525 onward) that the Insular dialects became isolated from the Continental dialects which have come to enjoy continuous contact; there is now a language barrier between Insular and Continental Scandinavian.

EUROPE

There has been no major phylogenetic regrouping among Indo-European languages in recent years, other than the regrouping of Hittite (or proto-Anatolian) from a position coordinate with proto-Indo-European (reconstructed from languages in the various well-attested branches or their reconstructions: all but two or three of the branches of I-E are represented primarily in Europe today—the Romance subgroup of the Italic branch, Greek, Germanic, Celtic, Slavic, Baltic, beside Albanian and Armenian). The coordinate position of Hittite beside I-E was known as the Indo-Hittite hypothesis. But now Hittite is taken by Puhvel (37) and others to be one of the older Indo-European languages descended from proto I-E, albeit less inflected than the other older Indo-European languages. The shift in position from coordinate with I-E to subordinate to proto I-E for Hittite apparently reflects a shift in American classification from the Indo-Hittite hypothesis which never won favor among European comparativists; hence, what was a regrouping in classification on this side of the Atlantic was merely an appreciation of the position always held in Europe.

Europe as an area, in contrast to Indo-European as a family, is certainly not characteristic of the major regions or areas of the world in its low degree of genetic diversity. There are fewer language families in Europe than in any of the other major regions into which the world may be divided. Aside from a language isolate (Basque), not one of the three major language families found in Europe is represented exclusively in Europe. Though many Indo-European languages are spoken outside of Europe, in South and Southwest Asia, almost all of the languages of the Finno-Ugric branch of the Uralic family are spoken there (besides Hungarian there are several Lappish and several Finnic languages in Europe, not to mention Volgaic and Permic languages in European Russia). Of the three branches of Indo-Iranian that are not primarily represented in Europe, there is one Indic language that is widely spoken in Europe (Romany, the language of Gypsies), and one Iranian language (Ossetic) a dialect of which was spoken in Hungary until it became extinct in the 16th century; but Nuristani, the third branch of Indo-Iranian is not represented in Europe at all. Beside the Indo-European and Uralic families, the Turkic family of the Altaic phylum also extends into Europe—e.g. as far as the Balkans for Turkish; besides Turkish there are several other Turkic languages in European Russia.

Questions of internal relationships within Indo-European concern the possibility of special interrelations of Baltic and Slavic to Germanic, as discussed by Senn (39); and of Italic to Celtic, as discussed by Watkins (47), who doubts the reconstructability of Italo-Celtic; and of extinct Phrygian and Thracian to Albanian and Armenian, respectively, as discussed by Hamp (28).

External or phylum relations between the Indo-European family and other families, as Uralic and Semitic, continue to be claimed, most recently between I-E and Egyptian in Afroasiatic by Levin (30).

SOUTH ASIA, EAST ASIA, AND SOUTHEAST ASIA

The characteristic language families for each of the three regions that are considered here have long been recognized; what is new in recent phylogenetic groupings is the production of more or less extensive cognate support for external relations of one language family with another, thereby leading to wider or phylum affiliations which transcend the three regions under consideration.

It is possible to distinguish between two types of claims of genetic relationship. First are those which present evidence of lexical or sound correspondences between the languages for which wider relationships are claimed. The second type are those which make claims without examination of sound correspondences among cognates. A good example of the former is the renewed proposal for the Austroasiatic phylum in which Munda may now be grouped with some confidence. Examples of the latter are claims without adequate support, as the claims that Dravidian, though unrelated to any other language family in South Asia, is still related to one or another language family in some major region more or less adjacent to South Asia. Despite the fact that such claims are unsupported or inadequately supported, it is not possible to disprove them; it is only possible to dismiss them, as Krishnamurti (29) does for some: "Attempts to trace genetic connections between Dravidian on the one hand and other languages such as Caucasian, Korean, Egyptian, or Sumerian on the other may be passed over in silence, since the methods and materials used in their support have been unimpressive."

Beside the external phylum affiliations, an occasional reconsideration of an internal classification within a traditional language family has led to alteration in classification; such changes of internal relationships are possible in consequence of obtaining data in depth on daughter languages and reexamination, rather than any change in the theory or method of comparative work. The changes in external or phylum relationships—the wider affiliations between language families—do not always flow from an application of the comparative method; they may be postulated on the basis of lexicostatistical comparisons of presumed cognates, or on grammatical as well as lexical similarities, without benefit of detailed reconstruction by the comparative method.

The typical language families cited for South Asia include Dravidian and Munda; both are represented exclusively in South Asia, as is the Indic branch of Indo-European, except for Romany, while languages of the Iranian branch extend to the west beyond South Asia. Until recently, Indo-Iranian was dichotomized, with the subgroup of Dardic languages (spoken mostly in Afghanistan) classified by Grierson (24) as part of Iranian. The Dardic languages have now been reclassified by Morgenstierne (35) and by Emeneau (13) as members of the Indic rather than the Iranian subgroup of Indo-Iranian; and Nuristani or Kafiri, instead of being taken as a subgroup of Iranian (24), is now taken as a third coordinate subgroup of Indo-Iranian with Indic and Iranian (Strand 41a). Sino-Tibetan languages of Assam and the border states of India are more widely represented in East and Southeast Asia than in South Asia. At least one language of Assam is recognized as having Kam-Thai affiliations. Burushaski in Pakistan and Nahali remain without known affiliations, while Khasi of Assam is now counted as a western representative of the Austroasiatic phylum.

The typical language families traditionally cited for East Asia (between North Asia and Southeast Asia) include Ainu, as a language isolate, Japanese and Korean, and Miao-Yao, which includes languages extending into Southeast Asia. In contrast, Sino-Tibetan representatives, except for Chinese, are found mostly beyond East Asia. Less typical of East Asia are a few intrusions from each of the three Altaic families: Turkic (e.g. Uighur in Sinkiang and Kansu), Tungus (Manchu), and Mongol. Two additional intrusions from North Asia may be counted if Japanese and Korean are accepted as members of the far-flung Altaic phylum.

Except for languages in the north of India and in the border states of Nepal, Sikkim, and Bhutan, almost all Tibeto-Burman groups of Sino-Tibetan are found in Southeast Asia, where also are found a number of other language families. The older conception of the Sino-Tibetan phylum was in terms of two major parts: Sinitic (Chinese, Kam-Tai, Miao-Yao) as opposed to Tibeto-Burman. The latter is accepted in the modern conception, while the "Sinitic" part of Sino-Tibetan is discredited; and the rejection of Sinitic is now in danger of discrediting the whole concept of Sino-Tibetan.

Shafer (40) was the first to reject the bifurcation within Sino-Tibetan between Sinitic and Tibeto-Burman. Bodman (8) grants that Tibeto-Burman constitutes a natural assemblage of major constituents within Sino-Tibetan, but he is uncertain how Chinese is related to which constituent in Tibeto-Burman. Past comparisons have largely focused on comparing Chinese with Classical Tibetan, without broader exploration in Tibeto-Burman.

Any special relationship of Kam-Tai or Miao-Yao to Chinese within "Sinitic" has been rejected or questioned by, among others, Benedict (1, 2). Kam-Tai has been claimed to have special relationship to Austronesian rather than to Chinese. This leaves the status of Miao-Yao open for further research, but the relationships of Miao-Yao are expected by some to be found in Asia and by others in Oceania.

All that remains secure in Sino-Tibetan is Chinese and Tibeto-Burman; first Kam-Tai and now Miao-Yao are being seriously proposed by Benedict as members of an Austro-Tai phylum. With the abandonment of "Sinitic" as a major branch within Sino-Tibetan, Benedict finds new hope for affiliating the Miao-Yao family together with Kam-Tai in his superordinate phylum known as Austro-Tai (the Austronesian languages of Oceania plus the two Southeast Asian families mentioned).

With the increase of available information on languages of South and Southeast Asia, the postulation of an Austroasiatic phylum has been gaining wider acceptance. A decade ago it was considered premature to attempt a phylum grouping in the face of a lack of consensus among researchers. Even as late as 1966, Zide (51) says "no new overall classification is offered" because the opinions of the contributors "are not simply unifiable into one consistent and comprehensive system."

The classification of Austroasiatic given here follows Thomas & Headley (42), supplemented by that of Pinnow (36); it includes four language families formerly considered to be unrelated by many linguists: Mon-Khmer, Malacca, Munda, and Nicobarese. That Austroasiatic is primarily a Southeast Asia phylum is clear from the fact that, except for Munda in India (and Khasi in Assam), all its constituents are found in Southeast Asia.

Following the recent classification of Thomas & Headley (42), based upon "lexicostatistic and other supporting evidence," Mon-Khmer is a much larger group than previously believed, comprised of seven branches and two ungrouped languages. These include all the groups of languages listed by Pinnow as Mon-Khmer, plus Pinnow's Northeast or Palaung-Wa, including Khmuic, and North or Khasi subgroups of his East group of Austroasiatic. In addition, Thomas & Headley's Mon-Khmer includes Viet-Muong, which Pinnow excludes from Austroasiatic; Viet-Muong is now expanded to include three previously undiscovered languages of North Vietnam.

The inclusion of the three Malacca groups (Semang, Sakai, and Jakun) by Pinnow as a division of Austroasiatic is not firmly established, but there is a general acceptance of the three groups as related to each other; all except a few Semang speakers in Thailand are found in mainland Malaysia, and are geographically noncontiguous with other Austroasiatic languages.

The eight or more Khmuic languages are spoken mainly in Laos in numerous enclaves scattered in all directions from Luang Prabang and extending into Thailand.

The nine languages now classified as Palaung-Wa—i.e. excluding Khmuic, classified as an eastern branch of Palaung-Wa by Pinnow—are spoken primarily in Burma and Thailand.

The Munda languages are spoken in three areas of India, and an outlier of one of them (Kharia) is found in the Andaman and Nicobar Islands.

Nicobarese of the Nicobar Islands consists of a group of a half dozen languages (rather than one as formerly thought) according to Stampe (41) and others.

The superordinate phylogenetic groups in Southeast Asia are accordingly Sino-Tibetan, Austroasiatic, and possibly Austro-Tai. In addition to the Kam-Tai languages, a low number of languages of the possibly related Austronesian family (formerly known as Malayo-Polynesian) are found in mainland Southeast Asia (Malay and the nine Chamic languages of Vietnam and Cambodia), while beyond the mainland a very large number of Austronesian languages are spoken in insular Southeast Asia, in Melanesia, Polynesia, and Micronesia.

No single classification of Austronesian languages has compared all of the languages on the same basis, and hence argreement on subgrouping does not always exist. Using ten of the languages of Melanesia, Micronesia, and Polynesia, Dempwolff (9) set up Ur-Melanesisch as the common parent language of the languages of Polynesia and Melanesia (including Micronesia, except Palau and Chamarro), on the basis of common phonological developments not found in Indonesian languages. Grace (18) proposed that this group—later called Oceanic—includes all the languages of Melanesia east of the boundary between West Irian and Australian New Guinea, as well as the languages of Polynesia and Micronesia (except Palau and Chamorro). Dyen (11) argues that the setting up of Oceanic has been largely by inspection since "traditional comparative procedures have been applied superficially," and Dyen (12) points out that Oceanic "contains many languages and groups of languages that ... cannot be united by a lexicostatistical argument." However, Grace (20) argues that Dyen's lexicostatistical classification "appears to be fundamentally incompatible with any classification based upon the sound correspondences as they are now understood," and also that grouping based on "similarity of grammatical structure is not always associated with a corresponding degree of lexical similarity." Though no evidence has been published to show that Eastern Oceanic forms a group apart from other members of Oceanic, it is generally agreed that Polynesian and certain languages of eastern Melanesia are affiliated as an Eastern Oceanic division, and comparative work is being advanced in this area. However, since comparative work has been done for only a few of the many possible candidates for affiliation in eastern Melanesia, the exact membership of Eastern Oceanic is still uncertain (Biggs 3, Grace 19). Milke's (33) subclassification of Oceanic, based on the reflexes of proto Oceanic *1, *d, and *R in the daughter languages, yields three subgroups, one of which is equivalent to Eastern (with certain modifications from Grace), one of which consists of the languages of the southeastern Solomons, and the third adds to the remaining Oceanic languages the Austronesian languages of Geelvink and Humboldt Bays in West Irian. Grace (20) agrees that some of the languages of West Irian belong to Oceanic, namely, the Sarmic languages, which Dyen classifies with the languages of the Moluccas. Dyen's lexicostatistical comparisons of word lists from 317 Austronesian languages yielded a division into one major branch, Malayo-Polynesian, with many subdivisions, and over 40 minor branches, many of which are single languages. Most of these other branches, however, are grouped by one or another scholar with languages of various subgroups of Dyen's Malayo-Polynesian. Only those languages of South Halmahera-West New Guinea not classified by Dyen with the languages of the Moluccas and the Lesser Sundas remain as not clearly subgrouped by anyone with other Austronesian languages.

NORTH ASIA AND SOUTHWEST ASIA

The three superordinate phylogenetic groups of languages found in North Asia (from Bering Strait to the Ural Mountains) and Southwest Asia (from Afghanistan to Saudi Arabia, inclusive, and west to the Mediterranean, Black, and Caspian Seas) are (a) the Afroasiatic phylum which is further represented across North Africa; (b) the Ural-Altaic phylum which is further represented in East Asia, and in Europe to the west; and (c) the Indo-European family which extends from Europe to South Asia. Some classifications have claimed that the Ural-Altaic phylum could be extended to include Indo-European, which in turn is also sometimes thought to have genetic affiliations with the Semitic family. However, recent classifications have turned their comparative interest to the relationship of Semitic to Ancient Egyptian and other Afroasiatic languages (rather than to Indo-European), and of the traditional Ural-Altaic languages to Japanese and Korean (rather than to possible connections with Indo-European). Indo-European includes the extinct Tocharian languages of North Asia.

In addition to these three phylogenetic giants, there are two more or less preliterate groups of languages—Caucasian and Paleosiberian—whose genetic relationships in each restricted area are still not firmly established. Of the three groups of languages spoken in the Caucasus between the Black and Caspian Seas, the Northwest and Northeast Caucasian languages are now conceded to be descended from a single proto language, but the same is not always said for the three South Caucasian languages, including the literary language, Georgian. Whether or not there is a relationship between South Caucasian and the northern Caucasian languages is still uncertain.

One or another of the groups of Paleosiberian languages is sometimes claimed to have genetic affiliations with non-Paleosiberian languages, as with Altaic languages or with Eskimo, or to be genetically related to another Paleosiberian group; but both types of claims remain undemonstrated and are possibly indeterminate. So also is the claim that Korean and Japanese are descended from proto Altaic; and even the basis of proto Altaic reconstructed from Turkic, Tungus, and Mongolian languages may turn out to be indeterminate, as also their relationship to Uralic (but Uralic itself can be surely reconstructed).

All instances of indeterminacy mentioned here result from the same alternative possibilities in interpreting similarities between languages which are or have been in some sort of direct or chain-like contact—either descent from a single proto language attested by cognates among the languages compared, or else an interpretation of a borrowing process between the languages compared, a process that can utilize the same apparent "cognates" in the comparison, and can involve diffusion of grammar and phonology as well as lexicon. *Japanese and the Other Altaic Languages* by Miller (34) favors the first of these two possibilities, and succeeds in assembling an impressive list of "cognates" without at the same time finding a breakthrough in respect to the distinction between the first and second alternative interpretation mentioned, as Mathias shows in his review (31).

A third possibility often mentioned by Edward Sapir is "drift," whereby similar changes (not directly dependent on borrowing) occur in daughter languages after the break-up of a proto language; thus, in the case of the Altaic phylum, parallel "drift" among daughter languages might result in the same typological features (e.g. vowel harmony, agglutination, or special kinds of syntactic constraints) which would not have been necessarily present in the proto language. All three of the alternative possibilities mentioned—but especially drift—may reflect the universal tendency toward rule simplification.

PARTS OF OCEANIA THAT ARE NON-AUSTRONESIAN

There are at least two superordinate phylogenetic groups of languages in non-Austronesian parts of Oceania: the Australian phylum and the Papuan (Indo-Pacific) phylum.

There is now general agreement that the couple of hundred Australian languages are all related. The Australian linguistic situation can be stated as follows: 28 out of 29 families are found in the restricted north-northwest area of Arnhemland and the Kimberley District; the one exception is the twenty-ninth family, the Pama-Nyungan family of 160 languages which are spread over the rest of Australia. This means that most of the remaining 40 languages or so that are not Pama-Nyungan are divided among 28 families in the restricted northern area, yielding a total of 1, 2, or 3 languages per family to account for the main genetic diversity within the Australian phylum.

No one has recently postulated an Australian genetic relationship with the two or more languages which were formerly spoken on Tasmania, nor have suggestions that Tasmanian languages might be related to languages within the Indo-Pacific phylum been supported.

Hundreds and hundreds of Papuan (Indo-Pacific) languages—if "Papuan" or "Indo-Pacific" turns out to be a viable phylum accommodating much diversity—extend from Santa Cruz through the Solomons and the Bismark Archipelago, and the large island of New Guinea into insular Indonesia as far west as Alor. Not long ago the languages in this area were supposed to represent the world's greatest genetic diversity for any area of comparable size, exceeding the diversity of Californian Indian languages or even the languages of West Africa. The publications on New Guinea Highlands languages from 1960 on began to change this perspective (of superlative diversity) with the recognition that a fairly large group of languages in the Highlands are genetically related; this subsequently could be said of an even larger area containing languages of the Central New Guinea phylum.

This is the background of what Wurm (50) calls "the Papuan linguistic situation." For most linguists (then as now) there remain some families and isolated languages which are not yet demonstrated to be related to any others. Those engaged in survey work here among non-Austronesian languages identify some 75 families with usually not more than half a dozen languages in each family; most of such families and an equal number of language isolates (single languages genetically parallel to such families) are then grouped together on the basis of lexical similarities (as well as typological similarities in grammar)—an incipient but not yet full blown comparative method. This yields a low number of phylum-like groups of languages, possibly even a single phylum group which Greenberg (23) would name "Indo-Pacific" rather than "Papuan" in order to accommodate the inclusion of Andamanese in the Bay of Bengal.

AFRICA

The classification of all African languages into four "ultimate" phyla (often referred to as the Greenberg classification) has an interesting history of recognition for each phylum (and possibly a promise of some further reduction to even fewer phyla).

Thus, the Afroasiatic phylum was during the nineteenth century first based on a recognition of a genetic affiliation between the extinct Egyptian-Coptic in Africa and Semitic in Africa and Asia and thereafter expanded by the inclusion of Berber and Cushitic. The non-Semitic members were generally grouped together as Hamitic. Cohen (Meillet & Cohen 32), however, considered his Chamito-Sémitique to consist of four coordinate branches with no special status for Semitic. The full inclusion of Chadic was first proposed by Greenberg in 1950, and it is he who renamed the phylum Afroasiatic (22). Finally, the sixth member of this phylum, Omotic, was proposed by Fleming (14, 15), who amends the distinction between Cushitic and Partially Chushitic of Tucker & Bryan (44) by making a complete split of the former single family, Cushitic (recognized as Afroasiatic since Meillet & Cohen), into two families: Omotic and Cushitic.

At least two opposing positions have been held in respect to the Khoisan phylum: (a) the "preclassical" position, echoed by Bloomfield (7), who avoided the term "Khoisan" and instead spoke of non-Bantu languages that fall into "two unrelated speech areas"; and (b) the "classical" position founded by Dorothea Bleek (4–6), who recognized that Hottentot languages are somehow related to Bushman languages, a position accepted by Greenberg, with slight modification. In Westphal's (49 and earlier) divergent classification, Bushman is taken to represent five "unrelated" groups of languages, with Hottentot taken as a sixth group, unrelated to any Bushman group.

In contrast to Khoisan, with the least genetic diversity of the four African phyla, Niger-Kordofanian comprises the greatest number of different language families (and especially of individual languages); in this sense, it represents the maximum genetic diversity for any one phylum of Africa. In fact, it is almost too good, or too big, to be true; but all that can be given, briefly, is a report rather than an appraisal of the Niger-Kordofanian postulation.

For Kordofanian languages, Greenberg first supplies the group names Koalib, Tegali, Talodic, in the place of the group names used by Tucker & Bryan (43); next he treats the remaining languages of Niger-Kordofanian as a Niger-Congo superordinate group.

The following are the major constituent groups of Niger-Congo languages with most major groups being of phylum rather than of family scope: Adamawa-Eastern, West Atlantic, Benue-Congo, Gur=Voltaic, Kwa, and Mande. Thus, for example, under Benue-Congo five groups are incorporated: Bantoid, Bantu, Cross River, Jukunoid, and Plateau; under Kwa are twelve groups: Akan, Edo, Ewe, Ga-Adangme, Idoma, Igbo, Ijo, Kru, Lagoon, Nupe-Gbari, Central Togo, and Yoruba.

If Afroasiatic is the best established phylum, Khoisan the smallest, and Niger-Kordofanian the largest, then Nilo-Saharan can be said contrastively to be neither very well established, nor very large, nor very small. Much as the vast majority of languages in Niger-Kordofanian are subclassified under Niger-Congo, so most Nilo-Saharan languages (aside from three small groups—Koman, Maban, Saharan) are subclassified by Greenberg under Chari-Nile, and further under two main branches of Chari-Nile, Central Sudanic and Eastern Sudanic.

Of the four phyla set up for Africa, Nilo-Saharan is the least conclusive, according to Fodor (16). Some of the eastern languages classified under Niger-Congo might be related to languages now classified under Nilo-Saharan, and if so, says Greenberg, they "display a connection of a more remote nature." Nonetheless, this weak concession hints at the possibility of a greater reduction of phyla in Africa—in other words, of an expansion of the fantastically large Niger-Kordofanian phylum to engulf Nilo-Saharan also. Beside such a giant there would then remain the pigmy, Khoisan, and the relatively well established phylum, Afroasiatic.

NORTH AMERICA, IBERO-AMERICA, AND THE CARIBBEAN

The objective of Sapir (38) was to classify language families not by inspection but by their probable maximum phyla (or most remote relationships). Before this century, languages were classified by inspection of obvious similarities, as in the Powell classification of scores of language families. It was in reference to this that Sapir was given credit for reducing the diversity of a half hundred language families to a half a dozen language phyla, as though the families once incorporated in phyla were no longer relevant. But not so: the families supply a measure of internal diversity, and the phyla of external diversity. Powell's families were established on the basis of pedestrian cognates among the daughter languages, while Sapir's "phyla" are in effect brilliant hypotheses which might, however, not be supported in subsequent research. But the credit given to Sapir confused external relationships with internal ones.

When the salient points of Sapir's classification of external relationships among language families are compared with those of subsequent phylum research (up to 1964)—as by comparing the 1946 American Ethnological Society map (45) representing Sapir's hypotheses for North America with the revised version that represents a consensus among Americanist linguists in 1964 (Voegelin & Voegelin 46)—it turns out that four types of alterations were made in the 20-year interval between the two wall maps:

1. Reduction of a larger phylum, Hokan-Siouan, by means of dichotomizing it into a Macro-Siouan phylum and a Hokan phylum. There is a long history involved

in the postulation of external relations among language families in the east and west to account for Hokan and Macro-Siouan, respectively. The latter brings together as genetically related three language families (Siouan, Caddoan, and Iroquoian) and a couple of language isolates (Catawba and Yuchi); the Hokan phylum includes several small language families (Pomo, Shastan, Chumash, Salinan, Palaihnihan, Yanan, Yuman, Tequistlatecan, Tlapanecan, Coahuiltecan) and several language isolates, as Washo, generally known to belong to the Hokan phylum but not known to be affiliated with any particular language in Hokan; Seri is a quasi-isolate, for it appears closer to Yuman than to other Hokan families.

2. Expansion of a language family into a phylum by combining the language family with at least one more family. Thus, Haas (25–27) postulates for Macro-Algonquian that a language isolate in Texas (Tonkawa) and four Gulf isolates (Atakapa, Chitimacha, Natchez, and Tunica) enjoy a remote genetic relationship with two remotely related language families, Algonquian (with its quasi-isolates, Yurok and Wiyot in California) and Muskogean.

3. Recognition of unresolved problems. In contrast to the Sapir classification which did not leave any language or any language family unclassified, the 1964 Conference concluded that the Salish and Wakashan families remain to be externally classifed since their present status leaves them without recognized phylum affiliations.

4. The Sapir classification for North America was largely limited to languages north of Mexico by the limitation of knowledge of languages to the south. Since 1929, comparative work has shown that one phylum, Oto-Manguean, has all its relationships confined to Middle America; that most other language families in Middle America, as Mayan, have external or phylum relationships with languages north of Mexico; that these external relationships, as in the case of Penutian, may extend from North America north of Mexico, through Mexico and Middle America, deeply into South America, as in the case of the Chipaya-Uru family.

Phylum linguistic work concerned with external relations between language families in North America began with Dixon & Kroeber's (10) classifications of California languages in 1913 and reached two culmination points: Sapir in 1929 and the major consensus of revision at the First Conference on American Indian Languages in 1964. Attention among comparativists in North America is now turning to internal relationships within language families; this is reflected in papers offered to the conferences on particular language families, such as the successive Salish, Algonquian and Uto-Aztecan conferences, and to the general conferences on American Indian languages held in connection with the annual meetings of the American Anthropological Association for the last decade.

In contrast to the North American shift of interest from external or phylum linguistic comparisons to studies of internal relationships within a given language family, there appears in South America a shift from classifying individual languages into a hundred or more language families to classifying languages, as by Greenberg (21), into three phyla—Andean-Equatorial, Macro-Chibchan, and Ge-Pano-Carib. It can be expected that Greenberg's classification will induce a revision similar in scope to the earlier revision of Sapir's classification.

Literature Cited

1. Benedict, P. K. 1942. Thai, Kadai, and Indonesian: A new alignment in Southeastern Asia. *Am. Anthropol.* 44:576–601
2. Benedict, P. K. 1973. *Austro-Thai Studies.* New Haven: Human Relations Area File
3. Biggs, B. 1965. Direct and indirect inheritance in Rotuman. *Lingua* 14:383–415
4. Bleek, D. F. 1927. The distribution of the Bushman languages in South Africa. In *Festschrift Meinhof.* Glückstadt, Hamburg: Friederichsen
5. Bleek, D. F. 1929. *Comparative Vocabularies of Bushman Languages.* Cambridge Univ. Press
6. Bleek, D. F. 1956. *A Bushman Dictionary.* New Haven: American Oriental Society
7. Bloomfield, L. 1933. *Language.* New York: Holt
8. Bodman, N. C. 1971. *Some Phonological Correspondences Between Chinese and Tibetan.* Presented at 4th Int. Sino-Tibetan Conf., Bloomington, Ind.
9. Dempwolff, O. 1937. *Deduktive Anwendung des Ur-Indonesischen auf austronesische Einzelsprachen. Z. Eingeborenen-Sprachen* Suppl. 17
10. Dixon, R. B., Kroeber, A. L. 1913. Relationships of the Indian languages of California. *Science* 37:225
11. Dyen, I. 1964. Comment on "Movement of the Malayo-Polynesians: 1500 B.C. to A.D. 500." *Curr. Anthropol.* 5:387–88
12. Dyen, I. 1965. *A Lexicostatistical Classification of the Austronesian Languages. Indiana Univ. Publ. Anthropol. Ling. 19*
13. Emeneau, M. B. 1966. The dialects of old Indo-Aryan. In *Ancient Indo-European Dialects,* ed. H. Birnbaum, J. Puhvel. Berkeley, Los Angeles: Univ. California Press
14. Fleming, H. C. 1969. The classification of West Cushitic within Hamito-Semitic. In *Eastern African History,* ed. D. F. McCall. New York: Praeger
15. Fleming, H. C. 1972. Classification of Cushitic and Omotic languages. In *Language in Ethiopia,* ed. M. Bender et al. London, Addis Ababa
16. Fodor, I. 1969. *The Problems in the Classification of the African Languages.* Budapest: Center for Afro-Asian Research, Hungarian Academy of Sciences
17. Garvin, P. L., Ed. 1970. Introduction. In *Method and Theory in Linguistics.* The Hague: Mouton
18. Grace, G. W. 1955. Subgrouping of Malayo-Polynesian: A report of tentative findings. *Am. Anthropol.* 57:337–39
19. Grace, G. W. 1959. *The Position of the Polynesian Languages within the Austronesian Language Family. Indiana Univ. Publ. Anthropol. Ling. 16*
20. Grace, G. W. 1970. *Languages of Oceania.* Prepared for Lang. World Conf., Center Appl. Ling.
21. Greenberg, J. H. 1960. The general classification of Central and South American languages. In *Selected Papers of the Fifth International Congress of Anthropological and Ethnological Sciences,* ed. A. F. C. Wallace. Philadelphia: Univ. Pennsylvania Press
22. Greenberg, J. H. 1966. *The Languages of Africa.* Bloomington: Indiana Univ. Res. Center Anthropol., Folklore, Ling.
23. Greenberg, J. H. 1971. The Indo-Pacific hypothesis. In *Current Trends in Linguistics,* ed. T. A. Sebeok, 8:807–71
24. Grierson, G. A. 1919. *Indo-Aryan Family, North-Western Group: Specimens of the Dardic or Pisācha Languages* (including Kāshmiri). *Linguistic Survey of India,* Vol. 8, part 2. Calcutta: Govt. Print. Off.
25. Haas, M. 1958. Algonkian-Ritwan: The end of a controversy. *Int. J. Am. Ling.* 24:159–73
26. Haas, M. 1958. A new linguistic relationship in North America: Algonkian and the Gulf languages. *Southwest. J. Anthropol.* 14:231–64
27. Haas, M. 1960. Some genetic affiliations of Algonkian. In *Culture in History, Essays in Honor of Paul Radin,* ed. S. Diamond. New York: Columbia Univ. Press for Brandeis Univ.
28. Hamp, E. 1966. The position of Albanian. See Ref. 13, 97–121
29. Krishnamurti, Bh. 1969. Comparative Dravidian studies. See Ref. 23, 5:309–33
30. Levin, S. 1971. *The Indo-European and Semitic Languages.* Albany: State Univ. New York Press
31. Mathias, G. B. Review of Roy A. Miller, *Japanese and the Other Altaic Languages.* In press
32. Meillet, A., Cohen, M. 1952. *Les Langues du Monde.* Paris: Centre national de la recherche scientifique
33. Milke, W. 1958. Zur inneren Gliederung und geschlichtlichen Stellung der ozeanisch-austronesischen Sprachen. *Z. Ethnol.* 83:58–62

34. Miller, R. A. 1971. *Japanese and the Other Altaic Languages.* Univ. Chicago Press
35. Morgenstierne, G. 1961. Dardic and Kâfir Languages. *The Encyclopaedia of Islam,* 2:25. New ed. Leiden: Brill
36. Pinnow, H. J. 1959. *Versuch Einer Historischen Lautlehre der Kharia-Sprache.* Weisbaden: Harrassowitz
37. Puhvel, J. 1966. Dialectal aspects of the Anatolian branch of Indo-European. See Ref. 13, 235–47
38. Sapir, E. 1929. Central and North American Indian languages. *Encyclopaedia Britannica* 14th. ed. 5:138–41
39. Senn, A. 1966. The relationships of Baltic and Slavic. See Ref. 13, 139–51
40. Shafer, R. 1955. Classification of the Sino-Tibetan languages. *Word* 11:94–111
41. Stampe, D. 1966. Recent work in Munda linguistics. IV. *Int. J. Am. Ling.* 32: 390–97
41a. Strand, R. F. Notes on the Nūristānī and Dardic languages. *J. Am. Orient. Soc.* In press
42. Thomas, D., Headley, R. K. 1970. More on Mon-Khmer subgroupings. *Lingua* 25:398–418
43. Tucker, A. N., Bryan, M. A. 1956. *The Non-Bantu Languages of North-Eastern Africa. Handbook of African Languages,* part III, I.A.I. Oxford Univ. Press
44. Tucker, A. N., Bryan, M. A. 1966. *Linguistic Analyses, the Non-Bantu Languages of North-Eastern Africa. Handbook of African Languages,* I.A.I. London: Oxford Univ. Press
45. Voegelin, C. F., Voegelin, E. W. 1946. *Map of North American Indian Languages. Am. Ethnol. Soc. Publ. 20*
46. Voegelin, C. F., Voegelin, F. M. 1966. *Map of North American Indian Languages. Am. Ethnol. Soc. Revised Publ. 20*
47. Watkins, C. 1966. Italo-Celtic revisited. See Ref. 13
48. Westermann, D. 1953. African Languages. In *Encyclopaedia Britannica*
49. Westphal, E. O. J. 1971. The click languages of Southern and Eastern Africa. See Ref. 23, 7:367–420
50. Wurm, S. A. 1971. The Papuan linguistic situation. See Ref. 23, 8:541–657
51. Zide, N. H., Ed. 1966. *Studies in Comparative Austroasiatic Linguistics.* The Hague: Mouton

ON THE ADEQUACY OF RECENT PHONOLOGICAL THEORIES AND PRACTICES[1]

♦ 9524

John G. Fought

Department of Linguistics, University of Pennsylvania, Philadelphia

Whether they are linguistic specialists or not, anthropologists have a professional concern with the nature of language, its relation to the human organism, and its role in culture and society. From this point of view, the most important developments in linguistics as a whole and in phonology in particular over the past decade or so have been the rise to prominence of Chomskyan transformational theory in the late 1950s and early 1960s and the development, from largely independent roots, of a fresh perspective on some fundamental issues of linguistic theory through sociolinguistic research.

Systems of descriptive phonology must all meet certain basic standards of accuracy and scope if they are to be considered adequate even in principle. In dealing with the nonrandom distribution of the elements of a phonological inventory (the *sound pattern* of a language), the treatment of novel or "unused" combinations is an important gauge of the adequacy of a theory. This issue was raised, for example, by Chomsky (10) and by García in her excellent review (21) of Saporta & Contreras (46); it has been much discussed over the last decade. This only makes it more difficult to compress a survey of it into the space available here.

[1]Having accepted the editor's invitation to comment on developments in phonology during the past 10 years or so within 10 printed pages, I chose to concentrate on a single theme, the notion of adequacy, rather than to give an annotated guide to writings across the whole spectrum of the field in that period. Even so, the space limitation has forced me to leave out important contributions I would have liked to discuss at length. To those whose work deserves notice in a survey of this kind but who do not receive it here, I offer my apologies. I particularly regret having to leave out a number of fine descriptive and historical studies whose authors have helped set high standards of adequacy for all of us.

I wish to thank Paul Friedrich, Dell Hymes, and Michael Silverstein for their comments on an earlier version of this paper. The responsibility for the views expressed here is mine alone, however.

153

After first outlining the notion of sound patterns from the broadly structuralist point of view current in the late 1950s, I will discuss the development of the subject since then, giving special attention to notions of adequacy and the problem of novel sequences, and finally, I will consider a different dimension of phonotactics, sociolinguistic variability, and its implications for the adequacy of phonological theory and practice.

SOUND PATTERNS IN LANGUAGE

Within the grammar of a language, the principal tasks of phonology are to describe the phonetic elements of the sound system and to state their combinatory patterns, both within and across the boundaries of meaningful forms, accurately, completely, and economically.

Considered as sound, the speech of a community can be described as a system of recurring features and patterns of phonetic elements. Redundancy in the patterning of the elements allows for economical description without loss of accuracy, since the occurrence of some elements can be predicted by reference to the occurrence of others. The coherence of the system is such that phonetic details can be filled in if the outlines and the rules are known.

Some of these descriptive rules specify phonetic features implied by simultaneous groupings of other features; some specify features implied by sequential groupings. Some simultaneous combinations of features, such as labio-uvular closure, are excluded by the limitations of the human vocal apparatus; however, most sequential constraints and many simultaneous ones reflect patterning specific to the particular language. All are statable regardless of grammatical segmentation. Within an English syllable, for example, obstruent clusters are voiced or voiceless throughout: one finds / ts / and / dz /, but neither */ tz / nor */ ds /; the second elements of / pl / and / tr / are voiceless, and those of / bl / and / dr / are voiced. The distributional pattern of the phonological elements of a language, of which these illustrations are but a small part, is the phonotactics of the language. Describing it is a natural and important part of the linguist's task.

When speech acts are viewed as arrangements of meaningful forms, the pronunciation of many forms is observed to vary according to their linguistic or situational context of occurrence. There is redundancy in these patterns too, and many of the same combinatory regularities are found both within meaningful forms and bridging the boundaries between forms in combination. In English, for example, regular sibilant plurals end in / ɨz / after a sibilant (including the sibilant components of the affricates / č / and / ǰ /), in / z / after a voiced nonsibilant, and in / s / after a voiceless nonsibilant. Notice that the voicing conditions are in part a special case of the phonotactic regularity of voicing in consonant clusters noted just above; the rest of the statement of the alternation is not strictly phonetic or phonemic in content, since not all plurals are marked by a sibilant suffix, and not all that are so marked are regular (*dice* / days / is not). These variations in phonological form at or across morphological boundaries are collectively known as the morphophonemics of a language.

Sapir's Sound Patterns in Language (45), though nearly 50 years old now, is still an excellent introduction to the systems of phonetic and distributional constraints which interact to form the patterns he described as "resulting from all the specific phonetic relationships (such as parallelism, contrast, combination, imperviousness to combination, and so on) to all other sounds. These relationships may, or may not, involve morphological processes . . ." (45, p. 42).

TRANSFORMATIONALIST PHONOLOGY

In 1959, Halle's *Sound Pattern of Russian* (23) appeared, breaking sharply with descriptivist phonology on several vital points. It is interpretive, converting strings of lexical representations, boundary markers, and grammatical elements produced by the syntactic component into phonetic representations by means of a system of partially ordered rules, at least some of which are transformational in type. It explicitly rejects both the phonemic level and the item-and-arrangement mode of description then in favor, claiming greater simplicity and generality for the transformationalist approach. Indeed, many traits characteristic of it and of its successors are directly motivated by Halle's conception of simplicity or economy. Lexical representations, for instance, which are matrices of distinctive features, have a minimum number of features specified in the lexicon, and a maximum number specified by morpheme structure rules in the phonological component. Halle explained why:

> Since we speak at a rapid rate—perhaps at a rate requiring the specification of as many as 30 segments per second—it is reasonable to assume that all languages are so designed that the number of features that must be specified in selecting individual morphemes is consistently kept at a minimum (23, p. 29).

Recent experimental work has not dealt kindly with such simple-minded notions. Kim's survey (30) of experimental phonetic research finds evidence to support the syllable, rather than the segment or the morpheme, as the natural unit of speech production. Such findings complement the persistent tradition of interest in the syllable as a descriptive framework for phonotactics, a position taken very early and very persuasively by Haugen (25) and developed in various ways by Brown (9) and Fudge (20) within a transformational approach.

Another salient feature of Halle's work has been the requirement that segments be characterized in terms of a specific and universal list of binary features, originally those proposed in Jakobson, Fant & Halle (31). In his Russian study, Halle claimed a great deal for this system:

> Systematic reviews of the available evidence from a great variety of languages have shown that the binary distinctive feature framework is adequate to the task. No examples have been adduced by various critics that would seriously impair the validity of the binary scheme. On the contrary, the imposition of the binary structure on all features has supplied a satisfactory explanation for a number of 'puzzling' phonetic changes and made possible the formulation of an evaluation procedure for phonological descriptions (23, p. 20).

After nearly 15 years of polemics, sudden revisions, and disagreements concerning the universal binary feature system, the self-assurance of this passage seems laughable. Harms (24) surveys the developments of new features and the replacement of old ones through 1967; in 1968 an entirely new system was presented in *The Sound Pattern of English* (14), and since then there have been fresh challenges to it. Lisker & Abramson (42) criticize an important group of these features. Ladefoged (37) reviews the subject and presents an alternative system of features, some binary and some not. Bailey (2) presents a system of ternary features, and Parker & Bailey (43) a view of markedness to go with it. Contreras (16) challenged the foundations of Halle's views.

It is very difficult to read the history of the binary feature systems as a cumulation of experimental evidence and wisdom. Instead, it would seem to justify abandoning the requirement of binary structure entirely in favor of a more flexible system like Ladefoged's (37), supported as it is by impressive empirical work (e.g. 36). More generally, the history of the phonetic basis of transformational phonology should encourage a degree of prophylactic skepticism about the other claims of adequacy made on behalf of this approach.

The adequacy of transformational theory and the accuracy of its application in descriptive work have been persistent issues. Ferguson's review (17) of Halle (23) makes interesting reading today in this connection. He questioned the distinctive feature analysis and the claim of universality made for it, doubted the wisdom of relying on segments at all in the transformational format, deplored the lack of discussion of moot points, and warned that such complex notations and rules would make inconsistencies and errors more likely than they need be. All these points have been raised over and over since then; they remain telling criticisms of transformationalist work, in my opinion.

A more recent body of work provides a better basis for judging the adequacy of transformationalist phonology. In Chomsky & Halle (14), stress levels are assigned to American English constructions according to the principle of the transformational cycle: phonological rules apply in sequence first to the smallest or inmost constituent of a grammatically segmented and labeled string (a surface structure), and then reapply in sequence to the next larger constituent, of which the first is a part, and so on. The principle of the cycle was first formulated in Chomsky, Halle & Lukoff (15); the authors of *The Sound Pattern of English* note in their preface that it is the fruit of more than 10 years of work, and cite other works directed or influenced by them employing the principle of the cycle to predict accent elements. Although they note the existence of exceptions to their rules and predict (correctly, it seems) that the theory will be subject to revision, they are willing to present their "interim report" (14, pp. vii–ix). The cyclical rule system for English stress prediction can be taken seriously then, if anything can.

A comparison of the papers which have criticized and defended the 1968 analysis does nothing to increase one's confidence in it. A close study of Akmajian & Jackendoff (1), Baker (3), Beaver (4), Berman & Szamosi (5), Bolinger (6), Bresnan (7, 8), Lakoff (39), Ladefoged & Vanderslice (38), Lee (40), Schmerling's incisive papers (47–50), and their supporting bibliographies would reveal the extent of the empirical and theoretical difficulties raised by the treatment of stress in *The Sound Pattern of English.*

The transformationalist literature appears to focus on a notion of adequacy *in principle,* whereas many of the critics of this approach have sought to establish a notion of adequacy *in fact* in evaluating linguistic work. Thus Chomsky's definition of levels of adequacy or success in phonology in his Ninth Congress paper (10) and in the publications derived from it (11, 12) was challenged by Householder (27), who contended that the definition of observational adequacy as "merely . . . an account of the primary data . . .", said by Chomsky to be the highest level attainable by 'taxonomic' linguistics, was evidence of a certain "animosity which Chomsky feels toward this principle" (27, p. 14). In their reply, Chomsky & Halle (13, p. 138) rejected this, calling for evidence that they have "no regard for linguistic fact and fail to meet common standards of accuracy and seriousness." As evidence, one could cite today the studies of the transformational cycle mentioned above. Here I will provide evidence that was available at the time they wrote, and that is relevant to the discussion of adequacy in the exchange of papers between Householder and Chomsky & Halle. The statement of three levels of adequacy cited by Householder (27, p. 14) makes reference to the second of two abstract devices described in an earlier paper by Chomsky (11, p. 61):

> . . . we can take as an objective for linguistic theory the precise specification of two kinds of abstract device, the first serving as a perceptual model and the second as a model for acquisition of language.
>
> utterance $\longrightarrow$ $\boxed{\text{A}}$ $\longrightarrow$ structural description   (1a)
>
> primary linguistic data $\longrightarrow$ $\boxed{\text{B}}$ $\longrightarrow$ generative grammar   (1b)

In terms of this device, the adequacies were defined as follows (11, p. 63):

> . . . a grammar that aims for observational adequacy is concerned merely to give an account of the primary data (e.g. the corpus) that is the input to the learning device (1b); a grammar that aims for descriptive adequacy is concerned to give a correct account of the linguistic intuition of the native speaker; in other words, it is concerned with the output of the device (1b); and a linguistic theory that aims for explanatory adequacy is concerned with the internal structure of the device (1b); that is, it aims to provide a principled basis, independent of any particular language, for the selection of the descriptively adequate grammar of each language.

/ brik /, / blik /, and / bnik /

In an effort to clarify what they mean by levels of adequacy, Chomsky and Halle introduced a discussion of / brik /, / blik /, and / bnik / as English forms into their answer to Householder. It is an important step in the deployment of Chomsky's argument in favor of his own views and against those of "taxonomic" linguistics to claim that the ability shared by all speakers to identify totally novel sequences as acceptable or unacceptable, as in the cases of / blik / and / bnik /, or *colorless green ideas sleep furiously* and *furiously sleep ideas green colorless* can be accounted for or "explained" by transformational theory but not by "taxonomic" theory. Their discussion is most instructive (13, p. 101):

Thus in English there is a form *brick* (/brik/), but no /blik/ or /bnik/. Nevertheless, a speaker of English knows that /blik/ is an admissible form in a sense in which /bnik/ is not. This distinction is, furthermore, not a matter of universal phonetics. [. . . .] A description of English will achieve the level of observational adequacy, in this case, if it distinguishes /brik/, as an occurring form, from /blik/ and /bnik/, as non-occurring forms. Thus a lexicon—a list of all occurring forms—meets the level of observational adequacy. It correctly presents the data available to the child, the input to the acquisition model AM. The description will meet the level of descriptive adequacy if it distinguishes /brik/ and /blik/, as admissible forms, from /bnik/, as an inadmissible form. In this case, it will state what the speaker knows (unconsciously—cf. note 2) to be true; it gives correctly the output of AM. To meet the level of explanatory adequacy, a linguistic theory must justify the descriptively adequate grammar on internal grounds. That is, it must show on what basis the device AM (or the linguist) selects a grammar admitting /blik/ and excluding /bnik/. It must, in other words, justify the inclusion in a grammar of English of the rule (1) but not the rule (2):

(1) Consonantal Segment $\longrightarrow$ Liquid in the context: #Stop _ Vowel
(2) Consonantal Segment $\longrightarrow$ /r/ in the context: #/b_ik/.

It is implicit in the foregoing discussion of / blik / and / bnik / that a speaker's judgments of acceptability in phonology, as in grammar, reflect and in some sense employ the "internalized rules" of a generative grammar. The passage just quoted is a typical example of the special pleading and fallacious argument offered in place of experimental evidence to support this contention. For example, Chomsky & Halle insist that we choose either rule (1) or rule (2) to account for the occurrence of / brik / and the nonoccurrence of / blik / and / bnik /. To make the choice easy, they state rule (2) as narrowly as possible. Why not this rule (2')?

(2') Consonantal segment $\longrightarrow$ / r / in the context #Stop _ Vowel

It is amusing that rule (1), their choice, achieves observational inadequacy by generating / tl / and / dl /, perhaps the most hackneyed of all examples of nonoccurrent initial consonant clusters in English.

This failure is especially striking in an article offered in part as an answer to the charge that "mere mistakes of fact, no matter how gross and glaring, tend to be looked upon as trivial, and no votary would admit publicly that he spends any time avoiding them" (Householder 27, p. 14), and immediately before the claim that "both rules (1) and (2) are true of English, at the level of observation. That is, both correctly state facts about occurrence and nonoccurrence." (Chomsky & Halle 13, p. 101). Of course, rule (1) could easily be "corrected" by additional rules suppressing its unwanted outputs, but that is not the point: instead, it must be emphasized that in seeking to rebut Householder's charge that they do not care much about observational adequacy, Chomsky & Halle have unwittingly provided the strongest possible confirmation of it.

Postal (44, pp. 137–38) went farther than Chomsky & Halle, basing his predictions of acceptability judgments on particular features in rules as formulated in a transformational grammar, and outlining a remarkable four-way classification of phonological sequences, as possible and actual (English *big*), possible but not actual (*plig*), impossible but actual (*sphere*), and impossible and not actual (*fnes*). He suggested the use of 'exception features' in the underlying representation of forms like *sphere*. These features would protect the forms from the application of rules which would otherwise block or change them. Similar use has often been made of abstract "features" in transformational work. By the time Postal wrote, a psycholinguistic experiment conducted by Greenberg & Jenkins (22) had already rendered his position untenable. He does not mention this or any other experiment relevant to his claims, however, nor do Chomsky & Halle.

Greenberg & Jenkins found that the acceptability of a form to English speakers correlates very well (their lowest figure was +0.94) with the number of points in it where the substitution of a different phoneme produces an actually occurring form. Their procedure is difficult to summarize, but it leads to an index number showing the relatedness of a sequence to English forms. The intuitive judgments implied by Postal's categories do not match well at all with their findings.

It may be helpful here to examine the distributional facts and to state the observed pattern of English syllable onsets by means of a structuralist analysis into distinctive articulatory components so as to demonstrate that this approach is indeed capable of descriptive adequacy.

The active articulator(s) used in the production of a segment are among the distinctive components which characterize it in this approach. The components relevant to this example are the labial, frontal, and dorsal articulators; both the lips and the dorsum are involved in the production of back rounded vowels, and the lips and the tongue front in the production of front and central rounded vowels. In many kinds of American English, including mine, so-called back vowels are often central; this includes the glide elements in diphthongs. Defining / w / as a labial and not as a labiovelar then, and assigning the components frontal and labial to / r /, allow one to state that in syllable-initial clusters, the segments / w, y, r, l / occur after stops which differ from them by one or more articulator components. Thus one finds / tw, kw / but not */ pw /, / py, ky / but not */ ty /, / pl, kl / but not */ tl /, and / pr, tr, kr /, since / r /, with two articulator components, differs from any stop by one or two components. For some Midwesterners, this is the pattern for all syllable onsets; for others it holds only after pause. Naturally, different dialects call for different descriptions; other patterns of stop-continuant distribution may not be so neat. It is worth adding that this pattern of articulatory differences became evident through the operations of observation, segmentation, and classification. The rare exceptions to the pattern (e.g. *bwana, Tlingit*) are late accretions to my vocabulary, and of course must be listed.

There is a still more general approach to the distinction between acceptable and unacceptable nonoccurring syllables. It was originally developed by Bernard Bloch; an extended version is presented here. For English the test may be applied as follows: list the attested syllables twice, in terms of suprasegmental (stress, for English), consonantal onset, if any, nucleus, and consonantal coda, if any. From one list delete all onsets, and from the other delete all codas. The acceptable syllables are those generated by matching each occurrence of a given stress-and-nucleus combination from one list with all occurrences of the same stress-and-nucleus combination from the other list, adding any associated syllable margins. Schematically:

$$S + O + N$$
$$S + \quad N + C$$
$$\overline{S + O + N + C}$$

Thus / blik / is acceptable not because of intuitions but because of / blimp /, / blik /, etc, and / pik /, / slik /, etc; and */ bnik / is unacceptable because there are no */ bn / onsets (and in fact, no stop + nasal onsets) at all.

Since acceptability is a gradient attribute, even in phonology, it is worth observing that Bloch's test neatly segregates those syllables which are marginally acceptable to an informant: some are generated by the test when it applies to a sample of the speech community's productions, but not when it applies only to the informant's own usage—/ dup / is a case in point for speakers like me; it exists in the speech community but not in my own speech. Other syllables are generated by only a relative few of the paired constituent combinations in the informant's usage, and for that reason are presumably accepted with some reservations.

Conclusions

Neither structuralist nor transformationalist phonological practice responded adequately to the full range of phonological patterning. Each approach tended to slight what the other did best. Friedrich, in a recent paper which should provide a new departure for descriptive phonology, notes that the former school has typically been devoted to "listing the allophones, relevant contexts, and articulatory characteristics of phonemes, and then, as theory, to reducing the number of phonemes . . ." (19, p. 864). I would add that while structuralists continued to supply tables and formulae for phonotactics as an adjunct to their phonemic inventories, their reasons for doing so were not always made clear. Morphophonemics, under a program widely followed by structuralists, was moved from the phonology to the lexicon, where regular and irregular alternations were handled according to the same principles.

In transformationalist phonology, according to Friedrich (19, p. 864):

> . . . the typical and primary concern has been with ordering and abbreviating rules—to the neglect of patterning that is not necessary for a minimally redundant, maximally brief statement of such rules. In practice, the generativist goal often appears to be various formal mechanisms of 'representation' and 'abbreviation', rather than the characterization of features and their interrelations in terms of an optimal fit between externally and internally motivated criteria.

The patterning which attracted the interest of followers of Halle's program was almost entirely morphophonemic, and until very recently, proposals to incorporate language-specific but morphophonemically irrelevant phonotactic patterning into grammar in a visible and recoverable way have attracted very little attention from the leaders of this school. But even within the scope of morphophonemic patterning, there is a notable weakness of transformationalist doctrine.

Transformationalists have often reproached structuralists for an excessive concern with heuristic or "discovery" procedures. Their own excesses, on the other hand, have been in the area of algorithms, which they tend to mistake for theory. In phonology, particularly, Chomsky and Halle have provided not a theory, but only a powerful notation. It is so powerful that one can reach a given descriptive result in any number of ways, and this has lately raised questions. Lightner's recent survey of generative phonology (41), for instance, raises questions so fundamental and so far from being resolved within transformationalist doctrine that they should be deeply disturbing to its followers. Among these issues one stands out: what criteria decide whether two forms are to be related by the phonological rules? A moment's reflection will bring home the significance of these decisions in the hundreds of specific and often far from obvious cases which confront a linguist describing any language; Lightner presents a few himself. From the aggregate of these decisions arises the system of phonological rules itself and the pattern of alternations it generates. Yet while there is a body of doctrine and principles of structural linguistics worked out to handle these cases consistently, nothing corresponds to it in transformationalist writings. There is a needlessly powerful notational system with which to implement analysts' decisions, but no guidance at all in reaching them.

Indeed, as Friedrich put it (19, pp. 864–65): "Both of these models . . . lead to indifference to, or even rejection of, many kinds of rich, complex, and demonstrable patterns of covariation and intersection between units, subsets, and levels within one sound system." It is a great merit of Friedrich's paper that it restores all these kinds of patterning to a place of importance in linguistics they have not held since Sapir. In so doing he prepares for fresh answers to what he calls ". . . one of the more interesting and often neglected questions in phonological theory: what is the over-all gestalt of a phonology, what are the ways in which the diverse components of the diverse subsystems are put together?" (19, p. 864).

Sociolinguistic Variation

Among the kinds of patterning long neglected by both structuralists and transformationalists, the importance of those alternations governed by the circumstances of the speech act or of its participants has recently begun to be widely understood. Within the essentially fixed, static linguistic structures described by Saussure and his heirs in both these schools, language change and diversity within a speech community are anomalies; they pose profound theoretical problems. How can such structures change at all without some period of incoherence or disruption of the communicative fabric? How can the members of a demonstrably close-knit social group display the diversity commonly observed in their speech patterns without any apparent hindrance to their communication? And how is linguistic theory to integrate the answers to these questions with the notion of structure already worked out in descriptive and historical linguistics?

The answers to all these questions, as sociolinguists have begun to argue with great force, are to be found by abandoning the conception of a homogeneous and static linguistic code altogether (Labov 33, pp. 42–43): "Once we dissolve the assumed association between structure and homogeneity, we are free to develop the formal tools needed to deal with inherent variation within the speech community." Such tools are becoming available. The notion of the sociolinguistic variable and the variable rules which incorporate it into linguistic descriptions has enormous significance for the theory and practice of linguistics. The *th* variable is the initial consonant of *think, thumb,* etc in New York City English. There are three types of onset in these forms: an apicodental voiceless fricative [θ], standard in most dialects; an apicodental voiceless affricate [tθ]; and an apicodental voiceless stop [t]. Labov (32) found that the affricate and stop variants are stigmatized. For all classes, increased formality of speech is accompanied by decreased frequency of the stigmatized variants. Moreover, speakers from lower classes use them more frequently than speakers from higher classes.

On the other hand, the use of postvocalic *r* in New York City speech is positively valued. For all classes, the frequency of use of constricted *r* (hereafter, just *r*) increases as the formality of the style of speech increases. Moreover, the lower middle class, that most insecure of social groups in the sample, shows a radical shift in frequency, from less than the norm for upper middle class speakers in informal styles to considerably higher in formal styles, in a direct reflection of their insecurity. This crossover or hypercorrection pattern is one of the most dramatic findings of sociolinguistic research. It seems quite straightforward to interpret this distribution of *r* as a pattern of emulation of upper middle class usage by upward-mobile speakers superimposed on a pattern of emulation of national norms by outward-oriented upper middle class speakers.

Labov's variable rules (cf. 32–35) assign a coefficient ranging from 1.00 to greater than 0.00 to each rule (or in some cases to certain features of a rule). This coefficient determines the proportion of actual applications to possible applications: a value of 1.00 implies that the rule is applied whenever its conditions are met, and lower coefficients mean less frequent application. Since the rules typically interact in complex ways, it is not easy to arrive at appropriate coefficients for a set of rules. What is interesting in all this is the finding that the variation is orderly and rather easy to describe once the data are available. A numerical value can be assigned to style, social class, age, or other relevant factors whose sum is the coefficient of a phonological or grammatical rule; in this way such "nonlinguistic" factors can be built right into the grammar.

The same techniques can be used to account for stylistic or rhetorical variation in ethnographically relevant circumstances, as long advocated by Hymes (cf. 28, 29). In (18), Fought showed that morphophonemic fusion of sequences of basic vowels was least frequent in relatively language-conscious settings, and most frequent in dialog within the Chorti narratives examined. Frequency of fusion (indicated by the coalescence of two syllabic stresses into one) was a reliable indicator of the total morphophonemic activity in a given style or passage.

PROSPECTS

Today a system of phonological description which makes serious claims to adequacy in principle must go beyond even those standards of completeness laid down by Sapir and Friedrich. It must account not only for the phonetic details and the familiar types of phonotactic and morphophonemic patterning, but also for the sociolinguistic variation in these patterns, which itself forms a significant pattern.

There is now no fully worked-out model one can follow to reach these objectives, but there is a growing awareness that the familiar approaches are basically inadequate. As sociolinguistics develops, the next few years may be a period of growth and enrichment of linguistic theory more rapid and intense than we have experienced before. It is plausible, I think, that if 1968 is to be an important year in the history of linguistics, it will be more for Weinreich, Labov & Herzog's masterful survey of the place of diversity and variability within the history of linguistic theory (52) than for Chomsky & Halle's *Sound Pattern of English* (14).

It would be wise to remember, amid the perfectly legitimate enthusiasm surrounding sociolinguistics, that many of its fundamental notions are not new. Hoenigswald's careful distributionalist presentation of language change (26) is based on a clear understanding of the vital role of competing alternative elements as a precondition for change (cf. 26, p. 66). Weinreich's survey of the linguistic scene in 1960 (51) pointed clearly to the importance of diversity within the speech community as a theoretical issue. The list could easily be extended. What is new, and most important, is the interest now taken in these positions. Sociolinguistics has moved from the periphery of linguistics to its very center.

Literature Cited

1. Akmajian, A., Jackendoff, R. 1970. Coreferentiality and stress. *Ling. Inq.* 1:124–26
2. Bailey, C.-J. N. 1970. Ternary feature list. *Working Pap. Ling.* 2.4:125–30. Honolulu: Dep. Ling., Univ. Hawaii
3. Baker, C. 1971. Stress level and auxiliary behavior in English. *Ling. Inq.* 2:167–81
4. Beaver, J. C. 1970. A note on the ordering of the nuclear stress rule. *Pap. Ling.* 3:405–9
5. Berman, A., Szamosi, M. 1972. Observations on sentential stress. *Language* 48:304–25
6. Bolinger, D. L. 1972. Accent is predictable (if you're a mind-reader). *Language* 47:257–80
7. Bresnan, J. 1971. Sentence stress and syntactic transformations. *Language* 47:257–80
8. Bresnan, J. 1972. Stress and syntax: a reply. *Language* 48: 326–42
9. Brown, G. 1969. Syllables and redundancy rules in generative phonology. *J. Ling.* 6:1–17
10. Chomsky, N. 1964. The logical basis of linguistic theory. *Proc. 9th Int. Congr. Ling.*, 914–1008. The Hague: Mouton
11. Chomsky, N. 1964. Current issues in linguistic theory. In *The Structure of Language: Readings in the Philosophy of Language,* ed. J. A. Fodor, J. J. Katz, 50–118. Englewood Cliffs, N.J.: Prentice-Hall
12. Chomsky, N. 1964. *Current Issues in Linguistic Theory.* Janua Linguarum, Series Minor, 38. The Hague: Mouton
13. Chomsky, N., Halle, M. 1965. Some controversial questions in phonological theory. *J. Ling.* 1:97–138
14. Chomsky, N., Halle, M. 1968. *The Sound Pattern of English.* New York: Harper & Row
15. Chomsky, N., Halle, M., Lukoff, F. 1956. On accent and juncture in English. *For Roman Jakobson,* 65–80. The Hague: Mouton
16. Contreras, H. 1969. Simplicity, descriptive adequacy, and binary features. *Language* 45:1–8
17. Ferguson, C. F. 1962. Review of (23). *Language* 38:284–97
18. Fought, J. G. 1973. Rule ordering, interference, and free alternation in phonology. *Language* 49:67–86
19. Friedrich, P. 1971. Distinctive features and functional groups in Tarascan phonology. *Language* 47:849–65
20. Fudge, E. C. 1969. Syllables. *J. Ling.* 5: 253–86
21. Garcia, E. C. 1963. Review of (46). *Word* 19:258–65
22. Greenberg, J. H., Jenkins, J. J. 1964. Studies in the psychological correlates of the sound system of American English. *Word* 20:157–77
23. Halle, M. 1959. *The Sound Pattern of Russian.* The Hague: Mouton

24. Harms, R. T. 1968. *Introduction to Phonological Theory.* Englewood Cliffs: Prentice-Hall
25. Haugen, E. 1956. The syllable in linguistic description. See Ref. 15, 213–21
26. Hoenigswald, H. M. 1960. *Language Change and Linguistic Reconstruction.* Univ. Chicago Press
27. Householder, F. W. Jr. 1965. On some recent claims in phonological theory. *J. Ling.* 1:13–34
28. Hymes, D. H. 1970. Linguistic theory and the functions of speech. In *International Days of Sociolinguistics,* 111–44. Roma: Istituto Luigi Sturzo
29. Hymes, D. H. 1972. Introduction. In *Functions of Language in the Classroom,* ed. C. Cazden, V. John-Steiner, D. H. Hymes. New York: Teachers College Press
30. Kim, C.-W. 1971. Experimental phonetics. In *A Survey of Linguistic Science,* ed. W. O. Dingwall, 16–128. College Park: Univ. Maryland Linguistics Program
31. Jakobson, R., Fant, G., Halle, M. 1952. *Preliminaries to Speech Analysis.* Acoustics Lab. Tech. Rep. 13. Cambridge: M. I. T.
32. Labov, W. D. 1966. *The Social Stratification of English in New York City.* Washington, D.C.: Center Appl. Ling.
33. Labov, W. D. 1970. The study of language in its social context. *Stud. Gen.* 23:30–87
34. Labov, W. D. 1971. Methodology. See Ref. 30, 412–91
35. Labov, W. D., Cohen, P., Robins, C., Lewis, J. 1968. *A Study of the Non-Standard English of Negro and Puerto Rican Speakers in New York City.* Coop. Res. Proj. 3288, Off. Educ., US Dep. HEW. Philadelphia: US Regional Survey
36. Ladefoged, P. 1964. *A Phonetic Study of West African Languages.* West Afr. Lang. Monogr. 1. Cambridge Univ. Press
37. Ladefoged, P. 1971. *Preliminaries to Linguistic Phonetics.* Univ. Chicago Press
38. Ladefoged, P., Vanderslice, R. 1972.

Binary suprasegmental features and transformational word-accent rules. *Language* 48:819–38
39. Lakoff, G. 1972. The global nature of the nuclear stress rule. *Language* 48:285–303
40. Lee, G. 1969. English word stress. *Pap. 5th Reg. Meet. Chicago Ling. Soc.,* 386–406
41. Lightner, T. 1971. Generative phonology. See Ref. 30, 499–564
42. Lisker, L., Abramson, A. S. 1971. Distinctive features and laryngeal control. *Language* 47:767–85
43. Parker, G. J., Bailey, C.-J. N. 1970. Ternary markedness values? An approach to the measurement of complexity in the operation of phonological rules. *Working Pap. Ling.* 2.4:131–42. Honolulu: Univ. Hawaii
44. Postal, P. M. 1968. *Aspects of Phonological Theory.* New York: Harper & Row
45. Sapir, E. 1925. Sound patterns in language. *Language* 1:37–51. Reprinted 1968 in *Selected Writings of Edward Sapir,* ed. D. G. Mandelbaum, 33–45. Berkeley: Univ. California Press
46. Saporta, S., Contreras, H. 1962. *A Phonological Grammar of Spanish.* Seattle: Univ. Washington Press
47. Schmerling, S. F. 1971. Presupposition and the notion of normal stress. *Pap. 7th Reg. Meet. Chicago Ling. Soc.,* 242–53
48. Schmerling, S. F. 1971. A stress mess. *Studies in the Linguistic Sciences* 1.1:52–66. Urbana: Univ. Illinois Dep. Ling.
49. Schmerling, S. F. 1972. Two questionable assumptions concerning sentential stress. In manuscript
50. Schmerling, S. F. 1972. A reexamination of 'normal stress.' In manuscript
51. Weinreich, U. 1960. Mid-century linguistics: attainments and frustrations. *Romance Philology* 13:320–41
52. Weinreich, U., Labov, W. D., Herzog, M. 1968. Empirical foundations for a theory of language change. In *Directions for Historical Linguistics,* ed. W. Lehmann, Y. Malkiel, 97–195. Austin: Univ. Texas Press

DIALECTOLOGY ❖ 9525

Gillian Sankoff

Département d'Anthropologie, Université de Montréal, Montréal, Québec, Canada

For this first chapter on dialectology in the *Annual Review of Anthropology,* I have taken two liberties in defining the scope of the review: first, to cover roughly the work of the last decade rather than only the past year; and second, to be selective in emphasis within this work, concentrating particularly on trends that will be of most interest to anthropologists.

DIALECT GEOGRAPHY AND STRUCTURAL DIALECTOLOGY

Dialectology has its roots in the tradition of dialect geography and linguistic atlas work, well established in France and in Germany by the end of the 19th century and spreading rapidly to the rest of western Europe and America, where the bulk of the dialect atlas work has been done. Classics include Bach (12) on German work, Dauzat (38) and Pop (132) on the French tradition, Kurath (94) and Kurath & McDavid (95) on the United States. Brook (22) summarizes research on English, both in the United Kingdom and elsewhere. In reporting on dialect atlas work, I have chosen to limit myself to publications with a particular theoretical or methodological interest, as well as review articles summarizing dialect geographic work in a particular country or area. Recent bibliographies can be obtained from these sources, and the interested reader is advised to consult the journal *Orbis,* which regularly contains numerous descriptive articles on the geographic distribution of particular linguistic features.

Most of the papers with a methodological focus concentrate on problems of questionnaire construction (e.g. Galffy 63, Davis & Davis 40) or of mapping (e.g. Obrecht 125, Heicke & Schindler 77). Other methodological developments deal with quantitative methods, to be discussed in the last section. Theoretical papers will also be discussed according to topical areas.

In terms of regional work, Arabic dialect studies are the subject of a bibliography edited by Sobelman (156). Barczi (17) reports on Hungarian dialect work, Chao (33) on Chinese, and Aldus (4) on Anglo-Irish dialect studies. Japanese dialect work is treated in review articles by Tokugawa & Kato (164), Fujiwara (62), and Kandori (89). Weijnen & Hagen (178) report on an interlingual dialect atlas project in

165

Europe. A number of important publications resulted from the innovative Yiddish Language and culture project (Weinreich 180, 182) whose direction was assumed by Herzog after Weinreich's death (Herzog et al 79). Weinreich himself contributed many important insights to the whole field of dialectology (e.g. 181, 183). In Australia, Ramson (134) edited a collection of papers on Australasian English. Finally, 19 papers on dialect geography were published as part of the Proceedings of the Tenth International Congress in Bucharest (151).

American dialect atlas work continued to be carried out throughout the period under review (cf. for example Pederson 128). Several of the recent publications in American dialectology review (e.g. Davis 42) or consolidate previous work. Thus McDavid edited and abridged Mencken's classic, *The American Language* (122); the work sheets of the dialect atlas were published (Davis et al 39); Reed (135) summarized existing knowledge on American dialects, and several new collections appeared. A book by Williamson & Burke (188) contains 50 papers and 29 dissertation abstracts; the compilation by Allen & Underwood (5) contains 41 papers and an up-to-date bibliography. Though both include some material on social dialects, they represent principally a traditional dialect geographical approach. The collection by Griffith & Miner (66) contains seven rather diverse papers presented at a 1968 conference on dialectology. Finally, a Festschrift for Raven McDavid (Davis 43) brings together a number of important papers representing both dialect geography and social dialectology.

Following on two classic articles of the 1950s by Weinreich (179) and Stankiewicz (158), structural dialectology was developed in a number of studies, including Heiser (78), Ivic (85-87), Jongen (88), Kohler (93), Moulton (124), and Pulgram (133). The essential contribution of structural dialectology has been to stress the importance of comparing corresponding units in structured systems rather than studying the distribution of features whose status within the local system is not taken into account. Thus the systematic status of features being plotted on a map or compared with others over a particular area becomes a crucial factor in the analysis. This is a fundamental principle which has been retained in more recent developments, the most important of which have been in the area of social dialectology and sociolinguistics (cf. e.g. Rona 139).

During the 1960s, in addition to seeing some of their methods and insights extended and extrapolated within new theoretical orientations, dialect geographers themselves developed a greater awareness of the importance of social factors in the differentiation of speech varieties. A number of programmatic statements on the need to incorporate social factors into dialectological work appeared in a wide range of journals in several countries. These included Hammarstroem (73), Hutterer (82), Marcellesi (119), Spangenberg (157), Theban (163), and Vulpe (175). Some authors, e.g. Althaus (7), Schrader (150), Shanmugam (152), Ullrich (170), and Wells (185), did indeed take social factors into consideration in their analyses of particular cases.

DIACHRONIC LINGUISTICS AND THE BOUNDARY PROBLEM

Interestingly enough, many problems raised and relationships seen by sociolinguists and social dialectologists in the late 1960s and early 1970s had already been noted and discussed within the field of dialect geography. For example, the close relationship of dialectology to diachronic linguistics, long a tenet of dialect geography and noted in the period under review in work by Canfield (25), Delbouille (49), Fairbanks (55), and Gregg (65), has been paralleled by the important work of sociolinguists on the problems and mechanisms of language change. Friedrich (60) combined historical botanical study with reconstructive techniques in investigating a semantic system of Proto-Indo-European. The most important modern classic is the 1968 paper by Weinreich, Labov & Herzog (184), in which they provide the foundations for an empirically based theory of language change. The continuing groundbreaking research of Labov in this area has resulted in a number of publications and reports (97, 99-101, 106, 107, Labov et al 110). Other recent work includes that by Anshen (10), Bailey (15), Cedergren (30), Chen & Hsieh (34), Cheng & Wang (35), Cook (37), Gumperz (68), Hsieh (80), Laberge (96), and Traugott (165).

Another area in which dialectologists led the way, later to be investigated by sociolinguists, has to do with the discreteness of dialects and the use of subjective or reception rather than production criteria as an aid in establishing boundaries. Stankiewicz (158) wrote on the discreteness-continuity issue, and there were a number of attempts to apply some variant of the methods originally proposed by Voegelin & Harris (172) to judge intelligibility and establish subjectively viable language and dialect boundaries.

Perception of dialect differences was the subject of studies by Bender & Cooper (18), and Bush (23), Kirk (92), Scholes (149), Wendell (186), Willis (189), and Yamagiwa (193). Agard (2), Grootaers (67), Haugen (75), Mase (120), Sankoff (144), Stieber (160), and Weijnen (177) addressed themselves more specifically to the boundary problem. Smith (155) discussed the phonological bases for the folk view of Sedang dialect differences.

Another area having to do with subjective perception of dialect differences uses perceived speech differences as indicators of social, ethnic, and racial stereotypes. Recent work in this field includes studies by Lambert and associates, who pioneered the "matched guise" experimental technique (e.g. Anisfeld & Lambert 8), as well as by Williams et al (187) and a review article by Lee (112).

GENERATIVE GRAMMAR: RULE ORDERING AND DIALECT DIFFERENTIATION

Despite the lack of homogeneity encountered by basically empiricist traditions [structural linguistics in successively seeking homogeneity at the language, dialect, and idiolect level (cf. discussion in Labov 103, 104) and dialectology in continuing to document diversity], generative linguists began by assuming Chomsky's now famous ideal speaker-hearer in a homogeneous speech community. During the 1960s there began to appear articles dealing with dialect differences explained in terms of differences in rule ordering, following Kiparsky's (91) treatment of language change. Papers by Butters (24), Davis (44), Rulon (141), Saltarelli (143), Saporta (148), T'sou (168), and Vasiliu (171) were written from this theoretical perspective, as was Keyser's (90) review and reformulation of some of the American dialect atlas work. For the most part, however, the data base for such analyses was by no means explicit. This permitted linguists to talk about "my dialect" in a somewhat cavalier and referent-less fashion, not making clear whether the dialect in question was assumed to be idiosyncratic, or shared by some other group of people defined in terms of geographical, social, or other boundaries.

An important exception was the work of Guy Carden (26-28) in empirically investigating the intuition of American speakers regarding the distribution of rules involving the interaction of negatives and quantifiers. For a sentence such as "All the boys didn't arrive," Carden referred to the reading "None of the boys arrived" as representing the 'NEG. V' dialect, while the reading "Not all of the boys arrived" represented the 'NEG. Q' dialect. In 1972, Carden (29) and Labov (108) came to similar conclusions regarding this particular problem, in the light of the fact that people's interpretations differ under different testing circumstances. Thus it appears that virtually everyone is capable of either interpretation. Further problems arising from variability within the usage (and competence) of single individuals are discussed in the section on social dialects and variability below.

BLACK ENGLISH

The debates on American Black English of the late 1960s (cf. Kernan's review in the chapter on language in the *Biennial Review of Anthropology 1971*) brought to the fore specific questions relating to several classic issues in dialectology. The first had to do with the boundary problem—the relationships between the English spoken by black and white Americans, whether the dialects in question are discretely different and at what level of their structures, what the extent of differences are, and to what extent they are obscured by regional and class factors. A sampling of articles presenting divergent views on this subject include those by Davis (41), Dillard (51), Labov (102), Loflin (117), Stewart (159), and von Raffler Engel (174).

The boundary problem led naturally to the question of historical interpretation and genetic affiliation of Black English (to English or to West African languages) and its relationship to the Caribbean creoles. On this question cf. Alleyne (6), Bailey (14), Dillard (52), and references contained therein. DeGranda (48) reviews the problem for Spanish-speaking Latin America.

The last two questions had to do with the homogeneity issue. Educators who had been shown that the English spoken by lower class black children was a legitimate variety and not simply "bad English" still needed advice and direction about the English to be taught in the schools. There ensued the controversy over the issue of "bi-dialectalism"—should black children be taught standard American English as another variety, should they first be taught to read in their own dialect, to what extent is this feasible and desirable, and from whose point of view. Writings on this general issue include a collection of papers edited by Fasold & Shuy (59), Legum et al (113), and Tarone (162), as well as a great number of articles appearing in the *Florida FL Reporter* in the years 1969 and 1970 in particular.

Lastly, there arose the fundamental descriptive issue of just how homogeneous a system Black English is as it is presently spoken by any given speaker (cf. Anshen 9; Labov 102, 109; Legum et al 114; Pfaff 129; Riley 137). This question was even more pressing and difficult in communities which showed a greater range of diverse forms ranging from pidgin or creole to standard, such as Hawaii or Jamaica. The variation in any one speaker's forms led Bailey (13), for example, to decide to describe an idealized creole system for Jamaica which represented not the speech of any individual speaker, but the system most divergent from standard English, postulated to have been spoken in Jamaica in the past. DeCamp (46), on the other hand, experimented with the use of Guttman scales to describe what he called the "post-creole continuum" in Jamaica, and Tsuzaki (169) discussed coexistent systems in the case of Hawaii. Labov (105) wrote on the notion of system in creole languages in general.

Attempts to account for variation among individuals as well as variation in the speech of any one individual in cases like Black English, Jamaica, and Hawaii were, however, only examples of a general attempt in the late 1960s to try new frameworks and methodologies in attempting to understand the relationship among speech varieties. There existed a number of traditional solutions for neglecting variation and setting it outside of the "system" linguists were attempting to elucidate (cf. discussions of this in Labov 103, 104), including the liberal application of labels such as "free variation," "dialect mixture," and "stylistic variation," but for the first time linguists began to make such phenomena the object of study, and to examine them as they actually occurred within speech communities.

SOCIOLINGUISTICS, SOCIAL DIALECTS, AND VARIATION

In 1968, a classic review article by Gumperz (69) surveyed the interinfluence of geographic and social factors in the creation and maintenance of diverse linguistic repertoires in speech communities of various kinds. By the end of the 1960s it was thus well established that geography (geographic distance) alone was not sufficient to explain linguistic and dialect diversity, and that social differences among people living in the same geographical area were the basis of many systematic speech differences. Thus social and geographic factors were shown to be interrelated in differentiating speakers' "dialects." It is important to note that degrees of geographic distance in dialectology have been traditionally equated with relative lack of contact of populations or speakers, in itself a social factor, and work showing isoglosses spreading out from centers of prestige and influence (cf. e.g. Malkiel 118) has brought out very clearly the influence of social parameters. Though criticisms of dialectology based on its supposed reliance on geography alone and lack of attention to social factors (e.g. Dillard 50) are exaggerated, it is probably fair to say that the social assumptions underlying much of the work in dialectology were taken for granted and not investigated in any systematic way. Friedrich (61) has recently contrasted the characteristic European and American pattern of waves radiating out from urban centers with the different kinds of distribution of features occurring where relations between neighboring communities are essentially egalitarian.

Several authors attempted to reexamine some of the postulates of typological studies and their implications in terms of genetic and diffusionist types of explanation (cf. Afendras 1, Haugen 76, Pierce 130, Sherzer & Bauman 153). The sociolinguistic dimensions of the problem and their intimate connection with linguistic detail were brought into sharp focus by Gumperz & Wilson's (72) discussion of convergence in North India.

By the late 1960s, sociolinguistic work had also begun to show that most, and probably all, normal individuals possess a range of speech styles, registers, dialects, and even languages, such that the locus of the "homogeneous dialect" the linguist might wish to study also became problematic (Hymes 84). Descriptions of "dialects" and even "idiolects" thus had to incorporate considerations of cultural appropriateness, usually thought of in terms of contextual and situational factors (Ervin-Tripp 54, Hymes 83) and social meaning, construed as the interactional force and implication of register and code choice (Gumperz 70, Gumperz & Hernandez 71). Social roles and relationships were seen as important in the study of linguistic variation (Hannerz 74).

A number of descriptive studies of particular urban areas showed the complex interrelationships between the class, age, sex, ethnic, racial, and religious factors tending to differentiate the population in terms of speech varieties, and the stylistic variation socially defined in terms of type and function of speech event. Labov (98) again provided a model for many of these studies with his pioneering research in New York City, though there were earlier works of merit [e.g. Blanc (21) on Baghdad and Reinecke (136) on Hawaii]. More recent studies include Albo (3) on Cochabamba, Berntsen (19) on Phaltan, Cofer (36) on Philadelphia, Cedergren (31) on Panama City, Fasold (57) on Washington, Lavandera (111) on Buenos Aires, O'Cain (126) on Charleston, Sankoff & Cedergren (147) on Montreal, Trudgill (166) on Norwich, Wald (176) on Mombasa, and Wolfram (190) on Detroit. Levine & Crockett (116) and Pahlsson (127) also document systematic variation, and Shuy et al (154) published a field manual for urban language work.

The problems of how to deal theoretically with the kinds of variation these studies have demonstrated has been a key issue in the past several years. Labov (102) proposed the concept of "variable rules," demonstrating that phonological, syntactic, and social constraints have regular effects on the operation of rules, effects which are better construed as variables than as constants. Labov was criticized by Bickerton (20), who claimed that most of the variability Labov could not reduce to categorical behavior was an artifact of grouping individuals. Bickerton's own analysis draws on Bailey's work on the "wave theory" model (15, 16). According to Bailey, the diffusion of linguistic rules across speakers and across environments produces a situation in which dialects (or idiolects) can be arranged such that each differs from the next by a single rule condition. Bickerton argues that this tends to create implicational orderings of rules and speakers. Others who have worked on the use of scales and implicational relationships include DeCamp (45-47), Elliot et al (53), Ross (140), and Sag (142). Labov (109) countered Bickerton's arguments by showing the regularly variable patterns found for individual speakers, and argued that grouping individuals was therefore not equivalent to making a number of categorical grammars look like one variable grammar. This view was supported by Sankoff (145) and by Cedergren & D. Sankoff (32) in an elaboration of the mathematical foundations of the variable rule approach.

Fasold (56) provided a relatively early review of alternate models of "socially significant linguistic variation," but the problem continued to be an important one and was discussed at some length by participants in a conference on New Ways of Analyzing Variation in English, convened at Georgetown in October of 1972. Papers included those by Anshen (11), DeCamp (47), Fasold (58), Robson (138), Trudgill (167), Sankoff (146), and Wolfram (191), among many others. All are to be published in a volume edited by C.-J. Bailey and Roger Shuy. The growing interest in variation apparent in studies such as those by Hurford (81), Lehiste (115), and Straight (161) was furthered by the appearance in 1972 of the *Lectological Newsletter,* edited by C.-J. Bailey of Georgetown University.

Quantitative methods of some sort were used in many of the studies of socially significant variation mentioned above. They were also used in work where dialect differentiation was studied in terms of the traditional regional or geographic dimension, e.g. Afendras (1), Gersic (64), McKaughan (121), Miller et al (123), Piirainen (131), Voegelin et al (173), and Wood (192).

DISCUSSION

The past decade has seen a marked growth in the cross fertilization between dialectology and various other traditions in linguistics. Linguists have generally become more interested in problems arising from a perspective which views language as a socially situated vehicle of communication, and have found dialectologists able to contribute insights of importance in this area. If I have concentrated in this review on the burgeoning field of social dialectology, with only a summary treatment of developments in dialect atlas and structural dialectological work, it is only partly because this field is of particular interest to anthropologists. More importantly, it is the area which has seen the most rapid and fertile development and which promises continued interest during the 1970s.

Literature Cited

1. Afendras, A. E. 1970. Quantitative distinctive feature typologies and a demonstration of areal convergence. *Rev. Inst. Appl. Ling.* 9:49–81
2. Agard, F. B. 1971. Language and dialect: some tentative postulates. *Linguistics* 65:5–24
3. Albo, X. 1970. The social constraints of Cochabamba Quechua. Latin American Studies Program, Cornell Univ.
4. Aldus, J. B. 1969. Anglo-Irish dialects: a bibliography. *Reg. Lang. Stud.* 2:1–17
5. Allen, H. B., Underwood, G. N. 1971. *Readings in American Dialectology.* New York: Appleton-Century-Crofts. 584 pp.
6. Alleyne, M. C. 1971. Acculturation and the cultural matrix of creolization. In *Pidginization and Creolization of Languages,* ed. D. Hymes, 169–86. London: Cambridge Univ. Press

7. Althaus, H. P. 1969. Ansaetze und moeglichkeiten einer kontrastiven Sprachgeographie. *Z. Dialektol. Ling.* 36, 2:174–89
8. Anisfeld, E., Lambert, W. E. 1964. Evaluational reactions of bilingual and monolingual children to spoken languages. *J. Abnorm. Soc. Psychol.* 69, 1:89–97
9. Anshen, F. 1969. *Speech variation among Negroes in a small Southern community.* PhD thesis. Univ. New York
10. Anshen, F. 1970. A sociolinguistic analysis of a sound change. *Lang. Sci.* Feb. 1970:20–21
11. Anshen, F. 1972. *Some data which don't fit some.models.* Presented at 1st Ann. Colloq. on New Ways of Anal. Var. in Engl. Georgetown Univ.
12. Bach, A. 1950. *Deutsche Mundartforschung.* Heidelberg: C. Winter. 335 pp.

13. Bailey, B. L. 1966. *Jamaican Creole Syntax: A Transformational Approach.* Cambridge Univ. Press. 164 pp.
14. Bailey, B. L. 1971. Jamaican creole: can dialect boundaries be defined? See Ref. 6, 341–48
15. Bailey, C-J. N. 1969–70. Studies in three-dimensional linguistic theory: (1) some implicational phenomena in dialectology; (2) implicational scales in diachronic linguistics and dialectology; (3) lectal groupings in matrices generated with waves defined along the temporal parameter; (4) meso-models of linguistic change; (5) building rate into a dynamic theory of linguistic description. *Working Pap. Ling. Hawaii* 1,8:105–38; 1,10:245–49; 2,4:109–24; 2,6:-149–56; 2,9:161–233
16. Bailey, C-J. N. 1973. The patterning of language variation. In *Varieties of Present-day American English,* ed. R. W. Bailey, J. L. Robinson. Macmillan. In press
17. Braczi, G. 1963. Les recherches dialectologiques en Hongrie. *Orbis* 12:141–56
18. Bender, M. L., Cooper, R. L. 1971. Mutual intelligibility within Sidamo. *Lingua* 27:32–52
19. Berntsen, M. 1973. *The speech of Phaltan: a study in linguistic variation.* PhD thesis. Univ. Pennsylvania, Philadelphia
20. Bickerton, D. 1971. Inherent variability and variable rules. *Found. Lang.* 7:457–92
21. Blanc, H. 1964. *Communal Dialects in Baghdad. Harvard Middle Eastern Monogr. X.* Cambridge: Harvard Univ. Press. 204 pp.
22. Brook, G. L. 1963. *English Dialects.* London: Heffer. 232 pp.
23. Bush, C. N. 1971. Temporal ratios of sound segments and the perception of English dialect differences. *Int. Congr. Phonetic Sci.* 7:101
24. Butters, R. R. 1971. Dialect variants and linguistic deviance. *Found. Lang.* 7:239–54
25. Canfield, L. D. 1964. The diachronic dimension of 'synchronic' Hispanic dialectology. *Linguistics* 7:5–9
26. Carden, G. 1970. A note on conflicting idiolects. *Ling. Inq.* 1,3:281–90
27. Carden, G. 1970. A problem with primacy. *Ling. Inq.* 1:527–33
28. Carden, G. 1971. A dialect argument for *not*-transportation. *Ling. Inq.* 2:423–26
29. Carden, G. 1972. *Disambiguation, favored readings, and variable rules.* See Ref. 11
30. Cedergren, H. J. 1972. *On the nature of variable constraints.* See Ref. 11
31. Cedergren, H. J. 1972. Interplay of social and linguistic factors in Panama. PhD thesis. Cornell Univ.
32. Cedergren, H. J., Sankoff, D. 1973. Variable rules: performance as a statistical reflection of competence. To appear in *Language*
33. Chao, Y. R. 1967. Contrastive aspects of the Wu dialects. *Language* 43:92–101
34. Chen, M., Hsieh, H-I. 1971. The time variable in phonological change. *J. Ling.* 7:1–13
35. Cheng, C-C., Wang, W. S-Y. 1970. *Phonological Change of Middle Chinese Initials.* Univ. California, Berkeley, Dep. Ling. Project on Ling. Anal., 2nd Ser. 10. CW1–CW69
36. Cofer, T. 1972. *Linguistic variables in a Philadelphia speech community.* PhD thesis. Univ. Pennsylvania, Philadelphia
37. Cook, S. 1969. *Language change and the emergence of an urban dialect in Utah.* PhD thesis. Univ. Utah
38. Dauzat, A. 1944. *La Géographie Linguistique.* Paris. 200 pp.
39. Davis, A. L., McDavid, R. I., McDavid, V. G. 1969. *A compilation of the work sheets of the linguistic atlas of the United States and Canada and associated projects.* Univ. Chicago Press. 105 pp.
40. Davis, A. L., Davis, L. M. 1969. Recordings of standard English questionnaire. *Orbis* 18:385–404
41. Davis, L. M. 1969. Dialect research: mythology vs. reality. *Orbis* 18:332–37
42. Davis, L. M. 1970. Social dialectology in America: a critical survey. *J. Engl. Ling.* 4:46–56
43. Davis, L. M., Ed. 1972. *Studies in Linguistics Presented to Raven McDavid.* Univ. Alabama Press
44. Davis, P. W. 1970. A classification of the dissimilative jakan'e dialects of Russian. *Orbis* 19:360–76
45. DeCamp, D. 1971. Implicational scales and sociolinguistic linearity. *Linguistics* 73:30–43
46. DeCamp, D. 1971. Toward a generative analysis of a post-creole speech continuum. See Ref. 6, 349–70
47. DeCamp, D. 1972. *What do implicational scales imply?* See Ref. 11
48. DeGranda, G. 1970. The creole dialects in Spanish-speaking areas. *Orbis* 19:72–81
49. Delbouille, M. 1966. Reflexions sur la genese phonétique des parlers romains. *Cah. Saussure* 23:17–31

50. Dillard, J. L. 1969. The dare-ing old men on their flying isoglosses, or dialectology and dialect geography. *Fla. FL Rep.* 7,2:8–10; 22

51. Dillard, J. L. 1971. Lay my isogloss bundle down. *Nat. Conf. Ling. Int. Ling. Assoc.* 16,3

52. Dillard, J. L. 1971. The creolist and the study of Negro nondialects in the continental United States. See Ref. 6, 393–408

53. Elliot, D., Legum, S. L., Thompson, S. A. 1969. Syntactic variation as linguistic data. In *Papers from the Fifth Chicago Regional Meeting,* ed. R. Binnick et al, 52–59

54. Ervin-Tripp, S. 1972. On sociolinguistic rules: alternation and co-occurence. In *Directions in Sociolinguistics,* ed. J. J. Gumperz, D. Hymes, 213–50

55. Fairbanks, G. H. 1969. Language split. *Glossa* 3,1:49–66

56. Fasold, R. W. 1970. Two models of socially significant linguistic variation. *Language* 46:551–63

57. Fasold, R. W. 1972. *Tense Marking in Black English.* Washington, D.C.: Center Appl. Ling. 254 pp.

58. Fasold, R. W. 1972. The concept of 'earlier-later': more or less correct. See Ref. 11

59. Fasold, R. W., Shuy, R., Eds. 1970. *Teaching Standard English in the Inner City.* Washington, D.C.: Center Appl. Ling. 141 pp.

60. Friedrich, P. 1970. *Proto-Indo-European Trees.* Univ. Chicago Press. 188 pp.

61. Friedrich, P. 1971. Dialectal variation in Tarascan phonology. *Int. J. Am. Ling.* 37:164–87

62. Fujiwara, Y. 1967. Une histoire de la dialectologie japonaise. *Orbis* 16:35–45

63. Galffy, M. 1969. Questionnaire et structure de l'atlas dialectal: observations basées sur les travaux de l'atlas dialectal sicule. *Orbis* 18:405–11

64. Gersic, S. 1971. Die Berechnung der phonetischen Variabilitat; ein Beitrag zum objektiven Vergleich phonetischer Texte. (The computation of phonetic variation; a contribution to the objective comparison of phonetic texts.) *Int. Congr. Phonetic Sci.* 7:110–11

65. Gregg, R. J. 1971. Linguistic change observed: three types of phonological change in the Scotch-Irish (SI) dialects. *Int. Congr. Phonetic Sci.* 7:113–14

66. Griffith, J., Miner, L. E., Eds. 1970. *The First Lincolnland Conference on Dialectology.* Univ. Alabama Press. 188 pp.

67. Grootaers, W. A. 1964. La discussion autour des fontières dialectales subjectives. *Orbis* 13:380–98

68. Gumperz, J. J. 1966. On the ethnology of linguistic change. In *Sociolinguistics,* ed. W. Bright, 27–38. The Hague: Mouton. 324 pp.

69. Gumperz, J. J. 1968. The speech community. *Int. Encycl. Soc. Sci.* 9:381–86

70. Gumperz, J. J. 1970. Verbal strategies in multilingual communication. *Georgetown U. Monogr. Lang. Ling.* 23:129–47

71. Gumperz, J. J., Hernandez, E. 1969. *Cognitive aspects of bilingual communication.* Working Pap. No. 28, Lang. Behav. Res. Lab. Berkeley

72. Gumperz, J. J., Wilson, R. 1971. Convergence and creolization: a case from the Indo-Aryan/Dravidian border. See Ref. 6, 151–67

73. Hammarstroem, G. 1967. Zur soziolektalen und dialektalen Funktion der Sprach. *Z. Mundartforsch.* 34,3–4: 206–16

74. Hannerz, U. 1970. Language variation and social relationships. *Stud. Ling. Lund* 24:128–51

75. Haugen, E. 1967. Semicommunication: the language gap in Scandinavia. *Int. J. Am. Ling.* 33,4:152–69

76. Haugen, E. 1970. Linguistics and dialinguistics. *Georgetown U. Monogr. Lang. Ling.* 23:1–12

77. Heicke, G., Schindler, F. 1970. Versuche zur Dialektgeographie Akustisch-phonetischer Messwerte am Beispiel Schlesischer Mundartaufnahmen. *Z. Dialektol. Ling.* 37,1:26–43

78. Heiser, M. M. 1971. A diasystem of four southcentral French dialects. *Nat. Conf. Ling., Int. Ling. Assoc.* 16,2

79. Herzog, M., Ravid, W., Weinreich, U., Eds. 1969. *The Field of Yiddish: Studies in Language, Folklore, and Literature.* Third collection. The Hague: Mouton. 327 pp.

80. Hsieh, H-I. 1972. Lexical diffusion: evidence from child language acquisition. *Glossa* 6:89–104

81. Hurford, J. R. 1968. The range of contoidal articulations in a dialect. *Orbis* 17,2:389–95

82. Hutterer, C. J. 1968. Sieben Thesem zur Dialektforschung. *Acta Ling. Acad. Sci. Hung.* 18,3–4:279–86

83. Hymes, D. 1967. Models of the interaction of language and social setting. *J. Soc. Issues* 23, 2:8–28

84. Hymes, D. 1968. Linguistic problems in defining the concept of 'tribe.' In *Essays on the Problem of Tribe.* Proc. AES Ann. Spring Meet. 1967, ed. J. Helm, 23–48

174   SANKOFF

85. Ivic, P. 1963. Importance des caractéristiques structurales pour la description et la classification des dialectes. *Orbis* 12:117–31
86. Ivic, P. 1964. Structure and typology of dialectal differentiation. *Proc. 9th Int. Congr. Ling.,* 115–21. The Hague: Mouton
87. Ivic, P. 1971. Review of J. Goossens' *Strukturelle Sprachgeografie: eine Einfuhrung in Methodik und Ergebnisse* (structural linguistic geography: an introduction to methodology and results). Heidelberg: Carl Winter, 1969. *Language* 47:685–91
88. Jongen, R. 1969. Vergleichende Untersuchung des Lautmaterials verwandter Mundarten: zur Methodik der strukturellen Lautgeographie, Teil I. *Leuv. Bijdr.* 58,1:25–44
89. Kandori, T. 1968. Study of dialects in Japan. *Orbis* 17,1:47–56
90. Keyser, S. J. 1963. Review of *The Pronunciation of English in the Atlantic States,* by H. Kurath, R. I. McDavid. Ann Arbor: Univ. Michigan 1961. *Language* 39:303–16
91. Kiparsky, P. 1968. Linguistic universals and linguistic change. In *Universals in Linguistic Theory,* ed. E. Bach, R. Harms, 171–207. New York: Holt, Rinehart & Winston. 210 pp.
92. Kirk, P. L. 1970. Dialect intelligibility testing: the Mazatec study. *Int. J. Am. Ling.* 36:205–11
93. Kohler, K. J. 1967. Structural dialectology. *Z. Mundartforsch.* 34,1:40–44
94. Kurath, H. 1949. *A Word Geography of the Eastern United States.* Ann Arbor, Michigan. 88 pp., 163 full-page maps
95. Kurath, H., McDavid, R. I. 1961. *The Pronunciation of English in the Atlantic States.* Ann Arbor:Univ. Michigan. 182 pp., 180 full-page maps
96. Laberge, S. 1972. *Observation d'un changement linguistique: les pronoms indéfinis dans le français montréalais.* Thèse de maîtrise. Dep. d'Anthropol., Univ. Montréal
97. Labov, W. 1965. On the mechanism of linguistic change. In *Georgetown Univ. Monogr. Ser. Lang. Ling.,* ed. C. W. Kreidler, 91–114
98. Labov, W. 1966. *The Social Stratification of English in New York City.* Washington, D.C.: Center Appl. Ling. 655 pp.
99. Labov, W. 1966. The effect of social mobility on linguistic behavior. In *Explorations in Sociolinguistics,* ed. S. Lieberson. *Soc. Inq.* 36:186–203
100. Labov, W. 1966. Hypercorrection by the lower middle class as a factor in linguistic change. In *Sociolinguistics,* ed. W. Bright, 84–113. The Hague: Mouton
101. Labov, W. 1968. On the mechanism of linguistic change. *Georgetown Univ. Monogr. Lang. Ling.* 18:91–114
102. Labov, W. 1969. Contraction, deletion, and inherent variability of the English copula. *Language* 45:715–62
103. Labov, W. 1970. The study of language in its social context. *Stud. Gen.* 23:30–87
104. Labov, W. 1971. Methodology. In *A Survey of Linguistic Science,* ed. W. O. Dingwall, 412–91. Univ. Maryland Ling. Program. 810 pp.
105. Labov, W. 1971. The notion of 'system' in creole languages. See Ref. 6, 447–72
106. Labov, W. 1972. The recent history of some regional dialect markers on the island of Martha's Vineyard, Massachusetts. See Ref. 43, 81–121
107. Labov, W. 1972. The internal evolution of linguistic rules. In *Linguistic Change and Generative Theory,* ed. R. P. Stockwell, R. K. S. Macauley, 101–71. Bloomington: Indiana Univ. Press
108. Labov, W. 1972. *For an end to the uncontrolled use of linguistic intuitions.* Presented at Ling. Soc. Am. Ann. Meet., Atlanta
109. Labov, W. 1972. Where do grammars stop? *Georgetown Monogr. Lang. Ling. No. 25.* In press
110. Labov, W., Yeager, M., Steiner, R. 1972. *A quantitative study of a sound change in progress.* Rep. Nat. Sci. Found. Contract GS-3287
111. Lavandera, B. R. 1972. *A syntactic variable: if-clauses in Buenos Aires Spanish.* Presented at Ling. Soc. Am. 47th Ann. Meet., Atlanta
112. Lee, R. R. 1971. Dialect perception: a critical review and re-evaluation. *Quart. J. Speech* 57:410–17
113. Legum, S. E., Williams, C. E., Lee, M. T. 1969. Social dialects and their implications for beginning reading instruction. *Southwest Reg. Lab. Educ. Res. Develop. Tech. Rep.* 14:1–40
114. Legum, S. E., Pfaff, C., Tinnie, G., Nicholas, M. 1971. The speech of young black children in Los Angeles. *Southwest Reg. Lab. Educ. Res. Develop. Tech. Rep. 33*
115. Lehiste, I. 1970. Grammatical variability and the difference between native and non-native speakers. *Ohio State Univ. Working Pap. Ling.* 4:85–94

116. Levine, L., Crockett, H. J. 1966. Speech variation in a Piedmont community: postvocalic r. See Ref. 99, 76–98
117. Loflin, M. D. 1969. Negro non-standard and standard English: same or different deep structure? *Orbis* 18:74–91
118. Malkiel, Y. 1964. Some diachronic implications of fluid speech communities. *Am. Anthropol.* 66,6 pt.2:177
119. Marcellesi, J-B. 1971. Linguistique et groupes sociaux. *Langue Française* 9: 119–28
120. Mase, Y. 1964. Une nouvelle tentative pour tracer les frontières subjectives des dialectes. *Orbis* 13:357–67
121. McKaughan, H. 1964. A study of divergence in four New Guinea languages. *Am. Anthropol.* 66,4,pt.2:98–120
122. Mencken, H. L. 1963. *The American Language.* Abridged by R. I. McDavid Jr. with assistance of D. W. Maurer. New York: Knopf
123. Miller, W. R., Tanner, J-L., Foley, L. P. 1971. A lexicostatistic study of Shoshoni dialects. *Anthropol. Ling.* 13: 142–64
124. Moulton, W. C. 1968. Structural dialectology. *Language* 44:451–66
125. Obrecht, D. H. 1965. Toward automated phonological mapping. *Linguistics* 17:21–36
126. O'Cain, R. K. 1972. *A social dialect survey of Charleston, South Carolina.* PhD thesis. Univ. Chicago
127. Pahlsson, C. 1972. The Northumberland burr: a sociolinguistic study. *Lund Studies in English* 41, ed. C. Schaar, J. Svartik
128. Pederson, L. 1971. Southern speech and the LAGS project. *Orbis* 20:79–89
129. Pfaff, C. W. 1971. A coding system for the study of linguistic variation in Black English. *Southwest Reg. Lab. Educ. Res. Develop. Tech. Rep.* 38:1–51
130. Pierce, J. E. 1965. Hanis and Miluk: dialects or unrelated languages? *Int. J. Am. Ling.* 31:323–25
131. Piirainen, I. T. 1969. Quantitative Methoden in der Sprachforschung. *Ling. Ber.* 3:22–30
132. Pop, S. 1950. *La dialectologie.* Aperçu historique et méthodes d'enquêtes linguistiques. I. Dialectologie romance. II. Dialectologie non-romance. Univ. Louvain
133. Pulgram, E. 1964. Structural comparison, diasystems, and dialectology. *Linguistics* 4:66–82
134. Ramson, W. S., Ed. 1970. *English Transported: Essays on Australasian English.* Canberra: Australian Nat. Univ. 243 pp.
135. Reed, C. E. 1967. *Dialects of American English.* Cleveland: World Publ. 119 pp.
136. Reinecke, J. E. 1969. *Language and Dialect in Hawaii: A Sociolinguistic History to 1935.* Honolulu: Univ. Hawaii Press. 254 pp.
137. Riley, W. 1968. Competence or performance? A problem for dialectology. *Working Pap. Phonetics, UCLA* 10: 200–5
138. Robson, B. 1972. *Not-quite-rule-governed variation.* See Ref. 11
139. Rona, J. P. 1970. A structural view of sociolinguistics. In *Method and Theory in Linguistics,* ed. P. Garvin, 199–211. The Hague: Mouton. 336 pp.
140. Ross, J. R. 1972. The category squish: Endstation Hauptwort. In *Papers from the Eighth Chicago Meeting,* ed. P. M. Peranteau, J. N. Levi, G. C. Phares, 316–28. Chicago Ling. Soc.
141. Rulon, C. M. 1970. Distinctive feature phonology, rule ordering, and dialectal variation. *Pap. Ling.* 3:65–72
142. Sag, I. A. 1972. On the state of progress on progressives and statives. See Ref. 11
143. Saltarelli, M. 1966. Romance dialectology and generative grammar. *Orbis* 15:51–59
144. Sankoff, G. 1969. Mutual intelligibility, bilingualism and linguistic boundaries. In *International Days of Sociolinguistics,* 839–48. Rome: Istituto Luigi Sturzo
145. Sankoff, G. 1972. *A quantitative approach to the study of communicative competence.* Presented at Conf. on Ethnography of Speaking, Austin, Texas
146. Sankoff, G. 1972. *Above and beyond phonology in variable rules.* See Ref. 11
147. Sankoff, G., Cedergren, H. J. 1971. Some results of a sociolinguistic study of Montreal French. In *Linguistic Diversity in Canadian Society,* ed. R. Darnell, 61–87. Edmonton: Ling. Res.
148. Saporta, S. 1965. Ordered rules, dialect differences, and historical processes. *Language* 41:218–24
149. Scholes, R. I. 1968. Perceptual categorization of synthetic vowels as a tool in dialectology and typology. *Lang. Speech* 11,3:194–207
150. Schrader, E. 1967. Sprachsoziologische Aspekte der deutschen Wortgeographie. *Z. Mundartforsch.* 34,2:124–36
151. Section 3: *Géographie linguistique.* Actes Xe Congrès Int. Ling., 1970, Bucharest 2:1–225
152. Shanmugam, S. V. 1971. Dialects in inscriptional Tamil. *Orbis* 20:90–98
153. Sherzer, J., Bauman, R. 1972. Areal

studies and culture history: language as a key to the historical study of culture contact. *Southwest. J. Anthropol.* 28: 131–52

154. Shuy, R. W., Wolfram, W. A., Riley, W. K. 1968. *Field Techniques in an Urban Language Study.* Washington: Center Appl. Ling. 128 pp.

155. Smith, K. D. 1969. Sedang ethnodialects. *Anthropol. Ling.* 11: 143–47

156. Sobelman, H., Ed. 1962. *Arabic Dialect Studies: A Selected Bibliography.* Washington: Center Appl. Ling. and Middle East Inst. 100 pp.

157. Spangenberg, K. 1967. Sprachsoziologie und Dialektforschung. *Wiss. Z.* 16, 5:567–75. Schiller Univ., Jena

158. Stankiewicz, E. 1957. On discreteness and continuity in structural dialectology. *Word* 13:44–59

159. Stewart, W. A. 1971. Observations (1966) on the problems of defining Negro dialect. *Florida FL Reporter* 9:47–49;57

160. Stieber, Z. 1968. Le problème de la frontière entre deux langues slaves. *Word* 24, 1–3:476–78

161. Straight, S. 1972. *Yucatec Maya pedolectology: segmental phonology.* PhD thesis. Univ. Chicago. 258 pp.

162. Tarone, E. 1969. A selected bibliography on social dialects for teachers of speech and English. *Florida FL Reporter* 7:23

163. Theban, L. 1968. Géographie linguistique; typologie, sociolinguistique. *Rev. Roum. Ling.* 13,6:659–63

164. Tokugawa, M., Kato, M. 1966. Introduction to the linguistic atlas of Japan. *Orbis* 15,2:388–96

165. Traugott, E. C. 1972. *Historical linguistics and its relation to studies of language acquisition and of pidgins and creoles.* Lectures at Univ. California Santa Cruz, August 1972

166. Trudgill, P. J. 1971. *The social differentiation of English in Norwich.* PhD thesis. Edinburgh Univ.

167. Trudgill, P. J. 1972. *Diasystemic rules and variation in Norwich English.* See Ref. 11

168. T'sou, B. K. 1972. Reordering in diachronic syntax. See Ref. 140

169. Tsuzaki, S. M. 1971. Coexistent systems in language variation: the case of Hawaiian English. See Ref. 6

170. Ullrich, H. E. 1971. Linguistic aspects of antiquity: a dialect study. *Anthropol. Ling.* 13:106–13

171. Vasiliu, E. 1966. Towards a generative phonology of Daco-Rumanian dialects. *J. Ling.* 2:79–98

172. Voegelin, C. F., Harris, Z. S. 1951. Methods for determining intelligibility among dialects of natural languages. *Proc. Am. Phil. Soc.* 45:322–29

173. Voegelin, C. F., Voegelin, F. M., Wurm, S., O'Grady, G., Matsuda, T. 1963. Obtaining an index of phonological differentiation from the construction of non-existent minimax systems. *Int. J. Am. Ling.* 29:4–28

174. von Raffler Engel, W. 1971. International and vowel correlates in contrasting dialects. *Int. Congr. Phonetic Sci.* 7:143

175. Vulpe, M. 1967. Fapt dialectal si fapt popular. *Stud. Cerc. Ling.* 18,4:369–77 (Rumanian)

176. Wald, B. V. 1973. *Variation in the system of tense markers of Mombasa Swahili.* PhD thesis. Columbia Univ.

177. Weijnen, A. 1968. Zum Wert subjektiver Dialektgrenzen. *Lingua* 21: 594–96

178. Weijnen, A., Hagen, A. 1967. Introduction a l' "Interlinguale Comparatieve Atlas (ICA)." *Orbis* 16:23–34

179. Weinreich, U. 1954. Is a structural dialectology possible? *Word* 10:388–400

180. Weinreich, U. 1962. Multilingual dialectology and the new Yiddish Atlas. *Anthropol. Ling.* 4:6–22

181. Weinreich, U. 1964. Four riddles in bilingual dialectology. In *American Contributions to the Fifth International Congress of Slavists,* 335–59. The Hague: Mouton

182. Weinreich, U., Ed. 1965. *The Field of Yiddish: Studies in Language, Folklore, and Literature.* Second collection. The Hague: Mouton. 289 pp.

183. Weinreich, U. 1969. The geographic makeup of Belorussian Yiddish. See Ref. 79, 82–101

184. Weinreich, U., Labov, W., Herzog, M. 1968. Empirical foundations for a theory of language change. In *Directions for Historical Linguistics,* ed. W. P. Lehmann, Y. Malkiel, 97–195. Austin: Univ. Texas Press. 199 pp.

185. Wells, J. C. 1970. Local accents in England and Wales. *J. Ling.* 6:231–52

186. Wendell, M. V. 1971. Relative intelligibility of five dialects of English. *Ohio State Univ. Working Pap. Ling.* 9: 166–91

187. Williams, F., Whitehead, J. L., Miller, L. M. 1971. Ethnic stereotyping and

judgments of children's speech. *Speech Monogr.* 38:166–70

188. Williamson, J. V., Burke, V. M., Eds. 1971. *A Various Language: Perspectives on American Dialects.* New York: Holt, Rinehart & Winston. 706 pp.

189. Willis, C. 1971. Synthetic vowel categorization and dialectology. *Lang. Speech* 14:213–28

190. Wolfram, W. A. 1969. *A Sociolinguistic Description of Detroit Negro Speech.*

Washington: Center Appl. Ling. 237 pp.

191. Wolfram, W. A. *On what basis variable rules?* See Ref. 11

192. Wood, G. R. 1970. On ways to examine the local language. *Computer Stud. in Hum. Verbal Behav.* 3:100–10

193. Yamagiwa, J. K. 1967. On dialect intelligibility in Japan. *Anthropol. Ling.* 10:1–17

ETHNOGRAPHIC FILM: STRUCTURE AND FUNCTION

❖ 9526

Timothy Asch,[1] John Marshall,[1] and Peter Spier

Anthropology Department, Brandeis University, Waltham, Massachusetts

> I call our world Flatland, not because we call it so, but to make its nature clearer to you, my happy readers, who are privileged to live in Space.
>
> —Edwin Abbott *Flatland*

Pad and pencil are the traditional tools of the anthropologist, but they are by no means the only tools. The use of camera and film, particularly over the last 5 years, has grown to the point where they might be considered as important as the notebook in any research project. However, taking pictures purely for the sake of taking pictures is next to useless. An anthropologist must understand the potential of the camera as a recording device, and he must have a clear understanding of why he is carrying all that extra weight into the field. This paper is an attempt to outline some of these principles and to explore ways in which film made by the ethnographic team can be used on its return from the field.

The value of the camera lies in its ability to do and record what the human eye cannot. Film can stop time, merely slow it, or compress hours into seconds. It can, in this way, view subjects as small, like gestures, facial expressions, and body synchronizations, or as large, like patterns of travel within a village, as the filmmaker desires. The camera will also, with special films, record phenomena beyond the visible spectra and discover patterns of motion or land use that the unaided eye could never see (4).

The aim of ethnographic film is to preserve, in the mind of the viewer, the structure of the events it is recording as interpreted by the participants. This is often a very difficult task, and is in many ways determined by the way in which the film is taken and by how it is handled after it is shot. The camera has position in both time and space, and therefore imposes a perspective on any action. Turning a camera on and off is an automatic structuring of events, as determined by the bias of the camera operator. Editing is another selection process and a second restructuring. Skillful editing can lead an audience to almost any desired conclusion. Finally, because each viewer possesses a different background, the significance attached to

[1]Co-Director of Documentary Educational Resources, Somerville, Massachusetts.

179

any particular segment of a film by one person will be different from that attached by another, restructuring the event for a third time for each viewer. For an ethnographic filmmaker to be successful he must thoroughly understand his people, and he must do his best to let the indigenous structure guide him in his recording efforts.

Traditionally, filmmaking has fallen into three basic methodological categories, as outlined on the opposite page:

Objective Recording

Objective records are characterized by a structure which is imposed by the action. The use of film records may be broken down into two main subcategories, descriptive and analytical. Descriptive film originated in about 1898, its predecessor being the use of still photography to preserve and demonstrate social and cultural forms. At first anthropologists collected only isolated images, and later, many images of the same subject taken in sequence. With the development of motion picture technology anthropologists began to bring movies back with them from the field. From 1900 to the early 1940s few of these films were ever edited, but were shown, like most home movies, as the original camera rolls. Editing gave the process a new sophistication, but the greatest advances in ethnographic film have come since 1965 with the development of easily portable sound-synchronous equipment (2).

Some descriptive films have attempted to record, from a remote view, as much data as one can get on a particular behavioral process. One example of such an enterprise is Marvin Harris' study of working class welfare families in the Bronx. In this study several hundred hours of video tape were made, at selected times, by remote control cameras placed in various locations throughout several apartments. Richard Sorenson has proposed a similar type of study with only one camera, which would photograph an entire New Guinea village for a brief time at fixed intervals. The aim of this kind of study is to record actual behavior, as contrasted with behavior described by the participants. Dr. Sorenson has also proposed an archive for the deposit of such film, and has further developed the idea into a National Ethnographic Film Archive where Data Films, consisting of all footage, synchronous sound, translation and commentary sound tracks, and written ethnographic material will be stored and made available to scholars to perform research on any aspect of the culture recorded (3). While the Archive's main intent is to store record films for research use, it is not restricted to this category, and films in all categories have already been contributed by several people.

The analytical film has shared the early development of the descriptive film and is, in some ways, an outgrowth of it. In this form the film is examined, often frame by frame, to discover patterns which cannot be seen without the ability to repeat the action over and over again. A classic example of this, done primarily with rapid-sequence still photographs, is Mead & Bateson's 1936–1939 study of parent-child interaction in Bali (1). More recently, people like Birdwhistell, Scheflen, Eckman, Kendon, Condon, Lomax, Bullowa, Byers, Hall, and Erickson have been able to use frame-by-frame film analyses to investigate the communication process. Occasionally, after the data analysis is complete, film is cut and assembled to

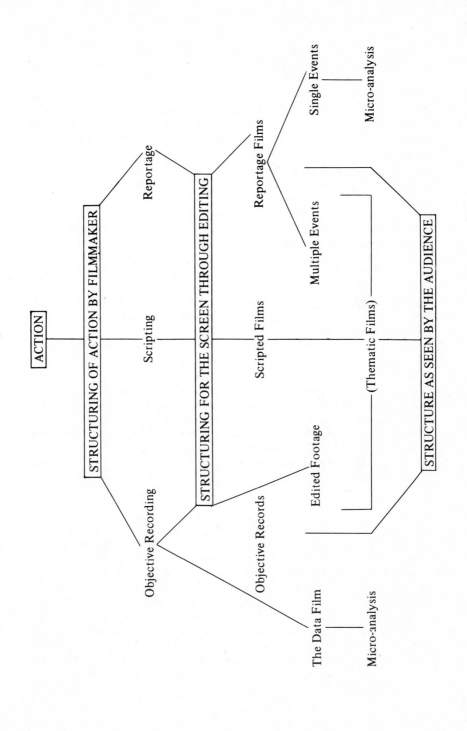

demonstrate the discovered principles, as in Birdwhistell's *Microcultural Incidents in Ten Zoos.*

Scripted Filming

The second category, scripted films, is characterized by a structure which is imposed by the filmmaker. These are often longer, feature films designed to illustrate a particular theme about the culture they depict. The fieldworker embarks on his expedition with an idea he wishes to illustrate, or he may discover an idea as his work progresses. On his return he will select only those segments, out of thousands of feet shot, which best fit his scheme. The remaining footage is unfortunately seldom seen by anyone else and is often thrown out after several years for lack of adequate storage facilities.

While many films of this genre were influenced by Hollywood traditions, ethnographic films have left their mark on Hollywood as well. Flaherty's classic, *Nanook of the North,* is one example. Films like *Nanook,* Cooper & Schoendsack's *Grass,* John Marshall's *The Hunters,* and Robert Gardner's *Dead Birds* offer excellent general introductory ethnographic material for teaching when backed up with appropriate additional presentations. However, one should always point out to students the internal bias inherent in any directed effort and explain the theme each film was made to illustrate.

Scripted films are also an excellent means of expressing ideas we have about our own cultures, as Jorge Preloran's *Imaginero* and *Ruca Choroy,* or even Ozu's *Tokyo Story* and Sembene's *Emitai* which, although they are entirely conceived and produced for a commercial audience, may actually be some of the best own-society ethnographic documents we have. Another interesting example in this regard is Sol Worth's experiment to allow Navajo Indians to film their own society (5).

Reconstruction projects, like Asen Balikci's Netsilik Eskimo films and Roger Sandall's Australian Aborigine studies, deserve special note in this category since, although they are scripted, they are attempts to record a vanishing culture before it is totally lost.

Reportage

Reportage film is the category which is probably best able to preserve the indigenous structure of an event as the footage goes through the restructuring process. While on the surface there is a great similarity between reportage and record films, the distinctions are crucial to anthropological work. The subject matter of reportage is always an event or a complete segment of life. A recorder can be turned on and off at any time, and can be focused on anything which appears significant. Records may be made by an untrained observer from the very moment he first enters a strange society. No one, however, can report a society, its values, life style, patterns of daily routine, cosmology, etc., until he has spent time in it and can approach a comprehension of its members as they comprehend themselves, or to put it in other words, until they share a cognitive map. This map is built on the analysis of experience, which includes any data in the records he has collected.

What this implies is that the anthropologist, when he enters a strange society, is at first shooting blind, if he is shooting at all. As he becomes familiar with his people he can see patterns in their lives, and he can find units of life, with definite beginnings and ends, with which the people will agree. It is the filming of these discreet units which constitutes reportage.

At present there are only a few people engaged in reportage, which is still in something of a developmental stage. An understanding of exactly how far the technique has come may be had through close examination of some of the work of John Marshall. *Debe's Tantrum* depicts a Bushman child, Debe, who is determined to accompany his mother on a gathering trip. When she refuses to take him he throws a tantrum, and in the end, gets his way. The film opens with the beginning of the tantrum. While the shooting is extremely tight, and the entire conflict is depicted, the sequence is incomplete in that it lacks the context (the gathering trip) and the trigger (his mother's refusal) which are added in Mr. Marshall's narrative introduction. In this sense it is a record, rather than a complete report. *An Argument About a Marriage* a slightly more complex film about a disputed marriage, suffers from some of the same problems, but a slightly less intimate shooting style does much to give the film a context.

Mr. Marshall's more recent work with the Pittsburgh police, notably *Three Domestics,* has done a great deal to correct the context problem. Filming is initiated somewhat sooner than with the Bushman studies, so that the police are actually seen to arrive at the scene of each quarrel, and filming is stopped only after they have left. While a great deal of understanding is gained simply by the fact that these films are made in our own society, it is the recognition that life segments include both causes and consequences, as well as the actual action, which enables these films to communicate with the audience.

Reportage is not limited to conflict, although conflicts are easy units to define, and sequences may easily be strung together to portray a broader theme. One good example is Jean Rouch's *Les Maitres Fous,* in which one event in the lives of members of the Hauca cult is examined in great detail and then placed in the larger context of modern Accra life. Other examples would be the films of Wiseman, Leacock, Pennebaker, and Drew.

Of course, the entire context of an event is not always available in real time for the anthropologist to capture on film. This is a genuine problem for teaching, which is probably the most important use of ethnographic film, and a problem which is not easily solved. It has been traditionally felt that film, the visual image, should be complete in itself. This, unfortunately, has seldom been possible. Filling in information with narration has been tried with varying success, but the more narration a film contains the more guidance it gives the audience, and the less opportunity it gives them to draw their own conclusions from their observations.

Karl Heider has proposed one possible solution, the written module, which would accompany the ethnographic film. This module would contain general ethnographic background for the event filmed, a shot by shot description of the action, and kinship charts, maps, and other materials to define the relationships between the participants in the action. This eliminates the need to include this material at the beginning of each film, and is actually a better way to give students background and a framework for viewing since they may read a module as many times as they like before viewing a film, and they may bring it to class and refer back to the charts as the action proceeds. This leaves the image free to convey the action as it happened, and it allows the student more room to draw his own conclusions from what he can observe in a type of in-class "fieldwork." Dr. Heider has already written the first of these modules, for *Dead Birds,* which is available from Warner Modular Publications.

While the module might be considered as a way out for the filmmaker, a sort of patent medicine which will cure all the ills he discovers in his film on his return from the field, a far more important aspect is to use it as a way into teaching. The foundation of anthropology is the field study. Unfortunately, most students are presented only with distilled data and conclusions, intermingled with theory. While it is indeed these ideas which are important, students do not get the opportunity, until they are forced to do their own fieldwork, to see where the data comes from or how the theories are formed. Film, when properly shot and presented, can actually bring the field to the classroom and allows for a sort of on-the-job training.

Reportage film, that is film shot using the sequence method, presents whole single units of behavior, the units trained anthropologists study. The written module presents background that the anthropologist has spent 18 months or more in the field gathering, and a perspective for viewing which 6 or 8 years of training has instilled in him. With all of this information the student is virtually thrown into the field situation, and when asked to draw conclusions he is faced with much the same problems as those encountered by the trained fieldworker.

The making of high quality ethnographic film sequences is a large job which requires the close cooperation of an anthropologist and a filmmaker. Napoleon Chagnon and Timothy Asch, working under a grant from the National Science Foundation, are developing a curriculum using this approach based on fieldwork done with the Yanomamö Indians of Venezuela and Brazil. Asch and Chagnon have 100,000 feet of color film, all shot in sequence style, which they are in the process of editing into approximately 50 short films, each of a single event, which may be used in any number and combination that a professor desires. Because they present no thematic viewpoint, these films in conjunction with the modules may be used to teach a great variety of anthropological principles. Chagnon and Asch hope that others will adopt this approach to ethnographic filmmaking so that similar materials will be available from other societies. They would also like to point out that sequence style shooting is the most efficient method for filming in the field for such things as kinesic studies, since each sequence may be distilled into its component parts. In addition to using independent units, one can use several such unit sequences in conjunction to present a general theme for classroom instruction.

At the 1970 Belmont Ethnographic Film Conference, the Anthropology Film Research Institute (AFRI) was established. At present it has a committee to set guidelines for making ethnographic film and a committee for the development of a world ethnographic film sample. However, for most of the members of the institute, the urgent task is the development of a National Ethnographic Film Archive, planned at present for the Smithsonian Institution in Washington. When an archive is established we can begin to properly gather, preserve, and use what footage we have which represents the way man has lived on this planet for thousands of years, and we can begin to develop standards for the production of ethnographic film which will be most useful for teaching and research. It is the opinion of many in this field that the camera can be to the anthropologist what the telescope is to the astronomer or what the microscope is to the biologist.

Literature Cited

1. Bateson, G., Mead, M. 1942. *Balinese Character, A Photographic Analysis. NY Acad. Sci.* 2
2. Pincus, E. 1969. *Guide to Filmmaking.* New York: New American Library
3. Sorenson, E. R. 1967. A research film program in the study of changing man. *Curr. Anthropol.* 8, 5:443–69
4. Vogt, E. Z., Ed. 1974. *The Uses of Aerial Photography in Anthropological Research.* Cambridge: Harvard Univ. Press. In press
5. Worth, S., Adair, J. 1972. *Through Navajo Eyes.* Bloomington: Indiana Univ. Press

letter. Washington, D.C.: Am. Anthropol. Assoc.

Wolf, G., Robineaux, R., Eds. *Research Film/Film de Recherche/Forschungsfilm.* Goettingen, W. Germany: Institut für den Wissenschaftlichen Film

Bibliographies

Bouman, J. C. 1954. Bibliography of Filmology as Related to the Social Sciences. *UNESCO Reports and Papers on Mass Communication* 9

de Brigard, E. R. 1974. *Anthropological Cinema.* New York: Museum of Modern Art. In press

McGrath, E. M. 1972. *Uses of Film in the Study of Human Behavior: The Social Scientist as Film-maker and Film Analyst.* Presented at African Studies Assoc., Philadelphia

Ruby, J. 1968. *Film and Anthropology.* Philadelphia: Temple Univ.

Trotter, R. T. 1972. *The Ethnographic Use of Film: A Review Article.* Dallas: Southern Methodist Univ.

SELECTED BIBLIOGRAPHY

Film Index

Comité International du Film Ethnographique et Sociologique 1967. Premier catalogue sélectif international de films ethnographique sur l'Afrique noire. Paris: UNESCO

Comité International du Film Ethnographique et Sociologique 1970. Premier catalogue sélectif international de films ethnographique sur la region du Pacifique. Paris: UNESCO

Comité International du Film Ethnographique et Sociologique 1973. Premier catalogue sélectif international de films ethnographique sur l'Asie et le Moyen Orient. In press (approximate title)

Heider, K. G., Ed. 1972. *Films for Anthropological Teaching.* Washington, D.C.: Am. Anthropol. Assoc. 5th ed.

Periodicals

James, C. A., Reining, C. C., Topper, M., Eds. *Media Anthropologist.* Largo, Md.: Prince George Community College

Williams, C., Ruby, J., Seltzer, J., Eds. Program in Ethnographic Film. *News-*

Books and Articles

Asch, T. 1972. *New Methods for Making and Using Ethnographic Film.* Presented to Research Film Committee, African Studies Assoc. Philadelphia

Asch, T. 1972. Making Ethnographic Film for Teaching and Research. Program in Ethnographic Film. *Newsletter* 3:2

Asch, T. 1974. Audio Visual Materials in the Teaching of Anthropology from Elementary School through College. In *Education and Cultural Process: Towards an Anthropology of Education,* G. Spindler. New York: Holt, Rinehart & Winston. In press

Asch, T. 1974. *Visual Presentation in the Classroom: Toward the Development of Pedagogy for the Use of Audiovisual*

Materials in Teaching Anthropology. To be presented at 9th Int. Congr. Anthropol. Ethnol. Sci. In *Visual Anthropology,* ed. Paul Hockings. The Hague: Mouton

Balikci, A., Brown, Q. 1966. *Ethnographic Filming and the Netsilik Eskimos.* Cambridge, Mass.: Education Services

Bateson, G., Mead, M. 1942. *Balinese Character, A Photographic Analysis.* NY Acad. Sci. 2

Bennett, J. W. 1960. Individual Perspective in Fieldwork: An Experimental Training Course. In *Human Organization Research Field Relations and Techniques.*

Birdwhistell, R. L. 1970. *Kinesics and Context.* Philadelphia: Univ. Pennsylvania

Birdwhistell, R. L. 1955. Kinesic Analysis of Filmed Behavior of Children. In *Transactions* (conference on Group Processes), ed. B. Schaffner, 141–45

de Brigard, E. R. 1974. *Anthropological Cinema.* New York: Museum of Modern Art. In press

Bullowa, M., Jones, L. G., Beber, T. G. 1964. The Development from Vocal to Verbal Behavior in Children. *Monogr. Soc. Res. Child Develop.* 29:1

Byers, P. 1966. Cameras Don't Take Pictures. *Columbia Univ. Forum* IX:1, 27–31. New York: Columbia Univ.

Calder-Marshall, A. 1963. *The Innocent Eye: The Life of Robert Y. Flaherty.* New York: Harcourt, Brace & World

Collier, J. 1967. *Visual Anthropology: Photography as a Research Method.* New York: Holt, Rinehart & Winston

Condon, W., Ogston, W. D. 1968. Sound Film Analysis of Normal and Pathological Behavior. *Neurol. Ment. Dis.* 142: 2–237

Dunlop, I. 1968. *Retrospective Review of Australian Ethnographic Films: 1901–1967.* Lindfield, Australia: Australian Commonwealth Film Unit

Ekman, P., Frieson, W., Taussig, T. 1969. II VID-R and SCAN: Tools and Methods for the Automated Analysis of Visual Records. *Content Analysis,* ed. G. Gerbner, O. Holsti, K. Krippendorff, W. Paisley, P. Stone. New York: Wiley

Gardner, R. 1967. Anthropology and Films. *Daedalus* 86:344–50

Griffith, R. 1953. *The World of Robert Flaherty.* New York: Duell, Sloan & Pearce

Heider, K. G. 1972. *The Dani of West Irian.* Andover, Mass.: Warner Modular Publ.

Heusch, L. de 1962. The Cinema and the Social Sciences: A Survey of Ethnographic and Sociological Films. *UNESCO Reports and Papers in the Social Sciences* 16

Hitchcock, J. T., Hitchcock, P. 1960. Some Considerations for the Prospective Ethnographic Cinematographer. *Am. Anthropol.* 62, 4:656–74

Hockings, P. 1968. *Ethnographic Film at UCLA.* Presented at the Am. Anthropol. Assoc. Meet., Seattle

Jablonko, A. 1964. *Ethnographic Film as Basic Data for Analysis.* Presented at 7th Int. Congr. Anthropol. Ethnol. Sci., Moscow

Jablonko, A. 1968. *Dance and Daily Activities Among the Maring People of New Guinea. A Cinematographic Analysis of Body Movement Style.* PhD thesis. Columbia Univ.

Lomax, A. 1968. Folk Song Style and Culture. *Am. Assoc. Advan. Sci.* 88:248–73

Lomax, A., Bartenieff, I., Paulay, F. 1969. Choreometrics: A Method for the Study of Cross-Cultural Pattern in Film. *Res. Film* 6:6–505

Lomax, A. 1971. Toward an Ethnographic Film Archive. *Filmmakers Newsletter* 4:4–31

MacDougall, D. 1969. Prospects of the Ethnographic Film. *Film Quart.* 23, 2: 16–30

Mead, M., MacGregor, F. C. 1951. *Growth and Culture: A Photographic Study of Balinese Childhood.* New York: Putnam

Mead, M. 1963. Anthropology and the Camera. In *The Encyclopedia of Photography,* ed. W. D. Morgan. New York: Nat. Educ. Alliance. 2nd ed.

Metraux, R. 1955. Five illustrations of Film Analysis. In *The Study of Culture at a Distance,* ed. M. Mead, R. Metraux. Chicago Univ. Press

Michaelis, A. R. 1955. *The Research Film in Biology, Anthropology, Psychology and Medicine.* New York: Academic

Notcutt, L. A., Latham, G. C. 1937. *The African and the Cinema.* Edinburgh House Press

Pincus, E. 1969. *Guide to Filmmaking.* New York: New Am. Libr.

Polonin, I. 1966. *Visual and Sound Recording in Ethnographic Field Work.* Presented at 11th Pac. Sci. Congr., Tokyo

Regnault, F. 1931. Le Role du Cinema en Ethnographie. *Nature* 2866:304

Rouch, J. 1955. Cinema d'Exploration et Ethnographie. *Connaissance du Monde* 1: 69–78

Ruby, J. 1971. Towards an Anthropological Cinema. *Film Comment* 7, 1: 35–39

Sandall, R. 1972. Observation and Identity. *Sight and Sound* 41:4, 192–96

Scheflen, A. E. 1964. The Significance of Posture in Communications Systems. *Psychiatry* 27:316–31

Sorenson, E. R. 1967. A Research Film Program in the Study of Changing Man. *Curr. Anthropol.* 8, 5:443–69

Sorenson, E. R., Gajdusek, D. C. 1963. *Research Films for the Study of Child Growth and Development and Disease Patterns in Primitive Cultures: A Catalogue of Research Films in Ethropediatrics.* Bethesda: N. I. H. Nat. Inst. Neurol. Dis. Blindness

Sorenson, E. R., Gajdusek, D. C. 1966. The Study of Child Behavior and Development in Primitive Cultures. *Pediatrics* 37, 1:2

Spannaus, G. 1955. Theoretische und Praktishche Probleme des Weissenschaftlichen Films (Theoretical and Practical Problems of Scientific and Ethnographic Films). In *Von fremden Volkern und Kulturen* (Foreign Peoples and Cultures), ed. W. Lang, W. Nippold, G. Spannaus. Dusseldorf: Hans Plischke zum 65 Geburtstage: Droste Verlag

Speed, F. 1970. The Function of the Film as Historical Record. *African Notes* 6, 1:46

Stoney, G. C. 1971. Film, Videotape and Social Change. *J. Univ. Film Assoc.* 23, 4:108

Vogt, E. Z., Ed. 1974. *The Uses of Aerial Photography in Anthropological Research.* Cambridge: Harvard Univ. Press. In press

Williams, C. W. 1968. *The Future of Moving—Image Communication in Anthropology.* Presented at Soc. Motion Pict. Telev. Eng. Tech. Conf., New York

Wolfenstein, M., Leites, N. 1950. *Movies: a Psychological Study.* Glencoe, Ill.: Free Press

Wolfenstein, M. 1955. Movie Analyses in the Study of Culture. In *The Study of Culture at a Distance,* ed. M. Mead, R. Metraux. Chicago Univ. Press

Worth, S., Adair, J. 1972. *Through Navajo Eyes.* Bloomington: Indiana Univ. Press

Worth, S. 1968. *Toward the Development of a Semiotics of Ethnographic Film.* Presented at Am. Anthropol. Assoc. Meet., Seattle

Zimmerly, D. 1968. *Ethnographic Filming.* Presented at Colo.-Wyo. Acad. Sci. Meet., Laramie

MATHEMATICAL ANTHROPOLOGY ❖9527

Michael L. Burton

School of Social Sciences, University of California, Irvine

This review is written at a time of great activity in mathematical anthropology, including the recent publication of edited volumes by Kay on mathematical anthropology (35), by Romney, Shepard & Nerlove on multidimensional scaling (50), and by Buchler & Nutini on game theory (8). In addition there have been recent reviews of the field by White (63) and Hoffman (31). Space does not permit a complete discussion of all instances where mathematics may have a place in anthropology, so I have chosen to emphasize some topics which have not been fully discussed in the other two review articles. These are measurement problems, some probabilistic topics in social organization, and spatial analyses.

MEASUREMENT MODELS IN ANTHROPOLOGY

Basic Concepts

Hoffman (31) discusses some of the basic mathematical concepts which are relevant to measurement, such as the concept of a distance metric. A good introduction to the theory of scaling is Torgerson (61), who distinguishes among nominal, ordinal, interval, and ratio scales. A nominal scale is simply a categorization; an ordinal scale is a rank-ordering; an interval scale has real-number measures of distance; and a ratio scale is an interval scale with a zero point. A distance metric must satisfy three conditions: positivity, symmetry, and the triangle inequality. The first states that all distances are non-negative, and that distinct entities have non-zero distance. The second says that $d(x,y) = d(y,x)$ for any y and x. The third states that for any entities x and y, and any third entity z, $d(x,y) \leq d(x,z) + d(y,z)$; in other words, a direct path between x and y cannot be longer than a path through some third point. A special case, the ultrametric inequality, is of interest for the study of hierarchical structures, such as taxonomies: $d(x,y) \leq \max(d(x,z), d(y,z))$.

Distances may be measured either on a straight line or in a space of several dimensions. Multidimensional scaling procedures solve problems having to do with the placement of points in such spaces. A theorem due to Young & Householder (67) is the underpinning for much of the later work in multidimensional scaling. It specifies conditions under which a symmetric N by N array of numbers may be represented as distances in a space of r dimensions, where $r \leq N-1$. Torgerson (61) includes a good description of the multidimensional scaling problem. Recent advances in multidimensional scaling due to Shepard (52, 53), Kruskal (39, 40), and Young (66) have resulted in the ready availability of computer programs which do multidimensional scaling analyses. These are called nonmetric multidimensional scaling procedures because they assume only a monotonic increasing relationship between dissimilarities in the input data and distances in the scaled configuration. Whitley (64) makes a comparative discussion of three such computer programs, with some cautions about their robustness. A multidimensional scaling analysis produces an r-tuple for each point, where r is the number of dimensions of the space. The investigator has to choose the value of r. For each dimension, $k, X_{i,k}$ is the value of point i on that dimension. The usual distance metric is the Euclidean metric,

$$D(i, j) = \sqrt{\sum_{k=1}^{r} (X_{ik} - X_{jk})^2}$$

which is a generalization of the Pythagorean theorem. The things which are represented as points in the space are any kind of cultural objects, such as words, beliefs, sentences, groups of people, or individual actors.

Goals of Measurement

Measurement problems are ubiquitous in anthropology. They range from the simple task of counting a single frequency, as with content analysis of text (17), to the construction of structures which contain multiple, interrelated measures. The goal can be to describe a single observation with greater accuracy than is possible solely with words, or to build a complex model with many parts. Although it is natural to contrast discrete mathematics to continuous mathematics, many structures from discrete mathematics have natural representations in continuous distance models. The tree structure is a good example.[1] Johnson (32) has published a procedure for measuring distance on tree structures, utilizing the ultrametric inequality. This makes possible the construction of tree structures from continuous measures of similarity or dissimilarity, obtained from judgments such as the triads test. So anthropologists, who have long been interested in hierarchical models of semantics, now have available to them mathematical treatments of such models both as discrete and continuous phenomena. Another mathematical entity which mixes discrete and continuous notions is the network, which is a directed graph with some value on each line. This value can be a continuous measure, such as the rate of flow. Examples are the flow of traffic on highways or the flow of fluids in pipelines.

The most popular topics for measurement in anthropology seem to be the study of cultural evolution, models of semantics, and measurement of social organization variables such as the rate of divorce (2) or the propensity to endogamy (47).

[1]Kay (36) has recently produced an elegant formalization of the concept of taxonomy.

Similarity Measures for Nominal Data

A wide variety of anthropological data takes the form of a matrix of zeros and ones. These cases include: cross-cultural data where societies (the rows of the matrix) are rated on the presence or absence of traits (the columns); and semantic data where sentences (the rows) are judged for the semantic appropriateness when different words (the columns) are substituted into slots or judgments are made about the assignment of beliefs to diseases (23). A problem common to all these cases is the measurement of the similarity of row items to other row items based on their distribution across columns. For example, beliefs can be considered to be similar if they are believed to be true for similar sets of diseases, or cultures can be considered to be similar if they have the same traits.

The general form of this kind of data is that each row item is judged as to the truth or falsity of a number of propositions. These propositions are of the forms "X culture has trait i," or "Y belief is appropriate to disease j." Let X and Y be two row items whose similarity is to be computed. Let $n(X)$ be the number of propositions which are true for X, $n(Y)$ be the number of propositions which are true for Y, $n(XY)$ be the number of propositions which are true for both and N the size of the total set of propositions. Stefflre, Reich & McClaran-Stefflre (57) define the measure

$$S_{x, y} = \frac{2(n(XY))}{n(X) + n(Y)}$$

Majone & Sanday (41) argue against the use of correlation coefficients for this kind of data, and propose two distance measures which satisfy the metric axioms:

$$D_1 (X, Y) = \frac{n(X) + n(Y) - 2n(XY)}{N}$$

$$D_2 (X, Y) = \frac{n(X) + n(Y) - 2n(XY)}{n(x) + n(Y) - n(XY)}$$

Both sets of authors use the derived measures as input to a cluster analysis procedure.

The Guttman Scale Model

The Guttman scale, or scalogram, is a model for categorical data (27, 61). The data may have to do with beliefs which are held by different people, with the presence or absence of various possessions in households (34), with the ascription of social taboos to kintypes (29), or with the rating of cultures by institutions (14–16). The Guttman model assumes an underlying unidimensional continuum, a set of attributes and a set of actors. Each attribute is a nominal scale which partitions the continuum into two or more categories. Each actor occupies a point on the continuum. The actor's response to each attribute depends upon the category into which he falls on the continuum. Guttman scaling is often done with binary attributes, coded as the presence or absence of some trait. In this case, the data matrix contains zeros and ones. However, it should be noted that Guttman scaling is not restricted to binary attributes. The Guttman model is a deterministic model. It is unlikely that real data will fit the model exactly. The coefficient of reproducibility measures the degree of fit of data to the model. The Guttman model is not appropriate as a model of multidimensional variation, so there are many scaling situations which it cannot handle.

Kronenfeld (38) discusses applications of Guttman scaling to anthropology. He suggests caution in the interpretation of coefficients of reproducibility. For certain kinds of data, the minimum possible coefficient of reproducibility for any ordering may be as high as .80. To obtain a high reproducibility coefficient does not guarantee the existence of a "true" unidimensional scale. Kronenfeld discusses Buchler's scaling of Crow- and Omaha-type kinship terminologies (7) in light of this caution.

Carneiro (14–16) has published a series of studies on the evolution of cultures, using the scalogram technique. His latest model uses 354 culture traits (16). His Index of Culture Accumulation is a measure of how many traits a culture has. It correlates strongly to population size (14). Thus, for Carneiro, evolution is seen as an increase in the number of culture traits. The traits which he includes in his sample fall very neatly into a Guttman scale, with high reproducibility So far, all is fine. However, there are some difficulties with Carneiro's model. The first is that his list of traits does not include the kind of traits which are known to be associated with societies with simple technologies and small community populations. Some of those traits are totemism, section systems, belief in soul travel during sleep, shamanism, mother-in-law avoidances, menstrual taboos, male puberty rites, the couvade, and postpartum sex taboos. The exclusion of those traits adds a bias towards the conclusion that technologically advanced societies are also more complex culturally. In addition, Carneiro purposely excludes traits which do not accumulate with time. An example is slavery, which seems to be most frequent in cultures on the middle of Carneiro's scale. The point here is that some procedure for random sampling of traits is as important as a procedure for random sampling of cultures. Unfortunately, the universe in this case is the set of all possible culture traits, which is an ambiguous concept. A final problem is that some of the relationships in Carneiro's Guttman scale are tautological. For example, his scale of 33 traits in Anglo-Saxon kingdoms (15) includes the items "communities of 100 or more," "towns of 2000 or more," "city of 10,000 or more," and "two or more cities." There is only one possible ordering of these four items. It is obvious that kingdoms with towns of 2000 or more will also have communities of 100 or more, as the former are the latter by definition. Another example is the traits "craft specialization," "full-time craft specialists," "state/church employs artisans," which also have only one possible ordering, by definition.

A recent paper by D'Andrade (22) suggests a procedure for the analysis of beliefs which could be used to replace Guttman scaling with binary attributes. It is more general in that it allows for various kinds of partial orderings of traits as well as the complete ordering implicit in a scalogram. The idea is that if attribute A precedes attribute B on a scale, then a contingency table for the two attributes will have a zero cell. There will be no cases where B is present and A is absent. D'Andrade proposes to compute the contingency tables for all attribute pairs and isolate those with zero cells. A perfect Guttman scale would be represented as a chain of precedence relations which includes all attributes. This procedure will also find other interesting kinds of logical relations among attributes, such as complementary distribution.

Models of Preference or Rank Ordering

A useful task, particularly for studies of social organization and semantics, is the construction of rank orderings on evaluative scales, such as power, prestige, or wealth. Two possibilities are the rating of actual people on such scales as part of a study of social organization, and the rating of lexical items on such scales as part of a study of cognitive organization. For many items it becomes quite difficult for a person to make the judgments required in constructing a complete rank-ordering. An alternative procedure is the method of paired comparisons (61). In this task, the judge compares each item to each other item on the evaluative dimension. This focus on a specific discrimination between two items prevents the cognitive overload involved with a complete rank-ordering. It also allows the possibility of intransitivities. An early model of the judgment process, Thurstone's law of comparative judgment (61), allows the construction of interval scales from aggregated paired-comparison data. Freed (25) has an alternative procedure for aggregating paired-comparison data into a rank-ordering, which works well for his data on caste orderings in India. Since the number of pairs for N items is $N(N-1)/2$, the number of judgments required for a complete paired-comparison task can be large. Burton (10) uses a balanced incomplete design for the paired-comparison task to reduce the number of judgments, while maintaining the reliability of the final scale. This uses a method derived from Gulliksen (28) for constructing the aggregated scale from incomplete data.

Roberts, Strand & Burmeister (45) study cultural differences in preference patterns, using direct sum ratio scales (61). They take as an example preference for different combinations of shirts and shoes. Subjects are presented with combinations of different numbers of shoes and shirts, two at a time, and express their preference for one as a ratio from the set (1:9, 2:8, 3:7, 4:6, 5:5, 6:4, 7:3, 8:2, 9:1). An example would be the choice between (three shirts, two pairs of shoes) and (two shirts, four pairs of shoes). From this data, the authors construct an average preference value for each combination and draw indifference curves for the two kinds of goods. These curves vary markedly between cultures and have high concordance within cultures. Some of them have opposite curvature than would be predicted by standard economic theory. Myers & Roberts (43) extend this technique to study preferences of Puerto Rican women for different combinations of male and female children.

The Multidimensional Model

At the present time, multidimensional scaling models have found applications to research in cognitive anthropology, cross-cultural studies, archeology, and historical linguistics. The nonmetric multidimensional scaling techniques require proximities or dissimilarities measures as input. Since dissimilarities measures are simply some kind of inverse transformation of proximities measures, I shall refer only to the latter in the following discussion. How to measure proximities is a separate problem from the multidimensional scaling problem. Ideally, the proximities measures are based on some kind of theory of the data collection process (20). Burton (11) shows that different similarities measures on the same data can result in quite different multidimensional scaling configurations.

In archeology, Gelford (26) and Cowgill (21) suggest the multidimensional model for seriation. Cowgill measures similarity between sites based on the percentage of shared artifact types. The multidimensional scaling of that data in one dimension could order the sites in a time series. This is a possible substitute for existing methods for chronological ordering by computer (1). Gelford measures similarity between artifacts, where there is a k-tuple for each artifact of values on attributes. He uses a city-block metric to measure distance between artifacts.

In cross-cultural studies, Bowden (4, 5) uses a kind of multidimensional model, the latent-distance model, to represent cultural evolution. He transforms correlation coefficients among societies into distances, and scales the societies in three dimensions. Like Carneiro, he excludes from the sample all variables which do not accumulate with evolution. He also excludes variables which do not have a high loading on the first factor of a preliminary factor analysis. These two actions tend to bias the data towards the kind of structure he is seeking.

In historical linguistics, Kirk & Epling (37) use cluster analysis and multidimensional scaling to reconstruct a taxonomy of Polynesian languages, using cognate data. This interesting approach to the problem of language classification also includes a computer simulation of the dispersal of the Polynesian peoples.

In cognitive anthropology, proximities among lexemes, beliefs, or other entities are based on a variety of different judgmental tasks, including the triads test (49), sentence frame substitutions (23, 56, 57), word associations (58), construction of binary trees (24), and the Q-sort (9–12, 42). Typically, data for the different tasks on the same entities have moderately high correlations (58). Two purposes are possible in scaling of cognitive anthropological data. The first is to test a particular model, as with Romney & D'Andrade's test of a componential analysis of English kin terms (49). The second use is as a heuristic device for the construction of a model. In the former case, the model is often some kind of feature model of semantics, and the investigator is searching for an alignment of axes in the multidimensional space which maps onto the hypothesized features. In the second case, the investigator observes the clusters of points in the space and attempts to find a reasonable interpretation for them. The multidimensional analysis is often done in conjunction with a cluster analysis (10, 23) such as Johnson's hierarchical clustering method (32). Several different kinds of structures may be represented by multidimensional configurations. These include cluster structures resulting from hierarchies, circular structures as with Romney's study of color terminology (48), componential paradigms (24, 44, 49, 62), and rank-orderings along evaluative dimensions. As an example of the latter case, Burton (10) tests the hypothesis that aggregat ed Q-sort data preserves information about the prestige ranking of occupations, and that the ranking implicit in a scaling of similarities data will be the same as the rank-ordering obtained from paired-comparison data.

With the triads test, subjects respond to three stimuli at a time. In one version of the test they pick the stimulus which is most different. In the complete method of triads they also pick the two stimuli which are most different from each other. This provides a complete rank-ordering of distances among the three stimuli; but does not provide a complete rank-ordering of all distances among all stimuli. The proximity measure for two stimuli is simply the frequency with which they are classified together. The number of possible triads out of N stimuli is proportional to the cube of N, so that it is not practical to utilize all possible triads for N greater than about 12. Burton & Nerlove (13) propose the use of balanced, incomplete block designs for the triads test. With such a design, each pair of stimuli occurs in the same number of triads. Such designs appear to provide stable data when that number is two or greater. Balanced designs make possible the use of the triads test for up to 25 stimuli.

Miller (42) uses the Q-sort to collect data on similarities among items in general vocabulary. With this task, words are written on cards which subjects sort into piles. The piles may each have different numbers of words, from 1 to N. They induce a partition on the set of words, each pile constituting a cell of that partition. Miller defines a distance measure based on aggregated Q-sort data. Burton (11) defines three more distance measures and shows that all four measures satisfy the ultrametric inequality. These measures differ in the amount of weight they assign to fine discriminations, as opposed to high-level contrasts.

Most multidimensional scaling analyses are done on data which are aggregated across individuals. This glosses over individual variability. It is possible to define similarity measures for pairs of individuals. Wexler & Romney study individual variability on triads responses for English kinship data (62), and Boorman & Arabie (3) define similarities measures on individuals for Q-sort data. Wish, Deutsch & Biener (65) study individual differences in perceived similarity of nations.

An interesting alternative procedure for the analysis of proximities data can be found in Sade (51), where a clique analysis is used to cluster interaction frequency data. This same technique could be used to do cluster analysis of semantic similarities data.

SOCIAL CATEGORIZATION SYSTEMS

Anthropological studies of social categorization have focused mainly on kinship. In that area, Boyd, Sailer & Haehl (6) have carried applications of algebraic group theory a step further by proposing the inverse semigroup as the natural model for the representation of genealogical systems.

There has long been some interest in information measurement theory as a device for the study of social categorization systems. Collier & Bricker (19) compute information measures of the efficiency of six different name codes for Zinacantan. Thompson (60) does an information theoretic analysis of choice of compadres in Ticul, Yucatan. In the first case, the object is to find which name code is most specific in the sense that there are few instances of two or more people sharing the same name. The authors assert that this name code, which has highest entropy, is also the one which is used most frequently. In the second case, Thompson finds that people who marry patrilocally have a 50–50 chance of choosing nonkin as compadres, but that people who marry matrilocally have an 80–20 preference for kinsmen as compadres. He measures the information content of those two probabilities. A problem with this is that it seems unlikely that any people in Ticul are actually cognizant of the two probabilities. Thus the information content of the two "messages" is known only to the anthropologist.

Hoffman (30) and Thompson (59) do Markov process studies of the probabilities of people making transitions from one social category to another. The Markov model assumes that there is a constant probability of a transition from category i to category j in one time period: P_{ij}. Given an initial distribution of people across categories, it is possible to predict that distribution for the next time period. It is also possible to predict a steady-state distribution of people across categories for the distant future. Hoffman treats the Galla age-grade system as a three state Markov chain, where the states are youth, adult, and senior citizen. The transition probabilities measure the likelihood that a person whose father entered the system in state i will himself enter the system in state j. Thompson obtains a categorization of people in Ticul into six named social classes through elicitation techniques, and has native judges rate fathers and sons for social class identification. From this he can measure the probabilities of a transition from class i to class j in one generation. A crucial question with this study is whether the transition probabilities are indeed constant over time. To ascertain this would require observations of considerable time depth.

Romney (47) develops a model for measurement of the probability of endogamous marriage among members of two or more social categories. This model assumes a two-stage marriage process. In the first stage people meet, and in the second stage they decide whether or not to marry. The probability of meeting is determined by the relative sizes of the two groups. The marriage decision is determined by relative preferences for endogamy or exogamy. For two groups of the same size, Romney defines a measure of endogamy

$$ e = \frac{d - \bar{o}}{d + \bar{o}} $$

where d is the total number of endogamous marriages in the sample, and o is the total number of exogamous marriages. For cases where the two groups are of different sizes, this measure cannot be computed until the data have been normalized for group size. Romney develops an iterative procedure for transforming marriage data for unequal group sizes to equivalent data for equal group sizes. The endogamy measure is computed on the latter data. He also does a computer simulation which tests the accuracy of the iterative procedure. Using the iterative procedure, he is able to show that the Purum data has only two departures out of 128 marriages from a perfect connubium, after adjustment for group size.

MODELS OF SPATIAL PROCESSES

There has been increasing anthropological interest in interrelationships among communities. A manifestation of this is the recent interest in peasant marketing systems. Skinner (54) uses the central-place model from mathematical geography to explain the location of Chinese peasant market centers. In a recent work along the same lines, Smith (55) develops a model of the market networks for much of Guatemala. A second topic with strong potential for anthropological studies of spatial relations is diffusion theory, which has had rapid growth as an independent topic in social science. Rogers (46) summarizes many of the findings of diffusion research. Coleman (18) has a mathematical treatment of diffusion, including a derivation of the logistic curve for adoption of innovations. A good survey of potential anthropological models of diffusion has been done by Jordan (33). The few recent efforts in anthropology to do mathematical studies of spatial phenomena demonstrate the usefulness of borrowing from the other mathematical social sciences to improve model building in anthropology.

Literature Cited

1. Ascher, M., Ascher, R. 1963. Chronological ordering by computer. *Am. Anthropol.* 65:1045–52
2. Barnes, J. A. 1967. The frequency of divorce. In *The Craft of Social Anthropology,* ed. A. L. Epstein, 47–100. London: Tavistock
3. Boorman, S. A., Arabie, P. 1972. Structural measures and the method of sorting. See Ref. 50, 1:226–48
4. Bowden, E. 1969. An index of sociocultural development applicable to precivilized societies. *Am. Anthropol.* 71:454–61
5. Ibid. A dimensional model of multilinear sociocultural evolution, 864–70
6. Boyd, J. P., Haehl, J. N., Sailer, L. D. 1972. Kinship systems and inverse semigroups. *J. Math. Sociol.* 2:37–61
7. Buchler, I. R. 1964. Measuring the development of kinship terminologies: scalogram and transformational accounts of Crow-type systems. *Am. Anthropol.* 66: 765–88

8. Buchler, I. R., Nutini, H. G. 1969. *Game Theory in the Behavioral Sciences.* Univ. Pittsburgh Press
9. Burton, M. L. 1968. *Multidimensional Scaling of Role Terms.* PhD thesis. Stanford Univ.
10. Burton, M. L. 1972. Semantic dimensions of occupational names. See Ref. 50, 1:55–71
11. Burton, M. L. 1972. *Similarity Measures for a Sorting Task.* Working paper 7, Sch. Soc. Sci., Univ. California, Irvine
12. Burton, M. L. 1972. *A model for the semantics of behavior concepts in English.* Presented at Ann. Meet. Southwest Anthropol. Assoc., Long Beach
13. Burton, M. L., Nerlove, S. B. 1970. *Brevity with balance: an exploration of a judged similarity test.* Presented at workshop on cognitive organization and psychological process, Huntington Beach, California
14. Carneiro, R. L. 1967. On the relationship between size of population and com-

plexity of social organization. *Southwest. J. Anthropol.* 23:234–43
15. Ibid 1968. Ascertaining, testing, and interpreting sequences of cultural development. 24:354–74
16. Carneiro, R. L. 1970. Scale analysis, evolutionary sequences, and the rating of cultures. In *Handbook of Method in Cultural Anthropology,* ed. R. Naroll, R. Cohen, 834–71. Garden City: Natural History Press
17. Colby, B. N. 1971. The shape of narrative concern in Japanese folktales. See Ref. 35, 117–26
18. Coleman, J. S. 1964. *Introduction to Mathematical Sociology.* New York: Free Press
19. Collier, G. A., Bricker, V. R. 1970. Nicknames and social structure in Zinancantan. *Am. Anthropol.* 72:289–302
20. Coombs, C. H. 1964. *A Theory of Data.* New York: Wiley
21. Cowgill, G. 1968. Archeological applications of factor, cluster and proximity analysis. *Am. Antiq.* 33:367–75
22. D'Andrade, R. G. 1971. *A propositional analysis of U.S. American beliefs about illness.* Presented at Math. Soc. Sci. Board Workshop on Natural Decision Making, Palo Alto, 1971
23. D'Andrade, R. G., Quinn, N. R., Nerlove, S. B., Romney, A. K. 1972. Categories of disease in American-English and Mexican-Spanish. See Ref. 50, 2:9–54
24. Fillenbaum, S., Rapoport, A. 1971. *Structures in the Subjective Lexicon.* New York: Academic
25. Freed, S. A. 1963. An objective method for determining the collective caste hierarchy of an Indian village. *Am. Anthropol.* 65:879–91
26. Gelford, A. E. 1971. Seriation methods for archeological materials. *Am. Antiq.* 36:263–74
27. Goodenough, W. 1951. *Property, Kin and Community on Truk.* Yale Univ. Publ. Anthropol. 46. New Haven: Dep. Anthropol., Yale Univ.
28. Gulliksen, H. 1956. A least squares solution for paired comparisons with incomplete data. *Psychometrika* 21:125–34
29. Hage, P. 1969. A Guttman scale analysis of Tikopia speech taboos. *Southwest. J. Anthropol.* 25:96–104
30. Hoffman, H. 1971. Markov chains in Ethiopia. See Ref. 35, 181–90
31. Hoffman, H. 1969. Mathematical anthropology. *Bien. Rev. Anthropol.* 6: 41–79
32. Johnson, S. C. 1967. Hierarchical clustering schemes. *Psychometrika* 32: 241–54

33. Jordan, B. 1971. *Diffusion, Models and Computer Analysis.* MA thesis. Sacramento State Coll.
34. Kay, P. 1964. A Guttman scale model of Tahitian consumer behavior. *Southwest. J. Anthropol.* 20:160–67
35. Kay, P., Ed. 1971. *Explorations in Mathematical Anthropology.* Cambridge: MIT Press
36. Kay P. 1971. Taxonomy and semantic contrast. *Language* 47:866–87
37. Kirk, J., Epling, P. J. 1972. *The Dispersal of the Polynesian Peoples.* Working Papers in Methodology 6, Univ. North Carolina, Chapel Hill
38. Kronenfeld, D. 1972. Guttman scaling: problems of conceptual domain, unidimensionality and historical inference. *Man* 7:255–76
39. Kruskal, J. B. 1964. Multidimensional scaling by optimizing goodness of fit to a nonmetric hypothesis. *Psychometrika* 29:1–27
40. Ibid. Nonmetric multidimensional scaling: a numerical method, 115–29
41. Majone, G., Sanday, P. R. 1971. On the numerical classification of nominal data. See Ref. 35, 226–41
42. Miller, G. 1969. A psychological method to investigate verbal concepts. *J. Math. Psychol.* 6:169–91
43. Myers, G. C., Roberts, J. M. 1968. A technique for measuring preferential family size and composition. *Eugen. Quart.* 15: 164–72
44. Nerlove, S. B., Burton, M. L. 1972. A further examination of cognitive aspects of English kin terms. *Am. Anthropol.* 74:1249–53
45. Roberts, J. M., Strand, R. F., Burmeister, E. 1971. Preferential pattern analysis. See Ref. 35, 242–68
46. Rogers, E. M., Shoemaker, F. F. 1971. *Communication of Innovations, A Cross-Cultural Approach.* New York: Free Press
47. Romney, A. K. 1971. Measuring endogamy. See Ref. 35, 192–213
48. Romney, A. K. 1972. Multidimensional scaling and semantic domains. *The Study of Man* 1:1–19. Univ. California Irvine, Sch. Soc. Sci.
49. Romney, A. K., D'Andrade, R. G. 1964. Cognitive aspects of English kin terms. In *Transcultural Studies in Cognition,* ed. A. K. Romney, R. G. D'Andrade, 146–70. *Am. Anthropol.* 66(3):part 2
50. Romney, A. K., Shepard, R. N., Nerlove, S. B., Eds. 1972. *Multidimensional Scaling, Theory and Applications in the Behavioral Sciences.* New York: Seminar Press. 2 vols.

51. Sade, D. S. Sociometrics of *Macaca mulatta. Folia Primatol.* In press
52. Shepard, R. N. 1962. The analysis of proximities. *Psychometrika* 27:125–40
53. Shepard, R. N. 1966. Metric structures in ordinal data. *J. Math. Psychol.* 3:287–315
54. Skinner, G. W. 1964. Marketing and social structure in rural China, part 1. *J. Asian Stud.,* 3–43
55. Smith, C. 1971. *The Marketing System in Western Guatemala.* PhD thesis. Stanford Univ.
56. Stefflre, V. J. 1972. Some applications of multidimensional scaling to social science problems. See Ref. 50, 2:211–43
57. Stefflre, V. J., Reich, P., McClaran-Stefflre, M. 1971. Some eliciting and computational procedures for descriptive semantics. See Ref. 35, 79–116
58. Szalay, L. B., D'Andrade, R. G. 1972. Scaling versus content analysis: interpreting word association data from Americans and Koreans. *Southwest. J. Anthropol.* 28:50–68
59. Thompson, R. A. 1970. Stochastics and structure: culture change and social mobility in a Yucatec town. *Southwest. J. Anthropol.* 26:354–74
60. Ibid 1971. Structural statistics and structural mechanics: the analysis of Compadrazgo. 27:381–403
61. Torgerson, W. S. 1958. *Theory and Methods of Scaling.* New York: Wiley
62. Wexler, K. N., Romney, A. K. 1972. Individual variations in cognitive structures. See Ref. 50, 2:73–92
63. White, D. R. 1972. Mathematical anthropology. In *Handbook of Social and Cultural Anthropology,* ed. J. J. Honigmann. Chicago: Rand McNally. 1232 pp.
64. Whitley, V. 1971. *Problems in Multidimensional Scaling.* PhD thesis. Univ. California, Irvine. 121 pp.
65. Wish, M., Deutsch, M., Biener, L. 1972. Differences in perceived similarity of nations. See Ref. 50, 289–313
66. Young, F. W. 1967. TORSCA, A FORTRAN IV program for Shepard-Kruskal multidimensional scaling analysis. *Behav. Sci.* 12:498
67. Young, G., Householder, A. S. 1938. Discussion of a set of points in terms of their mutual distances. *Psychometrika* 3:19–22

CURRENT DIRECTIONS IN SOUTHWESTERN ARCHAEOLOGY[1]

❖ 9528

William A. Longacre

Department of Anthropology, University of Arizona, Tucson

INTRODUCTION

In 1924 I thought I knew a good deal about the Southwest . . . how very wrong I was. But, . . . I was not nearly as wrong as was he who advised me, just 50 years ago, to take up work in another field because, he said: "The Southwest is a sucked orange." I only wish I could return to that wonderful country and wet my aged lips once again in the rich juice of a fruit which a half-century of research has little more than begun to tap (Kidder 90, p. 322)

Today we can look back upon nearly 100 years of archaeological research in the southwestern United States, but Kidder's description still holds true. The archaeology of the Southwest is probably better known than that of any other comparable region in the world. And yet the tempo of prehistoric investigations seems to be increasing there rather than diminishing.

The reason for the increased tempo of research, I submit, lies in the fact that so much is already known about the development of culture and the specifics of culture history in the Southwest. This along with the development of fine-scale chronological control through dendrochronology for many parts of the area presents the anthropological archaeologist with an ideal region in which to test hypotheses that go beyond developing regional chronologies and reconstructing the lifeways of presently extinct peoples. The Southwest seems to be an optimum laboratory for the archaeologist interested in developing the theory and methods for describing and *explaining* processes of cultural change and stability that operated over long periods of time in the past. The fact that so much is known about the prehistoric Southwest means that archaeologists are, perhaps, freer to concentrate on questions of more cross-cultural relevance, to test hypotheses that are atemporal and aspatial that are of concern to general anthropology.

[1]See NAPS document No. 02100 for 30 pages of supplementary material. Order from ASIS/NAPS, c/o Microfiche Publications, 305 E. 46th St., New York, NY 10017. Remit in advance for each NAPS accession number $1.50 for microfiche or $5.00 for photocopies up to 30 pages, 15¢ for each additional page. Make checks payable to Microfiche Publications.

In the past 15 years or so, there does seem to be an increasing concern on the part of Southwestern archaeologists to go beyond reconstructing culture history, a development that is, of course, not restricted to the American Southwest. Some writers have referred to these developments as the advent of the "new archaeology" or "processual archaeology." Martin (114), evaluating the impact of these developments on Southwestern archaeology, labeled them revolutionary, and Leone (96) recently reviewed the issues for archaeology in general. Part of my task in presenting this discussion of current directions in Southwestern archaeology will be to assess the impact of these recent developments in the field.

In order to undertake this task, I have decided to focus upon the more recent publications reporting the results of archaeological research in the Southwest. I arbitrarily chose 1967 as a base date and I have not included many materials published before that date. In going through the literature, I have tried to uncover themes underlying diverse research endeavors and to discover common directions that might be useful in predicting future research interests that we might expect in the Southwest.

To support the argument that the Southwest is certainly not a "sucked orange," I need only point out that since 1967 there have been more than 500 articles, monographs, reports, and books published on Southwestern archaeology. Indeed, between 1967 and 1972, 39 doctoral dissertations in this country were written on problems in Southwestern archaeology. This large number of publications precludes my discussing each contribution or any one of them in any depth. Rather, I will organize my review in terms of themes and directions. First, I will turn to see what seem to be important new directions in Southwestern archaeology, presenting a critical review of some of the newer developments. Of particular interest here is the recent development of the Southwestern Anthropological Research Group (Gumerman 57, 58), which I discuss in some detail. Then I turn to continuing directions in Southwestern archaeology, including the publication of the results of excavations (description), areal syntheses, and recent contributions to culture history in the Southwest. Emphasis is upon those contributions that deal with relatively less well known parts of the Southwest, or contributions that suggest new interpretations or are in other ways controversial. The final section of the review attempts to summarize our present position and points out what seem to me to be likely future directions in Southwestern archaeological research.

NEW DIRECTIONS

One of the more interesting of the new directions in Southwestern archaeology has been the appearance over the past decade of a series of studies that can be described as examples of the "new archaeology" (Hammond 65). In the most general sense, these studies represent new directions in that they focus upon organizational and behaviorial aspects of extinct societies and attempt to *explain* changes in these extinct societies within an ecological frame of reference (Martin 113). Many of the questions that are being asked are not necessarily new (Longacre 108), but many of the methods and certain aspects of the theory structuring these investigations do represent new or changed directions. The application of the scientific method in a more formalized way as a means for testing hypotheses and discovering cross-cultural regularities or laws is an important dimension of these recent developments (Fritz & Plog 45, Hill 72, Schiffer 134, Tuggle, Townsend & Riley 150).

An increased concern with demonstration, including the testing of alternative hypotheses, is one important aspect of these recent studies. For example, there have been several attempts to deal with prehistoric social organization beyond arguments of plausibility based largely in ethnographic analogy with modern Southwestern Pueblo peoples. One study was undertaken in east-central Arizona at the Carter Ranch site, dating at about A.D. 1150 (Longacre 105, 106). The distribution of 175 design attributes on pottery was analyzed, using a multiple regression technique that measured the covariation among the attributes and their provenience at the site. The clustering of stylistic phenomena taken in conjunction with the architectural pattern of the site and the highly patterned cemetary suggested the presence of at least two residence units. These units were maintained for several generations, and inheritance of some things (rooms, access to a cemetery, and certain ceremonial activity) seems to be in the female line.

Broken K Pueblo, a site in the same area dating around A.D. 1250, was studied by Hill (71, 73; Martin, Longacre & Hill 115). He employed a factor analysis in his research and was able to suggest both continuity and change in behavioral aspects compared to the earlier Carter Ranch site. The size of the residence units had remained constant but they were combined into larger social units. Changes such as this were related to a changing environment (Hill & Hevly 75).

These studies have received a great deal of criticism. Most of the criticism has been constructive, and among the most useful have been the comments by Stanislawski (145, 146). His arguments are based largely upon his recent and continuing studies of modern potters at several of the Hopi villages in Arizona. Although some of his arguments do not seem particularly relevant to an interpretation of these prehistoric communities, he does suggest some interesting alternative models that might produce a similar array of stylistic variability in a prehistoric pueblo. One should be able to generate more formal test implications for these alternative models and test them on prehistoric data. To date, Stanislawski has based his criticisms largely upon what his informants have told him and not upon a detailed analysis of the actual distribution of design attributes in the modern Hopi context. I would hope that his research includes plans to undertake such analyses that would make his study more comparable to those undertaken thus far in prehistoric pueblo villages.

There have been several other studies that have focused upon aspects of prehistoric social organization in the Southwest. Some of these are summarized in a recent book specifically designed to explore the nature of social organization in the Pueblo area (Longacre 107). Dean (29–31) reports the results of a carefully controlled analysis of late Pueblo III sites in Tsegi Canyon, northeastern Arizona. He undertook an analysis of the pattern of architectural growth at several sites but with primary emphasis on two of the largest, Betatakin and Kiet Siel. Augmenting the architectural study with a systematic dendrochronological analysis, Dean was not only able to identify the households that make up the communities, but he was also able to point out the dynamics of the founding and growth of these pueblo towns. He was able to argue that the basic structural unit of the village was the extended family and that postmarital residence was probably matrilocal. His study demonstrates the critical nature of refined chronological controls in the study of extinct social systems.

Vivian (151, 152) has undertaken a series of studies of water control systems and social organization in Chaco Canyon, New Mexico. Noting the association of massive water control systems and even prehistoric roads with the larger towns in the canyon, and the lack of such systems at the contemporaneous villages, he is able to argue that a different form of organization was operative in the two forms of communities. DiPeso (32, 33) has suggested that the towns in Chaco Canyon were drawn into a formalized trading network organized in Mexico and that the dynamics of that economic interaction must be understood in order to interpret the complex developments in Chaco Canyon. A massive, long-range research project has been started in Chaco Canyon by the National Park Service and the University of New Mexico under the direction of Robert Lister. We can look forward to the testing of the hypotheses raised by Vivian and DiPeso as this project matures.

Lipe (98, 99), reporting a long-term investigation of Anasazi communities in the Red Rock Plateau, southeastern Utah, was able to conclude that the basic social unit was the extended family household. Schwartz (138) reports on his investigation of a community that migrated from an upland location to the Unkar delta at the bottom of the Grand Canyon. He was able to predict and test for economic and social changes in the postmigration community.

Social and economic change was also the focus of an interesting study carried out by Leone (94, 95) in east-central Arizona. He tested the hypothesis that as economic autonomy increased in farming villages, so did social autonomy. His analysis suggested decreasing social interaction among villages as they became more dependent upon agriculture. Likewise, Tuggle (149) undertook an analysis of patterns of community interaction among Pueblo villages just below the Mogollon rim in east-central Arizona. Interaction was examined in terms of two processes: the movement of females among communities (village exogamy) and the circulation of ceramics by economic means such as trade. Tuggle's analysis supported the conclusion that there was increasing interaction after A.D. 1250 and that it was probably economic in nature.

In addition to an increased concern with aspects of social organization and patterns of village interaction, one can see growing interest in ecological studies and the analysis of sociocultural change in a framework structured by systems theory. One of the most important recent papers stressing a cultural ecological approach is an analysis by Schoenwetter & Dittert (136) of changes in Anasazi settlement patterns. They argue that Anasazi settlement patterns underwent only one major change in form, but a number of more minor shifts in type over the past 2000 years. They relate those transformations to economic change and to environmental shifts.

Several recent essays provide examples of systems theory and cultural ecology in attempts to explain prehistoric change in the Southwest. Plog & Garrett (124) face the problem of explaining variability in water control systems in different habitats.

They offer a model that focuses upon decision making in terms of variability in the habitat and a cost/benefit ratio for the prehistoric society involved. Glassow (48), adopting an explicit systems approach, argues that the transformation from Early to Late Basketmaker culture in the Anasazi area can be best understood in terms of a change toward increased economizing of energy (food, fuel) and human work. He raises a series of hypotheses centering on changes in the energy flow network through time in the Basketmaker area. On the basis of his analysis, he is able to suggest a cultural "law" or empirical generalization that may be operative in this case, ". . . with an increase in population density we would expect a concomitant increase in the amount of energy processed through facilities" (48, p. 299). A systems analysis has also been applied to a problem of taxonomy with highly useful results (Judge 86).

Systems theory, cultural ecology, and the search for laws of cultural evolution are playing an ever-increasing role in Southwestern studies. Several exciting recent studies illustrate this theme. Plog (122) focuses his attention on the change from Basketmaker to Pueblo in the Anasazi area as an example of major cultural transformation. After pointing to regularities that occur in major change of this magnitude, he uses the Anasazi example as a test case in evaluating a general explanatory model of major cultural change. Similarly, Glassow (47) attempts to explain observed variability in the distribution of prehistoric settlements in northeastern Mexico.

One byproduct of the systems approach is the increased utilization of modeling techniques and the application of game theory as analytic tools in archaeological interpretation. For example, Zubrow (162, 163) has employed a simulation model to test alternative models of population dynamics and ecologically defined carrying capacity in a valley in east-central Arizona. Cordell (26) used a simulation model in attempting to explain changes in settlement patterns at Wetherill Mesa, Mesa Verde. The "computer revolution" is having significant impact on archaeology, and Southwestern archaeology is no exception (Martin 112).

Thus far I have concentrated on current research focusing on extinct cultural systems postdating the time of Christ, the agricultural, pottery-making peoples that have been labeled the Anasazi and Mogollon cultures in the Southwest. There have been significant advances in research dealing with the Paleo-Indian and preceramic, Archaic periods as well. Irwin-Williams & Haynes (80) undertook a cultural ecological analysis of population dynamics and climatic change in the Southwest for these periods. They demonstrate the great effect of changes in available moisture upon the areal distribution of peoples and the economic adjustments that the various cultural systems made from approximately 9500 B.C. to A.D. 700. Similarly, Judge & Dawson (28, 87) were able to relate the distribution of Paleo-Indian site locations to the changing distribution of water sources upon which the megafaunal forms being exploited depended. Their work focused upon the central Rio Grande River valley in New Mexico, and they were able to define a typology of settlements based upon topographic associations and inferences about the activities carried out at the sites based upon analyses of surface artifactual materials.

In two stimulating essays, Gorman (49, 50) explores the composition of Clovis task groups and the activities they carried out. Inferences about the activities, division of labor, and other aspects of early hunters and others in the Southwest were the focus of two other studies based on the analysis of controlled surface collections from Cochise sites in southern Arizona (Agenbroad 1, Whalen 156). Studies by Wilmsen (157–159) focus on a number of Paleo-Indian sites in North America including several in the Southwestern United States. His careful analyses of tool technology, materials, and functional attributes of implements permit him to draw inferences on social organization, seasonal variability in group size, activities, and territory.

A major theme that is clearly becoming increasingly important in Southwestern archaeology is the appearance of long-term, multidisciplinary research projects. Such projects are specifically problem-oriented and involve participants from a variety of other disciplines than archaeology. Some of these projects are designed to last up to 20 years (Longacre 109). To date, nine such projects are under way in Arizona, New Mexico, and Utah.

The major themes that typify the new directions in Southwestern archaeological research of the past decade include a concern with explanation which has led to increased emphasis upon cross-cultural regularities, multidisciplinary research, systems analysis, and explicit problem formulation. Some of these developments are, of course, not new but are intensified versions of longer standing concerns. In any case, one senses an atmosphere of ferment and a spirit of new direction in the field of Southwestern archaeology. These developments have logically produced an important innovation in archaeological research endeavors represented by the founding of the Southwestern Anthropological Research Group (SARG) in 1971.

SARG consists of a group of cooperating Southwestern archaeologists devoting at least a part of their research time toward the testing of hypotheses of central interest to the group. The primary research question that the group has adopted is, "Why do people live where they do?" Ancillary themes are: "Why do population aggregates differ in size; why do the locations differ through time; and why does a single population aggregate (or individual site) grow or decrease in size?" (Gumerman 57, 58).

SARG has adopted three interrelated propositions that are interesting and testable and has developed a research design that structures the research (Hill 74, Plog 123, Plog & Hill 125, 126). The three propositions that the members of SARG are now testing are: (a) sites were located with respect to critical on-site resources; (b) sites were located so as to minimize the effort expended in acquiring required quantities of critical resources; and (c) sites were located so as to minimize the cost of resource and information flow between sites occupied by interacting populations. The members of SARG do not expect to be able to explain the distribution of all population aggregates in terms of these propositions, but they do hope to be able to assess the importance of critical resources in the distribution of sites. If SARG can determine the importance of resource availability in the determination of human settlement, then a level of explanation and prediction will have been reached.

In order to accomplish this, the members of SARG have agreed upon the critical variables they must measure in order to test these propositions. They have agreed upon the data they will collect, the format of those data and also upon a workable computer code for recording the data (Green 53).

The development of SARG is an important new direction in Southwestern archaeological research and has interesting implications for problem-solving endeavors in other parts of the world. If the group is successful, the approach may be developed beyond its current areal focus. It seems to me that a coordinated research endeavor attempting to solve an interesting problem might well be carried out by cooperating archaeologists working in a variety of places throughout the world.

Recently, Chang (23, pp. 20–22) criticized the research design and the propositions that are being tested by SARG. In his discussion I feel he has seriously misrepresented the nature of the research design and its operational aspects. He suggests (23, p. 20) that the members of SARG have "answered" the question of why people live where they do by generating the three propositions that SARG is trying to test. I fail to understand his argument concerning this point. He seems to suggest that the "proper" way to solve such questions is to begin with "the evidence" and work up from there to the level of explanation. Chang seems to be arguing for an inductive approach to the doing of science, which at best is an inefficient way to solve problems.

This is clearly not the place for a lengthy rebuttal to the arguments Professor Chang has raised. His discussion reflects, I feel, a rather different theoretical and epistemological stance in archaeology from that of the members of SARG. In any case, it is far too early to evaluate the success or failure of the SARG research program as another decade of work is planned. This research is not destructive in the sense Chang (23, p. 20) has implied, as no excavation is essential to the measurement of the variables of concern to the tests being carried out by the members of SARG.

Other new directions that typify Southwestern research include applications of new techniques from the physical sciences, major advances in dendrochronology, and new insights in the nature of past climates as a result of interesting new research in dendroecology and palynology. Remote sensing techniques have been applied to locating prehistoric sites and to identifying features of sites in the Southwest (Gumerman 56, Gumerman & Lyons 59). Trace element analysis has been applied to the identification of sources of obsidian tools in prehistoric sites located in northern Arizona (Jack 81, Schreiber & Breed 137).

Major advances have occurred in dendrochronology. At the Laboratory of Tree-Ring Research at the University of Arizona, Ferguson (40, 41) has been successful in developing an annual tree-ring chronology for Bristlecone pine that extends back more than 7000 years. This chronology has had an important impact on the radiocarbon chronology, causing some major revisions. The Laboratory of Tree-Ring Research has also completed a number of other important projects. Perhaps the most important of these is the review of nearly 100,000 tree-ring specimens that took 8 years to complete. The use of a computer-assisted dating technique helped Bannister and his colleagues to produce approximately 15,000 dates in this project and publish the results (9–14).

Recent work at the Laboratory of Tree-Ring Research has also resulted in important new studies of past climates. Sensitive measurement of variables affecting the growth of trees was undertaken and multivariate statistical analysis of tree-ring variation and climatic variation was accomplished. These studies have enabled Fritts and his colleagues to map moisture clines at 10 year intervals backward into the past for the western portion of North America (43, 44, 147). Palynology has also made significant progress in developing a picture of past climates in the Southwest as well as in paleoecological studies of particular sites and functional interpretations of features and facilities within sites and even intra and inter site dating (Bohrer 15–17; Hill & Hevly 75; Mehringer 118; Schoenwetter 135.)

CONTINUING DIRECTIONS

Many of the developments that I have described as new directions in Southwestern archaeology are, of course, innovative attempts at solving problems of long standing interest. There is considerable continuity in the nature of major questions being posed by researchers in the Southwest. The major changes that represent departures from the nature of past research have to do more with the development of new methods and techniques and more specific theoretical and epistemological directions rather than new questions or problems. It will be some time before we can evaluate the relative success of these new directions in problem solving, but the results to date are certainly encouraging.

The advent of the "new archaeology" has had its greatest impact upon method-ological and theoretical aspects of the nature of Southwestern archaeological re-search. It should be clear from the brief review I have presented that the "new archaeology" is not a single, monolithic theoretical and methodological pose, but represents a wide diversity of interests and directions of research. The diversity is healthy and has led to creative efforts at problem solving on a number of fronts. Over the past decade or so, these efforts have received a great deal of attention and have had considerable impact upon a wide range of ongoing archaeological research. This impact can be seen in the adoption of many of the newer methods and techniques in research, addressing more traditional important concerns such as cultural histori-cal reconstruction, and in increasing numbers of archaeologists becoming more sensitive to the great potential of data that were not generally observed or collected in the past. Thus the "new directions" in Southwestern archaeology have had considerable impact upon the nature of archaeological research that I have labeled "continuing directions," and is perhaps most visible in the nature of modern "sal-vage" or, "emergency archaeology" as discussed below.

There are a number of kinds of continuing directions that typify modern South-western archaeological research. I label them "continuing directions" in that they do not reflect radical or marked departure from the kind of activities that have characterized Southwestern archaeology over the past 50 years or so. These would include the publication of basic descriptive studies in the form of site reports and short articles describing unusual or atypical artifactual material. Also included are attempts at cultural reconstruction in the form of areal syntheses and the presenta-tion of regional sequences of cultural development. By far the most numerous of these are descriptive monographs or articles representing a considerable proportion of the total of more than 500 publications postdating 1967.

Some of the recently published descriptive monographs and historical reconstructions are reporting field research that was carried out from 20 to 40 years ago. These represent only a small percentage of an immense backlog of unpublished results (e.g. Judd 85, McGregor 111, Smith 142, 143). Others report the results of more recent excavations. Some are reporting sites excavated as a part of long-term research projects, such as the ongoing investigations by the University of Colorado and the National Park Service at Mesa Verde (Lister 101–103, Lister, et al 104, Rohn 131, Swannack 148). Others report the results of recently completed long-term projects such as the Museum of Northern Arizona's research in the Glen Canyon area (Lindsay et al 97). A considerable number of descriptive reports are the result of salvage archaeology and reflect a growing concern with the prompt publishing of basic results [e.g. see Hammack (64) for a list of reports to date resulting from highway salvage archaeology carried out in Arizona]. Many of the shorter descriptive articles report unusual ceramic pieces (e.g. Lambert 91), or unique or atypical artifactual items (e.g. Gell 46, Lambert 92). And others discuss functional interpretations of specific classes of artifacts (e.g. Ellis 36) or add interesting historical observations to the literature (e.g. Judd 84).

The large number of descriptive reports and areal syntheses do tend to reflect the areas and time periods in the Southwest that are receiving the greatest amounts of attention. The relative numbers of reports on excavations or cultural historical reconstructions for various parts of the Southwest point to "where the action is" in terms of current research activities. It is quite clear, for example, that there is an emphasis upon those areas of the greater Southwest that are less well known archaeologically such as northern Mexico and the desert portions and the more northern parts of the Southwest. There is also considerable emphasis upon the earlier time periods of Southwestern prehistory, especially the Paleo-Indian and preceramic Archaic periods.

One area that has been the scene of an intensification of research activity over the past decade or so is the desert portion of the Southwest and especially the area of southern Arizona. Research here has tended to focus upon the development of the Hohokam culture. Following the initial work of the Gila Pueblo Foundation in the middle 1930s, there was relatively little work in the Hohokam area until the mid-1960s. During this time, however, there was growing controversy about the chronology of Hohokam cultural development and interpretation. This has led to an increase in the research activities carried out in the region with a number of interesting results.

The University of Arizona undertook a major excavation at the important Hohokam site of Snaketown under the direction of Emil W. Haury in the mid-1960s. A major monograph reporting this work is nearly completed and will be published by the University of Arizona Press in the near future. Some of the results have been summarized by Haury in a recent article (67). The chronology of the Hohokam developments at the Snaketown site has been firmed up as a result of Haury's work. He now sees the beginning of the Vahki phase at about 300 B. C. It appears at Snaketown with a fully developed ceramic industry and irrigation technology, which, among other traits, has led Haury to postulate a migration of peoples to the

Gila Valley probably from Mexico. Platform mounds and other data are cited as additional evidence of the strong ties to Mexico. In a recent popular synthesis, Dittert (34) seems to agree with this interpretation.

There have been a number of recent publications describing the results of surveys and excavations in the Hohokam area, especially the less well known portions (e.g. Chenhall 24; Dove 35; Grebinger 51, 52; Hammack 63; Hayden 70; Morris 120, 121; Wasley & Benham 154; Weed & Ward 155). In addition, a major survey of prehistoric Hohokam irrigation canals has been published (Midvale 119). Alternative suggestions concerning the origin of Hohokam culture have been presented. Hayden (69) has suggested the possibility that a group may have rapidly migrated to the Gila Valley from fairly deep in Mexico, perhaps as far south as the modern state of Jalisco. One author has gone so far as to suggest that there was diffusion from South America (Gritzner 54)! The archaeological survey conducted by the Arizona State Museum in Sonora during 1966–67 failed to locate any early Hohokam material; this raises some doubts about a possible migration through or from northwestern Mexico.

Several articles of a somewhat controversial nature have appeared recently dealing with the Hohokam culture. One of these presents an alternative hypothesis of the function of the Hohokam "ball court," a common feature of later Hohokam sites in the Southwest (Ferdon 39). Pointing to attributes of such structures that seem to preclude the playing of a ball game, and drawing upon ethnographic data from the Pima and Papago, Ferdon argues that they probably represent dance courts and not ball courts at all. His arguments are most logical and the alternative he presents seems quite tenable. Clearly, the function of the Hohokam "ball court" is testable, but as yet no one has undertaken such a test. Another recent article that should generate controversy is one by Rippeteau (130) in which he attempts a psychological appraisal of the Hohokam based upon an analysis of ceramic decoration.

Another region that has received a great deal of recent attention is the northern portion of the greater Southwest, especially the area of the Fremont culture. A considerable amount of research has been carried out in Fremont sites, and the interpretation of Fremont cultural history is an area of considerable current controversy. The original descriptions of the Fremont culture suggested it was the result of Great Basin peoples borrowing selected Anasazi culture traits, largely in Utah, and this area was often referred to as the "Northern periphery" of the Southwest.

Beginning in the mid-1960s, articles and reports began to appear that challenge that interpretation of Fremont culture history. In 1966, Aikens (2) was able to argue that the Fremont culture had a northwestern Plains origin and was perhaps an Athapascan phenomenon which became partially acculturated to an Anasazi puebloan culture. In that same year, Sharrock supported Aikens in the argument of a Plains origin of the Fremont culture (139), but an alternative interpretation was presented by Ambler (7). He argues that the Fremont culture is the result of the spread of traits from the Anasazi culture via the Virgin branch and divides the Fremont area into a number of regional variants. Thus the "Fremont question" was born, and the debate is continuing.

Aikens (3, 4) continued to point to the evidence suggesting a Plains origin, and Ambler emphasized the relations of the Fremont culture and the Anasazi culture to the south (8). Breternitz tends to agree with Ambler in the debate, suggesting that the Fremont culture probably developed from an archaic base with affiliations to the Great Basin (20). He also suggests that regional variation in the Fremont area may be the basis for these alternative interpretations. Marwitt (116) suggests a northwestern Plains origin and subsequent modification as a result of contact with Anasazi peoples.

By the early 1970s, a considerable amount of work had been done and a number of monographs and articles published (Husted & Mallory 76; Leach 93; Marwitt 117; Sharrock & Marwitt 140; Shields 141). A major excavation was carried out at Hogup Cave (Aikens 5) that shed additional light on the "Fremont question." Gunnerson (62) published a monograph describing his work on the Fremont culture, work he had done before the current debate. Aikens (6) presents an excellent review of the various interpretations and the nature of the evidence which should be consulted by anyone interested in the Fremont area.

In addition to the work undertaken in the Fremont area, there have been cultural historical reconstructions and areal syntheses presented for parts of Arizona, New Mexico, and northern Mexico. For the most part these contributions deal with Southwestern areas that are less well known archaeologically or relatively unknown. In Arizona these contributions would include syntheses of the prehistory of Puerco River Valley (Gumerman & Olsen 60) and the Central Little Colorado River Valley (Gumerman & Skinner 61). Both of these syntheses present new data for those areas and extend the known chronology back to Archaic and Paleo-Indian times. Similarly, a summary of the findings of the recent work on Black Mesa by Prescott College is available (Gumerman 55).

Several recent publications report the results of recent survey and excavations in the Flagstaff area of northern Arizona. A major archaeological survey of Sinagua sites is reported by Wilson (160, 161). Kelly presents a synthesis of the later Sinagua culture with a cultural ecological perspective (88). The early prehistory of the Coconino Plateau is synthesized by Jennings (83).

The relatively unknown Middle Pecos River Valley in New Mexico was the scene of a research project undertaken by Jelinek (82). He presents a synthesis of the valley's prehistory beginning with the evidence for Paleo-Indian and Archaic period occupations. This is followed by the initial appearance of sedentary communities about A.D. 800 and a pattern of increasing dependence upon agriculture from that time until perhaps A.D. 1250. The widest utilization of the valley and probably the densest population seem to occur toward the end of that sequence. Between 1250 and 1350 a drastic economic shift is evidenced. Apparently these populations abandoned a farming way of life and abruptly turned to intensive exploitation of bison herds at that time. This major change in subsistence strategy seems to accompany a slight climatic shift in the area. The valley was abandoned by permanent populations after A.D. 1350.

The results of a multidisciplinary study undertaken in the Chuska Valley and the Chaco Plateau in New Mexico are reported by Harris, Schoenwetter & Warren (66). The results of geological, ecological, and palynological analyses are presented as well as physical/chemical analyses on the artifactual materials recovered from a number of sites. Of special interest is Schoenwetter's study of modern pollen rain and the distribution of plant communities, fundamental research for the interpretation of fossil pollens in the archaeological record. Four alternative syntheses of later Puebloan prehistory are presented by Ford, Schroeder & Peckham (42) and Ellis (37).

Syntheses focusing upon the early prehistory of the Southwest have also appeared. These reflect a growing concern with the Archaic cultures of the area. A major research project attempting to trace the origins of the Anasazi culture, directed by Irwin-Williams, has now been completed. She has published several articles synthesizing the results (Irwin-Williams 77–79). In the first article, she recognizes a series of similar cultures in the Southwest during the 3000 years before the time of Christ and argues that the Southwestern culture area emerges during that period. To emphasize the similarities and interaction she infers among these early cultures and their continuous development, she suggests the term "Picosa" be adopted to refer to this initial or elementary cultural unit. Reinhart (127, 128) presents a synthesis of the culture history of late Archaic cultures of the middle Rio Grande valley in New Mexico.

Northern Mexico has also received considerable attention from archaeologists in recent years. The results of earlier excavations at the site of Casas Grandes in Chihuahua, undertaken by the Amerind Foundation, have been summarized by DiPeso (32). A multivolume report is under preparation and will be published by the Amerind Foundation in the near future. A synthesis of the prehistory of the Sierra Pinacate region of northern Sonora has been published (Hayden 68). A summary of the archaeology of the central coast of Sonora has been made available by Bowen (18, 19).

Interest in the nature and impact of postulated Southwestern and Mesoamerican interaction is evidenced by several recent publications (Ellis & Hammack 38, Kessler 89, Reyman 129). This current interest in Mesoamerica-Southwestern interaction has been greatly stimulated by the provocative suggestions offered by DiPeso (33) concerning systematic economic interaction and especially the role of the *Puchteca* in the Southwest. There is also interest in economic interaction and trade in cultural historical studies focusing on the Puebloan Southwest (Schaefer 133; Warren 153).

In addition to these studies, there are a number of miscellaneous publications that should be noted. Brown (21, 22) has surveyed the distribution of sound instruments in the Southwest and has discussed the implications for ethnomusicology. Ross (132) has argued the case for the practice of copper metallurgy in the prehistoric Southwest. A delightful photographic essay on Pueblo architecture has been published by Current & Scully (27). And Cook (25) has presented a clever study of the relationship of population size and density of ceramic debris for several Southwestern sites. A continuing interest in the history of Southwestern archaeology is reflected in the excellent biography of Earl Morris prepared by Lister & Lister (100).

FUTURE DIRECTIONS

It is probably folly to attempt to predict future trends in a field of study enjoying such healthy diversity as Southwestern archaeology. But as I approach the end of a lengthy review of the field, I find myself tempted! Of course, any prediction must be flavored with a certain amount of the bias of preference of the particular author. With that warning, let me undertake such a folly.

I suspect that the various themes discussed under New Directions will continue to intensify over the next decade or so and that the diversity of these new directions will increase. I predict that a general concern with explaining cultural processes of stability and change will gradually begin to dominate Southwestern studies. There will also be a similar impact upon "salvage" or "contract" archaeology in the Southwest (Longacre & Vivian 110).

A great deal of archaeological energy will be expended over the next several decades in problem-oriented salvage archaeology as required by the Environmental Policy Act of 1969. Over the 8 years prior to mid-1972, more than 160 sites were excavated in Arizona alone in highway salvage archaeological projects. The recent legislation passed by Congress will greatly intensify the tempo of this kind of research.

Cultural historical reconstructions and areal synthesis will continue, but I suspect they will be increasingly influenced by the method and theory of the "new archaeology," especially, by general systems theory and cultural ecology. This should lead to a healthy "feedback" situation.

Those current directions that I hope will be expanded include the development of the Southwestern Archaeological Research Group (Gumerman 57, 58) and the "ethno-archaeological" studies of workers like Stanislawski (144, 145). I hope the SARG development will flourish and extend to include additional areas of the Southwest. I would hope that ethnographic investigations of "material culture" will be expanded to encompass more of the Southwestern Indian peoples such as those at Zuni, Acoma, and the Pueblos of the Northern Rio Grande Valley.

The prognosis for Southwestern archaeology seems excellent. I anticipate an increase in the tempo of interesting and important research, and I expect Southwestern archaeology to make significant contributions toward the solution of a variety of anthropologically relevent questions. The Southwest certainly is not a "sucked orange." If anything it is a ripe fruit bursting with rich potential for a better understanding of the nature of culture and of cultural change. It is up to the archaeologists working in the Southwest to tap that potential and contribute toward the solution of major problems facing the world today.

ACKNOWLEDGMENTS

A great many people have been of special help to me in the preparation of this review. I should like to acknowledge their assistance and thank them for their help. Of course, I alone am responsible for any shortcomings.

Much of the research and all of the writing was undertaken during my fellowship year at the Center for Advanced Study in the Behavioral Sciences at Stanford, California. Members of the Center's staff were extremely helpful to me, in particular Mrs. Betty Calloway, librarian.

The staff of the Anthropology library, Arizona State Museum, University of Arizona, were particularly helpful in the preparation of the list of references published since 1967. I thank John V. Baroco and Judy Reis for their generous assistance. Other individuals offered advice or helped me in other ways for which I am extremely grateful: Keith H. Basso, George J. Gumerman, L. C. Hammack, Emil W. Haury, Robert F. Heizer, James N. Hill, Alexander J. Lindsay Jr., Paul S. Martin, Leon D. Prodon Jr., J. Jefferson Reid, Raymond H. Thompson, and Ezra B. W. Zubrow.

Of the more than 500 books, monographs, reports, and articles dealing with Southwestern archaeology that have appeared since 1967, I have been forced to select only a small segment for discussion or even reference. I apologize to those colleagues whose work is not mentioned in this brief review. I have made available a selected bibliography of titles that I found useful in compiling this review (see footnote to p. 201).

Literature Cited

1. Agenbroad, L. D. 1970. *Cultural implications from the statistical analysis of a prehistoric lithic site in Arizona.* MA thesis. Univ. Arizona, Tucson
2. Aikens, C. M. 1966. Fremont-Promontory-Plains relationships. *Univ. Utah Anthropol. Pap.* 82
3. Aikens, C. M. 1967. Plains relationships of the Fremont Culture: A hypothesis. *Am. Antiq.* 32:198–209
4. Aikens, C. M. 1967. Excavations at Snake Rock Village and the Bear River No. 2 Site. *Univ. Utah Anthropol. Pap.* 87
5. Aikens, C. M. 1970. Hogup Cave. *Univ. Utah Anthropol. Pap.* 93
6. Aikens, C. M. 1972. Fremont Culture: restatement of some problems. *Am. Antiq.* 37:61–66
7. Ambler, J. R. 1966. *Caldwell Village and Fremont Prehistory.* PhD thesis. Univ. Colorado, Boulder. Ann Arbor: Univ. Microfilms
8. Ambler, J. R. 1969. The temporal span of the Fremont. *Southwest. Lore* 34: 107–17
9. Bannister, B., Dean, J. S., Robinson, W. J. 1968. *Tree-Ring Dates from Arizona C-D: Eastern Grand Canyon-Tsegi Canyon-Kayenta Area.* Tucson: Lab. Tree-Ring Res.
10. Bannister, B., Dean, J. S., Robinson, W. J. 1969. *Tree-Ring Dates from Utah S-W: Southern Utah Area.* Tucson: Lab. Tree-Ring Res.
11. Bannister, B., Hannah, J. W., Robinson, W. J. 1970. *Tree-Ring Dates from New Mexico M-N, S, Z: Southwestern New Mexico Area.* Tucson: Lab. Tree-Ring Res.
12. Bannister, B., Robinson, W. J. 1971. *Tree-Ring Dates from Arizona U-W: Gila-Salt River Area.* Tucson: Lab Tree-Ring Res.
13. Bannister, B., Robinson, W. J., Warren, R. L. 1967. *Tree-Ring Dates from Arizona J: Hopi Mesa Area.* Tucson: Lab. Tree-Ring Res.
14. Banister, B., Robinson, W. J., Warren, R. L. 1970. *Tree-Ring Dates from New Mexico A, G-H: Shiprock-Zuni-Mt. Taylor Areas.* Tucson: Lab. Tree-Ring Res.
15. Bohrer, V. L. 1970. Ethnobotanical aspects of Snaketown, a Hohokam village in southern Arizona. *Am. Antiq.* 35: 413–30
16. Bohrer, V. L. 1971. Paleoecology of Snaketown. *Kiva* 36:11–19
17. Bohrer, V. L. 1972. Paleoecology of the Hay Hollow Site, Arizona. *Fieldiana: Anthropol.* 63:1–30. Chicago: Field Mus. Natur. Hist. Press
18. Bowen, T. G. 1969. *Seri Prehistory: The Archaeology of the Central Coast of Sonora, Mexico.* PhD thesis. Univ. Colorado, Boulder. Ann Arbor: Univ. Microfilms
19. Bowen, T. G. 1969. Seri prehistory: the archaeology of the central coast of Sonora, Mexico. *Colo. Anthropol.* 2:39
20. Breternitz, D. A. (assembler) 1970. Archaeological excavations in Dinosaur National Monument, Colorado-Utah, 1964–1965. *Univ. Colo. Stud. Ser. Anthropol.* 17
21. Brown, D. N. 1967. The distribution of sound instruments in the prehistoric southwestern United States. *Ethnomusicology* 11:71–90
22. Ibid 1971. Ethnomusicology and the prehistoric Southwest. 15:363–78

23. Chang, K. C. 1972. *Settlement Patterns in Archaeology.* Module 24. Reading: Addison-Wesley

24. Chenhall, R. G. 1967. The Silo site. *Ariz. Archaeol.* 2

25. Cook, S. F. 1972. Can pottery be used as an index to population? *Contrib. Univ. Calif. Archaeol. Res. Facil.* 14: 17–39

26. Cordell, L. S. 1972. *Settlement Pattern Changes at Wetherill Mesa, Colorado: A Test Case for Computer Simulation in Archaeology.* PhD thesis. Univ. California, Santa Barbara. Ann Arbor: Univ. Microfilms

27. Current, W., Scully, V. 1971. *Pueblo Architecture of the Southwest, A Photographic Essay.* Austin: Univ. Texas Press

28. Dawson, J., Judge, W. J. 1969. Paleo-Indian sites and topography in the middle Rio Grande valley of New Mexico. *Plains Anthropol.* 14:149–63

29. Dean, J. S. 1967. *Chronological Analysis of Tsegi Phase Sites in Northeastern Arizona.* PhD thesis. Univ. Arizona, Tucson. Ann Arbor: Univ. Microfilms

30. Dean, J. S. 1969. Chronological analysis of Tsegi Phase sites in northeastern Arizona. *Pap. Lab. Tree-Ring Res.* 3. Tucson: Univ. Arizona Press

31. Dean, J. S. 1970. Aspects of Tsegi Phase social organization: a trial reconstruction. See Ref. 107, 140–74

32. DiPeso, C. C. 1968. Casas Grandes, a fallen trading center of the Gran Chichimeca. *Masterkey* 42:20–37

33. DiPeso, C. C. 1968. Casas Grandes and the Gran Chichimeca. *El Palacio* 75: 45–61

34. Dittert, A. E. Jr. 1972. They came from the south. *Ariz. Highways* 48:34–39

35. Dove, D. E. 1970. A site survey along the lower Agua Fria River, Arizona. *Ariz. Archaeol.* 5:1–36

36. Ellis, F. H. 1967. Use and significance of the tcamahia. *El Palacio* 74:1:35–43

37. Ellis, F. H. 1967. Where did the Pueblo people come from? *El Palacio* 74:3: 35–43

38. Ellis, F. H., Hammack, L. C. 1968. The inner sanctum of Feather Cave, a Mogollon sun and earth shrine linking Mexico and the Southwest. *Am. Antiq.* 33:25–44

39. Ferdon, E. N. 1967. The Hohokam "ball court," an alternative review of its function. *Kiva* 33:1–14

40. Ferguson, C. W. 1968. Bristlecone Pine: science and esthetics. *Science* 159: 839–46

41. Ferguson, C. W. 1969. A 7104-year annual tree-ring chronology for Bristlecone Pine, *Pinus Aristata*, from the White Mountains, California. *Tree-Ring Bull.* 29:3–17

42. Ford, R. I., Schroeder, A. H., Peckham, S. L. 1972. Three perspectives on puebloan prehistory. In *New Perspectives on the Pueblos,* ed. A. Ortiz, 19–39. Albuquerque: Univ. New Mexico Press

43. Fritts, H. C. 1966. Growth rings of trees: their correlation with climate. *Science* 154:973–79

44. Fritts, H. C., Blasing, T. J., Hayden, B. P., Kutzbach, J. E. 1971. Multivariate techniques for specifying tree-growth and climatic relationships and for reconstructing anomalies in paleoclimate. *J. Appl. Meteorol.* 10:845–64

45. Fritz, J. M., Plog, F. T. 1970. The nature of archaeological explanation. *Am. Antiq.* 35:405–12

46. Gell, E. A. M. 1967. A pine gum thimble from Point of Pines. *Kiva* 33:30–81

47. Glassow, M. A. 1972. *The Explanation of Variability in Prehistoric Settlement Distribution in Northeastern Mexico.* PhD thesis. Univ. California, Los Angeles. Ann Arbor: Univ. Microfilms

48. Glassow, M. A. 1972. Changes in the adaptation of Southwestern Basketmakers: A systems perspective. See Ref. 96, 289–302

49. Gorman, F. 1969. The Clovis hunters: an alternative view of their environment and ecology. *Kiva* 35:91–102

50. Gorman, F. 1972. The Clovis hunters: An alternative view of their environment and ecology. See Ref. 96, 206–21

51. Grebinger, P. F. 1971. *Hohokam Cultural Development in the Middle Santa Cruz Valley, Arizona.* PhD thesis. Univ. Arizona, Tucson. Ann Arbor: Univ. Microfilms

52. Grebinger, P. F. 1971. The Potrero Creek Site: activity structure. *Kiva* 37: 30–52

53. Green, D. F. 1972. The computer code format. See Ref. 58, 21–24

54. Gritzner, C. F. 1969. Hohokam culture origin: the possibility of diffusion from coastal Peru and Ecuador. *Neara Newslett.* 4:69–72

55. Gumerman, G. J. 1970. Black Mesa, survey and excavations in northeastern Arizona, 1968. *Prescott Coll. Stud. Anthropol.* 2

56. Gumerman, G. J. 1971. Archaeology and aerial photography. *Proc. 2nd ARETS Symp. Tucson* 2:206–16

57. Gumerman, G. J., Ed. 1971. The distribution of prehistoric population aggregates. *Prescott Coll. Anthropol. Rep.* 1. Prescott Coll. Press

58. Gumerman, G. J., Ed. 1972. Proceedings of second annual meeting of the Southwestern Anthropological Research Group. *Prescott Coll. Anthropol. Rep.* 3. Prescott Coll. Press

59. Gumerman, G. J., Lyons, T. R. 1971. Archaeological methodology and remote sensing. *Science* 172:126–32

60. Gumerman, G. J., Olson, A. P. 1968. Prehistory in the Puerco valley, eastern Arizona. *Plateau* 40:113–27

61. Gumerman, G. J., Skinner, S. A. 1968. A synthesis of the prehistory of the central Little Colorado valley, Arizona. *Am. Antiq.* 33:185–99

62. Gunnerson, J. H. 1969. The Fremont Culture. *Pap. Peabody Mus. Archaeol. Ethnol., Harvard Univ.* 59:2

63. Hammack, L. C. 1969. A preliminary report of the excavation at Las Colinas. *Kiva* 35:11–28

64. Hammack, L. C. 1972. *7th Ann. Rep. Arizona Highway Salvage Archaeol. June 1, 1971–May 31, 1972.* Tucson: Ariz. State Mus.

65. Hammond, A. L. 1971. The new archaeology: toward a social science. *Science* 172:1119–20

66. Harris, A. H., Schoenwetter, J., Warren, A. H. 1967. An archaeological survey of the Chuska Valley and the Chaco Plateau, New Mexico, Part 1, natural science studies. *Mus. New Mexico Res. Rec.* 4. Santa Fe: Mus. New Mexico Press

67. Haury, E. W. 1967. The Hohokam: first master of the American desert. *Nat. Geogr.* 131:670–95

68. Hayden, J. D. 1967. A summary prehistory and history of the Sierra Pinacate, Sonora. *Am. Antiq.* 32:335–44

69. Ibid 1970. Of Hohokam origins and other matters. 35:87–93

70. Hayden, J. D. 1972. Hohokam petroglyphs of the Sierra Pinacate, Sonora and the Hohokam Shell expeditions. *Kiva* 37:74–83

71. Hill, J. N. 1968. Broken K Pueblo: patterns of form and function. In *New Perspectives in Archaeology,* ed. S. R. Binford, L. R. Binford, 103–42. Chicago: Aldine

72. Hill, J. N. 1970. Prehistoric social organization in the American Southwest: theory and method. See Ref. 107, 11–58

73. Hill, J. N. 1970. Broken K Pueblo, prehistoric social organization in the

American Southwest. *Anthropol. Pap. Univ. Ariz.* 18

74. Hill, J. N. 1971. Research propositions for consideration, Southwestern Anthropological Research Group. See Ref. 57, 55–62

75. Hill, J. N., Hevly, R. H. 1968. Pollen at Broken K Pueblo: some new interpretations. *Am. Antiq.* 33:200–10

76. Husted, W. M., Mallory, O. L. 1967. The Fremont Culture: its derivation and ultimate fate. *Plains Anthropol.* 12:222–32

77. Irwin-Williams, C. 1967. Picosa: the elementary Southwestern culture. *Am. Antiq.* 32:441–57

78. Irwin-Williams, C. 1968. The reconstruction of archaic culture in the Southwestern United States. *E. New Mexico Univ. Contrib. Anthropol.* 1: 19–23

79. Ibid. Archaic culture history in the southwestern United States, 48–54

80. Irwin-Williams, C., Haynes, C. V. 1970. Climate change and early population dynamics in the southwestern United States. *Quaternary Res.* 1:59–71

81. Jack, R. N. 1971. The source of obsidian artifacts in northern Arizona. *Plateau* 43:103–114

82. Jelinek, A. J. 1967. A prehistoric sequence in the middle Pecos valley, New Mexico. *Anthropol. Pap.* 31. Ann Arbor: Mus. Anthropol., Univ. Michigan

83. Jennings, C. H. 1971. *Early Prehistory of the Coconino Plateau, Northwestern Arizona.* PhD thesis. Univ. Colorado, Boulder. Ann Arbor: Univ. Microfilms

84. Judd, N. M. 1967. The passing of a small P. III ruin. *Plateau* 39:131–33

85. Judd, N. M. 1970. Basketmaker artifacts from Moki Canyon, Utah. *Plateau* 43:16–20

86. Judge, W. J. 1970. Systems analysis and the Folsom-Midland question. *Southwest. J. Anthropol.* 26:40–51

87. Judge, W. J., Dawson, J. 1972. Paleo-Indian settlement and technology in New Mexico. *Science* 176:1210–16

88. Kelly, R. E. 1971. *Diminishing Returns: 12th and 13th Century Sinagua Environmental Adaptation in North-Central Arizona.* PhD thesis. Univ. Arizona, Tucson. Ann Arbor: Univ. Microfilms

89. Kessler, E. S. 1970. *Mesoamerican Contacts in the American Southwest and Southeast.* PhD thesis. Columbia Univ., New York. Ann Arbor: Univ. Microfilms

90. Kidder, A. V. 1958. Pecos, New Mexico: archaeological notes. *Pap. R. S. Peabody Found. Archaeol.* 5. Andover: Phillips Acad.
91. Lambert, M. F. 1967. A Kokopelli effigy pitcher from northwestern New Mexico. *Am. Antiq.* 32:398–401
92. Lambert, M. F. 1967. A unique prehistoric Anasazi pipe. *El Palacio* 74:41–42
93. Leach, L. L. 1967. *Archaeological Investigations of Deluge Shelter, Dinosaur National Monument.* Publ. PB–176–960. Springfield: Clearinghouse Fed. Sci. Tech. Inform.
94. Leone, M. P. 1968. *Economic Autonomy and Social Distance: Archaeological Evidence.* PhD thesis. Univ. Arizona, Tucson. Ann Arbor: Univ. Microfilms
95. Leone, M. P. 1968. Neolithic economic autonomy and social distance. *Science* 162:1150–51
96. Leone, M. P. 1972. Issues in anthropological archaeology. In *Contemporary Archaeology,* ed. M. P. Leone, 14–27. Carbondale: S. Illinois Univ. Press
97. Lindsay, A. J. Jr., Ambler, J. R., Stein, M. A., Hobler, P. M. 1968. Survey and excavations north and east of Navajo Mountain, Utah, 1959–1962. *Mus. N. Ariz. Bull.* 45. Flagstaff: N. Ariz. Soc. Sci. & Art
98. Lipe, W. D. 1967. *Anasazi Culture and Its Relationship to the Environment in the Red Rock Plateau Region, Southeastern Utah.* PhD thesis. Yale Univ. Ann Arbor: Univ. Microfilms
99. Lipe, W. D. 1970. Anasazi communities in the Red Rock Plateau, southeastern Utah. See Ref. 107, 84–139
100. Lister, F. C., Lister, R. H. 1968. *Earl Morris and Southwestern Archaeology.* Albuquerque: Univ. New Mexico Press
101. Lister, R. H. 1967. Contributions to Mesa Verde Archaeology: IV. Site 1086, an isolated, above ground kiva in Mesa Verde National Park, Colorado. *Univ. Colo. Stud. Ser. Anthropol.* 13
102. Lister, R. H. 1968. Archaeology for layman and scientist at Mesa Verde. *Science* 160:489–96
103. Lister, R. H., Ed. 1968. Contributions to Mesa Verde Archaeology: V. Emergency archaeology in Mesa Verde National Park, Colorado, 1948–1966. *Univ. Colo. Stud. Ser. Anthropol.* 15. Boulder: Univ. Colorado Press
104. Lister, R. H., Hallisy, S. J., Kane, M. H., McLellan, G. E. 1970. Site 5LP11, a Pueblo I site near Ignacio, Colorado. *Southwest. Lore* 35:57–67
105. Longacre, W. A. 1968. Some aspects of prehistoric society in east-central Arizona. See Ref. 71, 89–102
106. Longacre, W. A. 1970. Archaeology as Anthropology: a case study. *Anthropol. Pap. Univ. Ariz.* 17
107. Longacre, W. A., Ed. 1970. *Reconstructing Prehistoric Pueblo Societies.* Albuquerque: Univ. New Mexico Press
108. Ibid. A historical review, 1–10
109. Longacre, W. A., Ed. Multi-disciplinary research at Grasshopper. *Anthropol. Pap. Univ. Ariz.* In press
110. Longacre, W. A., Vivian, R. G. 1972. Salvage archaeology. *Science* 178:811–12
111. McGregor, J. C. 1967. The Cohonina culture of Mount Floyd, Arizona. *Univ. Ky. Stud. Anthropol.* 5
112. Martin, P. S. 1967. Paleo-anthropological research and computers. In *Computers and Humanistic Research,* ed. E. A. Bowles, 40–46. Englewood Cliffs: Prentice-Hall
113. Martin, P. S. 1970. Explanation as an afterthought and as a goal. See Ref. 107, 194–201
114. Martin, P. S. 1971. The revolution in Archaeology. *Am. Antiq.* 36:1–8
115. Martin, P. S., Longacre, W. A., Hill, J. N. 1967. Chapters in the prehistory of eastern Arizona, III. *Fieldiana: Anthropol.* 57
116. Marwitt, J. P. 1968. Pharo-Village. *Univ. Utah Anthropol. Pap.* 91
117. Marwitt, J. P. 1971. *Median Village and Fremont Cultural Variation.* PhD thesis. Univ. Utah, Salt Lake City. Ann Arbor: Univ. Microfilms
118. Mehringer, P. J. Jr. 1967. Pollen analysis and the alluvial chronology. *Kiva* 32:96–101
119. Midvale, F. 1968. Prehistoric irrigation in the Salt River valley, Arizona. *Kiva* 34:28–32
120. Morris, D. H. 1969. Red Mountain: an early Pioneer Period Hohokam site in the Salt River valley of central Arizona. *Am. Antiq.* 34:40–53
121. Ibid 1970. Walnut Creek Village: a 9th century Hohokam-Anasazi settlement in the mountains of central Arizona. 35:49–61
122. Plog, F. T. 1969. *An Approach to the Study of Prehistoric Change.* PhD thesis. Univ. Chicago
123. Plog, F. T. 1971. Some operational considerations. See Ref. 57, 1:45–54
124. Plog, F. T., Garrett, C. K. 1972. Explaining variability in prehistoric

Southwestern water control systems. See Ref. 96, 280–88

125. Plog, F. T., Hill, J. N. 1971. Explaining variability in the distribution of sites. See Ref. 57, 1:7–36

126. Plog, F. T., Hill, J. N. 1972. The Southwestern Anthropological Research Group: Revisions of the Research Design—1972. See Ref. 58, 3:7–20

127. Reinhart, T. R. 1967. The Rio Rancho Phase: A preliminary report on early Basketmaker culture in the middle Rio Grande valley, New Mexico. Am. Antiq. 32:458–70

128. Reinhart, T. R. 1968. Late Archaic Cultures of the Middle Rio Grande Valley New Mexico: A Study of the Process of Culture Change. PhD thesis. Univ. New Mexico, Albuquerque. Ann Arbor: Univ. Microfilms

129. Reyman, J. E. 1971. Mexican Influence on Southwestern Ceremonialism. PhD thesis. S. Illinois Univ. Carbondale. Ann Arbor: Univ. Microfilms

130. Rippeteau, B. E. 1972. The need-achievement test applied to the Hohokam. Am. Antiq. 37:504–13

131. Rohn, A. H. 1971. Mug House, Mesa Verde National Park, Colorado. Archaeol. Res. Ser. 7–D. Washington: Nat. Park Serv.

132. Ross, S. H. 1968. Metallurgical beginnings: the case for copper in the prehistoric American Southwest. Ann. Assoc. Am. Geogr. 58:360–70

133. Schaefer, P. D. 1969. Prehistoric trade in the Southwest and the distribution of Pueblo IV Hopi Jeddito Black-on-yellow. Kroeber Anthropol. Pap. 41

134. Schiffer, M. 1972. Cultural laws and the reconstruction of past lifeways. Kiva 37:148–57

135. Schoenwetter, J. 1970. Archaeological pollen studies of the Colorado Plateau. Am. Antiq. 35:35–48

136. Schoenwetter, J., Dittert, A. E. Jr. 1968. An ecological interpretation of Anasazi settlement patterns. In Anthropological Archaeology in the Americas, ed. B. J. Meggers, 41–66. Washington: Anthropol. Soc.

137. Schreiber, J. P., Breed, W. J. 1971. Obsidian localities in the San Francisco volcanic field, Arizona. Plateau 43:115–19

138. Schwartz, D. W. 1970. The postmigration culture: a base for archaeological inference. See Ref. 107, 175–93

139. Sharrock, F. W. 1966. Prehistoric occupation patterns in Southwest and cultural relationships with the Great Basin

and Plains culture areas. Univ. Utah Anthropol. Pap. 77

140. Sharrock, F. W., Marwitt, J. P. 1967. Excavations at Nephi, Utah, 1965–1966. Univ. Utah Anthropol. Pap. 88

141. Shields, W. F. 1967. 1966 excavations: Uinta Basin. Univ. Utah Anthropol. Pap. 89:1–30

142. Smith, W. 1971. Painted ceramics of the western mound at Awatovi. Pap. Peabody Mus. Archaeol. Ethnol. Harvard Univ. 38

143. Ibid 1972. Prehistoric kivas of Antelope Mesa, northeastern Arizona. 39:1

144. Stanislawski, M. B. 1969. What good is a broken pot? An experiment in Hopi-Tewa ethno-archaeology. Southwest. Lore 35:11–18

145. Stanislawski, M. B. 1969. The ethno-archaeology of Hopi pottery making. Plateau 42:27–33

146. Stanislawski, M. B. 1973. Review of: Archaeology as Anthropology: A case study. Am. Antiq. 38:117–22

147. Stockton, C. W., Fritts, H. C. 1971. Conditional probability of occurrence for variations in climate based on width of annual tree-rings in Arizona. Tree-Ring Bull. 31:3–24

148. Swannack, J. D. Jr. 1969. Big Juniper House, Mesa Verde National Park, Colorado. Archeol. Res. Ser. 7–C. Washington: Nat. Park Serv.

149. Tuggle, H. D. 1970. Prehistoric Community Relationships in East-Central Arizona. PhD thesis. Univ. Arizona, Tucson. Ann Arbor: Univ. Microfilms

150. Tuggle, H. D., Townsend, A. H., Riley, T. J. 1972. Laws, systems, and research designs: a discussion of explanation in archaeology. Am. Antiq. 37:3–12

151. Vivian, R. G. 1970. An inquiry into prehistoric social organization in Choco Canyon, New Mexico. See Ref. 107, 59–83

152. Vivian, R. G. 1970. Aspects of Prehistoric Society in Chaco Canyon, New Mexico. PhD thesis. Univ. Arizona, Tucson. Ann Arbor: Univ. Microfilms

153. Warren, H. 1969. Tonque: one pueblo's glaze pottery industry dominated middle Rio Grande commerce. El Palacio 76:36–42

154. Wasley, W. W., Benham, B. 1968. Salvage excavation in the Buttes Dam site, southern Arizona. Kiva 33:244–79

155. Weed, C. S., Ward, A. E. 1970. The Henderson site: Colonial Hohokam in north central Arizona, a preliminary report. Kiva 36:1–12

156. Whalen, N. M. 1971. *Cochise Culture Sites in the Central San Pedro Drainage, Arizona.* PhD thesis. Univ. Arizona, Tucson. Ann Arbor: Univ. Microfilms
157. Wilmsen, E. N. 1967. *Lithic Analysis and Cultural Inference: A Paleo-Indian Case.* PhD thesis. Univ. Arizona, Tucson. Ann Arbor: Univ. Microfilms
158. Wilmsen, E. N. 1968. Lithic analysis in paleoanthropology. *Science* 161:982–87
159. Wilmsen, E. N. 1968. Paleo-Indian site utilization. See Ref. 136, 22–40

160. Wilson, J. P. 1967. Another archaeological survey in east-central Arizona: preliminary report. *Plateau* 39:157–68
161. Wilson, J. P. 1969. *The Sinagua and their Neighbors.* PhD thesis. Harvard Univ.
162. Zubrow, E. B. W. 1971. *A Southwestern test of an Anthropological Model of Population Dynamics.* PhD thesis. Univ. Arizona, Tucson. Ann Arbor: Univ. Microfilms
163. Zubrow, E. B. W. 1971. Carrying capacity and dynamic equilibrium in the prehistoric Southwest. *Am. Antiq.* 36:127–38

SOUTHWESTERN ETHNOLOGY: ❖ 9529
A CRITICAL REVIEW

Keith H. Basso[1]

Department of Anthropology, University of Arizona, Tucson

INTRODUCTION

Anthropologists have been investigating indigenous cultures of the southwestern United States and northern Mexico for three quarters of a century and have produced a body of literature on the subject which in terms of sheer magnitude and richness of detail probably surpasses that of any ethnographic region in the New World. Far more impressive than the bulk of this material, however, is the extent to which it reveals the decisive role played by earlier generations of Southwestern ethnologists in stimulating the growth of American anthropological theory. Following classic contributions to the study of kinship and social structure by Kroeber (92) and Lowie (102), there was a period of intense theoretical activity between 1930–1950 which resulted in the presentation of new hypotheses on a wide range of topics. These included the historical reconstruction of kinship systems (Kroeber 93, Opler 110), the relationship of kinship categories to social behavior (Eggan 46, Opler 111, Parsons 123), evolutionary changes in the form and function of religious institutions (Underhill 155, White 161), the concept of patterning in culture and the influence

[1]I would like to take this opportunity to express my gratitude to the many people who aided me in the preparation of this essay. The following individuals kindly responded to an early call for help in locating publications that otherwise might have escaped my attention: Clifford Barnett, Harry Basehart, William Bittle, David Brugge, Bruce Cox, Ross Crumrine, Henry Dobyns, Robert Euler, Michael Everett, Bernard Fontana, Robin Fox, Charlotte Frisbie, Theodore Graves, James Gunnerson, Robert Hackenberg, James Hester, Thomas Hinton, William Hodge, Louise Lamphere, Jerrold Levy, Shuichi Nagata, Morris Opler, Alfonso Ortiz, Mary Shepardson, Edward Spicer, Kenneth Stewart, Jack Waddell, Thomas Weaver, Robert Weppner. Using the references supplied by these colleagues, together with those secured from other sources, Judy Reis compiled an excellent bibliography. The task of reviewing the literature was shared with Thomas McGuire, whose careful work and critical insight contributed significantly to my own understanding of the present state of Southwestern ethnology. During the actual writing I profited greatly from conversations with Ellen Basso, Bernard Fontana, Thomas McGuire, Edward Spicer, Richard Thompson, and especially Jerrold Levy. Ellen Basso, Melody Brancato, and Jerrold Levy also made helpful suggestions concerning matters of presentation and style. My sincere thanks to all; blame to none but myself.

221

of pattern on personality development (Benedict 17, 18, Eggan 45, Goldfrank 62, Kluckhohn 87), cultural "themes" (Opler 112), the social and psychological functions of myth, ritual, and witchcraft (Kluckhohn 88, 89), and issues in the analysis of value orientations (Kluckhohn 90).

Shortly before 1950, the year in which Fred Eggan's masterful treatise on the Western Pueblos affirmed the value of combining both functional and historical principles in comparative studies of social organization, increasing numbers of anthropologists in the Southwest turned their attention to problems in the field of culture change, especially those bearing upon processes of acculturation, assimilation, and revitalization among American Indians (e.g. Aberle & Stewart 5, Adair & Vogt 7, Dozier 42, Rapoport 125, Spicer 137, Vogt 156). These and other aspects of change served as focal points for a great deal of research during the next two decades, but with a few exceptions—notably Edward Spicer's (138) massive synthesis of Southwestern culture history and David Aberle's (2) meticulous treatment of the rise and spread of Navajo peyotism—this work fell short of producing major theoretical advances. In the early 1960s younger scholars who had become dissatisfied with entrenched interpretations began to formulate new problems and attack them from fresh perspectives. This willingness to challenge and experiment has been responsible for some original and valuable contributions, but the introduction of new approaches, together with the persistence of more established ones, has also resulted in unprecedented fragmentation and compartmentalization within the field as a whole.

There is simply no one underlying theme—or two, or three—that can be adduced to integrate the diversity of interests, aims, and assumptions with which Southwestern ethnologists presently confront their data. At one end of the spectrum are staunch empiricists who locate structure in overt behavioral regularities and seek explanation through the use of statistical patterns and coefficients of probability; at the other end are equally enthusiastic "mentalists" who find structure in the cognitive codes that underlie behavior and seek explanation in the formal properties of conceptual oppositions and decision-making models. In between stand a number of scholars who lean one way or the other depending on the task at hand. Intersecting the behaviorist-mentalist continuum is another whose poles are defined by the presence or absence of an explicit emphasis on processes of adaptation and adjustment (psychological as well as cultural) and the effects these processes have upon changing social forms. The presence of a concern with adaptation tends to be accompanied by behaviorist methods and is clearly visible in recent studies of urban migration, social pathologies, political conflict, and systems of resource exchange and distribution; the absence of this concern, frequently coupled with mentalist strategies, is most conspicuous in studies of ritual, world view, and religious ideology.

Of course, the difficulty with pigeonholing is that there are inevitably more pigeons than holes. Consequently, it would be deceptive to claim that distinctions of the kind mentioned above do more than provide general points of orientation in a burgeoning literature characterized by immense variety. On the other hand, it would be just as misleading to pretend that this literature fails to provide evidence for the emergence of new trends as well as the continuation and demise of old ones. To wit:

1. Interest remains strong in the historical reconstruction of Southwestern Indian societies, the dynamics of their relations with the physical environment and other human populations, and their responses to successive waves of conquest and subjugation by the governments of Spain, Mexico, and the United States.

2. Studies of contemporary social structures continue to stress the importance of residence groups and kin-based associations at the expense of sodalities in which membership is defined by other principles.

3. The emphasis upon kinship and local communities is balanced to some extent by work in the area of social change which calls attention (often by implication only) to new organizational forms that have arisen as a consequence of the position of Indian societies in a regional and national hegemony.

4. Investigations of religion focus upon the structural analysis of symbol-complexes and their role in the ritual process. The theories of Claude Lévi-Strauss and Victor Turner have been particularly stimulating in this regard, and their application to Southwestern data in the future seems assured. In other work, the techniques of ethnographic semantics have been employed to disclose aspects of Indian world view, but, as Eggan (47) has recently observed, the potential of linguistic models has not yet been fully exploited.

5. In almost all spheres, there has been an increase in efforts to account for variation within single societies and a concomitant decline in cross-cultural comparisons.

6. Studies of value-orientations also appear to be on the wane, although the critical role of values in the lives of Indians attempting to adjust to changing social conditions is clearly apparent in several biographies and autobiographies.

7. Studies formerly grouped under the rubric of "culture and personality" (e.g. child socialization, personality formation, dream analysis, etc.) have come to a virtual halt.

These observations, together with others presented in the remainder of this essay, are based upon a sample of nearly 300 articles and books published between 1968–1972. It has not been possible to mention all of these contributions, much less discuss them, and I have selected for citation and comment only those pieces that seemed to me to accomplish one or more of the following objectives: (a) the presentation of substantial amounts of data that were previously unavailable; (b) the use of data (old or new) to derive, evaluate, or test explicitly stated hypotheses; and (c) the interpretation of test results in accordance with clearly articulated theoretical premises. I must also confess to an abiding weakness for simple, lucid, English prose. Where I have found complicated ideas neatly expressed I have tried to grasp them. Where I have found ideas expressed in language that is totally unintelligible I have ignored them altogether. Finally, I want to apologize to those colleagues whose work I have misinterpreted or failed to locate; my shortcomings in this respect have not been intentional.[2]

HISTORY AND ETHNOHISTORY

Anthropological contributions to the study of Southwestern culture history continue to appear at a steadily increasing rate. A number of recent publications, modestly conceived and unpretentiously intended, deal with the straightforward documentation of newly recovered ethnographic materials. Others, broader in scope and more concerned with matters of interpretation, integrate what is already known of particular groups and regions to produce descriptive overviews and syntheses. Comparatively few studies address themselves to theoretical issues of general significance, and fewer still confront problems of method and analysis.

In a short but important paper, Harry Hoijer (84) examines the historical relationships of the Apachean languages as well as their affiliation to the Athapaskan stock as a whole. Revising his earlier classification (83) on the basis of new lexicostatistical data, Hoijer finds that Navajo, Chiricahua, Mescalero, Lipan, and Western Apache are closely related dialects of a single language; Kiowa Apache is a second language equidistant from each of the six dialects. In turn, the Apachean family is more closely related to Athapaskan languages of northern Canada than those of the Pacific Northwest. James & Dolores Gunnerson (70) pick up the Apacheans after their migration southward (circa 1525 A.D.) and summarize what is known of the Plains-dwelling groups during the seventeenth and eighteenth centuries. Employing documentary sources, as well as archeological data secured from recent excavations in New Mexico (Gunnerson 68, Gunnerson & Gunnerson 69) and Texas (Tunnell & Newcomb 153), they conclude that by 1700 all of the eastern Apaches had shifted from a nomadic to semisedentary mode of existence as the result of repeated contacts with agricultural peoples on the eastern and western peripheries of the Plains. Central to the Gunnersons' argument is the association of so-called Dismal River sites with Athapaskan occupants, an assumption which Morris Opler (117) challenges in an article dealing with the manufacture of Jicarilla pottery. Opler observes

[2]The great amount of material that has become available in recent years on the "Greater Southwest" (16) has required that the scope of this essay be restricted in several ways. First, I have dealt solely with published writings. Second, I have limited myself to literature concerning American Indians, thereby excluding studies of Mexicans, Mexican-Americans, Blacks, and other cultural groups. Third, I have not included recent work in archeology and have touched only lightly on southwestern linguistics. The latter topic has been covered in detail by Carl and Florence Voegelin in an article entitled "Southwestern and Great Basin Languages" which will be published in a forthcoming volume of *Current Trends in Linguistics.* Recent developments in southwestern archeology have been reviewed in equally able fashion by William A. Longacre in an essay published in this volume. Finally, and regrettably, I have been obliged to omit from discussion a number of works dealing with southwestern Indian art and material culture. Of these the most significant are by Brody (23), Chapman (28), Dunn (44), and Kluckhohn, Hill & Kluckhohn (91).

that Dismal River complexes cluster in time within a 50–year period around 1680—the year of the Pueblo rebellion—and believes that they may represent a retrenchment of Pueblo refugees rather than a stage in the development of Apache culture. In contrast to the measured opinions of Hoijer, Opler, and the Gunnersons, M. Jean Tweedie's (154) account of the early history and ecological adaptations of Apache groups suffers from a number of unqualified assertions, a serious lack of documentation, and overly facile interpretations of the ethnographic literature.

Turning to studies of Apache peoples in more recent times, we have a detailed description by Opler (116) of the territories inhabited by the Jicarilla in the middle of the nineteenth century. Reliable data concerning this tribe have long been in short supply, and Opler's contribution, which also clarifies important aspects of Jicarilla economy and social structure, is a timely one. Western Apache raiding and warfare forms the subjects of a book edited by Keith Basso (15). Based upon the unpublished field notes of Grenville Goodwin, this volume contains lengthy narratives by Apaches who participated in raids during the 1850s and 60s as well as chapters on the leadership and organization of war parties, the role of shamans, weapons, and other related topics. Goodwin's materials do much to deflate the popular stereotype of the Apache as "bloodthirsty villains," and therefore should help to balance the recent work of some historians (e.g. Moorhead 106, Thrapp 150) whose chronicles of Apache military operations reflect an almost total ignorance of ethnographic facts. In a comparative study whose sample includes the Chiricahua Apache, Mary Helms (74) advances the hypothesis that during times of war, when adult males are frequently away from home for long periods of time, matrilocal residence rules function to assure the effective enculturation of children. This may very well be true, but it is not terribly illuminating since we may safely assume that the same function is also served by matrilocality in times of peace.

General trends in the development of Navajo culture have been concisely reviewed by Robert Young (169) and James Hester (75), but the more focused studies of David Brugge (24), Ronald Kurtz (95), and Lawrence Kelly (85), all of which report on original research, warrant special attention. Drawing upon information contained in burial and baptismal records of the Catholic Church, Brugge makes a number of empirical observations about the costs and conduct of Indian warfare in New Mexico between 1694–1875. Some examples: "Navaho losses were considerably higher than White losses, the overall ratio being 3:1 . . . The Apacheans were clearly the most successful in their wars, being identifiable as attackers in 434 deaths [n=607] . . . Both sides had effective techniques for invading the enemy's territory and doing damage there, but neither had marked success in holding any gains made in the process" (p. 137). Statements of this kind, backed by quantitative analysis, are rare in studies of Southwestern ethnohistory, and Brugge's work, careful and detailed, constitutes a praiseworthy exception.

Kurtz takes a different approach entirely in a tightly reasoned piece that shows how structural changes in the role of Canyoncito headmen promoted stability in other sectors of Navajo culture during periods of intense ecological stress in the eighteenth and nineteenth centuries. Kurtz's argument, which deserves to be read, not summarized, proceeds from the following basic premise.

... some positions in any society are more likely than others to bring their occupants into contact with members of other societies or to be involved in changes in the habitat. Such positions and their associated role-segments are more significant than others in accounting for changes in response to modifications in the external situation. Adjustive changes take place by means of such critical positions, and these changes then affect individuals performing other roles within the society (p. 86).

In a full-length study historian Lawrence Kelly attempts to account for Navajo reactions to some of the long-range goals imposed upon them by the federal government between 1900–1935, and how, in turn, federal Indian policy was influenced during this period by dealings with the Navajo. Although the first of these objectives is accomplished more effectively than the second, Kelly's analysis of the motives and aspirations of local interest groups (e.g. stockmen, merchants, farmers, etc.) as well as those of U.S. Congress and Bureau of Indian Affairs is consistently revealing and refreshingly unbiased. One is deeply impressed (yet again!) with the tremendous complexity of the situation and how intimately the fate of the Navajo has been bound to factors over which they had little or no control.

Henry Dobyns and Robert Euler (39) have written a monograph whose primary purpose is to establish the identity of aboriginal Pai society as a "tribal chiefdom." In addition to being somewhat vague, the authors' definition of this construct combines attributes that have been used by other typologists to distinguish *between* "tribes" and "chiefdoms" and therefore may serve to compound the present confusion in taxonomic circles rather than relieve it.[3] Dobyns & Euler are at their best when they examine the social and political structures that enabled the scattered Pai to unite militarily against the U.S. Army during the so-called Walapai War of 1866–1869. Here they focus squarely on the dynamics of cultural change, and their account of Pai society in crisis is both informative and rewarding. Other works of note concerning Yuman-speaking groups in the Southwest include articles by Kenneth Stewart (147, 148) on the history of Mohave Indians and the poorly known Chemehuevi (146).

The reconstruction of Pueblo prehistory is beset with difficulties at the moment, most noticeably in the Rio Grande region where archeological evidence conflicts with that afforded by linguistic studies and the latter conflict with each other. Ford, Schroeder & Peckham (55) grapple courageously with this dilemma, offering fresh interpretations of their own, but unfortunately touch only lightly upon what they consider to be the most basic problems of all—those of methodology. Schroeder (128) has provided an excellent distillation of Rio Grande ethnohistory from 1540–1846, and Ford examines Pueblo materials in two valuable papers that evaluate general hypotheses about the operation of systems of resource distribution. In one of these articles, Ford (54) finds that among the Pueblos, as among egalitarian societies elsewhere in the world, rituals function as "regulatory mechanisms" that circulate food when severe shortages threaten survival; in the other (53), he de-

---

[3]According to Dobyns & Euler, "The simplest definition of a tribal chiefdom is that it is the largest group habitually combining local-group forces for offensive and defensive military actions" (p. 80).

scribes the structure of Tewa intertribal trade networks during the nineteenth century, concluding that environmental variables, mediated by local adaptations, were responsible for determining the *forms* of economic transfer as well as the kinds of goods exchanged.

An outstanding contribution to Western Pueblo studies has been made by Maitland Bradfield, whose *The Changing Pattern of Hopi Agriculture* (22) stands as one of the most proficient ecological studies yet to appear on a Southwestern Indian society. Firmly conceptualized, thoroughly researched, and meticulously documented, this work is motivated by a sure and uncluttered sense of purpose and a deep appreciation of the delicate and complex relationships that link the fate of human societies to the natural settings in which they flourish. Bradfield begins by analyzing the geological, botanical, and hydrological factors that condition the selection of farm-sites near the village of Oraibi. The primary factor, he finds, ". . . is, and has always been, the availability of water in the form of surface run-off, either directly from an adjoining talus slope or indirectly via a tributary water course: and secondary to this, the capacity of the subsoil to retain the moisture that reaches it. Both factors are reflected in plant cover, and the Hopi know best where to make their fields by looking at the vegetation" (p. 36). The author then turns his attention to the climatic causes and social consequences of the dissection of the valley below Oraibi around the turn of the century. These consequences, he observes, were grave.

> At a blow, a third of the best farm land in the valley was lost, and this, I believe, was the immediate cause of the split of the old village in 1906 and of the lesser migration to Moenkopi that followed the split. Had the dissection of the wash taken place twenty to thirty years earlier, that is to say sooner after the introduction of burros and horses, the lost land might have been replaced by new fields at the head of the valley; but by 1905–6, the opening-up of new land that followed the introduction of draught animals had already been offset by a corresponding rise in population, so that by then there was no other source of cultivable land within the valley to turn to (p. 37).

Finally, Bradfield considers how Hopi farming patterns have been altered by draught animals and carts, and, more recently, by the introduction of tractors and pick-up trucks.

> . . . the introduction of draught animals had three main effects on the pattern of land use in the Oraibi valley. It led to the clearing of fields in the upper third of the valley, which took place between c. 1870 and 1900; by reducing the labour required for agriculture, it opened the way for the great increase in sheep-herding which characterised the first three decades of the present century; and when the effects of the climatic shift of the last thirty to forty years began to bite, the use of draught animals (and ploughs) facilitated the abandonment of 'marginal' land, the concentration of farming resources on those fields that best respond to Hopi farming methods (even when they were some miles distant from the village), and their grouping into larger and more economical holdings. The introduction of pick-ups and tractors in the last fifteen to twenty years had done little more, I think, than carry this last process, i.e. the grouping of fields into larger holdings at a distance from the village, a stage further (p. 37).

In northern Mexico there is a large desert called the Bolson de Mapimi, whose indigenous Indian inhabitants, the Chisos, Tabosos, and Salineros-Cabezas, were exterminated by the Spanish before 1750. William Griffen (66) has done an excellent job of piecing together the history of this process, but there are points at which his analysis of it is rather puzzling. For example, he asserts that the Indian cultures responded to Spanish domination with a series of ". . . adaptive modifications directly related to the survival of individuals who identified with the native social systems" (p. 150). Perhaps so, but the fact remains that the native systems were destroyed, and therefore it seems quite wrong to claim that changes preceding their extinction had "adaptive" value.

Edward Spicer (140, 143) continues his long-standing investigation of the history of Spanish-Indian relations with two studies that are separately concerned with processes of political incorporation in New Spain and contrasting forms of nativism which arose among the Yaqui and Mayo during the nineteenth century. In the latter piece Spicer concludes that while both groups suffered more or less equal amounts of deprivation at the hands of the Spanish, their distinctive reactions to it resulted from differences in cultural and social integration. A concern with integration also dominates Lynne Crumrine's (35) treatment of Mayo ceremonial exchange which attempts to show how the development of sodalities (or "cults") associated with Catholic saints created linkages between formerly autonomous Mayo communities, thus producing a variety of "mechanical" integration which approximates that characteristic of Service's ideal type of "tribal" society. Such a process may indeed have occurred among the Mayo, but reading this and other current works (e.g. Crumrine & Crumrine 38) it becomes apparent that the concept of integration is in serious need of remedial attention. The trouble is basic and familiar. Many anthropologists use the concept, either as a descriptive device or as an explanatory variable, but they use it in very different ways. More important, almost no one attempts to define integration or measure it with operationally explicit procedures. For scholars like Crumrine, who believe that ". . . the form of integration is, after all, the most important level of evolutionary development" (p. 48), problems such as these would seem to be of paramount importance.

KINSHIP AND SOCIAL ORGANIZATION

In 1963 David Aberle (1) called attention to the fact that Navajo social organization is characterized by a large number of culturally acceptable alternatives, a condition which imparts considerable "flexibility" to the system but at the same time imbues it with a "fuzzy" quality that has prevented anthropologists from defining basic patterns with clarity and precision. Today, 10 years later, the fuzziness Aberle described remains as conspicuous and troublesome as ever, but the tendency in recent years has been to regard it as the product of flawed ethnography rather than a property of Navajo culture that requires explanation. Consequently, a number of current studies are concerned with descriptive issues, chief among which is the identification and characterization of the kinds of groups that compose Navajo society.

For years ethnographers have acknowledged both the presence and importance of nuclear and extended families in Navajo social organization. However, debate continues over the principles that govern the combination of these units into larger domestic groups and the criteria according to which the latter should be defined. Gary Witherspoon (165) identifies what he calls the *subsistence residential unit,* a minimal "corporation" whose members reside in adjacent dwellings and combine their sheep into a single herd. Other criteria distinguishing this type of unit are discussed, but Witherspoon's most interesting contribution lies in his demonstration that all of them are intimately linked to, and ultimately derive from, Navajo symbols of motherhood. In a lengthier study that analyzes Navajo pastoralism as a form of ecological adaption, James Downs (41) also attaches primary significance to a social group which is ". . . composed of a number of related families living close together and sharing the responsibilities of a single sheep herd" (p. 31). It appears likely that this is the same kind of group identified by Witherspoon, for Downs emphasizes that women play vital subsistence roles and that the act of herding sheep symbolizes matrilineal affiliation with the group as a whole. Mary Shepardson and Blodwen Hammond (133) have completed the only full-length ethnography of a Navajo community to appear within the last decade. Largely descriptive and guided by what the authors themselves imply may be an out-dated form of "structural-functional analysis," it is nonetheless a valuable and informative study which presents large amounts of carefully collected data on a wide range of topics. In their discussion of social structure, Shepardson & Hammond define four types of membership groups—household, camp, lineage, and clan—but the most prominent attribute of each seems to be its "flexibility," which brings us right back to Aberle and suggests once again that Navajo social units are not so neat and tidy after all.

Nor is variation restricted to the composition of social groups; it crops up again and again in kinship terminology with the result that consistent patterns of usage remain extremely difficult to delineate. Shepardson & Hammond show that variation is greatest among terms labelling what Murdock has called "distant relatives," but the authors are unable to account for this finding except to say that it ". . . substantiates the claim, made by Navajos in their theoretical explanations, that distant positions are regarded as clan, rather than traceable consanguineal relationships" (p. 231). At a more general level the authors conclude: "Unfortunately, not enough data have been assembled through the use of genealogies and specific clan affiliations to make possible a definitive assessment of the changes and regional variations in Navajo kinship terminology today" (p. 231). Stanley and Ruth Freed (58) also confront the problem of indeterminacy in the use of kinship terms, but they, too, have difficulty explaining it. The Freeds speculate that a tendency for Navajos to reside near their place of birth may be instrumental in maintaining regional differences, although ". . . other factors would have to be involved, and what these are is not clear" (p. 1443). They also suggest that variation found among populations in the Low Mountain and Piñon regions may have been caused by contact with the neighboring Hopi. The question of what produces variation in areas where diffusionist hypotheses cannot be invoked is left unanswered.

In two stimulating papers dealing with nonterminological aspects of kinship, Louise Lamphere (97, 98) develops a model of Navajo social structure that departs in interesting ways from those outlined above. Challenging the fundamental premise that the social organization of these people is based upon a hierarchy of sharply defined groups, she argues that beyond the extended family Navajos move within unbounded social fields commensurate with extensive ego-centered kinship networks. Through an analysis of Navajo concepts of autonomy and cooperation, together with the use of excellent case materials, she goes on to illustrate how individual Navajos exploit and manipulate these networks to recruit collaborators in activities requiring the participation of large numbers of people. The important point is that for any given activity any given person can select from among many potential collaborators, a finding that simultaneously helps to explain why alternative social strategies are available to the Navajo and why fixed-membership groups of the kind so cherished by anthropologists are difficult to define. Lamphere also demonstrates that despite the matrilineal component in Navajo society models of cognatic descent systems and bilateral kindreds can be usefully applied. In sum, her work is provocative on several counts and warrants serious consideration by all concerned with Navajo studies.

It needs to be stressed, however, that the fundamental problem posed by Aberle in 1963 has not been satisfactorily answered. How should the high degree of variability in Navajo social organization be accounted for? The solution would not seem to lie in more elaborate typologies. Rather, as Aberle himself suggested, it will probably come from an analysis of the historical and environmental factors that have shaped Navajo society during the last few centuries. The time is right for Navajo specialists to embark upon such a project in earnest. The results of their research could be exciting indeed.

In other works dealing with Athapaskan groups, Harry Basehart (10) has provided a lucid study of Mescalero band organization and leadership which analyzes both ecological and cultural variables in relation to band movements, fluctuations in band size and composition, and the decisive role of chiefs in maintaining social solidarity. Leland Donald (40) describes leadership roles in a modern Navajo community, distinguishing two major types: "formal leaders" who obtain their position by election to office and are primarily charged with the regulation of extra-community affairs, and "informal leaders" who achieve eminence through expertise in ceremonial activities and are mainly concerned with mediating interpersonal disputes and supervising the community's ritual life. Basso (13) has written a short ethnography of a Western Apache community, and, in another study (14), analyzes the types of social situations in which Apaches refrain from speech. The absence of verbal communication, he finds, is associated with situations in which the social identity of at least one participant is ambiguous. Under these conditions, fixed role expectations lose their applicability and the illusion of predictability in social interaction is lost. In short, keeping silent among the Western Apache is a response to uncertainty and unpredictability in social relations.

Significant contributions to the study of Pueblo social organization have been made by Robin Fox (56), Edward Dozier (43), and Alfonso Ortiz (118). In a bold and provocative monograph which centers upon an analysis of modern Cochiti, Fox challenges Fred Eggan's hypothesis that Eastern Keresan kinship patterns represent modified versions of those found among the Western Pueblos. To the contrary, Fox contends, Cochiti is neither a diluted Crow-type system nor a bilateral imitation of Anglo, Spanish, or Tewa models. Rather, he says, ". . . it is an intelligible system in its own right, based on a form of double descent and dual affiliation, and an organization of extended families" (p. 187). Eyeing the evidence of linguistic distributions, Fox goes on to argue that the Keresans have evolved from an original social system all their own, traces of which are still apparent and provide the basis for historical reconstruction. At this point his reasoning becomes openly speculative, causing Eggan (47), who is willing to accept contemporary Keresan social organization as a distinctive type, to point out that the ancestral system Fox proposes—one based on exogamous patrilineal moieties intersected by matrilineal clans—is more complex than any found so far in the Pueblo area. If this raises doubts, they do not seem to worry Fox (57), who has subsequently modified his model of the Keresan prototype (i.e. the moieties need not have been exogamous) in a paper suggesting that his main concern is to formulate a set of *general principles* which will relate transformations in kinship structures to changes in their associated terminologies. What *causes* these transformations in particular cases, and why certain ones occur instead of others, appear to be matters of secondary importance.

Edward Dozier (43) reverses these priorities in a volume that synthesizes data from all the Pueblo groups and addresses itself to a number of topics besides social organization. With respect to the latter, Dozier argues for the chronological priority of the Tanoans in the Rio Grande area and supports the position, espoused by Eggan but rejected by Fox, that the major features of Keresan social structure developed in response to contact with these people. Dozier is careful to add, however, that "It was not so much the influence of these alien societies which is crucial in understanding the changes, but the adjustment to a new ecological environment, particularly to irrigation farming, which favors a society managed by nonkinship units . . ." (p. 143). More specifically, he believes, that ". . . as the demands of an incipient irrigation society made its impression on Keresan pueblos, medicine associations took over responsibility for communal tasks. This may have happened by equating Keresan medicine association with the special cosmological associations of Tewa moieties" (p. 153). Dozier does not explain why such an equation would have been necessary or, if it was, why this particular one took place. Neither does he present a detailed analysis of the organizational requirements of Rio Grande irrigation systems. Consequently, his theory rests somewhat precariously on the assumption that agricultural tasks in Rio Grande villages involve the participation of all adults, while those in the Western Pueblos are limited to the members of families and clans.

The Tewa World by Alfonso Ortiz (118) focuses on important issues in the study of social systems characterized by dual organization. Proceeding from a structural analysis of three pairs of hierarchically arranged categories used by the Tewa to classify human and spiritual existence, Ortiz explores the relationships of these categories to ritual, economic, and political activities as well as to the nonexogamous moieties that partition Tewa society. Drawing a sharp distinction between the *social* aspects of dualism (represented by the moieties) and its *symbolic* aspects (expressed chiefly in ceremonialism), Ortiz then advances to what he considers a more fundamental problem: how can a society such as the Tewa be divided and united at the same time? He finds the answer in a set of complex symbols which function to mediate the moiety division at crucial points in the life cycle, thus establishing a network of personal ties that overcome this opposition and, in so doing, provide a point at which "all paths rejoin" and the individual Tewa finds himself at one with all members of his society. If this recalls Lévi-Strauss, it is precisely because Ortiz wishes to show—and does so, quite successfully—that the most cogent interpretation of dual organizations thus far advanced can be improved upon. How? First, by admitting to the fact that moieties may have nothing to do with the regulation of marriage or, by extension, to systems of generalized exchange. Such is the Tewa case. And secondly, by acknowledging that Lévi-Strauss' model, which is based entirely on societies with unilineal descent, may be inadequate to account for structures in societies where this construct is absent. Lévi-Strauss has concluded that dual organizations do not really exist. Ortiz plainly believes they do. I wonder about a problem more mundane. Why, if Tewa pueblos are really as unified as San Juan is portrayed to be, have they been troubled by factionalism?

Joking relationships in Tarahumara society are examined by John Kennedy (86), who views joking as a form of "structural entertainment," the primary function of which is to provide euphoria and joy through laughter. Following a criticism of Radcliffe-Brown's interpretation of joking as a conflict-resolving device, the author proceeds to characterize this type of verbal behavior as a form of play which ". . . symbolically reverses life situations, permitting momentary escape from the imprisonment of fully accepted but chafing rules" (p. 60). This sounds very much like the kind of conflict-catharsis explanation to which Kennedy is opposed, and his assertion that joking is most highly institutionalized in societies lacking "sophisticated forms of entertainment" also strikes me as being open to question.

The recently published *Handbook of Middle American Indians* includes articles on the Huichol and Cora by Joseph Grimes and Thomas Hinton (67), the Southern Tepehuan and Tepecano by Carrol Riley (126), the Northern Tepehuan by Elman Service (131), the Yaqui and the Mayo by Edward Spicer (142), the Tarahumara by Jacob Fried (59), and the remnant tribes of Sonora (Opata, Pima, Papago, and Seri) by Thomas Hinton (78). Although all of these studies present data on social organization, most of it has been analyzed in greater detail by the same authors in other publications.

CULTURAL STABILITY AND CHANGE

Within the last decade growing numbers of Southwestern Indians have been drawn to Anglo towns and cities in search of employment. Simultaneously, members of reservation communities have intensified their efforts to gain control of local affairs. These trends are clearly reflected in the work of anthropologists who have become increasingly concerned with the analysis of native political processes, the social and psychological consequences of accelerated developmental change, and the adjustment of Indians to life in urban contexts.

Robert Hackenberg (71) has edited a collection of 11 articles that report upon selected aspects of "modernization" among the Papago. Utilizing data contained in the Papago Population Register, an extensive set of census materials compiled under the aegis of the Bureau of Ethnic Research at the University of Arizona, Hackenberg and his collaborators also share common methodological assumptions—a happy situation that lends overall unity to the volume without inhibiting the examination of specific hypotheses. Valuable papers are presented on demographic dispersion, the construction of modernization scales, changes in fertility and mortality rates, and shifts in breeding patterns, but the broadest conclusions are those reached by Hackenberg (72) himself in a paper outlining a descriptive model of Papago adaptation. The Papago are described as employing a "centrifugal" economic strategy which relies heavily on resources imported from communities off the reservation and involves only minimal dependence upon other Papago villages. This contrasts with the "centripetal" strategy of the U.S. government which is designed to develop resources on the reservation and engage all adult Papagos in local programs sponsored by the tribal administration. Hackenberg accounts for preference of the centrifugal strategy by arguing that in an environment characterized by scarcity and uncertainty it maximizes the range of economic opportunities while minimizing the risks of failure. This is a reasonable hypothesis, but its validity hinges on a key assumption that Hackenberg fails to document, namely, that the Papago are unable to stay at home and make a living at the same time. Until this is demonstrated the possibility remains open that they seek off-reservation employment for other than economic reasons, in which case the centrifugal strategy cannot be so easily explained in terms of its survival value.

Whereas Hackenberg's unit of study is the entire Papago population, Jack Waddell (157) focuses on a handful of individuals in a curiously inconclusive monograph which attempts to show that the demands of Anglo occupational roles precipitate modifications in personality structure and cultural values. In fact, few significant changes seem to occur, suggesting either that the author looked for them in the wrong places or, more likely, that Papagos purposely select jobs requiring a minimum of personal adjustment. In another study, Waddell (158) examines "condescending patronage" in a mining corporation which is attempting to reshape Papago goals and work habits so as to make them more congruent with Anglo bureaucratic standards. Padfield & van Willigen (120) compare the unemployment and income rates of Papago populations on and off the reservation, and James Simpson (134), an economist, comes to the conclusion that anthropological concepts are useful in analyzing Papago responses to programs of developmental change. Thank you, Mr. Simpson.

Contributions to the study of Navajo culture change cover a wide range of topics. William Adams (8) addresses himself to the role of values in Navajo economic life in a short but elegant piece that challenges strict materialist interpretations of cultural development. Adams shows that in the community of Shonto, where he worked until 1955, the preferential value accorded to various economic activities is in almost exact inverse order to their actual cash return. Thus, for example, off-reservation wage work pays well, but all but a very few Shonto Navajos reject it. Instead, the majority engage in agricultural and herding activities which, according to Adams, result in important social benefits but are distinctly less remunerative.

"In general," he concludes, "and regardless of actual material rewards, Navajos most value those forms of economic activity which preserve and reinforce the traditional fabric of their society and least value those activities which threaten or disrupt it" (p. 81). Adams continues:

> I prefer to offer the Navajo case as one more challenge to those cultural materialists who unhesitatingly identify economy and society as horse and cart respectively. We all acknowledge that up to the point where minimum biological necessities are satisfied we can hardly account for human behavior in other than materialist terms. We should also acknowledge that beyond that point necessity becomes a matter of cultural and not of biological definition. From here on a materialist explanation is really only appropriate to a materialist society; it is in fact as *emic* as any other ideological bias (p. 81).

Aubrey Williams (163) investigates the processes by which Anglo-American political institutions have been incorporated into Navajo society. He focuses on the "chapter," a community level organization that was modelled after the Anglo "town meeting" and introduced by the government in 1927. In comparison to two other imposed institutions which met with strong Navajo opposition—the Tribal Council and "grazing committee"—the chapter program was favorably received and implemented with little resistance. Williams chronicles the program's history in close detail, observing that its success stemmed from the willingness of Indian service personnel to permit the Navajo to operate chapters in accordance with their own standards of political selection and social control. Modern chapters continue to function as they did 30 years ago, providing ". . . a structure that allows the transfer of Anglo-American principles of government to the Navajo culture with a minimum amount of conflict" (p. 63). All is not placid and peaceful, however, as Mary Shepardson (132) shows in a concise study of Navajo political disputes which also proposes a set of general features for distinguishing "schismatic factionalism" from other forms of intragroup conflict.

Although the now famous Rough Rock Demonstration School has been widely praised as representing a major advance in both the philosophy and practice of Indian education, Erickson & Schwartz (49), who were commissioned by the Office of Economic Opportunity to evaluate the experiment, found that in terms of academic achievement and basic goals it was distinctly less than successful.

> The instructional programs were the least articulated and thought-out that we had seen in some time. Little discernible attention had been given to bringing the school's impressive ideas down to earth. The concept of adapting programs to Navajo culture is enormously appealing, but the adaptation will require months of effort. What Rough Rock needed more than anything else was a sustained attempt by teachers, administrators, dormitory workers, board members, parents, and even (at times) pupils to identify problems and unanswered questions, devise possible solutions, apply the solutions, obtain feedback, reconsider, refine, cope, revise evaluate" (p. 9.6).

In view of such thorough criticism, one is impelled to ask what the Navajo themselves think about the new school. Is it really as ineffective as the authors claim, or does it serve important covert functions of which they were unaware? Regardless, the picture is not entirely black. Erickson & Schwartz emphasize that the Rough

Rock experiment has had very positive effects on the attitudes of professional educators.

> The very act of publicizing Rough Rock's ideas may have had a major impact on American Indian education . . . Virtually everyone was familiar with the demonstration at Rough Rock and wanted to express opinions pro or con. The principal at Rock Point insisted that his freedom to experiment within the structure of BIA was greater because of Rough Rock. From this standpoint, at least, it is our judgement that the Rough Rock demonstration was a marked success . . . The schooling of Navajo children may be permanently the better for it" (p. 9.1 - 9.2).

In another evaluation of Anglo efforts to involve Navajos in programs of planned change, Adair & Deuschle (6) describe the rationale, implementation, and fate of the Navajo-Cornell Field Health Project, a program designed to improve the delivery of modern medical services to the residents of Many Farms, Arizona. One of the program's primary goals was to train bicultural Navajos as "health visitors" who would look in on Navajo families at regular intervals, inquire as to their health, and relay the findings to Anglo physicians. The health visitors experienced some difficulties adjusting to their new role, but on the whole performed ably and well. Eventually, however, and perhaps tragically, they were rejected—not by the Navajo, but by registered nurses in the Public Health Service who viewed the training of "subprofessionals" as a threat to their own positions. Refraining from even the slightest expression of moral outrage at this turn of events, Adair & Deuschle conclude—accurately no doubt, but lamely nevertheless—that the health visitor program failed because of insufficient attention paid by its architects to the beliefs and values of their own society. In fact, "The efficient inner working of the nursing service took precedence over what the [Cornell] University group saw as the ultimate need of training Navajos to participate in rural health service" (p. 147).

Levy, Kunitz & Everett (101) have made a detailed study of Navajo criminal homicide in which they test the familiar hypothesis that murder rates, serving as indices of social disorganization, can be expected to increase as the pace of acculturation and change accelerates. To the contrary, they find that from 1930 to the present homicide rates of the Navajo reservation have remained stable; in addition, they are unable to demonstrate any association, positive or negative, between the act of homicide and alcohol use. There is ample evidence, however, of a characteristic pattern of Navajo homicide which contrasts in significant ways with that reported for urban Black and Anglo populations. Levy & Kunitz (100) examine the same basic hypothesis in a subsequent paper, this time considering social pathologies other than murder and presenting data on the Hopi as well as the Navajo. Concluding once again that the hypothesis is untenable, they go on to suggest that in both groups ". . . the prevalence and patterning of these behaviors are largely explainable in terms of persisting elements of aboriginal culture rather than as responses to acculturation and social disorganization" (p. 97). This may well be true, but there may also be a basic flaw in the way Levy & Kunitz approach their problem. They *assume* throughout that acculturation is necessarily accompanied by social disorganization. Yet they make no attempt to demonstrate that this is so. The very persistence of the aboriginal culture elements upon which they place such heavy stress, together with the findings X of other ethnographers which attest to the adaptability of Navajo social organization, can easily be interpreted to mean that acculturation and disintegration do not go hand in hand. If so, what is at fault is not the careful and exacting work of Levy & Kunitz but the internal logic of the hypothesis they have sought to investigate.

What happens to Navajos who leave their reservation and migrate to urban centers in search of work? What kinds of problems do they encounter and by what means do they attempt to solve them? In short, how do they respond to a social environment that exerts pressures and holds out rewards radically different from those they have experienced before? These and a number of related questions were asked by Theodore Graves (63–65) and several of his students (e.g. 136 and 160) who recently completed a long-range study of variation in the personal adjustment of Navajo migrants to the city of Denver, Colorado. Graves' work is concerned with the abuse of alcohol among urban Navajos, and his primary aim is to discover the psychological and structural factors that contribute most directly to it. Through the use of complex statistical analyses, he shows that variables such as premigration educational training, parental role models, and marital status all play a part in explaining why some Navajos drink excessively and others do not. In general, he finds that ". . . better prepared Indians have far fewer drinking problems than less well prepared Indians, [and that] we can understand their high drinking rates in comparison to other urban groups by virtue of the fact that their preparation for successful, unstressful living is far poorer" (p. 50). This is hardly a startling conclusion, but it does not detract from the methodological sophistication of Graves' research or his convincing demonstration that explanations of intragroup differences can be achieved through the use of variables which have relevance beyond the boundaries of specific cultures. Reporting on another study of Navajo alcoholism, Frances Ferguson (52) draws a distinction between individuals who drink for essentially recreational reasons and those who drink in response to psychic distress. The latter, she observes, respond less readily to treatment in Anglo rehabilitation centers, but the most distinctive attribute of Navajo drinking ". . . is the presence of forces which promote additive recreational drinking [chiefly in the form of intense peer group pressures] without adequate counter forces to control it" (p. 167).

Having migrated to the city, what determines the Navajo's choice to remain there permanently or go back home? William Hodge (80, 81) seeks the answer in the operation of two sets of factors—"push and pull forces" he calls them—which compete simultaneously with one another to keep Navajos in urban areas and draw them back to the reservation. Hodge describes a number of these factors in commendable detail but unfortunately does not attempt to weight them, thus making it impossible to assess their relative significance or generalize about the conditions under which "push" forces dominate "pulls" and vice versa. Despite this shortcoming, Hodge approaches his problem in an interesting way, showing that Indian reservations and Anglo-American cities are subsystems within a larger whole and that passage between the two is inevitably mediated by a multiplicity of complex variables.

The reservation to which some Navajos return—and which the vast majority never leave—is in drastic need of economic development, and David Aberle (4), responding to a request from the U.S. Joint Economic Committee, has outlined a plan to help achieve it. Bold, expensive, and thorough, Aberle's proposal contains suggestions for improvement that range from the installation of better fitted windows in Navajo houses to the implementation of more profitable systems of resource processing and marketing. Throughout, Aberle emphasizes that the value and desirability of the changes he recommends must be judged by the Navajo themselves. It is they who must have the final authority in all such matters, and it is they, in turn, who must assume final responsibility for their decisions. In a brief concluding statement that all planners of development change would do well to remember, Aberle observes:

> Responsibility is not doing what someone else wants to do; it is being able to think about the consequences of one's acts, calculating the effects of those acts on others and on oneself, and being willing to live with the consequences. There is no such thing as preparing a *people* for responsibility. The capacity to deal with the group's affairs grows only by performance, not by rehearsal (p. 272).

In a useful article tracing the historical development of wage labor on the San Carlos Apache Indian reservation, William Adams (9) again draws attention to the importance of social and ritual values in shaping—and, in this case, retarding—processes of economic growth. Edward Parmee (122) presents a balanced description of the San Carlos school system as it operated in 1961 and concludes that it was woefully deficient in almost every respect. Nor surprisingly, Parmee found that the educational program was oriented towards the assimilation of Apaches into Anglo society, ". . . an aim which was diametrically opposed to the desires of most Apaches. Efforts to bring the goals of the program into more extended agreement with the needs of the Apache people were either weak or non-existent" (p. 81). Michael Everett (50) has examined the extent to which White Mountain Apaches tolerate different forms of socially disruptive behavior, and in a more recent study (51) investigates the kinds of information Apaches process when choosing between alternate types of medical treatment. Everett summarizes what is probably his most interesting finding as follows: "As Apache disease symptoms become more psychological in nature, their etiologies or causes assume greater significance, while a concern for symptoms and their relative intensity is increasingly minimized. Conversely, as physiological symptoms manifest greater intensity, considerations of cause become relatively insignificant" (p. 148).

In an analysis of Havasupai land tenure John Martin (103) suggests that patterns of inheritance, though affected to a limited degree by traditional normative principles, are more directly influenced by demographic and ecological variables which impinge upon the developmental cycle of extended families and precipitate conflict between fathers and sons. The impact of environmental factors upon social structure is also discussed by Thomas Hinton (79), who offers an explanation of variation in rates of acculturation among Cora villages in northern Mexico.

Few anthropologists paint upon as broad a canvas as Edward Spicer. His recent works include a discussion of developmental change as a form of cultural integration (139), an excellent case study of how clientele systems operate to destroy or subvert viable forms of social organization in communities of the poor (144), and a general statement describing the kinds of phenomena which, when properly analyzed, should contribute to a more sophisticated understanding of cultural persistence (145). Some of these phenomena have already been identified by other workers in the field, but Spicer is virtually alone among Southwestern ethnographers in calling attention to the need to study *ethnic boundaries* and the processes by which they are generated and maintained. Having resisted assimilation thus far, Southwestern Indians will almost certainly continue to resist it in the future, simultaneously affirming their distinctiveness in ways that create symbolic lines of demarcation between themselves and the members of other societies. It is essential that these boundaries be honored and respected, but before this can happen, as Spicer himself suggests, their content and structure must be made more intelligible.

For decades ethnologists have asserted that Pueblo societies are more impervious to change than any to be found in the Southwest. John Bodine (21) does not deny the impressive durability of the Pueblos, but he demonstrates clearly that significant modifications have taken place (especially in the sphere of demography) and that generalizations to the contrary must be viewed with skepticism. Emory Sekequaptewa (129) presents a clear review of the issues underlying the current Hopi-Navajo land dispute and gives a "Hopi historian's view" of the split that occurred at Oraibi around the turn of the century.

> The more sophisticated view is that the division itself was the substance of a prophecy, in that it was designed in deliberation or, in Hopi terms, *diingavi*. It held that such a division was necessary to the survival of the Hopis as a people, in that establishment of another Hopi community would secure to the Hopis the lands between it and Oraibi. It also held that the sanctity of the religious authorities had become subject to more and more abuse as Oraibi grew in size and social complexity ... (p. 247).

This is an important statement, not only for its intrinsic ethnographic value but because it suggests that Maitland Bradfield's interpretation of the Oraibi split is similar to the one held by the Hopi themselves: in short, an expanding population with not enough land to support it. In other works dealing with the Hopi, Bruce Cox (34) analyzes the functions of gossip in relation to "progressive" and "traditional" political factions, and Richard Clemmer (30) describes the causes of a recent dispute between U.S. government representatives and conservative Hopis over the erection of utility poles and lines to the village of Hotevilla.

Shuichi Nagata (108, 109) has written an extensively detailed ethnography of Moenkopi which focuses upon the adjustment of this Hopi colony to changing economic conditions and its close proximity to the agency town of Tuba City on the Navajo reservation in Arizona. Nagata's study proceeds from the premise that Moenkopi exemplifies a broad category of cases in which a segment of a native community moves to some other but operates initially as an offshoot of the parent village. Later it becomes an ethnic enclave within the new community and its dependence upon the parent village is greatly weakened; simultaneously, its social and economic institutions become more and more closely tied to those of the larger society. Nagata documents this process with liberal amounts of data, eventually concluding that Moenkopi's "modernization" vis-à-vis other Hopi villages can be attributed to two major factors. First, "Moenkopi, of all the villages in Hopiland, came under the strongest acculturative influence that emanated from Tuba City. Since the majority of governmental projects were initiated from this reservation community, Moenkopi became their first recipient" (p. 214). Second, "[Moenkopi's] location on the reservation of an enemy tribe placed the villagers in a competitive position with the Navajo and tended not only to tinge their economic behavior with aggressiveness but also to encourage cooperation with the government, which they regarded as their protector from the Navajo. This made them comparatively more receptive to economic opportunities present in the area" (p. 215). Nothing in the material Nagata presents contradicts these findings but both are very situation-specific, a feature that limits their usefulness in formulating more general statements about processes of economic change or the type of migrating populations with which the author is concerned. In my opinion, Nagata's most valuable contribution is his fine-grained description of Tuba City. It is far and away the best we have of the social structure of a modern agency community.

Summarizing the events of a recent election at Zuni, Triloki Pandey (121) notes that factional allegiances play a prominent part in such affairs and that the power of traditional Zuni theocracy is gradually being weakened by the Tribal Council. M. Estellie Smith (135) embarks upon an investigation of the ways in which Taos political institutions function to maintain social control but, for reasons that remain obscure, never gets around to applying a highly touted "processual model" which she claims would help to reveal them. Judicial procedures for resolving conflict at Taos are outlined by John Collins (32), who reaches the less than momentous conclusion that the native system is sufficiently flexible to cope with changing conditions at any given time. The most interesting contribution to the study of Pueblo law is contained in a brief paper by E. Adamson Hoebel (82), which compares Keresan legal systems to those of other nonliterate societies. Pueblo law is of special interest, Hoebel observes, because it does not conform to the model of British social anthropologists who view stateless societies as kept in balance through the opposition of lineages and clans in feud and threat of feud:

> Rather, it is unique in the fact that although lineages and clans are important in the social structure, they do not function in the legal process. There is no private law and not even a vestige of feud. There is no monarchy, such as characterizes many highly developed tribal systems with centralized authority. If we seek comparative analogies, our attention turns to totalitarian oligarchies and their use of coercive authority to maintain order and conformity in societies based on dogmatic ideology (p. 130).

Although Hoebel does not attempt to explain why Keresan law is so atypical, his comments point directly to real weaknesses in the British model and, to this extent, should serve to stimulate productive discussion.

The life history provides an excellent format for recording and assessing the reactions of individual personalities to changing cultural conditions, and recent autobiographies by Rosalio Moises (with Jane Kelly and William Holden), "Chris" (with Morris Opler), and Helen Sekequaptewa (with Louise Udall) take full advantage of it. *The Tall Candle* (104) is an engrossing chronicle in which Moises, a Sonoran Yaqui, describes his life during a vital period in Yaqui history (circa 1910–1965) when Mexican encroachment precipitated bitter internecine struggles and forced significant modifications in almost every sector of the Indian society. Kelly's lengthy introduction provides a detailed sketch of Yaqui culture and an excellent evaluation of Moises' testimony in light of known historical events. *Apache Odyssey* (113) is the story of Chris, a Mescalero man, who grew up at a time when the adult members of his tribe were just beginning to recover from the crushing impact of military defeat and the harsh indignity of confinement to a reservation. As Chris matured he learned to maneuver in Anglo society as well as his own, and his personal adjustment to the requirements of both systems constitutes the underlying theme of his narrative. Morris Opler's introduction and numerous footnotes contain a wealth of previously unpublished information on Mescalero life (especially on shamanism), and the book as a whole represents a solid addition to Apachean studies. Helen Sekequaptewa is a Hopi woman who was born at Old Oraibi in the late 1890s, received formal education at Anglo schools, married, and sent six of her ten children to college. In *Me and Mine* (130) she describes these episodes, emphasizing the reaction of traditional Hopis to her willingness to depart from established custom. Pueblo cultures may indeed be changing but the experience of Mrs. Sekequaptewa indicates that the costs of innovation are still very high.

> Living in Hotevilla was just like living in any little country town where everyone sees and knows and talks about what everyone else does, only more so. The keynote was "conform," and one who failed to do so felt the lash of disapproval. Our lives were a combination of what we thought was the good of both cultures, the Hopi way and what we had learned at school. Whenever we departed from the traditions, our neighbors would scorn us (p. 186) ... After many years, the enmity between ourselves and our relatives and neighbors has at last almost melted away. There is still some jealousy, mostly because our children did well at school, and we worked together and lived better. We were as stubborn about going back to the old ways as they were about changing their ways. A spirit of tolerance has gradually replaced the spirit of hostility (p. 203).

RELIGION, RITUAL, AND WORLD VIEW

One of the most outstanding contributions to Southwestern religious studies in recent years is Leland C. Wyman's *Blessingway* (167), a lengthy and meticulous description of the magnificent ceremonial around which so much of Navajo religious life revolves. Wyman provides extensive commentary on the functions of Blessingway and its associated mythology and sandpaintings, but the bulk of this enormous effort consists of three versions of the ceremony itself which were recorded by Father Berard Haile between 1930–32. After Father Berard's death in 1961, his texts fell to Wyman, who prepared them for publication. The long-awaited result is excellent in virtually every respect. Gary Witherspoon (164) observes that "*Blessingway* is undoubtedly one of the most important works ever published on the Navajo ..." and is certainly correct in his judgment that "As a sourcebook on Navajo culture and worldview only Gladys Reichard's *Navajo Religion* is in its class" (p. 1361). Wyman (168) has also published a study of the sandpaintings that accompany Shootingway, another major Navajo rite. Here the focus is on an analysis of graphic symbolism, and Wyman's careful and scholarly treatment is a model of completeness and detail. A third class of Navajo ceremonials—*kinaaldá* (the girl's puberty rite)—is described in a volume by Charlotte Frisbie (60) that centers upon an exegesis of chants and songs. Like Wyman, Frisbie provides rich supplementary information on myth, symbolism, and ritual procedure, but it is her painstaking analysis of *kinaaldá* musical texts that reveals most about the ceremony's meaning and significance. Sociolinguists will be interested in Frisbie's work for other reasons. Complex morphophonemic changes occur when spoken Navajo is transformed into song, and I can think of no case where this type of style shift has been documented in closer detail. Louise Lamphere (96) directs attention to the communicative aspects of Navajo ritual (Male Shootingway), describing how symbolic actions and objects are manipulated by singers to recreate a Navajo model of the universe, and, simultaneously, to transform the patient from a state of "ugliness" (illness) to a state of "pleasantness" (health). She then goes on to show that in contrast to the African Ndembu, who map concepts derived from body states and fluids upon the workings of the supernatural world, the Navajo accomplish exactly the reverse: concepts and meanings from supernatural phenomena are projected onto conditions of the body. In two papers dealing with related topics, John Collins (31, 33) describes a Taos peyote ceremony and suggests that the sequence of ritual events which composes it functions symbolically to transform participants from a "profane" state to a "sacred" one and back again.

Principles of Jungian psychology are applied to the Navajo emergence myth by Sheila Moon (105), who seeks to discover ". . . the content and symbolism of a great religious tradition and to discuss it as a source of illumination for the darkness in the spirit of man" (p. 3–4). Moon's basic assumption is that myths are created out of man's need to find significance and meaning in his life, and therefore may be viewed as expressions of a universal search for coherence and understanding.

> The paradox of the search as it appears in the Navajo myth, as well as in many other myths and in human experience, can be stated simply. Only through darkness, chaos, the unformed, the difficult, can light come into being. This is the vision of redemption. It is a vision with deep roots in the human psyche, a vision of true consciousness and wholeness, a vision of ultimate unity which contains within it the duality of existence (pp. 10–11).

If this calls to mind a certain Frenchman, it is not altogether fortuitous, for in some respects Jung's approach to the study of myth resembles that of Lévi-Strauss. Both men are fascinated with contradictions inherent in the human condition, and both view mythologies as complex symbolic instruments that embody "explanations" of these contradictions and serve to overcome them at an unconscious level. There is no way of telling whether Moon has hit upon the correct Navajo explanation because there is no way of testing it. This will probably disturb some anthropologists. Those who are Jung at heart will be less upset.

On the basis of data collected in interviews with 21 Navajo singers and 284 students in BIA schools, Chien Chiao (29) discusses the transmission and persistence of Navajo ceremonial knowledge. His most general finding, quoted below, concerns the effects of formal education upon the attitudes of young people towards their native ritual tradition.

Navajo girls [who have less difficulty adapting to change] tend to have more favorable responses to Anglo-American education than do the boys. Girls become more amenable to the teachings of Anglo-Americans as they progress in their education. Consequently, older girls (10th to 11th grades) tend to more readily accept the anthropological version of the Navajo origin than younger ones. Navajo boys have more difficulty adapting to changes and tend to have more resentment toward Anglo-American culture and more resistance to Anglo-American education. These attitudes are strengthened as the boys grow up. Acceptance of the Navajo story concerning their origin is a means of expressing their resentment and resistance. This is probably why older boys . . . are more willing to accept the Navajo story than younger ones" (p. 87–88).

An exchange between Aberle (3) and Opler (114, 115) has clarified certain aspects of the nature of ritual payment in Apachean cultures. Writing about the Navajo, Aberle proposes that just as objects received by a shaman on behalf of supernatural powers obligate the powers to cooperate in ceremonials so do goods given the shaman obligate him to officiate. These arrangements are further interpreted as links in an unbroken circle of reciprocal transactions that bind men to gods, gods to men, and, finally, men to men. Opler does not question the importance of reciprocity in some spheres of Navajo life, but he argues convincingly that gifts to supernaturals are conceptually distinct from shamans' fees, and that the latter, which can be refused, lack the compelling power attributed to them by Aberle. Drawing upon extensive materials from both published and unpublished sources, Opler goes on to demonstrate that this is probably a general Apachean pattern.

In an investigation of Western Apache witchcraft, Basso (12) draws upon the techniques of ethnographic semantics to construct a model of the behavioral and nonbehavioral attributes that distinguish witch suspects from other categories of persons. He then investigates the types of social relationships that obtain between victims of witchcraft and the individuals they accuse. In the Western Apache case, these relationships are found to be characterized by a lack of reciprocity, an unequal distribution of scarce resources, and an absence of mechanisms that operate to suppress or resolve interpersonal conflict. Basso concludes with the observation that in most studies of witchcraft "The basic question of 'who witches who' is hardly ever given explicit attention, and as a result, we know very little about the attributes of witch-accuser relationships in other societies. This is unfortunate because it is entirely possible that variation in these attributes might be discovered to correlate with variation in social organization" (p. 56). Florence Hawley Ellis (48) discusses witchcraft among the Pueblos in a discursive essay that contains some intriguing data on witchcraft beliefs and some interesting speculations about their historical origins. Unfortunately, however, she touches only lightly upon the kinds of social contexts in which these beliefs acquire significance and force, thus making it impossible to assess their adaptive and adjustive functions (the presence of both is implied) or the impact they have upon the conduct and organization of interpersonal relations.

Drawing directly upon the theories of Lévi-Strauss and, to a lesser extent, those of Victor Turner, Barbara Meyerhoff (107) analyzes the relationships of three key cultural symbols to the ecology and history of the Huichol Indians of northern Mexico. Myerhoff's basic premise is that the transition of Huichol society from a desert to mountain setting and from a hunting to agricultural subsistence base is not yet complete. This condition, she believes, generates a set of profound discontinuities in Huichol life that are reflected in, and ultimately resolved by, the symbols of Deer, Maize, and Peyote. Deer symbolizes the original Huichol, the Huichol as hunter, the richness of the Huichol past. Maize is a symbol of the modern Huichol, of the Huichol as cultivator, of the dull and ceaseless labor that dominates the Huichol present. Peyote is neither mundane like maize, nor exotic and exicting like deer. To the contrary, "It is that solitary, ahistorical, asocial, asexual, arational domain without which man is not complete, without which life is a lesser affair" (p. 72). Having postulated opposition at one level of meaning, Meyerhoff, like all good structuralists, must search for unity and reconciliation at another. And like all good structuralists she finds it. "When the Huichol juxtapose [these symbols] and consider each to be an aspect of the other, they are stating that there is a wholeness to being human, that man cannot live without a sense of his past, working for his living, or finding moments of solitary beauty. Surely this is an accurate statement of the life of man when it is healthy and whole" (pp. 72–73). At points such as this structural anthropology and academic theology come very close together, not in subject matter, of course, but because the acceptance or rejection of their findings depends upon something akin to an act of faith. Such acts are private affairs and do not lend themselves well to dispute in the public arena. I hope, but do not feel certain, that the Huichol universe is as tidy and consolidated as Meyerhoff has depicted it.

The subject of ritual clowns is taken up in papers by Ross Crumrine (36, 37) on the Mayo *capakoba* and by Louis Hieb (76) on the Zuni *koyemci*. Crumrine begins with the observation that Mayo clowns behave in exaggerated violation of cultural norms, and, in so doing, dramatize fundamental oppositions between conflicting social principles (e.g. "human" vs "non-human" and "sacred" vs "profane"). He then asserts that anomalies in the clown role function to mediate these oppositions, simultaneously serving the valuable purpose of encouraging adherence to the norms the clowns have so flagrantly challenged. This could be construed as a form of anthropological tricksterism were it not for Crumrine's awareness and understanding of recent work in psychology. Daniel Berlyne (19, 20) has conducted as series of sophisticated experiments indicating that mild collative cognitive conflict produces heightened awareness on the part of individuals who experience it. In this condition, they probe alternative solutions, and, when a workable solution is found, fixate upon it. This in turn helps them to learn and, in most cases, reinforces what is already familiar. Crumrine suggests that Mayo clowns produce exactly the kind of conflict Berlyne describes. As a consequence, "The blurred social relations and cultural structure portrayed by the *capakobam* and their confusing appearance reinforce traditional Mayo social relations and the cognitive structure of their universe" (p. 20). In contrast to Crumrine's presentation, which is reasonably direct and straightforward, Hieb's paper on Zuni clowns shoots out in all directions at once. Oppositions fly left and right, reversing each other, inverting each other, and doing other forms of scatological structural damage that only Hieb understands for sure. I confess there were portions of his paper which left me thoroughly confused. Hieb convinced me that *koyemci* are special, complex, and fascinating, but I was never completely sure why he thought so.

On the other hand, it is readily apparent why Dennis Tedlock (149) is interested in the stylistic aspects of Zuni varrative fiction.

A good deal of truth which Zunis see in their fictional narratives derives not from the final explanatory elements but from the efforts of the narrator to create the appearance of reality within the body of the story itself. The ability to create this appearance is the most important measure of the individual's narrative skill (p. 226).

Focusing upon a class of tales told only at night and in the winter, Tedlock discusses the ways in which Zuni storytellers enhance and augment verbal description so as to heighten its verisimilitude. The stylistic devices they employ range from sophisticated "framing" strategies to onomatopoeia, from physical gestures and quotation to the manipulation of paralinguistic phenomena such as voice quality and loudness. Ultimately, however, it is the storyteller's consummate ability to combine and juxtapose these cues that contributes most to the credibility of his narrative and the impact of his performance. Tedlock's study is an important one, opening up, as Eggan (47) has observed, ". . . a new dimension to Zuni oral literature" (p. 300). Simultaneously, it illustrates the rich rewards that await Southwestern ethnographers who turn their attention to problems in the field of sociolinguistics.

In *The Tewa World*, which is as much a study in religion as it is of social structure, Ortiz (118) presents an excellent description of Tewa ontological categories and goes on to relate them to cultural themes that find symbolic expression in public ceremonials. More recently, he has used the same approach to construct a generalized model of Pueblo world view (119). This latest work is useful for several reasons, not the least of which is a discussion of Pueblo attitudes towards the interpretation and regulation of deviant behavior. But it is elsewhere, I think, in a discussion of the "world view" concept itself, that Ortiz makes his most interesting remarks. To begin with, he notes, the concept has always been too generally defined; as a result, its value has been chiefly rhetorical. What is needed instead is a truly operational definition that serves to identify the constituent elements of world views wherever they are found. Although Ortiz does not claim to have formulated the ideal definition, he argues that categories of space and time are the most fundamental elements of all and the points at which analysis should begin. Why? Because categories of space and time provide man with his primary orientation to reality, and if, as Ortiz believes, conceptions of reality lie at the heart of world views, there is no other viable strategy.

Byron Harvey III (73) has written a helpful overview of Pueblo religion, and Don Roberts (127) has performed a similar task with respect to the ethnomusicology of the Eastern Pueblos. Naomi Ware (159) discusses survival and change in Pima Indian music, and Gertrude Kurath (94) provides what is easily the most thorough and exhaustive analysis yet to appear of Tewa chants and ceremonial dances. Although I lack the competence to assess the work of ethnomusicologists, it was intriguing to discover how economically some of Kurath's choreographic data could be generalized and restated in the form of ordered rules similar to those employed by transformational linguists. Accompanied by an explicit statement of contextual restrictions, such rules might be used to construct a "grammar" that would specify all (but only) acceptable dance-step sequences. This is probably not a novel idea in ethnomusicological circles, but even so it is one that could be pursued with extremely interesting results.

Recent studies in ethnoscience include an analysis of Uto-Aztecan color terminologies by Jane and Kenneth Hill (77) which calls into question the universality of one of the stages in the evolutionary sequence postulated by Berlin and Kay. Elsewhere, George and Felicia Trager (152) describe directional categories in two Tiwan languages, Felicia Trager (151) discusses concepts of time at Picuris, and William Leap (99) reports on recent changes in the semantic correlates of Tiwa noun classes denoting units of space. In a study of Maricopa food taxonomies, Jack Frisch (61) finds that the most pervasive distinction is between edibles which contain water (e.g. cactus and fruit) and those which do not (e.g. meat and bread). The importance of this distinction, Frisch suggests, may be related to the fact that the physical environment of the Maricopa is one of semiarid desert characterized by seasonal shortages of water. In aboriginal times, he believes, the water/non-water contrast may have been of prime importance to survival. Norma Perchonock & Oswald Werner (124) describe Navajo categories of food in a paper that directs attention to problems created by intersecting and overlapping lexical domains, the existence of different classificatory principles within single hierarchical taxonomies, and overly strict reliance upon highly structured eliciting techniques. In another article, Werner & Begishe (161) present a complete Navajo classification of parts of the foot, drawing upon this material to refine a set of general propositions about the structure and growth of folk taxonomies first advanced by Brent Berlin.

Basso (11) and Witherspoon (166) have published semantic analyses of Apachean classificatory verb systems. Basso's paper, which deals with Western Apache, is more explicit in the definitions it presents, but Witherspoon's, which deals with Navajo, is more complete. Witherspoon's analysis is valuable for other reasons as well. He adduces convincing evidence that traditional interpretations of number in the Navajo language are too simplistic. In addition, he shows that the dimensions of "grouping" (i.e. whether plural objects are considered to form a single group or more than one) and "patterning" (i.e. whether the items in a group are arranged randomly or in a straight line) are fundamental to the categorization of objects at rest. According to Witherspoon, Navajos recognize 15 general categories of this kind each of which is partitioned into one singular and fourteen plural categories, producing a total of 225; of these only 102 are lexically marked. Such complexity is impressive and Witherspoon seizes upon it to ask a familiar question.

Are the peoples whom we class as "primitive" really underdeveloped in abstract thinking or intellectual activity, or is it that we are just beginning to understand how they think? Do we call them simple because they really are simple, or because we only understand the simplest forms and ideas of their cultures? (p. 121)

Of all the works published by Southwestern ethnologists during the last 4 years none has reached a wider audience or met with such enthusiastic popular acclaim than Carlos Castaneda's recently completed trilogy (25–27) about his experiences in pursuit of "knowledge" with the Yaqui philosopher Don Juan. Indeed, so much has been written in praise of Castaneda's accomplishment that one could easily form the opinion that it is superior in every respect. In some respects it is. There can be no doubt, for example, that the Don Juan trilogy constitutes a major contribution to the literature on encounters with hallucinogenic drugs. It also provides an excellent account of the mutually enriching relationship that can develop when a willing anthropologist and an equally willing informant join forces to seek and exchange understanding. Finally, Castaneda describes in compelling fashion the sophisticated views of a not so primitive man, the remarkable Don Juan himself, whose personal vision of the universe rests upon a set of metaphysical assumptions so different from those of Western philosophers that at times the contrast is truly startling. In these ways the Don Juan experience is informative and illuminating. It should not, however, be mistaken for ethnography. Who, really, is Don Juan? Where does he come from? What is his background? How does he live? We are given only the barest of hints. When Don Juan is not instructing Castaneda he participates in a social and cultural system; he is a member of a community. But which one? Where is it? How does it operate? What are the constraints it imposes, the rewards it holds out? What concepts and values does it embody, and how if at all, have these influenced Don Juan's own thought? Again we are left uninformed. Consequently, as Spicer (141) has observed, the wisdom of Don Juan—and indeed Don Juan himself—exist in a "cultural limbo," a context that is really no context at all because it is lacking in historical substance, shorn of spatial parameters, and devoid of social form. Don Juan is obviously a person in society, and at times even *of* society, but never is he in or of any society in particular. Thus he is a man without cultural identity—never completely real and always slightly less than believable.

CONCLUSIONS

It should now be evident that between 1968–1972 Southwestern ethnologists have not been lacking for things to do. To the contrary, their enthusiasm has been unflagging, their energy quite enormous, and their published output just a little shy of prodigious. But the issue, of course, is not how much they have done but how well they have done it. What has been accomplished?

1. If the sole measure of achievement is explanation, then little has been achieved. Most Southwestern ethnologists, like most anthropologists working elsewhere in the world, have not been successful in accounting for the rich abundance of variation that social and cultural systems display. However, they have *attempted* explanation to a greater extent than ever before.

2. Southwestern ethnologists have critically examined a wide range of existing theories, and, in some cases, have refined them in important ways. However, they have formulated few original theories of their own.

3. Southwestern ethnologists have reached valuable conclusions about the development and operation of specific cultures. However, only rarely have they used these conclusions to construct (or test) cross-cultural hypotheses.

4. The descriptive and analytic strategies employed by Southwestern ethnologists have become more sophisticated. This is reflected in an increased concern with adequate sampling procedures, a growing use of multivariate statistics, and the adoption of techniques that facilitate the formal definition of cultural categories.

5. Culture historians have continued to learn more and more about key *events* in the Southwest's rich and exciting past. However, their understanding of the social and cultural *processes* that have shaped the region's present lags behind.

6. Students of social organization have done some excellent work, but in most cases have tended to ignore the structural relationships that link Indian institutions to those in the non-Indian world around them. This is unfortunate because it gives the misleading impression that modern Indian societies are closed systems and/or cultural isolates. In fact, of course, they are neither.

7. Studies of persistence and change rely more heavily than ever before upon models that define processes of environmental adaptation and psychological adjustment as the major determinants of cultural development.

8. Several Southwestern ethnologists have been called upon to devise, implement, and evaluate programs of planned change involving Indian communities. They have taken these responsibilities seriously and have discharged them with honesty and integrity.

9. Studies of religion and world view exhibit increased interest in structural analyses of cultural symbols and the value such analyses have for understanding the expressive functions of ritual in dramatizing covert social principles. Studies in ethnoscience have also increased, but few go beyond the presentation of specific findings to consider broader issues in linguistics or ethnography.

10. No single personality, theoretical model, or methodological strategy can be said to dominate Southwestern studies at the present time. Neither is there any sign of an overarching synthesis that can, or will, reconcile the diversity of aims, assumptions, and approaches currently being employed. If, as a number of scholars have observed, anthropology as a whole is now encumbered with a fractured paradigm, the field of Southwestern ethnology—no more or less than any other—reflects it clearly.

Literature Cited

1. Aberle, D. F. 1963. Some sources of flexibility in Navaho social organization. *Southwest. J. Anthropol.* 19:1–8
2. Aberle, D. F. 1966. *The Peyote Religion Among the Navaho.* Chicago: Aldine. 454 pp.
3. Aberle, D. F. 1967. The Navaho singer's "fee": payment or prestation? In *Studies in Southwestern Ethno-linguistics*, ed. D. H. Hymes, W. E. Bittle, 15–32. The Hague: Mouton. 464 pp.
4. Aberle, D. F. 1969. A plan for Navajo economic development. In *Toward Economic Development for Native American Communities*, 1:223–76. Joint Econ. Comm. Washington, D.C.: GPO. 320 pp.
5. Aberle, D. F., Stewart, O. C. 1957. Navaho and Ute peyotism: a chronological and distributional study. *Univ. Colo. Ser. Anthropol.* 6
6. Adair, J., Deuschle, K. W. 1970. *The People's Health: Medicine and Anthropology in a Navajo Community.* New York: Appleton-Century-Crofts. 188 pp.
7. Adair, J., Vogt, E. Z. 1949. Navaho and Zuni veterans: a study of contrasting modes of culture change. *Am. Anthropol.* 51:547–61
8. Adams, W. Y. 1971. Navajo ecology and economy: a problem in cultural values. In *Apachean Culture History and Ethnology*, ed. K. H. Basso, M. E. Opler, 77–82. Anthropol. Pap. Univ. Arizona 21. Tucson: Univ. Arizona Press. 168 pp.
9. Ibid. Wage labor and the San Carlos Apache, 115–28
10. Basehart, H. 1970. Mescalero Apache band organization and leadership. *Southwest. J. Anthropol.* 26:87–106
11. Basso, K. H. 1968. The Western Apache classificatory verb system: a formal analysis. *Southwest. J. Anthropol.* 24:252–66
12. Basso, K. H. 1969. *Western Apache Witchcraft.* Anthropol. Pap. Univ. Arizona 15. Tucson: Univ. Arizona Press. 75 pp.
13. Basso, K. H. 1970. *The Cibecue Apache.* New York: Holt, Rinehart & Winston. 106 pp.
14. Basso, K. H. 1970. "To give up on words": silence in Western Apache culture. *Southwest. J. Anthropol.* 26:213–30
15. Basso, K. H., Ed. 1971. *Western Apache Raiding and Warfare: from the notes of Grenville Goodwin.* Tucson: Univ. Arizona Press. 330 pp.
16. Beals, R. L. 1943. Northern Mexico and the Southwest. *El Norte de Mexico y el Sur de Estados Unidos*, 191–99. Mexico: Talleres de la Editorial Stylo. 362 pp.
17. Benedict, R. 1928. Psychological types in the cultures of the Southwest. *Proc. 23rd. Int. Congr. Am.*, New York, 572–81
18. Benedict, R. 1934. *Patterns of Culture.* Boston: Houghton Mifflin. 291 pp.
19. Berlyne, D. E. 1966. Conflict and arousal. *Sci. Am.* 215:82–87
20. Berlyne, D. E. 1966. Curiosity and exploration. *Science* 153:25–33
21. Bodine, J. J. 1972. Acculturation processes and population dynamics. See Ref. 119, 257–87
22. Bradfield, M. 1971. *The Changing Pattern of Hopi Agriculture.* Roy. Anthropol. Inst. Occasional Pap. 30. London. 66 pp.
23. Brody, J. J. 1971. *Indian Painters and White Patrons.* Albuquerque: Univ. New Mexico Press. 238 pp.
24. Brugge, D. M. 1968. *Navajos in the Catholic Church Records of New Mexico, 1694–1875.* Window Rock. 160 pp.
25. Castaneda, C. 1968. *The Teachings of Don Juan: A Yaqui Way of Knowledge.* Berkeley: Univ. California Press. 196 pp.
26. Castaneda, C. 1971. *A Separate Reality.* New York: Simon & Schuster. 317 pp.
27. Castaneda, C. 1972. *Journey to Ixtlan.* New York: Simon & Schuster. 161 pp.
28. Chapman, K. M. 1970. *The Pottery of San Ildefonso Pueblo.* Albuquerque: Univ. New Mexico Press. 260 pp.
29. Chiao, C. 1971. *Continuation of Tradition in Navajo Society.* Inst. Ethnol. Acad. Sinica, Monogr. Ser. B, 3. Nanking, Taipei, Republic of China. 101 pp.
30. Clemmer, R. O. 1969. The fed-up Hopi: resistance of the American Indian and the silence of the good anthropologists. *Steward Anthropol. Soc. J.* 1:18–40
31. Collins, J. J. 1968. Descriptive introduction to the Taos peyote ceremony. *Ethnology* 7:427–49
32. Collins, J. J. 1968. Law, function, and judicial process at a New Mexican pueblo. *Int. J. Comp. Sociol.* 9:129–31
33. Ibid 1969. Transformations of the self and the duplication of ceremonial structure. 10:302–7

34. Cox, B. 1970. What is Hopi gossip about? Information management and Hopi factions. *Man* 5:88–99

35. Crumrine, L. S. 1969. *Ceremonial Exchange as a Mechanism in Tribal Integration among the Mayos of Northwest Mexico.* Anthropol. Pap. Univ. Arizona 14. Tucson: Univ. Arizona Press. 64 pp.

36. Crumrine, N. R. 1968. Mayo ritual impersonations: the mask, arousal, and enculturation. *Anthropos* 63:976–77

37. Crumrine, N. R. 1969. Capakoba, the Mayo Eastern ceremonial impersonator: explanations of ritual clowning. *J. Sci. Study Religion* 8:1–22

38. Crumrine, N. R., Crumrine, L. S. 1969. Where Mayos meet mestizos: a model for the social structure of culture contact. *Hum. Organ.* 28:50–57

39. Dobyns, H. F., Euler, R. C. 1970. *Wauba Yuma's People: The Comparative Socio-political Structure of the Pai Indians of Arizona.* Prescott College Press. 98 pp.

40. Donald, L. 1970. Leadership in a Navajo community. *Anthropos* 65:867–80

41. Downs, J. 1972. *The Navajo.* New York: Holt, Rinehart & Winston. 136 pp.

42. Dozier, E. P. 1954. The Hopi-Tewa of Arizona. *Univ. Calif. Publ. Am. Archaeol. Ethnol.* 44:259–376

43. Dozier, E. P. 1970. *The Pueblo Indians of North America.* New York: Holt, Rinehart & Winston. 223 pp.

44. Dunn, D. 1968. *American Indian Painting of the Southwest and Plains Area.* Albuquerque: Univ. New Mexico Press. 429 pp.

45. Eggan, D. 1943. The general problem of Hopi adjustment. *Am. Anthropol.* 45:357–73

46. Eggan, F. 1950. *Social Organization of the Western Pueblos.* Univ. Chicago Press. 373 pp.

47. Eggan, F. 1972. Summary. See Ref. 119, 287–305

48. Ellis, F. H. 1970. Pueblo witchcraft and medicine. In *Systems of North American Witchcraft and Sorcery,* ed. D. E. Walker Jr., 37–72. Anthropol. Monogr. Univ. Idaho 1. Moscow, Idaho: Univ. Idaho Press. 295 pp.

49. Erickson, D. A., Schwartz, H. 1969. *Community School at Rough Rock: an Evaluation for the Office of Economic Opportunity.*

50. Everett, M. W. 1970. Pathology in White Mountain Apache culture: a preliminary analysis. *West. Can. J. Anthropol.* 2:180–203

51. Everett, M. W. 1971. White Mountain Apache medical decision-making. See Ref. 8, 135–50

52. Ferguson, F. N. 1968. Navaho drinking: some tentative hypotheses. *Hum. Organ.* 27:159–67

53. Ford, R. I. 1972. Barter, gift, or violence: an analysis of Tewa intertribal exchange. In *Social Exchange and Interaction,* ed. E. N. Wilmsen, 21–45. Anthropol. Pap. 45, Mus. Anthropol., Univ. Michigan. 147 pp.

54. Ford, R. I. 1972. An ecological perspective on the eastern pueblos. See Ref. 119, 1–18

55. Ford, R. I., Schroeder, A. H., Peckham, S. L. 1972. Three perspectives on puebloan prehistory. See Ref. 119, 19–39

56. Fox, R. 1967. *The Keresan Bridge: A Problem in Pueblo Ethnography.* London Sch. Econ. Monogr. Soc. Anthropol. 35. London: Athlone. 216 pp.

57. Fox, R. 1972. Some unsolved problems of pueblo social organization. See Ref. 119, 71–86

58. Freed, S. A., Freed, R. S. 1970. Notes on regional variation in Navajo kinship terminology. *Am. Anthropol.* 72:1439–44

59. Fried, J. 1969. The Tarahumara. In *Handbook of Middle American Indians: Ethnology,* ed. E. Z. Vogt, 8:846–70. Austin: Univ. Texas Press. 349 pp.

60. Frisbie, C. J. 1967. *Kinaalda: A Study of the Navaho Girl's Puberty Ceremony.* Middletown, Conn.: Wesleyan Univ. Press. 437 pp.

61. Frisch, J. A. 1968. Maricopa foods: a native taxonomic system. *Int. J. Am. Ling.* 34:16–20

62. Goldfrank, E. S. 1945. Socialization, personality, and the structure of Pueblo society. *Am. Anthropol.* 47:516–39

63. Graves, T. D. 1970. Personal adjustment of Navajo Indian migrants to Denver, Colorado. *Am. Anthropol.* 72:35–53

64. Graves, T. D. 1971. Drinking and drunkenness among urban Indians. In *The American Indian in Urban Society,* ed. J. O. Waddell, O. M. Watson, 274–311. Boston: Little, Brown. 414 pp.

65. Graves, T. D., Lave, C. A. 1972. Determinants of urban migrant Indian wages. *Hum. Organ.* 31:47–62

66. Griffen, W. B. 1969. *Culture Change and Shifting Populations in Central Northern Mexico.* Anthropol. Pap.

Univ. Arizona 13. Tucson: Univ. Arizona Press. 192 pp.

67. Grimes, J. E., Hinton, T. B. 1969. The Huichol and Cora. See Ref. 59, 792–813

68. Gunnerson, J. 1969. Apache archaeology in northeastern New Mexico. *Am. Antiq.* 34:23–29

69. Gunnerson, J., Gunnerson, D. 1970. Evidence of Apaches at Pecos. *El Palacio* 76:1–6

70. Gunnerson, J., Gunnerson, D. 1971. Apachean culture: a study in unity and diversity. See Ref. 8, 7–27

71. Hackenberg, R. A., Ed. 1972. Modernization research on the Papago Indians. *Hum. Organ.* 31

72. Hackenberg, R. A. 1972. Restricted interdependence: the adaptive pattern of Papago Indian society. *Hum. Organ.* 31:113–26

73. Harvey, B. III, 1972. An overview of Pueblo religion. See Ref. 119, 197–218

74. Helms, M. W. 1970. Matrilocality, social solidarity and social structure. *Southwest. J. Anthropol.* 26:197–212

75. Hester, J. J. 1971. Navajo culture change: 1550 to 1960 and beyond. See Ref. 8, 51–67

76. Hieb, L. 1972. Meaning and mismeaning: toward an understanding of the ritual clown. See Ref. 119, 163–96

77. Hill, J. H., Hill, K. C. 1970. A note on Uto-Aztecan color terminologies. *Anthropol. Ling.* 12:231–38

78. Hinton, T. B. 1969. Remnant tribes of Sonora: Opata, Pima, Papago, and Seri. See Ref. 59, 879–88

79. Hinton, T. B. 1970. Indian acculturation in Nyarit: The Cora response to mestizoization. In *The Social Anthropology of Latin America: Essays in honor of Ralph Beals,* ed. W. Goldschmidt, H. Hoijer, 16–35. Los Angeles: Univ. California Press. 369 pp.

80. Hodge, W. H. 1969. *The Albuquerque Navajos.* Anthropol. Pap. Univ. Arizona 11. Tucson: Univ. Arizona Press. 84 pp.

81. Hodge, W. H. 1971. Navajo urban migration: an analysis from the perspective of the Family. See Ref. 64, 346–92

82. Hoebel, E. A. 1968. The character of Keresan pueblo law. *Proc. Am. Phil. Soc.* 112:127–30

83. Hoijer, H. 1938. The southern Athapaskan languages. *Am. Anthropol.* 40: 75–87

84. Hoijer, H. 1971. The position of the Apachean languages in the Athapaskan stock. See Ref. 8, 3–6

85. Kelly, L. C. 1968. *The Navajo Indians and Federal Indian Policy,* 1900–1935. Tucson: Univ. Arizona Press. 221 pp.

86. Kennedy, J. G. 1970. Bonds of laughter among the Tarahumara Indians. See Ref. 79, 36–68

87. Kluckhohn, C. 1941. Patterning as exemplified in Navaho culture. In *Language, Culture, and Personality: Essays in Memory of Edward Sapir,* ed. L. Spier, A. I. Hallowell, S. S. Newman, 109–30. Menasha, Wis.: Sapir Memorial Pub. Fund. 298 pp.

88. Kluckhohn, C. 1942. Myths and rituals: a general theory. *Harvard Theol. Rev.* 35:45–79

89. Kluckhohn, C. 1944. Navaho witchcraft. *Pap. Peabody Mus. Am. Archaeol. Ethnol.* 22. Harvard Univ.

90. Kluckhohn, C. 1951. Values and value orientations in a theory of action: an exploration in definition and classification. In *Toward a General Theory of Action,* ed. T. Parsons, E. Shils, 389–433. Cambridge: Harvard Univ. Press. 506 pp.

91. Kluckhohn, C., Hill, W. W., Kluckhohn, L. C. 1971. *Navajo Material Culture.* Cambridge, Mass.: Belknap Press Harvard Univ. 488 pp.

92. Kroeber, A. L. 1917. Zuni kin and clan. *Am. Mus. Natur. Hist. Anthropol. Pap.* 18:39–205

93. Kroeber, A. L. 1937. Athabascan kin term systems. *Am. Anthropol.* 39: 602–8

94. Kurath, G. P., Garcia, A. 1969. *Music and Dance of the Tewa Pueblos.* Santa Fe: Univ. New Mexico Press. 309 pp.

95. Kurtz, R. J. 1969. Headmen and war chanters: role theory and the early Canyoncito Navajo. *Ethnohistory* 16:83–111

96. Lamphere, L. 1969. Symbolic elements in Navajo ritual. *Southwest. J. Anthropol.* 25:279–305

97. Lamphere, L. 1970. Ceremonial cooperation and networks: a reanalysis of the Navajo outfit. *Man* 5:39–59

98. Lamphere, L. 1971. The Navajo cultural system: an analysis of concepts of cooperation and autonomy and their relation to gossip and witchcraft. See Ref. 8, 91–114

99. Leap, W. L. 1970. Tiwa noun class semology: a historical view. *Anthropol. Ling.* 12:38–45

100. Levy, J. E., Kunitz, S. J. 1971. Indian reservations, anomie and social pathologies. *Southwest. J. Anthropol.* 27: 97–129

101. Levy, J. E., Kunitz, S. J., Everett, M. 1969. Navajo criminal homicide. *Southwest. J. Anthropol.* 25:124–52

102. Lowie, R. H. 1929. Notes on Hopi clans. *Am. Mus. Natur. Hist. Anthropol. Pap.* 30:303–60

103. Martin, J. F. 1968. A reconsideration of Havasupai land tenure. *Ethnology* 7: 450–60

104. Moises, R., Kelly, J. H., Holden, W. C. 1971. *The Tall Candle: The Personal Chronicle of a Yaqui Indian.* Lincoln: Univ. Nebraska Press. 251 pp.

105. Moon, S. 1970. *A Magic Dwells: A Poetic and Psychological Study of the Navaho Emergence Myth.* Middletown: Wesleyan Univ. Press. 206 pp.

106. Moorhead, M. 1968. *The Apache Frontier: Jacobo Ugarte and Spanish-Indian Relations in Northern New Spain, 1769–91.* Norman: Univ. Oklahoma Press. 309 pp.

107. Meyerhoff, B. G. 1970. The deer-maize-peyote symbol complex among the Huichol Indians of Mexico. *Anthropol. Quart.* 43:64–78

108. Nagata, S. 1970. *Modern Transformations of Moenkopi Pueblo.* Urbana: Univ. Illinois Press. 336 pp.

109. Nagata, S. 1971. The reservation community and the urban community: Hopi Indians of Moenkopi. See Ref. 64, 114–59

110. Opler, M. E. 1936. The kinship systems of the Southern Athapaskan-speaking tribes. *Am. Anthropol.* 38:620–33

111. Opler, M. E. 1937. An outline of Chiricahua Apache social organization. In *Social Anthropology of North American Tribes*, ed. F. Eggan, 173–239. Univ. Chicago Press. 456 pp.

112. Opler, M. E. 1945. Themes as dynamic forces in culture. *Am. J. Sociol.* 51: 189–206

113. Opler, M. E. 1969. *Apache Odyssey.* New York: Holt, Rinehart & Winston. 301 pp.

114. Opler, M. E. 1969. Remuneration to supernaturals and man in Apachean ceremonialism. *Ethnology* 7:356–93

115. Ibid 1969. Western Apache and Kiowa Apache materials relating to ceremonial payment. 8:122–24

116. Opler, M. E. 1971. Jicarilla Apache territory, economy, and society in 1850. *Southwest. J. Anthropol.* 27:309–29

117. Opler, M. E. 1971. Pots, Apache, and the Dismal River culture aspect. See Ref. 8, 29–33

118. Ortiz, A. 1969. *The Tewa World: Space, Time, Being, and Becoming in a Pueblo Society.* Univ. Chicago Press. 197 pp.

119. Ortiz, A., Ed. 1972. *New Perspectives on the Pueblos.* Albuquerque: Univ. New Mexico Press. 340 pp.

120. Padfield, H. E., van Willigen, J. 1969. Work and income patterns in a transitional population: the Papago of Arizona. *Hum. Organ.* 28:208–16

121. Pandey, T. N. 1968. Tribal elections in a southwestern pueblo. *Ethnology* 7: 71–85

122. Parmee, E. A. 1968. *Formal Education and Culture Change: A Modern Apache Indian Community and Government Education Programs.* Tucson: Univ. Arizona Press. 132 pp.

123. Parsons, E. C. 1939. *Pueblo Indian Religion.* Univ. Chicago Press. 2 vols. 1275 pp.

124. Perchonock, N., Werner, O. 1969. Navaho systems of classification: some implications for ethnoscience. *Ethnology* 8:229–42

125. Rapoport, R. N. 1954. Changing Navaho religious values: a study of Christian missions to the Rimrock Navahos. *Pap. Peabody Mus. Am. Archaeol. Ethnol.* 41. Cambridge, Mass.: Peabody Mus.

126. Riley, C. L. 1969. The southern Tepehuan and Tepecano. See Ref. 59, 814–21

127. Roberts, D. L. 1972. The ethnomusicology of the eastern pueblos. See Ref. 119, 243–56

128. Schroeder, A. H. 1972. Rio Grande ethnohistory. See Ref. 119, 41–70

129. Sekequaptewa, E. 1972. Preserving the good things of Hopi life. See Ref. 145, 239–60

130. Sekequaptewa, H. (As told to Louise Udall) 1969. *Me and Mine: the Life Story of Helen Sekequaptewa.* Tucson: Univ. Arizona Press. 262 pp.

131. Service, E. R. 1969. The northern Tepehuan. See Ref. 59, 822–29

132. Shepardson, M. 1971. Navajo factionalism and the outside world. See Ref. 8, 83–90

133. Shepardson, M., Hammond, B. 1970. *The Navajo Mountain Community: Social Organization and Kinship Terminology.* Berkeley: Univ. California Press. 235 pp.

134. Simpson, J. R. 1970. Uses of cultural anthropology in economic analysis: a Papago Indian case. *Hum. Organ.* 29: 162–68

135. Smith, M. E. 1969. *Governing at Taos Pueblo.* Portales: Eastern New Mexico Univ. 41 pp.

136. Snyder, P. Z. 1971. The social environment of the urban Indian. See Ref. 64, 206–43
137. Spicer, E. H., Ed. 1961. *Perspectives in American Indian Culture Change.* Univ. Chicago Press. 549 pp.
138. Spicer, E. H. 1962. *Cycles of Conquest.* Tucson: Univ. Arizona Press. 609 pp.
139. Spicer, E. H. 1968. Developmental change and cultural integration. In *Perspectives in Developmental Change,* ed. A. Gallaher, 172–200. Lexington: Univ. Kentucky Press. 263 pp.
140. Spicer, E. H. 1969. Political incorporation and cultural change in New Spain: a study in Spanish-Indian relations. In *Attitudes of Colonial Powers toward the American Indian,* ed. S. L. Peckham, G. R. Gibson, 107–35
141. Spicer, E. H. 1969. Review of C. Castaneda's *The Teachings of Don Juan: A Yaqui Way of Knowledge. Am. Anthropol.* 71:320–22
142. Spicer, E. H. 1969. The Yaqui and Mayo. See Ref. 59, 830–45
143. Spicer, E. H. 1970. Contrasting forms of nativism among the Mayos and Yaquis of Sonora, Mexico. See Ref. 79, 104–25
144. Spicer, E. H. 1970. Patrons of the poor. *Hum. Organ.* 29:12–19
145. Spicer, E. H. 1972. In *Plural Society in the Southwest,* ed. E. H. Spicer, R. H. Thompson, 21–76. New York: Interbook. 367 pp.
146. Stewart, K. M. 1968. A brief history of the Chemehuevi Indians. *Kiva* 34:9–27
147. Stewart, K. M. 1969. The aboriginial territory of the Mohave Indians. *Ethnohistory* 16:257–76
148. Stewart, K. M. 1969. A brief history of the Mohave Indians since 1850. *Kiva* 34:219–36
149. Tedlock, D. 1972. Pueblo literature: style and verisimilitude. See Ref. 119, 219–42
150. Thrapp, D. L. 1967. *The Conquest of Apacheria.* Norman: Univ. Oklahoma Press. 405 pp.
151. Trager, F. H. 1971. Some aspects of 'time' at Picuris Pueblo (with an addendum on the Nootka). *Anthropol. Ling.* 13:331–38
152. Trager, G. L., Trager, F. H. 1970. The cardinal directions at Taos and Picuris. *Anthropol. Ling.* 12:31–37

153. Tunnell, C. D., Newcomb, W. W. 1969. A Lipan Apache mission. *Texas Mem. Mus. Bull.* 14
154. Tweedie, M. J. 1968. Notes on the history and adaptation of the Apache tribes. *Am. Anthropol.* 70:1132–42
155. Underhill, R. 1948. Ceremonial patterns in the greater Southwest. *Am. Ethnol. Soc. Monogr.* 13
156. Vogt, E. Z. 1951. Navaho veterans: a study of changing values. *Pap. Peabody Mus. Am. Archaeol. Ethnol.* 41. Cambridge, Mass.: Peabody Mus.
157. Waddell, J. O. 1969. *Papago Indians at Work.* Anthropol. Pap. Univ. Arizona 12. Tucson: Univ. Arizona Press. 160 pp.
158. Waddell, J. O. 1970. Resurgent patronage and lagging bureaucracy in a Papago off-reservation community. *Hum. Organ.* 29:37–42
159. Ware, N. 1970. Survival and change in Pima Indian music. *Ethnomusicology* 14:100–13
160. Weppner, R. S. 1971. Urban economic opportunitites: the example of Denver. See Ref. 64, 244–73
161. Werner, O., Begishe, K. Y. 1970. A lexemic typology of Navajo anatomical terms I: the foot. *Int. J. Am. Ling.* 36: 247–65
162. White, L. 1928. A comparative study of Keresan medicine societies. *Proc. 23rd Int. Congr. Am.,* New York, 604–19
163. Williams, A. 1970. *Navajo Political Processes.* Smithson. Contrib. Anthropol. 9. Washington, D.C.: Smithson. Inst. 75 pp.
164. Witherspoon, G. J. 1970. Review of L. C. Wyman's *Blessingway. Am. Anthropol.* 73:1360–61
165. Witherspoon, G. J. 1971. A new look at Navajo social organization. *Am. Anthropol.* 72:55–65
166. Witherspoon, G. J. 1971. Navajo categories of objects at rest. *Am. Anthropol.* 73:110–27
167. Wyman, L. C. 1970. *Blessingway.* Tucson: Univ. Arizona Press. 660 pp.
168. Wyman, L. C. 1970. *Sandpaintings of the Navaho Shootingway and the Walcott Collection.* Smithson. Contrib. Anthropol. 13. Washington, D.C.: Smithson. Inst. 102 pp.
169. Young, R. W. 1972. The rise of the Navajo tribe. See Ref. 145, 167–237

CROSS-CULTURAL ANALYSIS: METHODS AND SCOPE

❖ 9530

Stanley H. Udy, Jr.

Department of Sociology, Dartmouth College, Hanover, New Hampshire

Any comparative study of social phenomena across two or more different societies is, in the broadest sense of the term, "cross-cultural." Current usage, however, ordinarily distinguishes "cross-cultural" from "cross-national" research, with the former referring only to comparisons among nonindustrial societies of the variety traditionally studied by anthropologists, and the latter, to comparisons among modern nations. It is also usually presumed that "cross-cultural analysis" is directed, at least in part, toward generalizations, and is thereby distinguished from piecemeal comparisons seeking only to describe one society by contrasting it with others, though this distinction has by no means always been approved (Lewis 14). The trend of recent years has thus favored an increasingly specialized conception of cross-cultural analysis, and for good reason. As a research activity, the comparative study of nonindustrial societies with a view to discovering or testing general principles is distinctive, and in fact quite different theoretically, conceptually, and methodologically from both cross-national research and piecemeal comparison. Our discussion will thus be confined to cross-cultural analysis, conceived in this narrower, more specialized, sense.

Despite the fact that the ultimate objectives of cross-cultural analysis would seem to be central to both anthropology and sociology, its basic patterns of operations, as well as the skills it demands, are very different from those of any other type of research habitually carried on in either field. The typical cross-cultural study is directed toward the analysis of a relatively small number of traits over a relatively large number of societies. The number and type of societies studied, as well as the range and kinds of data required from each society, are determined by the nature of the generalizations sought, rather than by a desire to study any society in particular. If only because several or many societies are involved, the cross-cultural researcher is almost always obliged to rely on secondary source materials for most of his information. Since the sample of societies is usually fairly large, it is likely to prove convenient, and possibly necessary, to manipulate the data through aggregative statistical techniques. Cross-cultural analysis therefore typically emerges as a scholarly and statistical enterprise carried on largely in the library, office, and

253

laboratory, rather than in the field. Generally speaking, it involves studying secondary ethnographic and historical sources in large numbers of nonindustrial societies, coding relevant data from these sources, and manipulating these data so that they will yield fairly abstract, theoretical conclusions.

There certainly would seem to be nothing terribly strange about all this. Indeed, if one wishes to develop general theories about the nature of human society from empirical data, it is difficult to imagine how else one could do it. Yet this "package" of activities does not contain very many things that anthropologists or sociologists have been, or are, normally trained to do. This situation seems rather curious, and the historical circumstances that brought it about lie at the root of many current problems faced by cross-cultural research. We shall thus begin our review with a brief discussion of these circumstances and the intellectual situation in which they have left us. We shall then be in a position to comment not only on the kinds of research problems to which cross-cultural analysis is appropriate, but also on its practical limitations in dealing with these problems. This discussion will lead us to a more explicit consideration of the difficulties currently faced by cross-cultural analysis, together with some suggestions as to how such difficulties might be resolved or at least coped with. Throughout the entire review, our references to the literature will be illustrative rather than exhaustive. Unlike many social scientists, cross-cultural researchers are frequently assiduous bibliographers, with the result that fairly complete bibliographies of this field are readily available elsewhere. We shall thus not replicate them here. Excellent, complete, current, and cumulative bibliographies are provided by O'Leary (27, 28). The journal, *Behavior Science Notes,* proposes to publish annual supplements to these bibliographies. A fine selective bibliography is provided by Textor (39, pp. 189–208). Marsh's *Comparative Sociology* (15, pp. 375–496) contains a comprehensive selection, not limited, however, to cross-cultural comparative research as that area is here defined.

THE HISTORICAL LEGACY

Cross-cultural analysis makes sense only in an intellectual context that stresses the fundamental general similarities among separate societies that are different in detail. "Classical" evolutionism provided such a context, (Tylor 40) as does—to some extent—contemporary sociological theory (Parsons 29), but what happened in between did not. As a result, the current theoretical situation of cross-cultural analysis is rather weak, and the data base from which such analysis must usually proceed is not especially well suited for comparative purposes.

Cultural Relativism

This situation had its origin in the severity of the cultural relativist reaction to classical evolutionism. Some of our humanist colleagues even today have never quite forgiven us for the excesses of nineteenth and early twentieth century social evolutionism. Nevertheless, whatever their faults, the evolutionists did emphasize cross-cultural research using a framework based on analytic similarities assumed to be universal to all societies. Unfortunately, in their righteous indignation at the frequently both grandiose and incorrect formulations of the evolutionists, the cultural relativists virtually cast out the comparative method along with evolutionism. Each society became unique. The comparison of different societies, therefore, made no sense. The proper task of social anthropology became the explanation of traits by tracing their configuration within a single, presumptively unique, culture.

The widespread acceptance of this position discouraged the explanation of culture traits not only by the general evolutionistic theories it was meant to avoid, but by any general theory whatever. Yet at the same time it provided a major stimulus to the development of a rich and valuable tradition of descriptive empirical field research in anthropology, a tradition which continues, and without which cross-cultural research would today be impossible for want of data. The cultural relativist reaction thus has the mixed consequence of making cross-cultural analysis possible today while at the same time being responsible for many of its most serious difficulties. It generated a veritable flood of ethnographic field studies. At the same time, its atheoretical and anticomparative bias meant that most of these studies were not carried on with a view to their possible use as sources in cross-cultural research, and they were quite likely to have been conducted with the underlying idea that they could not be so used (Eggan 6, pp. 747–49). As a result, the cross-cultural analyst today is likely to have to cope with fairly uneven data and must face some exceedingly difficult problems in adapting these data for comparative purposes without distorting them.

Mitigating Influences

The situation might be worse were it not for two more or less independent mitigating elements in the situation. The first was a lack of consistency among the cultural relativists in their insistence that each society is unique. Furthermore, this lack of consistency fortunately followed quite consistent patterns and thus laid some groundwork for later comparative taxonomy. The cultural relativists particularly stressed fieldwork and developed standard strategies for doing it, which resulted in some comparability, unintended or not, among different ethnographic reports. They also continued, by and large, to utilize fairly uniform sets of topical headings in presenting their findings. Certain entire models from the earlier comparative tradition were preserved as well and continued to be uniformly applied in different societies. The most elaborate and frequently used was Morgan's model of the kinship system (16), and it is noteworthy that the comparability of data thereby achieved subsequently made kinship one of the most fruitful areas of cross-cultural research. To be sure, these seemingly arbitrary, albeit systematic, deviations from a strict relativist doctrine imposed an occasionally odd structure of criteria of relevance on anthropology. The presumed centrality of kinship to social structure is a case in point. One wonders what anthropology might look like today had Morgan happened to write, for example, on Forms of Coordination and Authority in Human Work. What is important, however, is that some measure of uniformity and standardization was maintained in both research and reporting in the face of strong opposing pressures.

The second mitigating element in the situation was the fact that cultural relativism in the last analysis represented more a shift of emphasis than a total abandonment of comparison per se. Lewis (14) argues this point in some detail, pointing out that "comparison is a generic aspect of human thought rather than a special method of anthropology or of any other discipline." As part of this picture, comparative studies of even the extensive cross-cultural variety we have in mind here continued to surface from time to time. Perhaps the most notable examples were those of Hobhouse, Wheeler & Ginsberg (12) and of Sumner & Keller (37).[1] In the heyday of cultural relativism, however, such comprehensive efforts were neither particularly appreciated nor admired. To a great extent this still remains the case; a legacy of three decades is very difficult to escape, particularly if one is in the position of having to continue to depend on much of what it has left behind. However, the situation has basically changed. The current state of social theory is such that cross-cultural analysis again makes sense and at the very least is difficult not to tolerate in some form.

The "Return" to Comparative Research

Every systematic empiricist enterprise, if at all sophisticated, is soon in search of a theoretical rationale. Cultural relativism found such a rationale in functionalism. The effect of early functionalism, whatever may have been its intent, was not to generalize but rather to particularize by portraying any given culture as a unique network of interdependent concrete traits. In its actual application, however, the analytic procedure following from this position implied the presence of some general model against which the description of the society in question was being projected. In the course of time, therefore, functionalism did a complete about face, moving from a collection of discrete empirical systems of concrete traits, each describing a particular society, to a generalized model relating structural categories allegedly common to all societies (Levy 13). Whatever special problems this model may involve, it denies that each culture is truly unique and stresses general cultural similarities. It thus not only provides justification for cross-cultural analysis on a basis different from that of evolutionism, but also lends itself to the formulation of conceptual frameworks specifically designed for that purpose.

By the late 1940s, therefore, the stage had been set for the reconstitution of cross-cultural analysis as an intellectually respectable enterprise. Indeed, such reconstitution may be regarded as having been initiated by the publication in 1949 of Murdock's *Social Structure* (17), and has proceeded since that time. It has proceeded at something less than breakneck speed, however, for the legacy of cultural relativism is still very much with us. In many quarters, descriptive field research is still regarded as being much more important than comparative analysis. Of more significance, because it is more unavoidably durable, is the fact that most of the data available for use in cross-cultural research were collected under the influence of strongly anticomparative intellectual persuasions. At best, considerable adaptation, with many attendant risks and problems, is necessary to render these

[1]The latter eventually led to the establishment at Yale University of the Cross-Cultural Index, later to become the Human Relations Area Files (Ford 7).

data usable for comparative purposes. Finally, in view of the excursion away from theory for the better part of three decades, it is not surprising that contemporary cross-cultural analysis is likely to suffer frequently from ad hoc conceptualization and highly eclectic and opportunistic taxonomy. Placed in this context, our earlier observations that cross-cultural analysis is less popular than one might logically expect it to be, and that it involves a style of work quite different from the current norm in both anthropology and sociology, become more readily understood. Yet the fact remains that the objectives of cross-cultural analysis are not only central to both of these fields, but embody certain kinds of research problems that are very difficult to attack by any other method.

PROBLEMS APPROPRIATE TO CROSS-CULTURAL ANALYSIS

Cross-cultural analysis is not only appropriate, but in principle necessary, whenever one is studying phenomena whose total relevant range of variation exceeds the degree of variation ever found within any given society. This condition is regularly encountered in two research situations, and may be encountered in a third. The first situation occurs in very broadly conceived research designed to achieve generalizations about the nature of human society as such. The second occurs in the generalizing study of narrower institutional structures which, however, regularly permeate entire human societies. Both of these situations are similar in that entire societies are the basic units of observation—in the case of the first because society is itself the object of investigation, and in the case of the second because some of the boundaries of social institutions always at least presumptively extend to the boundaries of the society in which they are found. The third situation is different. It is the study of organizations of one type or another by means of cross-cultural analysis. The difference lies in the fact that the basic units of observation are organizations of the type being studied, rather than societies, with the latter along with institutional structures emerging as contextual rather than primary objects of investigation. Cross-cultural analysis in principle is always a possible response to this type of research situation, but it becomes essential only if the research problem requires the systematic introduction of more contextual variation than can be achieved in the context of a single society. In practice, the cross-cultural study of organizations is quite rare.

Almost any given cross-cultural study can be classified as primarily involving some one of these three research situations, on the basis of what it is essentially about (i.e. what the structural reference is of the dependent variables it is ultimately trying to explain). Such classification is useful because the precise nature of certain fundamental theoretical and methodological problems depends specifically on the locus of the ultimate dependent variables. It is not, however, uncommon for a given study to involve, in a secondary way, more than one of these research situations. Any cross-cultural study of organizations, for example, will almost invariably entail some analysis of the nature of institutions or entire societies in order to develop independent contextual variables (Udy 45). The basic problems encountered, however, will remain those of a study of organizations, rather than of institutions or societies.

The Study of Society

Though standard fare for the earlier evolutionists, comprehensive cross-cultural research about the general nature of human society is not too frequently encountered today as an end in itself. Rather, it usually appears as a means for developing independent contextual variables to aid in explaining something less general, such as institutions or organizations. Cross-cultural analyses focusing broadly on the nature of human society thus ordinarily appear as parts of studies primarily concerned with something else. Even those that stand alone usually clearly imply that they were carried out with the aim of systematizing the context of lower order phenomena to be studied in the future (Freeman & Winch 8, Schuessler & Driver 34). The only consistent exceptions are occasional comprehensive, neo-evolutionist efforts, though there are other unique examples (Carneiro & Tobias 3).

Although this variety of cross-cultural research may be explicitly directed toward stating general propositions and of course implicitly always involves doing so, it is more frequently carried on with a view to devising classification schemes or constructing taxonomies, given its usual purpose. It almost always follows one of two major approaches. The first seeks to discover principal dimensions of social structure inductively through the use of cluster or factor analysis. Relationships among the dimensions thus yielded can then be explored and propositionalized, with the end result, presumably, of a set of principles about the general nature of human society (Driver & Schuessler 5, Gouldner & Peterson 9, Gregg & Banks 11, Sawyer & LeVine 32, Schuessler & Driver 34, Stewart & Jones 36). Although this approach has yielded some extremely interesting pieces of work, it emerges with a final closed model of society consisting of interrelated basic dimensions of variation among the traits studied. One must therefore be prepared to argue that the list of traits studied is a theoretically defensible operational definition of "any society." The present state of theory combined with the highly empiricist character of most ethnographic materials make such an argument very difficult. Criteria of relevance for the selection of traits to be included in such an analysis are very likely to be insufficiently developed, and efforts to overcome this problem by an "everything but the kitchen sink" solution will not suffice. One is thus faced with a model describing a somewhat arbitrary collection of culture traits, purporting to be a model of any society, and constructed in such a way that traits cannot be added without, in effect, starting all over again. Reliable results are difficult to achieve; this approach yields an inflexible solution to a problem that, given the current state of the field, may require a more flexible solution. It has proved more useful as an exploratory aid to discovering contextual correlates of variation in particular institutions where "finality" of results may be exactly what is desired (Russell 31).

The second major cross-cultural approach to the study of entire societies is that of ordering societies on a Guttman scale according to whether or not they possess certain culture traits, or to utilize some other similar form of index construction. It has proved possible, at least empirically, to do this from a number of points of view, with the resulting scale, in one way or another, usually roughly indicative of variations in structural complexity (Carneiro 2, Carneiro & Tobias 3, Freeman &

Winch 8, Naroll 23, Schwartz & Miller 35). In principle, of course, this approach suffers from many of the same problems as the first. However, in our view, it has fared somewhat better in practice. It lends itself to evolutionistic formulations—most notably the "surplus" model of development—and can hence benefit from criteria of relevance derived from evolutionistic models. In this connection, it also has the fortunate capability of often yielding pragmatically fruitful results even when the model on which it is based proceeds from questionable or incorrect assumptions. For example, one of the controversies surrounding this approach is whether or not a scale so derived describes an actual developmental sequence. Our position, which we and others have argued elsewhere, is that one cannot answer this question on the basis of an inductive inspection of the scale pattern alone (Graves, Graves & Kobrin 10, Udy 43). The answer, however, may be quite irrelevant in many applications of this method. In fact, it may not even matter whether the resulting "scale" is really a scale at all, as opposed to a simple typology of qualitatively different kinds of societies which fit a pattern that merely looks like a scale. What is important is that through scaling one can systematically order societies according to degree of complexity, degree of affinity to the characteristics of industrialism, and so forth, in such a way as to generate independent contextual variables in connection with the study of institutions and organizations. To be sure, if one is interested in social change at the societal level, the developmental sequence problem remains. In such instances, scaling undoubtedly can be used to advantage, but, we would argue, only in combination with other historical evidence.

Social Institutions

The study of the general nature of human society is rather ambitious, and it is thus perhaps not surprising that the most frequent application of cross-cultural analysis lies in a less comprehensive area—the study of particular social institutions. By "institution" in this context we understand a more or less internally consistent system of values, norms, and folk models defining a pattern of aspects of social activity. An "institutional structure" is a complex of institutions, culturally defined as systematically interrelated, although occasionally this term is also used to refer to a single institution as well. These conventions of usage lead one to a superorganic view of culture; the totality of institutional structures in any society would constitute the "culture" of that society. One may thus think, for example, of "debt relations" as an institution, forming part of a broader institutional structure called the "economic system," which in turn combines with other similarly broad institutional structures such as the political and religious systems to form the culture of the society. It is apparent that some institutional structures are more comprehensive than others, and that the more comprehensive ones are frequently intertwined by virtue of the high probability that particular institutions may have simultaneous reference to more than one broader institutional structure. Debt relations, for example, are very likely to have political as well as economic relevance in any society. Since institutions define aspects of action rather than concrete unit acts, it is conceptually possible to assume that any given institution at least potentially permeates the entire society, and most cross-cultural studies make this assumption. It thus becomes possible for the researcher to discuss any social activity, or set of social activities, from the standpoint of potential relevance to any institutional structure.

It is likewise evident that the number, type, and arrangement of institutions may vary considerably from one society to another. In societies very close to the subsistence level, for example, the political system may emerge as essentially a substructure of the kinship system, or it may not even exist as a separate culturally defined entity. Such questions are ordinarily left to empirical determination, and, in one form or another, are often part of the cross-cultural research problem itself.

Institutional cross-cultural studies vary enormously in scope, as one might expect, since institutional structures themselves vary greatly in complexity and comprehensiveness. Some such studies focus narrowly on particular sets of customs, such as, for example, child-rearing practices, menstrual taboos, or specific forms of witchcraft. Others are broadly conceived and focus on comprehensive institutional structures, such as the economy, religious system, or kinship system. The bibliography of such studies is very extensive, and the reader is referred to O'Leary (27, 28) for references. Two particularly thorough examples which illustrate almost polar variations in scope are Whiting & Child (47) and Swanson (38).

The typical institutional research strategy seeks to explain variations in the institutional structure focused upon by concomitant variations in (*a*) other institutions, (*b*) physical environmental conditions, and/or (*c*) general measures of social-organizational characteristics. With dependent and independent variables thus conceptualized, their values are coded over a sample of societies, a correlational analysis of some type is made, and an explanatory causal model imposed on the results. The last step is potentially the most productive, yet at the same time often the weakest, as the researcher is here frequently obliged to draw on—and try to create—theoretical resources greater than the field realistically provides at the present time. Two general kinds of causal models are commonly found in the literature, sometimes separately and sometimes together. One is ecological and adaptive; an institution is structured the way it is, regardless of specific motivations involved, because no other adaptation would be viable in view of some presumed set of functional requirements or structural properties. The other is psychological and motivational; an institution is structured the way it is as a result of people being motivated by orientations to other institutions or organizational problems. Neither of these models can be applied except in conjunction with the other one, at least to the extent of making some assumptions, explicit or implicit, about its state. The mechanism implied by the first does not alone really provide a causal explanation. The mechanism implied by the second is likewise incomplete. It can operate only in a structural context and also invites questions about the consequences of its operations for presumed viable structural properties.

The fact that the cross-cultural researcher is forcibly pushed into confronting the causative problem in principle renders cross-cultural institutional analysis a potentially very powerful tool for theoretical development. In practice, however, it has proved extremely difficult to realize this potential, owing to the character of the data ordinarily at the disposal of the cross-cultural analyst. In order to trace social causation through both of these models simultaneously, it is necessary to move between the cultural, morphological, and interpersonal levels of social structure, at the very least (Udy 44). Most ethnographic sources available for cross-cultural research, however, report only cultural—and perhaps some morphological—data with any degree of consistency or completeness. Most cross-cultural analyses are thus constrained to predict to dependent variables deriving from prevailing normative patterns, folk models, or gross morphological characteristics, from independent variables in these same areas. Emphasis on kinship terminology, as such, is a case in point. Intervening behavioral or interpersonal structural patterns cannot consistently be "observed." One must therefore either make assumptions about them or remain content with no more than a correlational or cross-tabular description of what seems somehow to go with what.

This situation combines with the lack of a temporal dimension in most cross-cultural data to make it impossible to test hypotheses concerning specific causal mechanisms directly. Even with the lack of a temporal dimension, one could come closer to such a test if one could at least make some cross-sectional observations of presumed intervening mechanisms. Without this possibility, the researcher is reduced, at best, to observing the starting points and end points only. To be sure, this is not wholly without value, since it is of course possible to try imposing various models on such observations with a view to selecting those which seem best to relate the starting and end points. That potentialities are restricted by having to proceed in this manner, however, is evident.

Some Theoretical Problems

It is thus apparent that cross-cultural analysis is subject in practice to rather severe restrictions and requires certain quite far-reaching theoretical assumptions. This is especially true of the two general kinds of research situation just discussed; namely, where the object is to generalize about the nature of entire societies or the nature of institutional structures assumed potentially to permeate entire societies. Some of these restrictions result from the character of the data usually available. The lack of much material describing change through time, plus the lack of much information of even a cross-sectional nature on behavioral and interpersonal patterns, render assumptions about causal mechanisms necessary, as we have just seen. The entire cross-cultural enterprise further demands the assumption that separate societies exist as independent entities and that they are enough alike so that they can be meaningfully compared as different instances of essentially the same thing. In practice, if not necessarily in principle, this assumption is closely related to the first one about causal mechanisms, since both assumptions are satisfied by a general functionalist model of "any society" as a self-subsistent boundary-maintaining social system, which handles all of its functional problems internally. Such a model describes any society as an independent entity, and provides at least a formal "solution" to the problem of causality by stipulating a general tendency toward stable functional integration which—if it exists—makes knowledge of specific causal mechanisms somewhat superfluous. It is thus perhaps not surprising that this model underlies most cross-cultural research. It is also necessary to point out, however, that this model flies in the face of common sense and is in fact quite unrealistic much of the time. Given diffusion and an ongoing network of intersocietal relations, few if any societies are now or ever were actually independent. This model also does not allow for discontinuities in social structure; society is portrayed as culturally homogeneous. As a result, the similarities between very small and very large societies are almost certainly exaggerated. We all know, for example, that Tikopia and China are actually very different; they may be so different that they are not, in fact, by any reasonable standard, separate instances of the same phenomenon. It is likewise well known that societies are almost never functionally integrated stable entities. This assumption has, on the whole, probably proved more difficult to stomach than either of the other two, at least judging by the frequency and vigor of the criticism directed against it. But much of this criticism misses the mark. The real problem is that in the absence of the possibility of directly investigating causal mechanisms, some assumptions about structural tendencies are necessary, and this one is not demonstrably any more unrealistic than any similar alternative assumption might be, say, to the effect that all societies tend to be conflict ridden and to fall apart, which is not true either. Most societies, though, do change through time, and the systematic general study of societal change will remain difficult until more comparative temporal data, and more comparative data on behavioral and interpersonal process, are available. It will then be possible to develop alternative assumptions, or perhaps consider a different model altogether.

Meanwhile, cross-cultural analysis is stuck with a basically functionalist model, both as a way of identifying "society," and as a way of coping with problems of social causation. The problem thus becomes one of devising research strategies which will, insofar as possible, avoid the consequences of the defects of this model. One such strategy, which we are following in this discussion in response to a general trend in the field as a whole, is to separate "cross-cultural" from "cross-national" research. Whatever one might say about the functionalist model of "any society," it is generally conceded to fit the small—or even large—traditional society familiar to ethnography better than it fits any contemporary industrial nation. It thus seems prudent to pursue these two modes of comparative investigation separately, comparing and contrasting their results when appropriate, rather than trying to combine them in a single over-all analysis. A second strategy is to design one's sampling frame so as to result, insofar as possible, in the selection of societies known to be maximally independent of one another historically, and we shall have more to say about this presently. A third strategy, which obviously cannot be followed all or even most of the time, is to attenuate the effects of the functionalist model by defining one's research problem in such a way that the society is no longer the basic unit of observation. This strategy coincides with a third general type of research situation to which cross-cultural analysis is often appropriate, and which deserves special discussion.

The Study of Organizational Forms

The cross-cultural study of organizations is theoretically quite a different matter from the cross-cultural study of either societies or institutions. An "organization" is a bounded system of roles, existing within the context of some society, and performed at any given time by a specifiable group of persons. Unlike an institution, which is a concrete system of symbols on the cultural level defining aspects of action on the social level, an organization is a concrete unit on the social level oriented to aspects of different institutions on the cultural level. Just as an institution may be predominantly but not completely manifested in certain organizations, so may any given organization be oriented predominantly but not completely to some one institutional structure. In our own society, for example, the government is undoubtedly predominantly politically oriented, but it is also oriented to economic and other institutional considerations as well. The pattern of institutional orientations of a given organizational form is, furthermore, very likely to vary from one society to another. Work organizations in our own society are almost always predominantly economically oriented, but in other societies they may be predominantly oriented to political or kinship considerations, with economic considerations distinctly secondary.

Most organizational research is, of course, not cross-cultural. Indeed, there is every reason why it should not be if the research problem calls for holding institutional orientations constant. However, if one is interested in exploring the relationship of organizational structure to institutional orientation, a cross-cultural analysis may be called for as a means of introducing sufficient variation into the social context (Nimkoff & Middleton 26; Udy 41, 45). The resulting research situation is quite different from that of studying entire societies or social institutions, for in the last analysis, one is comparing organizations rather than cultures. Typically, one is faced with a complex of independent and dependent variables concerning internal organization structure, together with certain contextual control variables having to do with the social and ecological setting. The unit of investigation is the organization, not the total society; the aim in sampling societies is not really to sample societies as such, but to introduce systematic variations in those contextual control variables with which one is working. One is sampling contexts rather than units. Thus the possible consequences of some of the theoretical problems we have indicated earlier, stemming from possible lack of independence of societies from one another, and the kind of model of "society" one is obliged to use, are at least attenuated in practice, even if they are not formally resolved in principle. In almost any sample of societies, especially a very large sample, there is, as we have seen, always some question of whether the societies sampled are really independent of one another. But if one samples organizations by first drawing societies and then drawing one organization from each society, there is considerable chance that the organizations drawn will be independent in all relevant ways even where the societies are not. Furthermore, since most cross-cultural studies of organizations are concerned with exploring specified ranges of contextual variation on organization structure, it is much more important, and also likely to be much more arguable, that the societies sampled provide the desired range of contextual variation than that they be representative of some total population of all possible societies. The fact that one is studying the structure of organizations rather than the structure of societies also renders much less important the question of what model of "society" one is assuming. What is important is what model of organization one is using, and that is a problem of organization theory not of cross-cultural analysis. It is also more easily handled.

The cross-cultural study of organizations thus offers several theoretical and methodological advantages over the cross-cultural study of either entire societies or social institutions, if only because it enables one to duck some rather difficult questions. However, it involves some problems of its own. The fact that it operationally equates sampling relevant social and technical contexts of organizations with sampling societies is, we think, not terribly serious, although for some purposes it does render difficult the precise specification of what population of organizations one's eventual sample represents, even if one has followed an impeccable strategy in selecting societies. A much more difficult practical problem is that standard categories of ethnographic reporting generally have to do with culture and institutions, rather than with organizational forms. It is thus necessary to do much "cutting and pasting" to retrieve the necessary information needed to locate organizations in the first place, let alone to discover how they actually function or are basically structured. To some degree one is saved by the probability that organizations will be described under the headings of their predominant institutional orientations, but there are still gaps. In the study of work organization, for example, one seldom finds much information usable for comparative purposes about actual interpersonal behavior patterns, or even about the numbers of people present in a work situation. One is obliged, for the most part, to work with descriptions couched in terms of generalized cultural models. The range of areas researchable by this method is thus limited to rather broad problems. This does not mean that such research is without value. An abiding problem with conventional, non-cross-cultural, organizational research is that it often proceeds with no clear conception of total possible ranges of variation. General cross-cultural research can aid in providing some such conception, which can serve as a backdrop against which comparative organizational studies confined to one society, or case studies of particular organizations, can be projected. There is value in knowing the layout of the ball park.

Summary

Inherent in each of the three major applications of cross-cultural analysis discussed are several rather difficult theoretical and methodological problems. These problems are actually quite similar, with different kinds of applications varying largely in the precise forms the problems take and the probable severity of their consequences. In all cross-cultural research the investigator is tied to an essentially functionalist model of human society from which it is hard to escape, inasmuch as the available data seldom admit of adequate exploration of causal mechanisms operating through time and across different structural levels. The state of theory is such that most cross-cultural studies are perforce exploratory, not only with respect to relationships among variables, but with regard to exactly what the specific variables and categories should be in the first place. The data themselves derive from an almost radically empiricist tradition, are descriptive and qualitative, and are at best ordered according to criteria of relevance that are frequently arbitrary and sometimes downright whimsical. They were also almost always gathered by someone other than the cross-cultural researcher and for purposes utterly removed from those of any cross-cultural analyst. All of these data must be coded, not only to fit a cross-cultural research problem, but usually also in such a way as to be of exploratory assistance in defining the problem in the first place and in specifying the variables relevant to it. When one combines this situation with the fact that the peculiar library-cum-statistical character of cross-cultural analysis does not conform closely to the current training traditions of either anthropology or sociology, it is no wonder that cross-cultural research is considerably less popular than its apparent theoretical centrality might lead one to expect it to be. It simply entails too many barriers and pitfalls. Nonetheless, the fact remains that cross-cultural analysis is, in principle, central to both anthropology and sociology, to the extent that these fields involve interest in developing any very general theories about their subject matter. It is also possible, despite limitations, to do cross-cultural analysis and in fact achieve some results. The remainder of our discussion will be devoted to an appraisal of available methods for conducting such analysis.

METHODS

Most literature on cross-cultural methodology deals either with the problem of selecting a representative sample of independent societies or with the question of validity and reliability of coding. These two topics represent only a part of the picture, however, and we shall treat them in the more general contexts of sampling and analysis procedures, respectively.

Sampling

The first problem to be confronted in cross-cultural sampling is what the size of the sample should be. If one is so fortunate as to be working with a tight research model and conducting classical tests of hypotheses of relationships among known variables, one can readily achieve a retrospective experimental design, and the problem of sample size becomes trivial. One matches societies on control variables, systematically varies the independent variables with the number of societies required following mechanically from the complexity of the model and the dictates of statistical significance. Very few cross-cultural studies, however, do or can involve very much classical hypothesis testing given the current state of theoretical knowledge. Rather, most are exploratory and are directed toward trying to discover what relationships, if any, exist among very broad structural areas. Frequently, the relevant specific variables are not known; part of the problem is precisely to discover what the variables are, i.e. which ones will work the best in characterizing relationships among the broad areas being studied. Having inductively extracted from the data variables which work, one then investigates and describes their interrelations. The results, when stated in propositional form, may superficially resemble a set of tested hypotheses. In fact, they are usually a series or possibly a system of result-guided descriptions.

There is nothing wrong with this provided one does not forget it, but one must face the difficulty that little is known of the formal properties of exploratory research. It is thus often difficult to choose among alternative procedures; it is no accident that cross-cultural research exhibits so many different approaches. Despite occasional assertions to the contrary, it is impossible to accept the contention that simply because the research is exploratory, "anything goes." Some guidelines would appear desirable, even if they may later prove somewhat arbitrary, if only to enable readers of the research to know how it was done and to insure some degree of consistency. As regards sample size, it is of course impossible formally to "solve for n" in exploratory research, since one does not know exactly what relationships one will ultimately wish to explore. It therefore seems desirable to draw the largest number of societies possible, known to be independent and representative according to criteria to be described presently, and for which the desired data are available. If this number seems, or later proves to be, larger than feasible or necessary, an alternative procedure is to extract variables at intervals while drawing the sample in such a way as to maintain representativeness throughout, and to stop drawing societies at that point where additional societies are yielding no new information.

The next sampling problem faced by the cross-cultural researcher is that of assuring maximum independence among the societies drawn, together with some arguable modicum of representativeness of the sample.[2] Unlike the question of size, this problem is similar in both hypothesis testing and exploratory research. The central difficulty is that one is of course limited to societies that have actually been studied, and among those, to societies on which adequate data are available relative to one's research problem. Since there is no valid way of determining how this rather restricted population might relate to the total universe of all societies, a straight random sampling procedure is unrealistic. In order to maximize the probability of finding the total possible range of variation in the variables one is studying, it is necessary to resort to a planned "quota sample," wherein one's final sample is distributed as evenly as possible over ethnographically recognized world culture areas, choosing at random within areas or subareas, where a choice exists. In the process, one can also maximize independence by selecting societies from different areas preferably, or at least from different subareas if the former procedure would result in too small a sample. Fortunately, this problem has received a great deal of attention in the literature, most notably at the hands of Murdock and his associates. As a result, several excellent procedural guides are available, and the reader is referred to them for further information and assistance (Barry 1, Murdock 18–20, Murdock & White 22, White 46).

Analysis Procedure

Having drawn a sample, one next faces the question of precisely what categories and variables the data are to be ordered into. In the case of hypothesis testing, the answer to this question is of course already known, but in the case of exploratory analysis,

[2]The question of independence, under the heading "Galton's problem," though certainly important, has been discussed *ad nauseam* in the cross-cultural methodological literature, receiving a really incredible amount of attention particularly when one considers that other problems of equal or greater importance are scarcely discussed at all. For recent summary statements of the vast "Galton's problem" literature, see Naroll (25) and Schaefer et al (33).

it usually is not, and methods textbooks have little or nothing to say about precisely what to do in such circumstances. Given broad areas of interest, a useful general convention is to proceed as far as one can on theoretical grounds, and beyond that to aim for categories which reflect the widest ranges of observed variation in the data. Procedures such as factor analysis may be useful here, but, as we have seen, they have various practical limitations. It may be better simply to try one system of theoretically defensible categories after another, and to choose that system which gives the best empirical results. It is usually desirable to carry out such trials by initially using a small number—say six or seven—of ethnographic sources known to be especially accurate and complete, and then apply the results to one's larger sample (Udy 42). At this stage the Human Relations Area Files become a facility of inestimable value, because the data in them are already ordered according to a generalized, yet detailed, classification scheme (Murdock et al 21). To the extent that one's sample has been contrived to include societies processed in the Files, one can at this point, by dint of another series of trials, discover how the Files can be searched so as to retrieve the data one needs. One can then formalize one's procedures and collect one's data, using the Files whenever possible, saving countless hours of work thereby, as well as being enabled to make use of the special bibliographical and critical information the Files provide.

A word or two of caution, however, is in order about the Human Relations Area Files. Except in rare fortuitous circumstances, where one's own categories happen to coincide with those of the Files, one cannot just "look things up" in them. Rather, one must code initially from monographs on a few given societies, then discover that pattern of search in the Files which yields the same information, with a view finally to applying that pattern to other societies. It is a question of "translating" the categories of the Files into one's own system of categories. The raw category system of the Files itself is derived ultimately from Sumner & Keller's *The Science of Society* (37), plus an elaborate variety of systematic and ad hoc emendations, and is, in principle, open to an infinitude of theoretical criticisms. Nonetheless, in our experience it works surprisingly well when used as we have described. The only comment we can offer on this score is that Sumner & Keller, adumbrated by years of practical ethnographic experience, might well bear revisiting.

Armed with a system of categories one may now code one's data. The most serious problems encountered in the actual procedure of cross-cultural analysis, whether one is testing hypotheses or exploring the material, are those of data validity and coding reliability. Various ways of coping with both problems have been proposed, all of which, according even to the claims of the proponents themselves, are, at best, merely somewhat helpful. The Human Relations Area Files seeks to code sources according to their probable accuracy. Naroll (24) has set forth and demonstrated a rather elaborate method which in effect weights variables in any given study according to both probable validity and observed coder reliability with respect to the traits comprising the variables, and takes such weights into account in the analysis. Much can be said in favor of such schemes, but their rigorous use does involve a "trade-off" in that it materially reduces the number of potentially available sources, and at times seems to do so quite artificially. Restricting oneself to those societies offering several ethnographic sources is open to the same objection. A more usual procedure is to utilize two or more judges in coding the material, together with possible group discussions to achieve consensus about coding or throwing out the source in cases of doubt (Swanson 38, Udy 45). A particularly severe problem on this score occurs when one is attempting to code some trait as "present" or "absent," and encounters a source where the trait is simply not mentioned. Under such circumstances, the question is whether to code the trait as "absent" or "don't know." Given the empiricist character of much ethnography, consistently—and, in a way, properly—coding "don't know" will result in an overreporting of "present" cases if one then eliminates the "don't know" cases from the analysis. For our part, we have adopted the convention of consistently coding such cases as "absent" if the ethnographer discusses other matters related to the trait in detail without mentioning the trait itself. Obviously, none of the foregoing "solutions" is very satisfactory. At some point one is obliged simply to believe what the ethnographer says, resign oneself to gaps in the data, propose results as tentative, and embrace the dictum that the ultimate test of cross-cultural research results lies in their successful application in other areas.

If one has succeeded in coping with the problems of sampling, category and variable construction, validity, and coding, we would contend that the remaining analysis problems in cross-cultural research are trivial, in that they do not differ at this point from those of any social science research problem characterized by essentially rectangular data sets. One simply runs one's data by any suitable standard statistical procedure (Driver 4). If the sample is very small, one may instead choose to proceed with words rather than numbers. There is no essential methodological difference in doing so; one cannot avoid statistical problems by using words. It seems necessary to point this out, since at one time the "words vs numbers" option was a matter of some controversy, albeit for reasons which we confess we have never been able to understand. It should be pointed out, however, that in the case of exploratory analysis, statistical (or equivalent verbal) procedures merely summarize and describe the results, despite the fact that they may superficially resemble tests of hypotheses. Such devices as tests of significance are therefore, in such instances, open to various technical criticisms. They may perhaps be defended as providing descriptions of how the investigator was thinking about the material, in that they project the findings against a random model.

CONCLUSIONS

In this review we have tried to show that cross-cultural analysis is neither ideal nor impossible. It suffers from a plethora of theoretical and methodological problems, many of which stem from intellectual-historical accident, some of which arise from the current state of theory, and perhaps the most serious of which derive from the character of available data. Indeed, some of the last-named problems are unquestionably forever inherent, as many of these data cannot now be changed. Because of this situation, cross-cultural analysis suffers from intrinsic and probably permanent limitations. The methodological history of the field has in great part been a history of compiling and archiving data combined with a history of efforts to evade these limitations. The latter efforts have not always been wholly successful and, as we have seen, have often consisted of conventions rather than formally defensible procedures.

However, the fact remains that one can carry out cross-cultural research and achieve results. The fact that some of these results can be successfully tested in other ways lends confidence in other results that must stand alone. Furthermore, cross-cultural analysis, despite its problems, is essential if one wishes to develop general theories about social structure while remaining in touch with empirical data. On this score, cross-cultural analysis has achieved something that few other specialties in social science have; namely, cumulative findings. It is possible to merge cross-cultural studies together when their samples overlap, and thereby construct new studies. The most comprehensive and ambitious effort to do this to date is that of Textor (39). Aided by the development and application of new computer routines, such effort could well lead to new and fruitful theoretical perspectives. If nothing else, cross-cultural analysis is surely dedicated to the proposition that ethnography is good for something apart from its own sake.

Literature Cited

1. Barry, H. 1969. Cross-cultural research with matched pairs of societies. *J. Soc. Psychol.* 79:25–33
2. Carneiro, R. L. 1970. Scale analysis, evolutionary sequences, and the rating of cultures. *Handbook of Method in Cultural Anthropology,* ed. R. Naroll, R. Cohen, 834–71. Garden City: Natural History Press
3. Carneiro, R. L., Tobias, S. R. 1963. The application of scale analysis to the study of cultural evolution. *Trans. N.Y. Acad. Sci. Ser. 2* 26:196–207
4. Driver, H. E. 1961. Introduction to statistics for comparative research. *Readings in Cross-Cultural Methodology,* ed. F. W. Moore, 303–31. New Haven: HRAF Press
5. Driver, H. E., Schuessler, K. F. 1957. Factor analysis of ethnographic data. *Am. Anthropol.* 59:655–63
6. Eggan, F. 1954. Social anthropology and the method of controlled comparison. *Am. Anthropol.* 56:743–63
7. Ford, C. S. 1970. Human relations area files: 1949–1969. *Behav. Sci. Notes* 5: 1–61
8. Freeman, L. C., Winch, R. F. 1957. Societal complexity: an empirical test of a typology of societies. *Am. J. Sociol.* 62: 461–66
9. Gouldner, A. W., Peterson, R. A. 1962. *Notes on Technology and the Moral Order.* Indianapolis: Bobbs-Merrill
10. Graves, T. D., Graves, N. B., Kobrin, M. J. 1969. Historical inferences from Guttman scales. *Curr. Anthropol.* 10: 317–38
11. Gregg, P. M., Banks, A. S. 1965. Dimensions of political systems. *Am. Pol. Sci. Rev.* 59:602–14
12. Hobhouse, L. T., Wheeler, G. C., Ginsberg, M. 1915. *The Material Culture and Social Institutions of the Simpler Peoples.* London: Chapman & Hall
13. Levy, M. J. Jr. 1952. *The Structure of Society.* Princeton Univ. Press
14. Lewis, O. 1956. Comparisons in cultural anthropology. *Current Anthropology: A Supplement to Anthropology Today,* ed. W. L. Thomas Jr., 259–92. Univ. Chicago Press
15. Marsh, R. M. 1967. *Comparative Sociology.* New York: Harcourt, Brace & World
16. Morgan, L. H. 1870. *Systems of Consanguinity and Affinity in the Human Family.* Washington, D.C.: Smithsonian Inst.
17. Murdock, G. P. 1949. *Social Structure.* New York: Macmillan
18. Murdock, G. P. 1957. World ethnographic sample. *Am. Anthropol.* 59: 664–87
19. Murdock, G. P. 1967. *Ethnographic Atlas: A Summary.* Univ. Pittsburgh Press
20. Murdock, G. P. 1969. *Outline of World Cultures.* New Haven: HRAF Press
21. Murdock, G. P. et al 1969. *Outline of Cultural Materials.* New Haven: HRAF Press. 4th rev. ed.
22. Murdock, G. P., White, D. R. 1969. Standard cross-cultural sample. *Ethnology* 8:329–69
23. Naroll, R. 1956. A preliminary index of social development. *Am. Anthropol.* 58: 687–715

24. Naroll, R. 1962. *Data Quality Control.* Glencoe: Free Press
25. Naroll, R. 1970. Galton's problem. *A Handbook of Method in Cultural Anthropology,* ed. R. Naroll, R. Cohen, 974–89. Garden City: Natural History Press
26. Nimkoff, M. F., Middleton, R. 1968. Types of family and types of economy. *Man in Adaptation,* ed. Y. A. Cohen, 384–93. Chicago: Aldine
27. O'Leary, T. J. 1969. A preliminary bibliography of cross-cultural studies. *Behav. Sci. Notes* 4:95–115
28. Ibid 1971. Bibliography of cross-cultural studies: supplement I. 6:191–203
29. Parsons, T. 1966. *Societies: Evolutionary and Comparative Perspectives.* Englewood Cliffs: Prentice-Hall
30. Radcliffe-Brown, A. R. 1952. *Structure and Function in Primitive Society.* Glencoe: Free Press
31. Russell, E. W. 1972. Factors of human aggression. *Behav. Sci. Notes* 7:275–312
32. Sawyer, J., LeVine, R. A. 1966. Cultural dimensions. *Am. Anthropol.* 68:708–31
33. Schaefer, J. M. et al 1971. Sampling methods, functional associations, and Galton's problem. *Behav. Sci. Notes* 6: 229–74
34. Schuessler, K. F., Driver, H. E. 1956. A factor analysis of sixteen primitive societies. *Am. Sociol. Rev.* 21:493–99
35. Schwartz, R. D., Miller, J. C. 1964. Legal evolution and societal complexity. *Am. J. Sociol.* 70:159–69
36. Stewart, R. A. C., Jones, K. J. 1972. Cultural dimensions. *Behav. Sci. Notes* 7: 37–81
37. Sumner, W. G., Keller, A. G. 1927. *The Science of Society.* 4 vols. New Haven: Yale Univ. Press
38. Swanson, G. E. 1960. *The Birth of the Gods.* Ann Arbor: Univ. Michigan Press
39. Textor, R. B. 1967. *A Cross-Cultural Summary.* New Haven: HRAF Press
40. Tylor, E. B. 1889. On a method of investigating the development of institutions. *J. Roy. Anthropol. Inst.* 18:245–72
41. Udy, S. H. Jr. 1959. *Organization of Work.* New Haven: HRAF Press
42. Udy, S. H. Jr. 1964. Cross-cultural analysis: a case study. *Sociologists at Work,* ed. P. E. Hammond, 161–83. New York: Basic Books
43. Udy, S. H. Jr. 1965. Dynamic inferences from static data. *Am. J. Sociol.* 70: 625–27
44. Udy, S. H. Jr. 1968. Social structural analysis. *Int. Encycl. Soc. Sci.* 13:489–95
45. Udy, S. H. Jr. 1970. *Work in Traditional and Modern Societies.* Englewood Cliffs: Prentice-Hall
46. White, D. R. 1970. Societal research archives system. *A Handbook of Method in Cultural Anthropology,* ed. R. Naroll, R. Cohen, 676–85. Garden City: Natural History Press
47. Whiting, J. W. M., Child, I. L. 1953. *Child Training and Personality.* New Haven: Yale Univ. Press

THE ORIGINS OF AGRICULTURE

❖ 9531

Kent V. Flannery[1]

University of Michigan Museum of Anthropology, Ann Arbor, Michigan

> It is now becoming increasingly clear that the domestication of weeds and cultivated plants is usually a process rather than an event.
>
> Edgar Anderson (1, p. 766)

Perhaps no aspect of prehistory has received as much attention over the last 15 years as the origins of agriculture. Archeological expeditions in the Near East, in Thailand, in Mexico, in Peru, and elsewhere have unearthed specimens of man's earliest crops. Botanists have argued over what the specimens mean. Geographers have analyzed the ranges of the wild ancestors of today's crops, and told us where they should originally have been domesticated. Anthropologists young and old have presented models for the way agriculture might have begun—some reasonable, some preposterous. Surely at this stage we could declare the origins of agriculture a bandwagon.

I have already traveled many thousands of miles on that particular wagon, and I yearn to step down and tackle other problems. I agreed to undertake this final review, however, because I feel a critical, skeptical view of the whole bandwagon is badly needed. The first archeologists to work seriously on the origins of agriculture were a cautious and circumspect lot. Unfortunately, they were followed by a number of botanically naïve, sensation-seeking opportunists who were more concerned with finding "the oldest domestic plant" than with clarifying the processes by which agriculture began. Their ingenuousness spread even to the botanists who worked with them, and soon we had claims for domestication based on a single burned seed, a single trampled rind, or a single crumpled pod. In cases where the range of variation of the wild ancestor was not known (in fact, even in cases where the actual species of wild ancestor was not known), we had prestigious botanists assigning a single crushed specimen to a modern cultivated race—a race which, in

---

[1]A number of archeological and botanical colleagues contributed unpublished data to this paper. I would like to thank in particular G. Beadle, K. C. Chang, R. Drennan, R. I. Ford, W. Galinat, L. Kaplan, T. Lynch, R. S. MacNeish, B. Pickersgill, and C. E. Smith Jr. Any errors in the text, however, are my responsibility.

271

some cases, may have taken thousands of years to stabilize. These were botanists who, under normal conditions, would have argued that nothing less than 100 specimens—with a mean and standard deviation—was an adequate sample; but perhaps the search for agricultural origins is not a normal condition. And what the botanists claimed was usually nothing compared to what the archeologists claimed.

Thanks to Robert Braidwood and Richard MacNeish, I have been lucky enough to work in Iran, Mexico, and Peru with some of the best "paleoethnobotanists" working on the origins of agriculture: Hans Helbaek, Jack Harlan, Willem van Zeist, Paul Mangelsdorf, Walton Galinat, George Beadle, Earle Smith, Barbara Pickersgill, and Larry Kaplan, among others. Consequently, I have received "personal communications" and overheard comments which have never appeared in print. I have also been made aware of changes in opinion that have appeared in journals which archeologists ordinarily never read. I think that if all archeologists could have overheard the off-the-cuff comments I received from these botanists, they would have a more profound and healthy skepticism of what we know about early agriculture. When they see a chart showing "domestic beans" at 5000 B.C., and only one single cotyledon is indicated—separated by 2000 years from the next oldest bean—they might take it with a grain of salt.

In return, I wish I could explain to every botanist that while an archeologist looks the other way for one minute, a pack rat can bury an intrusive bean 50 centimeters deeper in his favorite dry cave. Of course, botanists who work in the field with archeologists do learn (from bitter experience) not to accept anything on faith; I would like to single out Barbara Pickersgill in particular for her outstanding skepticism.

In this review, I will not try to cover the whole world; that would be impossible. Nor will I try to cover every cultivated species. What I have done is to select four areas—two in the Old World, two in the New World—and discuss the current evidence for the major staples domesticated there. Where possible I have also reviewed the current hypothetical models for the way agriculture began in a given area. Please note that the model for each area is different; I do not believe that agriculture began the same way, or for the same reasons, in all four areas, nor do I believe one model can explain them all.

My coverage of all four areas (Southwest and Southeast Asia, Mesoamerica, and the Andes) will not be balanced, because we know far less about some areas than others; I have spent the most time on Mesoamerica because the new "maize vs teosinte" debate is one of the most exciting theoretical issues of 1973. But first let me begin with a discussion of two major types of early agriculture.

ECOSYSTEMS AND PRIMITIVE AGRICULTURE

Geographer David Harris has made a useful distinction between two types of "paleotechnic" or primitive agriculture. In his typology, Harris regards farming systems as "man-modified ecosystems" and analyzes them in terms of species diversity, productivity, and stability or homeostasis (Harris 26).

1. *Seed-crop cultivation*—including early wheat farming in the Near East or early maize agriculture in Mesoamerica and Peru—is a relatively simple ecosystem because it consists of very few species (often only one) growing in nearly pure stands composed of large numbers of individuals. It is highly productive (as the later discussion of wheat and maize will show) but also very unstable because of its low species diversity; it requires constant human attention.

2. *Vegeculture*—such as the cultivation of manioc in Amazonia or yams and taro in southeast Asia—is often a very complex ecosystem, because many different cultivated species may be grown in a single field. Although sometimes less productive than intensive seed-crop cultivation, it is far more ecologically stable because of its species diversity; it more closely approximates the complexity of natural vegetation.

Because most early centers for seed-crop farming were in arid regions with good archeological preservation, a great deal is known about early farming there. Moreover, morphological changes in the seeds following domestication can usually be detected. On the other hand, most early centers for vegeculture were humid tropical regions with poor archeological preservation; and since many of these crops are planted by cuttings, roots, or some other vegetative part which shows little or no morphological change after domestication, we know much less about early vegeculture. Archeologists like Donald Lathrap (40) have long bemoaned the fact that we know so little about the origins of root crops, and their importance is so frequently ignored.

That is, it is ignored by archeologists working in arid regions; but archeologists working in the tropics, in spite of the absence of data, frequently present theories of root crop cultivation which are at present untestable. For example, Lowe (45) has argued for early manioc cultivation on the Pacific Coast of Chiapas and Guatemala, citing as evidence small obsidian chips which are said to resemble those used in manioc graters in South America. Yet a sample of more than 50 preserved plants from 1000 B.C. on the Guatemalan coast, which Coe and I recovered in 1962 (Coe & Flannery 9), contains no manioc; it is, like all arid Mexican highland samples of the same time period, mostly maize. Complicating the picture still further is the fact that botanist Earle Smith (MacNeish 46) identified a seed of wild *Manihot* from one of MacNeish's Tamaulipas caves. The species was one which has never been domesticated (Smith 67), but overeager archeologists continue to cite it as an example of cultivated manioc. The result is that many archeologists in Mesoamerica ignore root crops, while others argue strenuously for them with no supporting data. I will try not to ignore them, but I have little concrete data to offer.

THE ORIGINS OF AGRICULTURE IN SOUTHWEST ASIA

Southwest Asia, one of the first regions of the world to have agriculture, is also the most intensively investigated area from the standpoint of early cultivation. Thanks to the pioneering efforts of archeologists like Robert Braidwood (Braidwood & Howe 6) and paleoethnobotanists like Hans Helbaek (28, 29), we probably know more about early farming in the Near East than anywhere else. One or two valleys in Mesoamerica have produced superb evidence for early agriculture; but in Southwest Asia we have carbonized plant remains from Israel, Jordan, Syria, Turkey, Iraq, and Iran, all antedating 5000 B.C. The group of sites shown in Table 1 is only a tiny sample of what could have been listed.

So much has been published on early agriculture in the Near East that I will give here only a short resumé of the archeological evidence, and briefly restate one current hypothesis for the way farming may have begun. A more extensive synthesis of the archeological data can be found in a paper by Jane Renfrew (61), and a more detailed statement of the hypothesis can be found in an earlier paper of my own (Flannery 15).

The Near East is one of those parts of the world where sedentary life—in "hut compounds" or actual villages—seems to have begun *before* agriculture (Flannery 16). The earliest permanent settlements there are either without evidence of domestic plants, or have only plants which are "wild" in the phenotypic sense.[2] Currently it appears that these early sedentary communities relied on a mixed strategy of harvesting wild cereal grasses (wheat, barley, and ryegrass), nuts (pistachios, walnuts, almonds, and acorns), and legumes (*Astragalus, Trigonella*); hunting herd ungulates (sheep, goat, and deer); and collecting a wide variety of smaller species like fish, water turtles, land snails, cockles, mussels, and crabs. This adaptation seems to have crystallized during the second half of the Würm glacial advance of the Pleistocene period (20,000–9,000 B.C.)—a period during which the Near East is now believed, on palynological grounds, to have been colder and drier than today (van Zeist & Wright 74).

There can be no doubt that this prolonged cold, dry period affected man's environment in southwest Asia. Areas of the Zagros Mountains in Iran and Iraq, which today would have oak and pistachio woodland (were it not for overgrazing and deforestation) became virtually treeless during the late Würm. This would not only have reduced wild nut crops like acorn, pistachio, walnut, and almond, but also wild cereal grasses which are part of the woodland floral community. Only in the Levant (Israel, Lebanon, Jordan) and the Ghab basin of Syria did relict woodlands of oak survive (Niklewski & van Zeist 54). It was probably from these relict populations that the rest of the Near Eastern uplands became reforested after the post-Pleistocene climatic amelioration. These woodlands were the ancestral home of wild wheat (*Triticum*), barley (*Hordeum*), lentils (*Lens*), vetch (*Vicia*), vetchling (*Lathyrus*), peas (*Pisum, Cicer*), linseed (*Linum*), and many of the other ancestors of Southwest Asia's staple crops.

Wild wheat, barley, and their relatives have a long history in Southwest Asia. Some of the hardier species surely weathered the cooling and drying of late Würm times; in the sediments of Lake Zeribar in the Iranian Mountains, some "cereal type" pollen was present before 12,000 B.C. (van Zeist & Wright 74). But several of

---

[2]That is, the plants do not differ morphologically from wild races. This does not prove they were not cultivated—it merely shows they had not yet undergone any genetic change in the direction of the domestic races.

Table 1 Some early occurrence of cultivated plants (and their wild ancestors) in the Near East and Southeast Europe[a]

Archeological sites	Approximate date	Wild 2-row barley	Domestic 2-row barley	Wild emmer wheat	Domestic emmer wheat	Wild einkorn wheat	Domestic einkorn wheat	Lentil	Field pea (*Pisum*)	Linseed	Bread wheat	6-row barley
Tell Mureybit, Syria	8050-7542 B.C.	X				X						
Ali Kosh, Iran	7500-6750 B.C.	X	?			X	X					
Hacilar, Turkey	7000-6500 B.C.				X	X		X	X			X
Jericho, Jordan	7000-6500 B.C.		X		X		X	X	X			
Jarmo, Iraq	6500-6000 B.C.			X	X	X	X	X	X			X
Ali Kosh, Iran	6500-6000 B.C.		X		X			X				X
Catal Hüyük, Turkey	5850-5600 B.C.	X			X		X		X		X	X
Tell es-Sawwan, Iran	5800-5600 B.C.		X		X		X			X	X	X
Tepe Sabz, Iran	5500-5000 B.C.		X				X	X		X	X	X
various sites in Greece	6000-5000 B.C.		X		X		X	X			X	X

[a] After Renfrew (61) with modifications. Cambridge University's find of emmer in Kebaran levels at Nahal Oren, Israel (reported verbally but not published at this writing) will push that cereal's history back many thousands of years farther.

the species most exploited by prehistoric man prefer warmer habitats, and would not have done well until temperatures began to rise toward the end of the Würm. By late Paleolithic times, when scattered oaks and pistachios were reinvading the Zagros, conditions for the cereals had significantly improved. After 12,000 B.C., over much of the Near East, the possibilities for extensive use of wild wheat and barley were not only good, but steadily improving.

There is no evidence, however, that this climatic amelioration *caused* agriculture to begin. Surely there had been periods just as favorable during earlier interglacials, without any resulting agriculture. Two factors, however, *were* different during late Würm: (1) the population of Southwest Asia was higher than it had ever been before and (2) for the first time human groups were using *on a large scale* a whole series of foods which had previously been ignored or insignificant in their diet: the snails, crabs, fish, mussels, and other "harvestable" invertebrates already mentioned. In such a context, even wild cereal grasses might have looked appetizing, in spite of the labor involved in their harvest and preparation.

It must be admitted that our evidence for the first use of wild wheat and barley is circumstantial. Not a single carbonized grain has ever been recovered from the periods we would *most* like to know about—not because the sites lack ash deposits, but because previous archeologists usually lacked interest in saving any. In addition, it appears that some late Würm ash deposits are so mineralized that the carbonized seeds cannot even be floated out with water, which is one common recovery method. These technical obstacles are gradually being overcome by techniques like Cambridge University's froth flotation (Jarman, Legge & Charles 32), which has now yielded some of the world's oldest cereal remains from Nahal Oren, Israel. But until such techniques are widespread, we must draw on other lines of evidence. These have been summarized as follows (Flannery 15):

1. To convert most wild cereals into a satisfying meal, you need processing implements and storage and cooking facilities which the previous Paleolithic peoples of the Near East do not seem to have had. *These implements and facilities appear with explosive rapidity after 10,000 B.C.*

2. The wild cereals come ripe at a wholly different season from the wild tree crops (acorn, almond, pistachio, walnut): nuts in the autumn, cereals in late spring. Moreover, the harvest season for wild cereals is much shorter and more restricted and cannot be approached with the casualness permitted by the long nut crop season. *An appropriate shift in settlement pattern and social organization was required in order to focus on wild cereals, and seems to have appeared by 10,000 B.C.*

An Introduction to the Wild Cereals

Now let us examine the characteristics of five cereal species of three genera— *Triticum, Aegilops,* and *Hordeum*—whose habitats and ranges have recently been outlined by botanists Jack R. Harlan and Daniel Zohary (25).

1. Wild barley (*Hordeum spontaneum*) is the most widespread of these cereals, tolerating the greatest range of environmental conditions. Its primary wild range is the uplands of the Lebanon-Judean, Taurus, and Zagros Mountains, where it forms an important component of the summer-dry deciduous oak woodland. Inhibited by

extreme cold, it only rarely occurs in the wild above 1500 meters (and during the late Würm period may have stayed even lower); hence it is unlikely that man would have found useful stands in the higher mountains or on the plateaus of Turkey and Iran. On the other hand, wild barley tolerates heat and aridity better than wheat, and will follow seasonal stream beds down from the mountains and out into the hot steppes and desert regions. In fact, a slender, small-seeded race occurs as an annual grass of wet stream beds in the barren Negev and Syrian-Transjordan deserts, while a much more robust race inhabits the moist uplands at the head of the Jordan Valley. In addition, wild barley does so well as a "weed" in disturbed habitats or wheat fields that its range has been greatly increased by agriculture; today, semiwild "weed" barley "grows in the mountain forest, on the coastal plain, in the shade of rock outcrops in semidesert areas, and as a weed in the fields of every conceivable cultivated crop" from Morocco to Turkestan (Helbaek 28, p. 112). Wild barley therefore flourishes rather than retreating under conditions of human exploitation.

2. Wild einkorn wheat (*Triticum boeoticum*), as its name implies, usually has "one grain" on each internode of its head; it is what geneticists call a *diploid* species, which in the case of wheat means it has 2 X 7, or 14 chromosomes. Actually, the name einkorn is not wholly apt, since one race has evolved a "two grain" internode to survive in arid regions: one grain of the pair germinates the first year, while the second is delayed until later in case the first fails.

Einkorn, in contrast to wild barley, tolerates cold conditions well. It grows above 1500 meters in Turkey and up to 2000 meters in the Zagros Mountains of Iran and Iraq. Its primary range seems to be the Taurus-Zagros Mountain arc and immediately adjacent steppe; it grows in the Levant only as a weed in disturbed habitats. It prefers basalt, marl, and limestone as substrata, and will form massive stands "as thick as a cultivated field" where it finds these conditions in the heart of its primary range.

3. *Aegilops speltoides,* known as "goat-face grass," is a wild cereal closely related to wheat; its natural range overlaps with wild einkorn. In the Tigris headwater region of Turkey's southern Taurus region, wild einkorn and *Ae. speltoides* form dense stands on basalt ridges and uplands where they can be harvested together. Botanists feel that at some time in the very remote past, diploid (2 X 7) einkorn and diploid (2 X 7) *Ae. speltoides* hybridized to produce a *tetraploid* (4 X 7, or 28 chromosome) wheat known as wild emmer (see below).

4. Wild emmer wheat (*Triticum dicoccoides*) is the most sensitive and demanding of all the wild cereals to be discussed here; it will not tolerate cold as well as einkorn, nor heat and aridity as well as wild barley. It is therefore the most localized in its "primary range," the area where it will form dense stands. To complicate matters, its range is split into two distinct segments, separated by a gap in the Syrian Mountains where no wild emmer will grow.

A robust, large-seeded race of emmer occurs in Palestine, where it forms massive stands on basalt and limestone slopes in Galilee, Mt. Hermon, and the Golan plateau. Here Zohary estimates that harvests of up to 500–800 kilograms of grain per hectare (450–700 pounds per acre) could be made from untended, native wild stands in a rainy year. A smaller-seeded race occurs sporadically in the lower oak woodland of the Zagros and Taurus ranges, where rainfall is between 300 and 500 millimeters. This smaller race, which seemingly never forms dense stands, could eventually prove to be a "weed" emmer which spread to disturbed habitats in the Zagros-Taurus arc following cultivation. This cannot as yet be shown, nor is it clear precisely how this eastern race is related to *Triticum araraticum,* another wild tetraploid wheat occupying the same region.

Perhaps most significant is the fact that the large-seeded Palestinian wild race forms consistently fertile hybrids with cultivated emmer (*Triticum dicoccum*), while the small-seeded Zagros race usually will not. This strongly suggests that the Palestinian race is the wild ancestor of today's domestic emmer, and it focuses attention on the Israel-Jordan-Lebanon area as an early center for emmer cultivation.

5. *Aegilops squarrosa,* another species of "goat-face grass," has its principal range along the Caspian sea coast and the Kopet Dagh mountains on the Iranian-Turkmenistan border; there are also sporadic occurrences in the Zagros, but these may be "weed" strains in disturbed habitats. *Aegilops* was eaten by prehistoric man in the Zagros, but seems never to have been as important as wheat. We mention *Ae. squarrosa* primarily because genetic evidence suggests that, long centuries after cultivation had begun, it was diploid (2 X 7) *Ae. squarrosa* which hybridized with tetraploid (4 X 7) emmer to produce a hexaploid (6 X 7, or 42 chromosome) wheat, *Triticum aestivum*—the world's first "bread wheat." In general, the wheats mentioned above are unsuitable for breadmaking, and tend to be eaten as porridge.

The Potential (and Problems) of Wild Grain Harvests

The tremendous productivity of wild wheat and barley within the heart of their "primary" range has recently been stressed by Harlan & Zohary (25). They comment that "over many thousands of hectares" on suitable basalt or limestone substrata "it would be possible to harvest wild wheat today from natural stands almost as dense as a cultivated wheat field." Zohary's estimates of 500–800 kilograms per hectare for mixed stands of wild emmer and barley in rainy years on the east Galilee uplands have already been mentioned. Under such conditions, a single hectare of land could provide more than two million calories—or about the number required by a family of three during the course of a year.

On a basalt mountain range near Diyarbakir, in the upper Tigris drainage of Turkey, Jack Harlan set out to find out just how much a prehistoric man might be able to harvest (Harlan 24). Diyarbakir lies almost directly in the track of the rain winds passing through gaps in the Syrian mountains, and in 1966 the basalt uplands were a sea of wild einkorn wheat mixed with goat-face grass. After five separate periods of hand-stripping the wild wheat heads from their stalks, Harlan found he was collecting an average of just over 2 kilograms of grain per hour. Such hand-stripping is still practiced by the Bedouin of Southern Jordan, but it takes tougher hands than the average university professor has; Harlan's were soon lacerated by the coarse and raspy exterior of the cereal heads. He then switched to harvesting by means of a "prehistoric" sickle, made from flint blades set in a wooden handle; this enabled him to harvest nearly 2.5 kilograms per hour with less wear and tear on his hands. In the end, Harlan concluded that a family of four, harvesting for the whole of the 3-week period during which the Diyarbakir einkorn came ripe, could easily harvest a metric ton—one year's supply. Let us hasten to add, however, that such a family would face many obstacles, not the least of which are the physical characters of the plants themselves.

Look now at Figure 1, Hans Helbaek's diagrammatic drawing of a cereal "spike" or head. The black, composite vertical column is the axis or *rachis* of the spike, composed of many individual internodes separated by white interstices. Each internode bears at its upper end a "spikelet," consisting of one or more mature cereal grains (shown in white), encased between tough "glumes" or husks (shown as stippled). When a cereal plant reaches maturity, the axis begins to disarticulate, starting at the top. One by one, individual internodes detach themselves at the white interstices and fall to the ground; the whole process takes 1 or 2 weeks on the average. Finally, only the stalk is left; each seed has buried itself in the ground where it waits, encased in its protective glumes, for the next rainy winter. The "brittle rachis" of the wild cereals thus acts to disperse the seeds one at a time, preventing the unfavorable condition which would result if the whole head of grain fell to the ground in one place. In the latter case, half the seeds would never be buried and the rest would sprout in a dense mass of competing seedlings.

The brittle rachis is of no help to the collector of wild wheat or barley, however. In the first place, he cannot harvest before the grain is fully ripe, or a dried, wizened, unpalatable head results. It is thus not surprising that carbonized archeological specimens show that mature heads were harvested (Zohary 80). On the other hand,

Figure 1 Diagram of a spike of wheat or barley. The black, composite column is the axis or rachis. Its component parts, the internodes, are separated by white interstices where, in the wild, the axis disarticulates. In domestic cereals the interstices toughen and do not disarticulate. Three internodes near the bottom of the drawing are shown as having mature florets (white ovals) enclosed between glumes (stippled areas); in domestic cereals these glumes become easier to remove from the floret, in which the fruit or grain develops (see text). After Helbaek (29, Figure 138).

the collector cannot wait too long after the cereals ripen, or else he will be greeted by a field full of empty stalks. Even during the latter part of the harvest season, the heads may be brittle enough to shatter at the slightest touch.

Here timing becomes critical, for final ripening is brought on by the onset of dry hot weather at the end of the growing season, and this is quite variable from year to year. Under ideal conditions, a family of cereal collectors might have 3 weeks in which to harvest their metric ton; but Zohary points out that if an extremely dry warm spell (known in Israel as the *hamsin*) happens to occur at maturation time "shedding of fruit can be completed in a matter of 2 or 3 days" (80, p. 57). Being in the right area at the right time is therefore far more important than for collection of wild nut crops, and the harvest may be a fast and furious affair.

Some of the problems facing prehistoric collectors might thus be listed:

1. *The brittle rachis,* which, combined with unpredictable hot dry weather, makes timing essential: a year's supply of grain could hinge on a crucial period of 3 days or less.

2. *The tough glumes* which hold each kernel in a tight grip long after the rachis had disintegrated. In the wild cereals, these inedible glumes adhere so strongly to the grain that conventional "threshing" will not remove them.

3. *The annual fluctuations in rainfall* characteristic of the Near East. Zohary's estimate of 500–800 kilos per hectare was based on a "rainy" year. In a "dry" year, the yield could be 100 kilos or even less—a reduction which could bring some families to the brink of starvation.

4. *The extreme localization of dense cereal stands.* Even in a rainy year, it is only certain limestone massifs or basalt plateaus which have had stands as dense as those described by Harlan & Zohary. In between there are alluvial plains, wadis, and uplands of less favorable substratum where the cereals, if present at all, grew very sparsely.

5. *Harvesting tools.* Hand-stripping is an efficient way of selecting only the ripe heads and keeping the brittle internodes from scattering, but it can be slow and painful. More efficient implements for cutting and facilities for transport were needed.

6. *Storage.* After all, where can you go with a metric ton of cleaned wheat seed? It requires storage facilities, and it requires that they be sufficiently waterproof so the grain does not sprout during the moist winter season.

Not all of these problems could be solved by the prehistoric cereal collectors of the Near East prior to domestication. But we know what a few of their solutions were, and we can make some educated guesses about the rest on the basis of archeological data.

1. *The development of harvesting tools.* Sickles made from flint blades set in slots in a wooden or bone handle and cemented with natural asphalt or gum became widespread in the near East after 10,000 B.C. Sickle blades can be identified by a characteristic "sheen" or luster which develops on the cutting edge through its use on grass stems.

2. *Collecting and transporting facilities.* On the basis of limited archeological evidence, we suggest that grain was collected and carried from the field in baskets.

One of our earliest clues, dated by radiocarbon to before 8500 B.C., consists of fragments of possible basketry from Level B_1 of Shanidar Cave in Iraq (Solecki 69). Somewhat later sites (6500–7500 B.C.) have produced clear fragments of twined baskets, sometimes waterproofed with bitumen (Hole, Flannery & Neely 30).

3. *The development of processing facilities.* Sometime around the end of the Pleistocene, man discovered that by roasting the grain he had collected he could render the glumes so dry and brittle that they could be removed by abrasion. At several sites this was accomplished by roasting the cereals over heated pebbles in a pit or subterranean earth oven (cf. van Loon 73).

Removal of the glumes by abrasion (either directly or after roasting) was apparently done first with mortar and pestle. Harlan, following the experimental harvest already mentioned, found he could effectively dehusk his einkorn wheat with the type of wooden mortar and pestle used by the Osage Indians of the central USA. Wooden mortars have not been preserved at sites in the Near East (they could have existed well back in the Paleolithic), but limestone or basalt mortars and pestles appeared at the end of the Pleistocene. They were joined, after no great interval of time, by shallow basin-shaped or saddle-shaped grinding slabs on whose upper surface grain could be abraded by means of a flat or loaf-shaped second stone held in the hands (like the *metate* and *mano* of New World archeology). Further grinding by mortar or slab reduced the cereals to "groats," or coarse grits of grain which could be cooked up into a mush or gruel. Such groats are present in some of the earliest carbonized grain samples (antedating 7000 B.C.), which even seem to have included the woody base of the cereal spikelet; evidently this nearly inedible part of the plant was ground up and eaten right along with the grain (Helbaek 29).

4. *The expansion of storage facilities.* Below-ground storage pits were already present in some Upper Paleolithic sites, but the Natufian people of Palestine (9000–7000 B.C.) made them widespread in the Near East. Conical or bell-shaped (wider at the base than at the mouth), these pits are extremely numerous at Natufian sites, where they are sometimes coated with lime plaster, presumably for waterproofing. The process of roasting or parching the cereals, already mentioned, besides weakening the glumes also kills the germ so the cereal will not sprout during the damp winter. A single Natufian site, Ain Mallaha, contains more storage facilities than are known from all previous sites in the Near East put together (Perrot 57).

5. *Harvesting along the altitude cline* represents one method of increasing the harvest in spite of the brief, rapid ripening season of the brittle-rachis wild cereals. It depends on the fact that differences in maturation time do exist between different cereals and between different altitude zones. Zohary points out that in Israel, for example,

in mixed stands, *H. spontaneum* matures from 1 to 3 weeks earlier than *T. dicoccoides.* Plants growing in sites with deep heavy soil mature somewhat later than those occupying shallow soils. Considerable differences in the ripening time occur, however, at different altitudes. Maturation of wild emmer at the sea level belt near the Sea of Galilee occurs around the end of April, while higher up in the Safad area (alt. 700–800 m) stands mature around 15th–20th May. In the adjacent east-facing slopes of Mt. Hermon (alt. 1400–1600 m), ripening occurs still later—in early June. Similar altitude clines occur in Turkey, Iraq, and Iran. Therefore, in regions with varied topography, altitudinal amplitude compensates for the abrupt shedding. Collectors can start their harvest in lower elevations and proceed gradually to climb the higher slope, and effective harvesting time is extended to last 4 to 6 weeks (Zohary 80, p. 57).

We do not know for sure if such a pattern was followed during the 10,000–7,000 B.C. period, but if so, it might be detectable in the settlement pattern: harvesting camps at higher altitudes should date to later in the year.

6. *Problems solved by domestication:* finally, we come to a series of problems which were not (indeed, could not be) countered purely by the stategy and technology of harvesting and processing. These include (*a*) the brittle rachis, and (*b*) the annual variability in rainfall which kept densities of cereal stands unpredictable. Only the beginnings of agriculture—which brought the cereals down from their rainfed upland habitats, placed them on permanently humid floodplain soils, and reduced selection pressures for the wild phenotype—directly attacked these problems. Although the exact nature of Natufian subsistence is poorly understood, at least one village of this period, Tell Mureybit, although yielding a large carbonized seed sample, seems to have only grain of the "wild" brittle-rachis type (van Loon 73).

An important genetic change following domestication—one controlled by perhaps as few as two genes—was the shift to a tough rachis, one that held together at maturity. Tough-rachis mutants must always have existed, but in the wild they would have been selected *against* because of their poor seed dispersal mechanism. Early farmers evidently selected *for* them, for shortly after 7000 B.C. tough-rachis strains of emmer wheat or two-row barley appear in archeological deposits from Jordan to Iran. In some cases, three internodes from a single spike have stayed together through threshing, carbonization, 9000 years of burial underground, and the rigors of archeological flotation!

Another genetic change—this one apparently controlled by a single gene (Stubbe 72)—was the shift to a "naked" kernel, one whose glumes did not adhere as strongly as do wild glumes. "Naked" barleys appeared sporadically as early as 7000 B.C., but did not become common until after 6000 B.C. This must have reduced the amount of labor in threshing by a considerable factor. Still a third change was the evolution of two-row barley into six-row barley of both "hulled" and "naked" strains. This change, which occurred sometime before 6500 B.C. and became widespread by 5500 B.C., converted the normally sterile lateral kernels in each barley spikelet to large, fertile kernels like the central spikelet. Such lateral kernels develop facets where they meet the central kernel, as well as a slight twist; these characters allow six-row mutants to be identified in the archeological plant remains.

Finally, domestication allowed man to plant cereals selectively on permanently humid soils where moisture in the ground would help them survive the fluctuations in annual rainfall characteristic of the Near East. At Ali Kosh in southwest Iran, early farmers planted their wheat and barley so close to swamp margins that seeds of the club-rush *Scirpus* were mixed with the carbonized cereals (Flannery 15). Since wild wheat and barley do not grow in such marshy habitats, the native vegetation must have been removed to make way for them—the first steps in man's deliberate modification of the Near Eastern landscape.

A Model for the Origins of Near Eastern Farming

If, as Lee & deVore (43) tell us, hunting-and-gathering was the most stable adaptation man ever had, why did he ever give it up for a life of toil in the wheat fields?

We may never know why agriculture began in the Near East. All we know is that it was initiated toward the end of a long, cool, dry climatic phase by people with a recently evolved tradition of "broad spectrum" resource utilization; that it probably began among people who were at least partly sedentary, and whose population density (although far from the highest in the world at that time) was probably higher than it had ever been previously; and that it began in a region of relatively great environmental diversity over a relatively small area.

Binford, Birdsell, Wynne-Edwards, and others (Binford 5) have argued that most hunting-gathering populations, once reasonably well adapted to a particular environment, tend to remain stable at densities below the point of resource exhaustion. Lee (42) has suggested that emigration was one of the main mechanisms for keeping human populations low during the two million years prior to 10,000 B.C. By 10,000 B.C., however, man had occupied virtually every major land mass in the world, from Australia to the southern tip of South America. In other words, after that point emigration probably decreased in importance as a population-limiting device, while other mechanisms—long lactation, infanticide, senilicide, and so on—increased in importance. Some groups may also have attempted to increase food supply relative to population density by cultural means: turning to previously ignored sources of food like small aquatic or invertebrate species, or attempting to increase local stands of useful plants. The latter could be one path to agriculture.

In 1968, in a paper on post-Pleistocene adaptations, Binford (5) proposed a "density equilibrium" model for cultural change which I later applied to the Near East (Flannery 15). Binford argued that adaptation would change only in the face of some disturbance in the equilibrium between population and environment, such as (a) a change in the physical environment which would bring about a reduction in the density of chosen plant or animal foods, or (b) a change in population density or distribution which would raise human populations too close to the carrying capacity of the immediate area. A change of the first kind does seem to be reflected in the palynological record in Southwest Asia—the cold, dry late Würm, which restricted woodland resources to relict areas. And there are changes in population reflected in the archeological record, which we understand only poorly, but which might be examples of the second kind of change. For example, judged purely on the basis of numbers of sites per period (a slippery statistic at best), some areas of the Lebanon coast would seem to have decreased in population in the very late Pleistocene, while certain areas of Israel and Jordan enjoyed increases (Copeland & Wescomb 10, Marks 53). However, such site distributions may actually reflect shifts in population from one region to another, without any real overall population increase.

The Near East is a mosaic of "favorable" habitats (e.g. oak-pistachio woodland) and "marginal" habitats (e.g. gravel desert); the wild cereals have definite "optimum" zones in which they grow densely and marginal zones in which they do poorly. If one follows Binford's model to its logical conclusion, the "optimum" habitats should have been the centers for population growth, with the marginal areas receiving the emigrant overflow. It is in these marginal zones that man-land disequilibrium and stress would have been felt first. Thus in 1969 I suggested that farming might have begun first, not in the optimum area of wild cereal growth (where, as Harlan and Zohary point out, wild wheat already does as well as it would in a cultivated field), but around the margins where it was necessary to raise the available food per capita. In the marginal zone, wheat and barley would only produce 500 kg per hectare if artificially planted in selected humid soils such as stream beds and swamp margins. Rather than repeat the whole argument in detail, I refer the reader to the original presentation (Flannery 15).

Let me now raise some objections to this model. First, although it has won an almost frightening acceptance among some of my colleagues, it is still unproven and highly speculative. Second, as my comments above indicate, our archeological data (such as they are) do not show strong population increases in "optimum" areas like the Lebanese woodland, but the very opposite—some of the most striking increases are in "marginal" habitats like the Negev! Clearly, there were a number of very interesting processes at work in the late Pleistocene Levant which could only be handled by a more multivariate model. Finally, the model comes too close to making population growth and climatic change into prime movers. It may be that the "demographic change" which made cultivation seem like a good idea in Southwest Asia was an increase in sedentary communities—and the latter may have begun in response to changes in socio-political organization which had nothing to do with either climate or population density.

THE ORIGINS OF AGRICULTURE IN SOUTHEAST ASIA

As far as the origins of agriculture go, China and the Far East are an enigma. It will surely be decades before we have more than a sketchy outline of what happened there, and I will touch only briefly on some of the latest discoveries.

East Asia has examples of both of Harris' artificial ecosystems, temperate seed-cropping and tropical vegeculture. In the north, the Hwang-ho River valley of China has been singled out as an early center for the cultivation of foxtail millet *(Setaria italica)* and perhaps broomcorn millet *(Panicum miliaceum)*. Although present archeological discoveries trace these cultivated grasses back to only the fifth millenium B.C. (Chang 8), earlier stages in their history will almost certainly be filled in some day. In addition, wheat and barley were introduced into China from western Asia to augment this temperate seed farming. It is by no means clear to what extent early Chinese agriculture was independent of neighboring regions, and I will offer no model for its origins.

Southeast Asia is an area of root crops—yam and taro—none of which have yet been preserved in archeological deposits of any antiquity. Nevertheless, it is tropical Thailand which has produced the oldest archeological plant remains from the Far East (see below). Southeast Asia could also prove to be the homeland of rice *(Oryza sativa),* and it seems to me, as an outsider, that the "64 dollar question" in the rise of Far Eastern agriculture is the origin of domestic rice. Asia has countless other domestic plants, but none comes close to rice in providing an economic base for the populations of the East. Sadly, we probably know less about the origins of rice than any other major cereal, although a few new data are now at hand.

Of the more than 20 species of *Oryza* distributed through the Old World tropics, one wild perennial form, *Oryza perennis,* is the likely ancestor of *Oryza sativa.* The latter, although not the only species of cultivated rice, is the one which feeds more Asians than any other (Peebles 56). Domestication has changed it to an annual grass, given it a tough rachis and larger grain size (Heiser 27). Specimens of *Oryza sativa* are known from archeological deposits of ca. 3000 B.C. at Harappa and Mohenjodaro in the Indus River Valley and of ca. 2500 B.C. on Formosa (Peebles 56); the history of rice on the Chinese mainland is still longer, going back to the fourth millenium B.C. Archeologist K. C. Chang (8) hypothesizes that rice was first domesticated by early yam and taro growers of Southeast Asia, who might originally have encountered it as a weed in their gardens. While the archeological data to test this suggestion are not yet available, Chang does focus attention on Southeast Asia, a region which has recently been the scene of several new breakthroughs in paleoethnobotany.

The oldest radiocarbon-dated plant remains from Southeast Asia come from Spirit Cave in northwest Thailand; they were recovered in 1966 by archeologist Chester Gorman and identified by botanists D. Yen and P. van Royen. Gorman's excavation through a complex series of living floors was masterful, and Yen and van Royen's analysis careful and circumspect; I stress this for reasons which will be apparent below. First let us examine the raw data from Spirit Cave as they originally appear in print (Gorman 23).

The plant remains come from layers 4, 3, and 2 in ascending order of stratigraphy. Associated radiocarbon dates are:

Hearth in layer 2: 8550 B.P. ± 200 (6600 B.C.)
Charcoal in layer 2a: 8750 B.P. ± 140 (6800 B.C.)
Charcoal in layer 4: 9180 B.P. ± 360 (7230 B.C.)

The plants themselves are identified as:

Almond (*Prunus*)
Butternut (*Madhuca*)
Candlenut (*Aleurites*)
Local wild nuts (*Terminalia* and *Canarium*)
Betel nut (*Areca*)
A bean (*Vicia* or *Phaseolus*)[3]
Bottle gourd (*Lagenaria*)
Water chestnut (*Trapa*)
Black pepper (*Piper*)
Cucumber *(Cucumis)*

In addition, some radiocarbon samples are said to be "charred bamboo."

Gorman's presentation of the Spirit Cave data was cautious and reasonable. He was well aware that none of the plants recovered had been shown to differ genetically

---

[3]Many authorities now feel that east Asian *Phaseolus* beans should be assigned to the genus *Vigna* (Heiser 27).

from their wild phenotypes; indeed, one "bean" might be a palm, and another could not be identified to genus. Conspicuously absent from the collection of nuts and condiments was rice—or any other real staple of the Far East. Such absence, however, in no way prevented this from being one of the most important collections of plant remains ever recovered from an archeological site. It was our first look at the way man had used the floral environment of Southeast Asia in that remote, pre-pottery, cave-dwelling period. To those of us interested in such things, it seemed that the Spirit Cave data needed no "window dressing": they were exciting enough at face value.

We were therefore surprised a few years later, by an article in a popular journal by W. G. Solheim, overall director of the Thailand project of which Spirit Cave was one part (Solheim 70). While conceding in one sentence that the material recovered might all be "merely wild species gathered from the surrounding countryside," Solheim spent various sections of the article claiming that "an advanced knowledge of horticulture" characterized the occupants of Spirit Cave "about 10,000 B.C."; and his chronology chart (70, p. 38) pushes "incipient horticulture" in Southeast Asia back to 20,000 B.C. Consequently, the subtitle of the article tells us that the agricultural revolution "began some 5000 years earlier" in Southeast Asia than in the Middle East. This seems to be a bit of an overstatement until we know, among other things, whether we are dealing with a pea or a palm! It is not, however, the only confusing aspect of the chronology chart; although Spirit Cave was still aceramic at 6800 B.C., the chart tells us that pottery was invented in Southeast Asia at 13,000 B.C. But then, as Solheim says, his reconstruction "is largely hypothetical."

The problem with this overstatement is that it has created a widespread "credibility gap" between an important and reliable excavation by Gorman (which everyone accepts) and the inflated claims in the popular press (to which professional archeologists react with skepticism). There is a real danger that the significance of Spirit Cave—our first solid evidence for the plants early man was eating at 7200 B.C. in the forested uplands of Thailand—will be lost somewhere in a smokescreen of exaggerated claims.

Let us turn now to the problem of rice. Here Solheim's Thailand project has contributed a major breakthrough. Imprints of cereal grains and husks of *Oryza sativa,* the widespread Asian cultivated rice, have been identified in potsherds from the site of Nok Nok Tha in central Thailand; as is frequently the case at prehistoric villages, rice chaff was probably mixed into the pottery clay to give it body. The potsherds involved are dated by radiocarbon to "before 3000 B.C.," to which Solheim adds *"possibly* before 4000 B.C." (emphasis mine).[4] Stated most conservatively, rice must have been domesticated some time after the preceramic occupation of Spirit Cave (6800 B.C.) and before the founding of Nok Nok Tha (4000 B.C.?). Its origins, of course, could go back still farther elsewhere.

Let me close this section on the Old World on an optimistic note. My criticism of Solheim's writings in the popular press should not be construed as a criticism of

[4]He shows "rice" on his chronology chart at 6000 B.C. (70, p. 38)

the archeological work itself, or as an underestimation of its importance. On the contrary, his project has transformed Southeast Asia into one of the most exciting frontiers for research on early domestication in the Old World, and I hope that political conditions permit him to continue his work there for many years to come.

THE ORIGINS OF AGRICULTURE IN MESOAMERICA

Sometime between the close of the Pleistocene and the start of the fifth millenium B.C., the Indians of Mexico first began the cultivation of a series of native plants which would later become the staple foods of ancient Mesoamerican civilization. For centuries these prehistoric inhabitants of the semiarid basins and valleys of Mexico, Puebla, Oaxaca, Morelos, Guerrero, and Hidalgo had lived off the land, learning the secrets of the wild vegetation—how to roast *Agave* to make it edible, how to make wooden tongs for picking the spiny fruit of the organ cactus, how to extract syrup from the pod of the mesquite, how to leach tannic acid from the acorn, how to find wild bean and wild onion flowers in the dense underbrush, and how to predict when they would be ready to harvest (Flannery 14). They survived on the basis of a collecting strategy with many alternate moves and alternate food sources, depending on whether the rains came too soon or too late, the spring was too cool or too hot, the deer were in the valleys or up in the forest, the pinyon nut crop was heavy or meager. Finally, by 5000 B.C., one of their ultimate strategies became the artificial increase of certain edible plants by selection and planting. Beans, squashes, pumpkins, amaranths, chiles, tomatoes, avocados (and perhaps even prickly pear, maguey, and a whole series of semitropical fruits for which we have only Indian names) came under cultivation not long after this date. But the most important of these was maize or Indian corn, which they so modified that in the words of George Beadle (3) these prehistoric Indians "can be credited with having produced the greatest morphological change of any cultivated plant (assuming I am right about its wild ancestor) and with having adapted corn to the widest geographical change of any major crop plant."

Not so very long ago, the whole period of earliest agriculture in Mesoamerica was hypothetical; it existed only on paper. Then Richard S. MacNeish, after years of work on the northern periphery of Mesoamerica, began to explore the dry caves of Tehuacán, Puebla, in the central Mexican highlands. In the years 1960–1964, these caves yielded the preserved remains of many of the stages in the development of Mesoamerica's most important crops, from wild plants to highly advanced domesticates. Since then, many of us who were lucky enough to work for MacNeish have radiated into adjacent regions of Mesoamerica to add some footnotes to the available data. Techniques of flotation, adapted to archeology by Stuart Struever in the midwestern United States, are now being used to recover carbonized seeds in regions where dry caves simply do not exist. At the moment we know a good deal about the *order* in which various plants were domesticated in several regions (Table 2). We still do not know *why* they were domesticated, and it will certainly be a long time before we do.

Table 2   The oldest archeological occurrences of some of Mesoamerica's important plants[a]

Name of plant	Oldest archeological occurrences	Comments	Subsequent archeological occurrences
Setaria (foxtail grass)	0.5 oz. in level XXIII (7000 B.C.?) Coxcatlán Cave, Tehuacán	Smith believed *Setaria* domestic at Tehuacán by ca. 6000 B.C.; Callen saw size increase by 3500 B.C. in Tamaulipas	About 45 oz. from later levels (7000-5000 B.C.) in Tehuacán caves
Zea mexicana (teosinte)	Pollen grains in levels B-C (7400-6700 B.C.) Guilá Naquitz Cave, Oaxaca	It is still disputed whether teosinte pollen can be distinguished from that of maize	Seeds from 5000 B. C. level at Tlapacoya, Valley of Mexico
Zea mays (corn)	18 cobs in Level XIII (5050 B.C.), Coxcatlán Cave, Tehuacán, Mexico	Good sample. Mangelsdorf says "wild"; Beadle says "domestic." (see text)	74 more cobs, later levels (5000-3000 B.C.) in Tehuacán caves
Cucurbita pepo (pumpkin)	1 "pepo-like" seed in level D ($\pm$8000 B.C.) in Guila Naquitz Cave, Oaxaca, Mexico; bigger sample at 7000 B.C. in Ocampo, Tamps.	All specimens are seeds (and should be treated with caution) prior to the first peduncle frags. Even so, most specimens look "wild" prior to 5000 B.C.	14 seeds and peduncles in levels B-C (7400-6700 B.C.), Guilá Naquitz; 1 "wild" specimen from level XIV (5200 B.C.?) Coxcatlán Cave
Cucurbita mixta (squash)	3 specimens (2 dubious) in levels XIV-XIII (5000 B.C.), Coxcatlán Cave	All specimens prior to 3000 B.C. should be treated with caution	5 specimens including peduncle from level VIII (3010 B.C.) Coxcatlán Cave
Cucurbita moschata (squash)	1 dubious specimen, level XII (4500 B.C.?) Coxcatlán Cave	All specimens prior to 4000 B.C. should be treated with caution	4 less-dubious specimens from levels XI (4121 B.C.) and IX-VIII (3000 B.C.) at Coxcatlán Cave
Wild runner beans	100+ in 8700-6700 B.C. levels, Guilá Naquitz; 14 between 7000 and 5500 in Ocampo, Tamps.	These wild varieties were gradually replaced by cultivars through time	

Phaseolus coccineus (domestic runner Bean)	?	When domesticated not sure; Kaplan believes Ocampo beans are wild runners.	1 from roughly 200 B.C. at Coxcatlán Cave, Tehuacán
Phaseolus vulgaris (common bean)	6 pod valves dating to between 4000 and 2300 B.C., Ocampo, Tamaulipas	Small sample but very similar dates from Tehuacán and Tamulipas. A convincing sample.	Single pods from levels XI (4000 B.C.?) and VIII (3010 B.C.), Coxcatlán Cave
Phaseolus acutifolius (tepary bean)	118 seeds from level VIII (3010 B.C.) Coxcatlán Cave		
Persea americana (avocado)	1 seed in level XXIV (7200 B.C.?) Coxcatlán Cave, Tehuacán, is wild type	Larger seeds show avocado to be domestic by 1500 B.C., but when first cultivated is not known.	31 seeds in later levels (7000-5000 B.C.) in Tehuacán Caves are also wild type
Capsicum annuum (chile)	1 pod from level XIX (6500 B.C.?), Coxcatlán Cave, probably wild	Smith feels chiles domestic by level XI (4121 B.C.) at Coxcatlán Cave on basis of pendulous fruit	7 more specimens from later levels (6000-5000 B.C.) at Coxcatlán Cave, probably wild
Amaranthus (amaranth)	1 oz. from level XII (4500 B.C.?), Coxcatlán Cave (& minute traces in earlier levels)	There is no firm data on just when amaranth was domesticated; only seed color distinguishes wild and domestic	1 oz. from level X (3075 B.C.) Coxcatlán Cave
Gossypium hirsutum (cotton)	2 bolls from level XVI (5625 B.C.), Coxcatlán Cave, Tehuacán	Both found in an area of disturbed stratigraphy; Stephens is skeptical	2 bolls from level D (3300 B.C.) San Marcos Cave, Tehuacán; earliest cotton yarn is a "questionable" frag. from level IX (3183 B.C.) at Coxcatlán Cave
Lagenaria (bottle gourd)	Rind fragments in levels B-C (ca. 7000 B.C.) Guilá Naquitz, Oaxaca and 7000 B.C. levels at Ocampo Tamaulipas	The rinds are less secure evidence than seeds.	1 rind in level XIII (5050 B.C.) Coxcatlán Cave

[a]Note comments on the nature and reliability of the evidence. After MacNeish (47), Smith (65), Kaplan (35), Cutler & Whitaker (12), Stephens (71), Smith & Kerr (68).

The Botanical Problems

One of the major problems in telling the story of agricultural beginnings in Mesoamerica is the fact that not even the botanists involved can agree on the origin of maize, Mesoamerica's most important economic plant. There are two conflicting views. The most recent theory—and that perhaps best known to archeologists—is that of Paul Mangelsdorf (50). Mangelsdorf believes that cultivated maize descended from a now extinct wild pod-popcorn in which individual kernels were enclosed in and protected by chaff rather than by a cupulate fruit case. An older theory, which has been vigorously revived in recent years by botanists such as George Beadle, Jack R. Harlan, and Walton Galinat, holds that maize *(Zea mays)* may be descended from the widespread Mexican grass teosinte *(Zea mexicana)*, its nearest relative. Most archeologists are now familiar with Mangelsdorf's views, since he has been involved in the truly heroic task of analyzing virtually every important collection of early archeological maize from Mexico or Guatemala (cf. Mangelsdorf, MacNeish & Galinat 52). Beadle's recent work, however, is known only from a 9-page paper in a popular museum bulletin (Beadle 4) and from "word of mouth" among the archeologists who are in correspondence with him. In view of this, I will try to sketch in the outlines of the argument from an anthropologist's point of view. In the course of this, I will refer to three recent articles which should be read by all anthropologists interested in the origins of maize.

The first of these articles is Garrison Wilkes' review of the wild relatives of maize (Wilkes 79), which has greatly helped me in drawing the following "thumbnail sketches" of teosinte and *Tripsacum*.

1. Teosinte *(Zea mexicana)* is the nearest relative to cultivated maize, having an identical chromosome number. Indeed, as Wilkes puts it, "to the casual observer, maize and teosinte are so similar in appearance, with nearly identical staminate flowers borne in tassels and pistillate flowers enclosed in a system of husks in a lateral position on the stem, that the most reliable characteristic separating the two is the pistillate fruit—a distichous spike in teosinte and a polystichous structure (the familiar ear) in maize." Teosinte is a native annual grass of the semiarid, subtropical zones of Mexico and Guatemala, from southern Chihuahua to near the Guatemalan-Honduran border. It is a "short-day" plant which likes no more than 12 hours of sunlight a day, combined with warm temperatures. The teosinte fruit has 7 to 12 seeds, enclosed in very hard cupulate fruit cases and set in sequence on a brittle rachis. Like the wild wheat in the Near East, it shatters naturally and is hence very difficult to harvest efficiently. Nevertheless, it is used by some Mexican Indians as a "starvation food." Parenthetically, I might add that its brittle rachis and short period of peak maturation make it most efficient to harvest by large work gangs or "macrobands" (MacNeish 47); small "microbands" or individual families would take too long to get the whole crop before it shattered.

It is this plant which Beadle suggests was the wild ancestor of cultivated maize. His evidence will be discussed in a later section. But before proceeding to Wilkes' description of *Tripsacum,* let me add the following observations which Richard Ford and I (17) were able to make in 1971 when we accompanied Beadle and Wilkes on their "wild teosinte harvest" in Guerrero, Mexico.

Teosinte is a weedy, pioneer plant which colonizes natural scars in the landscape; in Guerrero the landscape was a semiarid thorn forest with *Lucaena, Acacia,* and *Setaria.* When corn fields are abandoned today, they are rapidly invaded by teosinte; at one point we drove for 20 kilometers without losing sight of massive teosinte stands, up to 2 meters high. If a group of hunter-gatherers cleared a campsite in such a thorn forest, the following year they would return to find their former campsite a teosinte field. Moreover, to our surprise, wild runner beans (*Phaseolus* sp.) and wild squash (*Cucurbita* sp.) occur naturally in such fields, with the beans twining around the teosinte (Figure 2). The *Zea*-bean-squash triumvirate is thus not an invention of the Indians; nature provided the model.

Due to the long "dormant" period needed by teosinte seeds, dense stands would occur only about every 2 years. This would continue until regrowth of the thorn

Figure 2 Wild runner beans twine around a stalk of wild teosinte in second-growth vegetation near Chilpancingo, Guerrero, 1971.

forest eventually shaded out the teosinte. When this happens, relict populations survive on scree or landslide areas, and on patches cleared by accidental fire.

2. *Tripsacum*—a genus composed of nine diverse perennial grass species scattered from Texas to South America—is a more distant relative of maize, the two having different chromosome numbers. Although crosses between maize and *Tripsacum* can be accomplished in the laboratory, according to Wilkes "all evidence indicates that the recent evolution within the genus *Tripsacum* has been independent and distinct from that of maize." And although *Tripsacum* may share the same semiarid mountain habitat with teosinte, the two do not hybridize in the wild and have not yet been successfully hybridized in the laboratory. Nor is there any evidence that the Indians of Mesoamerica ate *Tripsacum* or, in fact, used it in any way (except possibly as grass for thatching). This evidence suggests that *Tripsacum* has not played as important a role in ancient Mesoamerica as was once thought, and that the frequently used term "tripsacoid maize" (Mangelsdorf, MacNeish & Galinat 52) is probably a misnomer.

Perhaps equally important, it now appears that *Tripsacum* has played no role in the origins of teosinte either. It was once believed that teosinte was a derivative of a maize-*Tripsacum* hybrid, rather than a true wild grass (Mangelsdorf 50). In a 1972 conference at Harvard, Paul Mangelsdorf withdrew his support from this theory of some 30-years' standing (64). It now seems clear that teosinte is a true wild grass, independent from *Tripsacum* and far more closely related to maize.

Teosinte and *Tripsacum* are wild species which can still be studied by botanists today. We must now, however, consider the possibility of a third "wild species" which has never been seen growing or collected by a botanist.

3. Wild maize—a presumably annual grass once native to Mexico—was the hypothetical ancestor of domestic maize originally proposed by Mangelsdorf (50). This wild maize was supposed to have had small (female) cobs from the top of which a small (male) tassel grew. It was supposed to have been a "pod" corn (in which individual kernels were enclosed in and protected by chaff rather than by a cupulate fruit case) and a "pop" corn—one which would explode when heated. After giving rise to domestic corn, it was thought to have become extinct, either by overgrazing from introduced European animals or by "swamping" from domestic corn pollen.

Mangelsdorf's theory was seemingly confirmed by the discovery of tiny corn cobs in a Tehuacán cave, dated to 5050 B.C., in which the tassel did grow out of the top of the cob (Mangelsdorf, MacNeish & Galinat 52). These and later cobs had a number of teosinte-like characters, but these Mangelsdorf explained as the result of (a) hybridization with *Tripsacum* to produce teosinte, and (b) subsequent backcrossing with the latter to produce "teosinte introgression."

The Mangelsdorf hypothesis was also seemingly confirmed by the discovery of 60,000-year-old *Zea* pollen in a lake core from the Valley of Mexico (Barghoorn, Wolf & Clisby 2). This pollen was assigned to maize because of its large size relative to teosinte pollen.

Although Mangelsdorf's hypothetical wild ancestor was widely accepted by archeologists, many botanists never believed in it. The skeptics included George

Beadle, Jack R. Harlan, and many others. In particular, Beadle was skeptical because his own cytological and genetic work suggested that corn and teosinte were in fact the same species. Over the last 3 years, Beadle's renewed laboratory research and field work on teosinte have led him to the following conclusions, which appear in the second of my three recommended articles (Beadle 4):

1. The number of significant independently inherited gene differences between maize and teosinte is "not great—perhaps 6 to 10." This is based on the rate of recovery of pure "parental" types among 30,000 second generation hybrids of corn and teosinte growing at the International Center for Maize and Wheat Improvement near Mexico City.

2. Teosinte—which can be eaten after grinding in a mortar or "popping" like popcorn—can be made a more easily usable food plant by just two mutations: "one to a non-shattering rachis, so the fruits will not be scattered and lost as food; the other to a soft fruitcase, so the kernels can be threshed free of them." It is not known how many genes control the toughening of the rachis, but a single gene—the so-called "tunicate allele"—can produce soft glumes and a lessened tendency to shatter. (Note the striking similarity between this model and the one Helbaek has presented for wheat in the Near East.)

3. The tiny, inch-long corn cobs from the Tehuacán caves, which have been interpreted as "wild maize", can as easily be interpreted as representing "stages in the transition of teosinte to corn through human selection." Cobs closely matching them are readily recovered in second (and later) generations of corn-teosinte hybrids. They are said to have "fragile" cobs—possibly a persistence of the brittle rachis of teosinte. Some of them are two-ranked (distichous), i.e. having two rows of kernels—another teosinte trait. Finally, the early cobs have long, soft glumes suggestive of a tunicate allele. For Beadle it is not necessary to propose "teosinte introgression" for these early corn specimens—merely "teosinte ancestry."

4. Mangelsdorf's postulated wild maize could not have survived in the wild because it had no seed dispersal mechanism; the cob is a "man-made monstrosity" which no other grass has, and this is one of the reasons domestic corn cannot survive without human intervention. Yet we are asked to believe that it survived until the Spanish Conquest and then became extinct within 400 years.

5. It should be pointed out that Mangelsdorf's theory has not remained static in the face of criticism. Whereas he formerly regarded teosinte as too different from maize to have been its ancestor, he now proposes that teosinte arose through mutation from wild corn (Mangelsdorf 51). To this Beadle replies "if corn could have given rise to teosinte, the reverse must also be possible—and I would say much more probable, for teosinte is a highly successful wild plant and corn is not."[5]

The third article which should be read by all archeologists interested in the origins of maize is Walton Galinat's recent synthesis in the *Annual Review of Genetics* (20). Galinat, a long-time associate of Mangelsdorf's and perhaps the leading authority on maize anatomy, makes the following points, which I have placed in quotes to distinguish them from my own comments:

[5]Readers interested in this controversy should also read Mangelsdorf's reply to Beadle (51).

1. "Teosinte and maize hybridize almost freely, and their hybrids are fully fertile on both selfing and backcrossing in either direction." Teosinte and maize have the same chromosome number ($n = 10$); as shown by R. A. Emerson and George Beadle as early as 1932, their chromosomes are of equal length and similar in arm ratios; their chromosomes pair closely at pachytene; they have essentially the same frequencies of crossing over; where known, the position of various genes on the chromosomes is similar.

2. Anatomical studies (by Galinat himself, 19) show a "clear-cut connecting link between the maize cob and the cupulate fruit case of teosinte." In other words, the cupule which holds the kernel in both archeological and modern maize cobs has almost certainly evolved from the cupulate fruit case of teosinte. This would strongly support the Beadle view, since Mangelsdorf's postulated wild maize did not have a fruit case.

3. It is simply not true that all maize has pollen which is larger than (and hence distinguishable from) teosinte pollen. This is true for only four out of ten teosinte varieties; other studies "not only show that the size of pollen in most races of teosinte overlaps that of the Chapalote maize but that one teosinte, Jutiapa, has significantly larger pollen than this race of primitive maize." Galinat refers to Chapalote (an "ancient indigenous race" of Mexican maize) because of its great genetic similarity to the earliest maize from Tehuacán, and he further refers to a demonstrated "correlation between pollen diameters and ear or style length in the races of maize in Mexico." Thus there is an inconsistency between the large size of the 60,000-year old "fossil wild maize pollen" found in the Valley of Mexico (Barghoorn, Wolfe & Clisby 2) and the smaller size of primitive maize pollen. Galinat points out that the various preparation techniques used for pollen analysis—glycerin, lactic acid, acetolyis, and so on—may have a great effect on grain size, making the results of two palynological studies noncomparable. More to the point, when a scanning electron microscope is turned on the surface of maize and teosinte pollen, no significant difference can be detected—so far, at least (Galinat 21). This strongly suggests they are the same species.

4. The idea that "wild maize" became extinct because of competition from domestic maize or overgrazing by animals introduced by the Spanish is shaky; it assumes that "the original wild maize was unable to adapt to forces that teosinte has so successfully resisted." Not only does teosinte survive in spite of heavy maize competion, but "livestock, far from completely destroying teosinte, tend to spread it through their fecal droppings" (cf. Wilkes 78).

5. "The results of recent studies of electrophoretic patterns of storage proteins are consistent with the hypothesis that maize is domesticated teosinte." This comment, based on work by J. G. Waines (Galinat 20, p. 475), is strengthened by recent work by Robson & Konlande (62) and Cowan (11), which show that maize and teosinte have similar nutritional makeup and amino acid balances.

6. "The oldest known archeological maize cobs from Tehuacán, Mexico, about 7000 years in age, which have been assumed to be those of wild maize, can also be interpreted as in the early stages of transformation of teosinte to maize. All of these

primitive cobs have cupules that could have evolved directly from the fruit case of teosinte and some of them are two-ranked and have cupulate interspaces as in the pistillate spike of teosinte."

This final comment, from a botanical anatomist who has handled every one of the most ancient maize specimens from Mexico, is perhaps the best statement of where we stand at the moment. If it ultimately turns out that maize is a domesticated, highly evolved descendant of teosinte, the history of maize becomes a good deal simpler (involving less hybridization to account for its teosinte-like characteristics), and it will no longer be necessary to postulate the complete extinction of its ancestor. But our troubles will still be far from over, since it remains to be shown what precise genetic changes led to recognizable prehistoric maize.

Whether, as now seems reasonable, teosinte is the ancestor of maize (or even if "wild maize" actually existed), it now appears that *Zea* was originally domesticated prior to 5000 B.C. By the fifth millenium B.C., human selection of rare or mutant genes had progressed so far that the occupants of the Tehuacán Valley had plants with distichous or polystichous cobs with soft glumes and a partially toughened rachis. Further selection and hybridization over the next 3000 years produced corn cobs which share many genetic characters with two surviving "primitive races" of maize, Chapalote and Nal-Tel. However, rather than assigning certain second-millenium corn cobs to either of those races, I would suggest that we simply say that modern Chapalote and Nal-Tel retain many characters of Formative corn—a corn that must have been very unstandardized and genetically diverse, with a whole spectrum of phenotypes from teosinte-like to Chapalote-like.

Where was *Zea* originally domesticated? Teosinte's former wild range includes much of the short-day, semiarid, semitropical uplands between Chihuahua and Guatemala. If we suggest that it may first have been domesticated on the margins of its best range—as we have for wheat in the Near East—the area is further increased. But were its "margins" the very arid highland regions (like Tehuacán) where teosinte does not grow today, or the edges of the humid lowlands where it gives way to tropical vegetation?

Some botanists feel that the large-seeded Chalco race of teosinte, a native of the Valley of Mexico, is the most closely related to maize, and that the Guerrero and southern Guatemalan races are least maize-like (Wilkes 79), while others attribute the Chalco race's resemblance to maize to hybridization with the latter. Seeds of Chalco-type teosinte have been found at the archeological site of Tlapacoya in the Valley of Mexico in levels dating to 5000 B.C. (Lorenzo & Gonzales 44); but by this time period there are already specimens of true maize from Tehuacán to the south. Small pollen grains believed to be those of teosinte occur in Guilá Naquitz Cave, Oaxaca, in levels dated to nearly 7000 B.C. (Schoenwetter 63); but there is no evidence of domestication at this time in the form of actual mutant plant material. Indeed, actual teosinte material from dry caves in Mesoamerica is hard to come by.

Equally serious is the possibility that surviving races of teosinte may not give a clue to the origins of maize because (like the Near Eastern cereals described by Harlan) they have become "weed" races. According to Wilkes (79), at 10,000 B.C.

wild teosinte may have been a more suitable ancestor than the sophisticated, surviving "weed" teosintes, which have had to specialize to survive, and which have become "maize-mimics" as they invaded the cornfields; the Chalco race is particularly maize-mimetic. And Galinat (20) points out that domestic maize and today's teosinte, having exchanged genes over thousands of years, have evolved together and are perhaps more similar than they would otherwise be. Contributing to this is the fact that, on the basis of archeological plant samples (Smith 66), prehistoric farmers apparently encouraged teosinte to hybridize with maize in their fields. In addition to a shot of hybrid vigor, this gave corn drought and frost resistance (Jones 33).

In sum, we have little data with which to pinpoint the origins of *Zea* cultivation, except the very early date of the corncobs from Tehuacán—an area where teosinte has never been collected in the wild. We know even less about *why* domestication began, as the tentative model below will show.

A Model for Early Maize Cultivation: Stage I

Suppose that teosinte (or even an equally unappetizing hypothetical wild maize) was the ancestral *Zea*. Why would such a plant have been domesticated in the first place?

I am reluctant to propose for Mesoamerica a "density equilibrium" model for early corn domestication, such as the Binford hypothesis I applied to the Near East. The fact is that, prior to 5000 B.C., human population densities in those parts of Mesoamerica which we have surveyed are very low. There is no area in which we can document a population expanding so fast that it might have affected the density equilibrium of adjacent regions; however, MacNeish (48) feels that some areas of northern Mexico (Nuevo León-Tamaulipas) did have preceramic populations greater than those of Puebla or Oaxaca. There is one other possibility which is raised by Richard Ford's work in the arid Southwest (Ford 18). Like the Southwest, highland Mesoamerica has great contrasts in wild productivity between wet and dry years. Cultivation might have arisen as an attempt to "even out" the difference between these extremes by increasing the range of weedy, pioneer annuals, but we just don't know for sure. Whatever the cause, the origins of *Zea* cultivation amount to a deliberate increase in the availability of an "emergency ration"—one of the few that could be increased on a yearly basis.

One of the important small biotopes of the semiarid valleys of the central and southern Mexican highlands is the tributary barranca. In these slightly more humid canyons, cut by streams which vary from seasonal to permanent, grow varieties of herbs and grasses which may be absent or less common out on the main valley floor. Two of the grasses which grow in such habitats are foxtail grass (*Setaria* sp.) and teosinte; both were harvested and eaten by prehistoric Indians. *Setaria,* which reaches maturity in the early autumn, was ground and threshed in mortars. Eric Callen (7), who analyzed the human coprolites from MacNeish's dry caves in Tehuacán and Tamaulipas, believed he could detect a selection for larger grain size in some regions, and perhaps even the first attempts at *Setaria* cultivation. Teosinte, which matures later in the fall, can be ground up to produce coarse but rather pleasant-tasting unleavened cakes when cooked on a hot, flat rock.

There is a good deal of roughage in teosinte—up to 53 percent—and it may be harder to prepare than *Setaria*. But Beadle has experimented on himself and his colleagues sufficiently to show that daily consumption of 150 grams of teosinte flour has no ill effect (Beadle 4).

Empirical archeological data suggest that such things as *Setaria* and teosinte were really a very minor part of a diet that emphasized prickly pear, roasted *Agave*, mesquite, acorns and pinyon nuts, hackberry, wild avocado, deer, cottontail, mud turtle, and dove (Flannery 14). In a wet year, however, food collectors could count on a good *Setaria* harvest in the tributary barrancas, and the coprolite data indicates that they did. In a dry year, on the other hand, the *Setaria* harvest could only be raised to its usual level by augmentation with teosinte, which matured slightly later in the same habitat. But no matter how much you select and plant *Setaria,* it stays the same unappetizing weed. Whereas, if Beadle is correct, teosinte responded to cultivation and selection with a series of favorable genetic changes which moved it in the direction of maize. And this may have tipped the balance in favor of increased attention to the genus *Zea* on the part of man.

A Model for Early Maize Cultivation: Stage II

In attempting to figure out why man would increase *Zea* cultivation, there are a number of variables which need to be quantified. These include (*a*) the productivity of wild teosinte; (*b*) the productivity of cultivated teosinte; (*c*) the productivity of early maize; (*d*) the productivity of the competing vegetation which would have to be removed in cultivation; and (*e*) the relative man-hours of work involved in clearing, cultivating, and so on. Various members of the University of Michigan's Human Ecology project in Oaxaca, Mexico, have tried (in collaboration with George Beadle) to quantify these variables. Our preliminary results, which should not be taken as gospel, are as follows.

1. In 1971, Richard Ford and I measured the productivity of wild teosinte sample plots during Beadle's "teosinte harvest" in Guerrero and Valle de Bravo, Mexico (Flannery & Ford 17). Our least productive plot—on a scree slope probably approximating natural wild conditions—yielded an estimated 305 kg per hectare. Since 50% of the seed is inedible roughage, this corrects to 152.5 kg per hectare or less than a wild mesquite grove produces (see below). Our most productive plot—on an abandoned (fallow) corn field probably approximating the best cultivated conditions—yielded an estimated 1254 kg per hectare, or a corrected yield (minus roughage) of 627 kg per hectare. This is comparable to the yields of wild Near Eastern cereals, but could probably only be achieved under exceptional circumstances.

2. Robert D. Drennan (13) supervised the cultivation of a field of Chalco teosinte in the Valley of Oaxaca in 1972 (Figure 3). The yield was 161 kg per hectare; corrected for roughage, the yield would be only 80 kg per hectare—roughly that estimated by Kirkby for the maize of 5000 B.C. (see below). Two factors, however, lead Drennan to believe that this is a substandard yield. First, 1972 was a drought year in which many maize crops in the area failed altogether. Second, in lieu of any model for prehistoric teosinte cultivation, plants were spaced as far apart as is typical for maize; in retrospect, the experimental field could have been planted twice

Figure 3   R. D. Drennan and Guadalupe Luna H. from Fábrica San José, San Agustín Etla, Oaxaca, standing in experimental cultivated teosinte field, 1972.

as densely. To this we might add the fact that Chalco teosinte, adapted to 2300 m elevation, might not do as well at 1500 m. Nevertheless, the experiment gives us some idea of the perils of teosinte cultivation in a dry year.

3. The native vegetation of river floodplains in the Mexican highlands—most frequently groves of mesquite (*Prosopis juliflora*)—would have to be cleared to allow cultivation. Near Mitla, Oaxaca, we measured the productivity of edible mesquite pods from such groves; the highest yield was 184 kg per hectare, with yields of 160-180 kg per hectare common. Thus, disregarding for the moment any nutritional differences between *Prosopis* and *Zea,* it would hardly seem worth clearing the native mesquite from the floodplains unless a yield higher than 180 kg per hectare could be expected.

4. Recent field studies in Oaxaca by Anne Kirkby (38) show that Zapotec Indian farmers do not consider cultivation and land clearance to be worthwhile unless a yield of at least 200 to 250 kg (shelled maize) per hectare can be expected.

5. Kirkby also discovered a linear regression relationship between mean corn cob length and yield in kg per hectare for Indian fields in the Valley of Oaxaca (Kirkby 38). Based on this relationship, and using figures on the mean length of corn cobs recovered by MacNeish's Tehuacán excavations (and ours in Oaxaca), she then calculated an "estimated yield" for various periods of prehistory.

These estimates are based on the assumption of a cob-to-plant ratio like today's, whereas Beadle suspects early maize may have had more cobs per plant (like teosinte); nevertheless, we offer them in lieu of any other estimates. The earliest cobs from Tehuacán suggest a yield of only 60-80 kg per hectare; later preceramic cobs (ca. 3000 B.C.) suggest yields of 90-120 kg per hectare. According to Kirkby's figures, maize did not cross the critical threshhold of 200-250 kg until sometime between 2000 and 1500 B.C. This is remarkably close to the actual period at which permanent villages on (or overlooking) good alluvial agricultural land became the dominant type of settlement in Mesoamerica. Yields of 500-800 kg per hectare (as in *wild* Near Eastern cereals) may not have become common until centuries after village life had been established in Mexico!

6. We do not yet have reliable data on the man-hours required to harvest a hectare of wild teosinte, cultivate a hectare of domestic teosinte, or clear a hectare of mesquite groves. We have only Drennan's figures from his Oaxaca teosinte farming (13), which indicate that the harvesting and threshing amount to about 50 percent of the labor input. Cultivation may therefore require twice the labor of collecting the plant in the wild. On the basis of his Guerrero harvest (see above), Beadle suggests that a man could harvest perhaps one liter of teosinte per hour by beating out the seeds on a blanket.

Our tentative quantification of some of these variables allows us to complete the second stage of our model. Let us assume that teosinte had been domesticated somewhere in the humid barranca-piedmont habitat it shares with *Setaria*. Only in the best of conditions, as a second-growth pioneer on well-watered alluvial fans, would it approach the productivity of the wild Near Eastern cereals, and teosinte is even harder to harvest and process, being half roughage. In many areas it would not have been worthwhile to remove the mesquite cover of the main river floodplains to cultivate such a plant. A more reasonable strategy would have been to leave the mesquite on the main valley floor to produce its 180 kg per hectare each year, while growing teosinte in the piedmont barrancas where it was at home. (Our figures suggest that teosinte probably could have yielded an average of 150-200 kg per hectare, reaching 600 kg under exceptional conditions but falling to below 100 in drought years.) That such a strategy was used is suggested by the fact that for thousands of years after *Zea* had been domesticated, no valley-floor villages appeared in Mesoamerica, although MacNeish (47) suspects pit-house settlements in the tributary barrancas. The Indians divided their time among these various biotopes and probably did not regard any one zone as more "crucial" than the others.

But gradual genetic change leading to larger cob sizes eventually raised the minimum productivity of *Zea* to 200-250 kg per hectare or more. At some point prior to 1500 B.C.—the exact date may vary from one valley to another—it crossed the "threshhold" which the Indians felt made it worthwhile to clear the mesquite groves for cultivation. By 1300 B.C., permanent villages of wattle-and-daub houses on (or overlooking) the main river floodplains were widespread from Puebla to Guatemala. And when the Indians brought maize out of the barrancas, they also brought its two pioneer companions—beans and cucurbits—with whom it had coexisted for thousands of years. If you add to this the cultivated avocado (*Persea americana*), also originally native to the piedmont barrancas, you have the four most common cultivated genera found throughout Mesoamerica at 1300 B.C. With maize providing the carbohydrate, beans and squash seeds the plant protein, and avocados the fats and oils, the early Mesoamerican villagers were on their way.

Other Mesoamerican Cultivars

There is no way to discuss all of Mesoamerica's early cultivars in an article of this length, but since beans and squash have already been mentioned, let us pursue them a bit farther. Some light has been shed on the early use of beans and cucurbits by analyses of plant remains from 8700–6700 B.C. levels at Guilá Naquitz, Oaxaca. During a study to be published later, the nonrandom association of various plant species with each other on cave living floors was demonstrated by means of an ordered matrix of Pearson's r values (Whallon 75). The results suggest that wild runner beans were collected with plants from the oak woodland zone, such as acorns and pinyon nuts, while wild cucurbits were collected in a somewhat lower thorn forest zone, along with cactus fruits and *Agave*. This is a helpful clue to some of the floral zones preferred by these wild plants within the piedmont-barranca area.

Three species of *Phaseolus*—common beans (*P. vulgaris*), runner beans (*P. coccineus*), and tepary beans (*P. acutifolius*)—have wild ancestors in Mexico. The oldest beans archeologically documented are wild runner beans from caves in Ocampo, Tamaulipas (7000–5500 B.C.) and the already mentioned specimens from Oaxaca (8700–6700 B.C.); those from Oaxaca belong to a species which was never domesticated, while the Ocampo runner beans are wild *P. coccineus*. Domestic tepary beans and common beans both make archeological appearances between 4000 and 3000 B.C. According to Kaplan (34), three of the critical changes accompanying the domestication of the common bean were (*a*) an increase in seed permeability, so the beans did not need to be soaked in water as long; (*b*) a change from corkscrew-twisted pods (which shatter when ripe) to limp, straight, nonshattering pods; and (*c*) in some cases, a shift from perennial to annual growth patterns. Because beans are intimately associated with maize, both in the wild (see above) and in the diet of ancient Mesoamerica, it is also worth noting that they are rich in the amino acid lysine. Since maize is deficient in lysine, the combination of corn and beans makes for a better plant protein (Kaplan 34).

Domestic beans are among the plants which are represented by very few actual specimens prior to 3000 B.C.; for example, six pod valves are scattered through levels in Tamaulipas spanning the period 4000–2300 B.C., and the oldest Tehuacán specimen (4000 B.C. ?) is a single pod. The situation is roughly similar with the genus *Cucurbita* (squashes and pumpkins), and is complicated still further by the fact that in most cases the wild cucurbit ancestors are not known for certain.

Botanists H. C. Cutler & T. W. Whitaker (12) regard certain changes in the peduncle or stem following domestication as crucial for identification, but many of the earliest cucurbit specimens are seeds, and isolated seeds at that. Little is known (or at least, published) about the range of variation in seed size and shape in any of the potential wild ancestors; based on specimens in the Ethnobotanical Laboratory at the University of Michigan, I am struck by the considerable size-and-shape range in seeds from a single wild cucurbit. To me this would suggest that one might really need a whole "population" of seeds (say, 100 specimens) before he could prove that an ancient sample was outside the wild range. To describe an isolated seed as "probably wild," "probably domestic," or "pumpkin-like, but too small to be a domestic" may simply be another way of saying that wild cucurbits (and probably early cultivated cucurbits as well) had a great deal of seed variability and did not yet belong to any of the standardized domestic races we know today.

Wild cucurbits, for the most part, have flesh which is either so bitter or so thin and dry (like a gourd) that it cannot be eaten; it was the seeds that were originally important, while the edible flesh is a product of domestication. Cucurbit seeds occur as far back as 8000–7000 B.C. in caves in Oaxaca and Tamaulipas (Table 2); these earliest specimens are probably all wild forms, or "weedy camp followers" (see below). Morphologically, some resemble seeds of the pumpkin (*C. pepo*), but Cutler & Whitaker (12) specifically state that the specimens from Tamaulipas, as well as a later seed from Tehuacán (5200 B.C.), are "wild." Since no one has ever seen a "wild pumpkin"—its ancestor is, in fact, not yet decided upon (Whitaker 76)—it is hard to know just what to call these seeds. I am not a botanist, but I would suggest: "seeds of an unidentified cucurbit, presumably wild, resembling *C. pepo* but constituting an inadequate sample for species identification."

When peduncles are present, one could presumably assign a species name with more confidence; but peduncles do not appear until much later in the archeological sequence. For example, three seeds (two of them marked as dubious) of *Cucurbita mixta* squash appear as early as 5000 B.C. at Coxcatlán Cave, but *mixta* peduncles do not occur until 3000 B.C. For which of these dates should the first domestication be claimed?

As Cutler & Whitaker point out (12, 77), cucurbits tend to be "weedy camp followers" which do well on disturbed soils, like the talus slope of an occupied cave. Their wild forms resemble the bottle gourd, one of the plants with the longest documented history of human use. It may be that they were originally domesticated by foragers who already knew and cultivated the bottle gourd and who therefore instantly recognized the cucurbits as potentially useful. At any rate, they are one of the oldest Mesoamerican plants whose use can be documented, from Oaxaca to Tamaulipas.

THE ORIGINS OF AGRICULTURE IN THE ANDES

Three very different major biomes contributed to the richness and complexity of Andean agriculture. The first of these was the Amazon jungle and the tropical eastern slopes of the Andes. This zone contains many of the wild ancestors of the Peruvian domesticates—manioc, peanuts, guavas, coca, and lima beans—but little is known of their history because of the poor archeological preservation in this humid area. The second zone is the mountains themselves, which contributed the wild ancestors of potato, quinoa (*Chenopodium quinoa*), oca (*Oxalis tuberosa*), olluco (*Ullucus tuberosus*), and other crops. Little is known of the history of these cultivars either, since dry caves are scarce in the Andes and preceramic archeology there is still in its early stages. Finally, there is the coastal desert to the west of the Peruvian Andes. The remarkable archeological preservation in this zone, caused by the dessicating effects of the cold Humboldt current, makes it the richest in ancient plant remains of any Andean region. Unfortunately, very few wild ancestors of any consequence are native to this desert, and most of the early cultivars which show up there were probably introduced from the mountains, the Amazonian forest, or Mesoamerica.

Once again, Richard S. MacNeish has been a major contributor to our knowledge of early domestication—this time through his 1969–1972 project at Ayacucho in the south-central highlands (MacNeish, Nelken-Turner & Garcia 49). The caves of Ayacucho, while not as dry as those of Tehuacán, appear to have settled at least one of the Andes' thorniest problems: whether maize was locally domesticated or introduced from Mesoamerica. Arguing for the latter alternative was the fact that neither teosinte (or any form of "wild maize") had ever been found in South America. Galinat & MacNeish (22) now report that *Zea* cobs from 3000–2500 B.C. levels at Rosamachay Cave, currently Peru's oldest maize specimens, belong to a teosinte-influenced race, most closely related to Mexico's Nal-Tel and presumably introduced from that region. It would thus seem to have taken maize about 2500 years to reach the Peruvian highlands after its initial appearance at Tehuacán; it seemingly did not reach the desert coast until sometime after 2000 B.C. (Table 3).

Another problem is the origin of the common bean *Phaseolus vulgaris*. According to Kaplan (36), it is not yet settled whether *P. vulgaris* has one center of origin or multiple centers, though he leans toward the latter. There is a wild *vulgaris* in Mexico, and the Andean wild form *P. aborigineus* is so similar to *vulgaris* that "you could conceivably lump them all as races of one species." Indeed, some varieties of *aborigineus* are less impermeable than wild *vulgaris,* and may possibly be escapes derived from cultivated *vulgaris*.

The available radiocarbon dates do little to resolve this problem. The oldest domestic *vulgaris* beans identified by Kaplan are from Thomas Lynch's excavations at Guitarrero Cave in the north highlands of Peru, dated to 5600 B.C. (Kaplan, Lynch & Smith 37); *vulgaris* first appears in the Ayacucho sequence about 2800 B.C. Its oldest occurrences in Mexico are about 4000 B.C. in Tamaulipas and Tehuacán (see Table 2). Thus it is presently impossible to argue for its introduction into Peru from Mesoamerica, and its diffusion in the opposite direction could be supported only by the most tenuous arguments.

Similar problems occur with cotton, chile peppers, and certain cucurbits which have radiocarbon dates that put them in Mexico some 1500 to 2000 years earlier than in Peru. Such dates may simply result from the vagaries of preservation, sampling, and intrusive rodent burrows, and they should not be relied on too heavily. Almost certainly, the archeological record pertains to different species: in the case of cotton, *hirsutum* in Mexico and *barbadense* in Peru; in the case of chiles, *annuum* in Mexico, *baccatum* and *frutescens* in Peru (59). Moreover, there are the problems of population size and range of variation which I mentioned earlier; if early domesticates were unstandardized and genetically diverse, isolated specimens which resemble one or another of today's "races" may contribute more to confusion than clarification.

My lack of first-hand familiarity with the Andes prevents me from proposing a processual model for the origins of agriculture there; I don't know why it began.

But let me present a tentative historical model which does nothing more than account for the fragmentary plants and radiocarbon dates we have.

The oldest reported archeological plant remains from the Andes are rind fragments of bottle gourd (*Lagenaria siceraria*) from 11,000 B.C. levels at MacNeish's Pikimachay Cave in Ayacucho (MacNeish et al 49). Botanist Barbara Pickersgill (59), whom I have already praised for her skepticism, feels that the wild bottle gourd was distributed pantropically before man came on the scene and that these few rind fragments do not necessarily prove either domestication or diffusion from another continent. Moreover, the fact that overlying levels of the same cave (falling in the 11,000–6,000 B.C. range) have no preservation of plant remains makes these early rind fragments puzzling. Is it remotely possible they came down a rodent burrow from the 6,000 B.C. levels, which *do* have good preservation? If not, we are faced with a surprising situation: a cave with preservation at 11,000 B.C., followed by 5000 years with no preservation.

Lynch's Guitarrero Cave shows us that by 5600 B.C. the occupants of the Peruvian highlands were cultivating common beans and lima beans. The latter had to have come from the eastern slopes of the Andes, where their wild ancestors live; and MacNeish's Jaywamachay Cave yielded a seed of achiote (*Bixa orellana*) which, if it proves not to have been intrusive, suggests that the Ayacucho highlanders were importing this red pigment from the eastern slopes by this time (MacNeish, Nelken-Turner & Garcia 49). I draw two conclusions from this: (*a*) agriculture began in Peru at too early a date to have been stimulated initially by diffusion from Mesoamerica, and (*b*) from the very beginning the Amazonian slopes must have played a significant role, in spite of our lack of direct data from that region.

By 3000–2500 B.C., domesticates from Mesoamerica were reaching Peru. Maize of Mexican ancestry reached the highlands, then spread to the desert coast; *moschata* squash may have been an introduction of the same period. During the millenium 2500–1500 B.C., numerous Amazonian or eastern slope products like guava (*Psidium guajava*), manioc (*Manihot esculentum*), peanuts (*Arachis hypogaea*), and lima beans became firmly established on the coastal desert (Lanning 39, Patterson 55). In turn, maize must have traveled to the Amazon basin, but we know little of the time period involved. And we know next to nothing of the early history of Peru's important high altitude crops, potato and quinoa, although they grow wild along the routes through which these exchanges between the Coast and the Amazon must have taken place.

What this all means in terms of process or developmental models is far from clear. One of the most fascinating aspects of the Peruvian coast has been the possibility that here, as in parts of the Near East, sedentary or semisedentary life may have been possible before agriculture. The enormous fishing and shell-fishing resources of the Humboldt current make it one of the most productive environments available to ancient man. Could this be another situation where village life began with a wild food base, populations rose, and agriculture began in response to disturbances of density equilibrium around the margins of an expanding coastal population?

Such a model cannot be supported by the archeological data. According to Patterson (55), the oldest site to be occupied year-round on the Peruvian coast dates to about 5000 B.C.; and this site was virtually unique because its "contemporaries

Table 3 The oldest archeological occurrences of some of Peru's important plants[a]

Name of plant	Oldest archeological occurrences	Comments	Subsequent archeological occurrences
Lagenaria (bottle gourd)	Rind frags (11,000 B.C.), Pikimachay Cave, Ayacucho, Peru	Probably not domestic (Pickersgill); could even be intrusive, as 11,000-6000 B.C. levels have no preserved plants	5500-4300 B.C., Ayacucho; 3000 B.C. (?) Chilca, Peruvian coast; used as floats, Huaca Prieta (2500 B.C.)
Phaseolus vulgaris (common bean)	5600 B.C. at Guitarrero Cave, C. de Huaylas, Peru	Not yet known whether locally domestic or introduced from Mexico (Kaplan)	4700 B.C., northern Chile; 2800 B.C., Ayacucho, Peru
Phaseolus lunatus (lima bean)	5600 B.C. at Guitarrero Cave, C. de Huaylas, Peru	Native to the Amazon side of the Andes	2500 B.C., Huaca Prieta, Peruvian Coast
Canavalia (jack bean)	Huaca Prieta (2500 B.C.) Peruvian Coast	An Andean domesticate, later introduced to Mexico	
Zea mays (corn)	Level D (3000-2500 B.C.) Rosamachay Cave, Ayacucho, Peru	A teosinte-derived, Nal-Tel-like race of Mexican origin	Huarmay, Peruvian Coast 1950 B.C.
Cucurbita moschata	Pampa site (>3000 B.C.?); Ayacucho (2800-1700 B.C.)	Possibly introduced from Mexico?	Huaca Prieta, 2500 B.C.
Cucurbita ficifolia	Huaca Prieta (2500 B.C.) Peruvian Coast	An earlier occurrence at the Pampa site (3000 B.C.?) is uncertain	1000-400 B.C., Ayacucho
Gossypium (cotton)	3000 B.C.? Chilca Site, Peruvian Coast	Exact level of earliest cotton is not yet clear	2500 B.C., Huaca Prieta, Peruvian Coast

Table 3 (continued)

Name of plant	Oldest archeological occurrences	Comments	Subsequent archeological occurrences
Capsicum (chile)	2500 B.C. on Peruvian Coast (Huaca Prieta, Punta Grande, Yacht Club)		
Chenopodium quinoa (quinoa)	2 seeds (5500–4300 B.C.), Pikimachay Cave, Ayacucho, Peru	Pickersgill recommends caution, as these are the only quinoa seeds from the whole sequence	
Lucuma (lucuma)	1 seed from level VII (3000 B.C.?), Pikimachay Cave, Ayacucho, Peru		2500 B.C., Huaca Prieta 1 seed from 1500–400 B.C. Ayacucho, Peru
Psidium guajava (guava)	2500 B.C., Huaca Prieta, Yacht Club, Peru Coast	Native to the Amazon side of the Andes	
Manihot (manioc)	1800–1500 B.C. on Peruvian Coast	Native to the Amazon side of the Andes	
Arachis hypogaea (peanut)	1800–1500 B.C. on Peruvian Coast	Native to the Amazon side of the Andes	
Solanum tuberosum (potato)	400 B.C., Chiripa, Bolivia?	Towle is not certain whether these tubers are potatoes or one of the other highland root crops	A.D. 1000, coastal Peru; as both unprocessed and freeze-dried (chuno) potatoes

[a]Note comments on the nature and reliability of the evidence. After MacNeish, Nelken-Turner & Garcia (49), Lanning (39), Patterson (55), Galinat (21), Pickersgill (58, 59), and Kaplan (36).

who lived 50 miles to the north . . . were unable to maintain year-round settlements because of the spacing of seasonal food resource areas in their territory." Even at 3500 B.C., most coastal populations are believed to have moved from summer camps near the sea to winter camps further inland.

The first striking increase in overall coastal population is said to have begun about 3000 B.C. (Patterson 55). Such a population increase is far too late to provide the initial stimulus for agriculture. Indeed, long before the founding of the oldest known year-round coastal community, the occupants of the highlands were growing beans from the eastern Andes. Even the introduction of cotton, squash, beans, and chile peppers to the coast did not initially break down the annual round from summer to winter encampments. In fact, Lanning (39, p. 53) cites one community—the Pampa site, dating to the fourth millenium B.C.—whose occupants "began as both fishermen and [squash] farmers, then gradually gave up their farming and adopted a diet consisting almost exclusively of sea food." Regardless of the priority of sedentary or semisedentary life on the Peruvian coast, I would have to conclude at this point that the forces leading to domestication must be sought in the highlands and the Amazonian slope of the Andes.

EARLY EXCHANGES OF CROPS BETWEEN THE VARIOUS CENTERS MENTIONED ABOVE

An important ethnobotanical question is, "How independent was early agriculture in Asia, Africa, and the Americas? Could one area have influenced the others by diffusion of early crops?"

All archeologists should read an article on this subject by Barbara Pickersgill & A. H. Bunting (60). After dismissing earlier arguments for pre-Columbian maize in Assam, peanuts in China, grain amaranths in the Himalayas, and so on, the authors critically examine the botanical evidence for the four plants—cotton, bottle gourd, coconut, and sweet potato—for which the strongest diffusionist case can be made. They conclude:

1. The bottle gourd in the New World is far too ancient to have been carried there from Africa or Asia by agricultural man. Bottle gourds are probably pantropical; they float and are resistant to sea water and probably reached South America long before man did.

2. The cultivated sweet potato (*Ipomoea batatas*) is a hexaploid which may have arisen by hybridization between a diploid and a tetraploid ancestor. Two species with both diploid and tetraploid forms, *I. tiliacea* and *I. gracilis,* occur *both* in Polynesia and the Americas. The hybridization leading to *I. batatas* may therefore have taken place independently in both areas.

3. Coconuts (*Cocos nucifera*) will survive 110 days floating in salt water, and could also have reached South America from Polynesia without human agents.

4. Cotton genetics is still a complicated business which has not been fully resolved. But on the basis of all available new genetic data, Hutchinson (31) feels that the "AA diploid" strains of cotton (which go into the makeup of "AADD tetraploid" *Gossypium* or New World cotton) spread from Africa to America well before

the start of agriculture and "perhaps before the continents drifted apart." Pickersgill and Bunting also cite Stephens' (71) correction of an earlier report which, like the "manioc" from Tamaulipas, has been largely overlooked by archeologists: the "earliest" cotton from Tehuacán (5800 B.C.) is from an area of disturbed stratigraphy and presumably intrusive.

My overall conclusion is that Old World-New World diffusion of cultivated plants in Pre-Columbian times was very limited, if it took place at all; and certainly it did not "cause" agriculture to begin in either area.

SUMMARY AND CONCLUSIONS

I said at the outset of this review that I did not believe one model could explain the origins of agriculture in all four regions discussed. Cultivation may have begun after village life was already established in some parts of the Near East and Peru. In Mesoamerica and Southeast Asia, cultivation probably began during a phase of nomadic hunting and gathering; and in Mesoamerica, at least, nomadism continued for thousands of years after farming began. What, if any, are the generalities which could be offered for the origins of agriculture all over the world? I will offer a few for one type of "paleotechnic" agriculture, Harris's "seed-crop cultivation."

Although hunters and gatherers know and classify hundreds of wild species in their environment, they do not necessarily use them all. For example, the Kalahari Bushmen (Lee 41, p. 35) can name some 223 species of animals, but they classify only 54 species as edible and hunt only 17 of these on a regular basis. Of the 85 plant species they recognize, 23 species provide them with 90 percent of their vegetable foods. In other words, they divide food resources into "first choice," "second choice," and "third choice" foods, turning to the latter only when they run out of the former. On the basis of archeological data, virtually all the important seed-crop cultivars were derived from species which were originally "third-choice" foods; they were, among other things, more work to harvest and prepare, often requiring grinding which Pleistocene hunters were ill equipped to do. Their wild ancestors were used little, if at all, by hunters at 20,000 B.C. in the Near East, at 8000 B.C. in Mexico or Peru, and so on.

But the ancestors of these seed crops had a number of characteristics which most of the "first-choice" foods of the Pleistocene hunter did not have. They are mostly annuals; they yield a high return (200-800 kg per hectare); they tolerate a wide range of disturbed habitats; they store easily; and they are genetically plastic. Thus they could be used to replace the "native" vegetation with a plant that in less than a year after planting would cover a disturbed patch with a dense growth of storable food. And as time went on, they responded with favorable genetic changes which made them either more productive, easier to harvest, easier to prepare, or all three. If what you want is a plant which will increase the carrying capacity of each hectare, and which can be stored to last out the year, they are your obvious choices. The disadvantages are that (a) farming may be more work than hunting, judging by the available ethnographic data, and (b) an unstable man-modified ecosystem with a low diversity index results. Since early farming represents a decision to work harder and to eat more "third-choice" food, I suspect that people did it because they felt they *had* to, not because they *wanted* to. Why they felt they had to we may never know, in spite of the fact that their decision reshaped all the rest of human history.

Let me close with Edgar Anderson's admonition: the agricultural revolution was a process, not an event. To search for "the first domestic plant" is to search for an event; it is poor strategy, it encourages bitter rivalry rather than cooperation, and it is probably fruitless. We should search instead for the processes by which agriculture began. To do that we need settlement pattern data; well-excavated living floors with the plants left *in situ;* and samples of 100 specimens with a mean, standard deviation, and range of variation. We need to maintain our enthusiasm, but to temper it with skepticism, not only for our own efforts but for those of the scientists in other disciplines with whom we collaborate.

Literature Cited

1. Anderson, E. 1956. Man as a maker of new plants and new plant communities. *Man's Role in Changing the Face of the Earth,* ed. W. L. Thomas, 763–77. Univ. Chicago Press
2. Barghoorn, E. S., Wolf, M. K., Clisby, K. H. 1954. Fossil maize from the Valley of Mexico. *Bot. Mus. Leafl. Harvard Univ.* 16:229–40
3. Beadle, G. W. 1971. Letter to Flannery
4. Beadle, G. W. 1972. The mystery of maize. *Field Mus. Nat. Hist. Bull.* 43(10):2–11
5. Binford, L. R. 1968. Post-Pleistocene adaptations. *New Perspectives in Archaeology,* ed. L. R. Binford, S. R. Binford, 313–41. Chicago: Aldine
6. Braidwood, R. J., Howe, B. 1960. Prehistoric investigations in Iraqi Kurdistan. *Studies in Ancient Oriental Civilization* 31. Oriental Inst., Univ. Chicago
7. Callen, E. O. 1967. The first New World cereal. *Am. Antiq.* 32(4):535–38
8. Chang, K. C. 1970. The beginnings of agriculture in the Far East. *Antiquity* 44:175–85
9. Coe, M. D., Flannery, K. V. 1967. Early cultures and human ecology in south coastal Guatemala. *Smithson. Contrib. Anthropol.* 3
10. Copeland, L., Wescomb, P. 1965, 1966. Inventory of stone age sites in Lebanon. *Mélanges Univ. St. Joseph, Beirut,* 41–42
11. Cowan, J. C. 1972. Personal communication to R. I. Ford
12. Cutler, H. C., Whitaker, T. W. 1967. Cucurbits from the Tehuacán Caves. *Prehistory of the Tehuacán Valley,* ed. D. S. Byers, 212–19. Austin: Univ. Texas Press
13. Drennan, R. D. 1973. Experimental teosinte farming in Oaxaca, 1972. Unpublished manuscript. Univ. Michigan, Ann Arbor
14. Flannery, K. V. 1968. Archeological systems theory and early Mesoamerica. *Anthropological Archeology in the Americas,* ed. B. J. Meggers, 67–87. Washington, D.C.: Anthropol. Soc. Washington
15. Flannery, K. V. 1969. Origins and ecological effects of early domestication in Iran and the Near East. *The Domestication and Exploitation of Plants and Animals,* ed. P. J. Ucko, G. W. Dimbleby, 73–100. London: Duckworth
16. Flannery, K. V. 1972. The origins of the village as a settlement type in Mesoamerica and the Near East: a comparative study. *Man, Settlement, and Urbanism,* ed. P. J. Ucko, R. Tringham, G. W. Dimbleby, 23–53. London: Duckworth
17. Flannery, K. V., Ford, R. I. 1972. A productivity study of teosinte (*Zea mexicana*), Nov. 22–25, 1971. Univ. Michigan Mus. Anthropol. (Mimeo)
18. Ford, R. I. 1968. *An ecological analysis involving the population of San Juan Pueblo, New Mexico.* PhD thesis. Univ. Michigan, Ann Arbor
19. Galinat, W. C. 1970. The cupule and its role in the origin and evolution of maize. *Mass. Agr. Exp. Sta. Bull.* 585:1–18
20. Galinat, W. C. 1971. The origin of maize. *Ann. Rev. Genet.* 5:447–78
21. Galinat, W. C. 1972. Personal communication
22. Galinat, W. C., MacNeish, R. S. The ancient maize of Ayacucho, Peru. *Bot. Mus. Leafl. Harvard Univ.* In preparation

23. Gorman, C. F. 1969. Hoabinhian: a pebble-tool complex with early plant associations in southeast Asia. *Science* 163:671–73
24. Harlan, J. R. 1967. A wild wheat harvest in Turkey. *Archaeology* 20(3):197–201
25. Harlan, J. R., Zohary, D. 1966. Distribution of wild wheats and barley. *Science* 153:1075–80
26. Harris, D. R. 1972. The origins of agriculture in the tropics. *Am. Sci.* 60(2): 180–93
27. Heiser, C. B. Jr. 1973. *Seed to Civilization: The Story of Man's Food.* San Francisco: Freeman
28. Helbaek, H. 1960. The paleoethnobotany of the Near East and Europe. See Ref. 6, 99–118
29. Helbaek, H. 1969. Plant-collecting, dry-farming, and irrigation agriculture in prehistoric Deh Luran. See Ref. 30, Appendix 1
30. Hole, F., Flannery, K. V., Neely, J. A. 1969. *Prehistory and human ecology of the Deh Luran Plain. Memoirs* 1. Univ. Michigan Mus. Anthropol.
31. Hutchinson, J. B. 1962. The history and relationships of the world's cottons. *Endeavour* 21:5–15
32. Jarman, H. N., Legge, A. J., Charles, J. A. 1972. Retrieval of plant remains from archaeological sites by froth flotation. *Papers in Economic Prehistory,* ed. E. S. Higgs, 39–48. Cambridge Univ. Press
33. Jones, V. E. 1970. Personal communication
34. Kaplan, L. 1965. Archaeology and domestication in American *Phaseolus* (beans). *Econ. Bot.* 19(4):358–68
35. Kaplan, L. 1967. Archeological *Phaseolus* from Tehuacán. See Ref. 12, 201–11
36. Kaplan, L. 1972. Personal communication
37. Kaplan, L., Lynch, T. F., Smith, C. E. Jr. 1973. Early cultivated beans (*Phaseolus vulgaris*) from an intermontane Peruvian valley. *Science* 179:76–77
38. Kirkby, A. V. T. 1973. The use of land and water resources in the past and present Valley of Oaxaca, Mexico. *Prehistory and Human Ecology of the Valley of Oaxaca,* Vol. 1. *Memoirs* 5. Univ. Michigan. Mus. Anthropol.
39. Lanning, E. P. 1967. *Peru Before the Incas.* Englewood Cliffs: Prentice-Hall
40. Lathrap, D. 1970. *The Upper Amazon.* New York: Praeger
41. Lee, R. B. 1968. What hunters do for a living, or, how to make out on scarce resources. See Ref. 43, 30–48
42. Lee, R. B. 1971. Personal communication

43. Lee, R. B., DeVore, I. 1968. Problems in the study of hunters and gatherers. *Man the Hunter,* ed. R. B. Lee, I. DeVore, Chap. 1. Chicago: Aldine
44. Lorenzo, J. L., Gonzáles Quintero, L. 1970. El más antiguo teosinte. *Boletin* 42:41–43. Inst. Nac. Ant. Hist., Mexico, D.F.
45. Lowe, G. W. 1967. Discussion. In *Altamira and Padre Piedra, Early Pre-classic Sites in Chiapas, Mexico,* ed. D. F. Green, G. W. Lowe. *Pap. New World Archaeol. Found.* 20:53–79
46. MacNeish, R. S. 1958. Preliminary archaeological investigations in the Sierra de Tamaulipas, Mexico. *Trans. Am. Phil. Soc.* n.s. 48(6). Philadelphia
47. MacNeish, R. S. 1964. Ancient Mesoamerican civilization. *Science* 143: 531–37
48. MacNeish, R. S. 1964. Personal communication
49. MacNeish, R. S., Nelken-Turner, A., García Cook, A. 1970. *Second Annual Report of the Ayacucho Archaeological-Botanical Project.* Andover: Peabody Found.
50. Mangelsdorf, P. C. 1947. The origin and evolution of maize. *Advan. Genet.* 1: 161–207
51. Mangelsdorf, P. C. 1973. Letter to the editor. *Field Mus. Nat. Hist. Bull.* 44:16
52. Mangelsdorf, P. C., MacNeish, R. S., Galinat, W. C. 1967. Prehistoric wild and cultivated maize. See Ref. 12, 178–200
53. Marks, A. 1971. Settlement patterns and intrasite variablity in the central Negev, Israel. *Am. Anthropol.* 73:1237–44
54. Niklewski, J., van Zeist, W. 1970. A late quaternary pollen diagram from northwestern Syria. *Acta Bot. Neer.* 19(5): 737–54
55. Patterson, T. C. 1971. Central Peru: its population and economy. *Archaeology* 24(4):316–21
56. Peebles, J. 1972. Rice. Unpublished manuscript. Univ. Michigan, Ann Arbor
57. Perrot, J. 1966. Le gisement Natufien de Mallaha (Eynan), Israël. *L'Anthropologie* 70(5–6):437–84
58. Pickersgill, B. 1969. The archaeological record of chile peppers (*Capsicum* spp.) and the sequence of plant domestication in Peru. *Am. Antiq.* 34:54–61
59. Pickersgill, B. 1972. Personal communication
60. Pickersgill, B., Bunting, A. H. 1969. Cultivated plants and the Kon-Tiki theory. *Nature* 222:225–27
61. Renfrew, J. M. 1969. The archaeological evidence for the domestication of plants:

methods and problems. See Ref. 15, 149–72

62. Robson, J. R., Konlande, J. 1972. Unpublished studies. Dep. Nutr. Public Health, Univ. Michigan, Ann Arbor

63. Schoenwetter, J. 1972. The pollen records from Guilá Naquitz cave, Oaxaca, Mexico. To appear in future volume of *Prehistory and Human Ecology of the Valley of Oaxaca* (see Ref. 38)

64. *Sci. Am.* (no author) 1973. 228(1):44–45. See also Mangelsdorf (51)

65. Smith, C. E. 1967. Plant remains. See Ref. 12, 220–55

66. Smith, C. E. 1969. Carbonized plants from San José Mogote, Oaxaca. To appear in future volume of *Prehistory and Human Ecology of the Valley of Oaxaca* (see Ref. 38)

67. Smith, C. E. 1973. Personal communication

68. Smith, C. E., Kerr, T. 1968. Pre-conquest plant fibers from the Tehuacán Valley, Mexico. *Econ. Bot.* 22(4):354–58

69. Solecki, R. S. 1955. Shanidar cave, a paleolithic site in northern Iraq. *Ann. Rep. Smithson. Inst. 1954* (Publ. 4190), 389–425

70. Solheim, W. G. 1972. An earlier agricultural revolution. *Sci. Am.* 226:34–41

71. Stephens, S. G. 1967. A cotton boll segment from Coxcatlán cave. See Ref. 12, 256–60

72. Stubbe, H. 1959. Considerations on the genetical and evolutionary aspects of some mutants of *Hordeum, Glycine, Lycopersicon,* and *Antirrhinum. Cold Spring Harbor Symp. Quant. Biol.* 24: 31–40

73. van Loon, M. 1968. The Oriental Institute excavations at Mureybit, Syria: preliminary report on the 1965 campaign. *J. Near East. Stud.* 27(4):265–90

74. van Zeist, W., Wright, H. E. Jr. 1963. Preliminary pollen studies at Lake Zeribar, Zagros Mountains, southwestern Iran. *Science* 140:65–69

75. Whallon, R. W. Spatial analysis of occupation floors I: application of dimensional analysis of variance. *Am. Antiq.* In press

76. Whitaker, T. W. 1970. Personal communication

77. Whitaker, T. W., Cutler, H. C. 1971. Pre-historic cucurbits from the Valley of Oaxaca. *Econ. Bot.* 25(2):123–27

78. Wilkes, H. G. 1967. *Teosinte: the closest relative of maize.* Cambridge: Bussey Inst., Harvard Univ.

79. Wilkes, H. G. 1972. Maize and its wild relatives. *Science* 177:1071–77

80. Zohary, D. 1969. The progenitors of wheat and barley in relation to domestication and agricultural dispersal in the Old World. See Ref. 15, 47–66

NEW DEVELOPMENTS IN HOMINID PALEONTOLOGY IN SOUTH AND EAST AFRICA

❖ 9532

Phillip V. Tobias

Department of Anatomy, Medical School, University of the Witwatersrand
Johannesburg, South Africa

Recent years have witnessed remarkable progress in the unraveling of hominid evolution. The main advances registered—and which are now crying out for provisional synthesis—may be grouped under the following broad rubrics:

(*a*) The discovery of further hominid fossils in East Africa [Omo, East Rudolf, Chesowanja (27) and Olduvai] and in South Africa (Sterkfontein and Swartkrans) and their demographic analysis (81, 87, 117).

(*b*) New studies on the morphology of many specimens, with a concomitant better appreciation of the "total morphological pattern" (71) and of the ranges of variation within populations and taxa.

(*c*) The time scale of hominid evolution in East Africa is becoming progressively clearer with new age determinations based upon the potassium-argon method (38), paleomagnetism reversals (44), fission tracking (39), and faunal correlations (8, 9, 32, 55, 82, 83).

(*d*) The long uncertain and disputed time parameters of the South African australopithecine sites are at last yielding to analysis by faunal correlations (31, 84, 132) and by geomorphological methods (24, 93).

(*e*) As a result, it is becoming possible to formulate tentative synoptic models of the chronological and phylogenetic relationships between the South and East African fossil hominids—and a single pattern of African hominid phylogeny.

(*f*) Some special implications of the recent work are the rejection of the concept that only one hominid species has existed at any one time (based upon the so-called Principle of Competitive Exclusion); the realization that hominid evolution has been cladistic in character and not predominantly phyletic (*pace* Dobzhansky 37, Buettner-Janusch 20, and Wolpoff 134); the illustration of mosaic evolution in the emerging pattern of hominid phylogeny; and a greater consciousness of the extent and the limitations of sexual dimorphism in higher primates, and especially the Hominoidea.

311

(g) Paleoanthropologists have begun to show a healthy, critical, and self-critical approach to the niceties of systematics and nomenclatural procedure. This is clearing the air for a less confused and confusing picture of hominid systematics, which is an essential prerequisite to the erecting of hypotheses on hominid phylogeny and on the selective mechanisms which could have operated in hominid evolution.

An attempt is made here to review the newer evidence under some of these headings and to limn a tentative reconstruction of hominid phylogeny over the late Tertiary and Quaternary.

NEW HOMINID DISCOVERIES AND STUDIES IN AFRICA

East Rudolf

The most spectacular set of discoveries have undoubtedly been those made by R. E. F. Leakey and his co-workers in the vast area known as East Rudolf in northern Kenya. The sequence of hominid discoveries began with 4 finds—2 from Koobi Fora and 2 from Ileret—in 1968. These were followed by 3 specimens found in 1969 and 16 in 1970 (64, 65, 68). The 1971 season added 26 more hominid specimens or sets of remains (66, 69), whilst the 1972 season brought to light 38 additional hominid fossils (67). The net yield over the 5 years is thus some 87 specimens, of which rather more than half are derived from the larger, southerly area known as Koobi Fora and the remainder from the smaller northerly zone called Ileret. At least 16 localities in East Rudolf have yielded hominid fossils, the richest being Koobi Fora localities 104, 105, and 131, and Ileret localities 01 and 8.

The fossils have been briefly described and provisionally assigned to two hominid genera, *Australopithecus* and *Homo* (65–67). The australopithecine remains include KNM-ER-406, a very complete crested cranium of highly robust structure (68), comparable in many respects with Olduvai hominid 5, the type specimen of *Australopithecus boisei* (116); and KNM-ER-732, a probable female cranium of the same taxon (65, 69). The remains provisionally assigned to *Homo* include a superb complete mandible with small teeth (KNM-ER-992) and a juvenile mandible with mixed dentition (KNM-ER-820) (66). The majority of the East Rudolf finds are of cranial and dental remains, but the area is unique among the African early hominid sites in having yielded a large number of postcranial bones. No fewer than 29 of the 87 discoveries (33⅓%) are of post-cranial remains, thus adding appreciably to the available samples of limb bones of early hominids (123). These include, in whole or in part, 15 femora, 7 tibiae, 6 humeri, and 3 tali. Since the cranial and dental remains clearly indicate the presence of at least two taxa, namely *A. c.f. boisei* and *Homo* sp., the allocation of the isolated limb bones to one or other taxon presents a difficult problem which is at present receiving attention (35, 130).

A remarkable discovery late in 1972 was of the cranium KNM-ER-1470 (67). On reconstruction it proved to have an endocranial capacity of over 800 cc, nearly twice as great as the mean for South African crania of *A. africanus* (50, 52, 106, 121) and 25 percent as much again as the mean for 4 Olduvai crania assigned to *Homo habilis* (121, 125). Yet despite its bigger brain size, the new East Rudolf specimen was found at a level *below* the KBS tuff dated to 2.6 m.y. and subsequently shown by paleo-magnetism readings to be about 2.9 m.y. It would seem thus to be 1 m.y. or more older than the Olduvai *H. habilis* sample and would point to an appreciably earlier appearance of the *Homo* tendency to marked encephalization than had earlier been suspected.

The studies on the stratigraphy (128), chronology, and vertebrate faunas have led Maglio (83) to propose four faunal zones in the East Rudolf succession. The earliest, the *Notochoerus capensis* zone, is represented in the Kubi Algi beds to the south of Koobi Fora: these beds have not so far yielded hominid fossils. The *Mesochoerus limnetes* zone has a "best fit" age of 2.3 m.y. (2.0–3.0 m.y., indicated minimum and maximum). It is represented in the Lower Member of the Koobi Fora formation and includes some of the hominids tentatively assigned to *Homo*. There follows the *Metridiochoerus andrewsi* zone with a "best fit" age of 1.7 m.y. (1.5 to 1.9 m.y., indicated minimum and maximum ages); this zone corresponds in age and fauna with Olduvai Bed I and lower Bed II. It is represented in the Upper Member of the Koobi Fora formation and includes many hominids, both *Australopithecus* and *Homo*. The latest of Maglio's four zones, the *Loxodonta africana* zone, has a "best fit" age of 1.3 m.y. (1.0–1.6 m.y., indicated minimum and maximum) and is repre-sented in the Ileret Member. It includes many hominid specimens, both *Australopi-thecus* and *Homo*. These faunal stages are of course still tentative at this stage.

Archaeological remains were discovered at East Rudolf by Behrensmeyer in 1969 (7, 56, 61, 64) on the outcrop of a tuff (KBS) dated at 2.61 ± 0.26 m.y. Subsequent excavations revealed worked stone objects together with, at one site, small but significant quantities of broken bones in relation to the KBS tuff. These signs of hominid cultural activities have set the archaeological record of occupation sites back from 1.8 m.y. at Olduvai to about 2.6 m.y. at East Rudolf. This early record of implemental activities is corroborated by even earlier finds at Omo (q.v.).

In sum, the newest evidence from East Rudolf indicates the presence there of hominid fossils provisionally assigned to *Homo* in strata from about 2.9 m.y. and extending up to about 1.0–1.3 m.y., and of others belonging to a very robust australopithecine like *A. boisei* in strata from about 1.7 or even 2.0 m.y. onwards to about 1.0–1.3 m.y.

Omo

Since 1966 the Omo research expedition, led by F. C. Howell of Chicago and Y. Coppens of Paris, has been systematically exploring the series of sediments in the Lower Omo Valley (3, 4, 11, 22, 25, 33, 53–55). Two of the formations in this area, the Usno (47) and the Shungura (18, 46), have yielded hominid fossils from close to 70 localities. The fossiliferous strata in the Usno formation have an estimated age of 2.5–2.6 m.y. (19) and have yielded some 20 isolated or associated hominid teeth. The Shungura formation extends in time from 3.75 m.y. (Member B) to 1.84 m.y. (Member I); its hominid fossils are found mainly in the upper members (C–I) of the sequence, corresponding to potassium-argon ages of about 2.5–1.7 m.y. Only a few localities in the lowest part of the Shungura sequence, dated to about 3.5 m.y., have yielded hominid remains—some isolated teeth. The overwhelming majority of all the Omo hominid remains are of isolated teeth; there are also some cranial and mandibular parts and a number of postcranial bones. Although detailed studies of these hominid remains are awaited, some of them, more especially the teeth, have been tentatively assigned to a very robust australopithecine like *A. boisei,* and others to one or more smaller toothed forms, *A. aff. africanus* and/or *H. habilis* (33, 53, 54).

Artefacts have been reported by Chavaillon (28), Bonnefille et al (11), and Howell (55), including sparse occurrences as low down in the sequence as Member C. They include stone artefacts and fragmentary bone and suggest that in the northern Rudolf basin, "hominid object-manipulation and modification must date back to about 3 m.y." (55, p. 349). This would push back the archaeological record to nearly 0.5 m.y. earlier than its hitherto revealed expression at East Rudolf.

Olduvai

Dr. M. D. Leakey (62) has continued to lay bare the archaeological and paleontological sequence in the Olduvai Gorge, and some 48 hominid individuals are now represented. Many of these specimens have received preliminary description and publication (63, 114, 115, 123, 124), while to date only the type specimen of the very large toothed. extremely robust australopithecine *A. boisei* has been described in detail (116). The detailed study of the other hominid cranial and dental specimens from Beds I and II is virtually complete and will be joined by M. H. Day's description of most of the postcranial remains in those beds to form another volume in the *Olduvai Gorge* series. It is intended to relegate the descriptive analysis of those Bed II remains ascribed to *H. erectus,* as well as of the hominid remains from Beds III and IV, to a subsequent volume, in which also M. D. Leakey will describe the Acheulean cultural remains. Meantime, it can be recorded here that, save for Olduvai 9 and one or two other hominid fossils from the upper part of Bed II, all the identifiable hominid cranial and dental remains from Beds I and II have been assigned to a very robust australopithecine *A. boisei* or to the ultragracile *H. habilis* first described by Leakey, Tobias & Napier (58). Thus from Beds I and II, remains representing 15 individuals have been assigned to *H. habilis,* 5 individuals to *A. boisei,* while 8 further cranial or dental specimens have not been identified taxonomically. This analysis excludes the postcranial bones of some 8 individuals from Beds I and II (see 5 for a recent study of some).

Studies on Olduvai 24, reconstructed by R. J. Clarke (63), have shed much further light on the structure of the cranium of *H. habilis.* In a number of respects it is nearer to later forms of *Homo* than to *A. africanus,* and these include mean dental size, the position of the foramen magnum on the cranial base, and the cranial capacity. A sample of four crania attributed to *H. habilis* has a mean cranial capacity (adult values) of 640 cc (121, 125), as compared with the mean for the South African *A. africanus* of 442 cc (52, 121).

There has been some modification in the subdivision of the Olduvai formations (45), and Bed V, as used by H. Reck and L. S. B. Leakey, has been abandoned, its place being taken by the Mesak, Ndutu, and Naisiusiu stratigraphic units. In addition, Bed I has been extended downwards to include the basal lava flows and the underlying tuffs and clays; thus, there is now a Lower Member, a Basalt Member, and an Upper Member of Bed I. The pioneering application by Evernden & Curtis (38) of the potassium-argon method to the dating of Bed I has now yielded two most important, consistent and reliable dates: 1.85 m.y. for the Basalt Member and 1.75 m.y. for Tuff I^B within the Upper Member of Bed I. Moreover, the lapse of time from the bottom to the top of Bed I (Upper Member) is much smaller than was formerly thought and probably does not exceed 100,000 years. These dates have received independent support from the fission-track method of Fleischer and his co-workers (39) and from studies of geomagnetic polarity (44). Thus the lapse of time between the Bed I fossils assigned to *H. habilis* and those of Bed II attributed to the same taxon is nowhere near the figure of about 1 m.y. which had previously been adduced as evidence militating against the possibility that these two groups of hominid fossils belonged to the same taxon.

Considerable progress has been made by M. D. Leakey (62) in the archaeological analysis of the Bed I-II sequence. The lithic industries into which the artefacts are classified are threefold: the Oldowan (once called "pre-chellean"), Developed Oldowan, and Acheulean. Throughout Bed I and Lower Bed II, the characteristic tool of the Oldowan is the stone chopper. "Proto-bifaces" come into the picture from Upper Bed I to Middle Bed II and "appear to represent attempts to achieve a rudimentary handaxe by whatever means was possible." No true bifaces occur before the upper part of Middle Bed II, where they form an integral part of both the Developed Oldowan B and the early Acheulean industries. Yet, while tracing a strong thread of continuity from the Oldowan into the Developed Oldowan, Mary Leakey finds the Acheulean seemingly intruding as a dissonant element from Middle Bed II upwards. The Developed Oldowan and the Acheulean seem to her to "represent two distinct cultural traditions, perhaps made by two different groups of hominids."

Of the makers of the implements themselves, Mary Leakey is prepared in the latest *Olduvai Gorge* volume to go beyond the cautious line she followed at the Burg Wartenstein symposium in 1965 (59). She has now adduced strong evidence that *H. habilis* was responsible for the Oldowan culture. From six localities, five in Bed I and one in the lower part of Middle Bed II, she has found remains of *H. habilis* directly associated with Oldowan tools. With the Acheulean remains at Olduvai, *H. erectus* is probably associated, although, as the late Dr. L. S. B. Leakey has pointed out in a posthumous paper (57), evidence from elsewhere that *H. erectus* was the maker of the Acheulean industries is poor or totally lacking. The maker of the Developed Oldowan remains problematical. Only Olduvai hominid 3 is directly associated with a Developed Oldowan assemblage, and this is represented by only a very large molar tooth (almost certainly deciduous) and a canine. The molar is generally regarded as belonging to a robust australopithecine (cf. *A. boisei*), but this brings one no nearer to unraveling the authorship of the Developed Oldowan industries, as *A. boisei* seems to have been present *throughout* the times of Beds I and II, along with one or more other hominids at any particular level in time.

If the claim that *H. habilis* is the maker of the Oldowan culture is correct, this adds another trait to the list of features serving to distinguish *H. habilis* from *A. africanus,* as Leakey and Tobias suggested some years ago (58).

Sterkfontein

Excavations were renewed by Tobias & Hughes (126) in 1966 at Sterkfontein, Transvaal, and have continued uninterruptedly ever since. A number of new hominid fossils have come to light, including a cranium (StW/Hom 12/13/17) and a mandible (StW/Hom 14), both with teeth, found in situ at approximately the same level as the famous skull of "Mrs. Ples" (Sts 5). There are also a maxilla with teeth, some 15 isolated teeth, and 4 articulated lumbar vertebrae. Most of these remains can be assigned provisionally to *A. africanus.* A fragment of jaw with teeth from the West Pit (formerly called "Extension Site") may belong to *Homo* sp., as is true of some of the dental remains previously recovered from that uppermost part of the cave deposit (104, 113).

Detailed studies have for some time been in progress on the Sterkfontein hominids. For comparison with *A. boisei,* Tobias recorded many new data on the Sterkfontein *A. africanus* (116). Wallace (131) and G. Sperber[1] have made new detailed studies on the dentition, the former emphasizing wear patterns and other functional aspects of the masticatory apparatus, the latter concentrating on morphology (including odontometry cf. 133) of the premolars and molars.

The cranial capacity of the Sterkfontein hominids has been subject to restudy and reanalysis (50, 52, 106), as a result of which it is clear that earlier estimates of the Sterkfontein capacities were somewhat too high. Thus the value formerly cited for Sts 71 [480-520 cc -(17)] has been recomputed as 428 cc (50); that for Sts 19/58 has "dropped" from 530 cc (16) to 436 cc; while the values for Sts 6ʋ and Sts 5 have remained largely unchanged. Thus estimates of the mean for these four Sterkfontein capacities have been lowered from 486 cc to 444 cc. A similar reassessment of the Makapansgat MLD 37/38 capacity has lowered it from 480 cc (34) to 435 cc (50). For the total sample of 5 *A. africanus* adult specimens from Sterkfontein and Makapansgat, the mean capacity estimate has been decreased from 485 cc to 442 cc. If the revised adult estimate for Taung (440 instead of 540 cc) is included, the estimated mean for 6 crania assigned to *A. africanus* drops from 494 cc (121) to 442 cc (50).

This lowered estimate for *A. africanus* throws into strong relief the estimated mean value for *H. habilis* of 640 cc ($n = 4$). The difference is highly significant as Pilbeam (97) and Campbell (26) have pointed out.

Aguirre (1, 2) has reexamined the mandibles of some South African early hominids. He suspects that more than one hominid is represented in the Sterkfontein sample (excluding the late specimens from the West Pit), namely, *A. robustus* as well as *A. africanus,* but he is not as convinced of this for Sterkfontein as he is for Makapansgat (see below).

[1]In progress.

Rosen & McKern (111) have been reexamining the values of some fossil hominid crania for Le Gros Clark's three cranial indices (70). They suggest that the supraorbital height index and a new supraorbital upper facial height index they have devised so effectively distinguish *A. africanus* (represented in their study by Sterkfontein 5) from the robust australopithecines (represented by Robinson's 1963 reconstruction of Swartkrans 48 and by Olduvai hominid 5) as to justify the generic separation of the two groups of australopithecines, a view Robinson has long held. However, the question of the relationship between the robust and gracile australopithecines still remains a point of high contention (107, 118). In a review of the problem, Tobias (125) has suggested that the morphological, temporal, and phylogenetic relationships between the two or three groups of australopithecines justify the following systematic grouping:

One genus *Australopithecus* comprising: (*a*) one superspecies consisting of *A. robustus* and *A. boisei;* (*b*) one polytypic species, *A. africanus.*

The postcranial bones from Sterkfontein have come in for a good deal of attention lately. In a recent restudy of the capitate bone from Sterkfontein, Lewis (74) has shown that this wrist bone, far from being essentially human in appearance, "conserves, with but little progressive modification, important biomechanical characteristics still found in *Pan.*" Oxnard (90) believes that the suggestion currently in the literature that the Sterkfontein scapular fragment is relatively less specialized than the corresponding region of the gibbon and the chimpanzee (89), may not be justified. The femur has been the object of a number of studies by Lovejoy & Heiple (48, 75, 76) and by Preuschoft (98). Lovejoy & Heiple have been led to reiterate the distinctly hominid position of *A. africanus* and, too, where comparable parts are available of *A. robustus* and *A. africanus,* how closely they conform to the same total morphological pattern. Likewise, the recent studies of the pelvis by Zihlman (137–139) and by Lovejoy et al (77) have served to emphasize the close resemblance between the South African species *A. robustus* and *A. africanus.* On the other hand, some studies have stressed the distinctive features of the australopithecine femur as compared with that of *Homo* (35, 130). I regret that at the time of writing this review, Robinson's new work on *"Early Hominid Posture and Locomotion"* (1972), including detailed descriptions of the locomotor apparatus of the South African early hominids, is not available to me. Leutenegger (72) has computed the size of the head of the newborn *A. africanus* in relation to the size of the pelvic inlet of Sts 14 and has demonstrated that even on a maximum estimate of head diameter at birth, the head would readily have passed through the pelvic inlet of Sts 14. From this he is led to suggest that "in the early stages of hominid evolution selective pressures for enlarging the pelvic canal to ensure parturition may have been minor or even absent; selective forces toward highly efficient construction of the pelvis for bipedalism could have been stronger . . ."

Another series of studies has lately attempted to assess the stature of the australopithecines (21, 49, 75, 80), but little agreement has so far emerged from these attempts, save perhaps that individuals attributed to *Australopithecus* seem, in general, to have been short in stature, shorter on the average than most populations of modern man.

Researches and discussions, some published and some not, have shed much light on the cave stratigraphy and extent (Edmund Gill, personal communication; Butzer (22) and personal communication; Partridge and A. B. A. Brink, personal communication; Hughes & Tobias, unpublished). These newer observations point to (a) continuous deposition of the breccia over a considerable period of time, running to hundreds of thousands of years; (b) the existence of an earliest bone-bearing breccia *under* the travertine "floor" of the main cave deposit; (c) a much greater east-west extent of the cave deposit than was formerly suspected.

Attempts at dating by radioisotopes, paleomagnetism reversals, and the racemization of isoleucine (6) have so far not been successful, but two other lines of investigation have provided clear-cut pointers. Partridge's (93) geomorphological approach has provided him with an estimate of the time period at which the Sterkfontein cave *first* opened to the surface: the date is 3.3 m.y. Meantime, new faunal comparisons have permitted H. B. S. Cooke (31) to suggest provisionally that the Sterkfontein breccias may be about twice as old as has hitherto been thought, possibly "in the vicinity of 2.5 to 3.0 million years old."

This tentative view is supported by V. Maglio (84 and personal communication), who has kindly permitted me to state that his inference is based on a comparison of fossil suids from Sterkfontein and Makapansgat, and of *Elephas recki* from the latter site (*pace* Wright & Skaryd 136), with their well-dated counterparts from East Rudolf and the Omo (Shungura formation). Although the faunal evidence is far from adequate and further studies are needed, we may at this stage note Maglio's tentative statement that both Makapansgat and Sterkfontein appear to correlate best with the East African faunal succession of about the middle Shungura and lowest Koobi Fora formations. In terms of absolute chronology, Maglio believes that 2.5 m.y. is a fair estimate for the age of these faunas.

Thus "faunal dating" points to 2.5 m.y. or 2.5–3.0 m.y. for Sterkfontein, while Partridge's earliest date for the opening of the Sterkfontein cave is 3.3 m.y. (93). It is at present not clear if this is a real discrepancy, a geomorphological methodological difficulty, or a faunal sampling problem. If it is a real discrepancy, it would suggest that the early stages in the accumulation of deposit in the Sterkfontein cave, when the recently exposed lowest breccia was forming, may have been far longer than we had imagined, since the identified fauna, which has been correlated with East African lineages, comes from much higher in the Sterkfontein deposit.

The Sterkfontein artefacts come from the uppermost parts of the deposit, just beneath the roof, in the area of the West Pit. Those recovered earlier and studied by Mason (88) have been restudied by Mary D. Leakey (60, 62), who is inclined to relate them to Developed Oldowan B assemblages of Olduvai Bed II. Her classification of the Sterkfontein material differs from that of Mason, mainly in that most of the specimens which he regards as cores she would class as either choppers or polyhedrons. These earlier studies were made on limited samples. The excavations of 1967–1973 have yielded many new artefacts from the area of the West Pit; these have been examined by Isaac and are being studied by Mason. The presence in only the uppermost part of the breccia of stone implements with fragmentary hominid remains, including teeth which are small by the standards of the main Sterkfontein assemblage of *A. africanus,* suggests that further excavation in the latest strata may reveal the presence of a tool-making *Homo* sp., such as *H. habilis,* as a late arrival in the apparently lengthy sequence represented in the Sterkfontein breccias.

Makapansgat

Detailed studies of the form, measurements, and function of the Makapansgat hominid teeth have been carried out by Wallace (131), G. Sperber, Wolpoff (133), and Tobias (116). In addition, the crania and mandibles have been reexamined by a number of workers. The Makapansgat hominids are usually classified in *A. africanus,* an assignment which is supported by the most recent morphological studies. Yet in 1967 Tobias drew attention to some "robust" features in some of the crania, jaws, and teeth from Makapansgat. He went so far as to state: "In these respects, the Makapansgat specimens seem to show a somewhat nearer approach to *A. robustus* than do the Sterkfontein specimens. This reduces the distinctness of the lineages and renders it less likely that they represented two clades, the members of which should be regarded as generically distinct from each other" (116, p. 244).

Since then, Aguirre (1) has studied the early hominid mandibles from South Africa. He has identified a constellation of morphological features characterizing the mandibles of *A. robustus* from Swartkrans. These features, he believes, are clearly shown by MLD 2 of Makapansgat which, he states, should be regarded as a young male *A. robustus.* To Aguirre it appears indubitable that there is more than one species of hominid at Makapansgat—a thought I had raised independently as a tentative suggestion in 1968 and 1969 (119, 120).

Perhaps another way of looking at the somewhat intermediate features shown by the Makapansgat fossil hominids is that they resemble a population closer to the point of speciation between *A. africanus* and *A. robustus.* In such a population, anatomical polymorphisms could have co-existed, foreshadowing the later speciation of the *A. robustus-A. boisei* lineage from the basic *A. c.f. africanus* ancestor.

In another study on mandibles from Makapansgat, Swartkrans, Olduvai, and Peninj, Tobias (122) showed that the *relative space width* of hominid mandibles is —without a consistent definition—of no value in deciding taxonomic status (*pace* Robinson 101, 105, 106), nor is there any hard and fast dividing line between australopithecines and hominines with respect to the disto-mesial pattern of variation of these relative widths. Robinson had attempted to use this feature to support his claim that Olduvai hominid 7 (the type specimen of *H. habilis*) was a member of *Australopithecus* and not a member of the genus *Homo.* Unfortunately, three different definitions of the position of measurement were offered by Robinson in 1953, 1965, and 1966. The diagnosis of any specimen varied according to where the measurements were taken, and Tobias showed that this criterion did not and could not disqualify Olduvai hominid 7 from a place in the genus *Homo.*

The endocranial capacity of MLD 37/38 had been estimated by Dart (34) as being approximately the same as that of Sterkfontein 5, that is, about 480 cc. Holloway (50, 51) has made a "quite provisional" (personal communication) recalculation of the capacity of this specimen and obtains a lower value (435 cc). He used the MLD 1 parieto-occipital part to compute the bone thickness of MLD 37/38 in various regions. This may impart a source of error into his recomputation as MLD 1, with its converging temporal crests leading, in all probability, to an anteriorly placed sagittal crest, may well have belonged to a young adult *male,* whereas MLD 37/38, with no comparable development of temporal crests, could have belonged to a young adult *female.*

MLD 1 with its probable sagittal crest is an interesting specimen. Although its median sagittal contour is similar to that of Sterkfontein 5 (102), its transverse dimensions are appreciably greater (unpublished original data). This suggests that its capacity was probably greater than that of Sterkfontein 5 (with 485 cc). This might well prove another feature relating MLD 1 to *A. robustus* with its capacity of 530 cc [based on a single specimen from Swartkrans and supported by 530 cc for Olduvai hominid 5, *A. boisei* (112)]. It contrasts sharply with the bigger-brained early hominids of Olduvai *(H. habilis)* in which a larger cranial capacity is accompanied by temporal lines placed much more widely apart on the calvaria.

G. Sperber (unpublished) has supplemented his odontoscopic and odontometric study by a radiological investigation. For the first time, practically every single maxilla and mandible of the South African early hominids has been X-rayed. The resulting skiagrams are throwing much new light on the size range of pulp cavities, the extent of the secondary dentine response to marked attrition, and details of root structure and number.

The search for dateable materials at Makapansgat has been no less rigorous than at Sterkfontein. Thus far, positive results have been yielded by Partridge's geomorphological assessment—3.7 m.y.—as the earliest date at which the cave opened to the surface (93) and Cooke's (31) and Maglio's (84) faunal comparisons with East African suids and *Elephas recki.* As mentioned under Sterkfontein, the faunal picture matches the East Rudolf and Omo faunas of 2.5 or 2.5–3.0 m.y. Noncalibrated faunal comparisons among the South African sites had already led Wells (132) to infer that both Makapansgat and Sterkfontein belong to the Sterkfontein faunal span, but that some of the many points of difference between the faunas of the two sites might plausibly suggest that Makapansgat is older than Sterkfontein.

The cercopithecoids of Makapansgat have been the object of new studies by Maier, Freedman, and Eck. Maier (86) has described some 20 further specimens, over and above the 70 specimens, belonging to 5 species, previously recorded from the Makapansgat limeworks. A beautifully complete male skull of *Cercopithecoides williamsi* has enabled him to amplify the available descriptions of this species, to confirm its membership of the Colobidae (so far the only colobid monkey described from the South African early hominid deposits), and to confirm the invalidity of *C. molletti.* The other species represented are *Parapapio jonesi, P. broomi, P. whitei,* and *Simopithecus darti.* Freedman (40, 41, 43) has shown that the three *Parapapio* species occur at Makapansgat in the same proportions as at Sterkfontein: *P. broomi* >50 percent; *P. whitei* least common.

In the light of Wells's inference, it is noteworthy that Partridge's geomorphological analysis also suggests that the Makapansgat cave was opened to the surface earlier than the Sterkfontein cave, the two dates being 3.7 and 3.3 m.y. respectively. Again, there is an apparent discrepancy between the date of cave opening and the "faunal date."

Butzer's (23) analysis of the Makapansgat cave fill indicated that it differed from those in the Krugersdorp area, inasmuch as it contains appreciable deposits constituted for the most part of insoluble cave residues and precipitates, as well as typical *limons rouges.* The other sites (Sterkfontein, Swartkrans, and Kromdraai) are apparently comprised largely of a sediment matrix typical of *limons rouges,* similar to those developed in limestones of the Mediterranean region.

On the archaeological side, there is little newly published on the osteodontokeratic objects of Dart. Foreign stone objects, including some artefacts, are clearly present in parts of the deposit (85, 92), but it has so far not proved possible to assign them to a specific cultural horizon which could be equated with either the Sterkfontein or the Swartkrans industries, or with any part of the cultural sequence established in East Africa (60, footnote to p. 1224).

Swartkrans

C. K. Brain's (13) excavation at Swartkrans has continued to yield new hominid specimens. Apart from the excellent endocast, the vertebrae, and other specimens reported earlier, the most recent finds include an isolated metacarpal which is being studied by M. H. Day. Detailed morphological studies have been carried out on the very rich assemblage of hominids from Swartkrans, as well as on the other South African early hominids, by Wallace (131) and G. Sperber on the teeth, Holloway (51) on the endocast, Wolpoff, Day, Wood, and Tobias on various features. Aguirre's (1) study on the mandibles of the South African early hominids revealed that out of 20 morphological traits investigated, the Swartkrans *A. robustus* jaws were characterized by a constellation of 14 of these traits. These same features occurred also in the mandible of Peninj (Lake Natron), as well as in some of the earlier discovered jaws from Omo and East Rudolf, and in MLD 2 from Makapansgat.

The superbly preserved endocranial cast SK 1585, found by Brain (14) on 17 January 1966, has a cranial capacity of 530 cc (51). This was the first secure evidence in support of the long held, though unsubstantiated, view that *A. robustus* from South Africa had a somewhat larger cranial capacity than *A. africanus* ($\overline{X} = 442$ cc); previously, it had been shown that the hyperrobust *A. boisei* of East Africa also has a capacity of 530 cc (112, 116). But of course these two estimates from Olduvai and Swartkrans give only a rough indication of the position: many more determinations are required before a confident claim can be made that the superspecies *A. robustus/A. boisei* (125) had a larger mean capacity than *A. africanus* possessed.

The composite cranium from Swartkrans assembled by R. J. Clarke in July 1969 has been examined in more detail (29, 30). These studies seem to be justified in attributing the specimen to a species of the genus *Homo* (*pace* Wolpoff 135). The new evidence is of such importance that Clarke is now devoting a detailed and comprehensive study to the specimen in comparison with other fossils assigned to early South and East African members of the genus *Homo.*

The postcranial bones of Swartkrans have received much further attention. The height estimates of Burns (21) have suggested that SK 82 and SK 97 were both short individuals. The height of SK 82 was predicted from the femoral head diameter as 151 cm (4 ft 11.5 in), the range of probable heights being 146–156 cm; that of SK 97 was estimated as 157 cm (5 ft 1.5 in), with a range of probable heights of 152–

161 cm. McHenry's most recent estimates (80), based on as many upper and lower limb bones as possible (78), confirm the generally short stature of *A. robustus*. He infers that it is clear that the gracile and robust forms of South African australopithecines were not very different in height, though the robust form does appear to have been "a good deal heavier," to judge by the size of the teeth and skulls. Robinson (108) has inferred, from his study of two new vertebrae from Swartkrans, that the females of the robust species and males of *A. africanus* were probably similar in robustness as well as in stature.

The most recent descriptions of the pelvic bones have led Zihlman (138) and Heiple & Lovejoy (48) to conclude that both *A. africanus* and *A. robustus* show essentially the same functional anatomical complex. While Zihlman tends to regard this complex as being *sui generis,* and not quite the same as that of *Homo,* the latter two workers recognize but little difference between the complex in *Australopithecus (sensu lato)* and the pelvi-femoral complex associated with the bipedal, striding gait of modern man. Robinson (109), on the other hand, holds firmly to the view that *A. robustus* had "a relatively long, pongid-like ischium, which appears to have been part of a power-oriented propulsive mechanism." *A. africanus,* on the contrary, he believes, "had an ischium proportionately shorter even than that of *H. sapiens* and had an elongated femur and thus a fully human speed-oriented propulsive mechanism (Robinson 1972). The anatomy of the two forms thus differed in a manner indicating considerable adaptive difference . . ." (109). Unfortunately, Robinson's 1972 book, mentioned above, in which he doubtless gives the detailed evidence for these statements, is not yet available to me. A discriminant analysis of the Swartkrans left first metacarpal, SK 84, has suggested to Rightmire (99) that this fossil bone may be functionally similar to that of the chimpanzee.

On the archeological and ethological side, Mary D. Leakey's (60) study of the Swartkrans implements convinced her of resemblances between them and the Developed Oldowan B assemblages from Bed II, Olduvai. However, the Swartkrans collection is still too limited for quantitative analysis. Brain (15) has continued his search for, and careful study of, evidences of early hominid behavioral patterns. In his latest work, he has critically reviewed the evidence for interpersonal violence. Following Roper's (110) comprehensive review of all the published claims for interaustralopithecine violence, especially those of Dart (34), Brain has reexamined all the original fossil hominids from the five South African australopithecine sites. He has stated that "In most instances invalid conclusions have been drawn because ante-mortem damage to specimens has not been isolated conclusively from postfossilization effects." He concludes that the question of the incidence of interpersonal violence in this group must for the time being remain an open one.

The reconstruction of the cave sequence at Swartkrans is continuing to receive Brain's attention, and a major study of it is at present under way. Meantime, Butzer (23) has analogized the Swartkrans deposit to the *limons rouges* developed in limestone of the Mediterranean region. He does not accept the inferences drawn by Brain (12, 13) that Swartkrans was characterized by moist conditions and Sterkfontein and Makapansgat by dry conditions. The Swartkrans fauna is regarded as defining a Swartkrans Faunal Span, younger than the Sterkfontein Faunal Span, but older than the fauna of Kromdraai and the Cornelia Faunal Span (from Cornelia, Orange Free State) (132). Vrba is making a detailed study of the bovid remains from Swartkrans and other South African sites; already she has added a number of new species to the available lists of mammals from the early hominid cave sites (129). Freedman's 1970 checklist of cercopithecoids shows that of the genus *Parapapio*, only *P. jonesi* is represented at Swartkrans, along with *Papio robinsoni, Simopithecus danieli, Dinopithecus ingens,* and *Cercopithecoides williamsi* (41).

Cooke (31) has suggested that on faunal comparisons Swartkrans is at least as old as Bed I, Olduvai (1.7–1.8 m.y.). Partridge's (93) geomorphological study has set a date of 2.5 m.y. as the earliest period for the opening of the Swartkrans cave. Again there is a discrepancy of about half a million years between the two estimates, but both estimates confirm what faunal comparisons have indicated, that Swartkrans is younger than Makapansgat and Sterkfontein.

Kromdraai

The hominid teeth from Kromdraai have been studied recently by Wallace (131), G. Sperber, and Tobias (116). Oxnard (91) has interpolated the talus into a matrix of extant species. He concludes that on generalized distances the Kromdraai talus, like that from Olduvai (36, 73), is "completely dissimilar from both African ape and modern human tali." On the other hand, McHenry's (79) study of early hominid humeri has shown that the Kromdraai humerus, like that of Kanapoi, closely resembles the humeri of modern man. McHenry (80) has estimated a stature of 154.1 cm (5 ft) for the individual represented by the Kromdraai humerus (TM 1517)— short, like the other australopithecines.

The Kromdraai fauna generally cited are those from the Faunal Site, not the Hominid Site. Freedman & Brain (42) have recently demonstrated that the cercopithecoids from the two Kromdraai sites are different and point to different ages for the two deposits. The Hominid Site contains *Papio robinsoni, P. angusticeps,* and *Cercopithecoides williamsi.* The Faunal Site includes the two species of *Papio* (though in different proportions), *Gorgopithecus major,* but not *C. williamsi.* From this and other evidence it is clear that the former practice of using the Faunal Site species as a guide to the faunal dating of the Hominid Site at Kromdraai will have to be abandoned. However, both Kromdraai sites are clearly younger than Sterkfontein and Makapansgat.

Taung

Recent geomorphological studies carried out independently and with different approaches by Butzer and by Partridge have suggested a much younger age for Taung than had been thought previously. In 1969, Wells drew attention to the uncertainty of the dating of Taung in relation to the other australopithecine sites. Long regarded as the oldest, or among the oldest of the South African sites, Taung has a fauna which—at least in respect to the species most closely connected with the type specimen of *A. africanus*—do not warrant the view that the Taung child is the earliest South African australopithecine. The hominid-associated fauna, Wells believed, could just as readily be equated with Swartkrans or even with Kromdraai.

He added, "Some of the animals recorded from Taung may however belong to parts of the deposit appreciably older than the *Australopithecus* breccia" (132).

The point had been raised at the Wenner-Gren Foundation Symposium in 1965, when Wells raised the question, "What, if any, is the justification for considering the Taung fauna as belonging to the Sterkfontein rather than the Swartkrans stage?" R. F. Ewer replied, "This is slight and is based on the smaller forms which *seem* to indicate closer resemblances to Makapansgat and Sterkfontein than to Swartkrans. However, the designation was very tentative and statistically the numbers present are not significant" (10). Wells added that the short-faced baboon *Papio wellsi* from Taung seemed to be close to one from Swartkrans. Freedman's 1970 checklist (41) shows the significant absence from Taung of *Parapapio broomi,* which is the commonest cercopithecoid at Sterkfontein and Makapansgat! There are two species of *Papio* at Taung, another two at Kromdraai and one at Swartkrans, but none at Makapansgat or Sterkfontein. It would certainly seem that the cercopithecoid fauna support the notion that Taung is younger than the Sterkfontein Faunal Span.

Partridge's geomorphological estimate indicates that the Taung fissure did not open until 0.8 m.y. (93). Butzer's separate estimate also points to a very young age for Taung (24). If there is no systematic error in these estimates, we are forced to the astonishing conclusion that, far from being the oldest hominid site in Southern Africa, Taung is much younger and, according to Partridge, is probably the youngest! It would compete with Kromdraai and Chesowanja as being the site of the most recent survival of an australopithecine anywhere in Africa. (Peninj is a little *over* a million years.)

The implications of this relatively recent date for the place of the Taung hominid in phylogeny and systematics will be considered below.

TENTATIVE SYNTHESIS AND CONCLUSIONS

We may now marshal the evidence for the existence of various kinds or taxa of hominids at various time levels and attempt to construct a model of the later stages of hominid phylogenesis. In doing so, we shall accept the provisional estimates for Makapansgat and Sterkfontein (2.5-3.0 m.y.), Swartkrans (2.0 m.y.), Kromdraai (late in the Swartkrans Faunal Span, ±1.5-2.0 m.y.), and Taung (0.8 m.y.), though in the full appreciation that these estimates are tentative and may well need subsequent amendment. We shall accept for purposes of our model the date of 2.9 m.y. for the large-brained cranium of KNM-ER-1470 of East Rudolf and the provisional assignment of this specimen as an early member of *Homo.*

On this basis, Figure 1 gives the distribution of site samples of hominids in time. The hominoid molar of Ngorora, *Ramapithecus* of India and of Kenya, and *Gigantopithecus* of China and Bilaspur are omitted, as are the early hominids of Indonesia.

The usefulness of this chart is that it permits one to see which hominids were living contemporaneously at each time level. Thus, at about 5 m.y. the available

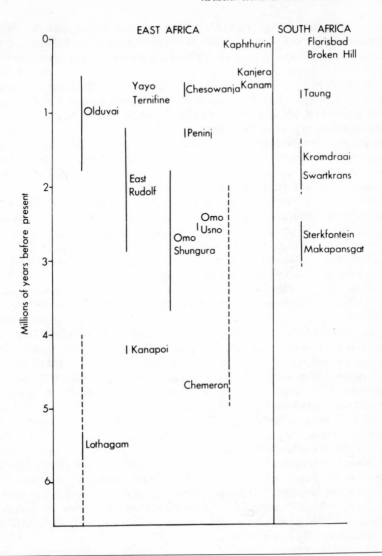

Figure 1 Provisional temporal distribution of early hominids in Africa (partly after Maglio 84). For each hominid-bearing site, the full duration in time of the deposit(s) at that site is indicated or suggested, even though hominid fossils may not necessarily have been found throughout the time sequence for the site. For example, the Chemeron deposits are shown as extending from ca. 2.0 to ca. 5.0 m.y., but the only hominid fossil thus far discovered there—the Chemeron temporal—may be at the 4.0-4.4 m.y. level.

sample comprises a single mandible from Lothagam: it resembles that of *A. africanus.* At just over 4 m.y. we have the humeral fragment of Kanapoi (*A. aff. africanus*) and perhaps the temporal of Chemeron, probably *Australopithecus* (94–96).

At 3.5-3.0 m.y. we have only some isolated teeth from the lower part of the Shungura formation: both a large-toothed australopithecine and a small-toothed early hominid (*A. aff. africanus* or *Homo aff. habilis*) seem to be present.

From 3.0-2.5 m.y. the series comprises *A. africanus* at Sterkfontein and Makapansgat and perhaps *Homo* sp. in the uppermost levels of these two sites; the superspecies *A. robustus/boisei* and a gracile hominid, probably *Homo c.f. habilis,* from Omo (both Usno and Shungura) and East Rudolf. This combination of *A. robustus/boisei* and *Homo aff. habilis* persists from 2.5 to 2.0 m.y.

From 2.0 to 1.5 m.y., we have in East Africa *A. boisei* and *H. habilis* (as represented at Olduvai, East Rudolf, and Omo) and in South Africa *A. robustus* and *H. aff. habilis* (the former "Telanthropus").

From 1.5 to 1.0 m.y., the form of *Homo* represented gives way from *H. habilis* to *H. erectus* (at Olduvai), while the very large-toothed *Australopithecus* (*A. aff. boisei*) lingers on at Olduvai, East Rudolf, and Peninj.

Below 1.0 m.y., *Homo erectus* is represented at Olduvai, Ternifine, probably Yayo, while the latest representative of the robust australopithecine line crops out at Chesowanja. If Partridge's claim that Taung is only 0.8 m.y. is correct, it would appear to have existed about two million years later than the youngest of the other hominids attributed to *A. africanus.* Its contemporaries are *Homo* (most probably *H. erectus*) and the last of the *A. robustus/boisei* lineage. Under these circumstances, it would appear on the face of it to be highly unlikely that the Taung child represents *A. africanus,* in the sense in which this taxon is defined from the Makapansgat and Sterkfontein hominid assemblages. The possibility of isolated relic populations of *A. africanus* having survived in the southerly cul-de-sac of the African continent for a million years after it had disappeared or given rise to the earliest *Homo* species elsewhere cannot, of course, be excluded at this stage of our knowledge. On the other hand, since its small brain size and dental characters would almost certainly exclude it from *H. erectus,* we must seriously consider whether it may be a late surviving *A. robustus.* Despite the lapse of almost 50 years since its discovery, it is an amazing fact that the Taung skull has never yet been fully analyzed and described. Such a study is now urgently necessary in the light of new discoveries and the newer dating evidence.

This analysis of the chronological dispersal of the African early hominids permits one now to draw a diagram based on a succession of cross-sections of the contemporaneous hominid populations (Figure 2).

In Figure 2, the flat ovals represent cross-sections of the putative populations at each time level. The horizontal distance between any two such ovals at the same time level is approximately proportional to the morphological, taxonomic, and phylogenetic distance between the two populations represented. Finally, in Figure 3, these cross-sectional population ovals are joined to provide a phylogenetic tree.

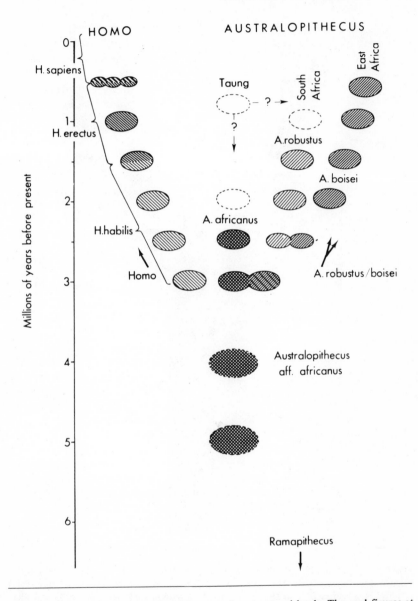

Figure 2 Hominid populations in Africa at various temporal levels. The oval figures at each time level represent the various systematically identified, synchronic hominid taxa living in Africa. The horizontal distance between a pair of ovals at any one time level is roughly proportional to the morphological and taxonomic distance between the populations or taxa represented by the pair of ovals.

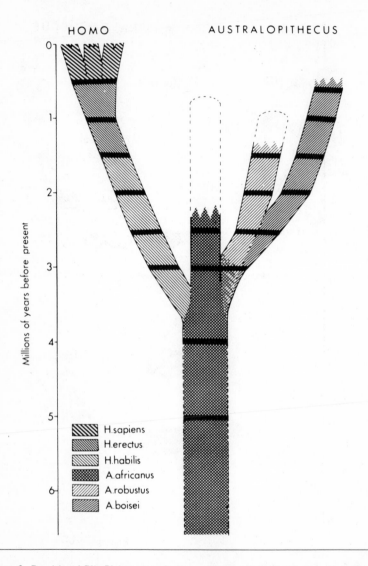

HOMO   AUSTRALOPITHECUS

Millions of years before present

H.sapiens
H.erectus
H.habilis
A.africanus
A.robustus
A.boisei

Figure 3 Provisional Plio-Pleistocene phylogenetic tree of the Hominidae. Note that the branching of *Homo* from *Australopithecus* is shown as an early event (3-4 m.y. B.P.) in order to accommodate in *Homo* the new East Rudolf specimen, ER-1470, which has been tentatively identified as an early *Homo* cranium (2.9 m.y. B.P.). The possible extension of *A. africanus* and/or *A. robustus* to a very recent period (<1.0 m.y. B.P.) is suggested to accommodate the Taung skull at its proposed new young date (0.8 m.y. B.P.).

This reconstruction of the hominid family tree supports the view that:

(a) The ancestral population was a gracile form of hominid, descended from *Ramapithecus* and increasingly resembling *Australopithecus africanus.*

(b) Sometime before 3 m.y., some East African populations diverged from the *A. africanus* lineage and, emphasizing cerebral enlargement and "complexification" as well as increasing cultural dependence, entered upon the very special and peculiar lineage of *Homo* with three time-consecutive species, *H. habilis, H. erectus,* and *H. sapiens.*

(c) The South African (and perhaps some East African) populations of *A. africanus* persisted for some time as such, even after the emergence of *Homo* in other parts of Africa. Just how long they persisted we do not know, possibly for another 2 m.y. (if Taung is correctly placed upon this lineage), or *A. africanus* as such may have died out soon after it had spawned the *Homo* lineage.

(d) Round about 3 m.y. (on present evidence), some populations of the ancestral australopithecine began to differentiate in another direction, emphasizing cheek-tooth expansion, bodily enlargement with a moderate degree of concomitant brain enlargement, but with no major cultural-implemental component. Thus was produced the "robust" lineage characterized by modest morphological and probably ecological and ethological specialization in South Africa (*A. robustus*) and extreme degrees of such specialization in East Africa (*A. boisei*); the lineage of the *A. robustus/boisei* superspecies was apparently sufficiently distinct in behavior and ecological preferences from the line of *Homo* as to have permitted the two lineages to coexist in Africa for something like 2 m.y. or even more.

The main difference between this reconstruction and that put forward in 1965 (114) is that the recent discovery in the Rudolf Basin of early hominids attributable to *Homo* has forced the division between *Homo* and *Australopithecus* back a million years earlier than was hitherto held necessary.

It is clear, too, that there was a major element of cladistic evolution in the Hominidae from 3-4 m.y. onwards. The apparently purely phyletic pattern shown earlier than those dates might well be an artefact stemming from the paucity of hominid remains between 4 m.y. and 12-14 m.y.

On this interpretation, the evolving hominid lineages between 5 and 2 m.y. were African phenomena; thereafter, *Homo* appeared in Asia at a stage when *H. habilis* was changing into *H. erectus* (cf. 127). [It is not yet clear whether *Australopithecus* accompanied *Homo* in Indonesia—as Robinson (100, 103) holds—or whether the robuster forms there were within the range of variation of *H. erectus*—as Le Gros Clark (71) believed.]

ACKNOWLEDGMENTS

I thank the Wenner-Gren Foundation for Anthropological Research, the University of the Witwatersrand, and especially its Bernard Price Institute for Palaeontological Research, as well as the Council for Scientific and Industrial Research, Pretoria, for financial assistance which made possible many of the studies cited above. I am indebted to Dr. C. K. Brain, Mr. A. B. A. Brink, Dr. K. W. Butzer, Mr. R. J. Clarke,

Dr. H. B. S. Cooke, Professor R. A. Dart, Professor M. H. Day, Mr. A. R. Hughes, the Leakey Family, Dr. C. O. Lovejoy, Dr. H. M. McHenry, Dr. V. Maglio, Dr. Margaret Marker, Dr. T. C. Partridge, Professor G. Sperber, Dr. A. C. Walker, Dr. J. A. Wallace, Dr. M. H. Wolpoff, Mrs. Kay Copley, Mr. P. Faugust, Miss Carole Orkin, and Miss Jeanne Walker.

Literature Cited

1. Aguirre, E. 1970. Identificacion de "Paranthropus" en Makapansgat. *Crónica del XI Congreso Nacional de Arqueologia, Merida 1969,* 98–124
2. Aguirre, E. 1972. Africa y el origen de la humanidad. *Documentacion Africana,* Madrid 15:1–36
3. Arambourg, C. 1969. La nouvelle expédition scientifique de l'Omo. *Riv. Sci. Preistoriche* 24 (1):3–13
4. Arambourg, C., Chavaillon, J., Coppens, Y. 1969. Résultats de la nouvelle mission de l'Omo (2e campagne 1968). *C. R. Acad. Sci.* 268:759–62
5. Archibald, J. D., Lovejoy, C. O., Heiple, K. G. 1972. Implications of relative robusticity in the Olduvai metatarsus. *Am J. Phys. Anthropol.* 37:93–95
6. Bada, J. L. 1972. The dating of fossil bones using the racemization of isoleucine. *Earth Planet. Sci. Lett.* 15:223–31
7. Behrensmeyer, A. K. 1970. Preliminary geological interpretation of a new hominid site in the Lake Rudolf Basin. *Nature* 226:225–26
8. Bishop, W. W. 1971. The late Cenozoic history of East Africa in relation to hominoid evolution. In *The Late Cenozoic Glacial Ages,* ed. K. K. Turekian, 493–527. New Haven/London: Yale Univ. Press. 606 pp.
9. Bishop, W. W. 1972. Stratigraphic succession 'versus' calibration in East Africa. In *Calibration of Hominoid Evolution,* ed. W. W. Bishop, J. A. Miller, 219–46. Edinburgh: Scottish Academic Press. 487 pp.
10. Bishop, W. W., Clark, J. D., Eds. 1967. *Background to Evolution in Africa.* Chicago/London: Univ. Chicago Press. 935 pp.
11. Bonnefille, R., Chavaillon, J., Coppens, Y. 1970. Résultats de la nouvelle mission de l'Omo (3e campagne 1969). *C. R. Acad. Sci.* 270:924–27
12. Brain, C. K. 1958. The Transvaal Ape-man-bearing cave deposits. *Transvaal Mus. Mem.* 11:1–125
13. Brain, C. K. 1967. The Transvaal Museum's fossil project at Swartkrans. *S. Afr. J. Sci.* 63:368–84
14. Brain, C. K. 1970. New finds at the Swartkrans australopithecine site. *Nature* 225:1112–19
15. Brain, C. K. 1972. An attempt to reconstruct the behaviour of australopithecines: the evidence for interpersonal violence. *Zool. Afr.* 7 (1):379–401
16. Broom, R., Robinson, J. T. 1948. Size of the brain in the ape-man, *Plesianthropus. Nature* 161 (4090):438
17. Broom, R., Robinson, J. T., Schepers, G. W. H. 1950. Sterkfontein ape-man *Plesianthropus. Transvaal Mus. Mem.* 4:1–117
18. Brown, F. H. 1969. Observations on the stratigraphy and radiometric age of the 'Omo beds,' lower Omo basin, southern Ethiopia. *Quaternaria* 11:7–14
19. Brown, F. H. 1972. Radiometric dating of sedimentary formations in the lower Omo valley, southern Ethiopia. See Ref. 9, 273–87
20. Buettner-Janusch, J. 1973. *Physical Anthropology: a Perspective.* New York/London: Wiley. 572 pp.
21. Burns, P. E. 1971. New determination of australopithecine height. *Nature* 232:350
22. Butzer, K. W. 1971. The Lower Omo Basin: geology, fauna and hominids of Plio-Pleistocene formations. *Naturwissenschaften* 58:7–16
23. Butzer, K. W. 1971. Another look at the australopithecine cave breccias of the Transvaal. *Am. Anthropol.* 73 (5):1197–1201
24. Butzer, K. W. 1973. Paleo-ecology of South African australopithecines: Taung revisited. *Curr. Anthropol.* In press
25. Butzer, K. W., Thurber, D. L. 1969. Some late Cenozoic sedimentary formations of the Lower Omo Basin. *Nature* 222:1132–37
26. Campbell, B. G. 1972. Conceptual progress in physical anthropology: fossil man. *Ann. Rev. Anthropol.* 1:27–54
27. Carney, J., Hill, A., Miller, J. A., Walker, A. 1971. Late australopithecine from Baringo district, Kenya. *Nature* 230:509–14

28. Chavaillon, J. 1970. Découverte d'un niveau Oldowayen dans la basse vallée de l'Omo (Ethiopie). *C. R. Séances Soc. Préhist. Franc.* 1:7–11

29. Clarke, R. J., Howell, F. C. 1972. Affinities of the Swartkrans 847 hominid cranium. *Am. J. Phys. Anthropol.* 37: 319–36

30. Clarke, R. J., Howell, F. C., Brain, C. K. 1970. More evidence of an advanced hominid at Swartkrans. *Nature* 225: 1219–22

31. Cooke, H. B. S. 1970. Notes from Members: Canada: Dalhousie University, Halifax. *Soc. Vert. Palaeontol. Bull.* 90:2

32. Cooke, H. B. S., Maglio, V. J. 1972. Plio-Pleistocene stratigraphy in East Africa in relation to proboscidean and suid evolution. See Ref. 9, 303–29

33. Coppens, Y. 1970–71. Localisation dans le temps et dans l'espace des restes d'hominidés des formations Plio-Pléistocènes de l'Omo (Éthiopie). *C. R. Acad. Sci.* 271:1968–71, 2286–89; 272: 36–39

34. Dart, R. A. 1962. The Makapansgat pink breccia australopithecine skull. *Am. J. Phys. Anthropol.* 20 (2):119–26

35. Day, M. H. 1973. Elliot Smith Centenary Meeting, Zool. Soc. London, Nov. 1972. In press

36. Day, M. H., Wood, B. A. 1968. Functional affinities of the Olduvai hominid 8 talus. *Man* 3:440–55

37. Dobzhansky, T. 1969. *The Biology of Ultimate Concern.* London/New York: Rapp & Whiting/New American Library. 152 pp.

38. Evernden, J. F., Curtis, G. H. 1965. The potassium argon dating of Late Cenozoic rocks in East Africa and Italy. *Curr. Anthropol.* 6 (4):343–85

39. Fleischer, R. L., Hart, H. R. 1972. Fission track dating: techniques and problems. See Ref. 9, 135–70

40. Freedman, L. 1957. The fossil Cercopithecoidea of South Africa. *Ann. Transvaal Mus.* 23:121–262

41. Freedman, L. 1970. A new check list of fossil Cercopithecoidea of South Africa. *Palaeontol. Afr.* 13:109–10

42. Freedman, L., Brain, C. K. 1972. Fossil cercopithecoid remains from the Kromdraai australopithecine site (Mammalia: Primates). *Ann. Transvaal Mus.* 28 (1):1–16

43. Freedman, L., Stenhouse, N. S. 1972. The *Parapapio* species of Sterkfontein, Transvaal, South Africa. *Palaeontol. Afr.* 14:93–111

44. Grommé, C. S., Hay, R. L. 1967. Geomagnetic polarity epochs; new data from Olduvai Gorge, Tanganyika. *Earth Planet. Sci. Lett.* 2:111–15

45. Hay, R. L. 1971. Geologic background of Beds I and II: stratigraphic summary. See Ref. 62, 9–18

46. Heinzelin, J. de 1971. Observations sur la formation de Shungura (Vallée de l'Omo, Éthiopie). *C. R. Acad. Sci.* 272: 2409–11

47. Heinzelin, J. de, Brown, F. H. 1969. Some early Pleistocene deposits of the lower Omo valley: the Usno formation. *Quaternaria* 11:29–46

48. Heiple, K. G., Lovejoy, C. O. 1971. The distal femoral anatomy of *Australopithecus*. *Am. J. Phys. Anthropol.* 35: 75–84

49. Helmuth, H. 1968. Körperhöhe und Gliedmassenproportionen der Australopithecinen. *Z. Morphol. Anthropol.* 60:147–55

50. Holloway, R. L. 1970. Australopithecine endocast (Taung specimen 1924): a new volume determination. *Science* 168:966–68

51. Holloway, R. L. 1972. New australopithecine endocast, SK 1585, from Swartkrans, South Africa. *Am J. Phys. Anthropol.* 37 (2):173–85

52. Holloway, R. L. 1972. Australopithecine endocasts, brain evolution in the Hominoidea, and a model of hominid evolution. In *The Functional and Evolutionary Biology of Primates*, ed. R. Tuttle, 185–203. Chicago/New York: Aldine-Atherton. 487 pp.

53. Howell, F. C. 1968. Omo Research Expedition. *Nature* 219:567–72

54. Ibid 1969. Remains of Hominidae from Pliocene/Pleistocene formations in the Lower Omo Basin, Ethiopia. 223: 1234–39

55. Howell, F. C. 1972. Pliocene/Pleistocene Hominidae in eastern Africa: absolute and relative ages. See Ref. 9, 331–68

56. Isaac, G. L., Leakey, R. E. F., Behrensmeyer, A. K. 1971. Archeological traces of early hominid activities, east of Lake Rudolf, Kenya. *Science* 173: 1129–34

57. Leakey, L. S. B. 1973. Was *Homo erectus* responsible for the hand-axe culture? *J. Hum. Evol.* In press

58. Leakey, L. S. B., Tobias, P. V., Napier, J. R. 1964. A new species of the genus *Homo* from the Olduvai Gorge. *Nature* 202:7–9

59. Leakey, M. D. 1967. Preliminary survey of the cultural material from Beds I and II, Olduvai Gorge, Tanzania. See Ref. 10, 417–46
60. Leakey, M. D. 1970. Stone artefacts from Swartkrans. *Nature* 225:1222–25
61. Ibid 1970. Early artefacts from the Koobi Fora area. 226:228–30
62. Leakey, M. D. 1971. *Olduvai Gorge,* Vol. 3. Excavations in Beds I and II, 1960–63. Cambridge Univ. Press. 306 pp.
63. Leakey, M. D., Clarke, R. J., Leakey, L. S. B. 1971. New hominid skull from Bed I, Olduvai Gorge, Tanzania. *Nature* 232:308–12
64. Leakey, R. E. F. 1970. Fauna and artifacts from a new Plio-Pleistocene locality near Lake Rudolf in Kenya. *Nature* 226:223–24
65. Ibid 1971. Further evidence of Lower Pleistocene hominids from East Rudolf, North Kenya. 231:241–45
66. Ibid 1972. Further evidence of Lower Pleistocene hominids from East Rudolf, North Kenya, 1971. 237:264–69
67. Ibid 1973. Further evidence of Lower Pleistocene hominids from East Rudolf, North Kenya, 1972. 242:170–73
68. Leakey, R. E. F., Mungai, J. M., Walker, A. C. 1971. New australopithecines from East Rudolf, Kenya. *Am. J. Phys. Anthropol.* 35:175–86
69. Ibid 1972. New australopithecines from East Rudolf, Kenya (II). 36: 235–51
70. Le Gros Clark, W. E. 1952. A note on certain cranial indices of the Sterkfontein skull no. 5. *Am. J. Phys. Anthropol.* 10:119–21
71. Le Gros Clark, W. E. 1964. *The Fossil Evidence for Human Evolution.* Univ. Chicago Press. 201 pp. 2nd ed.
72. Leutenegger, W. 1972. Newborn size and pelvic dimensions of *Australopithecus. Nature* 240:568–69
73. Lewis, O. J. 1972. The evolution of the hallucial tarsometatarsal joint in the Anthropoidea. *Am. J. Phys. Anthropol.* 37:13–34
74. Lewis, O. J. 1973. The hominid os capitatum, with special reference to the fossil bones from Sterkfontein and Olduvai Gorge. *J. Hum. Evol.* 2 (1): 1–11
75. Lovejoy, C. O., Heiple, K. G. 1970. A reconstruction of the femur of *Australopithecus africanus. Am. J. Phys. Anthropol.* 33:33–40
76. Lovejoy, C. O., Heiple, K. G. 1972. The proximal femoral anatomy of *Australopithecus. Nature* 235:175–76
77. Lovejoy, C. O., Heiple, K. G., Burstein, A. H. 1972. The gait of *Australopithecus. Am. J. Phys. Anthropol.* In press
78. McHenry, H. M. 1972. *Postcranial skeleton of early Pleistocene hominids.* PhD thesis. Harvard Univ., Cambridge, Mass.
79. McHenry, H. M. 1973. Multivariate analysis of early hominid humeri. In press
80. McHenry, H. M. 1973. How large were the australopithecines? *Am. J. Phys. Anthropol.* In press
81. McKinley, K. R. 1971. Survivorship in gracile and robust australopithecines: a demographic comparison and a proposed birth model. *Am. J. Phys. Anthropol.* 34:417–26
82. Maglio, V. J. 1971. Vertebrate faunas from the Kubi Algi, Koobi Fora and Ileret areas, East Rudolf, Kenya. *Nature* 231:248–49
83. Ibid 1972. Vertebrate fauna and chronology of hominid-bearing sediments east of Lake Rudolf, Kenya. 239:379–85
84. Maglio, V. J. 1973. *Am. Phil. Soc.* In press
85. Maguire, B. 1965. Foreign pebble pounding artefacts in the breccias and the overlying vegetation soil at Makapansgat Limeworks. *S. Afr. Archaeol. Bull.* 20 (79):117–30
86. Maier, W. 1970. New fossil Cercopithecoidea from the Lower Pleistocene cave deposits of the Makapansgat Limeworks, South Africa. *Palaeontol. Afr.* 13:69–107
87. Mann, A. E. 1968. *The Paleodemography of* AUSTRALOPITHECUS. PhD thesis. Univ. California, Berkeley. 153 pp.
88. Mason, R. J. 1962. Australopithecines and artefacts at Sterkfontein, Part II. The Sterkfontein stone artefacts and their maker. *S. Afr. Archaeol. Bull.* 17 (66):109–25
89. Oxnard, C. E. 1967. The functional morphology of the primate shoulder as revealed by comparative anatomical, osteometric and discriminant function techniques. *Am. J. Phys. Anthropol.* 26:219–40
90. Ibid 1968. A note on the fragmentary Sterkfontein scapula. 28:213–17
91. Ibid 1972. Some African fossil foot bones: a note on the interpolation of fossils into a matrix of extant species. 37: 3–12
92. Partridge, T. C. 1965. A statistical analysis of the Limeworks lithic assemblage. *S. Afr. Archaeol. Bull.* 20 (79):112–16
93. Partridge, T. C. 1973. Geomorphological dating of cave opening at Makapansgat, Sterkfontein, Swartkrans and Taung. In press

94. Patterson, B. 1966. A new locality for early Pleistocene fossils in northwestern Kenya. *Nature* 212:577–78

95. Patterson, B., Behrensmeyer, A. K., Sill, W. D. 1970. Geology and fauna of a new Pliocene locality in northwestern Kenya. *Nature* 226:918–21

96. Patterson, B., Howells, W. W. 1967. Hominid humeral fragment from early Pleistocene of northwestern Kenya. *Science* 156:64–66

97. Pilbeam, D. R. 1969. Early Hominidae and cranial capacity. *Nature* 224:386

98. Preuschoft, H. 1971. Body posture and mode of locomotion in early Pleistocene hominids. *Folia Primatol.* 14:209–40

99. Rightmire, G. P. 1972. Multivariate analysis of an early hominid metacarpal from Swartkrans. *Science* 176:159–61

100. Robinson, J. T. 1953. *Meganthropus, Australopithecus* and hominids. *Am. J. Phys. Anthropol.* 11:1–38

101. Ibid *Telanthropus* and its phylogenetic significance, 445–501

102. Ibid 1954. The genera and species of the Australopithecinae. 12:181–200

103. Ibid 1955. Further remarks on the relationship between '*Meganthropus*' and australopithecines. 13:429–46

104. Robinson, J. T. 1962. Australopithecines and artefacts at Sterkfontein: Part I. Sterkfontein stratigraphy and the significance of the Extension Site. *S. Afr. Archaeol. Bull.* 17 (66):87–107

105. Robinson, J. T. 1965. *Homo 'habilis'* and the australopithecines. *Nature* 205:121–24

106. Ibid 1966. Comment on "The distinctiveness of *Homo habilis.*" 209:957–60

107. Robinson, J. T. 1967. Variation and the taxonomy of the early hominids. In *Evolutionary Biology,* ed. T. Dobzhansky, M. K. Hecht, W. C. Steere, 1:69–100. New York: Appleton-Century-Crofts

108. Robinson, J. T. 1970. Two new early hominid vertebrae from Swartkrans. *Nature* 225:1217–19

109. Robinson, J. T., Steudel, K. 1973. Multivariate discriminant analysis of dental data bearing on early hominid affinities. *J. Hum. Evol.* In press

110. Roper, M. K. 1969. A survey of the evidence for intrahuman killing in the Pleistocene. *Curr. Anthropol.* 10:427–59

111. Rosen, S. I., McKern, T. W. 1971. Several cranial indices and their relevance to fossil man. *Am. J. Phys. Anthropol.* 35:69–73

112. Tobias, P. V. 1963. Cranial capacity of *Zinjanthropus* and other australopithecines. *Nature* 197:743–46

113. Tobias, P. V. 1965. *Australopithecus, Homo habilis,* tool-using and tool-making. *S. Afr. Archaeol. Bull.* 20:167–92

114. Tobias, P. V. 1965. Early man in East Africa. *Science* 149:22–33

115. Tobias, P. V. 1966. The distinctiveness of *Homo habilis. Nature* 129:953–57

116. Tobias, P. V. 1967. *Olduvai Gorge,* Vol. 2. The cranium and maxillary dentition of *Australopithecus (Zinjanthropus) boisei.* Cambridge Univ. Press. 264 pp.

117. Tobias, P. V. 1968. The age of death among the australopithecines. *The Anthropologist* special volume, 23–28

118. Tobias, P. V. 1968. The taxonomy and phylogeny of the australopithecines. In *Taxonomy and Phylogeny of Old World Primates with References to the Origin of Man,* 277–318. Proc. round table at Inst. Anthropol. Centre Primatol., Univ. Turin, Italy. Turin: Rosenberg & Sellier. 323 pp.

119. Tobias, P. V. 1968. New African evidence on human evolution. Wenner-Gren Found. Supper Conf., New York City, April 1968

120. Tobias, P. V. 1969. Commentary on new discoveries and interpretations of early African fossil hominids. *Yearbook of Physical Anthropology 1967,* ed. S. Genoves, 24–30

121. Tobias, P. V. 1971. *The Brain in Hominid Evolution.* New York/London: Columbia Univ. Press. 170 pp.

122. Tobias, P. V. 1971. Does the form of the inner contour of the mandible distinguish between *Australopithecus* and *Homo?* In *Perspectives in Palaeoanthropology: D. Sen Festschrift Volume,* ed. A. K. Ghosh, 9–17. Calcutta: Firma K. L. Mukhopadhyay

123. Tobias, P. V. 1972. Progress and problems in the study of early man in sub-Saharan Africa. In *The Functional and Evolutionary Biology of Primates,* ed. R. Tuttle, 63–93. Chicago/New York: Aldine-Atherton. 487 pp.

124. Tobias, P. V. 1972. "Dished faces," brain size and early hominids. *Nature* 239:468–69

125. Tobias, P. V. 1973. Darwin's prediction and the African emergence of the genus *Homo.* In *L'Origine dell'Umo.* Rome. In press

126. Tobias, P. V., Hughes, A. R. 1969. The new Witwatersrand University excavation at Sterkfontein. *S. Afr. Archaeol. Bull.* 24:158–69

127. Tobias, P. V., von Koenigswald, G. H. R. 1964. Comparison between the Olduvai hominines and those of Java and some implications for hominid phylogeny. *Nature* 204:515–18

128. Vondra, C. F., Johnson, G. D., Bowen, B. E., Behrensmeyer, A. K. 1971. Preliminary stratigraphical studies of the East Rudolf Basin, Kenya. *Nature* 231:245–48

129. Vrba, E. S. 1971. A new fossil alcelaphine (Artiodactyla: Bovidae) from Swartkrans. *Ann. Transvaal Mus.* 27: 59–82

130. Walker, A. C. 1973. New *Australopithecus* femora from East Rudolf, Kenya. *J. Hum. Evol.* In press

131. Wallace, J. A. 1972. *The Dentition of the South African Early Hominids: a Study of Form and Function.* PhD thesis. Univ. Witwatersrand, Johannesburg. 244 pp.

132. Wells, L. H. 1969. Faunal subdivision of the Quaternary in southern Africa. *S. Afr. Archaeol. Bull.* 24:93–95

133. Wolpoff, M. H. 1971. *Metric Trends in Hominid Dental Evolution.* Case Western Reserve Univ. Stud. Anthropol. 2: 1–244

134. Wolpoff, M. H. 1971. Competitive exclusion among lower Pleistocene hominids: the single species hypothesis. *Man* 6:601–14

135. Wolpoff, M. H. 1971. Is the new composite cranium from Swartkrans a small robust australopithecine? *Nature* 230: 398–401

136. Wright, G. A., Skaryd, S. 1972. Do fossil elephants date the South African australopithecines? *Nature* 237:291

137. Zihlman, A. L. 1967. *Human locomotion. A reappraisal of the functional and anatomical evidence.* PhD thesis. Univ. California, Berkeley. 115 pp.

138. Zihlman, A. L. 1970. *The question of locomotor differences in* AUSTRALOPITHECUS. Presented at 3rd Int. Congr. Primatol. Zurich

139. Zihlman, A. L., Hunter, W. S. 1972. A biomechanical interpretation of the pelvis of *Australopithecus. Folia Primatol.* 18:1–19

REPRINTS

The conspicuous number aligned in the margin with the title of each article in this volume is a key for use in ordering reprints.

Available reprints are priced at the uniform rate of $1 each postpaid. Payment must accompany orders less than $10. A discount of 20% will be given on orders of 20 or more. For orders of 200 or more, any Annual Reviews article will be specially printed.

The sale of reprints of articles published in the Reviews has been expanded in the belief that reprints as individual copies, as sets covering stated topics, and in quantity for classroom use will have a special appeal to students and teachers.

AUTHOR INDEX

SUBJECT INDEX

CUMULATIVE INDEXES

CONTRIBUTING AUTHORS VOLUMES 1-2

CHAPTER TITLES VOLUMES 1-2